THE
APPROPRIATE
WORD

THE APPROPRIATE WORD

Finding the Best Way to Say What You Mean

J. N. HOOK

ADDISON–WESLEY PUBLISHING COMPANY, INC.

Reading, Massachusetts   Menlo Park, California

New York   Don Mills, Ontario   Wokingham, England

Amsterdam   Bonn   Sydney   Singapore

Tokyo   Madrid   San Juan

Library of Congress Cataloging-in-Publication Data

Hook, J. N. (Julius Nicholas)
   The appropriate word : finding the best way to say what you mean /
Julius N. Hook.
     p.   cm.
   ISBN 0-201-52323-X
   1. English language – Synonyms and antonyms.   I. Title.
PE1591.H66   1990   89-18616
428 – dc20

Jacket design by Marianne Perlak
Set in 10-point Bembo by DEKR Corporation, Woburn MA

ABCDEFGHIJ- MW-9543210
First printing, May 1990

to RGH

INTRODUCTION

"Is this the appropriate word?" is a question not often fully articulated, but writers may need to answer it one or more times in almost any sentence. The question is not new, although the answers change somewhat with each generation. Joseph Conrad and Gustave Flaubert spent hours searching for the exact word, Elizabeth Barrett Browning put pyramids of possible alternatives in her margins, and many literate people remember Mark Twain's often-quoted statement that the difference between the right word and the almost-right word is as great as that between lightning and the lightning bug.

As professional authors, these nineteenth-century writers had effective ways to find the words that were appropriate for their times, their topics, and their readers. *The Appropriate Word* is intended to help today's people who write, especially nonprofessionals, in making many of their choices. A reference tool alongside a dictionary and a thesaurus, it should be of help to office workers, students, beginning or would-be authors, and anyone else who hopes to write clear, effective, and concise modern English that fits the circumstances.

FF and SWE

Books on English usage typically tell their readers, "This is right, but that is wrong. Say this, but don't say that."

The Appropriate Word is different. It says:

- There are no absolutes in language. What is standard in this century may have been taboo in the past or may become nonstandard in the future.
- A word may be "right" in some circumstances but not necessarily in others. Some of the words that are quite satisfactory at home or at a party or a bar may be less suitable in other places and with other people.

I use repeatedly in this book the letters FF (for "family and friends") to represent the casual, unplanned, carefree, and frequently slangy expressions that most Americans employ most of the time in conversing with or writing to people they know well or other people with backgrounds similar to their own.

I use SWE to refer to "standard written English." Some people call SWE "edited writing" instead, because its usages are similar to those found in such well-edited newspapers as the *New York Times* and the *Christian Science Monitor* or such magazines as the *Atlantic* and the *New Yorker*.

FF must not be equated with "wrong." The idea that every word or phrase is right or wrong was long ago repudiated by linguists. "Levels of usage" superseded "rightness" and "wrongness," but even that concept suggests superior levels and inferior levels. The contention in this book is that *most* words are appropriate in both formal and informal contexts but that at this time, late in the twentieth century, *some* words and expressions are appropriate in informal family-friends contexts but are regarded as less appropriate or inappropriate in relatively formal writing (as well as speaking). A word used in an inappropriate context is a weed.

A weed is defined by some botanists as "a plant out of place." A weed is not right or wrong, but is inappropriately located, perhaps in the middle of your manicured bluegrass lawn. A word, similarly, sometimes appears in an inappropriate place. As a word, it is not right or wrong, but in its location it may be suitable or unsuitable, appropriate or inappropriate.

For example, one of my college undergraduates, praising Emily Dickinson, said that she was "an exceptionable woman." *Exceptionable* doesn't belong in that context, because it means "objectionable," and my student was in no way objecting to or taking exception to that great American poet. He meant, of course, that she was *exceptional*, defined as "unusual, extraordinary, possessing unexpected or uncommon attributes." The student's *exceptionable* is a perfectly good word, definitely not wrong, but it was a weed in his sentence. This book will assist in the continuing and many-fronted fight against such weeds.

Appropriateness, then, involves adapting language to circumstances and to the intended receivers of the message. Almost everyone does some adapting, usually without thinking about it. When Daddy tells a story to Karen and Jason, he uses different words and even somewhat different grammatical structures and sentence lengths from those he uses in talking with adult friends or in writing a report to be used in his business or profession. Mama talks differently to the children, her own mother, her husband, her close friends, her business associates, and the pediatrician, and she writes differently to an old college friend, now living in Europe, from the way she writes to the seafood company that doesn't work hard enough to avoid killing dolphins, or to the congressional representative who perhaps can do something about it.

FF draws from the same vocabulary that SWE does, and countless FF sentences, addressed to family and friends, are identical to those employed in more formal contexts. Both FF and SWE are "good English" if they convey whatever information and emotion the writer or speaker intends. But FF is contrastable to SWE in these ways and perhaps in others:

- FF is ordinarily spontaneous, off-the-cuff, unplanned. We seldom think much about choice of words when we are conversing with a spouse, our children, or a good friend. We know that the words will come when we start chatting, and that if something is not clear, we'll be asked, "Whaddaya mean?"

- To the user of FF, language is just a tool, employed as unthinkingly as a spoon or a toothbrush. The FF speaker or writer seldom asks himself, "Is this word exact, completely clear, and in conformity with what Miss Snyder taught us in junior high school?" FF tends to be relaxed – linguistically and stylistically unconcerned.

- Because it is unplanned, FF is less meticulous than SWE. SWE generally differentiates, for instance, between *less* and *fewer, enemy* and *adversary,* or *disapprove* and *reject,* but most users of FF pay little attention to such distinctions.

- FF often exaggerates and exclaims. It may praise a small achievement as "Great!" or describe a merely unpleasant experience as "Horrible!"

- Some, but not all, users of FF either do not recall or do not obey teachers' admonitions not to use *ain't,* double negatives, *my mother she,* and other nonstandard forms such as those in "He done his work real good."

- FF usages are less consistent, less predictable, than those of SWE. Some FF users may say "I saw it" in one sentence but "I seen it" a little later.

- FF adopts innovative language, especially slang, more quickly than SWE does. As a synonym of *excellent,* FF in one decade may use *swell;* in another, *boss;* in another, *real cool;* and in still another, *ba-ad* or *wicked good.* But SWE may stay unswervingly with *excellent.* (It is true, though, that SWE eventually does accept a small percentage of originally slang words, especially if they are shorter, clearer, or more expressive than their synonyms. See the entry on MOB as an example.)

- FF more frequently than SWE uses words commonly regarded as profane or obscene. Some servicemen in two world wars were said – although certainly not accurately – to have vocabularies of only seven words, all of them at that time unprintable.

- FF tends to be more repetitive than SWE. It contains many redundancies, wasted words. It is sometimes succinct, but more often not. It may say "in the neighborhood of a hundred dollars" instead of "about a hundred dollars," or "a huge, big, immense building" instead of settling for a single adjective.
- The vocabulary of FF tends to be more limited than that of SWE. A person whose usual FF vocabulary may be only a few thousand words may use several times as many in business or professional work. Because of the greater meticulousness of SWE, its users take time to find the word that comes closest to conveying his precise meaning.
- FF is more varied than SWE. Its users range from near-inarticulateness to the edge of SWE. Some FF users are more slangy, profane, exclamatory, or hyperbolic than others. Some are less repetitive, more succinct, more versatile in word choice, more colorful, or more often observant of Miss Snyder's linguistic precepts than others.

A few people never need SWE at all. These are persons who have almost no contact with people other than those in their own limited environment and rarely need to communicate in writing. In fact, unless the job demands SWE, a whole week, a whole year, may be spent largely in FF contexts.

At least occasionally, however, most people do need to write letters to strangers, an explanation to the IRS, a memorandum or even a report to the boss. In an age when communication is increasingly called "the lifeblood of business and industry" and when the livelihoods of millions of Americans require considerable amounts of communication, a high degree of precision and consistency of word choice is desirable and often essential. This means SWE, not the FF that is appropriate mainly in contexts that are unlikely to penalize rather imprecise and inconsistent language.

Although SWE means "standard *written* English," its characteristics are present also in much *spoken* English, typically outside one's own intimate circles. SWE is especially likely in discussions of relatively serious subjects. If we are ever called on to address a convention of meteorologists, we will probably use SWE, but in talking about the weather with a chance acquaintance on the golf course, we use FF.

To describe SWE in part, we need only to turn upside down what has already been said about FF. SWE is usually:

- somewhat planned, seldom just spontaneous; it is thoughtful in regard to language, considering it an instrument that can be finely tuned to help a writer attain whatever his or her purpose may be.
- fairly careful in word choice.
- seldom exclamatory or hyperbolic.

- in general accord with conventional modern standards (although today less constrained than before by rules that now seem artificial, such as most of those about split infinitives and *shall* vs. *will*).
- consistent in choice of verb forms, pronoun cases, and the like.
- not more than moderately slangy, or in some contexts not at all.
- unlikely to be profane or obscene (except possibly in direct quotations).
- not wasteful of words, not repetitious except when repetition serves a purpose.
- furnished with a sizable vocabulary from which may be selected the words that most accurately convey intended information, ideas, or emotion from writer to reader.
- less extreme in its variations than FF, although its users are certainly not like peas in a pod. They differ especially in degree of formality, with some almost always preferring a light touch, and others most often serious without being stiff. They also shift gears as necessitated by context and purpose; for instance, a lawyer may be constrained to use legalese in official documents but may try to talk in layman's terms to his clients.

It can be argued that a no-man's-land exists between FF and SWE, a shaded area that cannot be categorized. I accept this argument and so occasionally use such terms as "informal SWE" or "marginally SWE" or "moving toward SWE."

An occasional entry in this book uses the acronym SANE, perhaps as in this short example:

appear on the scene, arrive on the scene   SANE says, "Delete three words in each."

SANE is an imaginary organization, the Society for the Avoidance of Needless Effort. It especially dislikes writing, typing, or speaking more words than are needed and forcing readers or listeners to read or listen to more words than they must. SWE generally follows SANE's precepts, but sometimes I have felt the need to suggest a change that I consider mere common sense. Then I say, in effect, "SANE recommends . . ."

Toward More Natural Expression

English language usages change slowly but constantly, as any reader of Chaucer, Shakespeare, or even a nineteenth-century author can easily see. Perhaps the greatest change in this century has been a move away from stiffness, long sentences, and greater-than-necessary formality. On average, today's SWE is less formal than that of 1940 or even 1960 or 1970, although a few circumstances demanding considerable formality still exist.

Modern American usage reflects lifestyles that in this century have steadily become less structured, more relaxed. A writer in the nineteenth century at least figuratively donned his Prince Albert coat before dipping his pen into the inkwell. Today's writer is likely to sit in shirtsleeves in front of the word processor.

Modern good writing, such as that in the best-edited magazines and newspapers, is characterized by relatively short sentences and paragraphs, lively verbs, an occasionally surprising noun or adjective, and especially a lack of starchiness. It reflects the influence of journalism but not journalistic excesses; it combines the lively styles of good reporters with the care and verbal precision of literary craftsmen.

By no means, then, have all the usage bars been let down. "Anything goes" has not become the rule governing SWE. The lowest common denominator, the language of the high school dropout, has not taken over. Today's even moderately careful users of SWE do not write, for instance, "had took" or "Me and her wasn't to blame nohow," nor do most of them confuse *apex* and *nadir* or *bisect* and *dissect*. They still adhere to a degree of orthodoxy, as is suggested by the fact that each year they spend millions of dollars on word processors or typewriters that alert them to spelling misdemeanors or provide lists of synonyms to remind them of choices that may be available. But in their writing, despite this leaning toward orthodoxy, they try to avoid stodginess, stiffness, and any hint of being old-fashioned.

Not only journalists and authors and editors of magazine articles have become less rigid. So have many of the people who write or dictate the correspondence coming from the nation's multitudinous places of business. Writers of business letters, for example, long ago stopped saying things like "Yours of the tenth inst. rec'd and contents noted. . . . Yr. obedient servant." Symptomatic of the trend are most of the articles in the *Wall Street Journal, Nation's Business, Forbes*, or probably any other widely read business publication.

Even scholarly writing has become less stiff. Paul Halmos is one of the world's leading researchers in mathematics and the editor of the prestigious *American Mathematical Monthly*. He tells of an early article of his that while in draft stage was criticized by a colleague for its occasional use of contractions, such as *isn't* rather than *is not*. At that time the use of contractions, as well as almost any other hint of informality, was taboo in scholarly writing. Halmos ignored the criticism, his article was published, and two years later it was awarded the coveted Chauvenet Prize for mathematical exposition.

In his autobiographical *I Want to Be a Mathematician*, published in 1985 by the Mathematical Association of America, Halmos expressed this belief about writing, a point of view increasingly accepted by scholars in many disciplines:

Expository writing must not be sloppy in either content or form and, of course, it must not be misleading; it must be dignified, correct, and clear. Within these guidelines, however, expository writing should be written in a clear, colloquial style, it should be evocative in the same sense in which poetry is, and it should not be stuffy, but friendly and informal. The purpose of writing is to communicate, and style is a tool for communication. It should be chosen so as to put the reader at his ease and make the subject seem as easy to him as it already is to the author.

Halmos was not the first to make such a plea. During most of the first half of this century, *Publications of the Modern Language Association of America* (PMLA), which prints articles by literary scholars, was almost invariably dull and stodgy, sometimes described as "a thin trickle of text and a river of footnotes." Its authors tended to display polysyllables and Latinate prose, and even though many of them were no doubt likable and good-natured, seldom did a trace of their amiability show up in their weighty PMLA articles.

Then in the 1940s along came an eminent Milton scholar, William Riley Parker. He was MLA secretary and PMLA editor. Like Halmos, Parker realized that scholarly accuracy and dignified writing were not incompatible with readability, a moderate degree of informality, and at least a touch of friendliness. He described in detail the expository qualities that he would insist on, and because of his prestige and that of the journal, he was able to get them – although some struggles did occur. Scholarly writing as a whole has become much more readable because of the work of such people as Halmos and Parker, and its contributions to human knowledge have not decreased in amount or significance.

Much more widely read than scholarly journals are many of the hundreds of popular magazines that fill today's newsstands. I once made a quick comparison of articles in a modern *Harper's* and an issue of a century earlier. Modern sentences average about half the length of the older ones, each word is much more likely to have six or eight letters rather than ten or twelve, even fairly technical subjects are treated so that almost any interested layman can understand them, and the words *flow*. Most published authors, such as those who write for today's best magazines, are not afraid to show that they are human beings, even making use of occasional wit and humor.

The Entries

The number of entries in *The Appropriate Word* is over 2,300, not counting cross-references. The total number of words treated (since many of the entries deal with two or more words) is close to 4,000.

How were the terms chosen? Admittedly, I had to be both selective and subjective. The book could have been much fatter; some readers may moan about what they consider unforgivable omissions. From varied sources I chose terms that reflected wordiness or misinformation or provoked uncertainty. These sources were many thousands of pages of college student writing, freshman themes through doctoral dissertations; local newspapers bought during my frequent travels, papers ranging from the weekly *Corn Belt Sentinel* to most of the nation's metropolitan dailies and their bloated Sunday editions; TV commentators and sports announcers, whose attempts at liveliness and cleverness vary in success. My wife and I for years have read regularly the *New York Times* and a semirural Illini or Hoosier daily. Large numbers of books from the past couple of decades make our bookshelves sag. We subscribe to some forty magazines (not always the same ones), including the *New Yorker*, the quite different *New York*, and the *Atlantic*, through *Newsweek*, *Good Housekeeping*, hobby magazines, *Arizona Highways*, an occasional West Coast periodical, and *Harrowsmith* (a delightful New England journal of rural life). To see what many other people read, we now and then buy tabloids and other periodicals, some of which we find it judicious to hide in the shopping cart under a box of cornflakes.

And in our travels in fifty states, my wife and I like to listen to people talk. Some might call us shameless eavesdroppers. We enjoy the many dialects, and we tuck away in our minds and sometimes on paper countless instances of words and constructions that occur in speaking but only rarely, if ever, in *House Beautiful*, for instance.

In writing about each term that I selected, how did I decide whether it was FF or SWE, or both (as is not unusual)? How did I decide that a word or expression was formal, informal, slangy, stiff, old-fashioned, wordy, or something else? I recalled, with my wife's help, its customary environment(s), noting whether it thrives in a lively breeze or in calm air, what its neighbors are like, how high-class its surroundings are (the languages of corner bars and of ritzy hotel bars differ considerably), whether it sometimes seems discordant in a given context. My wife and I try to be constantly alert to what is happening in the language, noting words or usages new to us, and other words or usages that seem to be getting established or dropping out of sight.

My wife, more conservative than I, often tempers my premature enthusiasm for some of the more eccentric coinages and innovative, or at least uncommon, usages. She also begs me not to call *imply* and *infer* interchangeable in SWE, even though a few respected publications treat them as though they are. And she implores me never to get what she calls "too permissive" about *unique*. Precision, she says, is important, even though the *New York Times* and other reputable publications are sometimes imprecise. The language is weakened, she believes, when it loses a needed word for which there is no exact synonym. This is what happens, for instance, when *unique*, which means "pertaining to the only one of its kind," is used to mean merely "unusual," because the language then has no remaining short, clear way to say "the only one of its kind." My wife's reasoning is sometimes very convincing. It shows up in a few entries in which I say, in effect, "SWE does so and so, but it would make more sense to do it this other way. SANE recommends . . ."

Abbreviations Used in Entries

FF: family and friends

SANE: Society for the Avoidance of Needless Effort (a fictitious organization)

SWE: standard written English

References Mentioned in Entries

AHD: *American Heritage Dictionary*. Boston, Houghton Mifflin, 1981 edition.

Bernstein: Theodore Bernstein, *The Careful Writer*. New York, Atheneum, 1977.

Bryant: Margaret Bryant, *Current American Usage*. New York, Funk & Wagnalls, 1967.

Copperud: Roy H. Copperud, *American Usage: The Consensus*. New York, Van Nostrand Reinhold, 1970.

——, *Webster's Dictionary of Usage and Style*. New York, Avenel Books, 1982 edition.

Crisp: Raymond D. Crisp, *Changes in Attitudes Toward English Usage*. Unpublished doctoral dissertation, U. of Illinois, 1971.

Evans: Bergen and Cornelia Evans, *Dictionary of Contemporary American Usage*. New York, Random House, 1957.

Flesch: Rudolf Flesch, *Lite English*. New York, Crown Publishers, 1983.

Flexner: Stuart B. Flexner, *Listening to America*. New York, Simon & Schuster, 1982.

Follett: Wilson Follett, *Modern American Usage*. New York, Hill & Wang, 1966.

Fowler: H. W. Fowler, *Dictionary of Modern American Usage*. Oxford and New York, Oxford U. Press, 1950 edition.

Howard: Philip Howard, *The State of the Language*. New York, Oxford U. Press, 1985.

Lamberts: J. J. Lamberts, *Short Introduction to English Usage*. New York, McGraw-Hill, 1972.

Morris: William and Mary Morris, *Harper Dictionary of Contemporary Usage*. New York, Harper & Row, 1975.

Nicholson: Margaret Nicholson, *Dictionary of American-English Usage*. New York, Oxford U. Press, 1957. (American edition of Fowler)

OED: *Oxford English Dictionary*. London, Oxford U. Press, 1971. (micrographic edition)

Oxford: *Oxford American Dictionary*. New York and Oxford, Oxford U. Press, 1980.

Partridge: Eric Partridge, *Usage and Abusage*. London, Hamish Hamilton, 1959 edition.

RHD: *Random House Dictionary of the English Language*. New York, 1987. Second edition.

Strunk and White: William Strunk and E. B. White, *The Elements of Style*. New York, Macmillan, 1979. Third edition.

Webster III: *Webster's Third New International Dictionary*. Springfield, Mass., Merriam, 1961.

THE
APPROPRIATE
WORD

A

a, an/per Purists of the sort who have asserted that *television* is a bad coinage because it combines Greek and Latin roots and thus is horribly miscegenetic have also said that *per*, from Latin, should not be used as a companion for words from Anglo-Saxon. SWE discards such reasoning as nonsense. Countless comparable mixtures exist in English and other languages. In the sense of "for each" or "by each," *per* and *a* (or *an*) are usually interchangeable: "a dollar per (or *a*) gallon." *Per* is especially likely in scientific contexts. Sometimes *a* may cause some odd-sounding sentences that *per* does not. "Output a man" is harder to understand than "output per man." Bernstein found this delightful example: "Belgium is rated third, with a yield a cow a year of 3,760 kilograms of milk." SWE would prefer ". . . an annual yield of 3,760 kilograms of milk per cow."

a/some "Some man told us how to get to Staunton" is FF. SWE: "A man . . ."

abandoned/depraved/vicious Each suggests immorality, but of different sorts. The *abandoned* person indulges frequently in "sin" and is not repentant. The *depraved* person actively searches for unusual sexual experiences and goes to extremes in use of alcohol or other drugs. The *vicious* person tries to hurt others, but the most likely victim of the abandoned or depraved person is himself.

abdicate/abrogate To *abdicate* is to relinquish formally, to give up: "Edward VIII abdicated the throne." To *abrogate* is to nullify or cancel: "Spain abrogated the treaty."

ability (verb with) SWE uses *ability* plus an infinitive rather than *ability* plus *of* plus an *-ing* form: "ability *to speak*" rather than "ability *of speaking*."

ability/capacity **1.** *Ability* and *capacity* both refer to qualities enabling a person to accomplish something, and sometimes may be used interchangeably. With reference to performing a specific act, however, *ability* is more likely: "ability to solve problems," ". . . to jump high." *Capacity* is a little more general and is more likely to be inborn rather than developed: "mental capacity," "capacity for painstaking research." One definition of the word is "ability to contain." **2.** SWE tries to avoid the pompousness of sentences such as "In what capacity does he work?" It prefers "What kind of work does he do?" or "Precisely what is his job?"

abjure/adjure To *abjure* is to swear off, to renounce, to recant sol-

For meanings of abbreviations and full names of references, see page xvi.

A slash mark separating headwords indicates that they are contrasted. A comma between them indicates treatment as a unit. Capital letters signify a short general article rather than one on specific words.

emnly: "Her husband abjured drinking and gambling." To *adjure* is to command solemnly or to beg earnestly: "My father adjured me to stay out of bars."

able   For the most part, only animate beings have ability; inanimate things in general are not "able" in the usual sense of the word: "We were able to hear the ocean waves from our cottage," or "From our cottage the ocean waves could be heard," but not "From our cottage the ocean waves were able to be heard." The restriction to animate beings is usually not applied to complex or "intelligent" machines, electronic gear, and so on: "My car is able to smooth out many of the bumps." "My computer is able to produce elaborate graphics."

aborning   Used in SWE, though uncommon, for "getting started" or "while barely under way": "The strategy was yet aborning."

about (redundant)   SWE omits *about* when the context makes it unnecessary, as in "She estimated that the task would take (about) ten or fifteen hours" (*estimated* implies "about").

about/around/round (adverb or preposition)   *Around* or *round* emphasizes circularity more than *about* does. Thus "walked around (or *round)* the house" suggests a tour of the outer edges, but "walked about the house" suggests moving from one place to another but perhaps not following a circular path.

above (adjective, noun)   With the meaning "mentioned above," *above* is SWE as an adjective but may seem stiff or awkward, as in "The above accusation was impossible to prove." SWE often rephrases, possibly as "The accusation referred to earlier . . ." *Above* as a noun is also SWE, although it suggests legalistic writing: "Two witnesses confirmed the above." In most SWE, "confirmed that statement" or something similar is likely.

above/more than   SWE prefers *more than* in indicating time or measure: "more than five weeks," "more than a meter." *Above* more often suggests a physical location: "above the treetops."

abridged/unabridged   An *abridged* dictionary, such as the various editions of *Webster's Collegiate*, is shortened from a full-length, *unabridged* one, such as Webster III. To abridge is to shorten or condense.

abrogate   See ABDICATE/ABROGATE.

ABSOLUTE COMPARISONS   See **COMPARISON OF ABSOLUTES**; PERFECT.

abstruse/obscure   Something *abstruse* is difficult for most people to understand because it is complex or specialized. Most of us still consider Einstein's theory of relativity abstruse, but many scientists do understand it. Something *obscure* is perhaps not clearly understood by anyone at all. Alternatively, it may be expressed in an unclear way: "The causes of some diseases are still obscure." "Many explanations are obscure because badly written."

ABSTRACT AND GENERAL WORDS   Although abstract and general words are often needed to avoid endless lists of concrete and specific terms, many inexperienced writers use too many of them. To write effectively, one must make readers see, feel, hear, smell, and taste. *Oppression* brings forth no image, no pain, really no sensation except vague dislike and pity. But *sting of the lash* or *three years in a dank dungeon* makes readers see, feel, perhaps even hear. *Plant* draws little response, nor does *pretty flower* draw very much, but *purple petunia* evokes a colored picture and possibly the recollection of a pleasant odor. *Said* conveys only the idea that someone spoke, but *whispered* or *screamed* makes the speaker live.

The good poet and the experienced novelist and almost every other excellent writer think in concrete, specific terms. They have learned to observe, and they do not lack the power to abstract or to generalize. But because they want not merely to inform but also to portray and often to move, they generally express themselves concretely, specifically. They often use examples or metaphors to make an abstraction seem real. They frequently provide only what is needed for readers to draw their own conclusions. In doing so, they are likely to use specific language. Thus Shakespeare's King Lear, who has given his kingdom to his children and whose daughter Goneril has deprived him of most of his attendants, does not prate about "selfishness," or "unkindness," or "ingratitude." Instead Lear says, "How sharper than a serpent's tooth it is to have a thankless child!" *Sharper, serpent's tooth, child* – all relatively concrete and specific, but Shakespeare made them shape for him the abstract thought he wished to convey.

academic As in "The question is only academic." The implication of such usage may be resented by university scholars who each year considerably increase human knowledge and some of whom are responsible, intentionally or not, for inventions and discoveries that increase human comfort, add to the food supply, and prolong human life. To equate *academic* with *trivial* is insulting. To equate it with *truth-seeking* is accurate. All truths are worth knowing: that is the center of academic belief. Most SWE writing, but not all, reflects this practice: if something is unimportant or trivial, say so, but don't call it academic.

accent/accentuate In the sense of "emphasize," often interchangeable, although one or the other may sound better in context. *Accentuate* is more common with abstractions: "'Accentuate the positive' is a line from an old song," but "Accent the first syllable."

accept/except *Accept*, a verb, means "receive as satisfactory or at least passable": "She accepted her prize with a gracious little speech." *Except* is usually a preposition meaning "with the exception of": "None of the girls except Sue won a medal." *Except* may also be a verb for "to make an exception of": "Because of John's illness, the teacher excepted him from the requirement."

acceptive/receptive Someone willing to accept something may be called *acceptive*: "Today she was in an acceptive mood, believing everything he told her – in sharp contrast to yesterday's stubborn incredulity." Much more commonly used, however, is *receptive*, with about the same meaning. Some writers prefer to use *acceptive* for a general tendency to accept, *receptive* with reference to a particular thing: "receptive to the latest offer."

accessorize   A dubious modern coinage, most often used by advertisers and by salespeople suffering from inflammation of the vocabulary. Possible substitutes: *trim, add gadgets* (or *ornaments*) *to*. See also –IZE.

accident/mishap   Although an *accident* certainly may result from bad luck, *mishap* emphasizes the mischance. *Mishap* is likely to refer only to small incidents, involving perhaps the loss of a glove or stumbling over a rock but not loss of life or even a large sum of money.

accounted for by   Awkward as a synonym for *consists of*: "Most of his income consists of (or *comes from* or *is derived from*, but not *is accounted for by*) dividends from common stock."

accrue   Because of the financial and legal connotations, SWE usually avoids *accrue* in highly personal contexts. "Much happiness accrued from their marriage" suggests cold, automatic increase, like that of compound interest.

accumulative/cumulative   SWE prefers the shorter.

accustomed/inured   We become *inured* to unpleasant or perhaps painful things that keep happening to us, such as television commercials: "Prison inures convicts to boredom." We become *accustomed* to pleasures, luxuries, or even everyday events that are neither pleasant nor especially objectionable.

acme/apex/epitome   *Apex* and *acme* both refer to the highest point of something, but the former is generally used literally, the latter figuratively: "the apex of the cone," "the acme of pianistic attainment." *Epitome* has nothing to do with highest points. It may (rarely) mean a summary, as in "the epitome of this philosopher's beliefs." More often it means "an excellent representative of its type," as in "Sister Teresa is the epitome of selflessness."

acoustics (verb with)   With reference to the science, takes a singular verb: "Acoustics is the science of sound." With regard to the qualities of carrying, reflecting, or absorbing sound, takes a plural verb: "The accoustics in Avery Fisher Hall were not good at first."

acquaintanceship   SWE generally settles for *acquaintance*, and SANE applauds: "her acquaintance with Henri." The longer word still appears occasionally.

acquiesce   Usually followed by *in*: "acquiesced in the decision." Note that a person may acquiesce in a proposal even though not wholeheartedly agreeing with it. One may acquiesce merely by not opposing.

ACRONYMS   Acronyms are not mere initials but are pronounceable as words: AWOL (absent without leave), CARE (Cooperative Agency for the Relief of Europe), or SANE (which I use for Society for the

Avoidance of Needless Effort). In using an acronym that is not very well known, SWE normally identifies it when it first appears, perhaps like this: Mutual of New York (MONY).

ACTIVE VOICE   See **PASSIVE VOICE**.

activity   Overused, especially by some weather forecasters. One of them in four minutes used the word eleven times – usually preceded by *shower* or *thunderstorm*. He even predicted that "shower activity" would be "active" again the following day, when "fresh thunderstorm activity" might move into the valley. At least one viewer pushed a button to *deactivate* him.

actual, actually   SWE omits these words if no change of meaning results, as is true in these sentences: "He did not know the (actual) truth." "He (actually) sprayed paint on her."

actual fact   Because there are no "unactual" facts, SWE deletes *actual*.

acute/chronic   An *acute* illness is severe, one that may have serious consequences. A *chronic* illness is one that lasts a long time; it may or may not be severe.

A.D./B.C.   Customarily, A.D. precedes a year. *A.D. 962* means "in the year of our Lord 962" – more logical than "962 in the year of our Lord." With reference to a century, however, as in "the third century A.D.," the abbreviation follows *century*. (No one pays attention to the illogicality of "the third century in the year of our Lord.") B.C. customarily and logically follows a number: *47 B.C.* means "47 years before Christ."

ad   Short for *advertisement*. Frequently used in SWE, but most often in fairly informal contexts.

adage   An adage is an old saying, so SWE avoids the repetitiousness of *old adage*. *Old cliché* is similarly repetitious.

added fillip   Most SWE omits *added* unless a first fillip has already been named. (Few people seem to know that a fillip is a snap of the fingers, or a sharp tap, or anything that goads, stimulates, or excites.) "The ice dancers' costumes were startlingly ragged, and an added fillip came from their choice of ragtime music."

addicted to/dependent on   Addiction is generally harmful: "addicted to gin" but probably not "addicted to health foods." Dependency may be undesirable but is usually less difficult to overcome than addiction is: "He became dependent on prune juice as a laxative."

additional(ly), in addition   SWE omits any such word if the sentence already has *more, another, add*, or the equivalent: "(In addition), one more point must be made." "Add (an additional) window on this side."

address/lecture   Unlike a speech, an *address* is likely to be formal and most likely is delivered by a prominent person; it ordinarily concerns a topic of wide significance, such as an international treaty. A *lecture*, too, is likely to be somewhat formal or at least carefully prepared for, but it is more likely to concern a narrow or specialized topic:

5

"Today the topic of the professor's lecture was the mating habits of earthworms."

adequate This word is often used to damn with faint praise. Although the literal meaning is "sufficient to meet the need," it has come to suggest "barely enough," especially with reference to quality: "Her word-processing skills are adequate." (Use of this word might result in a decision not to hire the candidate for the job.)

adjacent/adjoining In a hotel or motel, *adjacent* rooms are usually next to each other. So are *adjoining* rooms, but they have a door connecting them. The distinction has been important in divorce suits in which infidelity has been the issue: did the defendants have unobservable access to each other? In other contexts, *adjacent* may mean either "next to" or "very near." *Adjoining* means "touching." Thus two plots of land touching at any point are adjoining.

adjure See ABJURE/ADJURE.

adjust/readjust Sometimes *readjust* is used when *adjust* would be more accurate. Unless there has been a previous adjustment, there cannot be a readjustment. In writing about adjustments or readjustments in pay or prices, SWE notes that such changes can be either upward or downward; too often only upward changes are considered, as in "Recent bad weather may result in price adjustments."

administer/minister A person given help or care is *ministered* to. The help (medicine, for example) is *administered* to him. Last rites are either administered or ministered.

admission/admittance Both are widely used in the sense of "permission to enter." Thus the signs "No Admission" and "No Admittance" are likely to be interpreted in the same way. However, the former *may* be interpreted as "No admission fee is charged." When any such ambiguity is possible, "No Admittance" is preferable.

admit to/confess to *To* is often redundant. A criminal may either *admit* or *confess* a misdeed. He or she may, of course, *admit* (something) *to* a police officer or *confess to* a priest.

adopted/adoptive Parents who get legal permission to rear a child are adoptive parents, and the child is an *adopted* child. (Some dictionaries now say that *adoptive* is possible for both senses but that a distinction is customary.)

adore FF often applies *adore* to a color of lipstick, a hairdo, a quiche, or any other relatively unimportant thing. SWE customarily restricts *adore* or *adoration* to worship or extremely high affection and respect.

advance/advanced *Advance* (adjective) indicates a time earlier than normal: "advance notice," "advance payment"; or a forward position: "the advance platoon." *Advanced* usually refers to figurative rather than actual time or position: "an advanced thinker," "socially advanced legislation," "advanced mathematics."

advance reservations, future plans Because reservations and plans necessarily involve the future, SWE omits *advance* and *future* with such terms.

advent/arrival   *Advent* is normally reserved for something of great or at least considerable importance: "the advent of better relations with Russia." *Arrival* is suitable for less significant things: "the arrival of the new spring fashions," ". . . of the mail."

adversary/antagonist/enemy/opponent   An *enemy* ordinarily shows deep and steady hostility and is regarded with strong dislike. The role of an *adversary, antagonist,* or *opponent,* however, is often of short duration: "the opponent in tonight's game," "The attorneys had been courtroom adversaries once before." An *antagonist* is especially likely to show overt hostility that may be or become physical: "The antagonists glared at each other and clenched their fists." One may like, respect, or even admire an adversary or an opponent and sometimes even an antagonist: "an antagonist (or *foe*) worthy of his steel," as the cliché has it. But one is unlikely to feel affection or admiration for an enemy, although respect may be present.

adverse/averse   A person is *averse* to something: "Mr. Willis is averse to taking separate vacations." *Adverse* is used to characterize opposing circumstances or anything else working against someone: "Adverse weather caused delays in harvesting corn." "Her adverse remarks surprised him." "He was averse to her making adverse remarks."

advice/advise   *Advice* is a noun: "to give advice." *Advise* is a verb: "The professor advised me." "The judge advised counsel that such a motion was improper." Old-fashioned business letter jargon: "Please be advised . . . ," "This is to advise you that . . ."

advisedly/intentionally   An act is performed *advisedly* if it follows careful investigation and thought. It is performed *intentionally* if it does not occur by chance. Partridge makes the point with this quotation from a professor: "Many intentional acts are not carried out advisedly."

affect/effect   To *affect* is to have an influence on or bring about a modification in: "Her illness affected her disposition." To *effect* is to cause or to bring about: "The new law effected a reduction in bankruptcy declarations." As a noun, *effect* means "result or outcome": "an unexpected *effect* of the medicine," "Whatever affects a wife has an effect on her husand." As a noun (a rare use), *affect* is largely a psychological term for "emotion."

affirmative/negative   SWE avoids these words if *yes* or *no* will suffice. It prefers "She said no" to "She answered in the negative."

affluent/opulent/rich/wealthy   *Rich* is the all-embracing and therefore least specific of these words. An *affluent* person is rich enough to buy almost anything possessable that he or she wants. The word often connotes comfortable but unostentatious luxury. An *opulent* person wants, buys, and especially likes to display possessions and

7

perhaps achieve social prestige. *Opulent* may also be used to describe things: "opulent furnishings." *Wealthy* implies a stability that may be less characteristic of the other words. A wealthy family, for instance, often has possessed wealth for two or more generations. SWE tends toward but does not uniformly observe these distinctions.

aforementioned Useful legalese. Too stiff in most other contexts.

after my own heart "A man after my own heart" means "a man I am fond of because we are alike in some important ways." The expression is a cliché, but it does have the advantage of brevity.

after the end of "After the end of the war" is longer but no better than the SANE-approved "after the war."

afterward, afterwards Interchangeable.

again See RE- + AGAIN OR BACK.

age, aged, ages These words can often be omitted: "a boy of twelve" rather than "a boy of age twelve" or "a boy aged twelve." Similarly, "children four to six" rather than "children of the ages of four to six." "At sixteen" is much better than the redundant "at the age of sixteen years old."

agenda (verb with) A Latin plural meaning "things to be done." But in English the meaning has shifted to "a list of things to be done," so *agenda* is now almost always treated as a singular. The plural *agendas* ("lists of things to be done") is also not uncommon in today's SWE, despite the anguish of people who know Latin and consider a double plural as bad as bigamy or a double negative. The singular *agendum* is rare. It refers to one item to be done.

aggravate/annoy, irritate Conservatives still insist that *aggravate* can mean only "to make worse," as in "The damp weather aggravated my cold." In SWE, however, the meanings "annoy, irritate, vex" are no longer rare, even though the usage aggravates (vexes) many people. The shift is one example of a formerly FF usage that has become frequent in SWE.

agnostic/atheist An *agnostic* does not know whether God exists. An *atheist* believes that God definitely does not exist.

agonize, agony Used in SWE only for acute pain and suffering, usually prolonged. Dubious: "When I first glanced at the examination questions, I was in agony."

ah/aw Although the distinction is not always made, *ah* goes with something pleasant, *aw* with the unpleasant: "Ah, what an aroma!" "Aw, this place stinks!" Both are FF, of course.

ahold FF says, "They took ahold of both ends." SWE says, "They took hold . . ." In sentences where *a hold* is needed, it is written as two words: "The swimmers secured a hold on the edge of the raft."

aid/aide Today the spelling *aide* is usual with reference to a person: "a military aide," "aide-de-camp," "an aide to the president." Sometimes the spelling *aid* is used for a person, but SWE customarily uses that form for something inanimate. There is an obvious difference between "a nurse's aide" and "a nurse's aid (*help* or *tool*)"; the choice of spelling makes the distinction clear. A disposable thermometer is an example of a nurse's aid. Another sense is illustrated in "An intern came to the nurse's aid."

aim to   As in "They aim to arrive before dawn," the expression was once regarded as nonstandard American dialect, but it is now SWE in both the United States and England. However, it still has a more folksy air than *intend to* or *strive to*.

ain't   Although used at least occasionally in the speech of many – perhaps most – Americans, *ain't* in most writing and in semiformal or formal speaking is still regarded as slovenly. It is sometimes defended because the contraction is brief and was used by some of the Founding Fathers, and because *amn't* is awkward and never has caught on. *See also* AREN'T I.

air (verb)   Sometimes used in SWE as a synonym for *broadcast*: "The network will air the program tomorrow." Journalists, however, tend to overuse the word in other senses, as equivalent to *discuss, explain, justify, explore, make clear*, or what have you: "Congressman Adams will air his views today."

a.k.a. (also AKA, aka)   An abbreviation for "also known as": "We added a spoiler, a.k.a. an air dam." Its use has grown in recent years, but it may still puzzle many people. SWE geneally reserves it and other abbreviations for space-saving purposes, but sometimes uses it where the more familiar *alias* would fit as well.

akin   See KIN.

à la   French for "in the," elaborated to "in the manner of." SWE in a few expressions such as *à la carte, à la king* (although *la* is feminine and *king* masculine), and *à la mode* ("in fashion" but now more frequently "with ice cream"). The *à* is now often printed without the accent mark. *À la* in recent years has been used tiresomely and not always clearly with people's names: "dresses à la Oleg Cassini," "poetry à la Edgar A. Guest," "smiling à la Ronald Reagan," "bats à la Hank Aaron."

albeit   This synonym of *although* once seemed to be dropping out of the language, then came part of the way back, but still is not frequent in SWE and is almost nonexistent in FF. *Although, though*, and *even if* do the job well enough, but *albeit* can impart an old-time touch reminiscent of a Dickensian lawyer's office.

alias   See A.K.A.

alibi (noun, verb)   Technically, an *alibi* is evidence that a person was elsewhere when a misdeed was committed. SWE says, "His alibi was that he was working on his novel when the bank was robbed." In FF and much less often in SWE the word is substituted for *excuse*, as in "His alibi was that his hand slipped." A rarer FF use, as a verb, is derived from that sense: "'My hand slipped,' he alibied."

all during   *All* may be redundant. Instead of "all during the year," SWE may prefer "during the year," "during the whole year," "throughout the year," "all year," or "all year long."

all ready (adjective)/already (adverb)   *All ready* means "completely prepared, completely available": "We are all ready to eat." (Note that *all* can be omitted without affecting the meaning.) *Already* means "previously" or "at this early time": "She has already spent the money." "She has already arrived."

all right/alright (adverb)   *Alright* often appears in FF letters and the like, but most SWE users consider it no better than *alwrong* would be.

all that (adverb)   FF in such expressions as "the news wasn't all that bad." SWE: "The news was less bad than they expected" or "Not all the news was bad."

all the farther   *As far as* appears more logical and is much more common in SWE: "This is as far as I can go." *All the farther* appears often in FF. Similar comments apply to "This is all the higher I can reach," "all the taller it will grow," and countless others. See also AS FAR AS; FARTHER/FURTHER.

all together/altogether   *All together* means "as a group": "Sheep often move all together, cows usually in a crooked line." *Altogether* means "in all" or "entirely": "Altogether there are three bushels in the two piles." "That is altogether too many potatoes for us."

all told   Equivalent to *in all* or *altogether*, as in "Her mother counted twenty-seven of Mary's excuses, all told." *All told*, however, is less widely used than its synonyms and has suffered from feeble jokes, such as "That night she kissed sixteen boys. All told." The origin of the phrase lies in an old meaning of *tell*, "to count," as in "A nun was telling her beads." *All told* thus is literally "counting all, counting everyone or everything."

all-around/all-round   SWE uses either one to mean "versatile," as in "an all-around athlete" and "an all-round athlete." See also ROUND.

allege   This verb suggests something bad: "He is alleged to have been a spy," but not "He is alleged to have been a good Samaritan." The journalistic "alleged murderer" is intended to protect the media against a possible libel suit, and perhaps does so to a degree, but by itself may not fulfill that purpose, especially if no grand jury or other authority has actually alleged the crime. In other words, SWE avoids writing that something has been alleged if it is impossible to prove an official allegation.

allergenic/allergic   People may be *allergic* to dust, chocolate, and so on, but the dust or chocolate itself is *allergenic* ("allergy-creating"). Some products are correctly advertised as *nonallergenic*.

allergic/antipathetic   A person may be *allergic* to pollen or many other substances. In FF (informally or humorously) many of us are also allergic to work, a person, a theory, or almost anything else. In SWE a more accurate word or expression is preferred: *antipathetic* (rather stiff), *against, averse to, not friendly toward*, and so on, unless an allergy is actually involved.

allision/collision Although *collision* is used for the forceful meeting either of two moving objects or of a moving and a stationary object, a valuable but seldom-used word for the latter is *allision*. Reporters and lawyers in particular should find *allision* useful in making distinctions. It refers, for instance, to an auto hitting a telephone pole or a parked vehicle: "Allisions in parking lots are frequent." The verb form of *allision* is *allide*: "The car swerved and allided with a stone wall."

ALLITERATION SWE avoids alliteration in most prose. Some readers of poetry applaud the humming *m*'s in Tennyson's "The *m*oan of doves in i*mm*emorial el*m*s,/ and *m*ur*m*uring of innu*m*erable bees," but in prose the repeated sounds call too much attention to themselves. Even in poetry, alliteration is less frequent than it once was.

allude/refer These words are often used interchangeably, but many careful writers of SWE use *allude* in the sense of "hint" or "mention indirectly": "She did not say so, but may have been alluding to a burglary." *Refer*, in contrast, names directly: "She referred to a burglary at the Ellisons'."

allusion/illusion An *allusion* (see also ALLUDE/REFER) is an indirect or brief reference: "Dr. Brady made only one allusion to previous research." An *illusion* is a mistaken impression or belief, or something imagined rather than real: "Millions of people still share the illusion that the world is flat."

ALLUSIONS Most good writers are allusive. They make many of their points by alluding or referring to people, events, ideas, or things that their readers are likely to know about and that help to clarify or brighten parts of their writing. Here are a few suggestions for selecting allusions:

- Keep in mind the prospective readers. If you mention Joe DiMaggio, can they identify him? Will they understand that "Milton's mighty line" has to do with blank verse, not with part of the football team of a small Wisconsin college?
- In writing for a large readership, avoid inside jokes, local references, or news events that may soon be forgotten.
- The Bible and Shakespeare's works are better known to the English-speaking world than any other books. For this reason they are still among the richest sources of allusions and quotations. Don't misquote or give even a slightly incorrect source. Verify, no matter what the source is or how sure you are of the wording.
- Choose no allusion that does not serve a useful purpose. Don't show off. Allusions should be relevant and enlightening.
- The best allusion is one that comes unbidden to your mind as a natural outgrowth of your thinking about the subject.
- In spite of the limitations just suggested, the whole world *is* your oyster. Everything you know is related to or at least parallel to

countless other things. Each time you use an allusion, you may help your readers to see one or more of those relationships and parallels.

almighty dollar Cliché. Now that the U.S. dollar is much less powerful than it was when Washington Irving coined the phrase in 1836, we may as well give up the adjective.

almost/most (adverb) In FF such expressions as *most all* and *most anybody* are customary, but in SWE *almost all, almost anybody,* and the like are usual. *Most,* however, has been crossing the line recently and has brevity to commend it.

almost, much, sometimes, somewhat (no hyphen after) In SWE no hyphen is placed after such adverbs when they modify a following adjective: "an almost uncontrollable temper," "a much debated question," "a sometimes unnecessary declaration," "a somewhat misleading statement."

alms The word has an *s*; not "an alm." Generally, the verb in SWE is plural: "His alms were generous," although the singular is occasionally seen.

along with, as well as, in addition to, together with None of these phrases determines whether the verb is singular or plural: "Horace, along with (*as well as, in addition to, together with*) other Roman poets, was (not *were*) popular in the eighteenth century" (the subject of the sentence is *Horace*). Contrast with "Several other Roman poets, as well as Horace, were (not *was*) popular . . . ," in which the subject is *poets*.

alongside (of) *Of* is not needed. Seldom SWE: "The car was abandoned alongside of a row of poplars."

aloud See OUT LOUD.

already See ALL READY/ALREADY.

already existing SWE usually deletes *already*, which generally is redundant.

alright See ALL RIGHT/ALRIGHT.

also *Also* is seldom used in SWE for *and* in a series. In: "Bolivian mines yield tin, silver, copper, zinc, lead, also a little gold," SWE usually would substitute *and* for *also*, or possibly insert it before *also*. *Also* is occasionally used, however, in a sentence such as "She is tall, also slender."

altar/alter An *altar* is likely to be in a church. To *alter* is to change or to castrate.

altercation An *altercation* is a quarrel or an argument but does not ordinarily involve physical force: "The altercation did not degenerate into a fistfight."

alternate/alternative Usually the adjective *alternate* refers to taking turns, changing back and forth: "Baseball teams have alternate turns at bat." *Alternative* refers to choices: "You may select from three alternative chemical processes." With reference to substitution, however, either word may be used: an alternative plan is the same as an alternate plan. See also ALTERNATIVE.

alternative Because *alternative* is derived from Latin for "another," some purists have argued that it must refer to one of only two choices. In real life, however, three or more choices (alternatives) are often possible. So SWE does not follow the purist line here, but writes, "She suggested four alternative plans," ". . . several alternatives." See also ALTERNATE/ALTERNATIVE.

although/though *Although* is a little more formal than *though* and is more likely to be the choice for the beginning of a sentence: "Although (or *Though*) Congress rejected a similar bill, the President expects this one to pass." *Though* more commonly introduces a later clause, especially if it is short and in a relatively informal context: "It may rain, though I doubt it." After *even, though* (not *although*) is required.

although/while *While* can be used to mean either "during the time that" or "although," with the former more common, as in "While the debate was going on, people outside the hall began to shout and mill around." The meaning "although" is illustrated in "While the debate was intended to present opposing views, the debaters seemed to be largely in agreement." A problem arises if readers cannot be sure which meaning is intended or at best are momentarily confused: "While the cloth is woven in Alabama, the sewing is done in Mexico." In such a sentence, SWE chooses *although*.

although See also ALBEIT.

alumna (and so on) *alumna*: female former student; *alumnus*: male former student; *alumnae*: female former students; *alumni*: male former students, or male and female former students as a group: "alumni of the University of Maine." Note that graduation is not a requirement for being an alumnus or an alumna. If completion of a degree program is to be shown, SWE uses *graduate*: "Graduates are fewer than alumni."

A.M./P.M. May be written with lowercase or capital letters. Printers often use what they call "small caps." SWE does not use these terms with *in the morning* or *at night* because of redundancy.

amateur/novice A *novice* is one just starting, usually in a kind of work or a game. He or she may be either an amateur or a recently turned professional: "a novice in (or *at*) tennis," "a novice printer." A religious novice is taking preliminary or probationary training. An *amateur* is a "lover" in the sense that he or she engages in something not for money but because of liking it. In sports an amateur is one who is not paid for participating, although possibly very proficient.

amazing/astounding These are strong words that in SWE are not cheapened to mean only "unusual." If the thing being described does not truly amaze or astound, a more workaday substitute can certainly be found. Prices of eggs or soap powders, for instance, are not likely to be amazingly or astoundingly low (or even high). Rents for apartments in large cities – well, maybe.

ambiance/environment *Ambiance* (also spelled *ambience*) ordinarily refers to atmosphere, tone, taste, and attractiveness as well as to strictly physical things. It is likely to be associated with wealth and man-made comforts, not with hovels or glades. *Environment* is a much broader term, applicable to any kind of surroundings.

AMBIGUITY Although William Empson's classic in literary criticism, *Seven Types of Ambiguity*, demonstrated that ambiguity in poetry is often important or even essential, in most prose a twofold meaning is undesirable and usually confusing.

Lexical ambiguity involves two meanings for the same word. Is a *fine* comb one that is expensive and perhaps bejeweled, or is it one with thin, closely set teeth? Does a sign that says "Fine for Fishing" tell the angler that he is likely to catch fish there or that he may be fined if he tries? Structural ambiguity, more common, appears in various forms, and sometimes a sentence that is clear when spoken is unclear when written. Thus "It was another moving day for the Allen family" may mean that the family was again transporting its belongings or that the day was a highly emotional one. The intonations of speech may show which meaning is intended. Professor Norman Stageberg, in articles in the *English Journal*, once classified structural ambiguities. Some of the following examples have been borrowed from him. He says that modifiers of nouns cause much of the trouble. Is "a wonderful cold morning breakfast" a cold breakfast or one for a cold morning? Is "modern English teaching" the teaching of modern English or the modern teaching of English? Is "a French teacher" French or a teacher of French? Is "a black man's hat" a hat of a black man or a hat that is black? Would you stay at the Little Charm Motel?

When several nouns follow an adjective, how far does the adjective reach? In "fat hogs, sheep, and cattle," are only the hogs fat or all three kinds of animals? "Antique lamps and pottery" probably means that both are antiques, but we cannot be sure. What is the Temporary Spouse Membership Card offered by a chain of motels?

Two or more words with the last followed by a phrase or a clause may cause the reader to wonder whether the modifier applies to one or to all. A catalog description says that shirts are available in "gray, blue, or tan with white stripes." Do the gray and blue shirts have white stripes? Stageberg quotes from students' papers: "Zola was able to describe the characters, the places they went, and the things they did very well." "He used an arm stroke and a kick which propelled him rapidly through the water." Phrases and clauses also cause trouble when they may conceivably refer to either one of two terms or to both. In "She sat looking at the children in the house," was she in the house, were the children, or were both? In "We went to a restaurant on Palm Street which was gaily decorated for the Christmas season," what was decorated? (The use of *which* in this example points up the fact that much ambiguity is caused by faulty reference of pronouns. Many a *he, she, it,* or *they,* and not only *which,* is impossible for readers to pin down.) Adverbial modifiers create their own share of ambiguity. Stageberg quotes "the bottle on the table there." Is the bottle or the table "there"? In "I hit the man with the bottle," who had the bottle?

Common sense and trying to put oneself in the readers' place can eliminate most ambiguities. See also **ANTECEDENT**; WHICH.

ambiguous/equivocal Both words describe statements that can be interpreted in two or more ways: "She enjoys interesting men." *Ambiguity* is usually unintentional, except sometimes in poetry or in humor. But an *equivocal* statement is an intentionally deceptive one. The advertising claim "All prices slashed up to 50 percent" is equivocal because it suggests large, storewide reductions, but it may mean that most items are reduced, say, 1 percent, and that perhaps no more than one or two items have a 50 percent reduction. See also WEASEL WORDS.

ambivalent Ordinarily, *ambivalent* in SWE means "having conflicting feelings and thoughts," such as simultaneous liking and disliking. But even in SWE the word has lost clarity, often being diluted to "different," as in "There will be ambivalent effects of the new tax." Such weakening can lead to the death of a valuable word.

ambivalent/vacillating (adjective) A person who cannot decide whether to favor one thing or another is *ambivalent*; he or she may see strong arguments on each side. The person is *vacillating* when changing his or her mind, especially when moving from one opinion or solution to a second, a third, or even more. The vacillating person is likely to seem wishy-washy and indecisive; the ambivalent person, thoughtful but not yet decided.

amend/emend *Emend* is a specialized term, used to refer to editing (making changes, corrections, improvements) in written or printed copy: "She emended the text by making the punctuation consistent and by correcting several factual errors." *Amend,* the more common word, may be used in various contexts, such as "amending ('adding to') the Constitution," "amending (or *mending*) one's ways," "amending earlier practices."

America, American *America* and *American* should cover North, Central, and South America. Generally, though, other nations resignedly accept the usurpation of the term by the United States. In important documents, however, *the United States* or *residents of the United States* should be used for absolute clarity, sometimes with *of America* added. Various replacements for *American* have been suggested, but none has caught on. One possibility: USan (pronounced you-*ess*-un).

amiable/amicable Usually interchangeable, although *amicable* emphasizes friendliness and peacefulness, and *amiable* suggests good nature and a smiling demeanor.

amid, amidst Interchangeable. Sometimes regarded in SWE as too literary for normal use, but either is a good, short substitute for *in the middle of* or *surrounded by*.

among/between In general, *between* is used in SWE with two persons, *among* with three or more: "the differences between you and me," "the differences among the five of us." However, when each of several participants acts individually, *between* is preferable: "A formal agreement between the six nations will be signed this week" (each nation agrees and signs, in effect, with each one of the other nations). "Between traveling, practicing, and performing, a musician may have little time for composing." FF often uses *between* where SWE prefers *among*: "Just between the four of us, I believe . . ."

amongst Often used in Great Britain for *among* but infrequently in the United States.

amoral/immoral An animal or a person with extremely low intelligence may be *amoral*, "without morals," "having no comprehension of moral standards." An *immoral* person comprehends the accepted standards but chooses to disregard them.

amount/number *Amount* is often used in FF when SWE chooses *number*. In brief, if something is countable, SWE prefers *number*: "the number of pages (*cans, apples*)," "the amount of paper (*soup, applesauce*)." Exceptions occur when actual counting is unlikely: "The amount of guns and gun parts was huge." "The amount of beans was about ten pounds." Sometimes even apples: "The amount of apples to be shipped is at least eight truckloads."

& (ampersand) See + (PLUS SIGN) AND/& (AMPERSAND).

ample Not "ample enough." *Ample* is enough. Both *ample* and *enough* mean "sufficient," but *ample* hints at more than sufficient. A man of "ample girth" probably should consider dieting.

amplify on SWE generally omits *on*.

amused See BEMUSED.

ANACHRONISM Anachronisms usually involve putting a thing or a person in the wrong historical period, but sometimes in the wrong place. An imaginary conversation between Washington and Lincoln would be anachronistic because Washington was dead before Lincoln was born. Shakespeare was anachronistic in referring to striking clocks in ancient Greece and to tigers in the New World. Language, too, can be anachronistic – for example, in the use of twentieth-century slang in a novel set in the eighteenth century.

ancestor/descendant Your *ancestors* are your parents, grandparents, and so on. Your *descendants* are your children, grandchildren, and so on. This newspaper sentence did not conform to SWE: "Ancestors of Civil War veterans can barely imagine the bitterness that once existed between North and South."

16

ancestress   *Ancestors* covers both males and females. If a special need exists to limit a statement to females, however, *ancestress* is available: "Many of our ancestresses gave birth to more children than most modern women do."

ancient   *Ancient* fashions in dress are those described by Homer or worn by the Assyrians, for instance. Ancient history is mainly that of the pre-Christian era. SWE avoids using *ancient* for something that happened last year or even five hundred years ago.

and (as sentence opener)   It's no crime or even a stylistic fault in SWE to begin an occasional sentence with *and*. Doing so is likely to suggest greater emphasis on what follows. But the use should be infrequent, because each repetition of a stylistic device reduces its force. Similar comments apply to *but*, *nor*, *or*, *so*, and *yet* as sentence openers.

and (for *to*)   FF says, "She came and saw him in June." Usual SWE says, "She came to see him in June."

and moreover   Ordinarily, SWE omits *and*.

and/or   If *and* or *or* alone will make the intended meaning clear, SWE avoids *and/or*: "There were no corrections or (not *and/or*) additions to the minutes." "Park visitors can enjoy fishing and (not *and/or*) boating." The expression is sometimes useful in business or law to indicate three possibilities involving two persons or things: *A* alone, *B* alone, or both *A* and *B*: "The CEO and/or the president must be notified at once." In ordinary prose a more graceful substitute is usually possible.

and which, and who, and whom   In SWE, used only after an earlier *which*, *who*, or *whom*; not "He was a brave leader, and whom his followers trusted implicitly" (SWE deletes *and*, or rewords). For another example, SWE may say, "Marian is a woman who works hard and who is completely honest," or, more concisely, "Marian is a hard-working, honest woman." As the examples show, a construction with *and who* and the like can often be avoided.

angle   Now SWE for "position, point of view, approach," as in "What is his angle?" "What angle shall we take in writing this news story?" "From my angle it seems that . . ."

angry with/angry at   Books on usage generally prescribe *angry at* for references to things: "angry at the table leg that broke his toe"; but *angry with* for persons: "Lois was angry with her mother." More and more, however, *angry at* seems to be taking over both functions, perhaps by analogy with the colloquial *mad at*, but perhaps also because *with* suggests reciprocity – that both persons shared the anger. Maybe Lois was the only angry person, and her mother did not reciprocate. SANE recommends *angry at*, although SWE usage is divided. You may, of course, be *angry about* SANE's recommendation.

angry/mad   A teacher once said, "I teach my students to say 'get angry' instead of 'get mad,' but I have to admit that I get mad when they disregard my advice." Older teachers insisted that *mad* necessarily means only "insane," ignoring the fact that many words have multiple meanings. Ultraconservatives still gnash their teeth when they hear or see *mad* where they prefer *angry*, but fortunately the gnashing is only figurative or their dentists' bills would be higher.

animals (*that* vs. *who*)   See DOG WHO.

annihilate, destroy, flay, manhandle, massacre, slaughter, slay, smash, thrash   Sports pages are filled with verbs of mayhem even in accounts of games in which no one suffered as much as a broken fingernail. Writers who tire of *beat, defeat, overcome, shut out*, and other accurate verbs often resort to bloody hyperbole. People who are not sportswriters can ordinarily use less violent language.

annoy   (see AGGRAVATE/ANNOY/IRRITATE.

annual   See BI-/SEMI-.

answer, reply, response; rejoinder/repartee/retort   *Answer, reply*, and *response* are used interchangeably, although *response* may suggest slightly more formal circumstances. The other three words differ somewhat. A *rejoinder* is moderately sharp and contradictory. *Retort* conveys not only sharpness but also some hostility: "His retort was, 'That's an outright lie!'" *Repartee* is quick, good-natured, and often witty.

antagonist   See ADVERSARY/ANTAGONIST/ENEMY . . .

ANTECEDENT   In grammar an antecedent is a word or group of words to which a pronoun refers. Some sentences are not clear because readers cannot be sure about the antecedents of *he, she, it, they, this, that, which, who*, or other pronouns. In "When you get the old chair out of the crate, throw it on the junk pile," is *it* the chair or the crate? In "He ordered me to build a fire under the mule, *which* I was reluctant to obey," the antecedent of *which* is unclear for a moment. The SWE principle: When you use a pronoun (especially those listed), you should ask yourself, "Will readers instantly know what this pronoun refers to?" Debate goes on about whether *which* may ever refer to the whole idea of a phrase or a clause. The modern SWE answer is "Yes, but not if any confusion is possible." This sentence is clear: "That the undertaking might be dangerous, *which* had not previously occurred to him, now became apparent." When a noun comes just before the *which*, however, the construction may be temporarily misleading. That is true of the sentence about the mule and also of this: "He disregarded the offer, *which* surprised his friends." Here, *offer* seems to be the antecedent, and readers are consequently confused for a moment.

anticipate/expect   Although *anticipate* and *expect* may often be used as synonyms, the former may seem a little pretentious, as in "We anticipate only a five-cent profit." *Anticipate* is needed, however, in the sense of doing something about whatever is likely to happen. In baseball, for example, a batter not only expects or awaits the next pitch but also may anticipate it by deciding ahead of time what the pitcher is likely to throw.

antipathetic   See ALLERGIC/ANTIPATHETIC.

anxiety/apprehension/care/concern/worry   *Anxiety* is normally longer lasting and perhaps deeper than *apprehension*. For example, one may suffer for years from anxiety about the possibility of cancer but is likely to feel apprehension about catching a cold. *Care*, often *cares*, is usually associated with responsibilities: "family cares." A *concern* most frequently is of short duration and usually has a specific cause: "Her concern was that the rain would start before two o'clock." *Worry* is likely to be long, persistent: "a farmer's worry that the coming summer will be as dry as the present one."

anxious/eager   *Anxious* is related to *anxiety*, *eager* to *eagerness*. We are anxious ("worried") about harmful things that may happen, eager about things we want to happen. In FF we may be *anxious* to see a movie, get home early, and so on, but in SWE the customary word for pleasant activities is *eager*.

any (redundant)   FF: "The apology didn't help him any." SWE generally avoids the unnecessary word: "The apology didn't help him."

any and all   SANE advises and SWE concurs: in sentences such as "Any and all offers will be considered," choose *any* or *all*, but not both.

any is/any are   *Any* may be either singular or plural, depending on context and intended meaning. In "Any of those cakes is eligible for first prize," the meaning is that any single one may win. In "If any of the pears are badly bruised, they must be discarded," the meaning is that all the damaged pears are not to be sold.

any more/anymore   In "There are not any more bills left to consider" and similar sentences in which *more* is an adjective, *any more* is written as two words. In adverbial uses, as in "Annie doesn't live here anymore," the meaning is "at present" or "henceforth, from this or that time." Both spellings are used, with *anymore* gaining. In SWE, adverbial *anymore* or *any more* appears only in negative contexts, as in the example, or possibly interrogative: "They never invite him anymore." "Will they invite him anymore?" In FF, however, especially in some dialects, it appears in positive contexts: "Young folks used to get drunk, but anymore they get high on dope."

anybody, anyone (one word or two)   As a pronoun, each is written as a single word: "Anybody (or *Anyone*) may bring a friend." In the rather rare nonpronominal use, each is two words: "The posse could not find any body ('corpse')." "If any one (single) theory seems most likely . . ." *Anybody* and *anyone* are interchangeable, although some people feel that *anyone* is slightly more formal.

anybody, anyone (verb or pronoun with)   As shown by "anybody (or *anyone*) is . . . ," each word is singular. "If anybody in these tenements is most endangered, it is the infants." Technically, and most often but not uniformly when a following pronoun refers to *anybody* or *anyone*, that pronoun also should be singular: "If anyone wants to object, *he* (or *she*, or *he or she*) should feel free to do so." In FF, however, *they* is far more widely used: "If anyone wants to object, *they* should . . ." (The reason for this widespread use of *they* is that it makes unnecessary a choice between *he* and *she*.) SWE users who are conservative or are addressing conservative readers generally choose a singular pronoun rather than *they*.

anybody, anyone (with *else*) Just as *other* is used in SWE in a sentence such as "Jack is younger than any other boy on his team," so *else* is needed in "Jack is younger than anyone (or *anybody*) else on his team." Clearly, Jack could not be younger than anyone on his own team.

anyone See ANYBODY/ANYONE.

anyplace (adverb) Divided usage is found in SWE, as in "She could not find such statistics (anyplace or anywhere)." About half of the writers on usage insist on *anywhere* in formal contexts, but the rest say, in effect, "Take your choice." So – take your choice. Similar comments apply to *everyplace, noplace, someplace*, which may be used interchangeably with *everywhere, nowhere, somewhere*.

any time/anytime *Anytime* is used adverbially: "Little Suzie answers the phone anytime someone calls." As a noun, two words are required in SWE: "Any time you select will be satisfactory."

any way/anyway/anyways *Anyways* is FF (dialectal) for *anyway*. *Anyway* (one word) is SWE for the meanings "nevertheless" and "at any rate": "They went ahead anyway." "Anyway, they did not get lost." For the meaning "in any manner," both *any way* and *anyway* are SWE: "Spell it any way (or, less often, *anyway*) you like." Obviously, two words are required in a context such as "We could not find any way through the dense thicket," in which *way* is clearly a noun.

anywhere See ANYPLACE.

anywheres This is FF; SWE drops the *s*.

apex See ACME/APEX/EPITOME.

apiary/aviary No, you'll not find apes in an *apiary*, but you will find bees. (The Latin for "bee" is *apis*.) Because the Latin for "bird" is *avis*, a place where birds are confined is an *aviary*. *Aviator* and *aviation* are from the same source.

APOSTROPHE (punctuation) Examples of SWE usage: In contractions: *I'm, he'll, she'd, doesn't, it's* (only when the meaning is "it is" or [more rarely] "it has"); the apostrophe occupies the place where one or more letters have been removed. In possessives of nouns: the Queen's English, this *doctor's* husband, these *doctors'* husbands. In decades: the *1990's* or the *1990s* or the *nineties*. In plurals of symbols, and of letters or words referred to as letters or words: +'s, two *c*'s and one *s* in *occasion*, too many *and*'s. Not in plurals of nouns: *Tomatoes* for Sale (not *Tomato's* or *Tomatoes'*); the *Browns* (not the

Brown's or the *Browns'* unless possession is shown, as in "the *Browns'* dog").

apparent   SWE checks for ambiguity. An apparent mistake, for example, can be either what appears to be a mistake (but may not be) or a mistake that is easily seen.

apparent/evident/obvious   These three words are virtually interchangeable, meaning "easily perceived or recognized." But *evident* and *apparent* do differ somewhat. Something is *evident* if clear, easily obtainable evidence (facts) can be obtained. It is *apparent* or *obvious* if it can be seen at a glance. *Apparent* and *apparently*, however, sometimes cast a little doubt on the accuracy of an observation. Thus "Apparently he is telling the truth" shows less certainty than does *evidently* or *obviously*. On a believability scale, *obviously*, *evidently*, and *apparently* rank 1, 2, and 3.

appealing   Headline: "Singer Tina Turner is Appealing." Many male readers no doubt agreed. But the story said that she was appealing a legal decision. SWE is wary of ambiguous words.

appear   Some danger of ambiguity when an infinitive follows: "She appeared to testify against the defendant." Does this mean that she seemed to testify against him, or that she made a court appearance in order to do so?

appear on the scene, arrive on the scene   SANE says, "Delete three words in each."

appendices/appendixes   Both these plurals are standard. Surgeons, however, remove *appendixes*, and books are likely to have *appendices* rather than appendixes.

appendix (verb with)   According to FF, "Her appendix *have* been bothering her again. *They* gave her trouble last year, too." Because the appendix is a single organ, SWE chooses *has* and *It*.

apply downward pressure   Hoity-toity. Why not *press down*?

APPOSITIVE   An appositive uses different words to rename something that comes just before it in a sentence: "My brother, *the captain of the team*, led the scoring." Most often an appositive is set off by commas, as in the example. When necessary for identification and not just for further information, however, it is not set off. In "Ward's son, *John*, accompanied him," the implication is that Ward has only one son, and we are told what his name is. But in "Ward's son *John* accompanied him, but his son *Frank* remained at home," *John* and *Frank* are both necessary for identification and are not set off. Other examples: "the painter *Rubens*," "Mark Twain's novel *Tom Sawyer*," "We *boys* won," "for us *boys*." If the appositive is a pronoun, it is in the same case as the word with which it is in apposition. Thus in "The two men, *Graham and he*, fled," the form *he* is in the same case as the subject, *men*. But in "A posse pursued the two men, *Graham and him*," the objective *him* is chosen because it is in apposition with the direct object, *men*. Bernstein has commented on the superiority of the "post-appositive" over the "pre-appositive." He objects rightly to the ungainliness of "Ohio Supreme Court Judge and former trial lawyer James Garfield." Much more gainly is "James Garfield, Ohio Supreme Court Judge and former trial lawyer." Even more ridiculous, Bernstein suggests, is such journalese as "West 135th Street scrubwoman and subway rider Anna Johnson" (for this, perhaps, even a normally placed appositive would not be very graceful).

apprehension   See ANXIETY/APPREHENSION/CARE . . .

approach   SWE uses *to* after the noun *approach*, but not after the verb: "The approach to the mansion was a long, narrow lane." "We approached the mansion slowly."

apt/liable/likely   Followed by *to* and referring to probability, *apt* and *likely* are interchangeable: "They are apt (or *likely*) to turn here." *Apt* may also refer to an inborn tendency, ability, aptitude: "an apt student of mathematics." Especially but not exclusively in FF, *liable* is often used as *apt* and *likely* are, to indicate probability: "They are liable to turn here." But in SWE *liable* refers most often to unpleasant or otherwise undesirable possibilities: "We are liable to encounter a blizzard," ". . . liable to lose money." In legal use, *liable* can mean "responsible": "She is liable for her husband's debts."

arbitrate/mediate   In labor negotiations a person who *arbitrates* is empowered not only to gather facts and discuss them with all disputants but also to make a decision that all are bound to accept (although some preconditions may apply). One who *mediates* has less power. He or she may serve as go-between, gather and share information, give advice, and make recommendations, but not impose a settlement.

ARCHAIC LANGUAGE   Language of a bygone period is generally avoided in SWE except when the writer is trying to reconstruct that period. A historical novelist, in writing about a medieval battle, may use old words for parts of armor (e.g., "a *greave* and a *cuisse* protected the calf and the thigh"), and the characters' speeches in the novel may be laced with archaisms typical of the era (*quoth*, *eftsoons*).

archetype/prototype   Often used interchangeably, but one distinction is frequent in SWE: An *archetype* is an early model (e.g., of a machine) that is followed with little or no change in later models. (Jungian psychology has a special definition, related to survivals of inherited characteristics.) A *prototype*, also an early model, may later be considerably modified. Thus early Fords were prototypes of the Fords driven today. The word is also used to refer to something or someone that is a typical representative of a class or group: "He was the prototype of the New Deal legislator."

area   Often can be omitted: "In the area of statistics, it is easy to mislead people." SWE here is likely to delete *the area of,* or to increase readability by writing, "Through misuse of statistics . . ." or "It is easy to mislead people by misusing statistics."

aren't I   This expression is illogical, for probably no one says "I are not?" or "Are I not?" But because the contraction *ain't* is widely condemned, *amn't* seems awkward, and *am I not* may sound forced and unnatural, *aren't I* is widely used in FF though rarely in SWE. Despite misgivings, SWE writers usually settle for *am I not*. See also AIN'T.

arguably   Overused. Dubious in "Charles is arguably a handsome young man" or "Cherry is arguably the best kind of pie." Something is arguable if it is worth arguing about or at least can be argued about intelligently. A court decision or a congressional bill is usually arguable, but such things as handsomeness and taste are likely to be considered more emotionally than thoughtfully. As the saying goes, "There can be no disputing individual tastes." *Inarguably* (or *unarguably*) means, in effect, "This is one question that has only one side."

arithmetic progression/geometric progression   1, 5, 9, 13 . . . represents an *arithmetic progression* or *arithmetic series*, in which the same number is added at each step. (The accent in the adjective is on *met*.) 3, 9, 27, 81 . . . represents a *geometric progression*, using the same multiplier each time. It is also called a *geometric series* and is related to a *geometric mean*. See also AVERAGE.

armed to the teeth.   Cliché. Few people today carry daggers or other weapons between their teeth – not even figuratively.

armed with   This expression is used in SWE mainly when referring to actual arms or something else usable in offense or defense. Satisfactory: "armed with a shotgun," "armed with convincing evidence of the defendant's guilt." Dubious: "armed with kindly words," "armed with a birthday cake."

arm-twisting   Used figuratively to mean "vigorously trying to influence; putting pressure on." Although still slightly informal in tone the expression is widely used in SWE: "The president may have to do still more arm-twisting to get his bill through the Senate."

around   See ABOUT; ALL-AROUND; ROUND.

arrest   Although *arrest* may mean merely "stop," as in "to arrest the flow of water," it more often means "to take into custody." A person who is stopped for speeding, jaywalking, or any other relatively minor infraction and who is merely given a ticket or a reprimand is not arrested in the legal sense.

arresting/impressive/striking   An *arresting* sight is one that catches attention and holds it for more than a moment. An *impressive* sight impresses the viewer by its size, majesty, or some other quality. A *striking* sight is unusual, surprising.

arrogance/conceit/haughtiness/pride/vanity   *Pride* has a good face and a bad. The good one reflects self-respect and justifiable satisfaction and pleasure; "pride in a job well done," "pride in one's children." The bad face of pride is an excessively high opinion of oneself or of one's accomplishments or possessions. This face may reveal *arrogance* ("insolent claim or show of superiority"): "the arrogance

23

of kings." Pride may also be *haughtiness*, not much different from arrogance but showing itself in supercilious looks, holier-than-thou words or insinuations, high-handedness: "the haughtiness of some wealthy dowagers." *Conceit* is false pride, the sort which "goeth before destruction," exaggerating one's own little abilities or triumphs. *Vanity* is similar to conceit but is more commonly associated with personal appearance. Arrogance, haughtiness, conceit, and vanity are snapshots of the bad face of pride, taken from different angles.

artifact An *artifact* is something made by human beings, often with the aid of tools. One does not speak, then, of dinosaur bones or similar archeological findings as artifacts, although shards (fragments of pottery) are. "Man-made artifact" is obviously a redundancy.

artificial/ersatz/fake/imitation/spurious/synthetic All suggest a replacement of a "real" or an "original" thing, and all include a hint of inferiority, although some replacements may actually be improvements. *Artificial*, as in "artificial diamonds," means "man-made, not natural." *Ersatz*, borrowed from German in World War II, means "substitute." Ersatz meat, for example, has been made from seaweed. *Spurious* and *fake* are used to refer to imitations passed off as genuine: "fake pearls," "a spurious property deed"; because of the deceptiveness, these adjectives are the most critical or pejorative. *Synthetic* means "developed in a chemical laboratory in imitation of something else": "synthetic sweeteners." *Imitation* is a broad term meaning "copied from or based on an original."

artisan/artist/artiste In today's usage an *artisan* is a skilled craftsman, such as a glassblower. An *artist* is usually engaged in the visual arts, such as painting, but anyone who does or makes attractive things can be so designated, for example, a cook, hairdresser, or dancer. *Artiste* is most likely to be applied to a performer, such as a singer, dancer, or possibly an actor. Webster III adds "often a woman," but other dictionaries make no mention of gender here. The word has a French flavor that some people like, but the *e* ending may carry a connotation of effeminacy.

as a whole/on the whole Not quite interchangeable. *As a whole* suggests that the statement is true of the whole group but not necessarily of each individual: "As a whole the police department gets more money now, but officers' salaries are down." *On the whole* is equivalent to *generally* or *for the most part*: "On the whole our national economy suffered little."

as . . . as/so . . . as Some purists prefer to use *so . . . as* in negative comparisons: "not so big as Indianapolis." SWE occasionally but not constantly draws such a distinction; more often it uses *as . . . as* in both positive and negative contexts.

as/because/since *As* or *since* may refer to either time or reason. Careful writers make clear which meaning is intended. Time: "As Roy was strolling past the edge of the crowd, he saw a female pickpocket at work." Reason: "As Roy was law abiding, he looked around for a police officer." Ambiguous: "As (*When* or *Because?*) Roy moved cautiously toward the suspect, she was unaware of her danger." Ambiguous: "Since (*After* or *Because?*) her first lift turned out successfully, she felt more sure of herself." In the ambiguous sentences, *because* or a time word is more likely than *as* or *since* to be chosen by SWE.

as concerns, as regards A sentence such as "As regards Judge Milligan, he is competent, thorough, and fair" may well be trimmed to "Judge Milligan is . . ."

as far as A weather forecaster might say, "Here's the picture as far as the clouds in the Midwest." SWE advises, "Add *are concerned* at the end to complete the clause." See also ALL THE FARTHER.

as good or better than Conservatives advise completion of the comparison more clearly by adding *as* before *or*: "Joyce's reasoning seemed as good as or better than his," or, less awkward, ". . . as good as his or better." Quality magazines, including a journal for professors of English, do often omit the second *as*, but sometimes include it. The SWE verdict: play it either way.

as/as if/like A noted author, Laura Hobson, once changed brands of cigarettes because she objected to the slogan "Winston tastes good like a cigarette should." Such strong feeling is shared by other conservatives, many of whom insist that *as* not *like* may be used as a conjunction, as in "Do (*like* or *as?*) I do." Most teachers and editors condemn conjunctive *like*, but the public uses it unhesitatingly. Shakespeare was not consistent in his choice, and sometimes preferred *like as*. So did the men responsible for the King James Bible. Fear of conservative opinion has driven some people to use *as* where it definitely does not belong: "She can run as a deer." Conjunctive *like* for *as if* or *as though* has been condemned similarly, as in "France acted like another war was imminent."

Perhaps Mrs. Hobson looks down from Heaven and thinks she might as well have stuck with Winstons or that the distinction isn't worth the fuss. She and SANE might advise other writers, "Unless you are especially eager to gain the approval of conservatives, use whichever of the words you prefer. Other folks won't notice at all." SWE wavers but still more often than not disapproves of the Winston slogan.

as if, as though Equally good. SWE uses the one that sounds better in a given sentence. In a sentence such as "It looked as if (or *as though*) it (*was* or *were?*) going to snow," SWE chooses *was* if it really did snow, *were* if it did not. The noncommittal *might snow* is also possible. See also AS/AS IF/LIKE; WISH I WAS.

as is Items that are damaged and not guaranteed are sometimes sold *as is*: at the buyer's risk. *As are* is not SWE even though several items may be involved.

as long as As an equivalent of *because*, *as long as* is most likely to appear in FF. Sometimes it is ambiguous, as in "As long as it's snowing so hard, you'd better stay in the house." (Does *as long as* here mean "because" or "while"?) In SWE *as long as* most often means "while" and less often "since" or "provided that."

as of (with a time word)   In "as of now," SWE usually deletes *as of* but may substitute "at this time." For "as of Tuesday," SWE often substitutes "on Tuesday."

as per   Largely outdated business jargon. Instead of "As per your order of June 6, we are shipping . . . ," a modern business person is likely to fax, "As you requested . . ."

as such   This expression usually can be omitted without affecting meaning: "Athletes (as such) constitute a sizable part of the entertainment industry." Possible: "Her letters as such were not masterpieces, but as portrayals of an unstable mind they were fascinating."

as the crow flies   This is a cliché. The ornithology is faulty. Crows and most other birds only occasionally fly very far in a straight line, unless perhaps on long migratory flights.

as to   **1.** SWE uses the term for "concerning" in sentences such as "As to the jewels, they have not yet been appraised." **2.** In both "as to whether" and "as to why," *as to* is usually cut in SWE: "They were uncertain (as to) whether the owner permitted hunting." "The president gave no explanation (as to) why he vetoed the bill." (More compact: "The president did not explain why . . .")

as was true of, as with   Often SWE substitutes *like* for brevity: "Male deer, as is true of some other antlered animals, shed their antlers annually." (Changing to *like* saves three words.)

as well as   See ALONG WITH, AS WELL AS, IN ADDITION TO . . .

as with   See AS WAS TRUE OF/AS WITH.

ascend up   *Up* is unnecessary. Neither does anyone *descend down*. See also UP.

Asians/Asiatics   Many people from Asia prefer being called *Asians*, not *Asiatics*. Similarly, Chinese people prefer *Chinese* to *Chinamen*.

ask/demand/inquire   *Inquire* is a slightly more formal word for *ask*, but the two are in effect interchangeable. To *demand* is to ask more vigorously, perhaps from a position of authority: "'Where were you?' the sergeant demanded." Unlike *ask* and *inquire*, it may also mean "order": "Her employer demanded an apology." See also DEMAND/ORDER.

assassin/murderer   An assassin is a murderer, but most murderers are not assassins. An assassin (1) kills a well-known person, and (2) does so for political reasons.

assay/essay (verbs)   To *assay* is to examine chemically or test or assess in some other way: "To assay gold is to determine its purity and value." To *essay* is to try or try out: "He essayed reopening the lawsuit." This verb is less often used than in the past.

assemblage/assembly   *Assembly* refers to a meeting of an organized group of people, such as a school assembly or the General Assembly of the United Nations. An *assemblage* is often less formally organized and need not consist of people: an assemblage of starlings, of wheels and bolts, of transoceanic passengers.

assert See CLAIM.

assignation/assignment Referring to a secret meeting between lovers, SWE uses *assignation*. *Tryst* and *rendezvous* are other possibilities. In legal use, the transfer of property, rights, or interest may be called either an *assignation* or an *assignment*. Although dictionaries give *assignment* or *the act of assignment* as synonyms of *assignation*, teachers and students always use *assignment* in referring to a prescribed academic task.

assume/presume SWE often uses these words interchangeably, but some writers attempt a rather subtle differentiation. With the meaning "suppose," *assume* includes the idea of taking something for granted, but with little supporting evidence: "She assumed that her husband, as usual, would call from the airport when he returned." *Presume* is more like *guess*; we presume something that we consider reasonable, even though there may be no evidence at all: "I've never met her young friend, but I presume that he is at least old enough to tie his own shoes, if not his own necktie."

27

assumed name/pen name/pseudonym *Assumed name* has connotations of criminality because newspapers often refer to the *assumed name* or *alias* of a criminal. *Pseudonym* (false name) is less likely to have such connotations. *Pen name* (French *nom de plume*) should be reserved for writers. See also A.K.A.

assure SWE insists on an object: "Congressman Myers assured (us, his hearers, his constituents, and so on) that he would not vote for new taxes."

astounding See AMAZING.

astronaut/cosmonaut These Greek ancestral words are translated respectively as "star sailor" and "space sailor," but the work of each person is approximately the same. Americans prefer the former term, Russians the latter (*kosmonavt*).

astronomical SWE does not use the word with relatively small numbers. Dubious: "She paid an astronomical price for those slippers."

at (unnecessary) 1. SWE omits *at*, but FF sometimes keeps it, in sentences such as "Where is it at?" 2. SWE checks to see whether *at* is needed in such expressions as "at about" or "at around." *At* is not needed in "The plane will arrive at about (or *at around*) three o'clock," but is needed in "The land was bought at about (or *at around*) a thousand dollars an acre."

at the corner (intersection). Wordy. Why not "at First and Maple" instead of "at the corner of . . . "?

at the present time/at this time Both often occur in SWE, but SANE says they waste words. The first is a rather stately way to say "now" or "today" or "this year." Good writers first note whether an expression of time is needed at all. If it is, they see whether a shorter substitute will do as well. *At this time* is not stately and usually is not superior to *now*. See also POINT IN TIME.

at the rear of Will *behind* suffice?

at this juncture SWE usually downshifts to *now* or *then*.

atheist See AGNOSTIC/ATHEIST.

athletic/athletics An *athletic* coach is one who himself or herself engages in sports. An *athletics* coach might be confined to a wheelchair; he or she coaches athletes who engage in athletic contests.

atrocious A strong word, related to *atrocity*: "an act of unspeakable cruelty." SWE uses it only when something deserves such strong condemnation. It ordinarily does not apply the word, except humorously, to jokes, stories, or somebody's looks.

attached hereto/attached together *Attached hereto* is a phrase from an old-fashioned business letter. In *attached together*, SWE deletes *together*.

attack/assault/rape The newspaper practice of using *attacked* or *assaulted* because they're "nicer" words than *raped* has almost disappeared, partly because frankness has increased, and partly because *attack* and *assault* have other, more common meanings.

attire This is a general word for *clothing*, but SWE often searches for a more specific word: perhaps *coat*, *dress*, *a ragged shirt*.

attorney/attorney at law/lawyer Technically, an attorney is any person, not necessarily a lawyer, legally authorized to represent someone else. But in the United States, *attorney* and *lawyer* are generally considered synonymous. Not all attorneys are attorneys at law. An attorney at law is one who is authorized to make court appearances on behalf of clients (not all attorneys have such authorization).

attorney general (plural of) Formally, *attorneys general* is the usual plural, but because this is out of step with, for example, *major generals* or *lieutenant colonels*, the usage is gradually shifting to *attorney generals*.

au naturel (1) Note the spelling. (2) Why not say *nude* or *naked* instead of resorting to a cutesy French phrase?

audience/congregation/spectators Basically, an *audience* hears (e.g., a concert or a lecture), *spectators* watch (e.g., an athletic event), and a *congregation* worships together. Obviously, hearing and seeing – and even worshiping – often occur simultaneously.

aught/naught These old-fashioned words are on rare occasions still seen in SWE in expressions such as "for aught he knew," "all for naught." See also NAUGHT/NOUGHT.

augment/supplement To *augment* means "to increase," "get more of the same thing": "The candy company augmented its supply of sugar by purchasing huge quantities of it from other Caribbean countries." To *supplement* means "to add something," usually of a different sort: "The candy company supplemented its supply of sugar by purchasing artificial sweeteners."

aural/oral *Aural* refers to hearing, *oral* to speaking.

authentic/genuine   Almost but not quite, interchangeable in SWE. *Authentic* suggests that experts can attest that the object is really what it is claimed to be: "an authentic signature, according to handwriting analysts." *Genuine* lacks the connotation of examination by experts but does not preclude such examination: "These look like genuine rubies."

author (verb)   Increasingly, a usage such as "She has authored seven books" is seen in SWE. Although some people object to this conversion of noun to verb, it is defensible on the ground that "authoring" involves not only writing but also gathering material, planning, revising, typing and perhaps retyping, and sometimes helping to sell.

automatic/pistol/revolver   A *pistol* is any handgun. One variety of pistol is a *revolver*, in which a cylinder holds the cartridges and revolves slightly after each shot, ejecting the spent shell and moving in a replacement. An *automatic*, another variety, has no cylinder; it uses recoil to eject a shell, insert a new one, and recock the weapon, which will fire again if the trigger is still being pulled.

automation/mechanization   When a job formerly done by one or more persons is done by a machine, we refer to *mechanization*. But if a machine or machines are controlled by a thermostat or by any sort of electronic device, the result is *automation*. A fully automated factory would have all its machines under the "supervision" of one or more electronic "brains," although sometimes human beings might have to repair both the brains and the machines.

avenge/revenge   The distinction is not clear-cut, but some writers believe that *avenge* usually has as its subject a person other than the one who was harmed: "He avenged his sister." "He avenged her death." The subject of *revenge* is most often the person wronged, and its object is likely to be *himself* or a similar word: "He revenged himself (or *gained revenge*) for Dora's being unfaithful to him."

aver   An increasingly rare substitute for *say, state, declare. Aver* suggests more force or confidence than does *say.* It is unlikely in informal contexts.

average   SWE omits *each* or *apiece* with *average.* An average is based on two or more items. Illogical: "These chickens each average three pounds" or ". . . average three pounds apiece." Logical: "The average weight of these chickens is three pounds" or "These chickens average three pounds." If the chickens consistently weighed three pounds *each* or *apiece, average* could be superseded by one of those words.

average/common, ordinary   *Average* is not a synonym of *common* and *ordinary* in SWE. The latter words mean "familiar, usual." But a description of an average man (if one existed) would result from arithmetical calculations based on size, age, intelligence, and all other characteristics of all the men in the world.

average/mean/median   All three words refer to averages, but of different kinds. To find the *average*, as the *arithmetic mean* is commonly called, of the five numbers 3, 4, 6, 13, and 14, add them and divide by five. (Answer: 8.) There is also a *geometric mean*, which is the *n*th root of a product of *n* factors. To find this for two numbers, multiply the two and take the square root. For instance, $4 \times 36 = 144$. The square root of 144 is 12, the geometric mean of 4 and 36. (The *average* would be 20.) For three numbers, the cube root of the product of the three is taken; for four numbers, the 4th root. Statisticians say that when highly disparate numbers are involved, the geometric mean is less deceiving than the arithmetic mean. For example, if populations of three places are 500, 14,000, and 7,000,000, the arithmetic mean is c. 2,338,167, but the geometric mean is 36,593. To find the *median*, arrange the numbers in order and see which is the middle one. For 2, 4, 7, 10, and 15, the median is 7. When the sequence consists of an even number of items, the median is the average of the two middle items. For 3, 4, 7, 11, 13, and 14, the median is 9.

averse   See ADVERSE/AVERSE.

avert/avoid/prevent   *Avert* may mean "turn away": "Marjorie averted her eyes from the horrible sight." It may also be a synonym of *prevent* or *ward off*: "Clyde averted a crash by making a sharp right turn." *Avoid* means "stay clear of, shun": "The best way to avoid being disbelieved is to tell the truth."

aviary   See APIARY/AVIARY.

avocation/vocation   An *avocation* is a hobby. A *vocation* is one's life work, or a "call," for example, to the ministry.

avoid like the plague   This is a cliché. SWE follows the advice.

avoid   See AVERT/AVOID/PREVENT.

aw   See AH/AW.

awake   SWE has a rich variety of choices for the past tense of a verb meaning "stop sleeping": *awoke, awakened, awaked, wakened, waked, woke*, or *woke up*.

award/reward   In general an *award* is given for "long and distinguished service," as the cliché has it. A *reward* usually is for a particular act, such as the familiar "$5,000 reward for information leading to the arrest and conviction of . . ."

awesome   This fad word is often used in FF to mean "big," "surprising," or "very (almost anything)." A young California boy used it in accordance with SWE after his family survived a moderately strong earthquake: "It was *awesome*." One dictionary definition is "filling with respect tinged with fear."

awful   The historic meaning of *awful*, "awe-inspiring," is now so little known that "God is awful" sounds blasphemous. The meaning has switched to "bad, extremely unpleasant," or in some dialects to "good, praiseworthy." In SWE those meanings are not objectionable, but in precise writing a less chameleonic term is desirable – perhaps *terrifying, horrifying, dreadful*, or *awe-inspiring* – to fit different contexts.

awfully The comments on *awful* apply here. *Awfully* in FF as a rule modifies an adjective and means "very": "awfully stupid." In SWE *awfully* may be omitted or replaced by *extraordinarily, unbelievably*, and so on.

awhile (adverb)/a while (noun) "Stay awhile" illustrates the adverbial use, comparable to "Stay here." "Stay for a while" is a noun use, comparable to "Stay for an hour." "Stay a while" is being used increasingly in SWE.

B

babe/baby In SWE *baby* is almost always used, although *babe* survives in hymns, the cliché *babe in the woods*, and elsewhere. *Babe* suggests even more innocence and lack of experience than *baby* does: "a mere *babe*." (Probable exception: the grown "babe" who is addressed as "Babe.") In talking to an infant affectionately, some adults may say, "Don't cry, babe."

baby boom/baby boomer After World War II (c. 1947–1955) an unusually high birthrate prevailed in the United States and many other countries. As a result the period was called "the baby boom." The term now appears unlabeled in dictionaries. So does *baby boomer*, for a person born during the boom. Both are SWE.

baby boy (girl) In expressions such as "gave birth to a baby girl," *baby* is redundant. All boys and girls are babies when they are born.

baby/child/infant In legal terms an *infant* is any minor, and a *child* is a son or daughter of any age whatsoever; *baby* is not a category in the eyes of the law. In customary SWE, with some exceptions, *baby* and *infant* are interchangeable, with *baby* being more frequent; each usually signifies a boy or girl from birth to the out-of-diapers or weaned age. *Infant* is often, but not consistently, used for a very young baby. *Child* is used for those between infancy and puberty.

bachelor Any unmarried man, even if previously married, is a *bachelor*. Some women dislike the fact that there is no feminine equivalent, although *single woman* may be used. *Bachelorette*, although listed in dictionaries, has never caught on because of the diminutive, condescending, "cute" sound, and *bachelor girl* doesn't sound appropriate for a woman of fifty. Perhaps we should start using *bachelor* for both sexes, as we do *officer, bartender*, and many other words.

back See RE-.

BACK-FORMATIONS See ENTHUSE.

back of/in back of *In back of* is mainly FF. *Behind* and (less often) *back of* are SWE.

bad These uses are FF: *Bad* (or *badly*) *off*: "His health is poor. He's really bad off." "Financially, he's not bad off." *In bad*: "She's in bad with the law" (SWE: *in trouble*). *Not half bad*: "This pie is not half bad" (understatement for "very good").

bad/badly   See FEEL (GOOD/WELL).

badmouth   FF (slang) for "speak unfavorably of." Sometimes hyphenated.

bag and baggage   Earlier, *bag* referred to items belonging to an entire military unit, and *baggage* to personal belongings. At that time it made sense to say that the unit moved out *bag and baggage*. Now the expression is a cliché, as dead as those old-time soldiers.

bag/poke/sack   The words may be used interchangeably, although *bag* seems a little more common than *sack* and much more so than *poke*. Some speakers use *sack* only for a cloth container also known as *gunnysack* or *burlap bag*. *Poke* is a vanishing dialectal term, formerly often heard in the South, Midland, and West. Perhaps most familiar is the advice "Don't buy a pig in a poke."

baggage/luggage   The words are usually interchangeable, although in airports the sign *Baggage* is more likely to be seen. Stores sell *luggage*, not *baggage*. The implication is that *luggage* means especially the suitcases and trunks themselves, but *baggage* includes their contents as well. (Dictionaries, however, do not make this distinction.) See also BAG AND BAGGAGE.

bagpipe(s)   The word is *bagpipe* in the United States, *bagpipes* in Scotland, its native home. SWE uses both.

bail/bale   These words have several meanings: *bale* of hay or cotton; to *bale* hay; to *bail* water from a boat; to *bail* out from a plane; to raise *bail* for a prisoner; the *bail* of a kettle or pail.

balance   In a checking account, *balance* is the standard word for what remains after checks have cleared. But *balance* to mean the remainder of something nonfiscal is a debated usage, appearing increasingly in SWE.

balance/remainder/rest (verb with)   Usually *balance* or a similar word requires a singular verb, but when countable things or persons are referred to, a plural verb is needed: "Some of the apples were delivered to children's homes, and the *balance (remainder, rest, others) were* distributed among elderly people."

balding   Although some writers on usage dislike *balding* for "becoming bald," it is concise and comprehensible, and besides, no one objects to the comparable *graying*. Both *balding* and *becoming bald* are found in SWE.

bale   See BAIL/BALE.

balmy   Weather may be balmy, but *balmy* as an FF (slang) term meaning "eccentric" or "slightly insane" is based on a confusion with British *barmy*, referring to the foam of ale or beer and to people too well acquainted with it.

band/orchestra   The traditional distinction is that an orchestra includes stringed instruments but a band does not. The distinction has blurred in this century, however. Jazz bands often have a string bass or two, and rock bands have a string bass and one or more guitars.

bank on   This substitute for "rely on," originally a gambling term, hovers between informal and formal, and occurs fairly often in SWE.

bank/shore   *Bank* is customary for the edge of a creek or small river; *shore*, for that of an ocean or a sea, lake, pond, or large river: "the banks of the Wabash far away," "Lakeshore Drive."

barbaric/barbarous   Often used interchangeably. *Barbaric* means "crude, typical of barbarians": "the barbaric custom of eating with the fingers." *Barbarous*, although it, too, suggests crude and uncivilized behavior, adds to it the idea of cruelty: "barbarous treatment of captured enemy soldiers." Note the spelling – no *i*.

barely . . . when   See HARDLY . . . THAN.

based on   In SWE, should have something to modify. What is based on what? Dangling: "Based on a few months at the United Nations, he has concluded that peace in the Middle East is unlikely in this century." "He" is clearly not based on anything. SWE prefers "Based on his few months at the United Nations, his conclusion is that . . ."or "After spending a few months at the United Nations, he has concluded that . . ."

bash   1. *Bash* is FF for "lively or wild party." 2. It is SWE, although informal in tone, for "strike a heavy blow": "A falling tree limb bashed his head." If the blow was crushing, ". . . *bashed in* his head." 3. Related to 2, but apparently a rather recent borrowing from England or Canada, *bash* is SWE for "criticize severely, condemn," usually in the form *bashing*: "In the 1930s Roosevelt-bashing was the favorite occupation of Republicans."

basis of (or *that*)   Often *the basis of* (or *the basis that*) is wordy and can be omitted: "The students' writing was judged on (the basis of) its content, organization, and clarity."

bath   See MATUTINAL ABLUTIONS.

BATHOS   1. Bathos is a sudden and unintentional descent from elevated language to the petty, mundane, or at least relatively unimportant: "For God, for Country, and for Yale!" (Yale graduates may substitute Princeton or Harvard.) 2. A second meaning is "general dullness and commonplaceness in content or style." For instance, a political speech full of clichés about the glories of the nation, the dignity of labor, and the sacredness of motherhood could be described as *bathetic*. 3. A third meaning is "false pathos," like that of the sob sister who tries to make readers cry over the sad lot of the millionaire actress who has just been divorced by her fourth husband.

batty   Once an eccentric, somewhat demented, or even violently insane person was said in slang to have "bats in his belfry." The no-less-slangy FF *batty* is probably derived from that expression.

bazaar/bizarre   A *bazaar* (also *bazar*) is a market of a specialized kind:

33

"a church bazaar," "the bazaars of India." *Bizarre*, an adjective, means "odd, fantastic in a generally unpleasant way": "bizarre acts of crime," "bizarre ice formations."

B.C. See A.D./B.C.

be being Sometimes logical but always awkward. "He must be being operated on by now," said a relative in the waiting room of a hospital. In those circumstances no one should be a critic of language, but usually in SWE *be being* is avoided: "The operation has probably begun by now." *Is being, were being*, and the like are not objectionable. See also BEING.

beat/beaten SWE prefers *beaten* as the past participle: "was beaten" "has been beaten," "will be beaten." The informal expression "can't be beat," however, is so well established that "can't be beaten" sounds strange. (Modern dictionaries list both *beat* and *beaten* as the past participle.)

beat (up) Although most likely to be seen on the sports page, *beat* ("defeat") is SWE. *Beat up* and *beat up on* ("thrash, harm physically") are informal but not rare in SWE.

beauteous Beauty shouldn't hiss as the last sound in *beauteous* does. *Beauteous* is an unpleasant and rarely used synonym of *beautiful*.

because/for Often interchangeable. *Because* clearly indicates cause or reason: "They stayed at home because it was snowing." *For* (after a comma) normally joins two independent statements and may suggest cause, reason, or evidence. Cause or reason: "They stayed at home, for it was snowing." Evidence: "They may have decided to drive into town, for faint tire tracks remain in their driveway."

because See AS/BECAUSE/SINCE.

become/get *Become* is a little more sedate than *get*, and is sometimes pretentious. Most folks get tired, get angry, get red in the face. *Become* is fine for people who aren't folks.

befall Has an archaic flavor.

before/no later than In SWE "before Friday" means "no later than Thursday midnight." "No later than Friday" means "no later than Friday midnight."

beget The past tense is *begot*; the past participle, *begotten*. The word is archaic or biblical, especially the alternative past tense *begat*, which today is often used humorously.

behest Old-fashioned for "command" (noun): "Sir Bedivere rode away at King Arthur's behest."

behold Somewhat archaic, but still used in SWE, mainly by preachers. *Lo and behold* is also rather old-fashioned.

beholden This word is old-fashioned for "indebted" or "obligated," but is still used now and then in SWE.

behoove "It behooves me" is Shakespearean English for "I ought."

being This word is overused by inexperienced writers: "Alicia, (being) the shorter of the two girls, could not remove the shelf, (it being) just an inch above her fingertips." See also BE BEING.

being as how/being that/bein's as how   FF for *because*: "Being as how she was only seventeen, she could not order a drink."

bells/o'clock   "Four bells" is not the same as "four o'clock." A day on a ship has customarily been divided into six four-hour watches, starting at twelve, four, and eight o'clock, with a bell sounding at half-hour intervals. So four bells would signify the midpoint of a watch – two, six, or ten o'clock.

belly   SWE or FF. For no good reason some people consider *belly* somewhat vulgar, although it has served the English language well since the Middle Ages. Modern writers sometimes choose a substitute out of deference to those people, but the substitutes offer problems of their own. *Stomach* refers to only one part of the alimentary canal. *Abdomen* and *intestines* bring up pictures of clinics or hospitals and white-clad people poking and kneading. The boundaries of *midsection* are uncertain, and *tummy* is baby talk. See also TUMMY.

belly-up   FF for "dead," "bankrupt," or possibly "defeated": "He started a publishing business, but it went belly-up." *Belly up to* (e.g., a bar) is sometimes used in FF for "stand close to."

below   Objecting to the redundancy of "fell to the ground below," the late *New York Times* editor Theodore Bernstein remarked wryly, "*Below* is where the ground usually is."

bemused (adjective)   Not at all like *amused* in meaning. A person lost in thought is *bemused*: "She sat bemused by the window for an hour." (An old sense of *bemuse* ["to stupefy or confuse"] has almost disappeared from the language.)

benedict   This is a vanishing word for "a confirmed bachelor who recently married." Some purists might spell it *benedick* because it may be based on Benedick in Shakespeare's *Much Ado About Nothing*. See also BACHELOR.

benefactor/beneficiary   Kindly Mr. Lavine paid George's way through college. Lavine was George's *benefactor*. George was the *beneficiary* of Lavine's generosity. The distinction is between the giver and the receiver.

beneficent/benevolent   A *benevolent* person is literally a "good-wisher": a kindly, considerate person. He or she can also become *beneficent*, "a good-doer," by being helpful and generous to those who need assistance. Note the last four letters of *beneficent*. It is sometimes misspelled and mispronounced as *beneficient*.

beside/besides   *Beside* means "alongside, at the side of": "Walk beside him." *Besides* means "in addition (to)": "Besides, they attended a Puccini opera." "Besides the opera, they heard a concert in Symphony Hall."

best of all/. . . of any/. . . of every   SWE most often chooses *best of all*, as in Voltaire's "best of all possible worlds."

best/better   According to one version of an old story, at a pep rally before a Yale-Harvard football game the Yale coach ended his remarks with "May the *best* team win!" The Harvard coach began by asking condescendingly, "Don't you mean the *better* team?" "No," said Yale, "I brought sixty-six players – six teams. May the *best* team win!" SWE ordinarily follows the conservative use of *better* when referring to two, *best* for three or more, but an occasional "best of the two" slips in.

better than/more than   In expressions such as "better (or *more*) than a hundred yards" or "better (more) than ten pounds," SWE usage is split, with *more than* somewhat ahead. The AHD usage panel split 69–31 for *more than*, with one panelist calling *better than* "rustic and illogical. Is anything *better*, or *worse*, than a mile?"

between/among   See AMONG/BETWEEN.

between . . . and/between . . . to A • B   Note that the dot is *between* A *and* B. SWE reasons that it is illogical to substitute *to* there, or to say, as at least one weather forecaster does, "Temperatures will range between the mid-sixties *to* seventy."

between every (or *each*)   SWE users consider it nonsense to say, "Ray paused between every word" or ". . . between each word." They prefer ". . . paused between every two words" or ". . . after each word." SANE agrees.

between you and (I, me)   In SWE, always *me*, as with other objects of prepositions: "from me, to you and me, for her and me, at you and him, toward them and us." When two objects are involved, each should be the same as it would be if the other weren't there.

beyond (or *outside*) the Pale   *Pale* is used here as "palings, a fence." In medieval times *Pale* referred to English or Irish holdings in Ireland, and anyone "beyond the Pale" (an imaginary border fence) was likely to be regarded as hostile. History suggests, then, that a serious context – not a trivial one – is most appropriate for the phrase. Even then, only rather well-schooled readers are likely to understand it.

bi-/semi-   To avoid confusion in references to time, SWE uses *bi-* to mean "two" and *semi-* to mean "half." A biweekly paper is published every two weeks, a semiweekly every half week. Dictionaries define *biannual* as "every half year" and *biennial* as "every two years" or "lasting two years." Life would be simpler if *semiannual* were always used for the first of those definitions. SWE usually but inconsistently follows that practice.

bias/partiality/prejudice   *Bias* represents an inclination rather than a judgment. It is a leaning toward or away from one side of an opinion, a controversial issue, or a person or a group. *Partiality* is based on a favorable opinion and is normally revealed in some sort of action: "Tom Smothers complained about the partiality toward Dick shown by their mother." *Prejudice* is literally "prejudging," making up one's mind without considering all evidence. One is usually prejudiced *against* something, although it is possible to be prejudiced *for*.

bid (principal parts)   For "to make an offer or a proposal" and in phrases such as *bid defiance, bid fair,* and *bid in,* the principal parts are *bid, bid, bid*. For "to command" or "to utter" (a greeting or farewell), the principal parts are *bid, bade, bidden*.

biennial See BI-/SEMI-.

BIG WORDS See MATUTINAL ABLUTIONS; **PRETENTIOUSNESS**.

billet-doux Apparently the telephone call has largely supplanted the love letter, the love note, and the French word for either of those, *billet-doux*. For people who still do such writing, the plural is *billets-doux*.

billiards Takes a singular verb: "Billiards is great fun."

billion In the United States, France, and Germany, a *billion* is 1,000,000,000 – a thousand million. The British call the same number a *milliard*. The British billion is a thousand times as much: 1,000,000,000,000.

bisect/dissect To *dissect* (pronounced dis-*sect*) is to cut into parts, usually for purposes of examination. The number of parts may vary – not necessarily just two – and the parts need not be equal. To indicate cutting into two equal or almost equal parts, *bisect* is standard. Redundant: "bisect in two."

bison/buffalo The true buffalo are Asian or African animals such as the water buffalo, but the name is widely applied to the American bison, not closely related. The misnomer has long been used and perhaps causes no serious harm. "Bison Bill" would pack less wallop than "Buffalo Bill." There is also a European bison, larger but with a shorter mane and beard than the American version.

bit (with an adjective) *A little bit* for "a small amount" is slightly informal but does occur in SWE, usually with *of*: "a little bit of attention." *A little bit tired* or the like is informal. *The whole bit*, like *the whole schmeer*, is FF (informal or slang). *Bit part* (as in a play), *a bit much*, *bit by bit*, and *do one's bit* are SWE.

bite the bullet Cliché, but occasionally used in SWE for "meet the situation bravely," "accept the consequences." The phrase originated in wars of long ago, when a patient undergoing surgery would bite a soft lead bullet to keep from screaming.

bitter/bitterly (cold) SWE uses both. John Keats's line "St. Agnes' Eve – Ah, bitter chill it was!" contributed to making *bitter cold* acceptable.

bizarre See BAZAAR/BIZARRE.

black/Black Although for a while some Americans of African descent insisted on a capital letter (Blacks), most later agreed that, as in *whites*, the lowercase should suffice.

black humor/sick humor Both kinds treat in a comic way serious subjects such as alcoholism, death, AIDS, criminality, or the assumed pointlessness of life. Sick humor, however, may be more macabre, grotesque, and perverted, and more concerned with depicting small incidents than with a sustained treatment. A sick joke might concern, for example, two homosexuals on a desert island – a man and a woman.

37

blame for, blame on   Some writers on usage, including the British Fowler, have called *blame on* wrong in sentences such as "The farmer blamed his crop failure on the heavy rains." Fowler would prefer ". . . blamed the heavy rains for his crop failure." Nevertheless, *blame on* has become SWE, which uses both the *for* and *on* alternatives.

blasé/sophisticated   *Sophisticated* no longer means only "urbane, worldly." With reference to tools, robots, weapons, and other technically advanced instruments – even electronically controlled houses – SWE often uses *sophisticated* in the sense of "complex," "state-of-the-art." A truly sophisticated *person* is worldly-wise, has "been around," is aware of the conditions of people in various economic and social circumstances, knows that all human beings have strengths and weaknesses, and is willing to forgive most transgressors. A false sophistication exists also – that of the jet set or others who equate it with wealth, travel, the superficial trappings of what they consider the good life. A *blasé* person may well be one of the false sophisticates. He or she is "tired of it all," has experienced too much too soon, and is likely to pretend that a new experience is really not new, or if it is, it isn't worth getting excited about.

blatant/flagrant   *Flagrant* carries a suggestion of wrongdoing that *blatant* may not. In basketball, for instance, a foul that seems avoidable and malicious is flagrant, not blatant. "He seduced his guest's wife – a flagrant breach of hospitality." *Blatant* often suggests something glaring and unpleasant to the ears or, less often, the eyes: "the blatant, drunken laughter," "blatant colors."

blaze/blazon   One may *blaze* a trial but not *blazon* one. To blazon is to decorate, display, or loudly make known. In olden days knights wore their coats of arms blazoned (or *emblazoned*) on their shields.

BLENDS (E.G., BRUNCH)   See SMOG.

blitz   A standard word, shortened from *Blitzkrieg* ("lightning war") as practiced by the Nazis in World War II. Now SWE uses the word (both noun and verb) to refer to any intensive campaign: "With their well-filled coffers, the Republicans can afford a television blitz in the final week before the election."

blizzard   Technically, a blizzard involves much snow, persistently high wind, and sustained temperature of $-10°$ F or below. Snow alone does not make a blizzard. Figuratively, *blizzard* means an extraordinarily large number or amount of something almost at one time: "a blizzard of applications for financial help."

bloc/block   *Bloc*, not *block*, is SWE for "group united in a common cause," such as a business or legislative bloc.

blond/blonde   Usage is inconsistent in SWE. *Blond* may refer to either a male or a female, but usually a male. *Blonde* is ordinarily SWE for female. SANE recommends *blond* for both sexes. See also BRUNET/BRUNETTE.

blood, sweat, and tears   What Winston Churchill really told the

British was that winning the war required "blood, toil, tears, and sweat." The shorter version is a misquotation.

bloom/blossom Essentially interchangeable, these words refer to a flower, and phrases such as *in bloom* and *in blossom* are often used without distinction. However, *blossom* is more common with regard to fruit trees: "apple-blossom time" rather than "apple-bloom time," "the scent of orange blossoms" rather than ". . . orange blooms."

boast **1.** In the sense of "be proud to possess," *boast* has been frowned on by many good writers but seems to be gaining ground in SWE. It may be misinterpreted to mean "brag about," however, in a sentence such as "This church boasts a membership of over a thousand." **2.** SWE accepts both *boast* and *brag*, but regards *brag* as slightly more informal. *Brag about* is more common than *brag on*, which may be classed as dialectal.

boat/ship People in navies as well as most landsmen insist that a *boat* is a small vessel, a *ship* a large one: "You can carry a boat on a ship, but you can't carry a ship on a boat." Some dictionaries, however, treat the words as synonymous. SANE advises: join the navy.

bogus Now SWE. An Americanism for "counterfeit, fake, sham:" "a bogus twenty-dollar bill." *Phony* is an equivalent.

boo-boo FF (childish) for a silly or careless mistake.

bookie/bookmaker Although most dictionaries label *bookie* as slang or informal for *bookmaker* ("one who takes bets"), SWE uses it frequently. Many readers think of a bookmaker as someone who assembles parts of books, and thus may be momentarily confused when *bookmaker* refers to gambling. *Bookie* is therefore preferable in its limited context.

boondocks Now SWE as a disparaging term for "backcountry." Used with *the* and a plural verb. FF (slang): *boonies*. (*Boondocks* is one of the few English words from the Filipino Tagalog language.)

born/borne These examples represent SWE usage: "Melba was *born* in Missouri. Her mother had *borne* two other children; one of them, a boy, was *born* deaf and crippled. Melba's mother has *borne* that burden with patience."

borrow See LEND/LOAN.

boss, bossy *Boss* for "employer, foreman, supervisor" or "leading politician" is SWE. So is the comparable verb, as well as the adjective *bossy*. The adjective *boss* in the sense of "first-rate," however, is FF (slang): "He's a boss guitarist."

both/each FF says, "Both fighters claimed that the other had fouled him." What other? SWE says, "Each fighter claimed . . ." and "Both fighters complained about the referee." So, of course, did each fighter. Unclear: "Both boys earned a thousand dollars." Clear: "Each boy earned five hundred (or *a thousand*) dollars."

both (redundant) Omitted in SWE when another word in the same sentence carries a similar meaning, as in these FF redundancies: "both went together," "both are equal," "both are similar." So SWE avoids sentences such as "Ralph and Walter both agree." FF says, "the both of you"; SWE deletes *the*.

bottom line This business term, relating to the profit-or-loss line in an official report, has been taken over in figurative use to mean any final result. The term is SWE but in recent years has been greatly overused.

bought/boughten SWE uses *bought* as both verb and adjective: "Antonia had bought a dress." "Antonia had a bought dress." Many Northerners and North Midlanders, however, dislike the sound of "a bought dress" and are likely to say (possibly write) "a boughten dress" or to evade the issue: "a manufactured (or *store-bought, tailor-made*) dress," "baker's bread" (instead of "bought [or *boughten*] bread").

bovine (and similar words) Conservatives prefer to restrict words such as *bovine, canine,* or *equine* to adjectival use: "an equine face." But most dictionaries now recognize a noun usage as also standard: "a bovine was . . . ," "two canines." SWE is still undecided but leans toward the conservative position.

boyish/puerile *Boyish* is more favorable than *puerile*: "a boyish grin," "boyish daring," but "puerile boastfulness and bravado," "puerile silliness." See also JUVENILE.

brag See BOAST.

brand/kind/variety Although *brand* seems to be moving toward general acceptance in SWE in such phrases as "her brand of humor," many writers still prefer to restrict it to commercial use: "a good brand of tapioca," and to say "her kind (or *variety*) of humor."

breach/breech/bridge *Breach* is historically related to *break*. So we refer to a breach of a law, in a dike, of promise, in good relations. As a verb, to *breach* is to make a hole in: "breach the enemy's line." "A whale breaches when it breaks through the surface of the water." *Breach the gap* is an amusing slip. There's not much sense in making a hole in a gap. It makes more sense to *bridge* a gap. A *breech* may be the back part of a firearm, the lower part of a pulley, or the buttocks. A *breechcloth* covers the loins. Other uses appear in *breech delivery, breeches* (slang *britches*), *breeches buoy, breechloader*.

break up In "His jokes break me up," the term means "to cause to laugh almost uncontrollably." It's FF, but sometimes appears in SWE because it packs more punch than "I find his jokes extremely amusing."

breakdown This word is used too often when *analysis, profit-and-loss sheet*, or something else may be preferable. Sometimes *breakdown* is momentarily ambiguous. Does "He gave me a breakdown" mean that he showed me a chart, caused my car to stop running, or disturbed me so much that I needed a psychiatrist?

breech See BREACH/BREECH/BRIDGE.

British Isles/England/Great Britain/United Kingdom *England* is one part of *Great Britain*, which also includes Scotland and Wales. The *United Kingdom* is Great Britain and Northern Ireland (before 1922, all of Ireland was included). The *British Isles* include the United Kingdom and the islands near it. Ireland (Eire) is included in the British Isles but is not part of the United Kingdom or Great Britain.

Britisher/Briton Residents of Great Britain prefer to be called *Britons* but may call themselves *Britishers* informally. In the United States, *Britisher* in the late eighteenth or early nineteenth century was a somewhat derogatory term, but that usually is no longer true.

broke (adjective) Although some dictionaries call *broke*, meaning "without money," informal, Bryant's well-researched study says, "In America the use of *broke* [in this sense] is standard English, as in '. . . any United States citizen, be he wealthy or broke' (The *New York Times*)."

broken down When using this term to mean "classified," SWE is careful not to get a result like this: "Mrs. Leigh presented a report on the pitiable condition of many of the town's elderly people, broken down by sex."

browse/graze **1.** If your cow is eating grass, she is *grazing*. *Browsing* is a more inclusive term, most often referring to eating leaves and soft twigs of trees or bushes, but also to eating grass or other low-lying vegetation. **2.** In FF, a person who chooses among various possible snacks and eats one or more may be said to be *grazing*. **3.** *Browsing* is SWE for looking leisurely at items in a shop or for glancing at or through printed material.

brunch See SMOG.

brunet/brunette *Brunette* applies to females, *brunet* usually to males but occasionally to females. If *blond* (rather than *blonde*) gains ascendancy, SANE recommends the comparable *brunet*.

buff SWE for "enthusiast": "rock music buffs," "computer buffs." A buff may be less knowledgeable about his subject than an aficionado is, but the difference is not great.

buffalo See BISON/BUFFALO.

bug **1.** (eavesdropping device) "Spies placed a bug inside a lamp." "They bugged the lamp." Originally considered slang, but now SWE as both noun and verb because no other short, convenient term exists. **2.** The verb *bug* for "annoy," as in "Don't bug me," is FF. **3.** *Bug off* (or *out*) and *Butt out* are FF (slang) for "Don't bother me" or "Go away." **4.** *Bug* is used loosely for *insect* in SWE and especially in FF. Entomologists generally restrict the term to hemipterous insects such as bedbugs or squash bugs.

building/edifice SWE uses *edifice* for an unusually large, expensive building. Although such structures are now numerous, the word appears less and less, perhaps because it suggests unnecessary extravagance. Builder Donald Trump has been said to have an "edifice complex."

bulk of SWE doesn't write "the bulk of the senators" unless the reference is to their physical size. It chooses *most* or *the majority of*. With noncountable nouns (rice, sand, water, and so on), either *bulk of* or *most of* is used, but *bulk* may cause some readers to think mainly of the amount of space occupied. *Most* will not be so misinterpreted.

bullet/cartridge/round/shell/shot Hunters usually refer to shotgun *shells*, not *cartridges*. A rifle or handgun fires *cartridges*, but (confusingly) these are sometimes called *shells*. A *bullet* is the (usually) lead part of a cartridge, the part that leaves the gun when fired. The small, round projectiles in a shotgun shell are called *shot*. In counting the number of shells or cartridges available or used, military people and some hunters say *rounds*, as in "fifty rounds of ammunition."

42 **bum idea (or *rap, steer*)** *Bum*, in the sense of "poorly chosen," "worthless," or "undeserved," is FF.

bump *Bump* is FF but moving toward SWE for "displace someone from a job or position": "The airlines bumped several passengers because the plane was too heavily loaded." "Today two drivers were bumped from the qualifiers for the Indy 500 because two others posted faster times."

bunch In SWE *bunch* refers to things that grow together, such as grapes, or that can be fastened together, such as roses. In FF it may refer to a small group of chairs, people, jobs, even love: "I love you a whole bunch."

bunk/bunkum *Bunk* for "foolish talk" is classified by dictionaries as slang or informal, and *bunkum* (alternatively *buncombe*) as standard. Yet *bunkum* or *buncombe* is almost never seen in print, while *bunk* is not infrequent. Consider *bunk* SWE.

bureaucracy, bureaucrats In most people's minds these words have unfavorable connotations. SWE writers use them sparingly, and not when they believe that their readers should like or be neutral toward these people. Middle-of-the-road designations are *government workers, federal employees*, and the like.

burglarize, burgle Both words are based on *burglar* and are now SWE, with *burglarize* more common and less informal.

burglary/holdup/robbery/theft *Theft* ("taking something belonging to someone else") is a general word encompassing the other three. *Burglary* is stealing from inside a building entered unlawfully. In legal use, forcible entrance, even without stealing, may be considered burglary. *Robbery* involves use of threats or force. (*Mugging*, somewhat informal, is a form of robbery.) A *holdup* involves a gun or other weapon.

burst/bust Pipes *burst*, they *burst* (not *bursted*) last night, they *have burst*. *Bust* in the sense of *burst* or *break* is FF and is often considered a mark of illiteracy. The term *drug bust*, however, is widely used informally and in magazine articles and books, since there is no other conveniently short term. Consider it SWE.

bus (verb) Although a few people still object to "They *bused* (or *bussed*) the children" and similar uses of a noun as a verb, the usage is SWE. It is comparable to "*shipped* the crates" or "*trucked* the melons."

bush, bush league   *Bush* as an adjective meaning "inferior, second-rate" is FF. So are *bush league* and *bush leaguer* for "minor league," "minor league player." They do appear on sports pages, especially in columns written by supercilious big-city residents.

bust   See BURST/BUST.

but (for *except*)   When *but* means "except," it is a preposition and takes an object: "all but (or *except*) me (*us, him, her, them*)," "All the guests but you and me were formally dressed." Some grammarians have said that in a sentence such as "No one saw it but I (or *me*)" *I* is "proper" because the last part is a shortened version of "but I did." That argument is weak, because for that meaning *else* would be added: "No one else saw it, but I did." SWE almost invariably chooses the objective case; "No one . . . but me."

43

but/however, nevertheless   *But* is a lighter connective than the rather ponderous *however* or *nevertheless*. Between clauses of a compound sentence, the punctuation reflects this difference: "Laboratory explosions are rather frequent, but usually no one is hurt" (note the comma). "Laboratory explosions are rather frequent; however, usually no one is hurt" (semicolon). Obviously redundant are *but however* and *but nevertheless*.

but that/but what   Both forms occur sometimes in SWE: "Most congressmen do not doubt but what (or *but that*) the president will sign the bill." The construction, though, is a variety of double negative; it is also ungraceful. In the example, *that* alone will suffice. "I don't know but what (or *that*) you are right" may be simplified to "I believe you may be right" or "Perhaps you are right."

but which, but who, but whom   See AND WHICH, AND WHO, AND WHOM.

but (with a negative)   When *but* means "only," it is not SWE to use it with a negative. Instead of "There aren't but six," SWE prefers "There are but six" or, more likely today, "There are only six." Instead of "I couldn't see but one," SWE chooses "I could see only one" or "I couldn't see more than one."

butt out   See BUG.

buy   1. FF for "believe" or "accept": "When a president becomes a lame duck, Congress is less likely to buy his recommendations." 2. (As a noun) Once criticized by people who dislike using one part of speech as another, *buy* is now SWE in expressions such as "a good buy."

by means of   Often *by* or some other preposition is enough, so why wear out the word processor? "Pioneers harvested their grain with (not *by means of*) crude tools."

by nature   This expression adds nothing to the meaning in sentences such as "By nature he is taciturn but not unpleasant," or a weather forecaster's "Precipitation, snow in nature, will fall over the Great Lakes."

C

cacao/coca/cocoa/coconut   The small, tropical *cacao* tree produces seeds from which *cocoa* (source of chocolate) is made. *Coca*, however, is a South American shrub or small tree whose leaves are the source of cocaine. Still different is *coconut* (*cocoanut*), a tree that provides the large, hard-shelled nut with white flesh used, for example, in coconut cream pies.

cactus (plural)   The late J. J. Lamberts of Arizona State wrote, "A member of a garden club in Indiana or Ohio will probably use the plural *cacti*, but a rancher in New Mexico who lives with them all the time may say *cactuses*." When in Rome . . . SANE sides with the rancher, and in general favors the anglicizing of foreign plurals.

cadge   SWE for "get by begging or by imposing on others": "Although not poor, he cadges every meal he can."

calculate/reckon/suppose   SWE generally reserves *calculate* and *reckon* for mathematical statements: "He calculates (*reckons*) his assets to be ten million dollars." *Reckon* is slightly old-fashioned. In the sense of *suppose*, both are FF (dialectal or informal).

caliber (or *calibre*)   Note the decimal point in reference to guns: "a .22-caliber rifle." The bore of such a rifle or handgun or the size of its cartridge is .22 inches.

Calvary/cavalry   *Cavalry* refers to military units employing horses or, more recently, motorized vehicles. *Calvary* is a place near ancient Jerusalem where Christ was crucified. A calvary (small *c*) is an artistic portrayal of the crucifixion.

can/may   In SWE, *may* is customary in regard to permission: "Only the Supreme Court may legally make that decision." *Can* in SWE normally refers to ability or possibility: "No human being can run a three-minute mile." In FF *can* is often used where SWE prefers *may*. A discourteous reply to "Can I park here?" is "You can, but you may not." See also CAN'T/MAYN'T.

canine   See BOVINE.

cannon/canon/cañon/canyon   The most common meanings are these: *cannon*: a mounted gun; *canon*: principle or law, group of books or other writings recognized as standard, type of musical composition, church official; *canyon*: deep valley (Americanized spelling of Spanish *cañon*).

cannot   1. *Cannot* is the usual spelling. *Can not* provides more emphasis. The contraction is *can't*. 2. *Cannot but*, as in "They cannot but be proud," has literary standing but is awkward and may be misunderstood. SWE prefers *can only* or *must*. *Cannot help but* (*agree*, and so on), although sometimes criticized, is SWE, equivalent to *cannot help*. **3.** *Cannot seem to* (*think straight*, and so on) appears in SWE, although *seem to* is generally omitted. *Seems unable to* may be substituted. Similar comments apply to *could not help but* and *could not seem to*.

can't hardly   SWE is *can hardly*. *Can't hardly*, a double negative, is widely regarded as an indicator of inadequate education, in that way similar to *doesn't have none*.

can't seem to   See CANNOT.

can't/mayn't   FF almost never, and SWE seldom, uses *mayn't*, even when permission is involved, although for permission the uncontracted form may be usual. In both FF and SWE, "Why can't towns make such decisions for themselves?" is customary. In "They can't (vs. *mayn't*) have more time," both FF and SWE often choose *can't*. *Mayn't*, like *may* and *may not*, is sometimes ambiguous, referring to either permission or possibility.

canyon   See CANNON/CANON/CAÑON/CANYON.

capable   The usual idiom is *capable of doing*, not *capable to do*. With a word such as *sufficiently* or *enough*, however, the *to*-construction is SWE. "Mrs. Larson is sufficiently capable (or *capable enough*) to manage the whole office."

capacity   See ABILITY/CAPACITY.

capital/capitol   The state *capital* is the city in which the *capitol* (building) stands. Some people remember the *o* in *capitol* by thinking of the *o* in *dome*.

carat/caret/carrot/karat   *Carat* or *karat*: a jeweler's term for 200 milligrams; *caret*: a mark (∧) showing a place to insert written or printed material; *carrot*: a kind of vegetable.

cardinal/ordinal   *Cardinal* numbers are 1, 2, 3, and so on. *Ordinal* numbers are *first*, *second*, *third*, and so on. The endings *st*, *nd*, *rd*, and *th* are used less frequently than formerly with ordinals: "June 1" or "1 June" rather than "*June 1st*." In SWE, it's "the seventh son" rather than "the 7th son." With long ordinals, *127th* is customary rather than *one hundred twenty-seventh*. In tables, *1st*, *2nd*, and so on are less likely than *1*, *2*, and so on.

care of   For the abbreviation, as in an address, SWE uses *c/o*, not %.

care   See ANXIETY/APPREHENSION/CARE . . .

careen/career   In earlier usage, *careen* was applied only to boats leaning to one side, and *career* referred to fast, erratic movement of wagons or cars. Now, however, perhaps because of other, quite different meanings of *career*, *careen* is used for wheeled vehicles and sleds as well as boats: "Two cars careened crazily toward each other."

career   Pretentious or humorous when used to refer to a job held only briefly. In SWE *career* signifies the major professional activity of a lifetime. References to "my high school career" or "my three-week career as a hosiery salesman" appear either highfalutin or funny.

careful (*close*) scrutiny *Scrutiny* by definition is careful and close. SWE most often omits the modifier.

caret, carrot See CARAT/CARET/CARROT . . .

cartridge See BULLET/CARTRIDGE/ROUND . . .

case This word is overused in the sense of "situation" or "circumstances." Partridge quotes this amusing example: "There was a greater scarcity of crabs than in the case of herrings."

cast/caste A playbill lists a *cast* of characters. In India and sometimes elsewhere a class of society is called a *caste*: "The four major Hindu castes are Brahman, Kshatriya, Vaisya, and Sudra."

casual/causal Frequently confused by typists. *Casual* means "occasional, incidental, haphazard, indifferent, or informal": "a casual visitor," "casual clothing." *Causal* is derived from *cause*: "the causal relationship between friction and wear."

casualty In military and accident reports a casualty may be a person either killed or severely injured. A military casualty list may also include names of seriously ill, captured, deserted, or missing personnel. Because definitions of *casualty* are not all alike, a term such as "twenty casualties" is often unclear; in some counts but not in others a broken toe or a severe strain may make one a casualty.

catalog/catalogue Two centuries ago Noah Webster advocated simplifying many spellings, including most of those with a final silent *ue*. Today both *catalog* and *catalogue* are SWE, as are *dialog, dialogue*, and some others. SANE admires Webster.

catch on fire *On* is unnecessary.

catch up This term is now SWE in these senses: **1.** Overtake: "The second platoon tried to catch up with the first." **2.** Bring up to date: "catch up with the news." **3.** Become involved in: "caught up in the excitement." **4.** Discover (and probably point out) minor errors or untruths: "caught his brother up in a fib" (chiefly British).

Catholic/Roman Catholic SWE uses *Roman Catholic* rather than *Catholic* if any likelihood of confusion exists about whether Roman, Greek, or some other variety of Catholicism is meant. Uncapitalized, *catholic* usually means "wide-ranging, broad, universal": "As a reader, she is catholic in her tastes."

Caucasian With reference to race SWE prefers *white* to *Caucasian* unless clarity suffers. *Caucasian* is often considered rather pompous, and comparable words for *black, brown*, or *red* may be unfamiliar or offensive. Anthropologists no longer use *Caucasian* as a scientific term.

causal See CASUAL/CAUSAL.

cause/reason A *reason* gives an explanation: "The reason the storage tank was believed safe was that state inspectors had approved its design." *Cause*, however, deals in some direct way with origin: "The cause of the failure of the storage tank was an improper weld."

cavalry See CALVARY/CAVALRY.

cease More pretentious than *quit* or *stop*.

celebrant/celebrator SWE commonly restricts *celebrant* to a priest celebrating a religious rite or any person taking part in such a rite. It uses *celebrator* to mean, for example, someone in Times Square on New Year's Eve.

celebrate/commemorate To *commemorate* is to honor the memory of someone or something. You may *celebrate* your birthday, but only after you are dead can anyone commemorate it or you.

Celtic/Gaelic *Celtic* is the more inclusive term; it does not refer only to the Irish, as some people assume. The Celtic languages are divided by linguists into two branches: the Brythonic, consisting of Cornish, Welsh, and Breton, and the Goidelic, consisting of Irish Gaelic, Scottish Gaelic, and Manx. The ancestors of the speakers of all these languages were Celts, who lived in western and central Europe before settling mainly in the British Isles. A Gael is a Scottish Celt or Highlander, or any Celt who speaks Gaelic. *Gaelic*, as an adjective, means "pertaining to the Gaels or their language."

cement/concrete *Cement* is one of the ingredients of *concrete*. Usually the greater part of concrete is sand or gravel, with cement used as an adhesive. SWE refers to concrete – not cement – sidewalks or roads.

censer/censor/censure A *censer* is an incense burner. To *censor* a book is to forbid its sale or to cut out parts of it for political, moral, or other reasons. To *censure* is to blame. Some persons may censure an author for something he or she has written – possibly a book that was censored.

centenarian/centurion If your grandfather, who fought in World War I, lived to be a hundred, he was a *centenarian*, but he was not a *centurion*, as one small-town newspaper would have called him. A centurion served in an ancient Roman army and was in command of one hundred men.

center (preposition with) It's not logical to say "The argument centered *around* (or *about*) the high cost," for a center is not really around anything. Logic demands centered *in*, *on*, or *upon*. So many reputable writers have written *center around* or *about*, however, that those usages have become SWE, along with *in*, *on*, and *upon*. Language often refuses to be the slave of logic.

center/middle *Center* is usually a more precise term. In a circle, for example, the center is the point equidistant from any point on the circumference. *Middle* may be synonymous with *center*, but is usually interpreted as more inclusive: the area including and close to the center. Sometimes, though, *center* is used in that same sense: "the center (or *middle*) of town." Similarly, a person may be in either the center or the middle of a controversy.

cents SWE writes "ten cents," "10 cents" (especially in journalism), or "10¢" (in a table or an advertisement), but not ".10¢," which technically means "a tenth of a cent."

centurion See CENTENARIAN/CENTURION.

century 1. SWE uses context to indicate whether "*the past* (or *last*) *century*" means "the hundred years before this year" (e.g., 1891–1990) or "the century before the present one" (1801–1900). 2. The first century A.D. lasted from A.D. 1 through 100, so the second century began in 101. The twenty-first century will begin January 1, 2001, the twenty-second in 2101, and so on.

ceremonial/ceremonious SWE restricts *ceremonial* to things: "a ceremonial occasion," "ceremonial robes." *Ceremonious* may be applied to either things or persons; it refers especially to the formality and pomp of ceremony, and may suggest a dislike of what appears to be excessive or meretricious, insincere, unwarranted showiness: "the ceremoniousness of a presidential inauguration," "a high-church ceremoniousness," "spoke in the ceremonious tones she considered desirable for a commencement address."

certain Overused by amateurs, who timidly and uncertainly refer to "a certain place," "this certain person," "one certain time." SWE usually deletes *certain* or names the place, the person, the time. An unintentional biblical flavor may come from *certain*, as in "A certain man had a fig tree . . . ." (Luke 13:6). "I know a certain little girl who hasn't washed her face" is arch and condescending.

certainly Often can be omitted. "His account is certainly true" may be less strong than "His account is true," because the latter does not raise any question of certainty.

chafe/chaff To *chafe* is to irritate or annoy: "Armor often chafed parts of a knight's body." To *chaff* is to banter, to tease lightly: "Did I see you staring at that blonde again?" she chaffed.

chain reaction For a *chain reaction* to occur, each action in a group must be caused by (linked to) the preceding one, as in a chain.

chair/chairman/chairperson *To chair a meeting* is SWE. In an attempt to combat sexist language, the National Council of Teachers of English experimented with *chairperson* and then settled on *chair* to signify a person who heads a committee or presides at a meeting. The NCTE considers *chairman* sexist, *chairperson* awkward, and *chairman or chairwoman* too long for repeated use. Many members, however, both female and male, dislike *chair*. NCTE's uncertainty reflects that of the public. Bold writers use whichever they prefer, aware that each choice will offend someone. Timid or cautious writers substitute *presiding officer* or *head*.

chaise longue The plural is *chaise longues* or (French) *chaises longues* ("long chairs"). Popular etymology, lacking a French education, metathesizes *longue* to *lounge*, *longues* to *lounges*. Odds are that the French form will gradually disappear from English; *chaise lounges* already appears, for example, in some catalogs.

character **I.** Sometimes can be omitted: "Incidents of an unpleasant character" are "unpleasant incidents." **2.** SWE uses expressions such as "a suspicious (or *likable, amusing,* and so on) character." **3.** Frequently in FF and occasionally in SWE, *character* is used for "eccentric person": "He's a real character."

character/reputation *Character* is what or who a person really is, deep inside; *reputation* refers to what people say he or she is.

characterized by This expression often seems wordy or high-flown. Instead of "Her knitting is characterized by neatness," SWE says ". . . is neat."

charisma From "blessings bestowed by God" or "a spiritual quality bestowed on a leader," *charisma* moved on to refer to the ability of leaders to attract devoted followers, and has been further extended to mean the attractiveness of some actors, actresses, athletes, and other entertainers such as politicians, and even to that of things: "charismatic jewelry (*clothing,* and so on)." The once rare word, along with its adjective, has thus become overused.

charlady American SWE prefers *charwoman.*

(the) charts Has become SWE in reports on the ratings of currently popular music: "'Clackety-Quack' is still fourth on the charts this week."

chauvinism Nicolas Chauvin was a seventeen-times wounded follower of Napoleon. His enthusiastic and perhaps foolhardy loyalty was enshrined in the word *chauvinism.* Loyalty to a leader became translated into fanatical patriotism, "my country right or wrong," and then to loyalty to any group. Almost any sort of patriotism or loyalty is sometimes miscalled chauvinism. More recently, *chauvinist* has been equated with *male chauvinist pig,* a man accused of regarding women as inferior beings. Often the accusation is accurate, but a few extremists apparently believe that all men are chauvinists – that *chauvinist = man.*

cherub/seraph (plurals of) The Hebrew plurals are retained in the line of the hymn "Holy, Holy, Holy" about *cherubim* and *seraphim,* as well as in other religious references. Elsewhere *cherubs* and *seraphs* are likely. Those rosy-faced, babylike beings that have often been used on greeting cards are cherubs.

chicanery/duplicity Both words refer to deception. However, *chicanery* has a suggestion of trickery and wiliness, and *duplicity* of double-dealing.

Chicano *Chicano* is preferred to *Mexican-American* by many residents of the United States who are from Mexico or of Mexican ancestry. Historically, *Chicano* means "Mexican." However, other such residents prefer *Mexican-American* on the ground that *Chicano* does not show that they are now or expect to become American citizens. Both terms are SWE. SANE prefers *Mexican-American* as parallel to *German-American* and other such terms.

chide *Chide* is a somewhat old-fashioned word for "reprove" or "scold." Its past tense (*chided* or *chid*) and past participle (*chided, chid,* or *chidden*) have never settled down. *Chided* for each might cause least trouble.

Chief Justice   The nation's top jurist is technically not Chief Justice of the Supreme Court. He or she is Chief Justice of the United States.

child   See BABE/BABY.

childish/childlike/infantile   *Childish* or *childlike* behavior is to be expected of children. In adults, however, "childish behavior" is considered immature in a spoiled-brat way. "Childlike behavior" is less likely to be reproached; it tends to be interpreted in terms of a child's innocence and lack of sophistication. Some old people behave in childlike ways.

Chinamen/Chinese   Use *Chinese* or *Chinese people*. Singular: a *Chinese*. See also ASIANS/ASIATICS.

chintzy   This word, derived from *chintz* ("a bright-colored cloth"), is an SWE substitute for *gaudy, tawdry, excessively ornate, trashy, cheap, inferior, stingy*. Because of such varied meanings, some good writers avoid it.

chiseling   Figuratively, *chiseling* is cheating repeatedly in small ways: "chiseling on one's expense account," "chiseling by not reporting tips." Since such a word is needed, the accurate image (a sculptor with a chisel) conveyed by *chiseling* makes it worthy of its SWE acceptance.

choosy   See PICKY.

chord/cord   The most common use of *chord* is in music, referring to a combination of notes. It may also mean "an emotional response": "a sympathetic chord"; or, in mathematics, "a straight line joining two points on a curve." Most other meanings require *cord*: "tie with a cord," "electric cord ('wire')," "the cord ('raised rib') on a piece of cloth," "vocal cords," "a cord of wood." A cord of wood is not just any load but is 128 cubic feet, usually 8′ × 4′ × 4′.

Christian name   This term may be offensive if applied to non-Christians. *Given* (or *first*) *name* is usually preferable. *Baptismal name* is appropriate if a ceremony of baptism has occurred.

chronic   See ACUTE/CHRONIC.

chummy   There's no obvious reason why some dictionaries treat *chum* as standard English, appropriate for all stylistic levels, but call *chummy* "informal." With reference to pleasant, continuing, but not deep relationships, *chummy* is useful in SWE.

chutzpah   Flesch comments that dictionary-makers have never found a perfect definition for Yiddish *chutzpah*, but that *Webster's Collegiate's* "supreme self-confidence" and *Webster's New World's* "shameless audacity" come closest. It may also mean "a lot of nerve." Because no single English word is equivalent, *chutzpah*'s rating is gradually changing from FF (dialectal) to SWE.

circle around   Anything that circles goes around. SWE deletes *around*.

circumstances (*in* or *under*) *In the circumstances* is more logical, but *under the circumstances* is also established.

cite/quote If we *cite* a passage (e.g., from a book), we refer to its source and possibly either summarize or quote it, especially as re-inforcement of what we are saying. To *quote* a passage from something either written or spoken is to use the exact words, unless the quotation is designated as indirect.

cite/sight/site *Cite*, as a verb, may mean "refer to someone else's words" but also "use as an example" or "accuse formally of a violation." *Sight* has to do with seeing or something to be seen. It may be a noun or a verb. *Site*, a noun but occasionally a verb, refers to location: "The site is a pleasant one." "The houses are sited along a ravine."

CITIES **1.** It is tautological to say "the cities of Oslo, Copenhagen, and Stockholm" except when writing for children who presumably haven't yet studied geography. SWE just names the cities if the expected readers have passed the eighth grade. **2.** Except in addresses, names of countries may be omitted with names of large cities. Not "Moscow, Russia, and Paris, France," but "Moscow and Paris." But with smaller cities: "Moscow, Idaho, and Paris, Illinois."

citizen/inhabitant/resident These words are somewhat interchangeable. However, *citizen* carries the connotation of "voter," "one who holds citizenship." People not born in the United States must meet certain requirements to become citizens. An *inhabitant* or a *resident*, however, must merely live in a place (although he or she *may* be a citizen). A person questioned by police is more likely to say, "I'll have you know that I am a citizen" than ". . . I am an inhabitant (or *resident*)."

clad This is SWE, but perhaps slightly old-fashioned, for *clothed* or *wearing*.

claim (for *assert, declare, maintain*) Once criticized almost groundlessly when used in sentences such as "The defendant claimed that he was asleep when the assault began," *claim* is now SWE.

clarify *Clarify* means "to make clear" or "explain further." It does not mean "answer." "I'll try to clarify your question" is not the same as "I'll try to answer your question."

classy *Classy* is informal SWE for "stylish, elegant," or sometimes for "associated with very rich people."

clean/cleanse *Clean* usually has the literal sense of "to free from dirt": "clean the stable," "clean house." *Cleanse* may have the same meaning but is often more figurative, suggesting "to free of defilement, to eliminate impure thoughts": "Cleanse my spirit of whatever is vile, O Lord."

clench/clinch *Clench* is a variant of *clinch* and is generally used with parts of the anatomy: "clench one's fists (fingers, lips)." It may also mean "hold tightly": "clenched the document in her right hand." Normally one *clinches* nails, a baseball team clinches the pennant,

51

pieces of evidence may clinch an argument, and boxers clinch or "go into a clinch" when they hold each other.

clever/ingenious/inventive All three are words of praise. A *clever* person does well in solving small problems. An *ingenious* person probably combines work with imagination to reach unusual solutions. An *inventive* person is most likely to produce something new, especially something concrete.

cliché See ADAGE.

climactic/climatic *Climactic* pertains to climax: "climactic moments in the play." *Climatic* pertains to climate: "excellent climatic conditions."

climax This word is not used in SWE to mean "lowest point" or "point of lowest intensity." Dubious: "The drop in college enrollments reached its climax in the 1980s."

clinch See CLENCH/CLINCH.

clippers/pincers/pliers/scissors/shears/tweezers (verb with) Customarily take plural verbs: *clippers*, *pliers*, *shears*, *tweezers*. Usage divided: *pincers*, *scissors*. When *a pair of* precedes any of these nouns, however, the verb is singular: "A pair of pliers is on the table."

clone (noun, verb) Now SWE for asexual reproduction or its results: "The large graduate colleges cloned young Wall Streeters who looked alike, spoke alike, and – worst of all – thought alike."

close proximity Redundant, so SWE deletes *close*. Instead of *in close proximity to* it chooses *near* or *close to*.

close scrutiny See CAREFUL (*CLOSE*) SCRUTINY.

close to With numbers, SWE but more informal than *nearly*: "Close to twenty thousand people attended."

closet Now SWE for "secret," "private," "secrecy." It's used in such expressions as "closet homosexual" or "came out of the closet."

clout Now SWE for "influence," "pressure": "President Johnson seldom hesitated to use his clout with Congress." It's also SWE for "a blow, especially with a fist." Sportswriters often call a home run "a mighty clout."

clover leaf (plural) *Clover leaves* grow on clover plants. For highway intersections of that shape the usual term is *cloverleafs*.

clunker FF for something almost worthless, especially an automobile.

coach (verb) Once Someone decided that *coach* shouldn't be used with the name of a sport as the object, as "to coach football," arguing that the players are coached, not the ball or the game. But the substitute expression, such as "to give instruction in football," was so long-winded and high-flown that Nobody listened to Someone. So today men and women happily coach players, teams, and football and other sports. It's simpler – and better – that way.

cockamamie FF, but now appearing in SWE for "silly, ridiculous, worthless": "a cockamamie plot." Perhaps it's related to *poppycock*, *cock-and-bull story*.

coca, cocoa, coconut See CACAO/COCA/COCOA/COCONUT.

codger/curmudgeon A *codger* is an elderly but perhaps strange-acting man sometimes fondly referred to, redundantly, as "an old codger." A *curmudgeon* is not necessarily male or elderly. He or she is a grouchy and probably stingy person. In an obsolete definition a curmudgeon is a miser.

cohort In Latin a cohort was a division of a Roman legion. For that reason conservatives dislike calling one person a cohort, as in "the gangster and several cohorts." AHD labels such language "not appropriate in formal use." The more liberal RHD uses as a legitimate example ". . . followed by his faithful cohort, his son-in-law." SWE usage here agrees most often with RHD.

coiffeur/coiffure A *coiffeur* (feminine *coiffeuse*) is a hairdresser. A *coiffure* is a hairstyle considered suitable for a person and her or his intended image. (But what's wrong with *hairdresser* and *hairstyle*?)

cold glass of milk/hot cup of coffee It's usual for the milk to be cold, the coffee hot.

collaborate (or *collect, cooperate, gather*) together SWE omits *together* in such expressions.

collect together See COLLABORATE (OR COLLECT, COOPERATE, GATHER) TOGETHER.

collective *Collective efforts* and *collective strength* make sense, but *collective* works less well with parts of the body. Dubious: "raised their collective hands," "shook their collective heads." The second example suggests heads in a basket, like a farm wife's eggs.

collision See ALLISION/COLLISION.

collude/connive Interchangeable to mean "act together secretly, conspire." *Connive*, however, often adds the sense "pretend ignorance." A governor, for example, may connive by pretending to be unaware of misdeeds of his aides, even though he himself may have profited.

collusion *Collusion* is used in SWE only when the purpose of working together is illegal or evil: "worked in collusion to evade taxes." For a legal or good purpose, *cooperation* is SWE.

colossal, colossally (and the like) Searching for emotional strength, careless or hasty writers frequently use adjectives and adverbs loosely and without strict attention to meaning. Writers of advertising and of "confessions" are among the worst offenders. The words in the following list, as well as their adverbial forms, are all good, respectable, and useful, but they have been employed so frequently and hyperbolically that they have lost much of their intrinsic strength.

amazing	gigantic	miraculous	stupendous
awful	great	petrifying	terrible
breathtaking	huge	remarkable	terrific
colossal	incredible	sensational	thrilling
fabulous	magnificent	spectacular	tremendous
fantastic	marvelous	splendid	wonderful

If a writer uses *colossal*-type words honestly (and seldom), readers will be likely to respect her or his judgment and believe that anything described as colossal or the like really is.

colt/filly/foal/gelding/horse/mare/stallion   A *colt* is a young male horse. Both he and his sister, a *filly*, are also *foals*, a term applied to a newborn horse or to one less than a year old. *Foal* may be used as a verb, too, meaning "to give birth": "The mare will foal in April." The young female horse, the filly, is generally no more than two years old; some races are specifically for two-year-old fillies. *Horse* can be used generically for any equine animal of any age, or more specifically for an adult male horse. A *stallion* is a horse that has not been castrated; a *gelding* has been. (One meaning of the verb *geld* is "to castrate.") A *mare* is a female horse, usually adult.

come aboard   Overused for "become a member of our company (*group*, *team*, or the like)."

come of age   Although "She will become eighteen in May" is SWE, "She will become of age in May" is not. SWE says *come of age*.

comes time   1. "When it came time for recess" is a dubious expression, if only because it is wordy. SWE says, "When recess came" or "At recess." 2. "There came a time when" and "Comes a time in every woman's life" are SWE but verbose and somewhat affected. "*Come a time* like that again, I'll be happy" and "*Come fall*, we'll be out of debt" are FF (localisms).

comeuppance (also *comeupance*)   This bouncily FF Americanism for "appropriate punishment" or "just deserts" is not ordinarily used for long-term or severe punishment. Sometimes it may be no more than a reprimand or an effective rejoinder. (A clever put-down may give someone else his comeuppance.)

comfy   A pleasant FF shortening of *comfortable* sometimes found in SWE. It may elicit a vision of a couch or soft chairs, somewhat worn rugs, a fireplace, and one or two people in bathrobes and snug slippers.

comic/comical   A *comic* book or opera is not quite the same as a *comical* book or opera. *Comic* means "pertaining to comedy," and *comical* means "laugh-provoking." The two words are sometimes used interchangeably, but *comical* is more likely to refer to something odd or even ludicrous. An actor in a comedy is likely to be called a *comic* actor, but a clown or anyone in a clownish role is probably *comical*.

comity   This word for "mutual civility, courteousness," especially between nations, churches, or other large organized groups, is sometimes misused to mean "league, association." In speech, it may be misunderstood as *comedy*.

commendation   See PANEGYRIC.

comment/observation/remark   All are often used interchangeably. A *remark* is likely to be the most casual, least carefully thought out of the three. A *comment* often is an opinion, but it may add information. So can an *observation*, which is frequently based on the speaker's or writer's experience.

commentate Not used for an ordinary comment, but is SWE to name what a professional or otherwise qualified *commentator* does. That is more than just comment; it includes or should include research into the background of the topic, interviews with informed persons, and hard thinking.

Commie *Communist* is a neutral term, and the usually FF *Commie* may be either friendly or hostile, depending on intention, point of view, or tone of voice.

common/mutual **1.** In conservative use, *common* refers to something shared by two or more persons, and *mutual* to something felt or done by each of two persons toward the other:

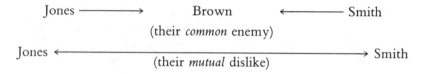

Jones ⟶ Brown ⟵ Smith
(their *common* enemy)

Jones ⟵ ⟶ Smith
(their *mutual* dislike)

Charles Dickens, however, in his novel *Our Mutual Friend*, did not maintain this distinction. Perhaps he, like others, avoided *common* because of its other meanings. **2.** Expressions such as *mutual friendship* (*exchange, cooperation*) and *mutually antagonistic toward each other* are redundant.

common See also AVERAGE/COMMON, ORDINARY.

company As a synonym of *guests*, *company* has a folksy air, but that does not disqualify it from being SWE.

compare/contrast To *compare* is to show a way or ways in which two or more things (persons, opinions, and so on) are alike or different. To *contrast* is to point out differences only.

compare to/compare with Often interchangeable. Many good writers, however, prefer *compare to* for a quick, undeveloped comparison, as in "Burns compared his beloved to a red, red rose." With *compare to*, the things are apparently dissimilar, as a sweetheart and a rose are. These precise writers use *compare with* in more fully developed comparisons, usually involving members of the same category: "The speaker compared the Russian variety of Communism with that of China." In the sense of "worthy of comparison," *compare with* is SWE: "In fragrance, roses do not compare with those of fifty years ago."

COMPARISON OF ABSOLUTES Some adjectives, such as *complete, dead, equal, final, full, impossible, perfect, round, total, unique,* and *vertical*, represent absolute conditions. If a man is dead, he cannot be deader. If a feat is impossible, another may be equally impossible but not more so. SWE generally avoids comparison of absolutes, saying, for instance, *more nearly round* rather than *rounder, more unusual* rather than *more unique*. But the comparative or superlative does sometimes appear, most often in figurative expressions: "the *deadest* party of all," "He's *straighter* than an arrow."

compendium Not used in SWE for a collection (of ideas, articles, and so on), *compendium* is a condensation or abridgement (e.g., of a speech, article, or book), or a full list or inventory, as "a compendium of the defense lawyer's objections."

complacent/complaisant A *complacent* person is self-satisfied, probably too contented. A *complaisant* person is amiable, glad to please others (this word is used infrequently).

complected FF (regional) for *complexioned* – but the region is spreading. Conservatives still prefer *dark-* (or *light-*) *complexioned*, arguing that *complected* means "interwoven." RHD, however, confirms that the word is used "occasionally in edited writing."

complement/compliment A *complement* is that which *completes* (note the first *e* in each word). Thus the complement of an angle is whatever needs to be added to complete 90°. A *compliment* is a statement made to praise or flatter. *Compliments* is now seldom used to mean "greetings": "Cap'n sends his compliments, Sir."

compliment See also PANEGYRIC.

compose/comprise SWE follows only at times the conservative view, which is that *comprise* is similar to *include, contain,* or *consist of:* "A baseball team comprises one pitcher, one catcher . . ." The converse is not true. Conservatives do not say "Nine players comprise a baseball team," because the players do not contain or consist of the team. SWE: "Nine players *compose* (or *make up, constitute*) a team." The distinction is slightly slippery, and only by a small margin did the conservative usage panel of AHD favor the "rules" just explained. SWE sometimes goes along with them but often not.

comprehend/understand *Understanding* is usually broader and deeper than *comprehension*. One may comprehend the meaning of a word by knowing its dictionary meaning and its basic uses and applications. But thoroughly understanding the word may necessitate knowing something of its derivation, changes in meaning, appropriateness in given situations, and especially its connotations – its overlay of associations. In addition, *understand* has a kindly, human touch that *comprehend* lacks. It's better to have understanding parents than parents who only comprehend.

comprise See COMPOSE/COMPRISE.

computerese This young word refers to the jargon used among computer operators. Much of it quickly became recognized in SWE, and new terms continue to be added.

con man FF for SWE *confidence man*, "a person who wheedles his way into one's confidence in order to obtain money or otherwise cheat." A *con man* today is anyone who uses fraud to achieve his ends. Con women also exist. *Con man* may eventually supplant the longer term.

conceit See ARROGANCE/CONCEIT/HAUGHTINESS/PRIDE/VANITY.

conceive/conceive of To *conceive* is to create; to *conceive of* is to understand or imagine: "He conceived the idea of extracting milk from milkweed." "I can't conceive of anyone's doing such a thing."

concern See ANXIETY/APPREHENSION/CARE/CONCERN/WORRY.

concerned about/concerned with If you are worried about something (or someone), you are *concerned about* it: "concerned about Jasper's health." A magazine article may be *concerned with* (may *deal with*, may *treat*) children, nuclear power, tsetse flies, or any other subject.

concert/recital Musicians prefer to limit *concert* to group performances (e.g., band, orchestra, chorus), and *recital* to solo performances or possibly those in which two or three persons perform singly and jointly – often called a *group recital*. In popular use, *concert* frequently applies to both group and solo presentations.

concertize SWE now occasionally uses this once condemned word meaning "to give concerts or recitals professionally." But see -IZE.

conclave Not just any meeting, but probably one held in secret by powerful people. Its participants are not a lad and a lass but a larger group with concerns that go beyond the personal: "Striking pro football players have just learned about a conclave of the team owners."

conclude/decide *Decide* is a general word for "choose between two or more alternatives," "make up one's mind." *Conclude* can mean the same thing but implies that considerable thought was expended before the decision. SWE usually prefers *that* instead of *to* after *conclude*: "We concluded that we should make one more attempt," not "We concluded to make . . ."

conclusion See FINAL COMPLETION.

concrete See CEMENT/CONCRETE.

concretize For "make concrete or specific," *concretize* is unpretty, as many *-ize* words are, but it's terse and is sometimes found in SWE. See also -IZE.

condition, conditioned Overused, especially in reference to illness or disease: "She has a nervous (or *muscular, intestinal,* or the like) condition." So do well people. SWE tries to be more specific. *Conditioned* is also overworked and may be unpleasant, but it's part of the jargon of many psychologists and educators. Instead of "He was conditioned to missing lunch," ordinary people and SWE say "accustomed to" or "used to," or "He generally missed lunch" or "He didn't mind missing lunch."

congenial/genial *Congenial* is often used when *genial* is more apt. A genial person is pleasant, affable, warm-mannered. Two persons or things are congenial if they get along well together. Thus desert conditions and cactuses are congenial, and many long-married couples live together congenially even though each may have personal quirks usually considered undesirable.

congregation   See AUDIENCE/CONGREGATION/SPECTATORS.

conjure   **1.** Accented on the second syllable, *conjure* means to beg, implore. The heroine in a melodrama sobs, "I conjure you, do not desert me thus!" **2.** Accented on the first syllable, *conjure* means to practice magic. In parts of the South and the West Indies a witch doctor may be called a *conjure man*. **3.** Accented on the first syllable and followed by *up*, *conjure* means to summon or imagine. Charles Lummis, holding a cigarette, overpraised it as a magic wand that "can conjure up tomorrow." Spiritualists supposedly conjure up the dead.

connect together, connect up   *Connect* is enough in SWE, but FF often wastes a word.

connive   See COLLUDE/CONNIVE.

CONNOTATIONS   The denotation of a word is its bare, unadorned, unemotionalized meaning, usually as in a dictionary. But most words other than *an*, *and*, *to*, *for*, and the like have connotations as well. These are fringe meanings. The denotation of *mother* is "female parent," but the connotations are various. They are normally in two not completely separable layers. In the first are one's personal reactions: what *I* associate with *mother*. Someone else, with a different mother, has different associations, and *mother* has different connotations for him. (Both my connotations and his may change as we get older and learn more about mothers.) The second layer consists of more generalized reactions – the associations that most people have. For *mother* the second-layer connotations tend to be favorable, because most people have good memories of mothers. They think of them as kind, helpful, generous.

   To influence readers as he or she wishes, a writer or speaker needs to think of the connotations of words, especially the second layer. An able prosecuting attorney chooses nouns, verbs, adjectives, and adverbs that through their connotations make the defendant seem despicable: "Ladies and gentlemen of the jury, this *ex-convict sneaked* down that dark, deserted street, waiting, *lust-driven*, for any *hapless female victim*." Political orators are adept at choosing emotion-laden words, words with "good" connotations for what they favor, words with "bad" connotations for positions held by the opposition.

   Insensitivity to connotations makes writing or a speech less convincing and persuasive. The word *socialistic*, for example, in the United States still has a generally unfavorable second layer. Knowing that, no Democrat or Republican will call socialistic a bill he or she is advocating, but may use it as a smear word to attack someone else's bill.

consciously/intentionally   SWE relates *consciously* to *consciousness*, *intentionally* to *intention*. People who consciously brag, for instance, are aware of what they are saying, but perhaps have no intention to be boastful, do not deliberately say to themselves, "Now I'll brag a little."

consensus A *consensus* is an opinion or agreement shared by all or most of the group. Both redundant: *consensus of opinion, general consensus.* SWE lets *consensus* do the job.

considerable/considerably SWE says, "She was *considerably* annoyed." "She helped us considerably." In each, a verb form is modified. FF often substitutes *considerable*, as in "She helped us considerable," a word used in SWE only to modify a noun.

considered judgment Any judgment should be considered, or else what good is a judge?

constitute See COMPOSE/COMPRISE.

constrain/restrain To *constrain* is to oblige or impel: "Her upbringing constrained her to tell the truth always." To *restrain* is to hold back: "Fear restrained her from telling the truth."

contact (verb) *Contact* as a verb has been inexplicably condemned by many persons who find no fault with the etymologically equivalent *get in touch with*. Extreme purists still shrink from *contacting* anyone, but despite their opposition the word is SWE. Indeed, it is overused. Frequently *call, make an appointment with*, or another specific term is preferable. The noun *contact* in the sense of "someone who can provide help or information" is also SWE: "Her contact was Shirley Rand, 555-4986."

contagious/infectious A *contagious* disease, such as scarlet fever, can be spread only by direct or indirect contact. The word comes from Latin for "in touch with." An *infectious* disease, however, can be spread in other ways, such as germ-bearing air or water.

contemporary This word does not mean "modern" only. Alexander Hamilton and Thomas Jefferson, for example, were "contemporary statesmen" or "contemporaries" – that is, they were contemporary with each other. *Contemporaneous* or *co-existent* may sometimes be more clear, for each means "existing at the same time."

contempt/disdain Both are varieties of scorn. *Disdain* has been defined as "aloof contempt" or "condescending contempt." If I have contempt for mice, I speak nastily of them, but if I disdain mice, I largely ignore them. The noun *contempt* is generally folllowed by *of* with reference to things or abstractions, or by *for* with people: "contempt of mice," "contempt of public opinion," "contempt for the neighbors."

contemptible/contemptuous *Contemptible*: "despicable, worthy of contempt": "To most people a rat is a contemptible creature." *Contemptuous*: "having contempt for": "The rat was contemptuous of our expensive cheese but nibbled on our bacon."

content/contents Often interchangeable: "the content(s) of the package." When the reference is not to anything concrete, however, *content* is more likely: "Read the article for its content, not its style." *Content* is also used for "volume, capacity": "The radiator's content is three gallons."

continual/continuous Sometimes used interchangeably. SWE, how-

59

ever, generally draws these distinctions: *Continual* describes things that go on almost steadily but with occasional and at least fairly regular lapses: "continual traffic on our busy street." *Continuous* means "unbroken, uninterrupted": "The need for continuous operation of a life-support system."

A visual aid: *continual*: --- -- ----- ---- -
           continuous: _____

continue/resume A man is digging a ditch. He *continues* ("keeps on") working until noon and then takes an hour off. He *resumes* ("starts again") at one o'clock and *continues* until five.

CONTRACTIONS Although contractions are regarded as informal, they often appear in relatively serious books and in articles in reputable magazines. They lighten the tone somewhat. For placement of the apostrophe, see APOSTROPHE.

contradict/deny/refute SWE avoids *refute* when *contradict* or *deny* is accurate. For example, a police officer charges that Brown committed a burglary. Brown *contradicts* the officer and *denies* the charge, but he cannot *refute* it unless he can provide proof that he is not guilty.

contrast See COMPARE/CONTRAST.

converse/inverse/obverse/reverse The face of a coin or a statue is the *obverse* side; the back of either is the *reverse* side. In general, *reverse* relates to "back" or "backward." *Converse* refers to the exact opposite of something else: "*Fearful* is the converse of *fearless*." *Inverse* is related to *inverted*, and means "upside down," although it has additional, technical meanings in mathematics and logic.

convince/persuade Sometimes interchanged. However, SWE usually assumes that one may *convince* by reasoning only, but may *persuade* by both reasoning and emotional appeal: "The accountant's figures convinced them that they were near bankruptcy." "Her husband's tearful pleading persuaded her to change her mind." "Her clenched fists persuaded him."

cool (lose one's) "When the bull charged, Glenn lost his cool." Conservatives would prefer "lost his composure," but in the example *cool* is not unlikely in SWE, which may reserve *composure* for more sedate situations, such as a courtroom trial.

coolth Why should this noun be treated as a joke? It follows the pattern of *warmth* and can become as useful. It's rare, though, in both SWE and FF.

cooperate together See COLLABORATE TOGETHER.

cop FF (slang) for "police officer," but also informal SWE. Likely to be used affectionately or neutrally rather than hostilely.

copacetic FF (slang) for "excellent."

cope A small skirmish is going on in SWE. May one cope in general rather than *with* or *against* something specific? Is "I can't cope" or

"He seldom copes very well" satisfactory, or must one say, for example, "I can't cope with my father's sarcasm"? Conservatives argue that undirected coping is like having a boxer in a ring with no opponent. Logic is on their side, but increasingly SWE allows an apparently unopposed *cope*, perhaps assuming that the enemy is all the things out there trying relentlessly to defeat us.

copout Based on an older slang phrase, *cop an out*, which meant "to seize an excuse," *copout* is today FF for "excuse, evasion, conciliatory compromise," or as a verb "to renege." Also, one who "cops out" may informally be called a copout.

copy/recopy See RE- + AGAIN OR BACK.

cord see CHORD/CORD.

corespondent/correspondent One may become a *correspondent* just by writing letters to someone. But one may become a *corespondent* in a divorce case by being accused of illicit relations with someone else's spouse.

corn, corny 1. To Americans, *corn* is a grain that grows on large ears and tall, thick stalks. To the British, it is wheat or oats, with shorter, thinner stalks. 2. *Corn* is FF (slang and outmoded) for "something old-fashioned or too sentimental." The adjective *corny* is an offshoot: "a corny joke."

coronary/heart attack/stroke A *coronary* (short for *coronary thrombosis*) is the closing of a heart artery by a blood clot. A *heart attack* is caused by failure of heart muscle. A *stroke* is a cerebral hemorrhage; a blood vessel in the brain bursts.

corps/corpse "Do your duty! Join the Ground Observer Corpse!" a newspaper advertisement urged. The request would have been more enticing if an *e* had been dropped. A *corpse* is a dead body. A *corps* is some kind of organized group. The plural of *corps* is corps (pronounced *cores*; the singular is pronounced *core*).

corpus delicti A Latin term popularly employed to mean "body of a murder victim." To a lawyer, though, it means "material evidence that a crime has been committed." That evidence is often a corpse, but not necessarily.

correspondent See CORESPONDENT/CORRESPONDENT.

corresponding/similar Here is dubious usage: "Robberies are most frequent at similar times in each December." If those times are approximately the same each December, *corresponding* would be more accurate than *similar*. In the example, *similar* suffers from vagueness. Are the times similar in dates, nearness to Christmas, weather, or what?

cosmonaut See ASTRONAUT/COSMONAUT.

couldn't care less Informal and overused for "don't care at all," "am indifferent." *Could care less* is vague but may mean that an unspecified degree of caring does exist. Both expressions are more likely in FF than in SWE.

council/counsel A *council* is an organization, for example, the National Council of Teachers of English, or a meeting such as a council of Indian chiefs. *Counsel* consists of advice or opinion: "Your counsel helped us to decide correctly." It may also be a lawyer, particularly one's representative in court: "Counsel for the defendant will approach the bench."

countless SWE employs this word only to refer to something actually uncountable, such as grains of sand on a beach. Dubious: "The room was filled with countless people."

couple **1.** This word is inaccurate for any number other than two. A minister marrying a couple doesn't marry three persons. Especially irksome are people whose "couple of minutes" turn out to be fifteen. **2.** Ordinarily *couple* takes a plural verb: "The couple *are* expecting their first child." In some instances, however, as in "This couple *is* next in line," when the word clearly refers to a unit, a singular verb is appropriate. **3.** "A couple weeks" is FF. SWE says "a couple of weeks," because *couple* is considered a noun, not an adjective.

(the) course of Can usually be deleted from phrases such as "during the course of the meeting."

courteous/polite Courtesy has more depth than politeness. A *polite* person says "Please" and "Thank you" and "May I help you?" A *courteous* person means them.

covet/envy If you *covet* your neighbor's wife, you probably also *envy* him for having her. To covet is to want something belonging to another, and to envy is to be sorry that someone has something that you desire.

crack down on Informal journalese (and to that extent SWE) for "enforce the laws strictly against (wrongdoers)."

crass Although some writers on usage say that *crass* should be used only as "stupid," in today's writing it almost always means "coarse, unrefined, insensitive, thoughtless." A crass remark, for example, is uttered by someone who pays no attention to the feelings of his or her listeners. In some instances it may have overtones of greed, money-grabbing: "the crass tactics of Wall Street."

crawfish *Crawfish* is what kids wading in a creek call the cretacean known to scientists as *crayfish*. Eaters of the delicacy are likely to look for *crawfish* on the menu. In Louisiana, crawfish lovers might not order at all if it were called *crayfish*, which might connote a high school biology laboratory. The verb *crawfish* ("to back out of an agreement or a position") is FF. But it's a picturesque metaphor suggested by the backward scurry of the creature.

credibility gap

What someone says	(credibility gap)	What we can believe

This is a useful term, and not only in politics, although SWE does often employ it in political contexts. Such gaps are perhaps even more numerous in business dealings. The ancient Romans showed that in their frequent use of *caveat emptor*, "let the buyer beware."

credible/creditable/credulous/discreditable/incredible/incredulous/uncreditable A *credible* story is believable; an *incredible* one, not believable. A *creditable* act deserves credit or praise; an *uncreditable* one does not; a *discreditable* one harms the reputation of the doer. A *credulous* person is too willing to believe anything heard or read; an *incredulous* one prefers to disbelieve.

crescendo Conservatives like the historically accurate definition: "gradual increase in intensity or volume": "Near the end of a long crescendo passage, the sounds of the percussion instruments became almost deafening." The conservatives dislike "The music reached a crescendo," in which the word signifies "peak, intense climax." Most classical musicians probably agree. The use in this sense is not rare in SWE, however.

criminally assaulted Nice-Nellie journalists use the term as a euphemism for "raped, sexually attacked." It's somewhat silly to do so, for almost every physical assault is a criminal act. See also ATTACK/ ASSAULT/RAPE.

criterion Almost always the SWE plural is *criteria*, but dictionaries do now also recognize *criterions*. *Criteria* is not SWE as a singular, however. SWE says "criterion," "the only criterion is . . ."

critical When referring to health, a writer of SWE may remember that the word comes from the same distant source as *crisis*. It concerns a turning point, a state in which the patient's physical or mental condition may become either much better or much worse. This is what hospital reports mean when they say, "Her condition is critical." Physicians and good writers distinguish *critical* and *serious*. The same principle applies to figurative uses, as in "The health of the national economy seems critical."

criticism Strictly speaking, criticism may be unfavorable, neutral, or favorable, or a mixture, but in the popular mind, and in most SWE, the word suggests more vinegar than honey. When the usual interpretation is not intended, SWE often resorts to "favorable criticism" or "comment" or another unambiguous term.

critique Increasingly used in SWE as a verb, not just as a noun: "Publishers' readers seldom have time to critique a manuscript thoroughly." Conservatives who dislike the noun-to-verb shift prefer *analyze*, *review*, or *criticize*. *Criticize*, however, is now often interpreted as basically negative, whereas a critique points out both good and bad qualities. See also CRITICISM.

crude/rude A *crude* man probably is too mentally handicapped or uneducated to realize when he is being rude. A *rude* woman probably knows that she is rude but doesn't care. An English saying: "A gentleman or lady is never rude – unintentionally."

culmination See FINAL COMPLETION.

cumulative See ACCUMULATIVE/CUMULATIVE.

curious Can be ambiguous. "She is a curious person" may mean either that she has curiosity and asks many questions, or that she is odd, peculiar, out of the mainstream. SWE tries to word sentences so that readers can easily determine which meaning is intended.

curmudgeon See CODGER/CURMUDGEON.

currently SWE omits this word unless it seems essential. Often a present-tense verb is enough. "She is currently writing a novel" is probably no better than "She is writing a novel."

cursive/cursory *Cursive* handwriting is flowing, connected writing as contrasted with manuscript writing as taught to many children, who first learn to print letters individually. *Cursory* means "rapid, hasty, superficial, perfunctory": "cursory inspection of our luggage," "cursory reading."

custom, custom–built Although originally these terms meant "especially built for each buyer," the meaning has gradually shifted to "more expensive than and slightly different from another model." SWE clarifies such terms by defining them or by choosing an unmistakable context, or it may substitute an undiluted, uncheapened expression such as *tailor-made*.

customary/habitual What "most people" do or say is *customary*: "It has long been customary to avoid wearing bright clothing at funerals." *Habitual* refers to what has become a habit, and it often applies to only one person: "his habitual discourtesy."

cut in half SWE, but so are the more logical *cut in halves* and *cut in two*.

cute Overused for "pretty," "delightful," "possessing qualities desirable in an attractive small child." Of late, *cute* has taken on added meanings; "arch," "mischievous," "pretending to be shy": "I'll answer you directly. I'll not be cute about it." Here is a rule followed by one writer of SWE: Use *cute* no more than once a day.

cyclone/tornado A *cyclone* is any system of rotating wind, ranging in size from a whirlwind to a hurricane or typhoon. A *tornado* (informally a *twister*) is one variety of cyclone. Its funnel–shaped cloud whirls with winds of high velocity and potential destructiveness, but a tornado is much smaller than a hurricane and lasts not nearly so long. In popular usage a tornado is often called a cyclone. That's what it is, but the more specific term is customary in SWE. See also HURRICANE/TYPHOON.

cynical/skeptical A *cynical* person distrusts people's motives and almost always suspects the worst. A *skeptical* person is less steadily and less broadly negative. He doubts the truth of someone else's assertion but does not make doubting a way of life.

D

dais/lectern/podium   A *dais* is a stage or platform where a speaker and perhaps others appear before an audience. A *podium* is a smaller platform, especially that where a conductor stands to be more easily seen by the orchestra. A *lectern* is a reading desk, usually with a slanted top on which a speaker may place notes.

damaged/injured   Things are *damaged*; people or animals are *injured*; parts of the body are injured, except for teeth, which are damaged: "damaged car, bicycle, apartment"; "injured boy, cat, wrist, paw."

Dame/Sir   In England, *Dame* is approximately the feminine equivalent of the knightly title *Sir*. Just as one refers to Sir Winston or Sir Winston Churchill but not Sir Churchill, one also does not refer to Dame Edith Sitwell as Dame Sitwell. (A once prominent English actress rejected American speaking invitations in which she was addressed as "Dear Dame.")

damsel   This once favored word of poets is now seldom used except jocularly: "Prithee, rescue yon damsel in distress."

dastardly   A *dastardly* act is not only despicable but also cowardly. The word is sometimes misused to mean despicable and bold.

data (singular or plural)   *Data*, a Latin plural, has gradually become treated in English more as a singular ("this data is"). The reason is that the meaning has shifted from "these figures" to "this set of figures." Most conservatives, scientists, and academic writers, however, are still likely to write "these data are." The Latin singular, *datum*, is rare. In its stead SWE generally prefers *this fact* (or *statistic*, or the like). See also AGENDA.

daylight-saving time   See SAVING(S).

dead body   "Three dead bodies were found in the wreckage of the plane." In such a context, we would be unlikely to say *bodies* unless they were dead. However, *dead* is defensible in "over my dead body" or other contexts in which death is not really meant.

deadbeat   Used occasionally in SWE for "loafer, no-good, one who does not pay his bills," *deadbeat* still seems slightly slangy, and for this reason some writers avoid it.

deadly/deathly   *Deadly* means "death-causing": "deadly weapon," "deadly carbon monoxide gas." *Deathly* means "like death": "deathly still," "His gray, emaciated face looked deathly."

deal   **1.** FF (informal and overused) in expressions such as "Big deal!" and "That's no big deal." **2.** "A raw deal" is also somewhat informal but does appear rather often in SWE. **3.** "A good (or *great*) deal of" appears frequently in SWE, although many writers prefer the shorter *much*. **4.** In SWE one deals *in* things, *with* persons or subjects: "Some brokers deal in junk bonds. They deal with both large and small investors. An article in *Money* deals with the topic."

deathly See DEADLY/DEATHLY.

debar/disbar *Debar* ("exclude, shut out, prevent") is giving way to *bar*: "The chairman debarred (*barred*) the topic of finance from the discussion." *Disbar* means only "officially expel a lawyer from the profession or from practice in a particular jurisdiction": "After being convicted of grand larceny, Lane was disbarred."

debut (as verb) SWE occasionally produces sentences such as "The soprano debuts in Carnegie Hall tonight," although strong conservatives prefer "makes her debut." Unlikely in SWE: "Auto dealers are debuting their new models" or "New-model Fords debut this week."

decease(d) Except in legal use, *die* is usual in SWE, not *decease*. *The deceased*, meaning "the dead person," is also mainly legal or at least largely impersonal. A person delivering a funeral eulogy, for instance, is likely to call the dead person by name rather than "the deceased." SWE carefully distinguishes *deceased* from *diseased*, "having a disease."

decide See CONCLUDE/DECIDE.

decimate Roman military officers sometimes enforced discipline by *decimating* troops – casting lots and killing one man in ten. Purists say that in modern use of the word the one-in-ten ratio should be preserved; if the population is decimated by AIDS, for example, about a tenth die. Modern dictionaries, however, define *decimate* as "destroy or kill a large part of," purposely leaving *large* vague. SWE writers, especially sportswriters, sometimes use the verb in that way. FF says, "The Denver Broncos decimated the hapless Houston team" (Denver did not kill or destroy the Oilers or even a substantial number of them).

declare See CLAIM.

decomposed/discomposed Anything *decomposed* is rotten. When things are *discomposed*, they are disarranged, disordered. A discomposed person is upset, agitated, but not quite distraught.

deduce/deduct/induce To *deduct* is to subtract: "Deduct line 9 from line 8." To *deduce* is to draw a conclusion: "She quickly deduced his motives, as any woman could." Although some dictionaries give *deduce* as a synonym of *deduct*, confusion may arise if no distinction is made. To *induce* is to persuade or to cause or in logic to move from particular instances to a generalization. Some people fail to distinguish *induce* from *deduce*. When you deduce, you start with a broad principle and then reason that certain specific points can be derived from that principle. For example, if the general principle is that most Swedes have blond hair, you may deduce that Lars, a Swede, probably has blond hair. But when you induce, you start at the other end, with a number of specifics from which you attempt to draw a general principle. For example, if you know several hundred Swedes, most of whom have blond hair, you may induce from those specific cases the generalization that most Swedes have blond hair.

defamation/libel/slander   *Defamation* is a general term meaning the stating of something harmful to someone's reputation. *Slander* and *libel* are two different kinds of defamation. Slander is always oral. Libel is usually printed but may be in handwriting, pictures, effigies, or even recorded oral language. So if *X* says of *Y* in a speech, "He is a liar and a thief," she may be guilty of slander unless she can prove the truth of her assertion. But if she says it in a recording that is played somewhere, or prints it, or shows it in caricature, she may be guilty of libel.

defective/deficient   Something *defective* has a flaw of some sort, such as a starting mechanism that does not work or a law that is ambiguously worded. Something is *deficient* if a part is missing. Perhaps a connection is missing in the starter or there is an oversight in the law.

definite/definitive   Something is *definite* if it is exact, certain, clearly defined: "a definite answer," "a definite meeting date," "definite steps toward a solution." *Definitive* means "final, best, authoritative." Thus a definitive edition of Poe's poetry is supposedly complete, accurate, and impossible or at least highly unlikely to be improved upon.

DEFINITIONS   See **CONNOTATIONS**; IS WHEN, IS WHERE.

defuse/diffuse   To *defuse* is to remove a fuse from, or in some other way make discharge impossible. We hope that a bomb is *defused*, not *diffused*. In diffusion its parts would be widely scattered – probably by the force of the explosion.

deliverance/delivery   Although *delivery* has several meanings ranging from "conveying a package" to "giving birth," *deliverance* is restricted in SWE to (1) a rescue from danger or bondage, or (2) (much more rare) a jury verdict or other publicly expressed decision. Example of (1): "In *Huckleberry Finn*, Tom Sawyer concocts an elaborate scheme for the deliverance of Jim from his confinement."

demand/order   To *demand* is to ask strongly and peremptorily that an action be taken: "Signers of the document demanded that political prisoners be released." Only a person with authority may legitimately *order* that an action be taken: "The president (*general*, or the like) ordered that political prisoners be released." *Order*, but not *demand*, may have a personal pronoun as an object. Instead of "He demands you to return the money," SWE requires "He demands that you return the money" or "He orders (or *commands*) you to . . ." See also ASK/DEMAND/INQUIRE.

deny   See CONTRADICT/DENY/REFUTE.

depend (on vs. upon)   Either *on* or *upon* is SWE after *depend*, but *upon* is slightly ponderous. Sometimes the sound or rhythm of a sentence may affect the choice. See also ON/UPON.

dependent on See ADDICTED TO/DEPENDENT ON.

deplete/reduce A depletion is normally greater than a reduction. To *deplete* is to use all or almost all of: "Mother Hubbard's cupboard was depleted." To *reduce* is to lessen, to use or eliminate part of: "Our food supply was reduced by a third."

deplore/lament/regret/repent Both *deplore* and *lament* express higher or more conspicuous emotion than *regret* does. To *deplore* is to regret strongly, but simultaneously to show disapproval: "Elizabeth Barrett Browning deplored the use of children as mine workers." *Deplore* does not take a personal object: you may deplore my actions but not me. To *lament* is to mourn deeply, and often loudly: "The mourners beat their chests and cried, lamenting almost hysterically." To *repent* is to be contrite about one's misdeeds: "Repent, ye sinners!" One who repents hopes to do better in the future.

depraved See ABANDONED/DEPRAVED/VICIOUS.

deprecate/depreciate To *deprecate* someone or something is to disapprove, belittle, disparage, make fun of: "She deprecated the usefulness of her own efforts." To *depreciate* is to reduce in value or to make a deduction for wear, age, or the like: "The IRS allowed us to depreciate the property over a five-year period." Confusingly, however, SWE sometimes uses *depreciate* in the sense of "belittle, disparage." Most often, though, SWE keeps the two words separate. See also SELF-DEPRECATION/SELF-DEPRECIATION.

desalinate/desalt When a long and a short word have the same meaning, SANE and SWE ordinarily choose the short one.

descend down See ASCEND UP.

descendant See ANCESTOR/DESCENDANT.

description SWE tries to avoid vague or ambiguous phrases such as "horses of this description." Is the meaning "such strong horses" or "horses that look like this" or "wild horses," or what?

desegregation/integration Although the readily apparent results of either process may be the same, the words have different emphases and perhaps different psychological effects. *Desegregation* stresses getting rid of something – a rather negative idea. *Integration* emphasizes developing something – a positive idea. SWE users are aware that neither of these words applies to racial matters only. For example, large companies may integrate (combine) or segregate (separate) parts of their operations, such as sales and consumer relations.

desert(s)/dessert (nouns) A barren, dry area is a *desert* (pronounced *dez*-urt). What a person *deserves* are his *deserts* (pronounced de-*zurtz*). In "He got his just deserts," *just* is redundant. *Dessert* (pronounced de-*zurt*), with an extra *s*, refers to the last course of a meal – the "extra" course that puts on unwanted weight.

designed/intended Although the two words are often interchangeable, *designed* is preferred in SWE when some actual designing (drawing, inventing, creating) is involved. Dubious: "The hay was designed to feed hungry caribou" (the hay was *intended* for the caribou, but nobody designed it).

desire Sometimes pretentious. "I have a desire for a Seven-Up" means only "I want . . ." or "I'd like . . ."

desperate/hopeless A *hopeless* person has no hope left. A *desperate* person has little hope but feels that there is a slight chance if reckless (desperate) measures are taken. A desperate criminal, for example, may try to drive through a police barricade, but may be less likely to do so if there is no hope of escape.

despite the fact that Wordy. SWE usually shortens it to *although* or *even though*.

dessert See *desert(s)/dessert*.

destroy The old order saith that *destroy* means "ruin completely, eliminate," and that therefore "destroy completely" or "partly destroy" is wrong. But the old order changeth. The distinguished conservative panelists of *Harper's* split their votes almost evenly, with Leo Rosten arguing that *completely* adds emphasis, and with several panelists saying that partial destruction is possible – say, two rooms in a five-room house. SWE also is somewhat split, but generally avoids "destroy completely" and is ambivalent about "partly destroyed the house" vs. "destroyed part of the house." See also AN-NIHILATE, DESTROY, FLAY. . . .

develop/invent To *invent* something is to create it. To *develop* something is to elaborate or improve upon what already existed. Bell invented the telephone, but many later workers have developed the phones that we have today. See also DISCOVER/INVENT.

device/devise *Device* is a noun: "This device
Catches mice.
Ain't that nice?"
Devise is a verb: "We'll devise a plan
To catch a man."

devilry/deviltry To use as a synonym of *mischief*, most British prefer *devilry*, most Americans *deviltry*. *Devilry* sounds more wicked.

devil's advocate In the Roman Catholic Church a *devil's advocate* is a qualified person designated to show why someone should not be canonized or beatified. In other contexts, a devil's advocate presents arguments against a proposal, not necessarily because of dislike but simply to make available the evidence on all sides. More loosely, the term means someone who is hostile to what is generally considered a good cause; SWE seldom follows this definition.

devise See DEVICE/DEVISE.

diagnose SWE says, "The illness was mistakenly diagnosed as malaria," but not "She was mistakenly diagnosed to have malaria." A condition may be diagnosed, but not the person who has it.

dialectal/dialectical *Dialectal* means "pertaining to dialect": "Professor Reeder is studying dialectal differences between North and South Carolinians" (*Dialectical* is occasionally used for this meaning but can cause misunderstanding.) *Dialectical* means "pertaining to dialectics ('methods of argument')": "Philosophers often have dialectical differences."

diaphanous/translucent/transparent   Thin, see-through clothing such as artists assume that houris wear is *diaphanous*. Anything that lets light through but denies a clear view of the houri is *translucent*. Clear glass, being *transparent*, does not interfere with the view. See also OPAQUE/TRANSLUCENT.

dice/dies   In games, the usage is one *die*, two or more *dice*; with reference to machinery, one *die*, two or more *dies*.

diction   Two meanings are usual for *diction*: "choice of words" and "degree of clarity in enunciation." These two meanings, however, may result in ambiguity. Does "Her diction is excellent" mean that she chooses words well or speaks (or sings) clearly? To avoid such ambiguity, some writers choose not to use *diction* at all unless something else in the sentence clarifies the meaning: "Her diction suggested a large vocabulary." "His diction – every word distinct – impressed the audience more than his ideas did." Other writers prefer to limit *diction* to "choice of words," and substitute *articulation, enunciation*, or *distinctness* for the other meaning.

die (*from* vs. *of*)   FF "She died *from* cancer." SWE says, "She died *of* (or *as a result of*) cancer."

die (noun)   See DICE/DIES.

differ from/differ with   The more common expression is *differ from*, meaning "to be unlike": "Peas differ from beans." "A child sometimes differs from both parents." "I differ from you in that I prefer chocolate to vanilla." In the sense of "disagree," however, *differ with* is SWE: "Mrs. Raleigh differed with her husband about the principles of child-rearing."

different   Often redundant, as in "They sampled fifteen (different) varieties of cereal."

different from/different than   *Different from* is the usual SWE, although *different than* sometimes appears and is prevalent in FF. When a clause follows, *different than* is SWE: "The quality of asparagus is different than it was last week." Using *from* would here require adding *what*. A beautiful example of differentiation is in this sentence by Adam Clymer in the *New York Times Magazine*: "Americans think of Russians as quite different from themselves, much more different than the British, Germans, or Japanese [are]." British people often use *different to*.

differential   In expressions such as "the differential between *A* and *B*" or "the differential is small," *difference* has the same meaning and is unpretentious. *Differential* is needed in some technical contexts.

diffuse   See DEFUSE/DIFFUSE.

dilemma   Historically, a *dilemma* is a situation in which two choices appear equally satisfactory (or unsatisfactory). More recently, it has been used to mean any troublesome situation: "One of today's greatest dilemmas is drug use." Since many other words exist for *problem* or *trouble*, it would be good (SANE believes) to hold *dilemma* to its historical meaning. The battle, however, seems unlikely to be won; SWE is moving toward the loose definition.

dimensions/proportions SWE often uses the words interchangeably, although many careful writers choose *dimensions* for measurements and *proportions* for comparisons or relationships. If the dimensions of a box are 4″ × 6″ × 4″, the proportions are 1 to 1.5 to 1. Less careful writers may say, "The dimensions of the disaster are unknown," when *extent* or *gravity* is probably better. Or they refer to "the proportions of the Grand Canyon," even though the canyon is measurable; *vast size* or a similar expression may be more accurate. See also DISASTER PROPORTIONS.

diplomacy/tact Sometimes used interchangeably, although *diplomacy* has a connotation of higher importance. Nations, for instance, engage in diplomacy, but individuals have more need of tact. *Diplomacy* also suggests adroit management, but *tact* is more often reflected in choice of words or small deeds. Diplomacy may have great things at stake, even the fate of a corporation or a nation, but the goal of tact may sometimes be only to avoid hurting someone's feelings. And, even though tact is not the same as diplomacy, diplomats must use a great deal of it.

direct/directly The adjective *direct*, like other adjectives, tells something about a noun: "a direct shipment," "a direct answer." The adverb *directly* is used in SWE especially in these senses: exactly – "Aim directly at the bullseye"; immediately, quickly, by the shortest route – "Go directly home"; positively, straight – "Evidence points directly at the butler as the murderer." In a sentence such as "We deliver _____ to your home," *directly* is usual in SWE, but *direct* is not questioned in advertising or other commercial contexts.

disapprove/reject Although SWE may use the words interchangeably, *reject* is stronger. For example, a parent may disapprove of a child's choice of friends but may be wise enough not to reject them.

disassemble/dissemble To *disassemble* is to take apart: "We disassembled the big clock." To *dissemble* is to conceal one's actions, intentions, or feelings: "Not wanting her husband to know where she had been, she dissembled by murmuring something about shopping."

disassociate/dissociate The simpler *dissociate* has almost pushed out *disassociate*.

disaster proportions Journalists sometimes write, "Damage has reached disaster proportions," or the like. The use of a noun as an adjective is often awkward, as it certainly is here. Usual SWE: "a disastrous amount."

disbar See DEBAR/DISBAR.

discerning/discriminating According to SWE, when you look at something with a *discerning* eye, you attempt to see the details. Art appreciation classes, for example, help viewers to discern things normally overlooked in a Rubens or a Monet. If you are *discriminating*, you again look at details but you also evaluate and compare, and especially you reject some things. An art expert may be discriminating enough to distinguish between a Monet and a Monet imitation.

disclose/divulge/reveal SWE uses each only with reference to something that has been hidden, not as a synonym of *say* or *tell*: "The secretary of state revealed (or *divulged, disclosed*) today that a secret meeting was held last month with . . ." Dubious: "The secretary of state revealed today that he will hold a press conference next Tuesday." Here *announced* or *said* is preferable unless the official had previously kept secret the upcoming conference.

disclosure/revelation In SWE *disclosure* is a neutral word, meaning "making known what was unknown." *Revelation* is more striking, perhaps even sensational. For example, an officeholder may make a disclosure of his income, but a revelation may occur if someone finds that some of that income derived from illegal activities.

discomfit/discomfort When SWE uses the verb *discomfort*, the idea of loss of comfort is present: "The move into a single room discomforted her." *Discomfit*, however, suggests becoming discontented or dejected: "Word of his cousin's injury discomfited Eric for several days."

discomposed See DECOMPOSED/DISCOMPOSED.

discontinue/disemploy/release Business and government use several such verbs for "discharge, fire." The intent is kindly, and the euphemism may be less damaging to the worker when he or she tries to get another job. In general, though, SWE prefers a more direct word. See also EUPHEMISM/EUPHUISM.

discourage/frustrate In SWE *discouragement* often suggests longer duration than *frustration*, which is usually a temporary or even momentary condition. For example, I may be frustrated but not discouraged by a balky can opener.

discover/invent People have *discovered* gold but *invented* radios. We discover what already exists but invent what was previously unknown. See also DEVELOP/INVENT.

discreet/discrete *Discreet* means "prudent, cautious, tactful": "A discreet editor insists that reporters check names and addresses carefully." *Discrete*, a comparatively rare word, means "separate, distinct": "There are many discrete species of bees."

discriminating see DISCERNING/DISCRIMINATING.

discrimination The emphasis on *discrimination* in references to unjust treatment of minorities has hidden the fact that discriminating people realize that discrimination of other sorts is desirable, for example, discrimination between politicians' words or smiles and politicians' substance and actions.

disdain See CONTEMPT/DISDAIN.

disemploy See DISCONTINUE/DISEMPLOY/RELEASE.

disinterested/uninterested The usual dictionary definition of *disinterested* is "impartial," and conservative editors still follow that. An umpire should be disinterested – fair to both sides – even though he or she has great interest in the game. But *disinterested* is used so widely to refer to loss of interest ("I soon became disinterested") that the battle to preserve the conventional definition seems all but lost. A sentence such as "The umpire was disinterested" is now often understood to mean that the umpire lost interest or had no interest. SWE frequently substitutes *impartial* for *disinterested* and uses *uninterested* in the usual meaning, "not interested." Some editors accept the "loss of interest" meaning for *disinterested*, but others (stubbornly or loyally) reject it.

dismiss against "Both charges against Gray were dismissed" is obvously more logical than "Both charges were dismissed against Gray." SWE realizes that the charges (not the dismissal) were against Gray.

disorganized/unorganized Ordinarily, in SWE, something *disorganized* was formerly organized but no longer is. *Unorganized* means "not organized, not systematically arranged."

disqualified/unqualified A person who has been disqualified was once qualified or was thought to be so. A person who is *unqualified* lacks the education, strength, skill, or other qualifications required for a position.

disremember/misremember *Misremember* is SWE as the equivalent of *remember incorrectly*: "I misremembered the number and touched a 7 instead of a 6." However, it is FF (dialectal) for "forget" or "fail to remember." *Disremember* is FF.

dissect See BISECT/DISSECT.

dissemble See DISASSEMBLE/DISSEMBLE.

dissimulate/simulate You *dissimulate* if you hide your thoughts, feelings, or motives: "She was angry, but had enough self-control to dissimulate." You *simulate* when you pretend: "My father often simulated dislike for my jokes, but he could not repress the laugh lines near his eyes."

dissociate See DISASSOCIATE/DISSOCIATE.

distinct/distinctive Something *distinctive* has an individual touch that differentiates it from most other things in the same category, but it is not necessarily unique: "This pitcher is distinctive because an unusual design has been etched in the Finnish glass." Something *distinct* either may be dissimilar to anything else or may be clear and unquestionable: "Platinum is distinct from silver." "His enunciation is always precise and distinct." The adverbs *distinctively* and *distinctly* are differentiated similarly.

distinctive/distinguished That which is *distinctive* is out of the ordinary (see DISTINCT/DISTINCTIVE). *Distinguished*, used chiefly of people, refers to accomplishments, eminence, or dignified appearance: "Senator Laramie's record is distinguished: he has sponsored much ecologically significant legislation."

dive (noun) FF (slang) for a disreputable place, often one where liquor, narcotics, or prostitutes are available and where robbery and other misdeeds are likely. Increasingly, however, the term appears in SWE: "in a dive in Bangkok."

dived/dove Both are standard, but *dived* is more likely in SWE. It is the older form, *dove* having developed by analogy with *drive, drove*. As a past participle, *dived* is usual, *dove* only occasional: "She had dived from an eight-meter board."

divide off (out, up) *Divide* is usually enough.

divorce (verb with) **1.** SWE often draws several distinctions. If Helen was the plaintiff: "Helen obtained (or *got*) a divorce." "Helen divorced Tom." If Helen was the defendant: "Helen was divorced." "Tom divorced Helen." If the divorce was "no fault": "Helen and Tom (or *Tom and Helen*, or *The couple*) were divorced." To indicate present status, regardless of who brought the suit: "Helen is divorced." "Helen is a divorcée." **2.** Purists say that *divorce* is only a transitive verb, as in "She divorced him," "He divorced her," "They were divorced." But in recent years sentences such as "They divorced in 1988" have become as common as divorce itself, and modern writing treats the verb as both transitive and intransitive.

divorcée A *divorcée* is "a divorced woman." Some dictionaries and most newspapers print the word without the accent mark. There's also *divorcé*, "a divorced man," but that word is infrequently used because of confusion with *divorce*.

divulge See DISCLOSE/DIVULGE/REVEAL.

do time This term is now SWE for "serve a prison sentence": "He has done time. He did ten years." Note that *do* is standard in many expressions for everyday tasks, such as doing chores, housework, homework, dishes, hair, exercise, problems.

dock/pier/wharf Technically, a *dock* is the space filled with water in which a ship remains when in port. A passenger boat or ship is tied to a *pier*, a freighter usually to a *wharf*. The three terms have been confused so frequently, however, that most dictionaries treat them as virtually interchangeable. Even seamen now refer to *dockworkers*, although such workers labor on a wharf (or *wharfside*) rather than out in the water. Some SWE writers follow the technical distinctions, but probably few people notice when they do not comply. See also HARBOR/PORT.

dog who (or *that*) A longtime controversy: should an animal be referred to as *that* or *who*? For people who have a beloved pet, the answer is clear: their pet deserves *who*-dom as much as a person does, so "our dog, who died last year," but "the cows that are grazing in the pasture" – unless the cows are personal friends.

dogma/tenet Each means "a principle, belief, or opinion." A *dogma* is more likely to emanate from an organized group and so to be regarded as authoritative: "Christian dogma." It may also mean "a system of principles or tenets." *Dogma* is the basis of the adjective *dogmatic*, which suggests unproved and perhaps arrogant assertions. A *tenet* is a firm belief held by either an individual or a group: "One of my political tenets is that . . ." Several or many tenets may be components of a dogma.

dollars SWE avoids the combination of $ and the word *dollars*, choosing one or the other; not any of these: "$45,000 dollars," "$45 thousand dollars," "the dollar-value is $45,000."

domicile Used in law, but in other contexts seems superelegant. Usually *house, apartment,* or *home* – or even *place* – is better. (Does anyone ask, "Your domicile or mine?")

dominating/domineering Both refer to controlling, to exertion of power by a superior. Neither is regarded as kind or gentle, but *domineering* is the more unpleasant term. A domineering person is haughty, arrogant, overbearing, even tyrannical and cruel.

donate SWE uses *donate* especially for charitable giving, not for gifts to friends and relatives: "She donated fifty dollars to the Christmas Basket Fund."

done, done with *Done* in the sense of "finished" is slightly informal but does appear in formal contexts as well: "The work of the committee is now done." SWE is careful, though, to avoid ambiguous sentences such as "The work of the committee will be done next Thursday," in which *done* may mean either "finished" or "performed." *Done with*, meaning "finished with," also hovers between formal and informal, leaning toward the latter: "She declared that she was done with him forever."

donnybrook A part of old Dublin called Donnybrook was the locale of fairs where savage fights often occurred. The word is now SWE for any fierce, no-holds-barred brawl involving several or many combatants. Loosely, it is also applied to angry, loud oral arguments with numerous participants on each side. The word is occasionally still capitalized.

don't 1. Like other contractions, *don't* is generally informal. However, it often appears in moderately formal SWE, sometimes to lighten the tone slightly, sometimes in imperatives such as "Don't underestimate the influence of letters to Congress." 2. *Don't* with a third-person singular subject is FF except in reporting conversations: "He (*She, It*) don't." SWE: "He (*She, It*) doesn't." 3. *Don't let's* is FF for *let's not*. 4. The plural of the noun *don't* ("a negative rule") is written *don'ts*. See also **CONTRACTIONS**.

dope FF for "narcotics, habit-forming drugs." See also DRUGS.

double entendre This French borrowing is SWE. It refers to a phrase or sentence that has two possible meanings, one of which is likely to be sexy or improperly suggestive. An old example is Mae West's "Come up and see me sometime."

DOUBLE NEGATIVE See NOT (AND OTHER NEGATIVES); NOT UN-.

doubtless(ly) SWE prefers *doubtless*. Oddly, both words often imply that some doubt does exist, as *no doubt* also does: "No doubt (or *Doubtless*) Harry will be late again" is similar to "Probably . . ."

dove (verb) See DIVED/DOVE.

downplay Although some dictionary editors seem not to have noticed it, the verb *downplay*, meaning "pay little attention to," or "de-emphasize" is rather widely used in both formal and informal contexts. It is no better, however, than the more conventional *play down*.

drag The past tense and past participle are both *dragged* (not *drug*) in SWE: "The terrier (has) dragged in a dead opossum."

drama/dramatic Strong words associated with literature and with high emotion. SWE avoids trivializing them. It chooses other words in, for example, accounts of most Little League baseball games.

drastic *Drastic* means "extreme, severe, violent." SWE avoids use in matters of relatively small importance: "Just because I misspelled a few words, the teacher lowered my grade from B to C. That was a drastic thing to do." SWE might rewrite: "That reduction seemed excessive" or "I thought that I still deserved a B−."

draw a conclusion Often can be shortened to *conclude*.

dreadful/horrible These words are too often used to describe trivial things or events, such as a large but harmless barn spider, misty weather for a picnic, or a sweater of an unstylish color. Something truly *dreadful* should fill us with dread; something *horrible*, with horror. See also AWFUL; COLOSSAL, COLOSSALLY; TERRIBLE, TERRIBLY.

dribble/drivel When a baby drools or slobbers, it may be said to *dribble* or *drivel*. The saliva is also called *dribble* or *drivel*. (*Drivel* is more likely as both verb and noun, *drool* still more likely.) A person talking stupidly *drivels*, and what he or she says is *drivel*.

drivel See DRIBBLE/DRIVEL.

dropout Now SWE for one who leaves school, employment, and so on, earlier than usual or perhaps earlier than desirable: "Even in kindergarten he wanted to be a dropout." "Our dropout rate is lower than most." To use it as a verb, SWE breaks the word in two: "to drop out of the race."

drought/drouth These alternative spellings are both SWE, but *drought* seems less desirable because in other words (*bought, ought, sought, thought*) *ought* is not pronounced like *out*. SANE pleads, "Don't further complicate English spelling." But SANE may be losing this one.

drowned/was drowned In a long debate, some persons argued for "Henry was drowned," saying that Henry himself did not perform the act. Opponents said *was drowned* meant that someone drowned him. Today, *drowned* and *was drowned* are interchangeable, with *drowned* more common because it is shorter. Note that *drowned* has only two *d*'s. The pronunciation and spelling *drownded* are nonstandard.

drugs This is now a standard shortening of "illicit drugs," even though most of the drugs sold in a drugstore are not illicit. If any misunderstanding is likely, SWE substitutes a more specific term, such as *heroin* or *narcotics*. *Drug addict* and *drug peddler* are also SWE, and *drug pusher* often appears in SWE.

drunk **1.** *Drunk* is FF (informal) in such expressions as "became a drunk," "the town drunk." *Drunkard* is slightly more likely in SWE. **2.** Conservatives prefer "drunken driver" to "drunk driver," but to a victim of such a driver the distinction is unimportant. "Drunk driver (*driving*)" is common in newspaper writing, and there is an organization called Mothers Against Drunk Driving (MADD). **3.** *Drunken* is now used only before a noun: "a drunken woman." *Has drunken* is an outworn form.

due to An unquestioned usage is "Her hospitalization was due to a fall" (*due* used as an adjective). Conservatives dislike *due to* as equivalent to *because of*: "Due to a fall, she was hospitalized." "She was hospitalized due to a fall." RHD, however, informs readers that *due to* for *because of* has been in use since the fourteenth century and says it is now "standard in all varieties of speech and writing." Most writers of SWE agree.

due to (owing to) the fact that SWE usually shortens the expression to *because* or *since*. Instead of "The reason is due to the fact that . . . ," SWE prefers "The reason is that . . ."

duel Dubious: "Four National League East teams are dueling for the championship." A duel involves only two teams, groups, or contestants.

duff This is FF (slang or highly informal) for "rump, buttocks, seat," but good writers and speakers sometimes use the word publicly. Carl Sagan, in a CBS interview, said, "The world will get better only if we get off our duffs and make it so."

dumb/ignorant/stupid An *ignorant* person may have only a small supply of general knowledge or have no knowledge in a particular field: "ignorant of the world outside his section of Chicago," "ignorant in music." A *stupid* person is dull, unintelligent, perhaps foolish: "too stupid to learn simple arithmetic." An ignorant person can usually be taught. A stupid person perhaps can be taught only a little. *Dumb* is an FF synonym of *ignorant* or *stupid* or both. In SWE it is ordinarily used to mean "unable to speak": "She is a deaf and dumb child."

duplicity See CHICANERY/DUPLICITY.

during the course of, during the time that *While* is usually enough.

dwarf, midget, pygmy A *dwarf* is a small person, usually one whose growth has been arrested by a pathological condition. Snow White's companions are the best-known dwarfs (or *dwarves*). A dwarf's physical proportions are distorted in some way. A grown *midget*, however, is well proportioned, a miniature man or woman. Tom Thumb was a midget famous in British folklore before someone given that name became a favorite P. T. Barnum attraction. Capitalized, Pygmy (or *Pigmy*) refers to a member of an African or Asian tribe whose heights range from four to five feet. Uncapitalized, *pygmy* (*pigmy*) may mean any unusually small person, and as an adjective may refer to some animals.

dwell/live/reside An ordinary family *lives* at 1136 Elm Street. A wealthy or pretentious family *resides* at 1101 Elmwood Circle. *Dwell* is old-fashioned, surviving mainly in poetry of yesteryear. Wordsworth's Lucy "dwelt among the untrodden ways."

E

each (verb and pronoun with) FF: "Each of the girls were trained to do their work well." SWE: "Each of the girls was trained to do her work well." The reason for SWE's preference is that *each* refers to one person or thing, as do the verb *was* (*is*, *walks*, and so on) and the pronoun *her* (*his*, *its*, and so on). The presence of the plural *girls* in the example confuses some writers, but *each* is the governing word.

each and every one *Each* or *every one* should be enough.

each/either Here is a dubious usage, from a catalog description: "The handbag has two outside pockets on either side." *Either* suggests "one or the other," but the catalog picture shows two pockets on *each* side. "Two pockets on both sides" would be ambiguous, probably meaning "two plus two" but possibly "one plus one."

each/every The essential meanings of "Each boy brought his rifle" and "Every boy brought his rifle" are the same, but the emphasis with *each* is on individual action, while *every* stresses that the group was unanimous.

each other/one another Interchangeable in most usage, although many SWE writers prefer *each other* for two persons, *one another* for more than two: "The boxers battered each other unmercifully." "All the members of the winning team were congratulating one another." SWE possessive forms are illustrated in "The two women admired each other's dresses" and "The three women admired one another's dresses." Note the placement of the apostrophes.

each See BOTH/EACH.

early beginnings SWE deletes *early*, or for *beginnings* substitutes *days*, *years*, or the like.

early on A relatively recent American borrowing from England, now SWE although not in general superior to *early*. It may be a little smoother and clearer as a sentence opener: "Early on, man had no tools at all."

easily/easy　SWE uses *easily* to modify a verb: "He could easily lift two hundred pounds." "She can do most of her work easily, but lifting is difficult." In a few idiomatic expressions *easy* has become SWE where *easily* might be expected: "Take it easy." "Please go easy on me."

Easter Sunday　This term has become SWE even though *Sunday* is unnecessary (Easter is always on a Sunday – the first one after the full moon on or next after March 21). One defense of *Easter Sunday* is that *Easter* is now often taken to include the period before and after the Sunday, as in "Easter vacation."

easterly/eastern　*Easterly* is used especially in "easterly winds" and "in an easterly direction." *Eastern* appears in most other contexts. Similar distinctions apply to the other points of the compass. An east wind comes from almost straight east, but an easterly wind is shifty, although it tends toward one direction. Each of the *-ly* words may also be a noun referring to a wind or a storm: "A northerly hit us hard."

easy money　SWE for money obtained by deception or with little effort – usually the latter.

easygoing　This word is SWE.

eaves　SWE chooses a plural verb: "the eaves are . . ." The form *eave* is rare, although SANE considers it logical when only one is meant. (*Eavesdrop* originally referred to standing under the eaves to hear what was being said inside a building.)

eccentric/erratic　An *eccentric* wheel rotates on an axle that is somewhat off center; in consequence the movement, while predictable, is not what is customary for wheels. Similarly, an eccentric person is "off center," not like us well-balanced folks. If there were such a thing as an *erratic* wheel, it would have many notches into which its axle could slip at random. Its rotation would be bumpy, unpredictable. An erratic person is also unpredictable, causing us to ask, "What on earth will he say or do next?" See also EROTIC/ERRATIC.

ecology/environment　*Environment* means "surroundings," "everything within one's surroundings": "The Arctic environment is unsuitable for most plants and animals." *Ecology* is the relationship between organisms and their environment, or the study of such relationships: "The ecology of an area is greatly affected when land is cleared and parts of it are cultivated." See also AMBIANCE/ENVIRONMENT.

economic/economical　*Economic* is a broad term referring to material wealth, finance, economics, the economy: "economic conditions," "the family's economic well-being." *Economical* means "not wasteful": "Economical buying is essential for most families." Although *economic* for *economical* does appear, SWE almost always differentiates to avoid possible confusion. See also ECONOMICAL/FRUGAL/ THRIFTY. . . .

economical/frugal/thrifty/miserly/stingy In SWE the first three are words of praise for not spending carelessly or foolishly. *Miserly* and *stingy*, however, refer to excessive saving, extreme unwillingness to spend. *Miserly* has the added connotation of hoarding: "Silas Marner was miserly; he buried his gold coins." See also ECONOMIC/ECONOMICAL.

edgeways, edgewise/endways, endwise/lengthways, lengthwise/ sideways, sidewise The words in each pair are interchangeable, although SWE usually prefers the form with *-wise*. See also -WISE.

edifice See BUILDING/EDIFICE.

edition/impression, printing A new *edition* of a book involves extensive revision. A new *impression* or *printing*, however, is only a reprint made without alteration (although very minor corrections are sometimes made).

educational/instructive *Educational* is overused and pretentious in the sense of "instructive." Exploration of a cave, for example, or playing with toys, might better be called *instructive*. *Educational* may refer to methods of teaching, a type of philosophy, or a system rather than to something relatively small in extent and effect.

educationese, pedagese These interchangeable disparaging names are applied to the language used by some educators, especially in their speeches and articles. Typically, it includes many passive verbs and vague, abstract, or cumbersome nouns, and is verbose.

educationist SWE seldom uses this word, preferring *educator*. When it does appear, it is as a disparaging term for an educator, or to describe educational policies disliked by the writer.

educator Most likely to be used in SWE for a school administrator or a professor of education. Miss Hanson in the third grade probably insists proudly that she is a *teacher*.

-ee This suffix normally refers to the one done to rather than to the doer, for example, *donee* vs. *donor*, *trainee* vs. *trainer*. Few people like *-ee* words. All the world loves a *lover*, but the word *lovee* may not have been used since 1894. *Hatee* seems never to have been used at all, thank goodness.

e'er/ne'er Contractions for *ever* and *never*, used mainly in poetry of a bygone time.

effect See AFFECT/EFFECT.

effective This word is used as business or military jargon in sentences such as "Effective May 12, these prices will be ten percent higher." In ordinary English, *on* or *beginning* is more likely.

effective/efficient *Effective* describes something that can produce a desired result: "Rat-Rid is effective in killing rats." *Efficient* is similar but suggests that the product can be used with comparatively little effort and perhaps at low cost: "Kill rats with efficient Rat-Rid: no traps, no mess, no odor, no danger to pets."

effeminate/female/feminine/womanly *Effeminate* in SWE is used to describe men whose appearance, actions, or other qualities seem more characteristic of a woman: "an effeminate way of walking." *Female* means only the opposite of *male* and is not at all judgmental: "Female breasts are larger than male." *Feminine*, the opposite of *masculine*, refers in a usually commendatory way to the delicate qualities, mannerisms, and so on of a woman: "He marveled at her softness and her feminine grace." *Womanly* suggests greater maturity than does *feminine* (although feminine qualities are also womanly): "womanly in her understanding."

effete Something strange has happened to *effete* in the twentieth century. It has moved from "exhausted, barren" to "self-indulgent, decadent," and is now most likely to refer to rich people such as those characterized by Spiro Agnew as "effete Eastern snobs." At one time, an unfruitful tree could be effete; hens, people were told in 1774, "after three years become effete and barren." SWE, of course, is unlikely to write about trees or hens as effete. Its effete people are likely to be degenerate or at best lacking in vigor.

efficient See EFFECTIVE/EFFICIENT.

e.g./i.e. *E.g.* means "for example" (from Latin *exempli gratia*). *I.e.* means "that is" (Latin *id est*). Both abbreviations are appropriate in technical writing or reference books but seldom appear in literary works. Punctuation before and after *e.g.* is the same as for *for example*; with *i.e.*, the same as for *that is*.

egoist/egotist Interchangeable, although a shade of difference is worth noting. An *egotist* is more likely to brag about himself; in his opinion he's the greatest. An *egoist* may think just as highly of herself and work selfishly toward her own goals, but she usually doesn't trumpet her abilities or accomplishments. (The term *egoism* is used in philosophy and ethics for the belief that morality is based on self-interest.)

egregious Originally meant "outside the flock, extraordinary," but now it means "unusual in an extremely bad way." Thus egregious lies are likely to be worse than ordinary lies.

either See EACH/EITHER.

either/neither (with more than two) Ordinarily, *either* or *neither* refers to one of two: "Either (*Neither*) of the two coats is satisfactory." For more than two, SWE usually chooses *any one* or *no one* (*none*). In sentences such as "I must buy either oranges, apples, or bananas," however, *either* is SWE even though three or more alternatives are given.

either . . . or/neither . . . nor (verb with) With two singular subjects, SWE uses a singular verb: "Either (or *neither*) Roy (n)or Sue is . . ." With two plurals, it uses a plural verb: "Either (*Neither*) the Poles (n)or the Czechs are . . ." With a singular and a plural, it uses a verb that agrees with the one that comes later: "Either (*Neither*) the boys (n)or Sue *is* . . ." "Either (*Neither*) Sue (n)or the boys are . . ."

elder, eldest/older, oldest *Older* and *oldest* may refer in SWE to either persons or things, *elder* and *eldest* to persons only. SWE now seldom uses *elder* and *eldest* except in referring to members of the same family or business firm: "the elder Mr. Craig," "the eldest member of the family," "The elder Mr. Lamson is a vice-president, the younger an office manager." Even in these examples, *older* or *oldest* may be used. *Elder* and *eldest* appear to be dying. *Elder statesman*, however, survives.

elderly No one knows for sure when elderliness begins, but suddenly it's there. *Middle-aged* quietly grays or balds into *elderly*. *Elderly* is a little kinder than *old* and considerably younger than *aged*.

electric/electronic *Electric* means "pertaining to, producing, derived from, or operated by electricity": "electric lights, vacuum cleaners," and so on. *Electronic* refers to devices or systems in which electrons flow in a vacuum, in a gaseous medium, or in semiconductors: "A computer is an electronic device."

ELEGANT VARIATION An ironic term coined by Fowler for a needless shift from a noun to its synonym; for example, from *woman* to *lady*, or from *Achilles* to *the son of Peleus* (yes, Homer did it often). Sportswriters may be the greatest American offenders, saying in one line, "Carter hit a home run," in the next that "Schmidt countered with a four-bagger" before "Elster decided the issue when he skied one to left." Perhaps only a close follower of baseball realizes that each of the three hit a home run. In general, SWE avoids such elegant variation.

elegy/encomium/eulogy An *elegy* is "a poem, especially a lament for the dead." An *encomium* is "a tribute or high praise to someone, usually living." A *eulogy* is "a speech or written prose praising someone, not necessarily a dead person."

elemental/elementary *Elemental* may refer to forces of nature: "an elemental force, such as gravity," or it may mean "simple but powerful": "the elemental fury of a hurricane," or "essential": "an elemental part of the process." *Elementary* means "introductory, basic, pertaining to basics." An elementary school provides an introduction to formal education, and when Sherlock Holmes said, "Elementary, my dear Watson!" he meant, "basic, simple." An elementary step, sometimes miscalled *elemental*, is a beginning step.

elevated Often too big a word for "high" or "tall." SWE prefers "high temperatures" and "high (or *tall*) hills." For moving up to a more responsible and better-paying position, "Hawkins was promoted to the vice-president's office" is more appropriate than *was elevated* (which suggests that the Otis Company was involved).

elicit/illicit *Elicit*, a verb, has the figurative meaning of "draw out" and usually refers to information of some sort: "Officers elicited the admission that Conrad had been drinking." *Illicit*, an adjective, means "illegal" or sometimes "not approved by public opinion": "an illicit love affair."

eliminate/prevent   These words are not interchangeable in SWE. Rust can be *prevented*, but it can't be *eliminated* unless it's already there. For example, this is not SWE: "Eliminate formation of rust by using No-Rust." See also AVERT/AVOID/PREVENT.

ellipse/ellipsis   An *ellipse* is an oval with both ends alike. Many racetracks are ellipses. In grammar, an *ellipsis* is the omission from a sentence of one or more words that can readily be "understood" by the reader or hearer. In "Call your mother" the elliptical word is *You*. In "I voted, but you did not," it is *vote*. The plural of each word is *ellipses*, but the plural of *ellipsis* is pronounced e-*lip*-seez rather than e-*lip*-suz. Three dots (. . .) to indicate an omission are called "marks of ellipsis." (Four are often used if the omission is at the end of a sentence, but the first is a period.)

83

elope   SWE is aware that a young woman should be careful if a man asks her to elope. An elopement does not necessarily include marriage. When a couple run away together, they are eloping, but marriage may not always follow.

eloquent/grandiloquent/magniloquent   An *eloquent* speaker speaks fluently, persuasively, movingly. A *grandiloquent* or *magniloquent* speaker uses too many flowery or polysyllabic words, seems pompous, and is not likely to be convincing even though he or she puts on a good show.

else's   SWE uses *somebody else's, nobody else's*, and so on. *Who else's* is also SWE: "Who else's answer is correct?" If no noun follows, either *who else's* or *whose else* is used: "Who else's is correct?" "Whose else is correct?" To obviate a choice, SANE recommends *who else's* in both instances.

emblazon   See BLAZE/BLAZON.

emend   See AMEND/EMEND.

emigrant/immigrant   If your ancestors came to the United States from Ireland, for example, they *emigrated* and were *emigrants* from that country (*e-* means "out"). From the standpoint of the United States, they *immigrated* and were *immigrants* (*Im-*, a variant of *in-*, means "in" or "into").

eminent/imminent   *Eminent* means "well-known, prominent, famous." It is more likely to be applied to statesmen or members of a profession than to actors, athletes, or tradespeople. *Imminent* means "coming soon," especially in time: "A flood seemed imminent." "Triumph was imminent."

emolument   Highfalutin for "wages, pay."

emote   Some dictionaries say that this word for "speak emotionally or theatrically, overact" is only to be used informally, but most do not attach a label. SWE uses it but realizes that it connotes effusiveness or excessive dramatics.

empathy/sympathy   The usual meaning of *sympathy* is "sharing the feelings of another – most often feelings of sadness or loss." *Empathy* is a stronger word, suggesting identification with another person or possibly an animal: "His empathy with the deer was so great that he could feel the sharp, cruel arrow in his own side." A less common meaning of *empathy* is pretending that inanimate beings share human feelings and qualities. Statements showing such empathy (also called "pathetic fallacy") include "The clouds began weeping gently" and "This crazy cliff is trying to kill us."

enact into law SWE deletes *into law* because *enact* means "make into law."

encomium See ELEGY/ENCOMIUM/EULOGY; PANEGYRIC.

end (come to an) This expression is wordy: "At last the struggle came to an end." Usually better is ". . . ended." *Put an end to* is similarly wordy.

end result/end product SWE deletes *end* unless some noteworthy preliminary or intermediate results have been named or at least have existed.

endemic/epidemic/pandemic An *endemic* disease almost constantly exists in an area or in one part of the population: "Swamp fever was endemic in the marshlands, especially among the white settlers." An *epidemic* strikes many people about the same time but is not customarily prevalent: "the 1918 flu epidemic." *Pandemic* diseases affect everyone or almost everyone in an area: "Tuberculosis became pandemic in the tribe." *Endemic* in the sense given here is almost always an adjective, seldom a noun, but *epidemic* and *pandemic* may be either adjectives or nouns.

ending See FINAL COMPLETION.

enemy See ADVERSARY/ANTAGONIST/ENEMY.

enervate Sometimes mistakenly thought to refer to nerves, and occasionally confused with its near-opposite, *energize*, *enervate* means to weaken, to reduce strength or vigor. An enervated person is debilitated: "Clancy's two months in a military prison camp had enervated him unbelievably."

enough See AMPLE.

endways, endwise See EDGEWAYS, EDGEWISE/ENDWAYS, ENDWISE/ LENGTHWAYS, LENGTHWISE . . .

engage in/indulge in Both mean "take part in, occupy oneself with." *Indulge in*, however, means "take part in (something) to a great extent or excessively." The "something" may lead to unpleasant results. Thus two persons in an office may engage in gossip for a few minutes, but if they indulge in gossip for a couple of hours each day, they may lose their jobs.

engine/motor Steam-powered: engine. Gasoline-powered: engine if large, engine or motor if small. Electric-powered: motor. Nuclear-powered: engine. Liquid-fueled rocket: engine. Solid-fueled rocket: motor.

engineer/scientist/technician *Scientists* search for principles or scientific truths, and *engineers* and *technicians* apply them. The technicians are especially concerned with day-to-day use and maintenance.

England See BRITISH ISLES, ENGLAND/GREAT BRITAIN . . .

engraving/etching Cutting tools are employed in making an *engraving*. For an *etching*, acid substitutes for the tools.

enigma/riddle Listed in some dictionaries as synonyms. *Riddle*, however, is more often used to mean a trivial or amusing question or problem: "What did the boy angle say to the girl angle?" "You're acute angle." An *enigma* is usually more obscure and is more likely to refer to serious matters. "The enigma is this: 'Why does so much poverty exist in the world's richest nation?'" Sir Winston Churchill's famous statement incorporates both words: "Russia is a riddle wrapped in a mystery inside an enigma."

enigmatic Not used in SWE to mean "doubtful" or "questionable." The meaning is "puzzling, like an enigma": "The wording of the new tax laws was so enigmatic that even IRS agents differed greatly in their interpretations."

enormity/enormousness For the meaning "great size," *enormousness* is more common in SWE: "the enormousness of the Sahara." In general, SWE restricts *enormity* to "extreme wickedness, something horribly offensive": "the enormity of this brutal crime," "the enormity of the Holocaust." *Enormity* for "great size" is gaining ground in edited writing. Nevertheless the distinction is worth maintaining, because confusion may arise when the two words are used interchangeably.

enough (*that* vs. *to*) SWE prefers *enough to*: "They have enough money to live on comfortably." More wordy: "They have money enough that they can live on it comfortably." (In general, a phrase is preferable to a clause if it is shorter and no less clear.)

enough See AMPLE.

enraged/incensed/infuriated Each refers to a different degree of anger. *Incensed* describes somewhat controlled anger, often justified: "I realized that my father was incensed by Hugo's insult, but his appearance remained calm." *Enraged* means "strongly angered": "Kate was so enraged that she stamped her foot hard enough to break off the heel of one of her dainty slippers." An *infuriated* person has lost even more emotional control, is "in a fury": "Kate was so infuriated that she threw two of her Royal Copenhagen plates at her husband."

enthuse A back-formation is usually a verb shortened from a noun. Some writers object to each new one but later may come to accept it, as is true of *edit* (from *editor*) and *reminisce* (from *reminiscence*). At present, *enthuse* (from *enthusiasm*) is still in the transitional stage. It is informal but appears increasingly in SWE: "She enthused every time another volunteer appeared." Many writers may not yet be happy with that sentence, but others prefer it to "She waxed enthusiastic."

entitle/title   In the sense of "give a name or title to," the words are synonymous: "Sarah entitled (or *titled*) her book *Retrieval*." The former is more common.

entomologist/etymologist   An *entomologist* studies insects; the word comes from Greek for "insect." An *etymologist* studies the origin of words. Greek *etumon* means "the true sense of a word." "The etymologist looked into his Latin dictionary to find an appropriate name for the insect that the entomologist had discovered." *Entomology* and *etymology* are the fields associated with each term.

enviable/envious   People who are happy are *enviable*, "to be envied." Those who do the envying are *envious*: "envious of other people's happiness." See also ENVY/JEALOUSY.

environment   A general word, and sometimes pretentious. If *home, family, neighborhood, community,* or *city* will express the meaning clearly, SWE chooses that because of its greater specificity. Pretentious: "In the baby's immediate environment were only his mother and sister." SWE says, "In the house at that moment were only the baby, his mother, and his sister." See also AMBIANCE/ENVIRONMENT; ECOLOGY.

envisage/envision   *Envision* is the more imaginative verb, as its relation to *vision* suggests. One envisions great and perhaps impossible things such as universal peace or a building grander than the Taj Mahal. To *envisage* is usually to form a mental picture that is not excessively unrealistic: "The college president envisaged a science building twice as large as the existing one, and much better equipped."

envy/jealousy   These are not synonyms in SWE. One may be *envious* of another's possessions or qualities but *jealous* of a rival: "Bartram envied the older attorney's poise in the courtroom." "Bartram was jealous of his wife's first husband, who often came to see his child and – Bartram suspected – also his ex-wife." See also ENVIABLE/ ENVIOUS.

epic   In SWE this word describes only great events such as might be the subject of epic poetry. It is not applicable to games or anything else not involving truly heroic deeds. A clutch home run or a strikeout that wins a World Series can be exciting or dramatic but is hardly epic.

epicure/epicurean/hedonist   A *hedonist* believes that pleasure is the chief goal of living. The small *-e epicurean* does also but differs from other hedonists in placing most emphasis on food and comfortable living. A capital *-e Epicurean* follows the philosophy of Epicurus, who believed in avoiding pain and worry and rejected most of the religious beliefs and practices of his contemporaries. An *epicure* has refined taste in food and wine.

epidemic   See ENDEMIC/EPIDEMIC/PANDEMIC.

episode/event/incident/occurrence   *Event* is the general term for any happening: "a pleasant event." An *episode* is one in a series of events: "Most novels consist of many connected episodes." An *incident* is a relatively small event: "Little Jerry scratched his finger — only one of the day's many incidents that Alicia would save to tell Tom about." *Occurrence* is often used for *event*, especially when the event is rather ordinary: "a daily occurrence."

epithet   Not necessarily an unfavorable word. In "Louis the Sun King" and "Stan the Man Musial," *the Sun King* and *the Man* are favorable epithets; but in "Ethelred the Unready," the epithet at least appears to be unfavorable (it may, however, be translated as "the Cautious"). *Epithet* may also mean "a term of abuse or contempt": "Members of the street gang shouted epithets at us." Today that meaning is probably more frequent than the other, although some conservatives consider it a misuse.

epitome   See ACME/APEX/EPITOME.

eponym/namesake   An *eponym* is a real or imaginary person from whom a place, tribe, institution, era, and so on, takes its name: "The perhaps mythical Romulus was the eponym of *Rome* and *Roman*." "George Washington was the eponym of thousands of American places." A *namesake* is on the receiving end: "Uncle Henry was very proud of the nephew who was his namesake, Senator Henry Lake." A namesake is a person named for someone else or – less often – a person who by chance has the same name.

equable/equitable   *Equable* means "uniform," "relatively unchanging," "unemotional": "States' penalties for the same sexual violation are far from equable, ranging from short sentences to life imprisonment." "She has an equable temperament, seldom showing even traces of anger." *Equitable* means "fair, just, right" but not necessarily "equal." An equitable division of property is one fair to all, even though the claimants may get different amounts.

equal (in comparisons)   Although George Orwell's *Animal Farm* told readers that some animals are more equal than others, SWE reasons that equal is equal and can't be any more or less so. See also COMPARISON OF ABSOLUTES.

equally as   Generally, one or the other word can be deleted: "The second cake tasted equally (as) good." "The second cake tasted (equally) as good as the first."

equitable   See EQUABLE/EQUITABLE.

equivocal   See AMBIGUOUS/EQUIVOCAL.

equivocate/lie/prevaricate   Each verb refers to deceiving, to telling a falsehood. *Lie* is the strongest, referring to what is definitely untrue: "He lied about his age, saying that he was thirty-nine instead of forty-five." *Equivocate* and *prevaricate* resemble each other in suggesting evasion of the truth rather than outright falsehood. One who equivocates often resorts to ambiguities: "She is thirty-nine, but equivocates by calling herself 'thirtyish.'" "He equivocated by saying

'Mistakes were made' rather than 'I made mistakes.'" *Prevaricate* is closer to *lie*: "He prevaricated, calling himself 'about forty' although he is forty-five."

-er, -est In general, adjectives of two syllables do not have comparative and superlative forms with *-er* and *-est* if they have any of the following endings:

-al (formal)	*-ile (agile)*
-ed (muddled)	*-ive (pensive)*
-en (rotten)	*-om (random)*
-ent (lucent)	*-ose (verbose)*
-ful (sinful)	*-ous (porous)*
-ic (frantic)	*-que (antique)*
-id (candid)	*-st (unjust)*
-il (tranquil)	*-ure (mature)*

Most other two-syllable adjectives do take *-er* and *-est*, although in some sentences *more* or *most* may sound better. Most dictionaries list the *-er* and *-est* spellings when appropriate.

erotic/erratic A newspaper story reports the following: "Police said that the suspect, John Doe, was walking down the street in an erotic manner." Well, maybe, but Doe's walking was probably *erratic* – stumbling, unpredictable. Male strippers, rather than poor Mr. Doe, are likely to walk in an erotic manner.

erotic/exotic *Erotic* means "sexually suggestive": "an erotic dance (movie, swaying of the hips)." *Exotic* means "foreign, strange," but has connotations of warmth, beauty, and imagination – like something out of the *Arabian Nights*. An exotic dance is one not native to or customary in our region. Technically, an ugly, barren foreign place can be exotic, but most modern readers will interpret the word to mean "charmingly unusual to Americans." SWE chooses a different word for an unattractive place.

errata (verb with) The plural of *erratum* ("error, especially in print") is *errata*. *Errata* usually means a list of errors not noticed or corrected before a book was printed. In this sense, like *agenda* and *data*, the word is often followed by a singular verb: "The errata is at the end of the book." Strong conservatives, however, would substitute *are* in that sentence, and SWE uses the plural in clearly plural senses: "Many errata were not corrected in the second edition."

erratic See ECCENTRIC/ERRATIC; EROTIC/ERRATIC.

error/mistake Although these words are often interchangeable, *error* is more likely to suggest blame, a failure to follow a course generally believed right or wise: "a serious error in judgment." A *mistake* may result from a rather small misinterpretation or a failure to remember: "a mistake in conjugating a Latin verb." In baseball, *errors* are strictly defined and are counted in the box score. *Mistakes*, probably much more numerous, may result from many small causes, such as throwing the wrong kind of pitch or playing too deep for a hitter. Such mistakes are usually less obvious than errors and do not appear in the box score.

ersatz   See ARTIFICIAL/ERSATZ/FAKE . . .

escalation   Often another word is more exact: *increase, enhancement, growth, invigoration, freshening, intensification, extension.*

especial/special   Interchangeable, with *special* the usual choice. *Especial,* if used at all, generally means "exceptional, superior in some way": "my especial friend," "my especial favorite."

especially/specially   *Specially* means "for a particular reason" or "in a particular way": "specially chosen," "specially prepared." *Especially* means "more than anyone or anything else," "more than ever": "Patience is especially needed now." "Patience is needed now especially." SWE avoids the redundant *more especially.*

espresso   The term is *espresso* coffee (not *expresso*).

-ess   Although no one objects to feminine-gender words such as *lioness* or *tigress,* recent decades have driven into disfavor people-oriented words such as *poetess, postmistress,* and *stewardess,* as well as other forms that for no good reason make gender distinctions: *aviatrix, usherette, salesgirl,* and so on. See also HOSTESS; STEWARDESS.

essay   see ASSAY/ESSAY.

essential/indispensable/necessary/requisite   Almost interchangeable, especially *essential* and *necessary.* To many writers, however, the order from strongest to weakest appears to be *indispensable, essential, necessary, requisite.* In SWE, *more* (or *less, least*) is seldom employed before any of these words, because if something is indispensable, no one can do without it. One thing cannot be more indispensable than another. In FF, however, one frequently says things such as "For her, admiration is more indispensable than food." See also COMPARISON OF ABSOLUTES.

essential . . . must   In "It is essential that children must learn more geography," *essential* and *must* carry the same meaning. *Must* here is omitted in SWE, or the sentence is shortened to "Children must learn more geography."

-est   See -ER, -EST.

-est, -eth (verb endings)   Only feeble humor results from use of archaic verb forms – feeble humor or sometimes pity of the ignorant. A horrendously garbled invitation to a college dance read, "Bringeth thou thine wench or thine squire to ye olde Don Quixote Ball." If it is ever necessary to write in the style of the King James Bible, rereading a few chapters may refresh memory. *Dost,* for example, is second person, *doth* third; *leadest* and *prayest* are second, *leadeth* and *prayeth* third: "thou dost," "thou leadest," "he doth," "he leadeth." *-Est* and *-eth* verbs are not imperative. The following is not King James: "Prithee prayeth thou for all who sinnest thus."

estate-size(d)   This term is used loosely in real-estate ads describing pieces of land. *Estate-size* or *estate-sized* lots may vary from less than a quarter-acre to enough for a small plantation. The small print is generally more precise.

estimate/estimation Although the words are often used interchangeably as nouns, SWE treats *estimate* as a reasoned guess about profit, cost, and so on, but treats *estimation*, like *estimating*, as the act of making such an estimate: "The assessor's estimate was $20,000." "The estimation took only ten minutes." *Estimation* can also mean "esteem, regard": "His behavior caused him to rise in my estimation."

estimated at about "The number of casualties is estimated at about thirty." SWE deletes as redundant either *estimated at* or *about*.

-et/-ette When a choice exists, as in *cigaret*, *octet*, and so on, SWE is inconsistent. SANE chops off the useless *te*.

etc., et cetera **1.** Since *et cetera* means "and other things," SWE does not duplicate *and* by writing "and etc." **2.** SWE avoids the term unless readers can easily fill in some of the "other things." Poor: "The speaker discussed waste, pollution, etc." Acceptable: "She labeled the displays *A*, *B*, *C*, etc." **3.** *Et cetera* or *etc.* is unlikely to be used of persons. Poor: "Committee members who were absent included Jane Colwell, Marcia Babcock, etc." **4.** SWE avoids frequent use. **5.** Some SWE writers use "et cetera" or "and so forth" in full, disliking the abbreviation, but the shortened form is more common.

etching See ENGRAVING/ETCHING.

eternal In SWE this word is not modified by *more* or *most*. Nothing can be more eternal than eternal. See also COMPARISON OF ABSOLUTES.

-eth See -EST, -ETH.

ethic/ethical/ethics *Ethic* means "principle, rule of conduct": "The work ethic requires one to work at least enough to support oneself and one's own dependents." *Ethics*, referring to morals or moral choices, ordinarily takes a plural verb: "Her ethics have never been questioned." But with reference to a branch of philosophy, it takes a singular verb: "Ethics is sometimes called moral philosophy." *Ethical* is an adjective: "Is deception ever ethical?" To a doctor, an ethical drug is one that requires a prescription.

ethnic Actually, everyone is *ethnic* – that is, belongs to several racial, cultural, religious, or national groups. The word is generally limited in SWE, however, to mean "belonging to a racial group other than the one predominant in the area." In that sense, whites in Africa are ethnics. The word is descriptive, not a slur. It may be used as noun or adjective.

etymologist See ENTOMOLOGIST/ETYMOLOGIST.

eulogy See ELEGY/ENCOMIUM/EULOGY.

euphemism/euphuism A *euphemism* is a gentle, kindly expression used instead of a more direct one that might hurt or offend someone: "passed away" for "died." *Euphuism* (often capitalized) is a literary term, from *Euphues* by John Lyly (1579). It is a highly artificial prose style, characterized by elaborate comparisons, balanced sentences, antitheses, and alliteration.

eve Now rarely used for "evening" except in such terms as *Christmas Eve* (December 24), or *New Year's Eve* (December 31), or the *eve of battle* (the evening before a battle).

event See EPISODE/EVENT/INCIDENT.

eventuate This is a fat, pompous word for "happen."

ever so often/every so often Although the two idioms are often used interchangeably, SWE uses *ever so* for "very," as the expression *ever so easy* clearly shows. "He called ever so often" means, then, "He very often called." SWE uses *every so often*, in contrast, to mean "now and then, occasionally," "once in a while": "Every so often the phone rings."

every Since *every* carries a singular meaning (similiar to that of *each one*), a pronoun referring to it should also be singular: "Every private or officer must obey his superiors." Informally, *their* often occurs in such sentences, probably because of the confusion between "every private" and "all privates." Eventually that usage may also become SWE, but at present it appears only occasionally. See also EACH/EVERY.

every day/everyday SWE uses the solid form as an adjective: "every-day clothing," "an everyday event." The meaning is "appropriate for ordinary days, usual, commonplace." When the term is not an adjective, SWE uses two words: "Every day is different from every other." "Every day they rise at dawn."

every other . . . except SWE avoids "every other family except ours" and the like because the meaning is duplicated in *other* and *except*. SWE: Either "every family except (but) ours" or "all other families."

every which way On the edge of SWE. Some writers still consider it an informal way to say "in all directions," "scattered about": "The ball bearings rolled every which way."

everybody/everyone Interchangeable. Since each of these words is singular, a singular verb or pronoun accompanies it in formal context: "Everybody (*Everyone*) in both houses *was* so alarmed that *he* (or *she*, or *he or she*) ran outdoors, fearing an earthquake." "Everybody must bring his (or *her* or *his or her*) own food." (FF uses *their*, which occasionally appears also in SWE.)

everyplace See ANYPLACE.

evidence/proof *Evidence* is data that may be used to show that something is true or false or to lead toward any other conclusion. Sufficient and strong enough evidence constitutes *proof*, which is defined as "conclusive demonstration": "After listening to many bits of evidence, the jury decided that there was no proof of Hardy's guilt."

evident See APPARENT/EVIDENT/OBVIOUS.

evoke/invoke *Evoke* means "elicit, draw or call out": "The speech evoked calls for the governor's impeachment." *Invoke* means (1) "ask for": "Let us invoke the help of God." (2) "put into effect": "Two aldermen requested that Ordinance 2607 be invoked."

exact same   SWE deletes *exact*. However, *exactly the same* may on rare occasions be useful to emphasize the sameness.

exam   SWE prefers *examination* but often uses *exam* in newspaper headlines and in informal contexts.

example/exemplar/ideal/model   Each word may mean "something or somebody worth imitating." An *example* may be good or bad: "set a good (bad) example for the boy." *Exemplar* is in some ways like *example* but stresses worthiness of being followed: "Horatio Alger's boy heroes were held up as exemplars for a whole generation." *Ideal* suggests something or someone that approaches perfection: "an ideal house," "When Sid was a boy, his ideal was George Washington." A *model* may be physical, as in "Visit our model homes," or a pattern worth emulating: "a model office," "His father was his model."

example/instance   *For example* and *for instance* are interchangeable.

example/sample/specimen   An *example* is something used to illustrate or represent a class of things or a principle: "One example of her bravery occurred yesterday, when a bear wandered into camp." A *sample* is usually a physical thing: "Try a sample of our new candy." *Specimen* is most likely to be used in scientific contexts: "urine specimen," "one specimen of crab."

except   See ACCEPT/EXCEPT; BUT (FOR EXCEPT); EXCEPTING.

excepting   In most instances, *except* is SWE but *excepting* is not: "All the claims, except that dated 07/14/90, have been paid." As a verb, *excepting* is possible but rare: "We are excepting ('excluding') the claim dated 07/14/90." "All claims, not excepting ('not making an exception of') the one dated 07/14/90, will be paid."

exception proves the rule   Cliché. The meaning is not "The exception proves that the rule is correct" – a generally ridiculous statement. The actual meaning is "The exception *tests* the rule to help us to discover whether or not it is correct." Some writers substitute *test* in the expression.

exceptional   Often confusing when applied to a child, for some persons think of it as meaning "precocious, unusually talented," and others think of it as meaning "retarded." SWE prefers an unambiguous adjective. The usual definition of *exceptional* is "unusual, extraordinary." Careful writers explain the way(s) in which the thing or person is out of the ordinary.

exceptional/exceptionable   Something unusual is *exceptional*: "exceptional apples that weigh a pound each." Something is *exceptionable* if one may take exception to it, object to it, on some rational grounds: "I found nothing exceptionable in his assertions." (Caution: So few people understand *exceptionable* that the word may be misunderstood.)

excess(ive) wordiness All *wordiness* (*verbiage, verbosity*) is *excess* (*excessive*). SWE deletes the adjective.

exciting/fascinating *Exciting* music may make us dance. *Fascinating* music almost hypnotizes us; it adds depth to our emotions or may make us philosophize. Outside of music, the distinction is essentially the same. See also COLOSSAL, COLOSSALLY; FABULOUS/INCREDIBLE.

exclusive/select Except in certain legal or business expressions, such as "exclusive rights" or "exclusive of sales tax," *exclusive* usually suggests snobbishness. Thus an "exclusive club" excludes as members people who do not meet an arbitrary qualification, such as wealth, and an "exclusive dress design" is one that you and I can probably not afford. The adjective *select*, however, refers to high quality, the sort that even ordinary folks would be likely to choose.

excuse/pardon (verbs) Interchangeable in the polite expressions "Excuse me" and "Pardon me."

excuse (noun) See ALIBI.

execute/kill, murder *Execute* is used in SWE with reference to killing only when a sentence of death has been imposed – by a court, for instance: "The convicted murderer will be executed in May." *Gangland execution* is a term sometimes used in newspapers. It is accurate when a "court" of gang leaders determines that someone is to be eliminated. Unless that is certainly the case, *gangland murder* (or *killing*) is preferable.

exemplar See EXAMPLE/EXEMPLAR/IDEAL.

exercise/exorcise One way to *exercise* spirits would be to put them on bicycles. What is more likely is that we would try to *exorcise* them – chase them away.

exhausted/fatigued/tired/weary *Fatigued* implies more weariness than *tired* does, and *exhausted* suggests such weariness that any action at all is impossible. *Exhausted* is sometimes misused of a person who is still working. Not SWE: "Although exhausted, she continued shoveling the snow." *Tired* and *weary* are interchangeable, although *weary* seems slightly bookish.

exhausting/exhaustive *Exhausting* means "making extremely tired, making worn out": "She endured an exhausting daylong physical examination." *Exhaustive* means "thorough, including almost all possibilities": "Her doctors said that an exhaustive examination was necessary."

exhibit/exhibition Often used interchangeably, although sometimes in SWE an *exhibit* is one part of the things displayed in an *exhibition*: "the Tom Thumb exhibit in the exhibition of model trains."

exist/subsist To *exist* is to be, to live. Although *exist* and *subsist* are sometimes used interchangeably, *subsist* followed by *on* indicates what one "lives on" (often something simple or minimal): "That winter they subsisted on cornbread and beans."

exit When *exit* is a verb, it is intransitive (takes no object): "He exited from the room" rather than "He exited the room." Better still: "He left the room," "He hurried from the room," or the like.

ex-murderer   *Ex-convict* is satisfactory, because the person is no longer a convict. But once a murderer, always a murderer. SWE deletes *ex-*, or is kind and calls the person something else – maybe his or her name, or *he* or *she*.

exorcise   See EXERCISE/EXORCISE.

exotic   See EROTIC/EXOTIC.

expatriate/ex-patriot   A book ad says, "Viertel's novel is a drama of ex-patriot high life." This is not SWE. Viertel's characters have not lost their patriotism, as *ex-patriot* suggests. Rather, they are *expatriates* – people who live outside their native land, voluntarily or not.

expect   FF for "suppose," as in "I expect you did well in calculus." In SWE, *expect* is generally used in the context of looking ahead, not back: "I expect that you will do well in calculus" or "I expect you to do well . . ." See also ANTICIPATE/EXPECT.

expectorate/spit   *Expectorate* seems too high-flown for so ordinary an act. Besides, many people would not understand a sign that says "No Expectorating."

expedient/politic   Something *expedient* is appropriate, as well as quickly accomplished: "Obviously the most expedient thing to do was to call the fire department." Sometimes it suggests "done for selfish reasons": "He saved money by doing what was expedient, not necessarily what was wise." The adjective *politic* refers either to what is prudent or to what is shrewd and perhaps artful and ingenious. It does not necessarily concern politics or politicians: "a politic decision, widely applauded for its good sense," "a politic decision, regarded as a clever stratagem," "a politic businesswoman."

expensive   Not SWE: "Prices are too expensive." In SWE, prices or costs are high or low, but not expensive. Cars, food, and other things that are purchased may be expensive.

expert   See QUALIFIED EXPERT.

explicit   A valuable word for "specific, clearly delineated, forthright." Unfortunately, it has been used so frequently in recent years to mean "fully detailed in its portrayal of sex" that some people now equate it with "X-rated." SWE does not abandon the word but shows from context that no sexual inference should be drawn. Possibly subject to misinterpretation: "This book is an explicit portrayal of life in an almost manless small Italian town in World War II" (*detailed*, *authentic*, or *no-holds-barred* might be better).

explore every avenue   Cliché. Politicians sometimes promise to "explore every avenue" to reduce poverty or correct some other problem. The figure of speech seems odd on the surface, since most people equate *avenue* with a broad, tree-lined street that would require no exploration. However, *avenue* may also mean "a way to a place, an approach."

explosion/implosion An *explosion* is a bursting outward. The related verb is *explode*. An *implosion* is a bursting inward, like that of a dropped light bulb. The verb is *implode*.

expose Because *expose* now often means "show one's nude body, 'flash,'" SWE makes certain that no ambiguity exists when the word is used. Dubious: "He exposed himself for what he was." Clear: "He proved what kind of person he was."

express/expressed An *express* purpose is one that is definite, clear, and perhaps single, exclusive: "The society's express purpose is to help the blind." An *expressed* purpose is one that has been stated. Often the word hints that the statement may not be true: "The expressed purpose is to help the blind, but most contributions are used to pay office expenses and salaries."

95

extended Some writers on usage object to "extended illness," saying that *extended* means "stretched out" and that probably no one would intentionally stretch an illness; they recommend *long*. However, the conservative AHD includes this definition of *extended*: "continued for a long period of time."

extra I. SWE avoids overuse in expressions such as *extra fine, extra plentiful, extra easy to operate*. If a modifier is needed, *uncommonly, unusually*, or some other adverb can often replace *extra*. **2.** In combinations such as *extracurricular*, no hyphen is needed unless to help a reader, as in *extraactive*, which should be *extra-active*. An *extra-base* hit is not the same as an *extra base* hit.

F

fable/legend/myth A *fable* is a fictitious story, often with animal characters, usually illustrating some principle of human behavior: "the fable of the fox and the grapes." A *legend* is a probably untrue story that usually concerns a real person or persons and that has been passed along for years: "the legend of George Washington and the cherry tree." A *myth* often has to do with gods or superhuman heroes such as Apollo, Juno, or Hercules. To social scientists it is a widely accepted but only partly true belief: "Hitler's myth of Aryan superiority in all things." Loosely, a myth is any made-up story.

fabricate One meaning of *fabricate* is "to speak an untruth, to lie," so it is redundant to say "fabricate falsely" or "fabricate an untrue story."

fabulous/incredible Overused, especially in fiction aimed at the semiliterate, to mean "thrilling, exciting, super," and the like, and to refer to almost anything – most often emotions and the "incredibly" handsome men who arouse them. See also COLOSSAL, COLOSSALLY.

facile May refer either to a task easily done or to anyone who performs a task easily: "facile writing," "a facile writer." The word carries a suggestion of superficiality, since important tasks are seldom easy.

facility Instead of using *facility* to mean something specific and tangible, such as an airport, a harbor, a building, or a part of a building, SWE usually names the structure: "He used the bathroom" rather than "He used the facility."

(of the) fact In sentences such as "You can be certain of the fact that this account is accurate," SWE omits *of the fact*.

factious/factitious *Factitious*, a comparatively rare word, means "contrived, not authentic, produced artificially rather than naturally": "a factitious rise in sugar prices, caused by crooked speculators," "a factitious appearance of thoughtfulness." *Factious* is related to the noun *faction* and means "factional, divisive": "Factious elements may once again split the Democratic party."

factor Overused by some writers, especially in phrases such as "one factor" and "an important factor." Among possible substitutes are *component, constituent, contributing fact, division, feature, ingredient, installment, integral part, item, member, part, piece, portion, section, sector, segment, share, slice.*

fair/fare The distinction is made clear in "The public insists that this fare increase is not a fair increase."

fair-trade agreement Before 1975, if you were on the side of a manufacturer who wanted all retailers to sell his product at a stipulated price, you referred to *fair-trade agreements* or *fair-trade laws*. But if you were a consumer who objected because the product was not available in a competitive market and perhaps at a lower price, you used a different term, *price-fixing*. Fair-trade agreements became illegal in 1975, but accusations of price-fixing still exist.

fairy/gay/pansy Today, it seems, fairy stories are found mainly in gay magazines. Thus two attractive words have become difficult to use in their earlier meanings. *Gay*, because of its brevity, is apparently here to stay in its meaning of "homosexual," "a homosexual person," and must be considered SWE. However, with increasing awareness and understanding of homosexuality, *fairy* and other ridiculing terms such as *pansy* are used less and less in that context and may yet be reclaimed by folklorists, children, and floriculturists.

fake See ARTIFICIAL/ERSATZ/FAKE . . .

fallacy A *fallacy* is an error in reasoning, not just any error. A mistake in judgment, for example, is not in itself a fallacy, although it may be based on fallacious reasoning.

false illusion SWE deletes *false*. An illusion does not exist and so cannot be true or false. See also ALLUSION/ILLUSION.

famous SWE doesn't bother to tell readers, unless they are children or uneducated people, that, for example, Napoleon was a famous general. It is perhaps satisfactory, though, to note that Nimrod, much less widely known than Napoleon, was a famous hunter in Old Testament times. See also NOTABLE/NOTED/NOTORIOUS.

fancy/imagination As the word *fanciful* or the expression *strike my fancy* may suggest, fancy is lighter and more whimsical than *imagination*. Fancy in the sense of "playfulness" may be part of imagination, but the latter may also include recall of past sights and sounds and other experiences, all blended with thought to attain a perhaps unexpected result.

fantastic See COLOSSAL, COLOSSALLY.

fare See FAIR/FARE.

farther/further An attempt has long been made to restrict *farther* to physically measurable distances, and *further* to nonphysical: "Harrisburg is farther from here than Allentown is." "Shall we discuss the question further?" Today *farther* and *further* are used almost interchangeably in sentences such as the first example, but only *further* is customary in SWE in the second and in other such instances as "further argument," "further preparation," "Further, I want to say that . . ." Conservatives still do not use *further* for physical distance. The superlative forms are *farthest* or *farthermost*, and *furthest* or *furthermost*. SANE prefers the shorter words.

fascinating See EXCITING/FASCINATING.

fatal/fateful A *fatal* event involves death. A *fateful* event has important good or bad consequences but ordinarily no deaths. SWE rarely uses the terms interchangeably. The distinction is worth keeping.

fatigued See EXHAUSTED/FATIGUED/TIRED . . .

fault (verb) As a substitute for *criticize* or *blame, fault* has been used occasionally since about 1850 and has finally attained SWE approval. The AHD usage panel split 52–48 in favor, and a 1988 *New York Times* headline read "New York Faulted on Tuberculosis."

favorable See OPTIMISTIC, PESSIMISTIC; FAVORABLE, UNFAVORABLE.

faze Note the spelling of this word meaning "bother," "make uncomfortable": "The presence of his ex-wife did not *faze* him." In SWE *faze* occurs mostly in negative statements, not in sentences such as "He was fazed by the presence of his ex-wife." In questions, it may take a form like "Did this faze him?" or "Didn't this faze him?"

feasible/possible An action is *feasible* if it is not only possible but also sensible, likely to bring the desired results. The action is *possible* if it can be performed, regardless of how sensible or worthwhile it may be.

feel Despite onetime opposition, *feel* is now SWE for "believe, think": "Senator South felt that the legislation went too far." *Feel*, however, still connotes more emotion, *think* or *believe* more rationality.

feel (good/well; bad/badly) *Feel badly* is sneaking up on *feel bad* in SWE, but *feel bad* still has a common-sense defense. An apple may taste good or bad, a perfume may smell good or bad, music may sound good or bad, and a person may look or feel good or bad.

Like *look, smell, sound,* and *taste, feel* is a verb referring to one of the five senses. The modifier after such a verb describes the subject: apple, perfume, or the like. Usually, then, in SWE a person feels *bad,* not *badly.* A person, however, may feel either *good* or *well,* because *well* can mean "in good health." There are two SWE exceptions to the *feel bad* generalization: A dog may *smell badly* if illness has decreased its smelling ability, or *smell well* if it is able to follow a faint trail, and people may *feel badly* if something is wrong with their sense of touch. Also, besides feeling well if their health is good, they may feel well if their sense of touch is unusually acute.

feisty Although some dictionaries label *feisty* as regional or slang, this word – meaning "active, spirited, small but lively" – is useful. When Congressman Claude Pepper became an octogenarian, the media frequently described him as *feisty.* The word deserves to be listed with no qualifying label. It is SWE.

feline See BOVINE.

fellow For the meaning "man," *fellow* is FF: "See that fellow over there?" For the meaning "beau, boyfriend," *fellow* is obsolete slang, used extensively in the first third of this century: "Who's your fellow now?" Although President Ronald Reagan sometimes addressed "my fellow countrymen," *fellow* is redundant.

female companion/girlfriend/mistress Newspapers sometimes report that an alleged criminal, a businessman, or someone else has been found in a hotel room with a "girlfriend" or "female companion." They avoid *mistress,* which can be libelous when not provable.

female, feminine See also EFFEMINATE/FEMALE/FEMININE . . .

feminist A person can be a *feminist* without being female. The author of this book is a reasonably good husband, a good-natured father, and a feminist. "I am proud to be a feminist," actor Paul Newman reportedly said.

(on the) fence Cliché. It is perhaps overused to mean "not yet having decided" but still a quick and rather picturesque phrase.

fever/temperature Dictionaries record *fever* as one synonym of *temperature.* Minority report: It would be good to preserve a distinction. Each of us has a body *temperature,* even if it is only 90°. We have a fever only if our temperature is above 98.6°, so there is a difference. If our temperature is 102.6°, we have a fever of 4°. Everybody, even a dead person, has a temperature, but only occasionally do most living people have fevers.

few(er) in number SWE deletes *in number,* just as it omits the in-phrases in "small(er) or large(r) in size," "circular in shape," "taller in height," and so on.

fewer/less In FF, *less* is used almost exclusively for both countables and uncountables: "less vehicles," "less sugar." SWE, however, ordinarily requires *fewer* for countables: "fewer vehicles," "fewer members than last year." Apparent exceptions are references to time: "less than four months"; distance: "less than ten miles"; money: "less than twenty francs"; weight: "less than twelve ounces"; and percentage: "less than three percent." The reason for each exception is that the unit (e.g., four months) is considered a collective – a single period of time, a single amount.

fiancé, fiancée Masculine and feminine, respectively. The accent mark is increasingly disregarded outside France.

fictional/fictitious A *fictional* person is someone, such as Scarlett O'Hara, who exists in fiction but not in real life. A *fictitious* person is also unreal but is not in a novel, short story, or other fiction. For example, many children have fictitious (imaginary) playmates. A false name is also fictitious, and if you lie about having money in the bank, you are referring to a fictitious bank account.

fiddle/violin Itzhak Perlman and other great violinists may refer affectionately or humorously to their *fiddles*, but you and I had better call them *violins*. All of us, however, may refer to the fiddles and fiddlers at the old-time barn dance or its modern equivalents. There are violins in the New York Philharmonic and fiddles in the Grand Ole Opry.

field 1. Overused. If all the traveling salespeople and educators who talk about spending time *in the field* were laid end to end and side by side, they would cover 8,732 acres. If *the field of* were omitted before every reference to chemistry, photography, and so on, scientists could do more work and photographers could take more pictures. 2. SWE is wary of ambiguity in using *field*. The newspaper of a small college for teachers ran this item: "Professors Henry Eastman and Hilda Bogue spent last week together in the field." No, there was no hanky-panky. The professors were off campus visiting student teachers – the jargon for which was *in the field*.

fight with Ambiguous: "Jones fought with the English." Did he help them or try to hurt them? Unless the context clearly answers that question, SWE replaces *with* by choosing *against, beside*, or some other unambiguous preposition.

figuratively/literally "I was so tired after the long hike that I was literally dead." Only a ghost could honestly say that, because *literally* means "actually." Possible substitutions: "figuratively dead," "almost dead," "thought I was dying." *Figuratively* is related to *figure of speech*. Anything said figuratively is not to be considered a reflection of actuality. It may exaggerate or draw a comparison that is not to be interpreted as true except in a somewhat poetic sense.

figure FF for "predict," "conclude," or "believe" in sentences such as "He figured that the enemy soldiers would avoid the top of the ridge." *Figure* in SWE means "to calculate": "I figure the distance to be eighty miles."

figure out Overused by writers too lazy to figure out whether to say *understand, invent, solve, compute, calculate, decide, determine, contrive, comprehend, reason out,* or something else.

figurehead SWE says, "Although Rankin held the title of Chairman of the Board, he was actually a mere figurehead." As this example shows, a *figurehead* is only nominally important – conspicuous but little more powerful than the carved figurehead on the prow of an old-time ship. SWE does not use the word to mean "chief," "leader," or the like.

final analysis Often wordy or pretentious. "In the final analysis one must conclude that the procedures were ineptly chosen" may be better stated, "An observer must conclude that the procedures were inept" or "The procedures were inept."

final completion (conclusion, culmination, ending, upshot) SWE omits *final*.

finalize Although criticized by some writers on usage, *finalize* is listed without comment in most modern dictionaries. It appears mainly in business or political contexts: "finalized the deal." See also –IZE.

find/locate *Find* is the broader term, applicable to coming upon something either by chance or by intention: "While exploring the area farther west, Giles found a large, bubbling spring." "Drillers found oil near here." *Locate* emphasizes the place or location of something being searched for: "They finally located the missing child, still alive, in an abandoned cistern."

fine As an adjective of praise (a fine day, sweater, woman, boy, rain, or the like), *fine* is both vague and overused. A writer usually has time to think of a more specific word. *Fine* is also used excessively as an adverb, although that use seldom appears in SWE. Instead of "doing fine," "it works fine," "I can hear fine now," SWE chooses *well* or, when feasible, a more definite adverb.

fire (verb) SWE for "dismiss, discharge" but more likely to be found in informal contexts. See also DISCONTINUE.

firmly entrenched Although a cliché, the metaphor is clear and useful. *Firmly* is often deleted.

first and foremost An established idiom, but SWE omits *and foremost* unless the writer wants to stress the special importance of the point.

first annual This term is sometimes too optimistic. Maybe the "first annual" celebration (or whatever) will be so unsuccessful that it will never be repeated.

first-rate *First-rate* as an adjective meaning "of the finest quality" is SWE. In the sense of "in good health," however, it is more likely FF: "He feels first-rate today." The adverbial use, as in "He does his work first-rate," is FF.

first two/two first Today "the first two pages" and "the two first pages" are sometimes used interchangeably. Some writers dislike "the two first pages," however, arguing that there can be only one first page. SANE agrees. Similar comments apply to *last two* and *two last*.

firstly, secondly (and so on) These are SWE, but usually *first*, *second*, and so on are enough and are not pretentious. (Old-time preachers sometimes got at least as far as *fourteenthly*; the record-holder is unknown.)

fish/fishes Both are standard plurals, but the usual SWE choice is *fish* except with reference to different kinds or species: "caught a few fish," "Fishes of these waters include yellowtail, pompano, and grouper."

fishy Flesch lists eighteen definitions of *fishy*, including "suggestive of deception" and "casting doubt or suspicion." He asserts that "the word, with its unique blend of smelliness and slipperiness, simply can't be replaced by another." Consider it standard, he says, because "it's one of the great treasures of the English language." *Great* is probably an overstatement, but the word is indeed useful enough that it appears occasionally in SWE.

fit/fitted Interchangeable as the past tense, although when the verb is transitive, many writers prefer *fitted*: "The tailor fitted the jacket carefully," in contrast to "The jacket fit well." *Fitted* is the usual choice for a passive: "Each rod must be fitted precisely to its opening."

fix This is an overused word, both as noun and verb. For one of the noun meanings, *predicament, dilemma,* and *embarrassing position* are among the more specific substitutes. For the meaning "injection of an opiate," *fix* seems informal, but no short equivalent is available. In using *fix* as a verb, SWE checks context to be sure that the meaning is clear. "I fixed it" may mean, among other things, that I repaired it, made it immovable, made a chemical substance nonvolatile, prevented its discoloration, prepared it, prearranged its outcome, or castrated it.

flab Related to *flabby*, this word for "soft body tissue" is now SWE: "This rowing machine will get rid of your flab."

flabbergast This eighteenth-century synonym of *astound* sounds humorous, but modern dictionaries treat it as standard because it does occur in SWE, although infrequently.

flagrant See BLATANT/FLAGRANT.

flair/flare SWE: "Rosemary has a *flair* for politics." "The marooned sailors lighted a *flare*." *Flair* means "natural aptitude"; *flare*, "a burning light, such as a torch." (If Rosemary had a flare for politics, she might set the voters ablaze.)

flak In World War II *flak* was coined to refer to antiaircraft fire: "The planes encountered heavy flak over Berlin." Today the meaning is broadened to include "hostile criticism": "Senator Barnes has taken much flak because of his stand on abortions." Because of its vigor and brevity, the word is useful, and it does occur in SWE, usually in informal contexts.

flammable/inflammable SWE prefers *flammable. Inflammable* was once favored but was sometimes misunderstood to mean "not burnable." This misinterpretation could cause a serious problem. More drivers may be reluctant to cut in front of a truck labeled "flammable" than one labeled "inflammable." Figuratively, *inflammable* is frequent: "an inflammable temper."

flap   FF (slang) for "commotion," "dispute," "disorganization."

flare   See FLAIR/FLARE.

flaunt/flout   To *flaunt* is to show off, display ostentatiously: "He flaunted his wealth by purchasing a 150-foot yacht." To *flout* is to ignore or disobey in a scornful way: "Alec flouted the dormitory regulations by openly bringing in booze and girls from the town."

flay   A strong word, with the primary meaning "strip off the skin, for example by whipping." The secondary meaning, "criticize vigorously," is also SWE but ordinarily applies to extraordinarily harsh, even cruel remarks. See also ANNIHILATE.

flied   **1.** SWE as baseball talk. We can hardly say that a batter "flew out to left field" even if he is a Cardinal or a Blue Jay. So, "He flied out." **2.** In a theater, parts of the scenery may be flied (raised into the flies, the space above the stage).

flipflop, flip flop   Dictionaries treat either form as standard in the sense of "handspring" or "back somersault" but informal for "change of mind." It's a vigorous word, useful in vigorous prose, and deserves to be considered standard.

flotsam/jetsam/lagan   The legal difference is sometimes important to shipping and insurance companies. *Flotsam* is wreckage or cargo left afloat after a ship has sunk or been badly damaged. *Jetsam* is equipment or cargo thrown overboard to lighten a ship in trouble. The less familiar *lagan* refers to jetsam to which a buoy has been attached as a marker.

flounder/founder   A just-decapitated chicken or a live fish on shore *flounders*, "moves about wildly." A boat or ship that sinks because it's filled with water, or a business, marriage, or other enterprise that fails (figuratively sinks), *founders*.

flout   See FLAUNT/FLOUT.

folks   An SWE but informal ("folksy") word for "people," "relatives": "Folks around here will never believe this." "We went to visit my wife's folks."

following   In referring to quite ordinary events, *following* is a little high-flown for "after": "Following the meat and potatoes, we ate vanilla ice cream." It's better in more important contexts, such as "Following the debate on highway funds, the legislature turned to school appropriations."

foot, hour, mile, pound (in measurements)   An SWE writer refers to a twelve-*foot* ladder, but a ladder twelve *feet* long; a three-*hour* wait, but waited three *hours*; a two-*mile* walk, but walked two *miles*; a ten-*pound* weight, but weighs ten *pounds*.

foot speed   Sports analyst: "The fullback lacks foot speed." In contrast to what other kind of speed? SWE omits *foot* or calls the fullback "slow-moving."

for free   Widely used, and treated as standard in some dictionaries, although *for* adds nothing to the meaning, and the adjective *free* is needlessly used as a noun. Why waste space? Usual SWE is "This is free."

for the purpose of Usually can be replaced by *to*: "Such a map is drawn for the purpose of showing differences in barometric pressure." SWE says, ". . . drawn to show. . . ."

for the reason that SWE prefers *because*.

for . . . to Not customary in SWE: "Jansen wanted for his son to become a lawyer." SWE says, "Jansen hoped that his son would . . ." or "Jansen wanted his son to . . ."

for See also BECAUSE/FOR.

force SWE avoids using *force* as a verb unless the implication of power or strength is intended. Dubious: "They were forced to choose between cake and pie." Better: "Their only choices were . . ." 103

forced/forceful/forcible *Forced* means "caused by something outside one's control." For example, a pilot may make a forced landing because of engine trouble or ice on the wings. It may also mean "strained, unnatural": "a forced attempt at cheerfulness." *Forceful*, often used figuratively, means "giving the appearance of strength and energy": "a forceful courtroom pleader." Something is *forcible* if it is done through physical force: "forcible entry," "forcible rape."

foregoing/forgoing *Foregoing* means "going before, preceding": "as the foregoing example suggested." *Forgoing* means "abstaining, doing without": "Her forgoing lunch was extraordinary."

FOREIGN EXPRESSIONS Purposeless use of foreign terms is mere exhibitionism. Sometimes, however, a foreign expression is justifiable because it is the precise one a writer needs and has no exact English equivalent. The Spanish *simpatico*, for example, is variously equated with *attractive*, *congenial*, *compatible*, and *friendly*, but it comes closer to being all of these rather than one. Foreign words that have not become thoroughly anglicized are underlined (italicized), but those common in English, such as "laissez-faire," usually are not. Accent marks, the cedilla, the tilde, and special foreign uses of capitals are retained in formal writing until the terms are accepted as English.

foreseeable future Strictly speaking, no part of the future is foreseeable. Nevertheless, *in the foreseeable future* is a rather useful equivalent of "to the extent that is predictable."

foreword/forward Part of the front matter in a book or long essay may be a *foreword*. Note the spelling. Uses of the adjective or adverb *forward* are illustrated in "a forward cabin," "a forward girl," "walk forward," "forward-looking."

foreword/introduction/preface A book may have one, two, or (rarely) all three of these. Usually *foreword* and *preface* are interchangeable, although a foreword is sometimes regarded as less formal. Some publishers prefer *preface* if the book's author wrote it, *foreword* if someone else did. An *introduction* is usually but not always written by the author. Although a preface or foreword normally consists of some background information and gives credit to various people, an introduction actually gets into the subject matter of the book, presenting basic information to clarify or pave the way for what comes later.

former, latter   Most SWE writers use these words in referring to one of two things. For three or more, they use *first* and *last*, or if necessary repeat a noun. Some writers try to avoid *former* and *latter*, considering them stiff.

formulate   Often *form*, *devise*, or *invent* may be more suitable. *Formulate* is most useful if in some way a formula is involved: "to formulate a medicine that will be both effective and palatable."

fortuitous/fortunate   Something is *fortuitous* if it is entirely unplanned; it may be either good or bad but more often good. A one-day drop in stock market prices, for example, may not be due to anyone's machinations and may help some investors, harm others; it is a fortuitous drop. Something *fortunate*, however, is attributable to good luck, not bad; it brings good fortune. A fortuitous meeting may or may not be a fortunate one.

forward   See FOREWORD/FORWARD.

founder   See FLOUNDER/FOUNDER.

founding fathers   Careful, informed writers remember that founding mothers existed, too. Women's roles in the American Revolution were considerable; in fact, a number of women took part in actual fighting. So *founding fathers and mothers* may often be more appropriate.

FOUR-LETTER WORDS AND PROFANITY   Only rarely do writers of SWE use four-letter words and profanity except in quotations and, in fiction, when in keeping with the narrator or the character being depicted. The reason for the general avoidance is not that there is anything inherently "bad" or "wrong" about them or the actions they depict. The letters and sounds in *piss* and *goddam(n)* appear unchallenged in thousands of other words, and the bodily functions named in the four-letter words are not objected to when their Latinate versions are employed: *urinate*, *defecate*, *copulate*, and the like. The SWE stance is based on the fact that, with or without justification, large segments of the public do consider the four-letter words and the profanity vulgar or sacrilegious. Most SWE writers believe that giving offense alienates many readers and listeners rather than convinces or persuades them. FF, used mainly with a small and familiar audience, shows less restraint.

fraction   In an expression such as "a fraction of the time," meaning "a small part," *fraction* is not entirely logical because $19/20$ as well as $1/20$ is a fraction. Nevertheless the expression is generally accepted in SWE, although many writers substitute something more specific, such as "less than half the time."

Frankenstein   In Mary Shelley's story, Frankenstein was a scientist who created a monster. So many people have confused the two that some dictionaries now define *Frankenstein* as both the scientist and the monster. Most SWE writers, though, avoid risk of ridicule by saying "created a Frankenstein monster" or the like.

fraught Old-fashioned for "filled" or "laden," as in "fraught with pain."

free gift Obviously a gift is free. SWE omits *free*.

free rein Horses are sometimes given "free rein," with the reins relaxed so that they can go at their own pace in the direction they choose. The term should not be confused with *reign* or *rain*.

frequently/regularly Dubious: "Chickadees appear regularly at our feeder." *Regularly* means "at regular intervals, on schedule." Chickadees may appear *often* or *frequently*, but few birds except the swallows of Capistrano or the buzzards of Hinckley, Ohio, do much on a precise schedule. *Regularly* may be equally faulty in other contexts.

friable/fryable *Friable* has nothing to do with frying. It describes soil that is easily crumbled or powdered. *Fryable* means "capable of being fried": "a chicken too old to be fryable."

friar/monk With some exceptions, *monks* live in self-supporting monasteries and through meditation and prayer strive to make themselves morally and spiritually better. *Friars* normally live on alms, often move from place to place, and try to improve the lives of others.

friendlily Standard but awkward in expressions like "behaved friendlily toward us." SWE generally chooses *friendly*, which is standard as both adjective and adverb, or uses a phrase such as "in a friendly manner."

from . . . to In expressions such as "walks from eight to ten miles a day," SWE deletes *from*.

from where/from which *From which* makes good sense if a noun is present to serve as the antecedent of *which*: "This was a spot from which he could watch the entire valley" (*spot* is the antecedent of *which*). SWE uses *from where* when no antecedent is explicit: "From where he sat he could watch the entire valley."

frugal See ECONOMICAL/FRUGAL/THRIFTY . . .

frustrate See DISCOURAGE/FRUSTRATE.

fryable See FRIABLE/FRYABLE.

-ful (plurals) If you need two containers of flour, you probably fill one cup, empty it, and refill the same cup. So the plural is *cupfuls*, not *cups full* as it would be if you used two cups. Similarly, the plural is *spoonfuls, basketfuls, bucketfuls, armfuls*, and so on. However, if you actually use two or more containers, the model is "We raked up three *baskets full* of leaves." Many writers prefer *cups, baskets*, and so on to avoid a choice.

fulsome A somewhat risky word to use. Most dictionaries define it as "exaggerated, excessive, overdone": "Her compliments were so fulsome as to be unbelievable." Some dictionaries add a second definition (which is about 750 years old but is now often criticized): "abundant, copious, generous": "Her fulsome compliments were obviously heartfelt." A reader may not know which meaning the writer intends.

fun (as adjective)   "A fun time," "a fun game to play," and the like are relatively new expressions, with *fun* corresponding in meaning to *enjoyable*. The usage is still mainly FF but may become SWE because of its brevity and expressiveness.

function (noun)   Suitable name for a ceremonious event such as an inauguration or a formal dinner but rather high-flown for a club meeting or most parties.

funny   In the sense "strange, odd, unexpected, coincidental," *funny* is often considered informal: "It's funny that you and he arrived in town on the same day." Both AHD and RHD, however, consider this meaning standard. Nevertheless in SWE *funny* is usually associated with humor.

furlough   Now called *leave* by the U.S. armed forces.

further   See ALL THE FARTHER; FARTHER/FURTHER.

future plans   See ADVANCE RESERVATIONS/FUTURE PLANS.

fuzz   see COP.

FYI   A useful abbreviation in business correspondence is often penciled at the top of a note, letter, or copy of something. It means "for your information," and it brings the overworked recipient the messsage, "Here's one thing that probably won't cause you any labor, but you may find the contents useful, interesting, or amusing. No response is necessary."

G

Gaelic   See CELTIC/GAELIC.

gallon   A U.S. gallon is 231 cubic inches (3.785 liters). A British imperial gallon is 277.42 cubic inches (4.545 liters). A gallon of petrol will take you farther than a gallon of U.S. gasoline.

galore   Most dictionaries and writers on usage classify *galore* as informal. 'Tis a pity that this word, derived from Old Irish *co* + *leór*, "enough," is not generally recognized as standard in all contexts, for it adds a lively tone to statements about abundance: "chances (neckties, corned beef, shamrocks, and so on) galore." It does appear fairly often in SWE.

gambit   Conservatives prefer to use *gambit* in a sense comparable to that in chess: an opening in which a player sacrifices one or more pieces for the sake of a favorable position: "Often Lincoln's gambit was to grant the validity of one or more of his opponent's most credible or least important arguments and then to say, 'But the point really at issue is . . .'" SWE often uses the word to refer to any kind of strategic opening, however, even when no sacrifice is made: "His gambit was to win his listeners with a broad smile and an appropriate joke."

game (adjective)   **1.** SWE for "plucky," "resolute": "a game young man." **2.** It's also SWE for "considered suitable for hunting": "The pheasant is the leading game bird of South Dakota." **3.** FF for "willing" (especially if some risk is involved): "Are you game for some ice-fishing?"

gaping hole   That's what most holes are. SWE omits *gaping*.

garbage in, garbage out (gigo)   Perhaps overused by computerists, this term is still helpful as a reminder that computer (or word-processor) results are almost invariably wrong, poor in quality, or useless if the input is inaccurate, incomplete, or badly chosen.

gargantuan   Unlike *gigantic* or *enormous*, *gargantuan* does not refer to size in all its varieties. Named for a character invented by Rabelais, it suggests unusually large capacity for food or pleasure: "a gargantuan appetite," "gargantuan lust."

gas/gasoline   After almost three quarters of a century of being labeled "informal" in most dictionaries, gas (for *gasoline*) finally reached unlabeled dignity in the conservative AHD. SWE makes sure, however, to avoid any possible confusion between the liquid fuel (gasoline) and the airlike substance (gas). There's a difference between *gas lamp* and *gasoline lamp*, for example, and *gas-burning equipment* is ambiguous.

gather together   See COLLABORATE . . . TOGETHER.

gay   see FAIRY/GAY/PANSY.

gem/jewel   With regard to precious or semiprecious stones, *gem* and *jewel* are interchangeable. Also, an extraordinarily likable or helpful person may be either a gem or a jewel: "My wife's husband, I believe, is a gem (or *jewel*)."

gender   Used chiefly to refer to the sexual classifications "male" and "female," *gender* in grammar does not necessarily refer to sex at all. In some languages, word forms vary in gender to show differences in size, age, closeness of relationship, or almost anything else. In other instances the classification may seem to mix sexes, as in references to a no-sex ship as "she." The German *Mädchen* ("girl, maiden") is grammatically neuter in gender.

general consensus   See CONSENSUS.

general public   *General* is unnecessary unless you have just been discussing one part of the public and now want to compare or contrast that part with the whole. Satisfactory: "The racetrack owners objected to the new tax, but the general public raised no outcry."

generally always   FF. Because these two words contradict each other, SWE prefers *almost always*.

genial   See CONGENIAL/GENIAL.

genie   A supernatural being that supposedly will perform for its master any task, workaday or miraculous. The word is also spelled *jinn, djin(n), djinni, djinny.* In the *Arabian Nights* it is associated with a magic lamp. In other fiction it may remain patiently in a bottle until released.

genius (plurals of)   Plural *geniuses* except in regard to guardian spirits in Roman mythology or to demons in Moslem mythology. In those two senses, *genii* is standard.

genius/talent   *Genius* is regarded as the higher of the two qualities and is not used in SWE as equivalent to mere "skill" or "high ability." It usually implies extraordinarily great intellectual and creative power. *Talent* may be mental or physical and (unlike genius) is not necessarily inborn but may be acquired. An athlete may have great physical talent, and a musician a talent for playing well, but neither is ordinarily said to have genius unless he or she demonstrates it through intellectual or creative activity. Talent, however, can apply the products of genius. Marie Ebner Eschenbach said, "Genius points the way; talent pursues it."

genre   Use of this word (pronounced *zhahn*-ruh) for "variety" or "kind" is restricted in SWE almost entirely to the arts. Thus novel is a literary genre, sonata a musical genre, surrealist painting a genre in art. Basketball, however, is a game but not a sports genre, and the term is equally unlikely to be used in business or science.

genteel   Now rarely used for "fashionable, polite, refined" or "prudish." When it is used, it often seems sarcastic and implies artificiality and old-fashioned behavior.

Gentlemen: Feminists may be driving out this conventional salutation of business letters, yet few women are enthusiastic about *Ladies and Gentlemen:* and certainly not *Gentlepersons:* or the cold and legalistic *To Whom It May Concern:*. Frequently, today's letters to recipients not identifiable by name have no salutation at all. William Safire recommends *Greetings:*.

genuine   See AUTHENTIC/GENUINE.

genus   Plural *genera*. A genus is part of a family and usually consists of several or many species. *Homo sapiens* indicates that human beings belong to the genus Homo; the self-congratulatory *sapiens* identifies us as a thinking species. See also SPECIE/SPECIES.

geographic, geographical; geometric, geometrical   In each pair, take your choice. SANE, of course, recommends the shorter.

geometric progression   See ARITHMETIC PROGRESSION . . .; AVERAGE. See also GEOGRAPHIC, GEOGRAPHICAL . . .

gerund   See -ING; -ING (CASE PRECEDING).

gesticulation/gesture   As nouns, these words are sometimes used interchangeably, although *gesticulation* is more abstract, referring to the use of certain bodily movements rather than to the movements themselves: "He is fond of gesticulation (or *gesturing*)." "His gestures are numerous and sometimes almost violent."

get   A prominent American grammarian, the late C. C. Fries, had access to thousands of letters written to a governmental agency by

Americans of varying backgrounds. One of his findings was that less literate writers used forms of *get* much more frequently than others did. OED devotes five pages of small print to *get*, and other dictionaries define scores of phrases using it. *Get* is thus a valuable word, but SWE avoids using it unnecessarily or inappropriately. SWE is unlikely to employ, for example, *get it* for "receive a scolding," *get his hooks into* for "take control of," *get with it* for "become aware of or alert." Other uses of *get* may be intelligently questioned, although a fair proportion of them are worth keeping. See also GET/OBTAIN/SECURE; GOT.

get/obtain/secure Not quite synonymous. To *get* something, you may or may not exert any effort, but to *obtain* or *secure* something, you must ordinarily work, scheme, or take some other action. You can get a cold without effort, but you don't obtain or secure a cold. You may get money either by earning or stealing it or as a gift, but if you obtain or secure money, usually you must perform some act.

GI World War II slang, corresponding to the *doughboy* of World War I. It first meant "galvanized iron," some historians say, then "general issue" or "government issue," and finally "an enlisted person" in one of the U.S. armed forces. Not applied to commissioned officers. The term became SWE but now is used less and less except with reference to World War II.

gibe/jibe To *gibe* is to make fun of, to ridicule lightly: "He gibed her about her new hairdo." "Maybe that's a new hairdo," he gibed, "but I think it's a hairdon't – your hair don't look good." An alternative spelling is *jibe*. The other *jibe* is a nautical verb referring to a shift of a fore-and-aft sail, but more recently it has come to mean "harmonize, agree": "The account he gave the arresting officers did not jibe with what he said today." Some dictionaries call this use informal, but it appears fairly often in SWE.

gift "Sam said that he had gifted her with a new Porsche." Both Sam's language and his intentions may disturb her if she is doubly a purist. SWE does not use *gift* as a verb, especially because it necessitates using *with*. It chooses the appropriate form of *give*.

gimmick Nobody knows where this word came from, but it's useful for a trick or device to catch attention, sell something, or attain some other end in an uncommon way. It has become SWE.

gimpy A somewhat unkind or jocular FF (slang) word to describe someone who limps.

girlfriend See FEMALE COMPANION/GIRLFRIEND/MISTRESS.

give the cold shoulder Cliché. Fairly widely employed to mean "ignore, slight, pay no attention to." The cliché is more meaningful if writer and reader both know that in medieval castles the welcome guests were treated to choice hot roast beef and the less welcome ones were given cold shoulder of mutton – tallowy and unpleasant.

given Mathematical and, less often, scientific problems may begin, "Given (or *Given that*) $A > B$, how . . . ?" This use of participial

109

given is SWE. In the 1980s the use of *given* as a noun equivalent became frequent, as in "It is a given that . . ." The meaning is "what is granted, what is true, what must be admitted." Although relatively new, this usage has also become SWE.

gizmo Also spelled *gismo*. FF for "gadget" or for some whatchama-callit whose name is unknown or temporarily forgotten. *Widget*, *thingamajig*, and *doohicky* are among the other FF synonyms.

glance/glimpse Fowler and Nicholson best expressed the difference: "The glimpse is what is seen by the glance." For example, if you take a *glance* at a store window, you get a *glimpse* of what is in it. The verb *glance* means to look quickly; it takes no object: "She glanced in his direction." *Glimpse* does take an object: "She glimpsed a slight grin on his face."

glean Gleaners used to follow reapers (and in impoverished places still do) to pick up grains that were missed. The idea of gathering a small amount at a time is still implicit in the verb, which is seldom used as a substitute for *gather, collect, acquire, obtain, find*, or the like, except when the gathering is indeed done bit by bit.

glimpse See GLANCE/GLIMPSE.

glitch A word from outer space – or at least derived from American space ventures. Flesch says that Germans who aided our early efforts (Wernher von Braun and others) used the German *glitschig* ("slippery") in referring to certain pulsars, and that *glitch* came from that. It means "rather unaccountable interruptions, speedups," and the like. The useful word has become standard and has expanded from pulsars to mean any of the many mysterious little things that can go wrong in any operation. The sputters, pings, and other automobile eccentricities or the occasionally inexplicable behavior of a computer are examples. Authors and editors know that glitches in publishing are not infrequent.

glittering SWE uses this word as the equivalent of *sparkling* – the sparkles being either literal or figurative. Glitter, like sparkles, is evanescent and may suggest gaudiness rather than intrinsic beauty. Users of SWE are dubious about "the glittering wedding ceremony of Prince Andrew and his bride," because *glittering* hints at cheap glamor.

glitzy Related to *glitter*, German *glitzern* "glitter," and perhaps *ritzy*, *glitzy* describes something showy, shiny, expensive – like Hollywood movies based on Judith Krantz novels. It started as slang and is now SWE.

glorious A strong word, associated with *glory*. Not used in SWE if *delightful* or *unusually pleasant* is more honest.

glutton/gourmand/gourmet The *glutton* emphasizes quantity of food; the *gourmet*, quality. The glutton goes back for second helpings of roast beef while the gourmet is still savoring the *potage cressoniére* with the chef's special croutons. The *gourmand* ranks between the two. He enjoys food but is more choosy than the glutton, less so than the gourmet.

go all out   FF for "do wholeheartedly," "give one's best," "try with enthusiasm and hard work."

go him one better   FF or borderline SWE for "outdo him," "outperform him," "excel him in some way."

gobbledygook   The coiner of this pejorative name for "officialese, language of bureaucracy" (probably a former congressman, Maury Maverick) said that much of that language reminded him of the gobbledy-gobbling of turkeys, which usually ends in a "gook." It is characterized by long but vague words, passive voice, lengthy and convoluted sentences, and often uncertain meaning.

God rest ye merry, Gentlemen   That comma is in the right place – no comma after *ye*. The meaning is "God keep you merry, Gentlemen."

goes by the name of   Appears in SWE but less frequently than *is named, is called, is popularly called*, or (most likely) *uses the alias.*

(it) goes without saying, needless to say   Although the first reaction to either phrase may be "Then why say it?" each is a short way of telling the reader, "Presumably you are already familiar with the following bit of information, but you should keep it in mind in reading this passage." Occasional usage is found in SWE.

gofer   An FF (slang) term more picturesque than *errand-boy* or *errand-girl* but equivalent in meaning. It's not likely to rise high among users of SWE; puns seldom do.

going (modifier)   SWE for "current, prevailing, present": "the going rate of interest."

going on   A CBS television reporter was not illustrating SWE when, in telling of a fire in Yellowstone Park, she referred to "the plight that is now going on." SWE does not use *go on, occur, happen,* or other verbs of movement when the subject is a noun that suggests the status quo. A plight, condition, situation, or status, for example, *exists* but does not *go on*.

going-over (noun)   SWE, although most frequent in informal contexts, for (1) "inspection," (2) "scolding," (3) "rehearsing, repeating": "Give it a quick going-over." "Her mother gave her a real going-over." "Your story needs another going-over."

goings-on (noun)   FF, used disapprovingly for "behavior, conduct": "I won't put up with such goings-on."

gold/golden   As a rule, *gold* refers to the physical substance: "a gold coin." *Golden* is ordinarily figurative: "her golden hair," "a golden sunset."

good and ready   SWE omits *good and* in most writing, although the phrase is widely used in FF for "completely ready."

good and sufficient reason   One of the adjectives is usually enough, but both may sometimes be justifiable.

good benefit, good success Are there any bad benefits or bad successes? SWE customarily omits *good*.

good long time In expressions such as "a good many people" or "a good long time ago," *good* is equivalent to the adverb *very*. It only rarely appears in SWE.

good/well The use of *good* and *well* may be one touchstone by which some employers may judge candidates for positions in which making a good impression on the educated public is important. Maybe not so much should hinge on two little words, but a candidate who explains lateness by saying, "My car wasn't running good this morning," may have not one but two strikes against him. The distinction is simple. If the word describes the subject, *good* is standard: "Her work was good." "The report looks good." But when the verb shows action and a word is needed to describe that action, *well* is standard: "My car wasn't running well." "She plays the piano well." See also BAD/BADLY; FEEL (GOOD/WELL).

goodly Old-fashioned for "attractive" or "rather large": "a goodly appearance," "a goodly sum of cash."

goodwill It's one word: "a message of goodwill," "a goodwill message." Obviously, two words are necessary in "No good will come of this" or the old-fashioned "He worked with a right good will."

goof 1. FF for "blunder, mistake, error," but it's moving toward SWE because none of its synonyms are equally good-natured, forgiving, and rather humorous. 2. *Goof off* is FF (slang) for "waste time, loaf, do nothing of any importance": "Are you goofing off again?" 3. *Goof up* is also FF (slang) for "bungle, make a mess of": "I goofed up. I goofed up the whole job."

goofy This FF (slang) word describes rather affectionately a somewhat stupid person or silly mistakes of the sort that he or she may make.

gorgeous Overused for "resplendent, brilliant, splendid, delightful," and the like, this word may be restricted by purists to decoration or outward appearance. They may say, for example, that a dress is gorgeous but that some other word should describe the girl wearing the dress. Bernstein approved of "gorgeous peacock," however, saying that the adjective is understood to refer to the plumage. Nonpurists, including many good writers, seldom bother about the distinction. They use the word sparingly, though, because of its strength.

got A pseudonymous author in 1789 concocted a paragraph of about 150 words in which he used *got* 22 times and other forms of *get* six more. He started like this:

> I GOT on Horseback within ten minutes after I GOT your letter. When I GOT to Canterbury, I GOT a chaise for town. But I GOT wet through before I GOT to Canterbury, and I

HAVE GOT such a cold as I shall not be able to GET rid of in a Hurry.

Some teachers have foolishly ordered students never to use *got*. Instead of proscribing, they should prescribe: "For Occasional Use." See also GET; GET/OBTAIN/SECURE; GOT/GOTTEN.

got/gotten In British English the past participle of *get* is (*have*) *got*; *gotten* is rather rare. In American English (*have*) *got* and (*have*) *gotten* are both used but are not always interchangeable. "They've got enough food" is informal for either "They have enough food" or "They have obtained enough food," but "They've gotten enough food" has only the second meaning. In many other sentences, Americans use either word: "They've got (or *gotten*) together on several occasions." *Gotten* is less common in SWE than *got*.

gourmand/gourmet See GLUTTON/GOURMAND/GOURMET.

graduate (verb) FF says, "She graduated college." SWE says, "She graduated from college" or, now less likely, "She was graduated from college." The argument favoring the last example is that the institution does both the admitting and the graduating, but the reasoning has not convinced everyone. SANE favors "She graduated from college."

graffiti In Italian, *graffiti* is the plural of *graffito* ("crude drawing or inscription"). Theoretically, then, we should say, "The graffiti *were* ugly and offensive." Usage, however, is divided. Members of the Harper panel voted 51–49 in favor of *were*. Take your choice. Only seldom is there a need for the singular, "A graffito was . . ."

grammar school Used in the British Isles for a secondary school for academically superior students, but often in the United States for an elementary school. Most U.S. teachers and school officials, however, prefer *elementary school* to *grammar school*. There is a National Association of Elementary School Principals – not "Grammar School."

grand This was a strong word until weakened by overuse. Most "grand openings" are not really "noted for grandeur," "rich and sumptuous," or "stately, regal." A "grand time" is often no more than a pleasant evening. *Grand* deserves more grandeur than it is usually accorded. It has fallen into plebeian surroundings.

grandiloquent See ELOQUENT/GRANDILOQUENT/MAGNILOQUENT.

grandiose *Grandiose* started out well in life. For example, a writer in 1850 used it in describing Greek amphitheaters. But the word has sunk in reputation and now suggests pomposity, affectation, garish display, size but not solidity.

grateful/gratuitous Not related in meaning. A person who feels gratitude is *grateful*: "Ogden Nash said that if you are grateful for anything, it will probably be gone tomorrow." Something is *gratuitous* if it is freely given and probably unwanted: "gratuitous advice (*information, assistance*, or the like)."

gratuity/tip If your dinner costs more than most people can afford, you leave a *gratuity*; if less, a *tip*.

graze See BROWSE/GRAZE.

great Bernstein coined the term *atomic flyswatter* to describe unnecessarily powerful adjectives. *Great* is one of these. In SWE it is reserved for the "truly great" – something important, large, extraordinarily noteworthy, and probably even rare. SWE avoids *great* hairdos, detergents, ice cream bars, bird-calling devices, or even boyfriends.

Great Britain See BRITISH ISLES/ENGLAND/GREAT BRITAIN.

greenhorn Follett called *greenhorn* a "fine English coinage." Originally, it meant "a young animal with horns not fully developed" and was so used as early as the fifteenth century. Today it is an SWE synonym of *novice, inexperienced person*, or *recent immigrant* but is used most often as ridicule.

green house/greenhouse A *green house* has green paint. A *greenhouse* has green plants inside its glass walls and roof.

grind to a halt Criticized as a cliché, but what other rather dramatic way is there to suggest a slow, unpleasant process of stopping, like that of most trains?

grisly/grizzly *Grisly* means "horrible, gruesome, repugnant." Maybe that's how a grizzly bear looks to someone it is endangering. (In fact, its scientific name is *Ursa horribilis*.) *Grizzly*, however, really means "grayish, flecked with gray," and the grizzly bear's brown hair usually has gray or silver tips. A man's hair may be described as grizzly (or *grizzled*), but it is unlikely to be ugly enough to be called grisly.

groom Informal for *bridegroom*, but found sometimes in SWE. Some people don't like *groom* because of its association with stables. *Bridegroom*, incidentally, means "bride('s) man."

ground/grounds Usually interchangeable when the meaning is "reason, basis": "no ground(s) for making that statement." Lawyers generally use *grounds*: "grounds for legal action."

groupie Kings and other potentates have often traveled with entourages consisting of servants, friends, sycophants, advisers, lovers, and family. Modern entourages, most often the followers of popular music stars, may consist in part of *groupies* – a term most frequently applied to young persons of the opposite sex who believe they enjoy their dim share of the starlight. The word lingers on the boundary between FF and SWE.

grouse (verb) FF for "grumble, complain": "He groused about the too-soft boiled eggs."

grow smaller Sometimes condemned as a contradiction, this expression is SWE nevertheless. The reason: *grow* may mean "become," as in "grow tired," "grow faint."

guess Informal in the sense of "suppose, expect, believe," long regarded by the British as one of the most typical Americanisms but is now used often by them, too. In fact, Chaucer some six hundred years ago used "I guess" about as Americans do, except that he spelled it *gesse*. Perhaps partly because of British ridicule in the nineteenth century, *guess* in this sense still makes only occasional appearances in SWE.

guesstimate (also guestimate)   Although not yet listed in some dictionaries, *guesstimate* (or *guestimate*) is a valuable word for something more careful than a guess but less precise than an estimate.

guest   Needed: a word that means "paying guest," as in a hotel, because *guest* may now refer to one who pays or to one, such as a houseguest, whose food and lodging are provided without charge. "Be our guest" can be ambiguous in some contexts. SWE does what is needed to clarify the intended meaning.

guest host   Perhaps starting as a title for any of the numerous replacements for talk-show master of ceremonies Johnny Carson, *guest host* is an oxymoron (a union of contradictory terms, such as "the cheerful crapehanger"). It has been ridiculed and mocked, but applauded by a few who said, in effect, "OK, but what would *you* call the substitute host?" One answer: *substitute host* or, more informally, *substitute MC*.

guests   See COMPANY.

guilt feelings/guilty feelings   Interchangeable, with psychologists generally preferring the former. Linguistic conservatives advise *guilty feelings* or *feelings of guilt* to avoid using the noun *guilt* as a modifier. SWE uses both.

gumption   This useful word is most likely to be found in informal contexts. It means not so much "intelligence" as "enterprise" combined with "shrewdness," a dash of "imaginativeness" and a little bit of "chutzpah." It appears now and then in SWE.

guru   In Hinduism, a *guru* is a spiritual teacher, a holy man. In American, a (usually) respected leader who advocates rather specific points of view concerning finance, political science, ethics, or other serious and somewhat abstract fields: "Milton Friedman – the guru of the monetarists." The word is used in SWE – often, for example, in the Business section of the *New York Times*.

gut feeling, gut issue, gut reaction   FF and unattractive synonyms for "deep feeling," "basic issue," and "quick or instinctive reaction." The SWE *visceral* is unfamiliar to many people, so SWE often chooses *deep feeling* or the like.

guts   Although intended as praise indicating bravery or boldness in an expression such as "He's got guts," the word carries unpleasant connotations of disemboweled rabbits. Except in references to entrails and the like, it is generally FF but occasionally SWE.

guy   FF for "man" or less often "man or woman" or even "woman": "See those guys over there? The tall fellow and the blonde girl?"

H

hail/hale   In stories such as Westerns an old-timer may ask, "Where d'ye *hail from*, stranger?" This old-fashioned expression obviously means "come from." *Hail* may also mean "call, summon," as in "hail a cab." *Hale*, in a rather rare use, may mean "cause to come," used especially in the expression "hale into court." More frequently, it is an adjective for "healthy, vigorous," as in the phrase *hale and hearty*, which usually describes an old person, even though young ones are likely to be haler and heartier.

hairy   FF (slang) when used to mean "difficult, dangerous, harrowing,": "Driving for hours on icy roads is a hairy experience."

half   It is redundant to use both *a* and *an* (or two *a*'s) with *half*: not "We waited a half an hour" but "We waited a half hour" or "We waited half an hour."

half-mast/half-staff   With reference to a position of a flag, the terms are interchangeable.

handgun   See AUTOMATIC/PISTOL/REVOLVER.

handle in routine fashion   SWE prefers the shorter *handle routinely*.

hang in there   Because of the "moral sustenance" it may provide, Flesch calls *hang in there* "one of the great creative idioms of the English language." Probably Flesch is exaggerating, but this expression, although still somewhat slangy, has been increasingly used to lend encouragement to a skier in a crevasse, a patient in a hospital, a couple contemplating a divorce, and countless other people in harrowing circumstances. It is increasingly used in SWE.

hanged/hung   For the sense "executed legally by hanging," many SWE writers prefer *hanged*: "The murderer was hanged at dawn." The legal phrase is "hanged until dead." FF and often SWE use *hung* as both the past tense and past participle of *hang*, in all its meanings. "He hung himself" is standard, because legal execution is not involved.

hang-up   **1.** An imprecise informal term and perhaps for that reason not listed in the *Dictionary of Behavioral Science*, this term may mean "inhibition, fear, worry, concern, emotional disturbance, overenthusiasm," or any possible cause of any of those. Because of such vagueness, SWE either avoids *hang-up* or else makes it explicit. It is much more common in FF. **2.** It is SWE in the sense "something that can be hung from something else": "One of the hang-ups was a small mobile."

happening (noun)   Starting perhaps in the 1960s in Woodstock, Greenwich Village, and then at other celebrations that hippies called *happenings*, the term spread to television, often as a synonym for "variety show," and then sometimes shrank to designate a family gathering or even a birthday party. The peregrinations of a word are often fascinating to follow. This one has seldom been given the sanctity of an SWE context unless between the protective arms of quotation marks.

happiness/pleasure Although we often speak of "a moment of happiness," in general happiness is more lasting than pleasure. For that reason we refer to "a happy life" when we are talking about a lifetime, but "a pleasant life" when referring to a shorter period. In addition to having greater duration, happiness also is likely to be less sensual, more quiet and contented. The Founding Fathers did not write about "life, liberty, and the pursuit of pleasure."

harangue/tirade Each is a noisy speech. A *harangue* is usually delivered to several or many persons, but a *tirade* may have an audience of one or a few. The harangue is likely to be vociferously and unpleasantly argumentative, the tirade bitterly, almost uncontrollably assertive and angry.

harbor/port Often used interchangeably, although to a sailor a *harbor* is any place that provides safe or sheltered anchorage, and a *port* is in a harbor, but is equipped for the loading and unloading of freight or passengers. See also DOCK/PIER/WHARF.

hard hat Because hard hats are required in much construction work, *hard hat* is often used in both FF and SWE to mean a worker who needs such protection. The word is also used as a modifier: "a hard-hat job."

hard put An SWE idiom in such sentences as "The Democrats will be hard put to win the majority of Senate seats" (meaning that they will have great difficulty). The odd expression may come from equestrian competition and relate to "putting" a horse to a jump.

hardly no/hardly none Double negatives. SWE substitutes *hardly any*, *almost no*, or *very few*. *Scarcely* appears in similar FF double negatives: *has scarcely none*, *scarcely no money*, *didn't scarcely find any*; or even triple negatives such as *didn't scarcely find none*.

hardly . . . than, scarcely . . . than SWE prefers *when* to *than* in sentences such as "She had hardly (*scarcely, barely*) entered the house when (not *than*) she heard Clara sobbing softly." Because the relationship is one of time, *when* is more logical.

hard-nosed In sports, a *hard-nosed* player is one who is tough, fearless, determined, and perhaps merciless. From sports the term has spread to politics, business, and other fields. Like many other metaphorical terms, it is still classed in dictionaries as informal, but it is not infrequent in SWE.

hardware/liveware/software In computerese, *hardware* consists of the equipment itself – keyboard, monitor, printer, and the like. The *liveware* (an infrequently used term) is the operator. The *software* is the programs, instruction books, and so on used by the liveware as he works with the hardware. In education, hardware is again equipment – projectors, recorders, radios, television sets, and the like – and software is slides, films, tapes, manuals, or other items used in or with the hardware.

hardwood/softwood   A *hardwood* tree (oak, maple, cherry, and so on) is deciduous, with broad leaves that fall annually. The term *softwood* is used less often. It applies to coniferous trees (pine, spruce, and so on), which bear cones, have needle-shaped leaves, and are commonly called "evergreens."

hardy/hearty   Sometimes confused because of similarity of sound. *Hardy* means "robust," "long-lasting," "able to endure inclement weather": "hardy outdoor man," "a hardy perennial." *Hearty* means "pleasantly warm, outgoing" as in "hearty greetings"; "strong," as in "hearty support"; "nourishing," as in "a hearty lunch." (What would a *hardy* lunch be?)

harebrained   Since the meaning is "stupid like a rabbit," *harebrained* is preferable to *hairbrained*, given as a variant in some dictionaries. (*Hair-triggered* is standard, though: it suggests a trigger so sensitive that the weight of a hair can move it.)

harmony/melody   The *Oxford Dictionary of Music* explains the difference as "vertical" vs. "horizontal." Notes that are simultaneously blended, as in a chord, are in *harmony*, but the succession of musical sounds constitutes a *melody*.

hassle   Now becoming standard for "disagreement, small fight," *hassle* ordinarily is not used for a major confrontation.

haste/hasten   *Haste*, a noun, as in "Make haste!" is no longer used as a verb: "Haste!" The verb is now *hasten*, although *hurry* is much more common: "The butler hastened to bring in the tea." "The butler hastened the maid on her way."

haughtiness   See ARROGANCE/CONCEIT/HAUGHTINESS . . .

have reference to   Not always avoidable, but in unnecesssarily wordy expressions such as "the story I have reference to," SWE substitutes something like "the story I mean."

he (the _____)   "The clerk reported to the manager that he (the clerk) had unintentionally overcharged a customer." SWE tries to recast such a sentence to eliminate the awkward *he (the clerk)* or, of course, *she (the clerk)*. In the example, since no misunderstanding is likely, *(the clerk)* may be deleted. If misunderstanding might occur, one solution is to recast as "The clerk reported an unintentional overcharge to . . ." Another is to use direct address: "The clerk told the manager, 'I unintentionally . . .'"

he, him, his/she, her, hers/it, its/they, them, their, theirs   SWE tries to make sure that the reader immediately understands the antecedent. (Editors sometimes ask "Who he?" in margins of manuscripts. They may also do that when a named person should be further identified.) SWE avoids sentences like these: "Mrs. Claire Prior will be the hostess. He is the president of the Nu-Times Company." (Substitute *Mr. Prior* or *Her husband* for *he*, or omit the whole sentence as irrelevant.) "The Tim Ranch family have faith in education. She is a graduate of Wellesley." (Who she? Mrs. Ranch? A daughter?) "The lawyer told the doctor that he had made a mistake." (Who he?) "The fireplace was roaring because it was windy." (A windy fireplace?)

he is a man who . . . , she is a woman who . . . It's usually not necessary to identify or describe a person as a man or a woman. SWE omits four of the five words.

he or she Many feminists who disliked a historically standard sentence such as "Everyone should solve *his* own problems if *he* can," saying that it left women out of consideration, have now decided that there are more important battles to fight in order to attain completely equal rights. One reason for abandoning the skirmish is that a good revision is hard to find. Awkward: "Everyone should solve his or her own problems if he or she can." Ungrammatical but widely used: "Everyone should solve their own problems if they can." Changing the subject to *People* will work, but not if the writer wants to concentrate on individuals. One solution: Use *he* unless it is important to emphasize that both sexes are meant. Another: Alternate, sometimes using *he*, sometimes *she*. Of course, use *she* for a member of an all-female group, *he* when each is male. (I once used *heshe, himer,* and *hiser* on a trial run in a book, but they were stillborn. The book was distributed by two major book clubs, but nobody liked my pronouns.)

He, She SWE capitalizes a pronoun referring to God: "Our Heavenly Father, He who . . ." "Our Heavenly Mother, She who . . ." Some writers, but apparently not most, capitalize *He* and *She* in referring to Jesus and the Virgin Mary.

head up In "Ms. Grove will head up the committee" and the like, *head* is enough, or *chair, lead, direct,* or (for an investigation) *conduct.* SWE deletes *up.*

headquarter(s) 1. "The expedition headquartered near St. Louis." Conservatives ordinarily disapprove of a shift that makes a noun a verb, especially if the result is cumbersome, as this seems. But the alternative, "set up headquarters" or "located its headquarters," is longer. Some dictionaries and some authors of histories treat the verb as standard. 2. The verb with *headquarters* as its subject is usually plural, but sometimes SWE uses a singular.

healthful/healthy Probably the battle is lost, but there's a good reason for keeping *healthful* instead of making *healthy* do two unlike jobs. Conservatives say that *healthful* describes something that promotes health, *healthy* something (or someone) that has health. If we write, "These vegetables are healthy," the meaning is uncertain. Are we saying that the vegetables are vigorous or that they are good for us? Using *healthful* for the second sense would prevent misinterpretation. SWE sometimes but not uniformly differentiates between the words.

heap SWE for "a somewhat disorderly pile": "a heap of trash." When Edgar A. Guest wrote, "It takes a heap o' livin' / To make a house a home," he was using *heap* in the FF (informal) sense meaning "lots, a great deal." The plural is sometimes used similarly: "heaps of good wishes." *Heap* for "an almost worn-out car: is FF (slang).

hear/listen In a world filled with sounds, many strike our eardrums – are *heard* – but pass unnoticed. When we *listen* to any of these abundant sounds, we pay attention, trying to interpret or otherwise make sense of them. Obviously, then, we hear much that we do not listen to. Less frequently, we listen but cannot hear because our hearing apparatus is not sharp enough or because an expected sound does not materialize: "She listened for the friendly ring of the telephone, but it was inexplicably silent."

hear tell FF (dialectal) for "hear, be told": "I heard (or *heerd*) tell you was with Zeldie last week."

heart-rendering Sorry, but a movie (or anything else) is never *heart-rendering* unless a heart can be rendered ("clarified by melting") as lard is. SWE would describe the movie as *heart-rending*.

hearty See HARDY/HEARTY.

heavy Because *heavy* has more than a score of legitimate meanings, it can easily be overused. One way to avoid the problem is to substitute a different word in modifying an intangible, for example, *ponderous* style, *substantial* losses, *severe* cutbacks, *pungent* odor, *grave* matters of state, *oppressive* taxes.

Hebrew/Israeli/Jewish/Yiddish (language) *Hebrew* is the language of the Old Testament and (in a modern version) of many people in today's Israel. These people are *Israelis*, but there is no Israeli language. We may speak of *Jewish* customs, Jewish life, and the like, but there is no Jewish language. *Yiddish* is a blend of languages long spoken by many European Jews, including large numbers who emigrated to the United States. It is basically a German dialect to which some Hebrew and Eastern European words have been added. See also ISRAELI/JEW.

hectometer *Centimeter, meter*, and *kilometer* are widely known, but the useful *hectometer* (100 meters) is rarely seen or heard.

hedonist See EPICURE/EPICUREAN/HEDONIST.

heist Once slang, now called informal in dictionaries for "steal, rob, hijack," or, as a noun, "theft, robbery, hijacking." It's rare in SWE, except in newspapers.

helicopter (verb) Although the Germans manage long verbs in addition to their sometimes immense nouns, verbs of more than three syllables occur infrequently in English and so are likely to seem awkward. Sentences such as "We helicoptered from Midway to O'Hare" do exist in SWE, probably because "We flew by helicopter" is more wordy. *Chopped* would be ambiguous, and *choppered* is uglier than *helicoptered*.

hell of a As in "a hell of a lot of trouble." Informal for "serious."

Perhaps not suitable for a letter to Great-Aunt Matilda, but publications as highly regarded as *Time* and *Harper's* may occasionally comment on the "hell of a mess" somebody thinks the world, or at least part of it, is in.

helm/rudder/tiller In a boat a *helm* or a *tiller* is used to move the *rudder*, which is a metal or wooden plate under the stern. The movement causes the vessel to alter its course. The tiller is in the shape of a bar or heavy rod, but the helm, especially on a ship, is probably a wheel. Figuratively, *taking the helm* and *taking the tiller* are interchangeable for "taking charge."

help Once criticized when used to mean "avoid, refrain from," as in "Many drunkards don't like drinking, but they can't help doing it," *help* in this sense is now SWE, even though the meaning is far from the usual one. See also CANNOT BUT.

helpmate/helpmeet Interchangeable. The King James version of Genesis 2:18 says that God, looking at the lonely Adam, declared, "I will make an help meet [an old word for 'suitable'] for him." When *meet* was no longer understood to mean "suitable," ministers and others interpreted *an help meet* as *a helpmeet* ("helper"). But that, too, seemed to make little sense, so *helpmate* developed. Now both words are SWE.

hemlock Some Americans have wondered how a drink made from hemlock could have killed Socrates, since their own ancestors drank hemlock tea. The two hemlocks are of different genera. The European one is a poisonous plant of the parsley family, but the American one is a coniferous tree.

hence/thence/whence *Hence*, meaning "from here," *thence*, "from there," and *whence*, "from where," have an archaic flavor, reminiscent of "Get thee hence" or "Whence he came I know not." A writer of SWE who is not bothered by the old-fashioned air at least avoids using *from* with any of these words.

henceforth/thenceforth Seldom used today except in legal documents.

hereditary/innate A *hereditary* trait is inherited from earlier generations. This may also be true of an *innate* quality, but usually *innate* means simply "present at birth." Perhaps because it is not possible to tell exactly what was inherited and what was not, SWE does not invariably try to differentiate the two words, although geneticists say, for example, that eye, skin, or hair color is hereditary, not innate.

hereof/heretofore/hereunto/herewith/theretofore Legalese for "of this," "before this," "to this," "with this," and "before that," respectively.

heroic **1.** *A*, not *an*, usually precedes it. **2.** *Heroic*, not *heroical*, is usual in SWE.

heroics Requires a plural verb, is now often used mockingly: "Such congressional heroics should be told in song and story!"

her's   Never in SWE. See APOSTROPHE.

hew   *Chop* or *cut* (*down*) is usual, but *hew* is now rare in the United States.

hex   *Hex* comes by way of Pennsylvania German from German *Hexe* ("witch") and now is an SWE synonym for "magic spell, bad influence, nemesis" or as a verb "bewitch, cause bad luck." Most modern Pennsylvania Germans laugh good-naturedly at the old superstitions, but many take commercial advantage of them.

high/lofty/tall   *High* is the general term and often can be used for either *tall* or *lofty*. Unlike *tall, high* may be applied to abstractions: "high ideals." *Tall* means "higher than average" or "high in relation to breadth": "a tall woman," "a tall grandfather's clock." *Tall* is more likely than the others in references to living things: "tall trees" (although *lofty* is aptly applied to the giant redwoods). *Lofty,* seldom used, refers to impressive height: "Lofty Mt. Denali," "lofty ceilings." It is applied, often rather unbelievingly or semihumorously, to abstractions: "lofty ideals," "lofty thoughts."

high noon   In SWE, ordinarily used only for "precisely 12 M.," not 11:59 A.M. or 12:01 P.M.

highbrow/lowbrow/middlebrow   Although *middlebrow* is seldom seen or heard, *lowbrow* and *highbrow* are not rare, even in SWE. The alternatives are wordy locutions such as "a person of high intelligence and considerable culture."

highfalutin (also *hifalutin*)   An unpretentious word for "pretentious." It knocks the pomposity out of users of high-flown language, the glitz out of purchasers of hundred-dollar perfumes. From frontier slang of the sort used to discombobulate stuffed shirts it has moved up the stairway to a dictionary rating of "informal" and to occasional SWE use.

highlight (noun and verb)   Established for centuries as a noun, *highlight* is now widely – perhaps too widely – used as a verb: "highlighted today's news stories," "highlight the eyelashes," "highlights the congressional hearings today." Sometimes *emphasize, feature, stress, play up, are most prominent, add color to,* or something else may be substituted.

hijack, hijacker, hijacking   These words sound slangy, but since no short synonyms exist, they are now listed as standard in most dictionaries. *Highjack* is an alternative spelling.

hike   Now SWE for "increase," as in "wage hike." Most useful to writers of headlines.

hilarious   A strong word. A *hilarious* movie is not merely amusing, funny, humorous, witty.

hillbillies   Don't call us that when we can hear you!

hinder/prevent   To *hinder* is to present difficulties, to delay: "A few fallen branches hindered our progress along the road." To *prevent* is to stop completely, to keep (something) from happening: "Fallen trees prevented our driving farther."

hindsight/retrospect(ion) *Retrospection* is thoughtful recall, review, or evaluation of past decisions and events. (*Retrospect* is rarely used except in the phrase *in retrospect*.) *Hindsight* also refers to looking back but carries the connotation of critical evaluation often tinged with regret: "Hindsight told him that he should have resigned earlier."

hippie An SWE word, but now seldom used except nostalgically by former "flower children," most of whom have changed from long-haired, free-loving, pot-smoking idealists to kempt, married, relatively abstemious pragmatists.

historic/historical A *historical* event can be any in history, whether important or not. A *historic* event is an especially memorable one. A place, such as a battlefield, may be historic, is associated with historical events, but is not itself likely to be called historical. SWE uses either *a* or *an* before both words, with *a* perhaps moving ahead because the *h* is rather distinctly pronounced.

historic/momentous Both words are overused by sports announcers in describing a contest a little more important than most. Perhaps the very first World Series game or the ones postponed in 1989 by a California earthquake were historic or momentous or both, but the words are trivialized if used with regard to every World Series or Super Bowl. *Momentous* differs from *historic* mainly by especially emphasizing the consequences, the later impact, of the event. See also EPIC.

hit over the head This idiom is established, but *hit on the head* is more logical.

hither, thither, whither All three are bookish, obsolescent words, usually avoided unless an archaic flavor is desirable. One exception is "a come-hither smile," never out of date.

hitherto SWE prefers *previously, earlier,* or *up to that time.*

hobnob *Hobnob* is an SWE word. It was associated hundreds of years ago with companionable drinking and now means "to talk with companionably," "to mix with in friendly fashion."

hock SWE but informal for "pawn" (verb) or "state of being pawned" (noun). In recent years the image of the pawnshop has faded somewhat, so that someone who claims to be "in hock" simply means that he or she is in debt – probably not to a pawnbroker.

hocus-pocus **1.** An SWE word for "trickery, magic, nonsense." **2.** The verb *hocus* is also standard, although rarely used. It means "deceive," "cheat," "adulterate," or "conceal as a drug in food or drink": "He hocused me again." "She hocused the coffee with vodka." ". . . the vodka with water."

hog (verb) In such expressions as "trying to hog the show," "hog the camera," or "hogging the time of other speakers," *hog* means "use more than a fair share of." It dates back to as early as 1887 and is now SWE, though informal.

hoi polloi Since the expression means "the common people," SWE doesn't write "*the* hoi polloi." In fact, since the term is condescending, many writers avoid it.

hokey Probably derived from *hocus-pocus*, this adjective means "contrived," "unrealistic," or "too sentimental": "His first short story was a hokey account of bank robbers with hearts of gold," "a hokey movie about children who are never even mischievous." It is usually FF but does appear in informal SWE. See also HOCUS-POCUS.

hold (steady vs. steadily) It's usually *hold steady* in both FF and SWE. The meaning of "Hold it steady" is "Hold it so that it remains steady." *Hold steadily* is rarely seen, but it's possible in the sense of "constantly": "He held the pose steadily for an hour." Similar comments apply to *hold firm* vs. *firmly*.

holdup See BURGLARY/HOLDUP/ROBBERY . . .

hollow tube Has anyone ever seen an unhollow tube?

holocaust Capitalized, *Holocaust* has come to mean Hitler's attempt to exterminate the Jews, especially in the cinerators of concentration camps. Uncapitalized, *holocaust* most often means a tremendously destructive fire, but – in a use sometimes questioned – it may mean any great disaster. The derivation, from a Greek word for "entirely burned," suggests that the implication of fire should be retained (although admittedly many words have strayed from their historical meanings).

home/house Follett illustrates a distinction that real-estate agents ignore: "Homes are not bought and sold, houses are." A *house*, conservatives like Follett say, is a physical structure. A *home* is not merely a structure but also a place of kindness, affection, and shared work and play, a place where memories – both pleasant and less than pleasant – gradually accumulate. Follett and his friends have lost to commercialism.

homely Has different meanings in Great Britain and the United States. A woman called *homely* in London may be pleased, especially if she is proud of her homey charm – the sort of wife a man would be glad to come home to. A woman in New York may feel insulted, because she interprets *homely* as "unattractive."

homicide/manslaughter/murder *Homicide* includes both manslaughter and murder, as well as almost any other killing of one person by another (unless as a result of war, court action, or – debated questions – abortion or euthanasia). *Manslaughter* in U.S. law is the illegal killing of one person by another without intent to do injury – for example, by a negligent driver. *Murder* is like manslaughter but involves "malice aforethought," interpreted as a desire – perhaps a plan – to do injury even if not to kill.

homosexual Either a male or a female can be *homosexual*, although the word increasingly is applied to males only. The language needs a male equivalent of *lesbian*.

honkey, honkie, honky An FF (slang) word used by some blacks to disparage whites; the reverse equivalent of *nigger*. All such offensive expressions are generally avoided in SWE except in direct quotation.

hooked This is still FF (slang) in the sense of "addicted." The addiction need not be to drugs; it may be to gambling, computers, or classical or rock music.

hooker This word appears to be more widely used, in most kinds of context, than *whore, harlot, prostitute*, or any other such word. It may still be called slang or informal, but it is much less so than a hundred or so clearly slang words with the same meaning. It frequently appears in well-edited publications.

hope Fowler lists three problem constructions and includes examples parallel to these: **1.** Double passive, as in "A better result is to be hoped to be attained tomorrow." Better: "The designers hope to attain . . ." **2.** Analogy with *expect*: "We hope him to do well." Better: "We hope that he does well" or "We expect him to do well." **3.** Omission of a needed *it*: "Plans for what is hoped will be the city's greatest parade have been completed." Better: Insert *it* before *is hoped.*

hope I remember "I hope I remember (*find, see*, and so on) it" is a standard Americanism in which a present-tense verb is used for future time. Conservative British speakers are likely to say, "I hope (that) I will remember it" or "I hope to remember it."

hope, hopeful/optimism, optimistic *Optimism* and *optimistic* suggest a higher probability of a favorable outcome than *hope* and *hopeful* do. A person can be hopeful about winning a lottery without being optimistic.

hopeless See DESPERATE/HOPELESS.

horn To classical musicians, *horn* means "French horn." To others it may include any brass instrument, or possibly even woodwinds. Modern dictionaries treat both definitions as standard. An English horn is technically a woodwind, somewhat similar to an oboe.

horrible, horribly Like the similar *dreadful, horrible* has degenerated in meaning from "filling with horror" to the much weaker "very bad" or "highly unpleasant": "a horrible day at the office." Its substitutes, including *horrid, horrifying, ghastly*, and perhaps *grim*, are following the same downward path. Today, to express the idea that the sight of a bloody accident filled you with horror, that's probably the way you have to say it, unless you choose to substitute specific details. "Horrible accident" has been demeaned to signify (in some FF) no more than a scratch or a broken fingernail.

hostess Despite the gradual disappearance of *poetess, sculptress*, and other such words often considered sexist, *hostess* is still an active noun. The occasional verb use, however, as in "hostessing a party," seems to be vanishing.

hot cup of coffee See COLD GLASS OF MILK/HOT CUP OF COFFEE.

hot-water heater *Hot* is unnecessary.

hour See FOOT.

house   See HOME/HOUSE.

housewares   SWE retains the *s*. Although *silverware, earthenware*, and several other such words are standard without the *s*, each of those refers to a single variety of "ware," but *housewares* includes several kinds.

how come   Usually considered informal for "Why?" in sentences such as "How come the medicine has lost its effectiveness?" In a rare reversal, RHD calls the expression informal, but the conservative AHD defines it without comment. It's infrequent in SWE.

how ever/however   Written as two words in sentences such as "How ever did you stay so calm in that emergency?" The fact that two words are essential is indicated by the alternative phrasing, "How did you ever . . . ?" When the meaning is "no matter how" or "nevertheless," *however* is standard: "However wise they are, they cannot solve every personal problem." "However, they will try to help you."

hubris   OED gives an 1831 citation for the adjective *hubristic* ("insolent, contemptuous"), but the noun *hubris* ("arrogance, presumption") has been in wide use only since about 1960. Now it is fully established, although still not familiar to some readers.

huddle   A good word for a brief conference on the football field, but probably executives and other high officials *meet, confer*, or *hold a discussion*, even though journalists may say that "the three prime ministers huddled." Other SWE items use the word occasionally.

huge throng   Nobody has ever seen a small throng. SWE omits *huge*.

huh-uh   Some writers confuse the negative *huh-uh* with the affirmative *uh-huh*.

human (noun)   Is *human* a noun as well as an adjective? *Human* or *human being*? The argument has long continued, and differences of opinion still exist. Most dictionaries now treat both *human* and *human being* as standard. Some writers avoid a choice by using *person(s)* or *people*. See also BOVINE.

human/humane   Although once the same word, *human* and *humane* are now differentiated. *Human* refers to any characteristic – good or bad – of people: "That's only human." *Humane* has only good connotations. It means "kind, helpful, sympathetic, compassionate": "humane treatment of animals."

humanist/humanitarian   A *humanist* is a student of the humanities, often with emphasis on the classics, or a student of humans and their well-being. A *humanitarian* deals more with concrete cases than with theory. While a humanist makes a study of charity, a humanitarian leads the local food drive on behalf of the poor.

humble   1. Usually preceded by *a*, not *an*, because most people pronounce the *h*. 2. "In my humble opinion" is seldom said by a truly humble person, who (as Roy Copperud wittily notes) most likely will "humbly adopt the views of others."

humbug   An example of how a colorful word sometimes ascends from slang to complete acceptance. A boost from Ebenezer Scrooge helped. The word now means not only "nonsense," the Scroogean application, but also "hoax" or, referring to a person, "charlatan, impostor": "He's a humbug."

humongous   FF (slang) based on *huge* and *tremendous*: "At the top of the beanpole was a humongous giant." "I've got a humongous idea."

humor/wit   *Humor* is usually more kindly than *wit*. A humorous person looks with amusement on human foibles and on the absurdities that characterize much in life. Although "black humor" reflects an almost hopeless view of life, most humor is much more tolerant. The eighteenth-century humorist Joseph Addison, for example, poked gentle fun at coquettes, empty-headed young men, and many others. *Wit* is often more biting than humor and is based largely on verbal cleverness. Ambrose Bierce was the American wit who said that *belladonna* in Italian means "a beautiful woman" and in English "a deadly poison." That proves, he said, the identity of the two languages. See also BLACK HUMOR/SICK HUMOR.

hunch   *Hunch*, as in "having (or *playing*) a hunch," may sound like modern slang, but it has been common in American English since about 1900, and in different senses ("a thrust" or "a lump") in British English for several centuries.

hung   See HANGED/HUNG.

hurl   SWE uses *hurl* only when such a powerful verb is appropriate. Most people *throw* stones instead of *hurling* them. And a remark or even a curse that is hurled must be uttered with great vehemence. A strong-armed baseball player may justifiably be called a *hurler*.

hurricane/typhoon   A *hurricane* has spinning winds exceeding seventy-five miles an hour. It originates in the Caribbean or the warm waters of the Atlantic. A *typhoon* has the same description, but it occurs in the China Sea or the western Pacific. See also CYCLONE/TORNADO.

hurting   Now SWE even with subjects that can have no feelings, such as "Efforts to aid Bangladesh are hurting because most Americans know little about the country." Many writers, however, would substitute *being hurt* or *hampered*.

hype   Some hypodermic injections are stimulants. The shortened form of *hypodermic*, *hype*, has existed since about 1960 with the meaning "something that stimulates sales." Hype may be "socially accepted fraud," as Flesch defines it, but often it is only high-powered or gimmicky salesmanship. The word is slang or informal but sometimes finds its way into serious discussion, including SWE. It may be either a noun or a verb.

hyper-/hypo-   One way to remember the difference between these prefixes is to recall familiar words to remind you that *hyper-* means "above" and *hypo-* "below." For example, a hyperactive child is *above* average in activeness, and a hypodermic needle goes *below* the skin.

hypnotic Refers to hypnotism, not to normal sleep. A drug that assists falling asleep may be described as *sleep-inducing* or (at the risk of incomprehension) *soporific*.

I

I In most scholarly and scientific writing and in official corporate reports, news stories, or the like, use of the first person is not permitted or, at best, is unorthodox. In other writing *I* is usually preferable to *the author, the writer,* or *the present writer*. See also PRESENT WRITER.

I don't think This idiom, as in "I don't think the chief will consent," has been attacked because obviously the speaker *is* thinking. Purists insist on "I think (or *believe*) the chief will not consent," and obviously logic is on their side. But the idiom is firmly established.

-ic/-ical Many adjectives have both *-ic* and *-ical* forms with the same meanings, for example, *strategic, strategical; tyrannic, tyrannical*. Unless the longer word improves the rhythm of a sentence, SANE favors the shorter. See also GEOGRAPHIC, GEOGRAPHICAL . . .

ice water (*tea*, and so on) Purists ask for *iced water*, in a restaurant, believing that *ice water* can be only melted ice. But Americans have so persistently ordered *ice water* that the term is now standard. A battle is still going on between *ice* tea (or coffee) and *iced*, with *iced* ahead. *Iced drinks* is also SWE.

-ics Names of sciences ending in *-ics* are treated as singular: "Ethics is a branch of philosophy." "Acoustics is important to many architects." Some of these words may be used other than as names of sciences and then are usually treated as plurals: "Her ethics are questionable," meaning her standards of conduct. See also ACOUSTICS; ETHICS/ETHICAL/ETHICS.

idea A word broad enough to encompass almost any thought, any product of the mind. Often, however, a more precise word is preferable. Among the choices: *assumption, belief, conception, conviction, fancy, feeling, image, impression, notion, opinion, plan, principle, scheme, significance, solution, theory, view, viewpoint*.

ideal See EXAMPLE/SAMPLE/SPECIMEN.

IDENTIFICATIONS (PILING UP) "Well-known Sioux City soft-drink bottler Herman Schmidt" is journalese for "Herman Schmidt, a well-known soft-drink bottler from Sioux City." Certainly, journalists must identify people they write about, but putting two or more identifications before the name, or putting four or more of them in the same sentence, often results in awkwardness.

identified with Dubious for "in the employ of," as in "Mr. Rasmussen was identified with the Crown Corporation for thirty years."

SWE substitutes *was employed by, worked for, was an officer of,* or something similar.

identify with   "Some young people try to identify with favorite fictional characters." Conservatives ask for *themselves* after *identify,* but psychologists use the verb without an object (this applies even to conservative psychologists). SWE accepts both versions.

idiot/imbecile/moron   The *Dictionary of Behavioral Science* says that an *idiot* has an IQ below 25 and cannot learn to speak, read, or write. An *imbecile* has an IQ between 25 and 50, a mental age between two and seven years. A *moron* has an IQ between 50 and 70 and can usually perform simple tasks under supervision. In the United States, the term *feebleminded* includes all three groups, but in Britain it's synonymous with *moron.* All four of these terms are SWE, but because they unfortunately are often used by the unkind or unwitting as terms of ridicule, many writers prefer a euphemism such as *mentally retarded person* or *slow learner.*

idle (verb)   Long established as SWE in sentences such as "The strike has idled 350 workers."

idle rich   Some are idle, others not. Some may work harder than you or I. SWE generally tries to be fair and to avoid stereotypes of the rich, the poor, or anyone else.

i.e.   See E.G./I.E.

if and when   Usually either *if* or *when* will suffice.

if I were/if I was   More frequently needed is *were,* as in "if I were you," "if Janice Smith were president." The reason is that the statements are contrary to fact: I am not you, and Smith is not president. The subjunctive *were* is customary in *if*-clauses that refer to such unreality. However, in one instance *if . . . was* is standard: when the statement is *not* definitely contrary to fact. For instance, assume that we are not certain whether Pauline was or was not at a meeting. We say correctly, "If Pauline *was* at the meeting, she may have an answer for us." Another example: "If I was crazy, I'm not crazy now."

if need be   SWE, but sounds old-fashioned. *If necessary* is more likely today.

if that were the case   Wordy for *if so.*

if/whether   Either word is used in SWE as an opener in an indirect question. "Mrs. Thatcher asked whether (of *if*) the Conservative majority would agree." *Whether* is more likely than *if* to introduce two or more possibilities: "Whether we lose, tie, or win, we intend to play well."

iffy   A word often used by Franklin D. Roosevelt to mean "uncertain, problematic, doubtful, questionable, hypothetical." If it was good enough for him, it should be good enough for most of us. Dictionaries, however, insist that it is suitable only for informal contexts.

ignorant/illiterate   *Illiterate* basically means "unable to read and write" but is often used to mean also "uneducated, lacking in culture." The relatively recent term *functionally illiterate* means "not well enough educated to perform more than menial tasks." *Ignorant* is a broader term, although lack of formal education is usually a contributing cause of ignorance. All of us are mainly ignorant: most of the world's knowledge is unknown to us. On the other hand, as William Cobden said long ago, if a plowman "knows how to plow, he is not to be called an ignorant man."

ignorant   See DUMB/IGNORANT/STUPID.

ill/illy   Comparative forms are *more ill* or *worse*, superlative *most ill* or *worst*. Although usually an adjective, as in "an ill person" and "She is ill," the word may also be an adverb, as in "ill defined." *Illy* is rare and not needed: "an ill-defined (not *illy defined*) task." (Both Thomas Jefferson and Washington Irving, however, did use *illy*.)

ill/sick   Interchangeable in the United States, although in England *sick* almost always means "nauseated." Some Americans feel that *ill* is for some reason a "nicer" word.

illegal/illegitimate/illicit/unlawful   *Illegal* and *unlawful* both mean "forbidden by law." *Illegitimate* may have that meaning, too, but earlier meant "born out of wedlock," as it still does. Its meaning has expanded, though, to "fake, spurious," as in "illegitimate claims for reimbursement." *Illicit*, too, though synonymous with *illegal*, often adds a note of shame, as in "an illicit romance." Such a romance may be contrary to custom, law, or both.

illegal operation   Not many years ago journalists euphemistically referred to an abortion as an *illegal operation*. Now *spayed* is called *spayed* and *abortion* is called *abortion*.

illegible/unreadable   Not quite the same. A letter or document may be *unreadable* because the handwriting is *illegible*, "impossible to decipher," but in addition it (or even a printed book) may be unreadable because it is badly worded, too polysyllabic, poorly organized, extremely boring, or offensive, even though all parts are legible.

illicit   See ELICIT/ILLICIT; ILLEGAL/ILLICIT.

illiterate   See IGNORANT/ILLITERATE.

illusion   See ALLUSION/ILLUSION.

image   Now an SWE word for "public impression," *image* was not widely used in this sense until after 1950: "The president's aides try to protect and enhance his image."

imaginary/imaginative   An *imaginary* child is an unreal, perhaps dreamed-of or hoped-for child. An *imaginative* child is a real child with a lively, creative mind.

imagination   See FANCY/IMAGINATION.

imagine/suppose   In theory, *imagine* should be the verb-companion of the noun *imagination*. However, it also has been used for centuries in the sense of *suppose*, even in such unimaginative sentences as "I imagine you're hungry, John." As a result, some dictionaries give *suppose* as one of its synonyms. In scientific or other technical writing and other SWE, however, *suppose* is the more likely choice for "assume to be true."

imitation See ARTIFICIAL/ERSATZ/FAKE . . .

immature/premature Evans says that all babies are *immature* but only 6 percent are *premature*. An immature mind is not fully developed. A premature baby is born before the usual nine months are up. A premature plan is made before such a plan is needed. An immature plan is not thoroughly developed.

immediately Sometimes needs to be followed by *after* for clarity. "Immediately he fired the shot he was sorry." Without *after, Immediately he fired the shot* may be momentarily misunderstood to mean "Quickly he fired . . ." Note the different meaning when *after* is added.

immigrant See EMIGRANT/IMMIGRANT.

imminent See EMINENT/IMMINENT.

immoral See AMORAL/IMMORAL.

impact 1. This noun for *effect* is sometimes too strong. Many writers of SWE reserve it, for example, for head-on collisions, not sideswipes; for momentous influence, not for a tag in sandlot football. 2. The verb *impact* for "have an effect on" became a vogue word in the 1980s, appearing tiresomely in sentences such as "The holiday season impacts the lives of everyone."

impeach Often misused to mean "remove from office." In actuality an impeachment hearing is comparable to a grand jury investigation to determine whether charges should be brought. For a president or other officeholder to be removed from office, he or she must first be formally impeached and, after that, be tried and convicted. A second meaning, not necessarily defined in a legal sense, is "discredit, degrade, attack verbally": "Layton repeatedly impeached his former friend, calling him a liar and a thief."

impecunious Most poor people call themselves "poor." Some poor people with college degrees call themselves "impecunious." *Impecunious* shouldn't be confused with *penurious* ("stingy").

impel/incite/induce To *impel* is to drive something or someone forward: "Greed impelled the Hunts to try to corner the silver market." To *incite* is to urge on or to stir into action. It is often associated with a socially undesirable outcome: "incited to riot." To *induce* is to persuade, often to use sweet reason to lead someone to a decision or action: "Henry needed an hour to induce Joel to accompany him."

imperial/imperious Today these two words are quite different in meaning. *Imperial* is used in expressions such as "the imperial palace, robes, decrees" and means "relating to the emperor or the empire." *Imperious* means "commanding, demanding, domineering": "an imperious tone" ". . . gesture," or the like.

impertinent/impudent/insolent All three words refer to inappropriately rude words or action. *Impertinent* suggests lack of respect for one's elders or superiors in rank: "Private Lewis spoke impertinently to the captain." Although impertinence may sometimes be forgiven because of the immaturity of the offender, *impudence* is less likely to be. It is stronger, brasher than impertinence. *Insolence* is still more rude. It suggests open dislike and may come close to insubordination: "'You sure you want me to do that, Cap?' Lewis asked insolently."

impressive   See ARRESTING/IMPRESSIVE/STRIKING.

implant/inculcate/inject/instill (passive voice)   SWE seldom says, "Young Jefferson was implanted (*instilled* or the like) with the knowledge that . . . ," because Jefferson was not implanted at all. Instead, "The knowledge that . . . was implanted in the young Jefferson" or "Young Jefferson's father inculcated (*implanted*) in his son the knowledge that . . ."

implement (verb)   Used in SWE for "provide the tools or other means" to accomplish something: "The House funding bill would implement construction of the dam." In some contexts *provide, accomplish, execute, achieve* or simply *make* will be more accurate.

implement/instrument   An *instrument* is ordinarily more delicate, complex, or precise than an *implement*. Doctors and musicians, for example, use instruments, but farmers, carpenters, and tractor repairmen more often use implements or tools, although on some occasions they need instruments.

implosion   See EXPLOSION/IMPLOSION.

imply/infer   SWE uses *imply* to refer to the sending end: "The speaker implied that Congress should provide military aid." The movement is speaker → listener, or writer → reader. On the receiving end, the listener or reader *infers* that Congress should provide the aid.

important/importantly   Both are SWE in sentences such as "More important(ly), the jurors seemed impressed by the defendant's manner." SANE votes for *more important* and suggests that it is short for "what is more important."

impossible   "Jill is impossible!" Not really. If Jill exists, she must be possible. *Impossible* as used here is FF (slang) for "too funny (*serious, unpleasant,* or anything else)." Only someone who knows Jill and the speaker well can guess what is meant.

impression   See EDITION/IMPRESSION, PRINTING.

impracticable/impractical   Something *impracticable* cannot be done or is foolish: "It is impracticable to mix two quarts of lemonade in a one-quart pitcher." Something is *impractical* if it is unwise to do, especially as a regular thing: "It is impractical to prepare two term papers during the last week of the semester."

in (adjective)   On the edge of SWE but possibly faddish for "popular, stylish": "Short skirts are in," "the in thing to do." Sometimes *in* makes a phrase a little hard to read. It's impossible to say how long *in* will be in. *In* can be a noun, too – again on the SWE edge: "In politics the ins keep trying not to become outs."

in addition to See ALONG WITH, AS WELL AS, IN ADDITION TO . . .

in back of See BACK OF/IN BACK OF.

in/into "Mavis danced into the kitchen" means that she entered dancing. "Mavis danced in the kitchen" means that she danced while she was in that room. Informally, *in* is often used where *into* is the usual SWE, but sometimes that usage may be ambiguous.

***in* phrases** Writing can often be tightened by reducing a phrase to one or two words. Examples starting with *in*:

> *in addition to* – besides
> *in all probability* – probably
> *in a* _____ *manner* – solemnly, quietly, and so on
> *in any shape or form* – Omit?
> *in connection with* – concerning, about
> *in height* – tall. Omit?
> *in most instances* – often, frequently
> *in number* – Omit?
> *in order to* – to
> *in question* – Omit?
> *in regard (respect) to* – on, about, concerning
> *in spite of the fact that* – although, even though
> *in terms of* – about. Omit?
> *in that time frame* – then (see also POINT IN TIME)
> *in the area (vicinity) of* – about, in, near
> *in the belief that* – believing
> *in the course of* – during, while, at
> *in the event that* – if
> *in the final (last) analysis* – finally, I conclude that
> *in the majority of cases* – often, most often
> *in the midst of* – in, within, during, amid, among
> *in the nature of* – like, such as
> *in view (light) of the fact that* – since, because

133

in re Meaning "in regard to," *in re* or *re* may be used in legal documents or a business letter to notify the reader of the subject matter. It is underlined (italicized). SWE seldom uses it for other purposes. In many business letters, the word *subject* is used instead.

in receipt of Outmoded business phrase, as in "We are in receipt of your recent shipment, but . . ." Modern: "We have received . . ." or "Thank you for filling our recent order, but . . ." or "In checking your recent shipment we . . ."

in the shape of Objectionable if what is discussed has no shape. Possible: "in the shape of a T." Illogical: "in the shape of a letter to the editor."

in the wake of Needed in "smaller boats were rocking in the wake of the yacht," but usually replaceable by *after* or *following* in figurative expressions such as "in the wake of the disaster."

in to/into We walk *into* a building, turn into a frog, fall into a creek, crash into a tree. In each instance, *into* carries the notion of movement from one place or condition to another. We walk *in to* see a friend, turn *in to* get some sleep – using *in* followed by the infinitive *to see*, and so on. Instances without an infinitive are rare. Copperud gives the example "We dropped in to coffee with the Smiths," which would be ridiculous as "We dropped into coffee . . ." See also IN/INTO.

inasmuch as, insofar as These are the standard ways to write the two expressions – which, by the way, can often be shortened to *because* and *so far as*, respectively.

inaugurate SWE avoids use for trivial occasions. Although one definition is "to begin or start officially," *inaugurate* is a bit strong for an added bus route or a new perfume counter. *Open, begin, start,* or *commence* will do.

incapable/unable *Incapable* suggests an inborn lack of ability, but *unable* more often means only a temporary lack. Most of us would rather be unable to answer the phone rather than incapable of answering it.

incensed See ENRAGED/INCENSED/INFURIATED.

inchoate *Inchoate* means "just beginning, developing, immature." Because of confusion with *chaos*, it is sometimes misused as "disorganized, chaotic." In reality a fetus – an inchoate baby – normally is well organized, each part where it belongs and of appropriate size for its current stage.

incident Defined as "a relatively minor occurrence," but used rather oddly in some newspaper stories: "Members of the youth gangs met at First and Sudbury and exchanged epithets and brandished weapons before police intervened, but no incidents occurred." (No blood, no incidents!) See also EPISODE/EVENT/INCIDENT . . .

inclined to In the sense of "favorable toward," most logically applies to animate beings. A person or a dog may be inclined to be lazy, but a stone has no inclination to be anything; not "This kind of stone is inclined to flake off in strips." SWE prefers *has a tendency to* or *often flakes off*.

include Questionable: "The membership of the Budapest String Quartet included Joseph Roisman, Alexander Schneider, Boris Kroyt, and Mischa Schneider." Ordinarily *include* implies "among others," but here, obviously, all four are named. Better: "The members . . . were . . . ," or "Joseph Roisman [et al.] comprised . . . ," or "The Budapest String Quartet was composed of . . ." SWE also says, "The membership . . . included two Schneiders." See also COMPOSE/COMPRISE.

incognita SANE favors discarding *incognita*, a feminine form, along with *aviatrix, poetess,* and the like. *Incognito* can serve both sexes.

incomparable/uncomparable Although few people ever use *uncomparable* (accent on *par*), statements carrying the literal meaning of "not capable of being compared" would often be clearer if that word were chosen instead of *incomparable*. The latter could then be reserved for "matchless, unsurpassed": "Sales figures for the two years are uncomparable (or *not comparable*) because different methods of tabulation were used," but "The beauty of Helen of Troy is said to have been incomparable."

incredible! A vogue word for "Great!" "Wonderful!" An interviewer said to a young actor, "And so you two married and now have a baby?" "Yes." "Incredible!" It wasn't at all unbelievable. That sort of thing happens frequently. See also COLOSSAL/COLOSSALLY.

incredibly fantastic After tiring of this vogue term, some people have discovered *fantastically incredible* – no improvement.

indefinitely A catalog stated that an adjustable wrench was "guaranteed to last indefinitely." Since an indefinite time can be a second or almost forever, the manufacturer need never make amends for defective wrenches. *Indefinitely* does not necessarily mean "a very long time." *Almost indefinitely* or *somewhat indefinitely* is meaningless.

indexes/indices Take your choice. SANE recommends anglicized plurals (*indexes*) except for firmly entrenched foreign forms.

indicate Follett says rightly that *indicate* is often used when a more specific verb is preferable. He lists about thirty possible substitutes, including *hint, insinuate, imply, announce, specify, proclaim, propose, urge, point out, report, admit, declare*. He also understandably dislikes such passive-voice usages as "A good stiff drink is indicated."

indict/indite Pronounced alike, but quite different in meaning. A person who is *indicted* is charged with a crime (note that the indictment does not prove guilt). Most people never need *indite*. It's a stiff old word for "write."

indispensable See ESSENTIAL/INDISPENSABLE/NECESSARY . . .

individual (noun) Usually SWE prefers *person* (or *dog, cat*, and so on) to *individual* except in singling out one or a few for special attention. Dubious: "Several individuals were injured." Possible: "Study of two individuals in the group is not enough to justify a generalization."

indoor(s), outdoor(s) SWE uses *indoor* and *outdoor* before a following noun: "an indoor pool," "an outdoor party." Otherwise it uses *indoors* and *outdoors*: "walked outdoors," "stayed indoors," "the great outdoors."

induce, induction See DEDUCE/DEDUCT/INDUCE.

indulge in See ENGAGE IN/INDULGE IN.

ineffable A seldom-needed word meaning, in effect, "with no words sufficient to describe." Adequate words almost always exist; the problem lies in finding them.

ineffable/unspeakable Although both words mean "impossible to express," they are quite different in usage. Something is *ineffable* if it seems too splendid to be described: "the ineffable joy of a mother who can once more hold her kidnapped child." *Unspeakable*, in contrast, often connotes something too unpleasant or vile to be talked about: "an unspeakable crime," "the unspeakable filth of Rio's slums."

inept/unapt *Inept* usually means "clumsy" or "foolish": "played an inept game at shortstop," "an inept remark." Rather rarely it means "inappropriate." *Unapt* means "unlikely" or "inappropriate": "She is unapt (or *not apt*) to follow such a suggestion." "In those circumstances, his comment was unapt." (Rarely, *inapt* substitutes for *unapt*, but it is even more likely to be confused with *inept*.)

inequity/iniquity SWE is careful with these. *Inequity* is "unfairness, inequality of treatment": "The inequity of some tax regulations." *Iniquity* is "sin, wickedness, moral offenses": "Sons should not be judged by the iniquity of their fathers."

infant See BABY/CHILD/INFANT.

infantile See CHILDISH/CHILDLIKE/INFANTILE.

infectious See CONTAGIOUS/INFECTIOUS.

inferno Described in the *Inferno*, part of Dante's *Divine Comedy*, in which it represents a place of torment for lost souls, *inferno* can mean "Hell, a Hell-like place, or the fiery place that Hell is rumored to be." From these definitions has derived the use of *inferno* for a tremendous conflagration such as the skyscraper fire shown in the movie *The Towering Inferno*. SWE does not cheapen the word as some writers of modern "romances" do. Some stories describe a woman's heart or desires as "an inferno of emotions" or "a roaring inferno of passion." (Sounds painful!)

infinite(ly) *Infinite* means "having no knowable limits, immeasurably large." SWE avoids "the infinite heights of the Rockies" or "the infinite reaches of the prairies" unless trying to reflect a child's perceptions. A thesaurus offers several dozen substitutes besides the obvious *immense* and *far*. Similar comments apply to *infinitely*.

inflammable/inflammatory We refer to *inflammable* (or *flammable*) materials, but almost never to *inflammatory* materials except figuratively: "Thomas Paine's inflammatory articles sparked many Colonists' anger against the British." A second meaning of *inflammatory* is related to *inflammation* ("bodily heat or swelling"): "Several anti-inflammatory drugs are available." See also FLAMMABLE/INFLAMMABLE.

informal(ly) When context by itself suggests informality, this word is not needed. Redundant: "Lounging beside the pool, Sylvia Heart-throb spoke informally with reporters for several minutes."

informant/informer Often interchangeable. However, a person who supplies information to a pollster or researcher is usually an *informant*: "Thousands of informants supplied data for Professor Cassidy's monumental study of American dialects." *Informer* has as one of its meanings "one who informs on others (perhaps for pay)" or the slang "squealer": "a police informer."

information/knowledge Not synonyms. *Knowledge* refers to a body of facts and inferences, especially but not necessarily carried in one's head, as "Dickens's thorough knowledge of London." *Information* refers particularly to facts – many or few – sometimes gathered at random and not necessarily systematized mentally. It may be contained in one's head or in a book or other place. Information is the basis of knowledge but is less broad, deep, and patterned than knowledge itself.

infrastructure In a city the infrastructure is the system of streets, sewers, electric and telephone conduits, and the like on which smooth functioning depends. In a large business it may be both the physical necessities and the system of governance. It is SWE, not just a "vogue word," as Morris calls it.

infuriated See ENRAGED/INCENSED/INFURIATED.

-ing Verbs, which are usually action words, often enliven sentences. Nouns, being names, keep them standing still. Many writers suffer from noun-itis – relying too much on nouns. One cure is to make more use of *-ings*, which of course are verb forms. Examples:

> gradual reduction of excess weight – *gradually losing pounds*
> a disinclination toward payment of additional taxes – *hating tax hikes*
> approach to the point of saturation – *nearing saturation*
> calls for modification of – *calls for modifying*
> movements of wings – *flutterings*

-ing (case preceding) When an *-ing* word such as *dancing* is used as a noun, is *you* or *your* preferable before it? In FF it makes little difference. In SWE a possessive (*your, my, the boy's, Linda's,* or the like) is usual: "We enjoyed watching your dancing again," meaning that it was the dancing that we enjoyed. But suppose that the dancer has just recovered from a long illness. We are likely to say, "We enjoyed watching *you* dancing again," meaning "watching *you* able to dance again." In short, the choice of modifier can result in conveying a slightly different meaning.

ingenious/ingenuous An *ingenious* person is clever, but an *ingenuous* one is usually naive and artless, or possibly a little too frank and revealing. See also CLEVER/INGENIOUS/INVENTIVE.

in-group/out-group Both are SWE words, popularized by sociologists. Members of an *in-group* share beliefs, interests, and activities, but persons in an *out-group* differ from them in one or more significant ways. Many out-groups, such as Christian sects or denominations, become new in-groups, which develop new out-groups, which . . . , perhaps almost *ad infinitum*, illustrating multiplication by division.

inhabitant See CITIZEN/INHABITANT/RESIDENT.

inhibit/prohibit Sometimes interchangeable, but *inhibiting* usually is a slow process whereas *prohibiting* may be as quick as a vote by a city council. Also, a prohibition usually comes from an outside authority, as in "an ordinance prohibiting parking." But an inhibition generally comes from within; for example, a person may be inhibited from sexual intercourse by fear of disease.

inhuman/unhuman *Inhuman* means "brutal": "inhuman treatment of captives." *Unhuman* means "not like a human being." For example, a sound not like any normally produced by humans may be described as unhuman; such a sound may be pleasant or unpleasant.

injured See DAMAGED/INJURED.

in-law (plural and possessive) Examples of SWE plurals are *sons-in-law, mothers-in-law*; SWE singular possessive, *my son-in-law's opinion(s)*; SWE plural possessive, *my sons-in-law's opinion(s)*.

inmost/innermost These are interchangeable, so why not use the shorter?

innards Standard since about 1815 for "the inner parts of a body or a machine." Derived from *inwards*, which today is rarely used in that sense.

innate See HEREDITARY/INNATE.

inner man Once meant "soul," but now is a feebly humorous cliché for "stomach, digestive tract": "keeping the inner man happy."

innocent bystander Sometimes another word is more appropriate than *innocent*, which means "not guilty." If guilt is not in question, *chance bystander, coincidentally a bystander, a bystander by mischance, uninvolved bystander*, or something else may be more accurate.

innocent/not guilty A defendant in court may plead "not guilty" but not "innocent." American law does not require a person to prove innocence – only lack of guilt of specified charges.

innovation Not preceded in SWE by *new* or *old*. An innovation is necessarily new, cannot be old. *Modern* or *recent* may be defensible, however.

innumerable/numerous The grains of sand on a seashore are *innumerable* ("countless"). Gulls along a seashore may be *numerous* ("great in number"), but they probably are not actually innumerable, although a count is unlikely.

inoculate/vaccinate Often used interchangeably, although *vaccinate* is customary for smallpox.

input/output SWE, but the words are ugly and quickly become tiresome. Perhaps they're essential in computer work or other special fields.

inquirer/inquisitor An *inquirer* asks questions. An *inquisitor* asks penetrating, often harsh, unfair, or unreasonable questions for a prolonged period. Because of its association with the Spanish Inquisition, the word suggests cruelty, relentlessness, and often a predetermined conclusion.

insoluble/unsolvable These words are interchangeable for "incapable of being solved": "an insoluble ('unsolvable') problem." Only *insoluble* is used for "incapable of being dissolved."

instance See EXAMPLE/INSTANCE.

instant/minute/moment/second Some people use time words more accurately than others do. To careful souls, *instant, moment,* and *second* each refer to a single tick of a clock, and *minute* to sixty ticks. Other people, however, not only fail to distinguish *minute* from the other words but also from *quarter hour. Second* implies a more precise measurement than does *instant* or *moment.*

instinct, instinctive, instinctual/intuition, intuitive *Instinctive* and *instinctual* are interchangeable. An *instinct* is an inborn manner of behavior: lemmings' instinctual journey to the sea, birds' nest-building and migrations, babies' reactions to differing tones of voice. Instincts reveal themselves especially in physical acts. *Intuition* is likewise untaught. It refers to making a judgment or decision or taking an action on the basis of "feeling" that it is correct, without following the usual processes of reasoning. One may have an intuitive knowledge or belief (not inevitably correct) that a personal or governmental decision is unwise, or feel intuitively that something pleasant or dreadful will soon happen (although it doesn't always).

institution of higher learning Note the position of *higher.* It is the learning, not the institution, that is higher.

instructional/instructive *Instructional* materials are used in instruction, especially in schools. Those materials are supposedly also *instructive* ("informative"). However, many instructive things are not necessarily used in schools or in other intentional teaching-learning situations. Good newspapers or magazines, novels, trips, discussions, or even a night in jail can be instructive without being intended as instructional. See also EDUCATIONAL/INSTRUCTIVE.

insufferable Not clearly related to *suffer* in the usual modern sense, *insufferable* means "intolerable, not endurable": "an insufferable tyrant," "The wait for the bus was almost insufferable."

integration See DESEGREGATION/INTEGRATION.

intelligent/intellectual An *intelligent* person has a quick and retentive mind and as an adult can grasp the abstract, not just the concrete. An *intellectual* person must first be intelligent, but he or she likes to focus that intelligence on literary or political theory, philosophy, scientific theory, or other subjects (or combinations) requiring considerable abstract thought. (It must be recognized, though, that an intelligent longshoreman – such as Eric Hoffer – or an athletic coach can be or become an intellectual; lack of academic degrees in theoretical subjects does not rule out intellectualism.)

intend See AIM TO.

intended See DESIGNED/INTENDED.

intense/intensive *Intense* means "extremely high in degree, size, or strength," "felt deeply": "The strain was intense." "She is an intense person who can mourn the death of a pigeon." *Intensive* has some of the significance of *intense* but suggests greater concentration. For example, an "intensive care unit" in a hospital concentrates attention on a small number of patients – possibly only one. Fowler uses as an example *intense* vs. *intensive* bombardment. Both kinds are heavy, but the intensive sort delivers most of the bombs to a small area.

intentionally See ADVISEDLY/INTENTIONALLY; CONSCIOUSLY/INTENTIONALLY.

intents and purposes Wordy: "To (*For*) all intents and purposes, the feuding has stopped." The first five words may be replaced by *apparently, essentially,* or (before *stopped*) *almost* or *nearly,* or by whatever word best conveys the meaning.

intercourse Some people automatically think of sex when they see *intercourse*. That fact should not necessitate abandonment of the basic meaning: "Communication, interchange between persons or groups." Context usually shows quickly what the writer intends.

interesting A namby-pamby word, sometimes unavoidable. When possible, SWE is more specific, designating what the kind of interest is.

interface Although *interface* is older than computers, it has thrived with them. Defined only as a noun in older dictionaries, it is now even more often an intransitive or transitive verb. Operators interface with computers, computers with one another or with a network, a space suit with the cabin, a woman's dress with its accessories – almost anything with anything else. A meeting on a street corner can be an interface; perhaps even a lover's tryst can be. People who overinterface should start to deinterface.

interject/interpolate In a conversation one person – quickly or sometimes rudely – may *interject* a remark of his or her own. Less often the softer *interpolate* is used in the same way – usually to suggest a remark intended to clarify or strengthen what the other person is saying. An interpolation frequently occurs in writing; for example, a writer may interpolate a new sentence or paragraph within a passage composed earlier.

interpersonal Often can be deleted, as in *interpersonal friendships* (or *enmities, relationships*). Sometimes *mutual* can be substituted for clarity: "mutual ill feelings." See also COMMON/MUTUAL.

interpretative, interpretive/preventative, preventive The SANE refrain: Choose the shorter. SWE increasingly does so.

into Since the 1960s many people have been *into* things: into karate, philosophy, mud-wrestling. Apparently, the hippies were into things when they weren't laid-back. The word at least carries a suggestion of hippiedom. Many specific SWE substitutes are available, depending on what one is "into." See also IN TO/ INTO.

intrigue (verb) "The contradictions in the girl's account intrigued us." As a synonym of *fascinate* or *arouse interest, intrigue* has been criticized as too vague. But it is stronger than *interest*, and it appears frequently in reputable book-review magazines, among others.

introduction   See FOREWORD/INTRODUCTION/PREFACE.

inured   See ACCUSTOMED/INURED.

invaluable/priceless   *Invaluable* and *valuable* both mean "having considerable value" (one of the many confusing things about our beloved language). Something *priceless* also has value, this time so great that it cannot be measured in money: certain heirlooms, for example. (It puzzles some foreigners that a *worthless* thing, in contrast to *priceless*, has no value at all.) *Priceless* is obviously a strong word, not to be used of most household items, a 1930 Ford, or other things to which price tags may indeed be attached. Things of great sentimental value, however, are properly described as *priceless*. Modifiers such as *absolutely, perfectly, simply, more,* or *less* are redundant.

invent   See DISCOVER/INVENT.

inventive   See CLEVER/INGENIOUS/INVENTIVE.

inverse   See CONVERSE/INVERSE/OBVERSE . . .

invite   FF as a noun: "We received an invite to the dance." SWE: ". . . an invitation . . ."

invoke   See EVOKE/INVOKE.

inward(s)   SWE uses *inward* when a noun follows: "an inward path." It uses either *inward* or *inwards* after a verb: "driven inward(s)." In such an adverbial use, *in* often serves equally well. See also INNARDS.

ipse dixit   See FOREIGN EXPRESSIONS.

IQ, I.Q.   Both forms are SWE for the abbreviation of "intelligence quotient." The term refers only to an often-questioned specific manner of measuring intelligence by use of a test. A person's IQ should not be treated as a true indicator of knowledge, practicality, common sense, wisdom, creativity, or anything else not claimed by the test constructors. What constitutes intelligence is still debated.

iron/steel   *Iron,* one of the elements, occurs in an impure ore. Its most easily forged form, *wrought iron*, contains a very small amount of carbon and impurities. *Steel* is an alloy of iron and from 0.2 to 1.5 percent carbon, possibly with other constituents added. It is normally hard, malleable, and durable. *Stainless steel* has more chromium than most.

ironic, ironically   Both are so overused in so many contexts that the meanings are often vague or incomprehensible. They appear to mean "odd(ly), incongruous(ly), (by) chance, coincidental(ly), disappointing(ly)," or nothing at all. Usually a word like one of those just listed is more precise.

In a literary sense, *irony* means saying the opposite of what is meant: "Lovely day!" when the rain is pouring down. Jonathan Swift was writing ironically when he seemed to be advocating that poor Irish children be fattened and sold to rich English people for food. In drama a situation is ironic if the audience but not the characters understand the incongruity in a situation. *Socratic irony* is a pretense of ignorance, a tactic that Socrates often employed in conversations with his disciples.

irregardless   FF. Technically a double negative (*ir-* and *-less*). SWE uses *regardless.*

irreparable/unrepairable   Although dictionaries call these words synonyms (as well as their antonyms *reparable* and *repairable*), *unrepairable* is ordinarily used of physical things, *irreparable* of abstract ones: "This clock is unrepairable." "The administration has done irreparable harm to the economy."

is (are, was, were) to   A sentence like "He is to leave tomorrow" is ambiguous if not clarified by the context. It may indicate simple future, "He will leave tomorrow," or it may represent an order equivalent to "I demand that he leave tomorrow." SWE rewrites when the context is insufficient.

is when, is where   Often used in FF definitions: "Enteritis is when the intestines are inflamed." That construction is too illogical for SWE use, since nothing is a when or a where. SWE says, "Enteritis is inflammation of the intestinal tract." Note that a good definition of a noun shows the general class to which it belongs (e.g., "inflammation") and then the way(s) in which it differs from other members of the class (e.g., "of the intestinal tract").

ism   Because *-ism* is the ending of many nouns related to beliefs or systems (*atheism, Protestantism, Americanism,* and so on), *ism* is often used, even in fairly sedate writing, instead of *belief* or the like. In using it or its plural, *isms,* an SWE writer is aware that it may connote a slur, as in "She keeps switching from one ism to another."

Israeli/Jew   An *Israeli* is not necessarily a *Jew,* for many followers of other religions also live in Israel. Israelis are the inhabitants of Israel. Similarly, not all Jews are Israelis. Although interpretations differ, in general any adherent of Judaism or descendant of biblical Hebrews is a Jew, and Jews live in many countries. See also HEBREW/ISRAELI/ JEWISH . . .

issue   Seldom if ever is *controversial* or *noncontroversial* needed with this word. If something is an issue, it is by definition controversial. If it is noncontroversial, it is not an issue.

it   As a sentence opener, *it* is often needed but can be overused. Only occasional sentences should begin with "It is true (*certain, probable,* and so on) that . . ." As for "It is believed," SWE usually tries to tell who the believer is, or chooses *probably, perhaps, possibly,* or *may.*

it stands to reason that   A smug expression that may irk someone whose reasoning differs from that of the writer.

iterate/reiterate   Interchangeable, although *reiterate* seems more forceful and is generally chosen.

its   No apostrophe when used to show possession: "The dog ate its chow (*lost its patience, hid its bone*)." "Romanticism was losing its appeal." See also **APOSTROPHE**; IT'S.

it's The apostrophe shows the meaning to be "it is" or "it has": "It's ('It is') going to snow. In fact, it's ('it has') already started." See also **APOSTROPHE**; ITS.

it's I/it's me Standard formal usage is "It is (*was*) I," "It is (*was*) he (*she, we, they*)." Informal is "It's me (*him, her, us, them*)." Because in English we are accustomed to having an object after a verb, as in "John hit me," the tendency to use an objective pronoun is strong. For that reason it is probable that "It is me (*him, her, us, them*)" will eventually become accepted in all contexts. (Winston Churchill often wrote "It was me," and an earlier prime minister declared, "The navy is us.") "It was me" sometimes appears in American SWE in informal contexts.

-ize An unbeautiful verb ending, often criticized by writers on usage, yet frequently necessary, as *criticize* itself illustrates. It is least objectionable when it reduces wordage: *hospitalize* is short for "place in a hospital." Dubious: *secretize*, no fewer syllables than *make secret*. When tempted to use a word ending in *-ize*, some writers try to find a substitute with no more syllables. Thus *make final* may replace *finalize*, and *give priority, prioritize*. But they may keep *democratize* because each alternative is longer.

J

jail/prison A distinction is not quite fixed but is worth making. In general, a *jail* is a relatively small place of confinement for rather short periods of time: "the town jail," "overnight in jail," "in jail for vagrancy," "held in jail while awaiting sentence." A *prison* is usually larger, and its inmates normally are serving longer sentences and for more serious crimes: "a state (or federal) prison," "a prison sentence of ten years for armed robbery."

Japanese The adjective and the singular and plural nouns are the same: "Japanese customs," "a Japanese is," "several Japanese are." Many Japanese and others regard *Jap* as insulting or at best derogatory.

jealousy See ENVY/JEALOUSY.

jerk (noun) FF (slang) for "a foolish, incompetent, unreliable person."

jet lag Now SWE for the temporary psychological or physical discomfort or disruptions caused by crossing several time zones in a few hours.

jet set Informal term, but often used in SWE for persons financially, emotionally, and mentally equipped to travel long distances to attend insignificant social affairs. The term is used enviously by some writers, noncommittally by most, and pejoratively by others.

jetsam See FLOTSAM/JETSAM/LAGAN.

143

jew down "Bargain to reduce a price." Offensive not only to Jews. If a term like *german down* or *italian down* existed, it would be equally offensive.

jewel See GEM/JEWEL.

Jewess Considered derogatory, like many other nouns with *-ess* to indicate females.

Jewish See HEBREW/ISRAELI/JEWISH . . .

jibe See GIBE/JIBE.

job action An inclusive name is needed that covers strikes, slow-downs, absenteeism, and any other way to impede production. Unless a more descriptive term is coined, *job action* will have to do, although supposedly anything that one does on the job could also be called a job action.

job/position No clear difference. *Job* most often connotes relatively low-paying, although not necessarily menial, work: "a job as a clerk (*laborer, welder, police officer,* and so on.)" *Position* supposedly connotes white-collar work. Nevertheless many executives speak of their "jobs," although probably few ditchdiggers talk about their "positions."

jobless Interchangeable with *unemployed,* this term is preferred by headline writers.

jock This is FF (slang) for "male athlete" or, more recently, "man who flaunts his maleness."

john This word is a euphemism for "toilet, bathroom" or (sometimes capitalized) for "man who patronizes a prostitute."

join together A traditional wedding ceremony – with occasional small differences in wording – includes, "Those whom God hath joined together, let no man put asunder." There's no reason to tinker with that tradition; the phrasing has a fine resonance. In less sublime contexts, SWE omits *together.*

joint recital See CONCERT/RECITAL.

jocose/jocular/jolly/jovial *Jolly* is associated with broad smiles, an outgoing nature, good humor, and often large bellies like that of the "jolly old elf," Santa. *Jocose* and *jocular* come from the same Latin source as *joke,* and people so described do like to tell jokes. They exude informal cheerfulness. A *jovial* person is again hearty and good-natured, but his jests are likely to be more meaty, with an undercurrent of seriousness. The jovial person is often better educated than the jolly person.

judge/jurist *Jurist* is a designation for an eminent or somewhat eminent lawyer, a person unusually learned in the law, but not necessarily a judge. A *judge,* if well qualified, may deserve to be called a jurist, but that title is a little high-flown to be applied to everyone who gets elected to a minor judgeship.

judicial/judicious A *judicial* action (or judicial anything else) is related in some way to courts: "judicial branch of government," "judicial chambers (*decisions, issues*)." *Judicious* means "thoughtful, sensible, showing good judgment" and is not necessarily related to courts at all. For example, many parents try to give judicious advice and to behave judiciously and encourage judicious behavior in their children.

juncture   A juncture is a point in space or time at which two things meet. "At this juncture" is rarely used in SWE for "at this time" unless the reference is to a crisis or a turning point, perhaps like that in Robert Frost's "The Road Not Taken" – a moment of choice or decision that can make "all the difference."

junket   Although a junket can be any tour or trip for business or professional purposes, the term has so often been used to refer to costly and sometimes fun-filled excursions by politicians that it has acquired an unfavorable connotation. SWE usually avoids it unless it intends ridicule or denigration of a trip or the travelers.

junkie   FF (slang) for "drug addict" and more recently "person with extraordinary enthusiasm for one thing." So we have television junkies, basketball junkies, and others for politics, Latin, humming-birds, or you-name-it.

jury-rigged   Mainly a nautical term, *jury-rigged* sometimes is erro-neously thought to refer to "'fixing' a jury," or is confused with *jerry-built,* which means "built cheaply and flimsily." To *jury-rig* is to make temporary repairs, usually during an emergency.

just exactly   *Just* isn't needed, but the expression is so widely used that *exactly* may appear naked without it. SANE approves that kind of nudity. *Just merely* is undesirably redundant. SWE deletes *just.*

juvenile/puerile   *Juvenile* refers to girls and boys below voting age or possibly before some other specified age: "juvenile offenders (*pastimes,* and so on)," "juvenile books" (i.e., suitable for juveniles). *Puerile* is generally slightly derogatory and applies to boys only: "a puerile, ill-considered remark." As in that example, behavior by a man may be described as puerile if it seems immature.

K

karat   See CARAT/CARET/CARROT . . .

kibitz, kibitzer   An old German name, *Gibiz,* for a bird with an erratic flight and a strange cry, followed a devious path through Yiddish for "unwanted adviser of cardplayers" to useful, cheerful, but still informal English words for "meddle" and "meddlesome person." It is sometimes SWE.

kick   FF (slang or highly informal) for each of these meanings: com-plain – "I won't kick about that"; contribute (with *in*) – "Can you kick in a few dollars?"; stimulating power – "This whiskey's got a real kick!"; die (with *off* or *the bucket*) – "He kicked off (*kicked the bucket*) last night." *Kick off* is also informal, mainly but not exclusively journalese, for "begin," as in "The charity drive will kick off (or *be kicked off*) at a dinner tonight." Also there's "a kick-off banquet." These uses may be derived from the SWE football term: "The Giants will kick off."

kickback   If a person illegally withholds or is given for his or her own use part of the wages or salary of an employee, the amount is called a *kickback,* especially if without such payment some privilege (or even the job itself) might be removed. A rebate is also called a kickback, but usually only if given for suspect reasons. Some dictionaries label *kickback* informal or slang, but the length of the definitions proves that it is needed. Consider it SWE.

kidding   Should be SWE, although most dictionaries do not treat it as standard. No other carries quite the same combination of meanings: "teasing" plus "playfulness" plus "harmless deceit," tied together as in "You must be kidding!" The word itself is playful, like a capering young goat.

kids   This is a pleasant informality for "children, young people," not rare in SWE. Formally a kid may be a young goat, a small wooden tub for a sailor's mess, a kind of seed pod, or a bundle of twigs or heather.

kidult   The *New York Times* has used the word to mean "the child-adult whose capacities and interests are fixed at an early age." The word isn't widely used yet, but it deserves to be. It implies, for example, a person like John Updike's Rabbit, a grown man whose interests remained stuck in the period when he was a star high-school athlete. Movies aimed at kidults, says Vincent Canby of the *Times,* "render even basic reasoning skills superfluous."

kill (figurative)   Several figurative uses of *kill* have become SWE, or close to it, as illustrated by these expressions: "kill the engine," "kill a bottle of gin," "kill the taste," "kill a story" (journalism), "kill the ball" (tennis), "kill the lights," "My back is killing me."

kill time/pass time/spend time   All are SWE. *Spending time* is generally more worthwhile and profitable than *killing time* or *passing time.* When you are fighting against boredom, you are killing time. When you are amusing yourself but not completely wasting time, you are passing time. The distinctions are useful but not always observed by copy editors.

kill   See also EXECUTE/KILL, MURDER.

kilt   A man may wear *a kilt.* He is not wearing *kilts* unless he has on more than one kilt.

kin   Together, all your relatives are your *kin.* Infrequently, the word is used to refer to only one person, equivalent to *kinsman.* More often we find "one of my kin (or *relatives*)" "my cousin," or the like. *Kin* and *akin* may both be used as adjectives following a verb: "She is kin (or *akin*) to me." *Kinsfolk, kinfolk,* and *kinfolks* are all SWE variants of the same word, although some dictionaries call the last two informal. *Kissing kin* are cousins or other fairly distant relatives whom one knows well enough to kiss in greeting or farewell. See also KITH AND KIN.

kind of, sort of   These classifications apply to both *kind of* and *sort of*: **1.** FF for "rather," as in "kind of short." **2.** FF: One kind of *a* cloud is the cumulus. SWE: One kind of cloud . . . **3.** FF: Those (*These*) sort of cloud (*clouds*) . . . SWE: That (*This*) sort of cloud (*clouds*) . . . SWE: Those (*These*) sorts of *clouds* . . . **4.** FF: That (*This*) kind of clouds *are* . . . SWE: That (*This*) kind of cloud is . . . SWE: What kind of clouds are those?

kind   See VARIETY.

kindly   Old-fashioned for "please": "Kindly remit the amount due."

kingly/regal/royal   Often interchanged, although the words convey subtly different emphases. That which is *kingly* is especially suitable for or characteristic of a king (as *queenly* is of a queen): "kingly attire," "a kingly hauteur." *Regal* and *royal* apply to both kings and queens and sometimes to their immediate families. *Regal* refers to more outward, more visible manifestations of the office: "regal pomp," "assumed his proud regal posture." *Royal* is usually the most favorable of the three and can imply greatness of spirit, generosity, and the like; "royal family," "royal munificence," "royal welcome."

kinky   FF (slang or informal) for "highly unusual, bizarre." When applied to sex, some people equate it to almost anything sexual except the position approved by early missionaries. T. S. Eliot used *kinky* in *The Cocktail Party* to refer to slightly uncommon emotionalism. The word is likely to become SWE in one or more of its senses. It is needed – increasingly.

kith and kin   Old-fashioned but still used occasionally. *Kith* means "friends and neighbors" but is not seen except with *kin*. See also KIN.

knave/rascal/rogue/scoundrel   *Knave* is an old-fashioned word for the other three. All four are now used mainly in fun or even with more or less affection, as when a proud father calls his mischievous small son "you little rascal." A *scoundrel* is perhaps the worst of the four, most likely to behave criminally or to play dirty tricks. A *rogue* has few worthy principles and will probably cheat if given a chance. A *rascal* is sly and scheming but probably steals no more than a few chickens unless the farmer's daughter happens to show up.

knee-jerk   Without the hyphen, an SWE noun for the little kick you make when a physician taps your knee. With the hyphen, it is an informal adjective for "involuntary, automatic." A *knee-jerk* conservative, for example, is one who automatically and unthinkingly takes a conservative stance on almost every issue. *Knee-jerk* is seldom used to describe things or people approvingly. Since no other word has precisely the same meaning, it appears increasingly in SWE.

knocked up   In the United States, FF (vulgar) for "made pregnant." In England, it is often used to mean "awakened," as in "I knocked her (*him*) up at seven this morning," or "very tired," as in "He (*She*) seems knocked up." The expression should be used cautiously on both sides of the Atlantic.

knot (unit of speed)   SWE: "a speed of ten knots through the bay." FF: "knots an hour." A speed of ten knots is about 11.5 statute miles an hour. *Knots* is used only for speeds across (or under) water. Sailors do not use *knot* as a measure of distance. They do not say, for example, that a place is seven knots from here.

know as   FF (regional or dialectal) for *know that* or *know whether,* sometimes followed, but not improved, by *how:* "I don't know as (how) I believe you."

know-how (also knowhow)   The word is disliked by many conservatives, who prefer *knowledge, skill,* or *understanding the way to perform* (a task). But that last phrase is too long, *knowledge* is a broad term that pertains more to "know what" than to "know how," and *skill* refers to performing rather than understanding how to perform. SWE uses *know-how* when it fits the intended meaning. Useful but rare: *know-what, know-when.*

knowledgeable   Some people object to the word, preferring *well-informed.* SWE uses both.

kudos   This word for "acclaim, praise, fame, glory" is from a Greek word of the same meaning and spelling (the *s* is pronounced as *s,* not as *z*). It is singular: "His kudos is deserved." *Kudo* developed as an alternative early in this century but is often disapproved of. Caution: Few people know the meaning of either *kudos* or *kudo.*

L

labyrinth/maze   Often interchangeable, although *maze* is conventional for a kind of paper-and-pencil puzzle or a network of hedges. *Labyrinth* is more common for confusing caves or the intricate passageways in the dungeon areas of old castles or monasteries, or even in the Pentagon.

laconic/reticent/taciturn   President Coolidge reportedly summarized for his wife a sermon on sin by saying, "He was agin it." Coolidge was a *laconic* man. He liked to use as few words as possible. A hermit, however, more than likely prefers to remain completely silent if possible. A hermit may be described as *reticent,* which does not mean "reluctant" as some people believe. Somebody equally silent but possibly also a bit uncheerful is *taciturn.*

lady/woman   In years gone by, most American females were glad to be or hoped to be *ladies,* partly because of the high regard in England for lords and ladies. Gradually, though, *lady* came to vacillate between a suggestion of excessive primness and the great un-

primness of "lady of the evening." Today, except in a few contexts such as "Ladies and Gentlemen," *woman* has largely replaced *lady*.

ladylike/womanlike, womanly Comparatively rare, *ladylike* suggests refined femininity, the qualities and decorum once taught in "finishing schools." *Womanlike* is literally "like a woman," similar to *womanly,* but sometimes is used unfavorably to indicate supposed weakness: "her womanlike fear of mice and snakes." See also FEMALE, FEMININE.

lagan See FLOTSAM/JETSAM/LAGAN.

lama/llama One difference is in the number of legs – two vs. four. The *lama* is a high-ranking Buddhist priest or monk of Tibet or Mongolia. The *llama* is a South American beast of burden.

149

lame duck SWE, though somewhat informal, for an elected official completing a term of office to which he or she will not be returning.

lament See DEPLORE/LAMENT/REGRET . . .

languid/limpid *Languid* means "spiritless, lacking in energy." After an illness a person often feels languid. *Limpid* is not related to *limp*. It means "clear, transparent," and by extension "calm, untroubled, at ease": "a limpid pool," "the relaxed, limpid singing of Perry Como," "limpid prose." See also LANGUOR/LASSITUDE.

languor/lassitude Can be used as synonyms, but *languor* is the somewhat softer word associated with laziness, quietly doing nothing, lacking much energy. *Languid* is obviously related. *Lassitude,* slightly harsher, often is associated with numbness or exhaustion.

large (or small) number of *Many* and *few* are obviously shorter. For *a large portion of, much of* or *most of* can usually be substituted, and for *a small portion of, little* saves a dozen keystrokes.

lascivious/lecherous/licentious All three refer to immoral or excessive sexual thoughts or behavior. A *lascivious* person is lustful, and lascivious dress (or undress) is intended to incite lust. Only a man is usually described as *lecherous*. He is considered excessively desirous of sex and frequently yields to that desire. *Licentious* refers to commission of acts (usually sexual) that are considered both immoral and illegal. The sexual fondling of a young child, for example, is licentious because it is clearly immoral and also can be punished by law.

lassitude See LANGUOR/LASSITUDE.

last/later/latter **1.** In referring to the person or thing named at the end, SWE uses *latter* if only two names were given, *last* for three or more. **2.** *Latter* and *later* may sometimes be used almost interchangeably: "the latter (or *later*) part of her life." However, *later* refers specifically to time (not position) and implies a comparison not involved in *latter*: "later, during the night," "a later plane," "happened later." Also, *later* but not *latter* may be used as an adverb.

last/latest Often used interchangeably in SWE, as in "the last (*latest*) issue of *Newsweek*." Conservatives choose *latest* when the meaning is "most recent": "the latest issue," not *last* unless the magazine has ceased publication.

last two   See FIRST TWO/TWO FIRST.

late   Not "the late William Shakespeare." The term refers to someone who died in the recent past – *recent* being imprecisely defined. It is most useful in reminding or informing readers who may not be sure whether or not the person is still alive.

   Not "the widow of the late . . . " Having left a widow, the poor fellow must be dead. See also WIDOW/WIFE.

later on   SWE omits *on* unless it helps the rhythm or clarity of the sentence.

later, latest   See LAST/LATER/LATTER; LAST/LATEST.

latter   See FORMER; LAST/LATER/LATTER.

laudable/laudatory   When Mary says that Herbert is *laudable* or has laudable qualities, she is making a *laudatory* remark. The one who praises is being laudatory; the one who is praised is said to be laudable. The verb *laud* is bookish for "praise."

lawful/legal   Synonyms, although *legal* always pertains to man-made law, and *lawful* sometimes is concerned with the higher law – that of God. See also ILLEGAL/ILLEGITIMATE/ILLICIT . . .

lawman   A term used mainly in Western fiction or movies to refer to a sheriff or other law-enforcement official, *lawman* is not listed in some dictionaries. It can be useful in the plural to indicate several kinds of such officials, however, or in the singular when the exact title is unknown.

lawyer   See ATTORNEY/ATTORNEY AT LAW/LAWYER.

lay/lie   A college president once remarked that he could gauge roughly the amount of education a person has had by observing his use of *lay* ("to place") and *lie* ("to recline"). The distinction is simple and can be mastered in a few minutes by composing and saying aloud repeatedly several sentences like these: "*Lay* it on the table. I *laid* it on the floor. You had *laid* it in the wrong place. Now you are *laying* it in the right place." "*Lie* down, Rover. Rover is *lying* here. He *lay* (past tense) here yesterday. He has *lain* here every day. Why does he *lie* in this spot? He enjoys *lying* here. Yesterday I *lay* beside him. I have often *lain* there."

leading question   A leading question is not intended to entrap, as is the familiar "Have you stopped beating your wife?" Rather, it is a question so worded as to suggest the desired answer, such as a court lawyer for either side often asks. A prosecuting attorney may ask the defendant, "Then you opened the door to the closet where the gun was, didn't you?" The attorney for the defense may phrase the question, "Next, did you open the closet door to hang up your coat?"

leak   Both as noun and verb, *leak* is SWE for "anonymous and usually unauthorized disclosure of information": "a leak from the administration," "an aide may have leaked the news." The brevity of the word is in its favor.

least, less/littler, littlest/smaller, smallest *Littler* and *littlest* are rare but do occur in SWE. A well-known Christmas narrative is "The Littlest Angel." In most contexts, however, *smaller* and *smallest* are used with reference to size. *Less* and *least* refer to quantities. See also FEWER/LESS.

leastways/leastwise *Leastways* is FF (dialectal) for *leastwise,* which is informal for "at least, anyway." See also ANY WAY/ANYWAY/ANYWAYS; -WISE.

leave/let 1. Both "Let me alone" and "Leave me alone" are SWE for "Do not bother me," although many argue that "Leave me alone" is ambiguous because it can also mean "Leave me by myself." 2. For the meaning of "allow, permit," only *let* is SWE, as in "Let me do that," "Let it stay there." 151

leave/lief *Lief* has an old-fashioned tone and is associated with nineteenth-century expressions such as "I'd jest as lief go squirrel huntin'" or "I'd liefer set right cheer." As *lief* was dying, nonstandard *leave* replaced it in some dialects: "I'd just as leave work on my car." SWE: *just as soon.*

lecherous See LASCIVIOUS/LECHEROUS/LICENTIOUS.

lectern See DAIS/LECTERN/PODIUM.

led One of the most often misspelled words is *led,* the past tense of *lead:* "We led the horse to water." The word seems to be widely confused with the name of the metal.

lee/port/starboard/windward The *lee* side of a ship (or of anything else) is the side sheltered from the wind – opposite the direction from which the wind blows. *Windward* is an antonym of *leeward* and *lee.* The *port* side of a ship or plane is on one's left when one is facing forward. A familiar mnemonic device is "We left port." The *starboard* side is to the right. The name comes from an old word for "steerside": the rudder on an old Teutonic ship was on the right side.

leery SWE, though informal, for *suspicious, hesitant, doubtful, wary, fearful, distrustful,* or *somewhat afraid.* It is less specific than any of those near-synonyms. An infrequent variant is *leary.*

legal See LAWFUL/LEGAL.

lend/loan Dictionary makers now classify "to lend money" and "to loan money" as interchangeable. Conservatives, however, prefer not to use *loan* as a verb. The noun use, as in "ask for a loan," is SWE. To obtain something as a loan is expressed in SWE by *borrow,* not by *loan:* "May I borrow some money from you?"

lengthways, lengthwise See EDGEWAYS, EDGEWISE/ENDWAYS, ENDWISE/LENGTHWAYS, LENGTHWISE . . .

lengthy/long A conversation may be described as either *lengthy* or *long. Lengthy* is seldom used except with reference to time, but *long* is more versatile. For example, we are unlikely to refer to a "lengthy board" or a "lengthy distance." *Lengthy* sometimes, but not always, carries a suggestion of tediousness, as in "lengthy congressional debate."

lens   SWE: "A lens is broken," "Both lenses are broken." FF: *a len, two lens*.

less/lesser   As comparatives of *little, less* generally refers to quantity and *lesser* to degree of importance: "less ammunition (or *daylight*, and so on), "a lesser reason," "the lesser man." See also FEWER/LESS; LEAST, LESS/LITTLER, LITTLEST/SMALLER, SMALLEST.

lest   A bookish word, usually for expression of doubt or fear, as in "He was fearful lest he be found guilty" (note the subjunctive *be*, customary after *lest*). More likely today: "He was fearful (*afraid*) that he would be found guilty."

let   See also LEAVE/LET.

let/net (tennis)   A ball that hits the net and goes over is technically a *let* or a *let ball,* not *net.* Here *let* has the meaning "obstacle," as it has in the legal phrase "without let or hindrance." Most professional tennis players use *let.*

let's   **1.** As in "Let's you and me talk it over alone," *me* is SWE. Expanded, the sentence is "Let us – that is, you and me – talk it over alone." **2.** *Let's not* is standard. *Let us not,* unless in very formal context, sounds like James Fenimore Cooper. **3.** *Don't let's* and *let's don't* are FF. **4.** In *let's us, us* is redundant, because here *'s* signifies "us."

level with   Now SWE for "speak frankly with": "She leveled with her employer about what really happened."

lexicographer/linguist/philologist   A *lexicographer* writes, edits, or helps to prepare dictionaries. A *linguist* specializes in linguistics and may or may not speak several languages. A *philologist* has wide interest in and knowledge of words and their literary use – often extending into classical scholarship or other languages such as Old Norse or Old High German.

liable   See APT/LIABLE/LIKELY.

libel   See DEFAMATION/LIBEL/SLANDER.

license   Singular. "My license is lost. I don't know where it is."

licentious   See LASCIVIOUS/LECHEROUS/LICENTIOUS.

lie   See LAY/LIE.

lief   See LEAVE/LIEF.

lightening/lightning   "Thunder and *lightning,*" "It lightninged (or, rather ambiguously, *lightened*) in the west." SWE avoids both the awkward *was lightninging* and the ambiguous *was lightening,* substituting perhaps "Lightning was flashing . . . " One meaning of *lightening* is illustrated in "They were lightening the donkey's load." Another: "Although the sun was not yet up, the east was lightening."

like   Overused, as in "The place was like, you know, like you've never seen before, like a – even like a nightmare, like, you know." Rare in writing of any kind, this *like* is equivalent to "er" or "uh" in speaking.

like for FF (dialectal) in sentences such as "We'd like for you to come along." SWE omits *for*.

like See also AS/AS IF/LIKE.

likes of "People the likes of you should be in jail." Writers on usage differ, some approving *likes of*, others both *like of* and *likes of*, still others neither. Probable in SWE: "People like (or *such as*) you . . . "

likewise *Likewise* has a somewhat formal tone but does occur also in ordinary speech. Its standard use is as an adverb: "do likewise," "answered likewise." It is not standard as a substitute for *and* or *together with*. Unlikely in SWE: "His sister, likewise his aunt, met him at the airport."

limit/limitation Usually interchangeable. In law, however, *limitation* is often a technical term for a time limit beyond which legal action is not possible: "statute of limitations." In general use, *limitation* is customary in the sense of a handicap: "mental or physical limitations." To refer to specific conditions, *limit* is likely: "reached the limit of his strength."

limited/Ltd./small 1. *Limited* and *small* are not synonyms. The powers of the U.S. president are limited but not small. 2. *Ltd.,* following the name of a British company, signifies that in financial matters the liability of each shareholder or officer is limited to a specified maximum.

limpid See LANGUID/LIMPID.

linage/lineage For clarity, SWE writes *linage* (pronounced *line-ij*) when referring to the number of lines: "The linage of the news story." *Lineage* (pronounced *lin-ee-ij*) refers to heritage, ancestry: "Some American women were seeking husbands who claimed noble lineage."

line SWE tries to avoid overuse and vagueness. For example, "He is in the cosmetics line" may be changed to "He sells (*manufactures, speculates in*) cosmetics," "I don't like his line" to whatever is meant by *line*. *Along these lines* may become *like this, in a similar way*, or *similarly*.

linguist See LEXICOGRAPHER/LINGUIST/PHILOLOGIST.

liquid refreshment Ordinary people serve coffee, tea, milk, beer, whiskey, or maybe just "drinks."

lion's share This term is hackneyed but more colorful than *largest portion*.

listen See HEAR/LISTEN.

litany/liturgy A *litany* is a prayer or incantatory recital in which a phrase or sentence uttered by a leader is responded to by a congregation. By extension, such things as a sometimes repeated conversation between parent and child, or any familiar, tedious recital, may be called litanies. The *liturgy* of a church is the form followed in a worship service. It may also mean the Book of Common Prayer or the Rites of the Eucharist.

literally   See FIGURATIVELY/LITERALLY.

literature   "Write for free literature," an advertisement invites us. When the "literature" arrives, it is a colorful leaflet extolling the merits of an insurance plan or . . . The term is so widely used in this sense of "advertising" that dictionaries list it without comment. But conservatives, at least those who revere Euripides, Virgil, Racine, John Milton, or even John Updike, shudder at what they regard as desecration. Many writers of SWE avoid cheapened use of the word.

littler/littlest   See LEAST, LESS/LITTLER, LITTLEST/SMALLER, SMALLEST.

liturgy   See LITANY/LITURGY.

live audience   Except in a graveyard, this appears redundant. Radio and television people use the term, however, usually in the phrase "recorded before a live audience," to mean that laughter or applause we hear does not come from a re-recording of a laugh track.

live   See DWELL/LIVE/RESIDE.

liveware   See HARDWARE/LIVEWARE/SOFTWARE.

livid   Most members of a class of college juniors and seniors misdefined *livid* as "bright red," "reddish," or something similar. Dictionaries define it as "discolored, as from a bruise," or "pale, as with rage."

llama   See LAMA/LLAMA.

lo and behold   See BEHOLD.

loan   See LEND/LOAN.

loath/loathe   Note the spellings. *Loath* is an adjective meaning "unwilling, hesitant": "loath to disagree" (the *th* is pronounced as in *thin*). *Loathe* is a verb meaning "hate, despise, abhor": "Some people loathe squash, but I like it" (the *th* as in *this*).

locate   See FIND/LOCATE.

long   See LENGTHY/LONG.

lose   See MISLAY/LOSE.

lot/lots   1. In "a lot (*lots*) of food," "lots of fun," "a lot of birds," *a lot* (two words) and *lots* are SWE, although slightly informal. However, conservative writers prefer *many, much, large quantities* (or *numbers*), or the like. 2. When *a lot* or *lots* is used as an apparent subject, as in "A lot of corn *was* spilled," the noun following *of* determines whether the verb is singular or plural: "A lot of apples *were* spoiled." "Lots of flour is left." "Lots of flowers are left." The explanation is that *a lot* or *lots* is not a real subject but a modifier of the subject.

loud speaker/loudspeaker   A *loud speaker* is a person who speaks in a loud voice. A *loudspeaker* is an instrument for amplifying sound: "Music came booming from a nearby loudspeaker."

lousy   This means "louse-infested." In the sense of "bad, inferior, unpleasant," *lousy* is FF (slang). An old joke:

Teacher: "Two words you should never use. One is *swell* and the other is *lousy*."

Student: "What are the two words?"

love Historically, *love* suggests intense affection, but the word has been cheapened not only by its frequently being limited to sexual activity, as in "making love," but also by its use with relatively trivial objects, as in "I love persimmons." Obviously, the numerous senses of the word cannot be thrown out, but many careful writers tend to restrict it to such senses as God's love for humanity or the strong and often enduring affection between man and woman or parent and child.

lovely Overused to describe almost anything that a person likes.

low profile Philip Howard, an Englishman, calls *low profile* "Pentagonese, or American defence jargon." The Pentagon, for example, favors tanks that have a low profile, that is, are difficult to see from a distance. So far so good. But the expression has become too widely employed in too many contexts. Some corporation officers (even tall ones) are urged to maintain a low profile, and so (very often) are school administrators and teachers and anyone else not likely to be helped by publicity.

lowbrow See HIGHBROW/LOWBROW/MIDDLEBROW.

Ltd. See LIMITED/LTD./SMALL.

luggage See BAGGAGE/LUGGAGE.

lunch/luncheon Interchangeable, but *luncheon* is more probable for a planned, formal or semiformal occasion. Hamburgers are more likely for lunch, Salisbury steak (glorified hamburger) or even London broil for a luncheon.

lusty/lustful In modern usage, *lustful* is largely restricted to sexual appetite or desire: "He looked at her with lustful eyes." *Lusty,* however, although it does not rule out sexuality, means "vigorous, robust, active": "He looked athletic, lusty." It may also be used to describe a vigorous way of doing something: "lusty singing."

luxuriant/luxurious The usual meaning of *luxuriant* is "growing abundantly": "the luxuriant plant life of the tropics, "luxuriant hibiscuses." Unusually fertile soil on occasion is called luxuriant. A spin-off definition is "elaborately ornate": "a luxuriant, even florid room with colorful rugs, bright tapestries, and geegaws galore." *Luxurious* is related to *luxury*. It suggests riches and probably comfort and good taste: "the Queen's luxurious bedroom."

M

machismo/macho *Macho*, Spanish for "male, masculine," is usually an adjective but sometimes a noun equivalent to *machismo*. *Machismo*, a vogue word in the United States from the 1960s on, means "overtly expressed maleness," including exhibition of boldness or courage, aggressiveness, and (often) domination of women.

macro-/micro- These are combining forms with opposite meanings: *macro-* "large," *micro-* "small." For example, the *macroclimate* is the climate of a large geographical area, such as the Antarctic; the *microclimate* is that of a relatively small area, such as Chicago, in comparison with the climate of Illinois or the macroclimate of the Midwest.

mad See ANGRY/MAD.

magic/magical Sometimes interchangeable, *magic* as a modifier serves mainly to identify: "magic show," "magic lanterns." *Magical* describes things as being "like magic": "a magical change," "The effect of her words was magical."

magniloquent See ELOQUENT/GRANDILOQUENT/MAGNILOQUENT.

magnitude In most instances *size, significance,* or *importance* is preferable, especially if the topic is inconsequential. This sentence from a sports commentary illustrates dubious use: "The fact that the loss plunges the Chiefs into last place shows the magnitude of the defeat." When two teams are battling for next-to-last place, the "magnitude" of a loss or a victory cannot be very great.

maintain See CLAIM.

major SWE generally uses *major* in serious, important contexts. Dubious: "a major disagreement in the village council," "Are you faced with a major decision about tonight's dinner entrée?" *More major* and *most major* are even more questionable, because, at least historically, *major* (as well as *minor*) is already a comparative.

majority/plurality In an election no candidate with fewer than half of the votes may claim a *majority*. If 5,000 votes are cast, a minimum of 2,501 is a majority. In some circumstances a two-thirds majority or other large fraction may be required. If in the election with 5,000 votes *A* received 2,000, *B* received 1,600, and *C* received 1,400, *A* has a *plurality* of 400. No one has a majority. (In many elections only a plurality is required.)

make As a synonym of *earn* ("Mrs. Landon makes forty thousand a year"), *make* was long opposed by purists but has become so widely used that dictionaries now list it without comment. Color it SWE.

make a pass Now SWE, although somewhat informal, for "make a sexual overture." In transportation, it is standard for "make an approach": "The little plane made a pass at the runway but went up again without touching down."

make an investigation into SWE shortens to *investigate.* SANE notes that other phrases with *make* can also be reduced. Examples: "make a comment" – *comment*; "make a report" – *report*; "make a study of" – *study*; "make use of" – use.

make do SWE for "get along with a somewhat insufficient or otherwise unsuitable or unsatisfactory amount or variety": "The family had to make do with forty dollars a week." "She made do with her fraying coat for another year."

MALAPROPISM This book is about appropriate words. A malapropism is not appropriate. It is a word confused with another of similar sound or spelling. *Malapropism* dates back to 1775, when Richard Brinsley Sheridan's play *The Rivals* introduced Mrs. Malaprop. Her name, from French *mal à propos* ("not right for this purpose"), suggests her problem. She urges her niece Lydia to "illiterate" (obliterate) Beverley from her memory. She does not like a young woman to be a "progeny (prodigy) of learning" but thinks that a well-bred girl should "be mistress of orthodoxy" (orthography), and that she should "reprehend" (apprehend) the true meaning of what she is saying. She hopes that Lydia will be courted by a captain who will find her "not altogether illegible" (ineligible). In her own love affair she hopes to find "joy infallible" (ineffable). Mrs. Malaprop is a humorous character, quite unaware that she is making herself ridiculous. She has not learned that simple words which one is sure of are much safer and saner than polysyllables wrongly used.

male chauvinist pig See CHAUVINISM.

malevolent/malicious Sometimes interchangeable, but *malevolent* stresses intention, "wanting bad things to happen," while *malicious* more often refers to the hostile act itself: "malicious mischief."

maltreat/mistreat Although each word means "to treat badly," *maltreat* implies a higher degree of roughness and cruelty.

mammoth (adjective) Best restricted to huge things. The sales advertised by small-town department stores seldom qualify. Macy's sales – maybe.

man and wife Although long used in many English and American wedding ceremonies, in other contexts *husband and wife* is more appropriate because both words refer to marital status.

man (woman) of letters Pretentious and unspecific term for *writer, author, poet, literary critic,* and the like.

mandatory Perhaps because of executive privilege, former President Gerald Ford was entitled to say (and did say) "absolutely mandatory." The rest of us should be satisfied with *mandatory.*

manhandle See ANNIHILATE, DESTROY, FLAY . . .

-mania/-phobia The combining form *-mania* refers to an extreme eagerness or passion for doing something, either bad or good: *kleptomania* ("urge to steal"), *bibliomania* ("enthusiasm for using or collecting books"). The form *-phobia* refers to obsessive fear: *claustrophobia* ("fear of small enclosed areas"), *triskaidekaphobia* ("fear of 13").

mankind After a time when a few feminists wanted to eliminate all such words as *chairman, foreman,* and *mankind,* most modern women grant that *mankind* includes women, too, and need not be replaced by *people, humankind,* or something else.

manly/mannish *Manly* is a term of praise. The person described, often a boy, has qualities considered especially desirable in a man, such as bravery, strength, and courtesy. *Mannish* now usually applies to women or things associated with some women: "Women's suits this year have a mannish look."

man-made artifact See ARTIFACT.

manner born (to the) *Manner* is SWE, not *manor*. When Hamlet said that he was "to the manner born," he meant that he had spent his childhood learning the customs or "manners" of his native land. The spelling *manor* would have implied a boast about being born in a manor. If that had been Hamlet's intention, he might have used *palace* or *castle*.

manslaughter See HOMICIDE/MANSLAUGHTER/MURDER.

margin/score Football announcer: "The Saints lead by a margin of twenty to fourteen." No. The *score* is twenty to fourteen. The *margin* is six points.

marks of ellipsis See ELLIPSE/ELLIPSIS.

marriage/nuptials/wedding Many brides and some bridegrooms prepare elaborately for their *weddings* or their *nuptials* – a more highfalutin name for the ceremonies. Not nearly so many brides and bridegrooms prepare adequately for their *marriages* – in the sense of lasting unions.

marry/be married to When it was customary for a man to woo and the maid to accept or reject, society reporters and Aunt Harriet wrote that "John married Anne" or "Anne was married to John." But now that many women woo and many weddings are reached by alternating the role of pursuer, the distinction in form is not regularly observed. Now Anne may marry John, and John may be married to Anne.

martyr/victim A *martyr* accepts suffering or death willingly – may even seek martyrdom for a cause in which he or she passionately believes. A *victim*, in contrast, is usually unwilling, unacceptive. Some outside force brings suffering or death, and while still alive the victim struggles to avoid or overcome it. One exception: A person who endures great suffering – say, from cancer – is often called a martyr to the disease but obviously is also a victim.

marvel/miracle A *marvel* is an oddity, something to wonder at: "The Taj Mahal is an architectural marvel." The word ordinarily refers to a thing rather than an event. A *miracle*, although it, too, is something to wonder at, has qualities of the superhuman, the supernatural. We speak, for example, of the miracle in which Christ fed thousands with a few loaves and fishes. It is most often an event.

massacre See ANNIHILATE, DESTROY, FLAY . . .

massive Originally used to refer to physical mass, *massive* spread to include abstractions such as "massive campaigns," "a massive plot," "massive affirmation," and so on. Such a shift is legitimate and often occurs in SWE, but *massive* does seem overused.

masterful/masterly These two words are sometimes used interchangeably, but many people preserve this distinction: *Masterful* means "strong, demanding": "The overseer's masterful voice and dire threats frightened the workers." *Masterly* means "skilled, expert in a craft": "This cabinetwork is indeed masterly."

material/matériél Almost anything can be called *material*, but *matériel* is most often military gear. It also means "apparatus or machinery" (not personnel) used industrially.

materialize Pretentious for "happen." *Materialize* means "assume actual form, become real": "Their dream house was finally materializing." Dubious: "The feared accident materialized the following morning." (An accident itself is not a material thing, even though things are involved in it.)

matinee performance SWE omits *performance* because *matinee* means "daytime performance."

matutinal ablutions No, SWE wouldn't write that for "morning bath." But whenever inclined to use a polysyllable (whoops! big word) instead of an equally pertinent short one, a would-be writer of SWE may think about *matutinal ablutions*.

maudlin/mawkish *Maudlin* carries the connotation of tearfulness, sometimes mingled with sentimentality. It is based on (Mary) Magdalene, a symbol of tearful repentance: "The drunk became maudlin each time he mentioned his wife." *Mawkish* sentimentality is so effusive as to be nauseating. The word is derived from a Middle English word for "maggot."

mausoleum/morgue/mortuary A *mausoleum* is a large, stately tomb. A *morgue* is a place, often under police supervision, in which persons found dead are kept until identified or buried or cremated. The term is also used for a newspaper's reference library. A *mortuary* is a funeral home, once called an "undertaking parlor," where bodies are kept until time for burial.

maven (also mavin) Introduced from Yiddish as slang in the middle of this century, *maven* is now sometimes used in SWE for "expert, connoisseur," and often refers to things more commonplace than those shown in the Metropolitan Museum or heard in Lincoln Center: "a rhinestone maven," "mavens of Elvis Presley souvenirs."

mawkish See MAUDLIN/MAWKISH.

maximize/minimize To *maximize* an effect (or anything else) is to increase it to the greatest extent possible. *Minimize* has the opposite meaning. The definitions make clear that these verbs cannot logically be modified by such words as *somewhat*, *greatly*, or *considerably*, although *nearly* or *almost* is possible.

may possibly be See POSSIBLE/POSSIBLY.

may See CAN/MAY.

may/might *Might* started as the past tense of *may*, but the time distinction is now not emphasized. *May* suggests slightly greater probability than *might*, as illustrated in "We may (*might*) call you tomorrow."

maybe/perhaps Interchangeable, with *perhaps* a shade more formal.

mayn't See CAN'T/MAYN'T.

maze See LABYRINTH/MAZE.

meander/wander Each means "to wander idly and aimlessly." *Meander*, however, often has the sense of "winding." A meandering stream, for example, is very crooked. Unlikely: "Where is my meandering son tonight?"

meaningful Some writers assert that *meaningful* isn't meaningful, but lexicographers define it as "significant" and attach no label. Appears often in SWE.

meant to be In the advertising exhortation "See these islands from small boats, as they were meant to be seen," the reader wonders about who "meant them to be seen" in any specific way. Similar is a cereal manufacturer's claim "Breakfast as it was meant to be."

mechanization See AUTOMATION/MECHANIZATION.

media (verb with) Is *media* to be treated as singular or plural? The battle goes on. Conservatives favor *are* rather than *is*, on the ground that the media are newspapers, magazines, radio, television, and so on, and not a single entity. Liberals say that *data* and *agenda* have switched from plural to singular, so why not *media*? The conservative rebuttal is that *data* can mean one set of figures, *agenda* one list, but *media* does not mean one single thing. The conservative argument seems stronger. One more vote for *media are*. FF says *medias*.

mediate See ARBITRATE/MEDIATE.

medic Now SWE, although infrequent, for "physician, surgeon." Long established in the armed forces.

mediocre This word has worsened or weakened in meaning (a process called "pejoration"). What conservatives call its "true meaning" is "average, neither good nor bad," but it has been used so often to mean "below average, not good" that anything or anyone now described as mediocre is faintly damned. Too bad, because the language needs a word for "in the middle range, intermediate in degree of excellence." (The now rare *middling* has suffered the same pejoration.) See also AVERAGE/COMMON, ORDINARY.

meet/meet (up) with "I'll meet with you tomorrow" suggests a longer get-together than does "I'll meet you tomorrow." *Meet with* is standard when referring to experiences: "meet with disaster," "meet with unexpected opposition (or *offers of help*)." SWE deletes the useless *up* in *meet up with*.

melodic/melodious Although they are sometimes interchangeable, *melodic* is a somewhat more technical term. It means "pertaining to melody," and thus is differentiated from *rhythmic* and *harmonic*. *Melodious* is more often the word needed by the layman. It means "pleasant-sounding, tuneful, containing an agreeable succession of sounds": "the melodious anthems of our church choir."

melody See HARMONY/MELODY.

melt/thaw The basic distinction is that when something *melts*, it changes from a solid to a liquid, but when something *thaws*, it changes from a frozen to an unfrozen state. Thus heated lead melts, but we thaw a frozen turkey. Snow melts during a spring thaw. Figuratively, *melting* may refer to a softening of attitude: "Joyce's heart melted when the baby smiled up at her." *Thawed* would suggest that Joyce's earlier attitude was extremely hostile.

memorandum Standard usage is "one *memorandum*," "two or more *memorandums* or *memoranda*." SWE uses either form. Historically, the trend has been toward anglicizing plurals of foreign nouns.

memories of the past SWE deletes *of the past.*

mendacity/mendicity *Mendacity* is what a liar is guilty of, and *mendicity* is what a beggar engages in. *Mendicant* friars lived by begging. *Mendicancy* is a synonym of *mendicity.*

161

mental telepathy *Telepathy* is by definition "thought transference." SWE omits *mental.*

meretricious Not related to *merit.* Something meretricious is showy, tawdry, deceptive, and possibly conducive to evil: "the meretricious allurements of a circus sideshow."

Messrs. Americans seldom use the plural of *Mr.*, preferring "Mr. Brown and Mr. Lavel," but may use *Messrs.* before a long list or omit titles entirely.

meteor/meteorite/meteoroid A *meteoroid* is a tiny-to-large body that wanders the solar system and may happen to enter our atmosphere. Friction makes it burn, and we exclaim, "There's a meteor!" or "There's a shooting star!" If any of the meteoroid survives the fiery passage, the stony or metallic piece that strikes the earth's surface is a *meteorite.*

method/methodology *Method* is usually rather narrow, applied, for example, to a procedure in a chemistry class. *Methodology* can pertain to the set of principles and methods followed in an entire field of knowledge, such as chemistry, or in an elaborate scientific study. When in doubt, SWE tries *method* first.

meticulous/punctilious/scrupulous All refer to being careful about details. To be *meticulous* is to be unusually precise and painstaking – often anxiously so. *Punctilious*, from Latin for "point," means paying great attention to small points, even unimportant ones. For example, a punctilious person obeys even small rules of etiquette and insists on "approved" forms in wedding invitations. A *scrupulous* person has scruples about possible mistakes or misconduct, is especially conscientious about behavior: "a scrupulously clean politician, making no promises that she is unlikely to keep."

Mexican-American See CHICANO.

micro- See MACRO-, MICRO-.

middle-age(d)/teen-age(d) 1. Should a person be described as *middle-age* or *middle-aged*, *teen-age*, or *teen-aged*? Answers are not consistent. SWE uses both forms. 2. *Middle age* (no hyphen) as a noun is variously defined as the period in a person's life between ages forty and sixty, or forty-five and sixty-five. In a life span of seventy years, the middle third would be from twenty-three through forty-seven, but apparently no one accepts that as middle age. See also ELDERLY.

Middle English/Old English Even some college English majors say that Chaucer and Shakespeare wrote in "Old English." Those authors wrote "old" English but not "Old." Language historians say that Old English ended and Middle English began about A.D. 1100. Chaucer wrote in Middle English, which lasted until about 1500, when Early Modern English, used by Shakespeare, began.

middle See CENTER/MIDDLE.

midget See DWARF/MIDGET/PYGMY.

midnight Tuesday is ending, and Wednesday is beginning. The time is exactly twelve o'clock. Should we say "Tuesday midnight" or "Wednesday midnight"? Because the night started on Tuesday, the former is SWE.

might See MAY/MIGHT.

mighty Informal adverb for "very," as in "mighty happy," was more popular in the nineteenth century than it is now. It is rare in SWE as an adverb.

mile See FOOT, HOUR, MILE . . .

miles square See SQUARE MILES.

million (plural) As is true of *dozen, score, thousand,* and *billion,* the singular form is used when the number is specified: "eight million unemployed," "several million (or *millions*) of them." Otherwise the plural is customary: "millions of cicadas."

miniature Not a synonym for *small, miniature* is best restricted to a scaled-down version, as "a miniature plane, twelve inches long." Ordinarily, there is no "miniature lake," ". . . forest," and so on.

minimize See MAXIMIZE/MINIMIZE.

minister/pastor/preacher/priest/rector The first three are used interchangeably in many Protestant churches. *Minister* is the inclusive term. *Pastor,* from Latin for "shepherd," emphasizes caring for "the flock" by making pastoral calls, helping the poor and the unhappy, and so on. *Preacher* emphasizes sermon delivery. Episcopalian ministers are *rectors.* (This term is used in other senses by Anglicans, and also by Roman Catholics, whose ministers are called *priests.*)

minus As in "Because of the accident he is minus two fingers," the usage is unlikely in SWE.

minutia "A detail, a trivial thing." The word is generally employed as a plural, *minutiae.*

miracle See MARVEL/MIRACLE.

miserly See ECONOMIC/ECONOMICAL.

mishap See ACCIDENT/MISHAP.

mislay/lose If you *mislay* your keys, you have merely left them in an unaccustomed place, but if you *lose* them, your chances of getting them back are much smaller. See also MISS/LOSE.

misremember See DISREMEMBER/MISREMEMBER.

miss/lose In expressions such as *miss his opportunity* and *lose his opportunity*, *miss* sounds a little less serious than *lose*. *Miss* may have a subliminal association with shooting: if one misses a shot, he probably can take another. But *lose* has an air of finality. See also MISLAY/LOSE.

mistake See ERROR/MISTAKE.

mistreat See MALTREAT/MISTREAT.

mistress See FEMALE COMPANION/GIRLFRIEND/MISTRESS.

mob Has been SWE for years, although eighteenth-century authors such as Jonathan Swift and Richard Steele opposed this shortening of the Latin *mobile vulgus* ("fickle crowd"). Brevity often supersedes length.

mode/mood Interchangeable as grammatical terms: "subjunctive mood (or *mode*)." They are not synonymous otherwise.

model See EXAMPLE/EXEMPLAR/IDEAL . . .

modern/modernistic In general, SWE uses *modern* – shorter and less judgmental. *Modernistic* is related to *modernism*, which like many other isms is sometimes held in low esteem. To many people, including some who profess to like modern art, modernistic art is thought (mistakenly) to refer mainly to distorted figures, strange angles, and utter meaninglessness.

mom-and-pop (also *mom-'n'-pop*) An informal but often accurate way to characterize a small store or other business owned or directly managed by a couple or a family. It is rare in SWE.

momentous See HISTORIC/MOMENTOUS.

monastic/monkish *Monastic* means "pertaining to monks or to the monasteries in which they live": "monastic life," "monastic architecture." *Monkish* is a usually unfavorable term for "like a monk." It suggests narrowness, unworldliness, excessive piety, a withdrawn quality.

monk See FRIAR/MONK; MONASTIC/MONKISH.

monkey (verb) Informal SWE intransitive verb for "play idly, manipulate unsystematically," generally followed by *with*, *around*, or *around with*: "I was monkeying with my computer." A seldom used, although SWE, transitive verb, *monkey* means "imitate, ape": "She monkeyed her grandmother's limping walk."

monolog(ue)/soliloquy A *soliloquy* is talking to oneself, especially in a play, as Hamlet does. A *monolog* (or *monologue*) is a one-person discourse, generally humorous, addressed to others. In his television talk show, Johnny Carson over the years has delivered thousands of monologs.

mood See MODE/MOOD.

moonlight (verb) Dating back to the mid-1900s, *moonlight* has now become SWE for "earn additional income from a second job."

moot The usual SWE meaning is "debatable, undecided." A *moot question* is one about which considerable evidence can be presented on each side. Sometimes, confusingly, *moot* is used for "unimportant," "unnecessary," or "hypothetical." That usage makes *moot question* uncertain in meaning. SANE recommends against *moot* with any of those three definitions.

moral/morale   *Moral* (adjective or noun) has to do with the goodness or badness of human actions: "moral conduct," "the moral of the story." *Morale*, only a noun, refers to mental or emotional condition, spirits, willingness to work or to obey orders: "After the victory, the morale of the troops was improved."

moral/moralistic   A *moral* person is one who believes in and practices conduct that the general public considers "right." A *moralistic* person can accurately be described in the same way. However, the word has come to be associated with narrow definitions of "rightness" and with preachiness in attempting to induce others to accept those definitions. Polonius in *Hamlet* was a moralistic person but not necessarily moral.

morality/mortality   *Morality* pertains to moral standards or moral behavior: "No one questioned the morality of her views." *Mortality* refers to the fact that all things that live must someday die: "the mortality of man." The opposites are *immorality* and *immortality* ("living forever"). The importance of distinguishing is shown in the notorious distortion of the title of Wordsworth's "Ode on Intimations of Immortality," which a student called "Ode on Imitations of Immorality."

moratorium   This resounding word for "deferment, delay" is used in SWE only for consequential matters, such as granting a nation a moratorium in paying its debts. Dubious or humorous: "The coach called a time-out – a welcome moratorium in the trouncing by the Tigers."

morbid   Football announcer: "The punter has had a morbid afternoon." Probably he meant "unsuccessful," "poor," or "mistake-filled." *Morbid* means "diseased," "psychologically unhealthy," or "too preoccupied with unwholesome thoughts."

more preferable   SWE omits the redundant *more*.

more than   See also ABOVE/MORE THAN; BETTER THAN.

more than one (verb with)   Logic demands "more than one were," but logic is frequently defeated by usage. The SWE usage is "more than one was" but "more than two were."

more than/over   Interchangeable in such expressions as "more than (*over*) five dollars," "more than (*over*) a foot long."

mores   This word (pronounced more-*ayz* or mo-*rayz*) means "accepted views and customs" of a group. The spelling is an unchanged borrowing from Latin.

morgue   See MAUSOLEUM/MORGUE/MORTUARY.

mortality   See MORALITY/MORTALITY.

mortgagee/mortgagor   It may seem odd, but the *mortgagee* lends the money and the *mortgagor* borrows it. The explanation is that the mortgagor puts a mortgage on his or her property.

mortuary See MAUSOLEUM/MORGUE/MORTUARY.

most (for *very*) *Most*, as in "our most gracious hostess," is SWE even though no comparison is intended.

most number TV reporter: "The picture receiving the most number of Oscar nominations is . . ." SWE says "largest (*highest*) number" or "the most Oscar nominations." Although *most number* is not standard, its opposite, *least number*, is. Also standard: *smallest* (*lowest, greatest, smaller, greater, lesser*) *number*.

most See also ALMOST/MOST.

mostly FF (dialectal or highly informal) for "most of the time": "Mos'ly, he jes droops aroun' the house."

motif/motive SWE prefers *motif* for these meanings: (1) "recurrent theme in a literary or artistic work," (2) "recurrent phrase in music," (3) "repeated decorative or architectural figure or design." *Motive* for any of these meanings sometimes appears but may be confusing.

motor See ENGINE/MOTOR.

moving violation Police jargon for breaking the law while driving a vehicle; for example, disregarding a stop sign, driving left of center.

Ms. Unquestionably, the language needs *Ms*. It designates a female without regard to her marital status, just as *Mr.* serves for either a married or an unmarried male.

much in evidence SWE, but *conspicuous* or *apparent* is more direct.

muchly Not listed in most dictionaries. *Much* serves as both adjective and adverb.

mucus/phlegm *Mucus* is the useful lubricant that coats body channels. (The lining of the channels is *mucous membrane*. Note the different spellings: noun *mucus*, adjective *mucous*.) *Phlegm* is, in effect, worn-out or morbid mucus, such as may be coughed up or expelled through the nose.

mugging See BURGLARY/HOLDUP/ROBBERY . . .

munch A crunching sound accompanies munching. One can *munch* popcorn, but not most sandwiches other than crisply toasted ones.

murder See EXECUTE/KILL, MURDER; HOMICIDE/MANSLAUGHTER/MURDER.

murderer See ASSASSIN/MURDERER.

mushmelon FF (dialectal) for *muskmelon, cantaloupe*.

mushroom (verb) Real mushrooms grow with amazing speed. The verb has become SWE for almost anything that grows or expands rapidly: "A tent city mushroomed, soon covering several acres."

must (noun) "Flowered blouses are a must this spring." *Must* with the meaning of "an absolute requirement" dates back a couple of centuries. Some conservatives, however, prefer to use it only as a verb. In SWE the noun use is occasional and somewhat informal.

must needs See NEED.

mutual cooperation SWE deletes *mutual*. See also COMMON/MUTUAL.

my dear In the salutation of a letter, *My dear* may be variously interpreted as supercilious, affectionate, prissy, or old-fashioned. Used today less frequently than in 1910.

myriad Either a noun or an adjective: "A myriad of stars," "the myriad stars of the heavens." The original Greek meaning was "ten thousand," and dictionaries still list that as one English definition, but that sense is now only figurative.

myself SWE as a reflexive: "I hurt myself"; and as an intensive: "I myself saw it." Otherwise FF for *I* or *me*, frequently so used by the grammatically unsure: "My father and myself stayed up all night" (SWE: *I*). "It was a terrifying ordeal for my father and myself" (SWE: *me*).

myth See FABLE/LEGEND/MYTH.

166

N

nab The reputability of a word is often hard to predict. *Nab* ("to grab, catch a wrongdoer, arrest, snatch") has been used by reputable writers, including Dickens and Thackeray, since the seventeenth century, but dictionaries still list it as slang or informal. SWE now uses it as a light synonym for "capture, arrest."

nadir/zenith Some people write *nadir* when they mean its antonym, *zenith*. One who thinks of the words together is likely to recall that *zenith*, not *nadir*, refers to the highest point in the sky. Both terms are also used figuratively: "the nadir of her despair."

naked/nude Usually interchangeable, although obviously painters paint "nudes" and not "nakeds." One may refer to an unsheathed sword as "naked" but not "nude." A legal document still needing some additions to be complete is "nude" but not "naked." For the human body, *naked* is the more frank, honest, and shameless word. Some people regard *nude* as "nicer"; it often suggests careful posing rather than careless and accustomed intimacy.

name of the game, what it's all about Both expressions have been popularized by sports announcers and have spread, often in contradictory statements: "Defense (*Offense, Scoring*) is the name of the game (or *what it's all about*)." "Making (*Saving, Spending*) money is . . ." SWE writers try to write what they really want to say about defense, saving, and so on.

namely SWE writers may ask themselves, "Is *namely* needed?" It is not, for example, in "My sisters, namely Faye and Dorothea, were . . ."

NAMES OF PEOPLE When first using a person's name in an article or a book, SWE normally identifies him or her not as Patterson or L. Patterson but as L. N. Patterson, Louise N. Patterson, Louise Patterson, Dr. L. N. Patterson, and so on. Often a further identification is desirable: "of the Harvard Medical School." Subsequent references, unless far removed, may be only Patterson or Dr. Patterson, although the *New York Times* always uses a title – *Mr., Mrs., Miss, Ms., Dr.,* and so on.

namesake See EPONYM/NAMESAKE.

nary FF (dialectal, old-fashioned) for "no, neither, not a, not one": "I didn't have nary a drop to drink." *Nary* may still be heard in secluded Appalachian and other areas, as (more rarely) may its companion *ary,* for "any, some, either": "I don't like ary one." "Have you got ary apples?"

national (noun) Increasingly used, especially as in "a Mexican national," to show that a person's nationality is not American. *National* is not the same as *citizen:* the Mexican national is not necessarily a citizen of Mexico. See also CITIZEN/INHABITANT/RESIDENT.

native A *native* of San Francisco (or any other place) was born there. The term *natives* has largely lost the earlier connotation of illiterate, half-naked denizens of some largely unexplored area. In some U.S. tourist areas, *native* is used to differentiate permanent residents from transients, even though the residents may have been born elsewhere. The transients are often given uncomplimentary informal names such as "snowbirds."

naturalist/naturist A *naturist* is anyone who enjoys and wants to preserve the joys and beauties of nature; he or she may also be a nudist. A *naturalist* presumably enjoys nature, too, and conceivably may be a nudist but ordinarily is a botanist, zoologist, or other student of nature. To a literary critic a naturalist is a writer of naturalistic fiction.

nature 1. A more specific word is often desirable. For example, if a woman writes about nature, the reader needs to know whether her chief subject is owls, forests, wildflowers, human nature, or . . .
2. A phrase such as *in nature* or *by nature* can often be omitted, as is true in "Bobsledding is dangerous (in nature)" and "(By nature), Jens is shy."

naught/nought Variants for "zero" or "nothing," both words seem old-fashioned. "Went for naught" survives but is not thriving. See also AUGHT/NAUGHT.

nauseated/nauseous Traditionalists have a good reason for trying to preserve a distinction between these words because, if used in the standard way, they prevent misunderstanding. In SWE "I am nauseated" means "I am sick to my stomach," but "I am nauseous" means, "I make people sick (by my appearance or actions)." The boundary between the words, however, is rapidly disappearing.

naval/navel *Naval* means "pertaining to a navy." *Navel* is standard for "belly button."

n.b. This abbreviation of Latin *nota bene* ("note carefully") is seldom used today except in business correspondence and reports; even there, *Note* or *Note especially* seems more frequent.

Near East Now usually called "Middle East" or, less often, "Mideast."

near-record Bernstein criticizes a statement that voter registration "set a near-record," saying that that was like saying, "The team scored three near-touchdowns." For that example, the criticism is justified, for near-records are not set, and near-touchdowns do not appear on the scoreboard. However, "Temperatures reached a near-record high" is different, comparable to "almost matched the record."

near-miss Widely used even in SWE, although illogical. If a bullet strikes a tree three feet from you, isn't it really a *near-hit*?

necessary requirement (or *requisite*) SWE omits *necessary*. See also ESSENTIAL/INDISPENSABLE/NECESSARY . . .

necessity Sometimes a contributor to wordiness. "The necessity of hurrying annoyed her" might be better worded "Having to hurry annoyed her" or even "Hurrying annoyed her."

nee Now written without the French accent mark. "Lucy Snodgrass, nee Walker" means "Lucy Snodgrass, whose family name (or unmarried name) is Walker." Dubious: "Lucy Snodgrass, nee Lucy Walker," because *nee* means "born as," and the only name Lucy was born with was *Walker*.

need Some constructions with *need* have an archaic flavor, although they are still used occasionally: "He need not do (*agree, retire,* and so on)" means "He does not need to." "Need she have chosen (*decided, asked,* and so on)" means "Did she need to?" "If need be" means "If it is (*becomes*) necessary." *Needs must,* as in "She needs must heed her mother's words," is archaic. SWE omits *needs*.

need for/need of In some sentences *need of* is ambiguous. In "The need of nurses is well known," are the nurses needy or are they in short supply? Clear: "Nurses' low pay . . ." or "The shortage of nurses . . ." When not ambiguous, *need of* can be satisfactory: "Ann's need of (or *need for*) money was becoming acute."

needless to say See (IT) GOES WITHOUT SAYING/NEEDLESS TO SAY.

ne'er See E'ER/NE'ER.

negative See AFFIRMATIVE/NEGATIVE.

neglect/negligence *Neglect* usually appears worse than *negligence*, which may result from mere carelessness. A child suffering from parental neglect is more likely to be cold and hungry than one suffering from negligence.

negligent/negligible A *negligent* person is careless about something or fails to do something desirable. *Negligible* most often applies to things or actions; it means "not important, not worth attention": "a negligible sum of money (*contribution to the discussion, breeze,* or the like)." On rare occasions it may apply to persons: a negligible tennis player is one considered highly unlikely to win a tournament. More than likely, however: "his negligible chances of winning."

negotiate Fowler and his American reviser, Nicholson, say that *negotiate* in the sense of "tackle successfully" is so bad that it "stamps a writer as literarily a barbarian." Modern American dictionaries, however, accept "negotiate a sharp curve" as unquestioningly as "negotiate a union contract." SWE.

Negress   Regarded by many as offensive, perhaps because no comparable "Whitess" exists.

neighborhood/vicinity   Both words refer to a small area, but a *neighborhood* is usually smaller. In addition, the word suggests neighborliness or even warmth. The size of a *vicinity* is indefinite but sometimes is rather large: "in the vicinity of Omaha."

neither   See EITHER; EITHER . . . OR/NEITHER . . . NOR; NOR; NOT ONLY . . . BUT ALSO.

169

nepotism   Some medieval church officials euphemistically called their illegitimate sons "nephews" and helped them to get good jobs – a practice called *nepotismo* in Italian. Since that time, the English *nepotism* has acquired the meaning of favoritism toward not only "nephews" but also other relatives and even friends. The "patronage" given by politicians to their supporters is not much different.

net (tennis)   See LET/NET.

nether   Old-fashioned adjective for "lower" or "beneath the earth's surface": "her nether lip," "the nether regions."

never had it so good   This phrase is FF (informal) for "was never so prosperous (*well fed, comfortable,* or the like)." The uncertainty about what *it* is and the vagueness of *good* may exclude this expression from most SWE contexts.

nevertheless   See BUT/HOWEVER; NEVERTHELESS.

new beginner   If someone joins an existing group of beginners, he may legitimately be called "a new beginner." Otherwise, SWE omits *new*.

new/novel   *New* refers to time or condition: "The new version seems stronger." "Your coat looks new." *Novel* emphasizes creativeness, unusualness: "a novel interpretation of *The Mikado*," "novel decorative effects."

New York City   SWE uses all three words whenever *New York* can be misinterpreted to mean the state. (The legal name is *The City of New York*.)

newfangled   Perhaps because of its strange sound, *newfangled* is often considered slang or colloquial. However, it has long been established in SWE. Unlike *new*, it is uncomplimentary, meaning "needlessly or excessively new, faddish."

news (verb with)   An anecdote about the great newspaper editor Horace Greeley asserts that when he came into the office he customarily asked, "Are there any news?" A smart-alecky cub reporter once responded, "No, sir. Nary a new." If Greeley really did treat *news* as a plural, today's editors would disagree. To them *news* is always singular. The *New York Times* slogan is not "All the news that *are* fit to print."

nice Strunk and White call *nice* "a shaggy, all-purpose word, to be used sparingly in formal composition." Probably everything that somebody likes has been described by someone as "nice." SWE chooses the most appropriate of the hundred or more substitutes, such as *tasty, aromatic, kind, well-proportioned, moral, friendly, lovable, likable, wise, precise.*

nicely Overused. Some alternatives, to be chosen according to context, are *attractively, carefully, cleverly, evenly, pleasantly, precisely, satisfactorily, suitably, thoughtfully, well.*

nicety A nicety is not usually "something nice." It is most often a subtle point, a detail: "a nicety of grammar," "niceties of diplomatic (or *social*) manners."

nigh The word is seldom used in today's English.

nimrod It's no longer considered clever – certainly not original – to call a hunter a "nimrod." The term got its start in Genesis. Noah's great-grandson, Nimrod, was "a mighty hunter before the Lord."

nitty-gritty This FF (slang) expression means "details, basic but possibly unpleasant facts."

no. This abbreviation for *number* (Latin *numero*), useful in commercial descriptions such as "Part No. 426-B," is not standard in most other contexts. (The symbol # is also used for *number*: "Part #426-B.")

no-good Informal, but found occasionally in SWE, as an adjective: "a no-good loafer." In the sense of "worthless," *no good* is found sometimes in SWE: "This poem is no good." SWE generally prefers *not good, worthless, poor,* or a more specific word.

no later than See BEFORE/NO LATER THAN.

no problem Short for "There is (*was*) no problem (*difficulty*) in doing what is (*was*) asked" or "It will cause no problem for me to do that." The shortcut is used mainly in conversation but appears sometimes in business and other contexts: "XYZ Company wants Friday delivery of 4,800 widgets. No problem."

no sooner Followed in SWE by *than*, not *when*: "No sooner had Flo arrived than the party began to sparkle." An *as soon as* construction may save a word or two: "As soon as Flo arrived, the party . . ."

no such a As in "No such a story is credible," SWE usually omits *a*.

no thinking person A sentence such as "No thinking person will conclude that . . ." not only puts down many other people but also indirectly praises the writer, who seems to be boasting of his or her own thinking ability.

no use SWE in "There's no use arguing" or "It's no use to argue," in which the meaning is "There is no need for . . ." or "It will do no good to . . ." It is FF in the sense of "useless"; "His bicycle is no use" (*of no use* is possible here, but seems unnatural).

no way Now overused. A vogue expression that started as a shortening of "I see no way to do that" but broadened to other negative ideas: "Not at all," "Not essential," "Not now," "Not today," and so on. It has been worked, if not to death, at least to exhaustion.

nohow   FF (dialectal) in sentences such as "They couldn't raise the money nohow," in which it is part of a double negative. Questionable but possible although infrequent, in such sentences as "They could nohow raise the money," in which it is equivalent to "in no way."

noisome   SWE, but rarely used because many readers misinterpret it as "noisy." It means "harmful" or (especially with regard to odors) "offensive, putrid." It derives from the same root as *annoy*.

nom de plume   Unless referring to a pseudonymous French author, SWE is likely to choose *pen name*.

nomenclature   "A system of names or naming": "botanical nomenclature." SWE writes, "The society took its name from . . . ," not "its nomenclature." 171

nominal   Not the same as *low*, a *nominal* fee is so low that it is a fee in name only – for example, a fee of $1 for services worth $100. Sometimes for legal or other reasons someone sells property for a nominal amount (e.g., $5) when it may be worth thousands.

NON SEQUITUR   Latin for "it does not follow," this term is generally used in English for a statement or a part of a statement that has no apparent relationship to what preceded it: "A woodsman since his youth, he plays the violin in the local orchestra."

NONCE WORD   *Nonce* dates back to Middle English for *then one(s)*, meaning "for once." A nonce word is coined to fit a particular occasion and may possibly never be used again. For example, when Joe Louis was heavyweight boxing champion, one of his knocked-out opponents was said to have been sent on "a Louisana hayride." A writer who is lucky enough to think of a nonce word that fits the situation, is clear, and is clever or funny or both, should use it – even in moderately formal writing. Some nonce words should become standard, for example, that of the child who, not wanting to walk farther, said, "I don't feel walkative any more."

nonstandard/substandard   Many linguists prefer to call, for example, "he don't have none" *nonstandard* rather than *substandard*. They define *nonstandard* as "not ordinarily used *at this time* in edited writing." They realize that usage changes and that a double negative, for example, was once "correct" and may become so again. Because there are no permanent standards in language, they assert, *substandard* is illogical.

noon luncheon   SWE usually omits *noon*. However, it indicates the time if the luncheon is scheduled at a somewhat unusual hour, such as two o'clock. See also LUNCH/LUNCHEON.

nor   SWE if *neither* is its teammate, but ordinarily not in sentences such as "She does not want fame nor riches," where *or* is standard. Exception: In some sentences the fact that the second part is negative may not be clear unless *nor* is used, as in "The skater showed none of her usual grace or maintained her customary relaxed air" (SWE says, ". . . nor did she maintain . . ."); "Players on four teams have not voted, or is a vote expected before Monday" (SWE says, ". . . nor is a vote expected . . .").

nor none   An FF double negative, as in "No sales tax was added in Florida, nor none in Georgia." SWE says, ". . . nor was any . . ." Also SWE: ". . . nor was any in Georgia either" (not *neither*).

normalcy/normality   Interchangeable. *Normal* may also be used as a noun, as in "back to normal."

northerly   See EASTERLY/EASTERN.

northward(s)   Interchangeable, but *northward* has a strong lead over the *s* form, as is true of *southward, eastward, westward.*

nosh   FF (slang or dialectal) noun or verb, from Yiddish for "snack."

nostalgia   Once referring only to homesickness, and sometimes still so defined, *nostalgia* has broadened its meaning to "fond recollection of persons or places in one's past." Often suggestive, too, of a wish to revisit or relive parts of one's "good old days."

not (and other negatives)   Only one negative is customary in SWE in each of these sentences:

> FF: "He did*n't* take *none* of it." SWE: "didn't take any," "took *none.*"
>
> FF: "She does*n't scarcely* (or *hardly*) have time." SWE: "She *scarcely* has time."
>
> FF: "We did*n't* buy any, *neither.*" SWE: ". . . either."
>
> FF: "I would *not* be surprised if she did*n't* decide to go home." SWE: ". . . if she decided . . ."

not (placement)   (1) Not all of them are guilty. (2) All of them are not guilty. (3) They are all not guilty. Sentence 1 means "some are, some are not"; sentence 2 is ambiguous; and sentence 3 means that all are innocent. These examples show why SWE is careful about placement of *not.*

not about to/not all that   FF (informal, wordy): "I'm not about to tell the judge that I'm not all that certain about what happened." SWE says, "I'm reluctant (*unwilling*) to tell the judge that I'm not sure about what happened."

not anything like/ nothing like   These expressions are SWE in "Not anything like (or *Nothing like*) that had ever been seen in Dubuque." FF for "not nearly": "This brand costs nothing like as much."

not . . . but   In sentences such as "Don't take but one" and "I didn't see but six of the buffalo," the *not . . . but* construction is frequent in conversation. "Take only one" and "I saw only six" are more likely in SWE.

not only . . . but also   In SWE, constructions following *not only* and *but also* are grammatically similar. In

> The union

> not only *insisted on higher wages*
> but also *shorter working hours*

the italicized parts are obviously not grammatical equals, are not "parallel." In this revision they are:

The union insisted on

> not only *higher wages*
> but also *shorter working hours*

The same principle of parallel construction applies when the conjunctions are *both . . . and* or *neither . . . nor.* In conversation we may not have time to attain such parallelism consistently, but in writing we generally can take enough time to make one side balance the other.

not that tired (Also *not that much, . . . little, . . . strong,* and so on) Conservatives object to using *that* as an adverb, and also to its indefiniteness; how tired is *that tired*? The expressions are firmly entrenched in FF but seldom seen in SWE. See also NOT TOO BAD OF A.

not to exceed Appropriate in business and legal documents, but in other writing *no* (or *not*) *more than* is usual.

not to worry Frequent in British speech, occasional in prose, this short substitute for "There is (or *was*) no need to worry" has gained popularity in the United States. It is rare in SWE.

not . . . too Radio interviewer: "You haven't been in Chicago too long, have you?" Smart-alec interviewee: "No, it just seems too long." *Not . . . too,* if used for *not . . . very,* can be ambiguous. SWE either omits *too* or substitutes *very.*

not too bad of a FF *not too bad of a* and its variants with other adjectives (*good, strange,* and so on) are based on the standard idiom illustrated in *too much of a good thing.* However, it's not too bad of an idea to delete the *of.* In fact, it's a good one, according to SWE custom. Similar is *not that bad of a.*

not un- The *not un-* combination represents one of the few widely accepted double negatives. (Another is much more rare: "Nobody doesn't like Sara Lee" or "I can't endure not playing golf this week.") A *not unusual* occurrence may happen 10 to 50 percent of the time, but for a *usual* one the frequency is certainly above 50. A *not unlikely* story is fairly believable, but less so than a *likely* one. See also NOT (AND OTHER NEGATIVES).

notable/noted/notorious Most often misused of the three is *notorious,* which means "infamous, well-known for evil-doing." SWE: "John Dillinger was a notorious bank robber." FF: "Saint Francis was notorious for his kindness." The noun form of *notorious* is *notoriety.* *Notable* means "worthy of mention, important": "one of the notable events (*women,* and so on) of the late nineteenth century." *Noted* applies mainly to people and means "famous, eminent, celebrated": "James Baldwin was a noted author." You might conceivably be sued for calling someone "notorious" but not for "noted" or "notable."

notable/noticeable Something *notable* is likely to be important, prominent, newsworthy. Something *noticeable* can be seen but may not be of much size or significance.

notary/notary public Often used interchangeably, but conservatives prefer the full title, *notary public*. The SWE plural is generally *notaries public*, but *notary publics* is gaining.

notate Not a substitute for *note* or *annotate*. However, a composer who writes the notes that represent the music in his or her mind may be said to notate – even when using a computer to do so.

nothing, nothing but *Nothing* takes a singular verb even if a plural follows: "Nothing in the packages was (not *were*) what she had ordered. Nothing in them *was* almonds." In "Nothing but bull's-eyes ____ counted," should the missing verb be *is* or *are*? Because the subject appears to be *nothing*, conservatives argue for *is*. Most people, however, automatically say *are* because of the proximity of *bull's-eyes*. The more sophisticated of them argue that here *nothing but* means "only." Because both choices seem awkward, SWE often substitutes "Only bull's-eyes were counted" or "Nothing was counted but (or *except*) bull's-eyes."

NOUNS UPON NOUNS The Germans call it *Substantivseuche* ("the noun disease"). Most common in American headlines but present even in prose needing less compression, it is the tendency to string several nouns together, each modifying what follows: "The teacher lesson-preparation number decrease demand will probably not be granted." To comprehend that string of nouns a reader must start with *demand* and work backward to *teacher* to untangle the mess, perhaps emerging with "The teachers' demand for a decrease in the number of lesson preparations will probably not be granted." In general, SWE looks with concern at more than two nouns strung together, although occasionally the string is clear or unavoidable: "the Michigan State University Research Foundation." See also –ING.

novelty See REAL NOVELTY.

novice See AMATEUR/NOVICE.

now pending SWE omits *now*.

nowhere near As in "The new tank will cost nowhere near (or *not nearly*) so much," this is SWE.

nowheres This word is FF (dialectal) for *nowhere*.

no-win This term is often used in FF, but increasingly in SWE, as adjective or noun: "The president finds himself in a no-win situation." "This is certainly a no-win." Because of its shortness, the expression is useful. Contrast it with the wordy "The president finds himself in a situation in which victory is impossible."

nth degree *N* is not synonymous with *infinite* or *large*. SWE, however, occasionally uses *nth degree* to mean "an indefinitely (or *infinitely*) large degree or extent."

number (verb with) SWE: "The number of errors was small." Here the writer is referring to an actual number – say, six. That number is small. The subject is *number*. SWE: "A number of errors *were* overlooked." Here a *number of* means "several" or "many": "Several errors were overlooked." The subject is *errors*, not *number*. (Columnist James Kilpatrick has campaigned against such use of *a number of*, arguing that it can mean "one" or "a million." He is obviously right, but the phrase is so widely used even in the "best" prose that his campaign has had no visible effect.)

number   See also AMOUNT/NUMBER.

NUMBERS (UNNECESSARY)   "Our two children, Anne and Paul, were with us." Most people will realize that Anne + Paul = two. "Iran, Iraq, and Saudi Arabia are the three nations that will be most helped by the decision." The SWE writer deletes *three*, and then, thinking further, deletes *are the three nations that*.

numerous   Not a noun. SWE changes "Numerous of the new traffic regulations are still unfamiliar" by deleting *of the* or by starting with *Many of the new* or *Several new*.

numerous/populous   A newspaper story reports, "The populous Kansas alumni are mostly an affluent group." This is not SWE. Kansas alumni are *numerous*. The usual meaning of *populous* is "densely inhabited": "populous Mexico City."

nuptials   See MARRIAGE/NUPTIALS/WEDDING.

O

obligate/oblige   Usually interchangeable. When you are under compulsion to do something, you may say either "I am obliged" or "I am obligated" to do it. When you feel gratitude toward someone, you are more likely to choose *obliged*: "I am obliged to him for his kindness." (An old way to say "Thank you" is "Much obliged.")

obscene   American courts so far have not been able to agree on a satisfactory definition. It is unsafe to assume that most people will readily accept whatever one's own definition is. (In some societies kissing is regarded as obscene.) Although ordinarily the term is related to sexual behavior, one dictionary definition is "loathsome," and on that basis many people argue that cruelty, violence, terrorism, profiteering, or war is more obscene than display of sexual activity.

obscenity/profanity   *Obscenity* in speaking or writing is the use of "indecent" expressions referring to sexual or excretory functions – often but not always four-letter words. *Profanity* is use of expressions that seem to show contempt or irreverence toward God or sacred things.

obscure   See ABSTRUSE/OBSCURE.

observance/observation   *Observance* refers to (1) celebrating a holiday or a religious rite: "observance of Veterans Day, Hanukkah, and so on"; (2) complying with law or custom: "observance of her family's traditions." *Observation* is "seeing, watching, noticing": "to make weather observations," "a patient kept under observation," "Observation through a telescope revealed . . ." See also COMMENT/OBSERVATION/REMARK.

obsolescent/obsolete   *Obsolescent* means "going out of style or use," and *obsolete* means "now out of style or use." Many of today's fashions in women's clothing may be obsolescent in a few months and obsolete in a year or two.

obverse   See CONVERSE/INVERSE/OBVERSE.

obviate   Means "make unnecessary," as in "My mother's telephone call obviated our planned visit." Although that meaning is the same as "removed the need of," *obviate* is not used in SWE to mean simply "remove."

obvious   See APPARENT/EVIDENT/OBVIOUS.

occasional/sometime   Use of *sometime* in sentences such as "Gladys is a painter and a sometime (*an occasional*) sculptor" appears to be growing. Conservatives point out that *occasional* does well enough, and that *sometime*, in its rather rare use as an adjective, ordinarily means "former." Confusion may arise: Is Gladys now occasionally a sculptor, or is she a former sculptor? Here SANE sides with the conservatives.

occupation/profession/trade   *Occupation* is broadest in meaning. It is any activity by which one earns a livelihood. *Profession* is usually restricted to an occupation requiring advanced study in a specialized field, such as law or medicine. The distinction is not firm, however. Not nearly everyone in the acting profession, for example, has taken advanced courses in acting. A *trade* normally involves skilled labor or buying and selling. Plumbing and shopkeeping are examples. See also AVOCATION/VOCATION.

occur/take place   Generally interchangeable, but some stylebooks advocate restricting *take place* to prearranged events: "The concert took place on May 9, as scheduled." SWE often follows that usage. *Occur* most often means "happen," but it also occurs ("appears") in sentences such as "The word *placidly* occurs three times on one page."

occurrence   See EPISODE/EVENT/INCIDENT . . .

o'clock   See BELLS/O'CLOCK.

octopus (plural)   If you meet two of these, call them *octopuses* if you speak English, *octopodes* (*oktopoda*) if you speak classical Greek, or *octopi* if you speak no known language.

oculist/ophthalmologist/optician/optometrist   An *oculist* and an *ophthalmologist* are the same, a physician (M.D.) specializing in treatment of the eyes. The professionals prefer the longer word. An *optometrist* also examines eyes and may prescribe glasses but is not an M.D. An *optician* makes or sells glasses and other optical goods.

odd/peculiar/quaint/queer/strange   Often interchangeable, but these connotations are frequent: *Odd* – "not fitting in": "He was an odd student, not interested in sports or girls." *Peculiar* – "having qualities not shared by others": "His gait is peculiar." *Quaint* – "old-fashioned but not unattractive": "When Rip Van Winkle returned from his twenty-year nap, his clothing seemed quaint." *Queer* – "eccentric; (possibly) homosexual": "Her speech is queer – full of uncommon grunts and gurgles." *Strange* – "unfamiliar, inexplicable"; "strange behavior."

-odd SWE avoids *some* (or *about, approximately*) *twenty-odd*, in which either the modifier or *-odd* is redundant. SWE uses the hyphen. "Twenty-odd people" and "twenty odd people" are not necessarily the same.

of (as part of verb) *Of* is FF for *have* in "could of" "might of," and the like. The standard *have* sometimes sounds like *'ve* when spoken and so is misunderstood and miswritten as *of*.

of between/of from With numbers, as in "a deficit of between (or *from*) ten to fifteen thousand dollars," SWE deletes the redundant *between* or *from*.

of course Copperud's advice is usually followed in SWE: "Every *of course* should be weighed critically with a view to striking it out." SWE preserves it only if the reader definitely needs to be assured that the writer is aware that the reader knows. It is equivalent to *as is widely known.*

of/'s SWE: "John's brother," "a brother of John," "a brother of John's"; "the college's president," "the president of the college." The following are SWE but different in meaning: "A photograph of John won the prize." "A photograph of John's won the prize." (Bryant points out that "a dog's bone" and "a bone of the dog's" have essentially the same meaning, but that "a bone of the dog" does not.)

off from, off of SWE omits *from* and *of*.

offer/tender The verbs are often interchangeable, but *tender* is starchy in its formality: "I hereby tender my resignation," "tendered his services (or *regrets*)," but "offered a better deal." SWE: "They tendered all their stock certificates to be cashed in."

offhand/offhanded/offhandedly *Offhand* and *offhanded* are interchangeable as adjectives, and *offhand* and *offhandedly* as adverbs. If that's hard to remember, SANE says, choose *offhand* for either: "an offhand remark," "He commented offhand that . . ."

officer Should a patrolman who is not yet a sergeant, lieutenant, or captain be called an "officer"? A long battle over that question has been waged. The ayes apparently have won, mainly because the person on the beat is indeed an officer of the law. Besides, *officer* makes unnecessary any concern about whether to say *policeman, policewoman,* or (heaven forbid) *policeperson.*

official/officious The adjective *official* means "pertaining to a governmental or other authoritative post": "Her official duties include checking expense accounts." *Officious* means "bustling, overeager to help": "His officious manner annoyed the visitors."

offputting   An unpleasant-sounding word of various meanings, including "ugly," "objectionable," "disconcerting," "distressing." Sometimes confused with *putting off* ("delaying"). SWE prefers a more precise word.

offspring   Both singular and plural: "an offspring," "several offspring."

oft   Once used by poets who needed a shorter word than *often* or *frequently*. Now regarded as affected, although it occasionally appears in compounds such as *oft-heard* or *oft-told*. *Ofttimes* has been largely replaced by *oftentimes*. *Often* may usually serve as well, although *oftentimes* adds the connotation of "repeatedly."

-og/-ogue   See CATALOG/CATALOGUE.

OK   *OK* (plural *OK's*) is the most common of the several spellings, although *O.K.* and *okay* are not infrequent. Verb forms: *OK'd, O.K.'d,* or *okayed; OK'ing, O.K.'ing,* or *okaying.* SANE, always seeking compactness, recommends *OK, OK'd, OK'ing.* Regardless of its spelling, *OK* is considered informal by most dictionaries – an oddity for the American word most widely used in the whole world. RHD says, "It occurs in all but the most formal speech and writing." And George Will, usually as conservative linguistically as politically, wrote in his *Newsweek* column, "OK, some of those numbers may involve overreaching . . ."

old adage, old cliché   See ADAGE.

Old English   See MIDDLE ENGLISH/OLD ENGLISH.

older   See ELDER, ELDEST/OLDER, OLDEST.

old-fashioned   SWE doesn't forget the *-ed*. The term is increasingly written without the hyphen.

oldster   SWE for "elderly person." Considered derogatory by some, affectionate by others.

on account of   *Because of* usually works as well, but doesn't shorten the expression very much. *On account of* followed by a clause is FF, sometimes considered illiterate: "She worked all summer on account of she needed money to start college." SWE prefers *because.*

on Sunday (and the like)   Before names of days, *on* may usually be dropped: "Our guests will arrive (on) Tuesday."

on the basis of   SWE finds that *because of, by, for,* or *on* will often suffice.

on the lam   FF (slang) for "in flight, especially from prison or fear of prison."

on (or *in*) the order of   "The estimate of the fire damage was in the order of about $25,000." SWE deletes *five* words.

on the part of   In a sentence such as "More accurate shooting on the part of the team is essential," SWE replaces the phrase with *by*. Even *by the team* is not needed here if the context shows that meaning.

on the whole See AS A WHOLE/ON THE WHOLE.

on to/onto In "John walked on to Covington," John was obviously not on top of Covington. But in "John stepped onto the ladder" (or *stage, table*, and so on), John moved to a position on the ladder or whatever. Both sentences are SWE. Grammatically, the difference is that in the first example, *on* is an adverb: "John walked on." In "stepped onto the ladder," *onto* is a preposition.

on/upon Often interchangeable, although some people try to reserve *on* for a position at rest and *upon* for when motion is involved: "The cat leaped upon the mouse." SWE prefers *on* when possible. When *up* can stand alone (as an adverb) and happens to be followed by *on*, two words are used: "The bear stood up on its hind legs." The difference is noticeable in speaking. Contrast the difference in sound between *up on* in that example and *upon* in this: "The bear was standing upon a large rock."

one (impersonal) (1) You may feel ambivalent about impersonal *one*. (2) I feel ambivalent about impersonal *one*. (3) One may feel ambivalent about impersonal *one*. Sentence 3 illustrates the use treated here. It appears mainly in formal prose, and to some people appears affected, stilted. Both 1 and 2 are more natural, but sometimes 3 is needed to maintain detachment and impersonality, as in a business or scientific report. In British use, if one starts a sentence with *one*, one must continue using *one* until one reaches the end of one's sentence – or one's patience. In American use, the initial *one* may be followed either by *one* or by *he, him, his, she, her*, or *hers*, as appropriate.

one and the same SWE generally omits *one and*.

one another See EACH OTHER/ONE ANOTHER.

one of the When tempted to write "one of the (questions, answers, catfish, or what-have-you)," the SWE writer asks, "Can I dispense with *of the*?"

one of the only Awkward: "Ferguson is one of the only, if not the only, legislators favoring the increase." SWE says, "Ferguson is one of the few legislators favoring the increase, if not the only one."

one of those who (verb with) In "Idaho is one of the states that (is, are) certain to support the Lambo bill," opinion about the verb choice is divided. Logic says that several states *are* certain, and that Idaho is one of those that are certain. But the singular *Idaho* is the focus of the sentence, and Idaho *is* certain. Most TV news people seem to prefer *is*. SWE is ambivalent, although conservatives and all who believe that language should be as logical as possible prefer *are*.

oneself/one's self SWE uses both. SANE prefers *oneself* for its simplicity – seven keyboard strokes vs. ten.

one-upmanship Now SWE for "the practice of keeping a little ahead of someone else." It's great to pack all of that into one word!

ongoing Less bad than Strunk and White consider it, no better than *present, existing*, or *existent* for the meaning "now in operation": "The ongoing (or *present*) program is bringing better results than its predecessor." Often, however, either word is superfluous.

only (as connective)   As in "He would have offered John a beer, only John's wife would have objected." Although *only* sometimes appears in such sentences in SWE, either *but* or the too wordy *if it were not* (*for the fact*) *that* is more frequent. Logically, *only* makes little sense.

only (placement of)   Should you write "Smith only wanted one" or "Smith wanted only one"? A study by Bryant reported in 1962 that 86 percent of magazines placed *only* as in the second sentence. Logic supports that placement: it was *only one* that Smith wanted. Bryant added that in spoken English, sentences like the first predominated. Her findings, although dated, still appear valid.

only too   In sentences such as "I'll be only too happy to help," *only too* adds nothing and indeed is nonsensical. SWE generally omits it.

onward(s)   *Onwards* never is needed, although not "wrong" as an adverb: "The troops moved onwards." SANE recommends, and SWE usually prefers, *onward* as both adverb and adjective: "moved onward," "the onward movement."

opaque/translucent   Blame glassmakers' labeling for the occasional confusion. Some of them call glass "opaque" if it lets a small amount of light through. *Opaque*, from Latin for "dark," means "not penetrable by light." What the glassmakers mean is *translucent* ("letting light through but not permitting clear perception"). See also DIAPHANOUS/TRANSLUCENT/TRANSPARENT.

open up   See UP.

operate   In a hospital, a person is operated *on* or *upon*. FF: "My father was operated yesterday." A factory may be operated, but not a father.

operative word   Overused for "key word, important word."

ophthalmologist   See OCULIST/OPHTHALMOLOGIST/OPTICIAN . . .

opine   Although SWE for "hold or express an opinion," *opine* has somehow acquired a slightly humorous or derogatory connotation.

opinion/theory   A *theory* is more solidly based and carefully reasoned than an *opinion*. Dubious: "My theory is that the Giants are the best team in baseball this year." SWE refers to Einstein's theory of relativity but not to his opinion of or about relativity.

opponent   See ADVERSARY/ANTAGONIST/ENEMY . . .

opt for   SWE for "choose, select, take this action rather than that."

optician   See OCULIST/OPHTHALMOLOGIST/OPTICIAN . . .

optimism, optimistic   See HOPE, HOPEFUL/OPTIMISM, OPTIMISTIC.

optimistic/pessimistic; favorable/unfavorable   People, but not things, can be *optimistic*, because optimism is mental and emotional. So SWE prefers "a favorable economic outlook" to "an optimistic outlook." The same comment applies to *pessimistic* vs. *unfavorable*. See also HOPE, HOPEFUL/OPTIMISM, OPTIMISTIC.

optimize   Somewhat pompous for "use (or *do*) as efficiently as possible." But it *is* relatively short: "Robinson Crusoe optimized the few things he salvaged from the wrecked ship." See also -IZE.

optometrist See OCULIST/OPHTHALMOLOGIST/OPTICIAN . . .

opulent See AFFLUENT/OPULENT/RICH . . .

or See AND/OR.

oral/verbal SANE recommends that for clarity a distinction between these words should be observed; *oral* for "spoken," *verbal* for "in words, whether spoken or written." Why? Because, for example, "verbal contract (or *agreement*)" is ambiguous, but "oral contract" or "written contract" is not. *Verbal* is useful in contrast to *physical*, *financial*, and probably other words: "Brown's attack was verbal, not physical." "Green's response was both verbal and financial. He publicly criticized Brown and also raised his rent." SWE's use of *verbal* is inconsistent.

oral See AURAL.

orate To *orate* is not necessarily to give an oration; it suggests an oratorical, pompous method of speaking. Telling someone that he or she orates may damage a friendship.

orchestra See BAND/ORCHESTRA.

order See ASK/DEMAND/INQUIRE.

ordinal See CARDINAL/ORDINAL.

ordinance/ordnance An *ordinance* is a regulation or a law, usually in a city or town. In the Old Testament, it refers to a religious ceremony. *Ordnance* comes to English from the same French source but has a quite different meaning: "military weapons, ammunition, and equipment."

ordinary See AVERAGE/COMMON, ORDINARY.

orient (verb) orientate Both are SWE. The longer is no better than the shorter, which SANE prefers.

-oriented As in "business-oriented." Strunk and White call it "a clumsy, pretentious device," but in avoiding it they use an example with one-third more words. SANE says, "Use it, but not excessively. Avoid it in vague expressions such as 'a goal-oriented school.'" (All schools should have goals.) The term appears often in SWE.

ornery An old variant of *ordinary*, *ornery* is treated in some dictionaries as standard for "unpleasant in disposition, short-tempered, (perhaps) criminal," but it is rare in SWE. It has an old-timey or down-home touch, and is unlikely to be used to describe a corporation president or anybody who might be seen at a society ball.

oscillate/osculate To *oscillate* is to waver, vacillate, or move back and forth like a pendulum. *Osculate* is a mildly humorous substitute for the verb *kiss*. "He oscillated for a while, but then he osculated her."

ostensibly/ostentatiously Not at all similar in meaning. *Ostensibly* means "apparently but not certainly": "His testimony was forceful and ostensibly honest." *Ostentatiously* means "in a showy, pretentious way": "Some popular singers dress ostentatiously even when not performing." The adjectives *ostensible* and *ostentatious* are similarly differentiated.

other Needed after *any* in a sentence such as "Marie is taller than any (other) girl in her class." *Other* refers to persons or things in the same category. Since Marie is in the class, she must be compared not with *any girl* but with *any other girl* in the class. But *other* is not to be used in "Marie is taller than any girl on the opposing team."

ought FF usage includes *had ought, hadn't ought, didn't ought. Ought* suffices.

ourself **1.** An SWE writer uses *we ourself* only if he or she is a king or queen. The plural *ourselves* has no such limitation. **2.** *Ourselfs* is FF, as are *themselfs* and *hisself.*

out loud Slightly more informal than *aloud*, but both are used in SWE.

outcome (verb after) Questionable: "The outcome may become dangerous." More likely: "The outcome will be dangerous." Questionable: "The outcome may lead to long delays." More likely: "The outcome may be long delays."

outside (of) *Outside of* is more likely in conversation: "Spot was barking outside of the fence." *Outside* is probable in SWE: "That action was definitely outside the law."

outstanding Sometimes, as in the following phrases, a more specific substitute for this word of praise can be found: a *world-class* athlete, a *below-four-minute* miler, a *wealthy* businessman, a *philanthropic* businessman, a painter *favorably compared with Monet.* Note that *outstanding* is a feeble substitute for any of the italicized terms.

outworn/worn-out Often interchangeable, but in reference to what is out of date, *outworn* is more likely: "an outworn belief." Clothing, machinery, and other tangible things more often become *worn out*, although in some families outgrown clothing is also called *outworn.*

over (in comparisons) Illogical: "The unemployment statistics show a slight decline over last month's figures." A decline, drop, or reduction can hardly be "over." In the example, SWE chooses *from*; in other sentences, perhaps *below* or *down from.* Or sometimes rewriting is preferable: "This month's unemployment figures are below those for March." An advertising claim reads, "Save 20 percent over the regular price!" What does that mean? SWE may substitute *of* for *over*, or write, "Now 20 percent below the regular price!"

over again FF (redundant): "Sing the chorus over again." SWE deletes either *over* or *again*, or says, "Repeat the chorus."

over (or *under*) my signature Most things – letters especially – are written *over* ("above") one's signature. In law, however, *written under my signature* means "attested to or authorized by me."

over with SWE deletes *over.*

over See also MORE THAN.

overall SWE checks to see whether *overall* is needed. It often can be deleted. For example, "the overall total," "our overall conclusion," "the overall result of the trial."

overavailability   This is bureaucratic jargon for "glut, surfeit, surplus."

overexaggerated   SWE deletes *over*.

overlay/overlie   The uses are similar to those of *lie* and *lay*. To *overlay* is to apply a covering; to *overlie* is to lie upon. These examples illustrate SWE usage: "The cabinetmaker overlays (*is overlaying, overlaid, has overlaid*) the wood with cherry veneer." "Rich black soil overlies (*is overlying, formerly overlay, had overlain*) a mixture of sand and clay." A similar distinction exists between *underlay* and *underlie*.

overlook/oversee   Dictionaries give *supervise* as a synonym of both words. Theoretically, then, "The supervisor oversees the laborers" and ". . . overlooks the laborers" have the same meaning. The second, however, may be ambiguous, for *overlook* usually means "ignore, pay no attention to." Because of such ambiguity in *overlook*, SWE uses *oversee* for "supervise."

overly   An unnecessary word, *overly* for *over* doesn't increase clarity. *Overoptimistic* and the like have long been standard.

owing to   "Owing to a blizzard, Sally missed two examinations." Conservatives would replace *owing to* with *because of* in this sentence, although they approve of it in a sentence in which *owing to* is used as an adjective: "Sally's missing two examinations was owing to a blizzard," where the expression is equivalent to *attributable to* or *caused by*. Despite the conservatives, sentences like the first example are frequent in SWE as well as in FF. See also DUE TO (OWING TO) THE FACT THAT.

OXYMORON   See GUEST HOST.

P

pad   FF (slang, probably fading) for "a place to live." In the 1960s it was chiefly hippie talk, but it spread to include anything from one corner of a crowded room to a luxurious apartment, and so became increasingly vague.

pail/pale   A *pail* is a bucket. The most common meaning of *pale* is "whitish."

pair   Although "five *pairs* of slacks (or *socks*, and so on)" is usual, *pair* sometimes appears in SWE in similar phrases. When two people (or *animals*, *insects*) are performing as individuals, *pair* takes a plural verb: "The pair of tame rabbits were frolicking." See also SLACKS.

palate/palette/pallet   Illustrations of differing meanings: "The hot soup burned my tongue and palate." "You made a palate-pleasing dessert." "The artist is mixing colors on her palette" (*pallet* is a seldom-used alternative spelling). "This part of the watch is the pallet." "A potter's paddle is a pallet." "Lay the pallet on the floor here." "Bookbinders use a pallet for artistic work." "The bricks were loaded on a wooden pallet to be hauled away."

pale See BEYOND (OUTSIDE) THE PALE; PAIL/PALE.

paltry/petty/trivial All mean "unimportant, insignificant, slight." *Petty* and *trivial* are almost synonyms, but *petty* carries a note of contempt less evident in *trivial*. *Paltry* is the strongest of the three, expressing deep contempt. It is often used of small amounts of money: "A paltry sum to pay for murder!" However, it may show contempt of quality as well as quantity: "a paltry, imitative pedant" (Jonathan Swift).

panacea/remedy SWE reserves *panacea* for a so-far imaginary cure for *all* diseases or evils. FF: "a panacea for gout." *Universal panacea* is a redundancy. In contrast, a *remedy* is intended to cure or relieve a single disease or evil, or a related group of them.

pandemic See ENDEMIC/PANDEMIC.

panegyric Too formal and high-flown for ordinary "praise," *panegyric* usually refers to a speech or a written tribute. *Encomium*, also formal, is a synonym. Another, which may be slightly less formal, is *eulogy*. On most private or semiprivate occasions, *praise*, *commendation*, or *compliment* is more suitable. See also ELEGY/ENCOMIUM/EULOGY.

pansy See FAIRY/GAY/PANSY.

paradise Capitalized for the place where many hope to live after death, but not in sentences such as "This is a paradise." SWE uses context to make clear which place is meant: (1) the Garden of Eden, (2) a place where the righteous await the second coming of Christ, (3) a place where the righteous will spend eternity, (4) any especially delightful earthly place, (5) an extraordinarily blissful emotional state. Of the several attempts to form an adjective, *paradisal* is probably best – certainly better than the more common *paradisaical*. Fowler evades the issue, preferring *heavenly*.

parameter Howard offers an excellent discussion of this word, which he says is misused 99 percent of the time. He has coined the term *hyperparametritis* for addiction to its use and has explained the seven highly technical definitions (in conic sections, mathematics, astronomy, crystallography, music, medical writing, and statistics). The eighth, he says, is "usually no more than a grand and showy substitute for boundary, limit, framework, or condition." The word is apparently often confused with *perimeter*. It does appear sometimes in SWE in that sense, but some readers then lose respect for the writer.

paraphrase/summary A *summary* is shorter than the original; it usually presents the main points but omits most examples and other elaboration. A *paraphrase* may be shorter or longer than the original, although usually shorter. It is a restatement, generally intended to clarify or simplify.

pardon   See EXCUSE/PARDON.

partake   In "partook of a delicious repast," the verb and the words for the meal both have an old-fashioned flavor. With regard to social or athletic activities, *participate* or *take part* is usual, not *partake*: "participated in the fun."

partiality   See BIAS/PARTIALITY/PREJUDICE.

partially/partly   Dictionaries draw a distinction, saying that *partly* refers to physical things and the meaning is "in part," but that *partially* refers to conditions and the meaning is "to a certain degree." Because the dictionary distinctions are not easy to make, SWE inconsistently follows them.

particular   May contribute to wordiness. SWE deletes seven words from "on this particular occasion that I am telling you about."

parting of the ways   This is a cliché.

party   "A party of one?" the maitre d' asks in supercilious disbelief. "Please meet your party at the United ticket counter," an employee intones over the airport public-address system. Despite years of dictionary insistence that *party* and *person* are not interchangeable, usages like these remain in FF but are rare in SWE.

pass away/pass on   These expressions, like other euphemisms, are intended kindly. They are certainly not objectionable with reference to family members, friends, or anyone else regarded with affection. For other deaths, the forthright *die* is customary in SWE. See also EUPHEMISM/EUPHUISM.

pass-fail   Now a standard term in academia in expressions such as "a pass-fail course," "I'm taking it pass-fail," the term was at first received questioningly. However, it is less cumbersome than "for credit but without a specific letter or number grade."

pass out   FF for *faint*.

pass time   See KILL TIME/PASS TIME/SPEND TIME.

pass up   More informal than "refuse to accept" (an offer, opportunity, or the like), *pass up* is used frequently in SWE.

passed/past   *Passed* is only a form of the verb *pass*: "A car passed slowly." *Past* is used differently, as in "the past decade" (adjective), "in the past" (noun), "hurried past" (adverb), "walked past the house" (preposition). See also PAST EXPERIENCE/PAST HISTORY.

PASSIVE VOICE   Passive: "She *was given* a huge basket of red roses by her admirers." Active: "Her admirers *gave* her . . ." Although either version may appear in SWE, most good writers prefer the active voice, which follows the natural order of telling who did what to whom. The passive is useful when the doer is unknown, unimportant, or obvious: "Clark was murdered in 1987, but detectives failed to find enough evidence to arrest anyone." "Both winners were elected by comfortable margins." Scholarly writers, instead of saying "I did so and so," still often say "So and so was done" (or the active "The researcher did so and so"). Even in their writing, the passive seems less frequent than it once was.

past experience/past history *Past* is clearly redundant in *past history*, because by definition history is past. It is redundant, too, in *past experience* if the context indicates past time; however, experience may also be present or future. Redundant: "Past experience has shown us . . ." Satisfactory: "Past experience is not a sure forecaster of future experience." *Past* can be omitted as a modifier of *accomplishments*, *records*, or other words clearly referring to past time. See also RECORD.

pastor See MINISTER/PASTOR/PREACHER . . .

PATHETIC FALLACY See EMPATHY/SYMPATHY.

patsy, pushover No single standard word carries quite the meaning of these two words customarily considered slang: "a gullible person; one who is easily deceived, imposed on, or cheated; one who is too softhearted for his own good." Unless a "better" word comes along, *patsy* or *pushover* will continue in occasional use in SWE.

pavement/sidewalk **1.** To many English people and some Americans, *pavement* means the (often concrete) path where pedestrians walk beside a street. The usual American term for that, however, is *sidewalk*. These same Americans may refer to a paved road or other paved area as "the pavement" or sometimes "the concrete." Both words are SWE, but the context must clarify the intended meaning. **2.** *Pound the pavement* is FF (slang) for "walk the streets in search of work or some other objective."

pay boost/pay hike *Boost* and *hike* are good journalistic words that fit well into many headlines. Sedate writers not responsible for writing headlines prefer *increase in pay*. SWE is not always sedate.

peace/piece Columnist James Kilpatrick quotes from a West Virginia newspaper: "The residents there deserve a little piece and quiet at night." Probably the intended word is *peace* ("tranquillity, absence of hostilities or turmoil"). The basic meaning of *piece* is "a part of."

peaceable/peaceful A *peaceable* nation, such as Switzerland, is inclined toward peace and tries to promote it. A book called *The Peaceable Kingdom*, by Elizabeth Coatsworth, describes a place where "the child can walk unafraid in beauty and contentment." A *peaceful* nation is one that is not now at war. It may or may not always be peaceably inclined.

peculiar See ODD/PECULIAR/QUAINT . . .

pedagese See EDUCATIONESE, PEDAGESE.

pedal/peddle You *pedal* a bicycle, and *peddle* cosmetics or fresh fruit from door to door.

peer, peerless A *peer* is one's equal, not one's superior. Confusion arises because in England *peers* are the nobility, the *peerage*. A *peerless* person is so remarkable in some way that he or she has no equal.

pen name See ASSUMED NAME/PEN NAME/PSEUDONYM . . .; NOM DE PLUME.

Pennsylvania Dutch See DUTCH, DUTCHMAN.

penurious Has gradually shifted its meaning from "poverty-stricken" to "miserly." Although dictionaries include both definitions, most readers will interpret the word as equivalent to *stingy*. See also IMPECUNIOUS.

people/peoples/persons A rough distinction: If a count can be easily made or is important, SWE uses *persons*: "Only five other persons were in the house at the time of the murder." Otherwise, *people*: "Many people believe . . . ," "About forty people were present," "the people of Sweden." In some in-between instances, either word is appropriate: "a dozen or so people (*persons*) in the audience." *Peoples* is in a sense a plural of a plural. It refers to nations or other more or less homogeneous groups: "the peoples of Indo-European ancestry," "the peoples of Asia."

per each FF: "The fee is ten dollars per each enrollee." SWE prefers *per enrollee* or *for each enrollee*. See also A, AN/PER.

percent (110) Sports announcers and coaches like to say that an athlete "gave a hundred and ten percent." Impossible, says SWE, because no one can exceed his potential. Probably most of us perform at no more than 50 percent of potential, so maybe the announcer could say that the athlete "gave sixty (or even *one hundred*) percent."

percent/per cent/percentage SWE has a choice of *percent* or *per cent*. SANE recommends *percent*, which is similar in form to *percentage*. Examples of SWE: "7 percent" (not *seven*, except to start a sentence or report conversation). "Seven percent was considered a high rate." "Thirty percent of the people were poor" (note the plural verb). "A high percentage of the estate is taxable." "A high percentage of the children are in school." Note: *A high* (or *low*) *percentage of* is frequently only a wordy way of saying *many, much, few,* or *little*.

perfect Logically, nothing can be more perfect than perfect. For example, if a perfect score is 100, no score can be higher or "more perfect." The framers of the U.S. Constitution, however, referred to a "more perfect union," so insistence on banning that expression would be unconstitutional. In most minds, *perfect* means no more than "extraordinarily good," and dictionaries include one definition like "unusually delightful or excellent: 'a perfect day'." It is sad, though, that English has no single word that means "without blemish, fault, or error." Many writers of SWE do restrict *perfect* to that sense. SANE applauds. See also COMPARISON OF ABSOLUTES.

perhaps See MAYBE/PERHAPS.

persecute/prosecute To *persecute* is to harass persistently over a long period of time: "For years the Romans persecuted the Christians." *Prosecute*, a mainly legal term, means "to take action against, especially in court": "A prosecuting attorney leads the action against the defendant."

-person Words such as *chairman, fireman,* and *policeman* are misleading, because many women serve in such positions. But the once recommended *chairperson* is no better (try *chair*), and *fireperson* and *policeperson* are much less desirable than *firefighter* and *police officer*. See also CHAIR/CHAIRPERSON; PEOPLE/PEOPLES/PERSONS.

personal, personally SWE usually omits *personal* and *personally* from expressions like these: "I personally believe," "my own personal opinion," "during my personal visit to them," "my personal friend," "I myself personally," "personally, I think . . ."

persons See PEOPLE/PEOPLES/PERSONS.

perspective/prospective *Perspective*, a noun, means "point of view": "From my perspective, the Supreme Court's decision appears wrong." The word also has technical meanings in art, architecture, and other fields. *Prospective*, an adjective, means "in prospect, expected": "Prospective profits were in the thousands."

persuade See CONVINCE/PERSUADE.

peruse If you *peruse* a document, you read it more carefully than you do, say, today's paper.

pessimistic See OPTIMISTIC/PESSIMISTIC; FAVORABLE/UNFAVORABLE.

petty See PALTRY/PETTY/TRIVIAL.

phenomenal Too strong a word for occurrences or things that are merely strange or unusual. For example, despite the hyperbole of sports announcers and writers, only a few athletic accomplishments are *phenomenal*.

phenomenon The SWE plural is *phenomena*, which FF sometimes then treats as a singular. SWE: "A phenomenon is . . . ," "Several phenomena are . . ."

philologist See LEXICOGRAPHER/LINGUIST/PHILOLOGIST.

philosophy "Coach Ramsay likes the gang-tackle philosophy." *Philosophy* is too intellectual a word here. SWE uses *strategy, tactic, system, method*, or other down-to-earth words for such a down-to-earth result. *Philosophy* refers essentially to thoughtful analysis and classification of fundamental principles of human life.

phlegm See MUCUS/PHLEGM.

-phobia See -MANIA/-PHOBIA.

phony Once regarded as slang for "false, not genuine, pretentious," *phony* has moved to SWE.

picky Most dictionaries call *picky* informal. But "picky eater" has existed for over a century, and such terms as *fastidious* and *excessively meticulous* are too high-sounding for the things that people are usually picky about. SWE uses *picky* or *choosy* for small things such as scraping off the anchovies and refusing to eat any cheese other than Brie. For matters of greater moment, such as selecting a new car, a bigger word may be appropriate.

piece See PEACE.

piece of the action This is FF (slang) for "chance to make a profit," "chance to take part in a (possibly illegal) activity": "Deal me in, boys. I want a piece of the action."

pier See DOCK/PIER/WHARF.

pig This is a hostile FF (slang) term for *police officer*.

pincers See CLIPPERS/PINCERS/PLIERS . . .

pinch hit, pinch hitter Standard in baseball, and broadened occasionally in other SWE to mean "substitute, temporarily replace."

pistol See AUTOMATIC/PISTOL/REVOLVER.

pizza pie SWE omits *pie*, because a pizza is a kind of Italian pie.

place 1. In SWE one *goes to* a place. FF: "We went many strange places." 2. In SWE, one places a thing *in* (or *inside*) another, seldom *into* it: "Place the folders in the cabinet."

place/put *Place* implies greater meticulousness than *put*. We carefully place pieces of crystal on shelves in a breakfront, and we put everyday glasses in a cabinet above the kitchen sink.

play down See DOWNPLAY.

play (it) by ear A figurative way to say "improvise": "She did not know what arguments her opponent would use, so she had to play it by ear." It appears in informal SWE. To a musician the meaning is different: "play music after hearing it but without reading a score": "My fiddler uncle couldn't read a note, but he played by ear dozens of country tunes." It is not uncommon in SWE.

playwright Like *shipwright* or *wheelwright*, this word ends in *wright*. (A *wright* is a person who makes or builds something. The word is not related to *write*.)

pleasantry A *pleasantry* is a light, often joking or bantering remark. The word is not a synonym of *pleasure* or *pleasantness*.

pleasure See HAPPINESS/PLEASURE.

plenteous/plentiful Interchangeable, although *plenteous* is less common and sounds like a word from old-fashioned poetry.

plenty In SWE use, *plenty* is a noun: "She has plenty of money." "Eden was a land of plenty." Not likely in SWE is "She has plenty money," or "The day was plenty hot."

plethora A *plethora* of something is not merely enough or even plenty. It is an excess, an overabundance, a superfluity, a supererogation, an overkill – like the plethora of words in this list.

pliers See CLIPPERS/PINCERS/PLIERS.

plight/predicament/quandary A *predicament* is an embarrassing or troublesome situation, sometimes with a slight element of danger: "My predicament was that my wife had already made a firm dinner engagement before my boss invited us to have dinner with his family." A *plight* is usually more serious, as the expression "a sorry plight" suggests: "Because of the fire and their lack of money, John's parents' plight worried him." A *quandary* is a state of uncertainty, often with several ways out, none of them pleasant. A satisfactory solution may require much thought or even be impossible. See also DILEMMA.

plurality See MAJORITY/PLURALITY.

plus 1. Overused in advertising for "besides": "Plus, you will receive at no extra charge . . ." The extensive use is attributable to the favorable connotation. 2. Note the singular verbs in "One plus one

189

equals two" and "His boldness plus his strength endears him to hero worshipers." In the first the meaning is "One added to one is two." The second *plus* is equivalent to *in addition to*. But note the plural verb in "His good looks plus his strength *endear* him to women," in which the subject is *good looks*.

+ (plus sign)/and/& (ampersand)   SWE avoids using a plus sign or an ampersand as a substitute for *and*.

P.M.   See A.M.

podium   See DAIS/LECTERN/PODIUM.

poet laureate   The SWE plural is *poets laureate*, but *poet laureates* is gaining.

190   **poetry/verse**   Although *poetry* and *poem* are widely used for anything that is not prose – especially if it has rhymes and short lines – the terms are usually applied in SWE to writings of high artistic quality. *Verse* is what many of us write as children, or as adults who like to see our literary efforts printed in a weekly rural newspaper or other publication whose editor uncritically calls our stuff "poetry."

point in time   In the Watergate hearings several witnesses repetitively said "at this (or *that*) point in time" instead of the more compact *today, now, at this (that) moment, then*, or the like. Although ridiculed in the press, the expression became widely used and still may be heard (less often seen) with annoying frequency. SWE generally abstains. See also AT THE PRESENT TIME/AT THIS TIME.

point of view   Sometimes wordy. SWE often shortens "My point of view is . . ." to "My opinion is . . . ," and "From my point of view, it seems . . ." becomes "I believe . . ."

point out   SWE employs *point out* when a statement is known to be factual or definitely provable: "The defendant pointed out that he was in Pocatello at the time of the murder." This is correct if evidence is available to prove the defendant's alibi. Otherwise *said, stated, asserted, declared, swore*, or the like is the SWE choice.

pointy   Slightly informal for "pointed": "a dog with a pointy tail." *Pointy head* is FF (slang) intended to ridicule someone whose intelligence or common sense is questioned.

poke   See BAG/POKE/SACK.

police (verb with)   *Police* is plural: "Our police are usually courteous." But *police force* is singular: "Our police force is the best in the state."

polite   See COURTEOUS/POLITE.

politic   See EXPEDIENT/POLITIC.

politician/statesman   A *politician* is anyone involved in politics, particularly party politics. Less frequently, it is anyone unusually knowledgeable about government. A politician may be or become a statesman, but statesmen are few. Most politicians are active on local and state levels. A *statesman* usually has national or international perspective. Another difference is that the statesman traditionally works for the public good rather than for personal or partisan benefit.

politick   This verb for "engage in political activity" or "attempt to influence by political maneuvers" is now SWE.

politics (verb with)   Singular when referring to the science or art of government: "Politics is his greatest concern." It is plural when equivalent to *political beliefs*: "My politics are of no significance to anyone else."

polyandry/polygamy/polygyny   *Polyandry* means "having more than one husband or male mate at a time"; *polygyny*, "having more than one wife or female mate at a time"; *polygamy*, "having more than one husband, wife, or mate at a time."

pooch   Flesch says, "A dog is a dog, but a pooch is a beloved friend." The *pooch* may be a mongrel or an animal with a dozen AKC champions in its pedigree. It's the affection between dog and person that makes a dog a pooch. The word is most likely to be used in conversations with family, friends, or the pooch, and so it is FF. See also DOG WHO.

poorly   FF (dialectal) for "ailing, unhealthy, in poor health, not feeling well (at this time)": "Pa's real poorly now."

popular   Not used in SWE with reference to only one person. FF: "Walter was never very popular with Susan." SWE says, "Susan was never very fond of Walter." However, Walter may or may not have been popular in his class or some other group.

populous   See NUMEROUS/POPULOUS.

pore/pour   When you *pore* over a book, you study it carefully. If you *pour* over a book, you may be putting water, coffee, or syrup on it.

port   See HARBOR/PORT; LEE/PORT/STARBOARD . . .

portray   Sometimes misused for *exemplify* or *illustrate*. To portray is to describe or picture: not "This gaunt child portrays the many now starving in Bangladesh." SWE chooses *exemplifies*, *typifies*, or *represents*.

position   See JOB/POSITION.

possess   This is sometimes a bit stiff. Would you rather "possess charm" or "be charming"? *Is possessed of* is usually only a wordy way to say *has*: not "He was possessed of a small upstate farm" but "He had (or *owned*) . . ." *Possessed by* (or *with*) is similar in meaning to "obsessed or dominated by": "possessed with a demon," "possessed by the age-old urge of the do-gooder." *Possessed* may also mean "calm, self-possessed": "Through the whole storm, Adele remained possessed, apparently unconcerned."

possible   SWE avoids "We thank the Stiver family members who made this reunion possible." It would have been *possible* without them. Instead, SWE says something like "who did all the hard work." Dubious: "Two possible suspects are . . ." Every suspect is possible. Illogical: "The firemen damaged the premises no more than possible." SWE chooses *necessary*.

possible/possibly   1. Logic argues that such *possible*'s as these should be *possibly*'s: "a possible broken arm," "a possible serious (or *fatal*) accident," "a possible dangerous encounter." **2.** *May possibly be* is redundant. SWE deletes *possibly* or writes *is possibly*. See also FEASIBLE/POSSIBLE.

postal card/postcard *Postal cards* are printed by the government and sold in post offices. *Postcards* (or *post cards*) may be purchased in many places, require stamps, and often have pretty pictures.

posted Informal for "informed": "Keep me posted about events in Keokuk." Found occasionally in SWE.

pot Sometimes used in SWE as an informal substitute for *marijuana*.

potluck "My wife isn't expecting company for dinner, but we'd both be delighted to have you take potluck." Although a cliché and not highly formal – probably because the meal isn't – *take potluck* is more compact than "eat with us but realize that no special preparations for guests have been made, so that the food, although nourishing, may be lower in quality than you would expect at the Four Seasons." It is SWE, as are *a potluck*, *potluck supper*, and so on.

pound the pavement See PAVEMENT/SIDEWALK.

pound See FOOT, HOUR, MILE . . .

practicable/practical If an idea is *practicable*, it is physically possible to carry it out. If it is also *practical*, it is sensible to do it. It may be practicable, but not practical, to build a bridge across the English Channel. It is both practicable and practical to lay the carpet before bringing in the grand piano.

practically/virtually Usually interchangeable, with *virtually* slightly preferred for "in effect" or "nearly." However, *practically* but not *virtually* may carry the meaning "in a way that is practical": "Practically, this task will be difficult, but theoretically it is simple."

praise See PANEGYRIC.

preacher See MINISTER/PASTOR/PREACHER . . .

precedence/precedents *Precedence* refers to priority in rank: "Automakers now assert that in their factories quality and safety take precedence over everything else." *Precedents* are acts or instances that may serve as examples or models when similar situations or legal cases arise: "Lawyers seek precedents that have bearing on the case now being tried."

precipitate (adjective)/precipitous *Precipitate* means "moving rapidly and recklessly," "impulsive, hasty": "Precipitate decisions are not characteristic of the Supreme Court." *Precipitous* is associated with *precipice* (cliff): "A precipitous area has several or many precipices." "A precipitous road or path down a mountain is dangerously steep."

predicament See PLIGHT/PREDICAMENT/QUANDARY.

PREDICATE NOMINATIVE See IT'S I/IT'S ME.

predict See PROPHECY/PROPHESY.

predilection A *predilection* is always in favor of someone or something, never against. It is equivalent to *preference*. Washington Irving referred to "her predilection for my powerful rival." See also BIAS; PREJUDICE.

preface See FOREWORD/INTRODUCTION/PREFACE.

prefer (*rather than* **vs.** *to* **or** *over*) When followed by an infinitive, usage is "I prefer to watch golf *rather than* to play it." When followed by anything else: "I prefer tennis *to* (or *over*) golf." "I prefer swimming *to* (or *over*) hiking."

preference See PREDILECTION.

pregnant Before this age of sexual frankness, *pregnant* was almost as taboo a word as *intercourse*, except in talking with one's doctor or good friends. Kindly euphemisms such as "in a family way" were numerous, and coarser expressions such as the Americanism "knocked up" were not uncommon. Today squeamishness is regarded as absurd, and some pregnant women wear shirts boasting "Baby soon" or providing the information "It all started one night."

prejudice See BIAS/PARTIALITY/PREJUDICE.

premiere (verb) Formerly condemned, but now SWE in expressions such as "The play will premiere in April" or "They premiered the play in April."

premise, premises The singular means "basis underlying an argument": "His major premise is . . . ," "Your premise is incorrect." The plural refers to land or buildings: "These premises are closed to the public." (*This premise* is not used in SWE for this sense.)

premonition/presage/prescience/presentiment A *premonition* is a feeling which warns that something unpleasant may happen. Since it is a warning, action may yet be taken to avoid the trouble. A *presentiment* is similar but may lack the element of warning. It is a feeling that something (perhaps good) will occur and is unavoidable. *Prescience* is ordinarily based more on knowledge than on feelings. A stockbroker with prescience can often interpret clues showing what the market will do next. *Foresight* is a synonym. *Presage* may be a noun or, more often, a verb. Anything presaged is unpleasant – a foreboding, premonition, bad omen.

prepared to admit (or *deny***)** Lawyer: "My client is prepared to admit (or *deny*) being in the room." That shouldn't require much preparation. SWE recommends "My client admits (or *denies*) . . ." or ". . . will admit (or *deny*) . . ."

PREPOSITION AT END When an aide dared to question one of Churchill's sentences that ended with *of* or *with*, Sir Winston reportedly roared, "This is the sort of nonsense up with which I will not put." Questions such as "Where did he come from?" or "What did she work with?" are SWE because the alternatives are awkward. So are alternatives to many SWE statements, such as "That is what he hopes you will talk about." Two sorts of final prepositions are avoided in SWE: (1) Redundant: "Where is she going *to*?" "Where is it *at*?" (2) Resulting in weak endings: "That is the question that he hopes to find an answer *to*." SWE: "That is the question he hopes to answer."

PREPOSITIONS (OTHER TROUBLE SPOTS) **1.** Pronouns as objects: In SWE a pronoun as object of a preposition is in the objective case. Confusion sometimes arises, however, when a noun or a second pronoun is near the first. Actually, the added word makes no grammatical difference and should be ignored in choosing the case form. So *with Jim and me* and *from her and him* are standard, as is *between you and me*. Good teachers ask, "What pronoun would you use if *Jim and* were not in your sentence? That's the one you still need." **2.** Redundancy: Examples of redundant prepositions besides those in the entry above are "off *of*," "remember *of*," "opposite *to*," "inside *of*," "amount *up* to." SWE omits each italicized preposition. **3.** Verbiage: Some prepositional phrases, rather long and ungainly, are avoided in SWE; for example, "antecedent to" (*before*), "in connection with" (*concerning*), "in the case of" (*as to*), "previous(ly) to" (*before* or *earlier*), "with the intention of" (*intending to*). **4.** Omission: Often two or more words are to be related to another word. Logic determines whether more than one preposition is needed. In "They fired from the tower and the parapet," the preposition *from* may logically serve both *tower* and *parapet*. But in "The children played in the water and the beach," since the children did not play *in* the beach, the missing *on* should be supplied. There is a tendency in FF to omit a preposition after some verbs with which it is required in standard usage; for example, SWE prefers "She graduated *from* college," "He was operated *on* yesterday," "Our minister officiated *at* the ceremony." **5.** Strung-together phrases. Poor: "In theory, at the conclusion of an investigation of this sort made during unusual circumstances of stress and with immoderate delays, an investigator of normal honesty and with due regard to the ethics of his position . . ." Although sentences with six or eight prepositional phrases are not uncommon, stringing together as in this example makes for hard reading. SWE condenses and often divides.

prerogative/privilege A *prerogative* is a privilege officially granted to someone because of rank or accomplishment. An absolute monarch, for example, has or assumes some prerogatives that an ordinary king or a mere president does not have. A *privilege* is an advantage, consideration, or benefit that may be permitted with or without reason, fairly or unfairly. In school, some of a child's privileges may be withdrawn because of misconduct. Doing so is the teacher's or an administrator's prerogative.

present incumbent An incumbent is a person at present holding an office or position. SWE deletes *present* as redundant.

present writer "The present writer first saw this rare moth in Costa Rica." As a minimum, SWE deletes *present*. Unless for good reason it is necessary to avoid first person pronouns, it changes *the present*

194

writer to *I*. In a scientific paper, the passive voice is frequent: "This rare moth was first observed by the investigator in Costa Rica." See also **PASSIVE VOICE**.

presidential/president's SWE reserves *presidential* for reference to a president's official roles, acts, or demeanor, not to his or her private life: "a presidential pardon (or *decision, task*)." "The presidential daughter" becomes "the president's daughter."

presume See ASSUME/PRESUME.

pretense/pretext Although it is possible to use the words interchangeably, *pretense* in SWE generally means "the act of pretending, a bit of make-believe, affectation." It implies some sort of action: "the child's pretense that she is a great dancer." A *pretext* is an excuse; it is words, not acts: "His pretext for his absence was that his brother had needed help in moving."

195

PRETENTIOUSNESS Some writers hide little thoughts in big words. They distrust the simple and straightforward, admire the high-flown and the circumlocutious. Perhaps their houses are decorated with gingerbread; anyhow, their prose is. They say *due to the fact that* for *because, in company with* for *with* or *along with*. They *shed gobbets of perspiration* when other people *sweat*, their *lachrymal glands become active* when others *cry*, and they *keep an engagement at the studio* when others *go to get a picture taken*. They put on thick wigs and long cloaks to hide their littleness. See also MATUTINAL ABLUTIONS.

pretty (adverb) As in "pretty good," "pretty reasonable," *pretty* means "rather, somewhat." It is now SWE except in highly formal writing.

prevaricate See EQUIVOCATE.

prevent See AVERT/AVOID/PREVENT; ELIMINATE/PREVENT; HINDER/PREVENT.

preventative, preventive See INTERPRETATIVE, INTERPRETIVE/PREVENTATIVE, PREVENTIVE.

previously to/prior to Both are somewhat stilted for *before*, but they seem less so in references to important events and considerable periods of time: "Even prior (or *previous*) to the Civil War, disagreements between North and South had involved many issues besides slavery." (With *previously*, *to* can often be omitted.)

price (adjective with) In SWE a price is *low* or *high*, not *cheap* or *dear*. *Dear* is now seldom used with reference to cost. An item, but not its price, may be described as *cheap*: "a cheap pair of shoes," "a low price for these shoes."

pride See ARROGANCE/CONCEIT/HAUGHTINESS . . .

principal/principle *Principle* is always a noun. Some writers associate its *-le* with the *-le* of *rule*: "The principle underlying the operation of this machine is . . . ," "a woman with firm principles." *Principal* is an adjective or a noun. As an adjective it means "main, most important": "the principal reason (or *difficulty, player*)." As a noun, it still retains the idea of "most important": A school principal is the principal teacher. In banking, a principal is the principal sum of money, in contrast to the usually smaller interest.

printing See EDITION/IMPRESSION, PRINTING.

prior to See PREVIOUSLY TO/PRIOR TO.

prison See JAIL/PRISON.

privilege See PREROGATIVE/PRIVILEGE.

pro Informal for *professional, pro* someday may replace the longer word in most contexts. Headline writers are preparing the way.

proceed 1. SWE doesn't use *proceed* when *go* is meant. It's highfalutin in "Let's proceed to the shack for a sandwich." Normally *proceed* means "to move on after a stop, to go on": "The next morning the soldiers proceeded toward Arras." "After the judge admonished counsel for the defense, the trial proceeded." 2. SWE uses *proceed*, not *proceed on* (*ahead, onward*).

procure This is pompous for *get*; besides, it may carry a sexual connotation because of its kinship with *procurer, procuress.* (A university that had a sign saying "Procurer's Office" soon changed it to "Purchasing Office.")

prodigal Although the biblical prodigal son wandered around while spending his money foolishly, *prodigal* means "squandering" rather than "wandering." It refers to waste, extravagance, being a spendthrift: "Throughout our history we have been prodigal of our resources."

profanity See OBSCENITY/PROFANITY.

profession See OCCUPATION/PROFESSION/TRADE.

progenitor It is not accurate to say that clavichords and harpsichords were *progenitors* of pianos; they were precursors or early forms. Nor was the builder of the first true piano its progenitor; he was an inventor. A progenitor is an ancestor of something animate. Among your progenitors are your parents and grandparents. A progenitor of the modern horse was the eohippus.

progressive *Progressive* is ordinarily what semanticists call a "purr-word" (in contrast to a "snarl-word"), a vaguely commendatory word that seldom defines "progress" or indicates its features. Most politicians want to be considered progressive or "modern" – certainly not reactionary – but each defines the word for himself. SWE users of the word try to make clear the goal toward which they or someone else hopes to progress.

promptitude *Promptness* is a virtue.

prone/prostrate/supine *Prone* means "lying face down"; *prostrate,* "lying face down," but suggesting weakness, helplessness; *supine,* "lying face up" (the *up* in *supine* may be a reminder).

PRONOUNS (PERSONAL) See various entries for I, ME, WE, US; YOU, YOUR(S); HE, SHE, IT, HIM, HER, THEY, THEM.

proof The label on a liquor bottle says "Eighty proof." That does not mean that 80 percent of the liquor is alcohol. Divide by two. "Eighty proof" is 40 percent. See also EVIDENCE/PROOF.

propaganda   Although *propaganda* may be anything used to gain support for a belief or doctrine, it now almost always is interpreted to mean that the belief or doctrine is "bad" or at least is opposed to what we "good" people support. We say that the enemy spreads propaganda but that our side offers facts or information or "the truth."

prophecy/prophesy   *Prophecy*, a noun, means "a prediction": "The unbelievable prophecy was coming true." *Prophesy*, a verb, means "to predict": "The witches had prophesied that Macbeth would become king." *Predict* is preferable to *prophesy* for statements based on fact or logic rather than inspiration or supernatural help. Weather forecasters *predict* or *forecast*; they do not *prophesy*. Old Testament prophets, often claiming to be inspired by Jehovah, prophesied.

197

proponent/supporter   *Proponent* may mean either "one who proposes" (e.g., a legislative bill) or "one who advocates." A *supporter*, ordinarily less active, seldom proposes anything and usually makes few or no public statements. His or her support more likely comes from contributing money or small amounts of time, making statements to family and friends, or perhaps being just one face in a crowd that shares similar feelings or beliefs. See also PROTAGONIST.

proportions   See DIMENSIONS/PROPORTIONS.

proposal/proposition   It is useful for a woman (or, today, a man) to know the difference: a *proposal* of marriage vs. a *proposition* for a merely sexual relationship. In business a proposition is normally more detailed and specific than a proposal. Thus a proposal may suggest that two companies share the cost of developing a new product, but a proposition specifies the responsibilities of each partner. In FF, *proposition* may mean almost anything: "Baseball is sometimes a funny proposition." No, but it can be a funny game, says SWE.

prosaic   Although *prosaic* in its early uses meant merely "in prose rather than in verse," the word has pejorated to suggest dullness, lack of imagination. Even though novelists write prose, they do not want their creations described as prosaic.

prosecute   See PERSECUTE/PROSECUTE.

prospective   See PERSPECTIVE/PROSPECTIVE.

prostate/prostrate   The *prostate* gland, surrounding part of the male urethra, is often miscalled *prostrate*. *Prostrate* means lying face down, usually after an attack of some sort. See also PRONE/PROSTRATE/SUPINE.

protagonist   There can be only one protagonist ("leading figure") in a novel, play, or other activity. So "two protagonists" and "the main protagonist" are unlikely in SWE. SWE distinguishes *protagonist* from *proponent* or *advocate*. See also PROPONENT/SUPPORTER.

protestant The word associated with religion is capitalized and pronounced *Prot*-us-tunt. An identical word, with small *p* and pronounced pro-*tes*-tunt, means "protester," but it has almost died out because of confusion with *Protestant*. Let it die, says SANE.

prototype See ARCHETYPE/PROTOTYPE.

proved/proven Interchangeable as past participle: "Botanists have proved (or *proven*) that . . ." *Proved* is more frequent. SANE asks, Why perpetuate unnecessary irregular and therefore confusing forms?

proverbial A football announcer reports that "Smith is in the proverbial doghouse of Coach Paterno." Who has ever heard a proverb about that doghouse? Possible: *well-known, infamous* (or no modifier at all). Unless *proverbial* refers to an actual proverb, it is of little use.

provided that/providing that Interchangeable, although conservatives prefer *provided*, without *that*. Often *if* carries the same meaning. When that is true, SWE generally chooses *if*.

PRO-WORD Sometimes called a "counterword," and seldom listed in dictionaries, a pro-word is a readily available but vague word used instead of a precise term. Many slang words, much profanity, and some standard words are pro-words: "*lousy* weather," "a *cute* dress," "*damn(ed)* hot," "cold *as hell*," "great," "super," "neat," "some deal," "case," "aspect," "factor."

prude Not necessarily a woman.

pseudonym See ASSUMED NAME/PEN NAME/PSEUDONYM; NOM DE PLUME.

psyche/psych *Psyche*, standard as a noun, is pronounced *sy*-kee and means "soul or spirit but not body" (psychiatrists have a more technical definition). From the noun an FF (slang) verb *psych* (pronounced *sike*) has developed. Alone, it means "use psychology on": "He psyched me." With *up*, it means "increase readiness or excitement": "I was psyched up about my vacation." With *out*, it means "bother emotionally or mentally": "She psyched me out by claiming to be pregnant." Although *psych* and *psych up* or *out* occur rarely in SWE, their brevity makes them candidates for greater use.

psychedelic A relatively new word, now SWE, that became entrenched in the 1960s. The drug subculture defined this adjective as "consciousness-raising, mind-expanding, mind-blowing, mood-enhancing." The medical profession defined it as "causing hallucinations, distorted vision, and possibly psychotic states."

psychiatrist/psychologist Both study the mind. A *psychologist*, usually a PH.D., may give people personal advice or therapeutic help. A *psychiatrist*, usually an M.D., specializes in diagnosis and treatment or prevention of mental illness.

psychological moment Although the *Dictionary of Behavioral Science* has no entry for this term, other dictionaries define it to this effect: "the time when a person's mental [and emotional] state is especially likely to produce the desired effect." In this sense the term is useful. SWE does not employ it, however, when no one's mental or emotional state is involved. This is not SWE: "The factory had reached the psychological moment when almost half of the equipment needed replacement."

public (verb with) Today the verb is almost always singular, but earlier writers made a subtle and worthwhile distinction. They used a singular to refer to the whole group: "The public is wiser than the wisest critic" (historian George Bancroft). The plural was used to signify the many individuals: "The public have neither shame nor gratitude" (essayist William Hazlitt). See also GENERAL PUBLIC.

puerile See BOYISH/PUERILE; JUVENILE/PUERILE.

pull one's weight Cliché, but still SWE. The extended meaning of this rowing term is "do the amount of work that is fair in proportion to the amount of compensation." It is better to write "pull one's weight" instead of about fifteen words.

punch-drunk For "acting in a dazed manner," *punch-drunk* has been listed as standard in American dictionaries for twenty years or more.

punctilious/punctual A *punctilious* person is precise and careful, especially with matters of conduct and etiquette: "Martin kept his procedures manual always at hand and adhered punctiliously to every regulation." A *punctual* person is exact in timing, being especially careful not to be late: ". . . arrived punctually for her nine o'clock interview." see also METICULOUS/PUNCTILIOUS/SCRUPULOUS.

pupil/student As ordinarily used by most teachers, a *pupil* is a child enrolled in elementary school, or anyone studying music or another art under a master: "Franz Liszt was a pupil of Antonio Salieri." *Student* also has two chief definitions: (1) a person enrolled in a secondary school, college, or university, and (2) anyone studying a subject independently. Even an octogenarian can be a student – in either sense.

purebred/thoroughbred Used interchangeably by most people, although some stock raisers prefer *thoroughbred* for horses, *purebred* for other animals. On rare occasions, a person of high integrity or courage is called a "thoroughbred," but probably never a "purebred."

puritanic/puritanical SANE recommends *puritanic*. The word is capitalized only when referring to the specific group known as Puritans.

PURPLE PASSAGE Also called *purple patch*, this term refers to a short section of prose or poetry that exhibits a noticeably heightened style. An author who perhaps has been writing almost ploddingly comes to something that moves him deeply, and he flings himself through his whole show of rhetorical tricks: highly figurative language, emotionality, complicated parallelism and inversion, five-dollar words. True, a heightening of style or change in rhythm or manner of expression is often desirable for a special effect. If overdone, though, heightening becomes a purple patch that distracts the reader and lowers the quality.

purposefully/purposely   *Purposely* means "intentionally": "Craig purposely tripped an opponent"; *purposefully*, "having a strong purpose," "with determination": "Knowing that the peaches must be picked in one day, the crew worked purposefully, with almost no time out."

pusher   Dictionaries label *pusher* slang for "seller of illicit drugs." But what standard word carries that meaning? The frequency of drug sales has resulted in more-than-occasional use of *pusher* in SWE.

pushy   Occasional in informal SWE for "too forward or aggressive."

pushover   See PATSY, PUSHOVER.

put up with   SWE for "endure," "accept (something unpleasant) with resignation": "She learned to put up with her drunken husband."

put down   FF (slang) for "demean, deprecate, suggest inferiority": "Why do you always put me down in front of your friends?" The informal noun *put-down*, meaning "a belittling statement," is related: "He said she looked OK – a real put-down, she thought." *Put-down* is SWE for "the landing of an aircraft."

put (someone) on   FF (slang) for "tease, mock, deceive": "You must be putting me on." The related noun *put-on* means "hoax, deception."

put   See PLACE/PUT.

pygmy   See DWARF/MIDGET/PYGMY.

Q

quaint   See ODD/PECULIAR/QUAINT . . .

qualification(s)   SWE makes sure that readers can immediately understand which of two definitions is intended: (1) "reservation(s)," as in "I accepted the offer but with some qualifications," or (2) "background, experience, training, ability," as in "This candidate's qualifications are unusually good." Ambiguous: "Voters should cast their votes for this true son of Texas, George Jones, without any qualifications."

qualified expert   One cannot be an expert if not qualified. A similar comment applies to *trained expert*. SWE deletes the modifier.

qualitative   Does not mean "of high quality." "Qualitative tests" are not necessarily good tests; they are tests of quality – whether high, mediocre, or low.

quandary   See PLIGHT/QUANDARY.

quartet   *Quartet*, as well as *trio* and other such words, is used in SWE mainly when members of the group are trained to act together: "a string quartet," "the championship (basketball) quintet from Indiana," but not "the trio of escaped convicts," who probably had not received specific training.

queer See ODD/PECULIAR/QUAINT . . .

question as to whether Many sentences with this phrase should be shortened. For example, "Some Japanese legislators raised the question as to whether social science textbooks did not lean too far left" could be reduced to "Some Japanese legislators asked whether social science textbooks leaned too far left."

quick/quickly All modern dictionaries say that *quick*, like *slow*, is standard as either an adjective or an adverb. The adverb is most likely in short, conversational sentences: "Come quick!" but seldom occurs in SWE. *Quickly* is more common in longer, less conversational sentences: "Congress is moving quickly toward adjournment."

quieten Some British writers prefer *quieten*, but the verb *quiet* is more likely in the United States.

quite A few conservatives still insist that *quite* should be used only for "entirely, altogether," as in "quite correct." But a different meaning, "rather, fairly, moderately," has been added: "quite warm, quite studious." Unfortunately, the result is sometimes ambiguity. For example, is a "quite satisfactory report" altogether satisfactory or only moderately so? How low is a "quite revealing décolletage"? The damage has been done but is being somewhat repaired by the gradual decrease in use of the older definition. SWE makes sure that readers can understand which definition is meant.

quite a **1.** SWE usually selects more specific expressions than *quite a while, quite a game, quite an exciting time.* **2.** *Quite a few*, oddly, means "a lot." Because of the oddness, some writers dislike it, but it is established idiom, listed as standard in leading dictionaries. Like other *quite a* expressions, however, it is not very specific.

quiz Standard noun among students for "a short test." Standard verb, perhaps overused by some journalists, for "interrogate, question at length." It occurs occasionally in SWE.

quotation by SWE avoids "The United States is a society 'where it is safe to be unpopular.' This quotation by Adlai Stevenson suggests . . ." The sentence is not a quotation by Stevenson, because he wrote it – he didn't quote it. It is a *statement* by him, and as used here it is a *quotation from* him.

quote/quotes *Quote* is informal for "quotation": "Did you get a quote from the candidate?" *Quotes* is informal for "quotation marks": "You forgot to put quotes around this." For each, SWE generally uses the complete term. See also CITE/QUOTE.

q.v. Abbreviated from Latin *quod vide* ("which see"). Less used than before to indicate a cross reference; today *see* or *see also* is usual, even in much scholarly writing. A few reference books retain it: "Because of the Treaty of Utrecht (*q.v.*) . . . ," but others substitute an asterisk or other symbol.

R

rack/wrack   SWE customarily uses *wrack* in *wrack and ruin*, and with the meaning "a tangle of seaweed," but *rack* for all other meanings.

radical   Not necessarily an unfavorable word, *radical* in its original sense means, as a noun, "one who attempts to get at the root of a problem"; a radical solution may be an attempt to dig down to the roots. Some uninformed readers, it is true, will misinterpret the word to mean "left wing."

raise/rear   Older convention decreed that one raises animals, poultry, or grain, but rears children. Today most Americans *raise* children, although *rear* is still sometimes retained in SWE.

rambunctious   The word may have started as Irish slang or may have been derived from the Latin word for "robust." It became American slang and then informal American and is now also humorous SWE.

range   "A wide range of people" is almost meaningless. Is the range in age, income, health, geographic location, eye color, or what?

rap   FF (slang or dialectal) for "talk."

rape   See ATTACK; CRIMINALLY ASSAULTED.

rare/scarce   As a rule, only items of value and high quality are *rare*: "as rare as undiscovered Rembrandts." Things normally more common may become *scarce*: "Pork chops are scarce in the market right now." "Bargains in shoes are scarce."

rarely ever, seldom ever   FF (informal, illogical). SWE: *rarely, rarely if ever, rarely or never, hardly ever, almost never; seldom, seldom if ever, seldom or never.*

rascal   See KNAVE/RASCAL/ROGUE.

rate   For "deserve" as in "He rates a high mark for such a performance," or for "have influence" as in "He really rates in this office," *rate* hovers between informal and SWE. It is unlikely in highly formal contexts.

rather   Use of this word always – intentionally or not – reduces the strength of whatever is modified. A "rather pretty girl" is less attractive than a "pretty girl." With some words the weakening is so great that illogicality results: "a rather superb performance." *Had rather* and *would rather* are interchangeable.

rather than   What is on the right side of *rather than* in SWE ordinarily is grammatically parallel to what is on the left. So: "tried to *dodge* the question rather than *answer* it" (not *answering*); "tried *dodging* the question rather than *answering* it" (not *answer*). If awkwardness results from such parallelism, SWE rephrases. SWE avoids the combination of *more* with *rather than*: not "She tried more for financial success rather than for integrity in her writing." SWE omits either *more* or *rather*. See also PREFER . . . RATHER THAN.

rational/rationale   *Rational*, an adjective, means "able to reason," "sane," "able to talk rather sanely," "logical." *Rationale*, a noun, means "a logical basis": "She has a rationale for everything she does"; or "an expression of reasons or principles": "Where is the rationale underlying this decision?"

rattle (verb)   Long considered slang, *rattle* is now SWE, although informal, in the sense of "unnerve, fluster": "The mishap with the food processor rattled him."

ravage/ravish   To *ravage* is to destroy, devastate: "The invading army ravaged the crops and the farm buildings." Infrequently, *ravish* has the same meaning; historian John L. Motley wrote, "The Spaniards had ravished the city." Ordinarily, however, it means "to rape," "to carry away," or "to enchant, to entrance." So a criminal may conceivably ravish a woman in any of three ways, although *entrance* is least likely. If we say that a woman is a ravishing beauty, we mean that she is entrancing.

203

re   See IN RE.

re- + again or back   A student writes a rough draft of a paper, copies it, and – perhaps because of some smudges – recopies it. He does not *recopy* it *again* unless there is a second recopying. Similarly, one does not *repeat again* or *redo again* unless one has previously repeated or redone. *Back* is redundant in expressions such as *return back* and *revert back*; usually also in *refer back*, but in that expression *back* may sometimes aid clarity.

reaction/response   In careful use, a *reaction* is usually quicker, more automatic or more emotional, and less thoughtful than a *response*. A response often offers a reasoned opinion, but when a reaction is an expression of opinion, it is generally one that is preconceived or echoed.

real   **1.** Informal as an adverb: "real tired, (*happy, pleasant,* and so on)." SWE usually omits it, or substitutes *really, very, greatly, highly,* or another suitable adverb. **2.** In *real facts, actual facts,* or *true facts,* SWE deletes *real, actual, true*. See also VERY.

real novelty   Is *real* needed? Sometimes yes, sometimes no. If something is actually a novelty, nothing like it has been seen before.

realistic   **1.** *Realistic* means "true to life, seeing or describing things as they really are." It does not mean "ugly, sordid, unpleasant." Things that are ugly may of course be described realistically, but so may beautiful things. **2.** In bargaining sessions, the proposals we favor are always "realistic," but obviously those we dislike are "unrealistic."

realm, sphere, world   If tempted to write "in the realm (*sphere, world*) of business (or *sports,* and the like)" an SWE writer checks to see whether "in business (*sports*)" will suffice.

Realtor   By no means can all real-estate agents legitimately be called "Realtors." As a registered trademark, it applies only to members of the National Association of Real Estate Boards, which prefers also that the word be capitalized. Members of the public are more likely to misuse the term than are representatives of real-estate firms.

rear (verb)   See RAISE/REAR.

reason/cause   See CAUSE/REASON.

reason is because   Disliked by conservatives, this expression is gaining favor. The usual SWE is "The reason for the delay was that (not *because*) a train was blocking the street."

reason why   Concerning "that is the reason why," conservatives correctly point out that *why* is unnecessary. Yet Tennyson, a poet respected by many conservatives, wrote about the soldiers called "the six hundred": "Theirs not to reason why, / Theirs but to do and die." If it's good enough for Tennyson . . . ? *Reason why* is established in sentences such as "The reason why the secretary of state made the comment is that . . ." SWE with or without the *why*.

reasons   SWE dislikes a construction in which a noun modifies *reasons*: "for courtesy reasons," "for politics reasons." SWE substitutes "for reasons of courtesy" or, better, "to be courteous"; "for reasons of health" or "because of his poor health"; "for political reasons."

rebellion/revolution   A *rebellion* is an uprising or revolt designed to effect a change of rules or even of government. If the rebellion succeeds and does indeed bring about large changes, it is called a "revolution." A *revolution* often enlarges the scope of the original rebellion.

rebound/redound   *Rebound* ("to bounce back") is sometimes misused for *redound* ("to have a good or bad effect"). SWE says, "A politician's name-calling sometimes redounds to his opponent's advantage by building sympathy."

rebuff   Headline: "Governor's Proposal Rebuffed." This is possibly SWE, but ordinarily a person rather than a thing is rebuffed, and the verb carries a suggestion of contempt or scorn that may not have existed when the governor's proposal was rejected.

recap   I. SWE as noun or verb referring to a tire: "A recap is cheaper." "We cannot recap all tires." 2. It's informal but useful for *recapitulation* or *recapitulate*: "Here's a recap of the news." "Let me recap the story."

recapitulate/repeat/summarize   To *repeat* is to say or do something again. To *recapitulate* or to *summarize* is to repeat in a shorter form. The word is based on Latin for "head," and a recapitulation gives basically the "headings," the main points. *Summarize* may mean the same thing but instead may refer to some other method of presenting a concise version, such as combining several points in a sentence or two.

receive   Sometimes pretentious: "I got a bicycle for my birthday" is usually better than "I received . . ." "I received some cracked ribs in the accident" sounds silly. "Some of my ribs were cracked . . ." is more likely in SWE.

receptive   See ACCEPTIVE/RECEPTIVE.

recital See CONCERT/RECITAL.

recollect/remember Usually considered interchangeable, *recollecting* may require more effort than *remembering*: "I am trying to recollect what was said." Also, you may remember people in your will, but you do not recollect them.

recommend FF: "We recommend you to watch this program" (we are not recommending *you*). SWE says, "We recommend that you watch . . . ," "We recommend this program to you."

recondition/renovate Interchangeable, although *recondition* generally suggests mechanical items (cars, vacuum cleaners), and *renovate* often refers to nonmechanical things (sofas, fur coats, rooms). *Remodel*, *reconstruct*, and *restore* imply more thorough treatment than either of the other words.

recopy See RE- + AGAIN OR BACK.

record (noun) Although several writers on usage say that modifiers such as *new* should not be used with *record*, so many records are kept today that qualification is often needed. For example, we may have a February, seasonal, or all-time record; a local, county, state, national, or world record; or an old record that has just been supplanted by a new one. Of course, if *new* or another modifier is not needed for clarity, SWE avoids it. See also NEAR-RECORD; PAST EXPERIENCE.

rector See MINISTER/PASTOR/PREACHER . . .

redound See REBOUND/REDOUND.

reduce See DEPLETE/REDUCE.

refer See ALLUDE/REFER.

reform/re-form To *reform* is to make better, to reduce or eliminate flaws. To *re-form* is to form again: "She re-formed the clay to alter the shape of the nose." Words in which a hyphen makes a similar large difference include *re-claim*, *re-collect*, *re-cover*, *re-creation*, *re-dress*, *re-fuse*, *re-lay*, *re-mark*, *re-move*, *re-place*, *re-pose*, *re-present*, *re-search*, *re-sign*, *re-solve*, *re-sound*, *re-strain*, *re-treat*, *re-trench*, and some rare ones such as *re-tail* ("to re-tail a kite"). Some people prefer to write "claim again" and so on instead. See also RE- + AGAIN OR BACK.

refute Not the same as *deny*. In court a defendant may deny guilt, but denial alone cannot refute charges brought against him or her. Refuting requires proof. See also CONTRADICT.

regal See KINGLY/REGAL/ROYAL.

regret See DEPLORE/LAMENT/REGRET . . .

regular(ly) Not ordinarily required when another word in the sentence shows regularity: *hourly*, *daily*, *monthly*, and so on. See also FREQUENTLY/REGULARLY.

REIFICATION In allegory, characters such as "Good Deeds" put on human clothing and walk around for all to see. In old-fashioned poetic invocations, Inspiration was addressed as a living thing. In some metaphors, such as the familiar "Happiness is a warm puppy," an abstraction is again translated into something tangible. *Reification* (literally "the making of things") is the name given to any such alteration into something concrete. Reification is often a useful way to explain something difficult to grasp. One effective user of it is Robert Krulwich, who on television news programs clarifies economic concepts by showing such things as piles of thousand-dollar bills, partly filled containers, or people with funny hats or odd behavior. They may represent such abstractions as capital, scarcity or shortage, or greed.

rejoinder   See ANSWER, REPLY, RESPONSE . . .

relatively   Implies a comparison. In "Only a relatively small number of passengers can be accommodated," the smallness (or the number) is relative to what? SWE deletes *relatively* or (not helpfully) substitutes *rather*. More specific: "No more than twenty passengers can be accommodated." A satisfactory use, showing a comparison, is "After yesterday's frigid blasts, today's weather will be relatively warm and calm."

206

release   See DISCONTINUE/DISEMPLOY/RELEASE.

religious (noun)   Although a monk or a nun may accurately be called "a religious," the term may baffle some laypersons, as in "Several religious were in the audience." *Nuns* would be less likely to confuse.

relocated   "They relocated from Albany to Syracuse." Pretentious for *moved*.

remainder/rest   If *rest* is as clear as *remainder*, SWE prefers the shorter word. *Remainder*, suitable in business correspondence, elsewhere may have a rather cold, mathematical connotation. See also BALANCE.

remains (noun)   **1.** Outmoded (and unpleasant) for *corpse*: "His remains were dug up again." **2.** It is still used for "items left over": "The remains of her meal were (or *was*) still on the table." Not used with a specific number, such as "three remains," but is possible with *a few, some, many*.

remark   See COMMENT/OBSERVATION/REMARK.

remediable/remedial   "The problem is *remediable*" ("correctable"). "The child needs *remedial* instruction" ("intended to serve as a remedy").

remedy   See PANACEA/REMEDY.

remember   See RECOLLECT/REMEMBER.

remembrance/reminder/souvenir   A *remembrance*, when physical, is a token of a person generally recalled with affection: "She kept her aunt's Bible as a remembrance." A *reminder* is likely to be of temporary service: "She set the microwave oven for ten minutes, so that its beep would be a reminder to call Jerry." A *souvenir* (French for "memory") is usually a small item that serves to recall a place, occasion, or experience, now and then a person.

remunerate   SWE for "pay back, compensate for": "He will remunerate you for your loss." The word may also mean "pay," but here the shorter word is generally preferable: "I will remunerate (*pay*) you for the fruit tomorrow."

renaissance/renascence Each means "rebirth." However, *renaissance* (often capitalized) is the usual form for the "revival of learning" of A.D. c. 1300–1600, and *renascence* is usual for any other sort of rebirth or revival.

renovate See RECONDITION/RENOVATE.

renowned In the adjective, *-ed* is essential: "a renowned clarinetist."

reparable/repairable See IRREPARABLE.

repartee See ANSWER, REPLY, RESPONSE . . .

repast See PARTAKE.

repeat See RE- + AGAIN OR BACK; RECAPITULATE/REPEAT/SUMMARIZE.

repeat the same Redundant: "He repeats the same anecdotes whenever we see him." SWE prefers either "He tells the same anecdotes . . ." or "He repeats his anecdotes . . ."

207

repent See DEPLORE/LAMENT/REGRET.

repertoire/repertory Interchangeable. The French form is more likely in music: "Mehta's amazingly large repertoire."

replace This word is sometimes ambiguous. What does "Colonel Jordan replaced Major Armstrong" mean? Did the colonel take a post formerly occupied by the major? Did he give the post to another officer, or did he put Armstrong back on the job? In using *replace*, SWE tries to provide clarifying context.

replace/substitute (preposition with) One player, ingredient, and so on may be *replaced by* or *substituted for* another, but SWE does not interchange the prepositions: "Gray has been replaced by Johnson." "Johnson has been substituted for Gray."

replete Not just "full," but "abounding" or even "overflowing": "The kitchen was replete with the aromas of Christmas morning."

reply in the affirmative (or negative) Pretentious for *say yes* or *say no*.

reply See ANSWER, REPLY, RESPONSE . . .

reportedly "Over two hundred people reportedly died in the storm." This is standard journalese for "are reported to have died." Follett asks, "How does anyone reportedly die?" To avoid answering that difficult question, many careful writers say "may have died," or better, "Local officials estimate that over two hundred people died in the storm."

represent "Passenger pigeons represented a large part of the total bird population of North America." No. The pigeons did not represent anything. SWE is likely to choose *composed, constituted*, or even *were*.

reprisal/retaliation Both involve getting even, but *reprisal* is getting more than even. A *retaliation* may be a tooth for a tooth, but a reprisal adds a broken nose. Neither, of course, needs to be physical. For example, one nation may decide to impose higher tariffs on another as a retaliation for something, or impose even higher tariffs as a reprisal.

reputation See CHARACTER.

requisite See ESSENTIAL . . . MUST.

research Too often used for a simple action such as looking up a topic in an encyclopedia. Most high school or college "research papers" are, more accurately, "source papers" or "library papers." Research is scholarly or scientific investigation or inquiry. Only occasionally do young students' endeavors qualify.

reside See DWELL/LIVE/RESIDE.

resident See CITIZEN/INHABITANT/RESIDENT.

respectively "Ford, Mager, and Lamont live in Idaho, Wyoming, and Montana, *respectively*" means that Ford lives in Idaho, Mager in Wyoming, and Lamont in Montana. *Respectively* is sometimes meaningless and often unnecessary: "Her three daughters are Alice, Lucille, and Doris (respectively)." "The parrots flew to their (respective) perches."

response See ANSWER, REPLY, RESPONSE . . . ; REACTION/RESPONSE.

rest easy *Rest easy* has become SWE, not *rest easily*: "At last he could rest easy about money."

rest on one's laurels This is a cliché, but it is certainly more colorful than the equivalent "be satisfied without trying to accomplish anything more."

rest See REMAINDER/REST.

restive In earlier centuries *restive* meant only "obstinate, resistant to control": "a restive horse." In this century the word has come to signify mainly "restless, fidgety." Conservatives dislike the change, but it is here to stay.

restrain See CONSTRAIN/RESTRAIN.

resume See CONTINUE/RESUME.

retaliation See REPRISAL/RETALIATION.

reticent See LACONIC/RETICENT.

retire **1.** Slightly prim or stiff for "go to bed." **2.** *Retire back*, as in "The soldiers retired back from the outpost," is redundant.

retort See ANSWER, REPLY, RESPONSE . . .

retrospect(ion) See HINDSIGHT/RETROSPECT(ION).

return back See RE- + AGAIN OR BACK.

reveal See DISCLOSE/DIVULGE/REVEAL.

Revelation The name of the last book in the Bible is "The Revelation of St. John the Divine" – not "Revelations."

revelation See DISCLOSURE/REVELATION.

revenge See AVENGE/REVENGE.

Reverend Much disagreement here, but these classifications describe fairly well the present status: very formal – the Reverend Henry Blue; formal – Reverend Henry Blue, and Reverend Blue (for a later reference); FF – the reverend, the Reverend, Rev. Blue, the Rev. Blue; formal – the Reverend Blue and the Reverend White, the

Reverend Blue and White; informal or FF – the Reverends Blue and White; moving fast toward SWE – Rev. Henry Blue, Rev. Blue. In addressing a minister orally, Mr. or Dr. (when the title fits) seems to be replacing *Reverend* but not *Father*: "Good morning, Dr. Blue." "Good morning, Father Brown."

reverse   See CONVERSE/REVERSE.

revolution   See REBELLION/REVOLUTION.

revolve/rotate   Our moon *revolves* ("circles") around our planet, and Earth itself *rotates* ("turns on its axis") once in each twenty-four hours. The distinction is useful, but *revolve* is frequently used, both orally and in print, for both meanings.

revolver   See AUTOMATIC/PISTOL/REVOLVER.

reward   See AWARD/REWARD.

rhyme/rime   In the sense of "identity of sound," although *rime* is a variant of *rhyme*, most literary folk prefer the longer spelling. Both are SWE.

rich   See AFFLUENT/OPULENT/RICH . . .

riddle   See ENIGMA/RIDDLE.

right (adverb)   1. SWE for "precisely": "right here," "right now." 2. FF for "very": "right good," "right smart." 3. FF as a modifier of an adverb and with the meaning "somewhat" or "very": "right suddenly," "right sensibly." *Suddenly* or *sensibly* can do the job alone. 4. Sometimes found in SWE is *right away* for "soon" or "at once." FF for the same meaning: *right off.*

rile   Formerly regarded as a provincial pronunciation of *roil* ("to make angry, to vex"), *rile* now occurs occasionally in SWE: "Her frequent absences riled her employer."

rime   See RHYME/RIME.

Rio Grande river   Since *rio* means "river" in Spanish, SWE omits *river.*

rip-off   This slang noun or verb referring to robbery, fraud, profitable deception, illegal exploitation, and the like has moved from the underworld to the *Wall Street Journal* and the *New York Times*, where it generally refers to cheating by brokerage houses and big corporations. Dictionaries still call it slang, but it deserves at least a label of informal, and unless moneyed executives stop ripping people off, it will almost inevitably increase its presence in SWE.

rites   Any kind of ceremony, especially if solemn and religious, is a rite. The word is not a synonym of *funeral*: not "Rites will be held in the Baptist church," but "the funeral service," "obsequies" (a good nineteenth-century word), "funeral rites," or "last rites." *The service* or *services* also is not fully adequate as a synonym of *funeral.*

rob/steal   A person, bank, or store is *robbed*, but the money, clothing, or whatever is taken is *stolen.*

robbery   See BURGLARY/HOLDUP/ROBBERY.

209

rock/stone *Rock* and *stone* have a few specialized meanings, as in *bedrock* or *grindstone*. A diamond may be called a stone, but only in slang is it a rock. In general, however, the two words are interchangeable. There is no agreement, for example, about which is larger. Boys throw rocks at tin cans, but in the New Testament people threw stones at the woman taken in adultery.

rogue See KNAVE/RASCAL/ROGUE . . .

role/roll SWE: "a role in a play," "one's role in life"; "a roll of tape," "call the roll."

romance (verb) Informal in the sense "woo, make romantic love": "He romanced her with the usual flowers and jewelry." Its use is occasional in SWE.

rotate See REVOLVE/ROTATE.

round **1.** (adverb) Interchangeable with *around*, but the latter is more common: "stood around (less likely *round*) without talking." **2.** (preposition) Interchangeable with *around*, but perhaps slightly more informal: "sat round (or *around*) the campfire," "The earth moves round (or *around*) the sun." **3.** *Round* is written with no apostrophe. See also ABOUT/AROUND/ROUND; ALL-AROUND/ALL-ROUND; BULLET/CARTRIDGE/ROUND.

routine training exercise (or *mission*, and the like) Usually, *routine* can be deleted.

row (noun) For "a dispute, a quarrel," *row* is generally used for small altercations, not for major disagreements: " a family row" but probably not "a row between France and Germany." See also RUCKUS; SPAT.

royal See KINGLY/REGAL/ROYAL.

ruckus FF, occasionally SWE, for "a noisy disturbance." It refers to small commotions such as loud family quarrels or back-fence disputes. See also ROW; SPAT.

rudder See HELM/RUDDER/TILLER.

rude See CRUDE/RUDE.

rudimentary/vestigial A *rudiment* is the beginning stage of something: "Buttonlike projections on the young buck's head were rudimentary antlers." A *vestige* is a remaining trace of something that was once more fully developed: "The human vermiform appendix is a vestigial digestive organ."

rules and regulations One of the nouns is often enough.

rural/rustic *Rural* is a neutral word for "pertaining to the country or country people": "rural route (*atmosphere*, *life*)." *Rustic* has the same meaning but may carry either favorable or unfavorable connotations. Many people like rustic furniture, speak of "rustic charm," and believe that they would enjoy supposedly uncomplicated rustic life. But *rustic* is also used pejoratively to suggest backwardness, lack of education and sophistication, lack of awareness of "real life"; a person called a "rustic" is often regarded as a bumpkin.

S

Sabbath To most Christians: Sunday. To Jews and Seventh-Day Adventists: Saturday. To Muslims: Friday.

sack See BAG/POKE/SACK.

safe/vault A *vault* for safekeeping of valuables is ordinarily large enough to walk into, but a *safe* is almost always much smaller. Some hotels that promise to keep your jewelry in a vault have a safe instead.

sagacious/sage A *sagacious* person is shrewd, practical in judgment: "sagacious reasoning about the effect on the stock market." *Sage* comes from a different Latin source. It means "wise" and is often associated with the wisdom of age. (A sage is a wise old person): "Her grandfather offered sage advice about the worth of monogamy."

Sahara desert *Sahara* is Arabic for "desert." When you've seen one *desert*, you've seen enough.

said As in "the said contract," is appropriate mainly in law, less frequent than before in business. "Those wrenches were shipped last week" is more modern than "Said wrenches."

salary/wages Not clearly differentiated, but in general a person is paid *wages* for any manual work or any other in which payment is by the hour, day, or (perhaps) week. One is paid a *salary* for what is customarily called a white-collar position, and the salary is often quoted for a year, although sometimes for a month or a week. See also EMOLUMENT.

same Redundant in expressions such as "This is the same one I mentioned before." It is legalistic in "They found the Christmas tree they wanted and cut same." Outmoded: "Your order has been received and same will be filled at once." SWE uses *it*. See also REPEAT THE SAME.

same as SWE in expressions such as "Your answer is the same as mine." It is FF in "I solved the puzzle the same as you did," for which SWE would usually substitute "the same way you did" or "in the same way that you did." Also FF as the equivalent of *just as*: "He came out shooting, same as you said he would."

sample See EXAMPLE/SAMPLE/SPECIMEN.

sanction It is unfortunate that *sanction* as a noun has two almost opposite meanings: (1) "authorization, permission, or encouragement to do something" and (2) "penalty for doing something." If a synonym will not work, SWE makes sure that the context reveals the meaning intended. The verb *sanction* poses the same problem. It may mean "to encourage, permit, or encourage" or "to impose a penalty."

Follett quotes this example of lack of clarity: "The field of sanction law as we understand it is the entire process of sanctioning."

sanguinary/sanguine *Sanguinary* means "bloody," "bloodthirsty": "a sanguinary battle," "Many pirates apparently were sanguinary fellows." *Sanguine* is quite different. It may mean "having a ruddy complexion" or "cheerful, optimistic": "He seemed always to be smiling and happy – sanguine about his family's future."

sans The French *sans* is used by show-offs instead of the English *without*.

sate/satiate Interchangeable. Each indicates full satisfaction, having an abundance or even an excessive amount, usually of food or sexual pleasure.

save Obsolescent or obsolete for *except*, as in "All save honor was lost." Many modern readers may not understand such a sentence.

saving(s) SWE prefers *saving* in "a saving of five dollars," "an annual saving," "daylight-saving time." It prefers *savings* in "a savings account (*bank, bond*)," "a savings and loan association."

say In reporting a conversation SWE often repeats *say* or *said*. Switching to a different verb with each change of speaker may annoy readers more than repetition does. However, SWE changes when good reason exists for telling readers that someone shouted, insisted, whispered, declared, and so on. (A verb such as *asseverated* may be a reader-stopper.) Frequently, a conversation requires no more than occasional identification of the speaker and consequently few verbs of saying. See also **ELEGANT VARIATION**.

say/state SWE reserves *state* for important people saying important things, or ordinary people saying anything firmly and quietly.

scam This underworld slang for "dishonesty, fraudulent scheme, confidence game" rose rapidly to higher levels in the 1970s and 1980s, when some members of Congress and prominent businessmen were found guilty of scams. Enough of them cooperated, in fact, that the word became SWE.

scan/skim 1. Each may mean "to read hurriedly, superficially": "She scanned (*skimmed*) the help-wanted ads." But *scan* may also mean the opposite: "read carefully," so "She scanned the ads" may also mean that she read them with care. For this reason many people use *skim* for the first meaning, *scan* for the second. Others avoid *scan*, substituting *scrutinize* or *read with care*. 2. To *scan verse* is to make a metrical analysis of it or to read it aloud with emphasis on each stressed syllable.

scarce See RARE/SCARCE.

scarcely See HARDLY NO/HARDLY NONE; HARDLY . . . THAN/SCARCELY . . . THAN.

scenario The meaning of "a plot outline" is often extended to mean "an imagined or hypothesized chain of events": "One possible scenario for the next few years is for our company to open stores in . . ." The word is obviously useful but appears so often as to be tiresome.

schlock From Yiddish, this noun or adjective for "inferior or trashy merchandise, fashion, art, or almost anything else" is widely regarded as FF (slang), but is useful and often now appears in print, especially in metropolitan newspapers and artsy magazines, thus approaching SWE status. The adjective can be *schlock* or *schlocky*, and the spelling *shlock* is sometimes used.

scholar Although dictionaries still include as one definition "a pupil in elementary or secondary school," that meaning is almost passé. Today a scholar is usually a mature person regarded as highly educated and a specialist in a branch of the humanities. Anyone who holds a scholarship is also a scholar.

score See MARGIN/SCORE.

Scot (and the like) Most Scots prefer these forms: A *Scot* or *Scotsman* rather than a *Scotchman*; (plural) *Scots* or *the Scotch*; (adjective) *Scottish* or *Scots* rather than *Scotch*, exceptions being *Scotch* broth, whisky (note no *e*), terrier, Guards, and a few subject-specific words such as *scotch thistles*. Note that *Scotch tape*, although it has no clear association with Scotland, is capitalized because it is a trade name.

scoundrel See KNAVE/RASCAL/ROGUE/SCOUNDREL.

scrip/script *Scrip* most often designates a substitute for regularly authorized paper money. It is ordinarily issued only in emergencies. *Script*, a much more common word, is used as in these examples: "The document was in script, not type." "Script type resembles handwriting." "Each actor was given a copy of the script."

scrupulous See METICULOUS/PUNCTILIOUS/SCRUPULOUS.

scrutinize Because *scrutinize* means "to examine carefully," *carefully*, *closely*, and the like are not used with it in SWE. See also SCAN/SKIM.

sculpt/sculpture Interchangeable as verbs.

seasonable/seasonal Although these words are often used interchangeably, many careful writers differentiate them. *Seasonable* means "appropriate to this season": "In the North in January, seasonable high temperatures are usually below freezing." *Seasonal* ordinarily means "dependent on or controlled by the season or time of year"; "One seasonal difference in hiring is caused by the annual influx of job-seeking June graduates."

secondly See FIRSTLY, SECONDLY.

secret tryst It wouldn't be a tryst if everyone knew about it. SWE omits *secret*.

sectarian/secular *Sectarian* refers to religious sects: "Sectarian differences have divided many denominations." *Secular* means "worldly rather than spiritual": "Some members asserted that the priest was too much interested in secular matters."

secure See GET/OBTAIN/SECURE.

see if I can (*can't*) "See if you can (*can't*) borrow the money." Both are used, although *can* has logic on its side. Either way, it's FF. SWE: "Try to borrow . . ."

see, saw "Zoos see a bright future, conferees asserted today." "World

War II saw an end to fortifications such as the Maginot Line." How can things without eyes see anything? The usage is SWE, illogical though it seems.

see where FF for "see that." In SWE one does not "see in the newspaper where the telephone workers may strike." Instead one "sees that . . ."

seeing FF for *because* or *as*: "Seeing (*Seeing as, Seeing as how*) we're late already, we . . ."

seem **1.** Overused by the timid. Robert Frost wrote, "The woods are lovely, dark, and deep." The timid write, "The woods seem . . ." **2.** *Can't seem to* is FF, marginally SWE, for "seem unable to." See also CANNOT (3).

seldom ever/seldom if ever/seldom or never *Seldom if ever* and *seldom or never* are SWE idioms. Each means that something seldom happened if it happened at all. *Seldom ever* is FF. See also RARELY EVER/SELDOM EVER.

select See EXCLUSIVE/SELECT.

-self, -selves In SWE the pronouns ending in *-self* or the plural *-selves* have two legitimate uses: (1) as intensives: "She herself told the story," and (2) as reflexives: "She told herself that Pete would not get drunk again." Generally considered FF in their use as subjects, objects, or the like, the terms appear in FF in these ways: "Betty and myself easily got work." "Xerox hired Betty and myself." "This is for Betty and myself." SWE substitutes *I, me, me,* respectively. (The *-self* pronoun in such sentences is a resort of someone who is uncertain about *I* vs. *me.*)

self-confessed As in "self-confessed killer," *self-* is redundant.

self-deprecation/self-depreciation *Self-deprecation* is a form of modesty, disavowing a real accomplishment as unimportant: "Aw, shucks, fellas, I didn't do much." *Self-depreciation* is unrealistic and excessive claims of lack of self-worth: "Nothing I do ever turns out right. I'm a failure as a wife, as a mother, as a businesswoman, as a . . ."

sell, sold Marginally SWE in expressions such as "You can't sell me such a theory" or "I'm sold on that idea," these verbs are often used by members of Congress, among others.

semi- See BI-.

senior citizens Certainly SWE, the term is disliked by some older people who consider it condescending. But what is a short substitute? *Older people* is an unfinished comparison – older than whom? Because *oldsters* sounds rather slangy or "cute," it has never caught on, nor (so far) has *generians*, which suggests that these people have *generated* and are partly responsible for the world today. *Generians* calls to mind *sexagenarians* and similar decade words. *Old folks* suggests Stephen Foster and the Swanee River. So, unless *generians* or some other word unexpectedly takes hold, SWE settles for *senior citizens.*

sensibility/sensibleness/sensitiveness/sensitivity *Sensibility* is not "sensibleness." *Sensibility*, *sensitiveness*, and *sensitivity* all mean "being sensitive," but *sensibleness* is "being sensible."

sensual/sensuous   SWE has blurred a useful distinction between these words. The most careful writers use *sensual* for "fleshly, voluptuous," usually referring to sex or, in a somewhat uncomplimentary way, to gratification of the senses. They use *sensuous* in a neutral or favorable way to refer to what is experienced through the senses: "sensuous descriptions," "sensuous impressions." Our sexually liberated age has so intertwined the two words, however, that few people can now tell them apart. A best-selling book of 1969 dealt almost exclusively with female sexuality and was called *The Sensuous Woman.*

sentiment/sentimentality   *Sentiment* refers to honest but not overwrought tenderness. Carried to extremes, sentiment becomes *sentimentality* – shedding tears for every fallen sparrow, imagining that one's relatives and closest friends are perfect, remembering only the good in "the good old days."

separate   SWE checks on whether it is needed, as in "The ambassador had separate conversations with the vice-president and the secretary of state," or unneeded, as in "The ambassador made five separate requests."

seraph   See CHERUB/SERAPH.

series   Everyone knows that *World Series* is as singular as *Super Bowl*. So is *series* in other meanings, unless more than one series is meant: "A series of explosions was (not *were*) heard." "Several series of explosions were heard."

serious   See CRITICAL.

seriously consider   Is *seriously* needed?

serve/service   SWE usually says that maintenance people *service* automobiles, refrigerators, computers, and the like, but ordinarily prefers *serve* in other contexts: "This telephone company serves only a few thousand customers." "Our cab company does not allow us to serve Newark passengers." "We serve the entire city."

set/sit   To *set* means "to place"; to *sit*, "to take a sitting position." People confused by these verbs may compose and say *aloud* repeatedly sentences such as these: "*Set* it on the table." "I *set* it on the floor." "You had *set* it in the wrong place." "Now you are *setting* it in the right place." "*Sit*, Rover." "Rover is *sitting* here." "He *sat* here yesterday." "He has *sat* here every day." "Why does he *sit* in this spot?" "He enjoys *sitting* here." Oddities: Hens *set* or *sit* on their eggs to hatch them (at other times they may *sit*). The sun *sets*. We *sit* or *seat* a person.

several   Although *several* has no precise numerical value, it is about the same as *a few* but fewer than *fairly numerous*. Dubious: "During its history, England has had a role in several wars" (*numerous* or *many* would be more accurate).

sewage/sewerage   *Sewage* is what passes through sewers. *Sewerage* can mean either the system of sewers, as in "the sewerage of Dayton," or "the removal of waste matter through sewers," as in "Increasing problems with sewerage are likely." Although *sewerage* sometimes is used for *sewage*, confusion may result.

sexy　Now SWE. Of three dictionaries published between 1971 and 1981, one labels *sexy* slang, one says informal, and one treats it as standard. More recent ones appear unanimous in considering it standard. The word is relatively new, having been traced only to 1928, but the biblical King David and probably Adam and Eve themselves seem to have recognized the qualities it summarizes.

shake down, shakedown　The verb, noun, and modifier one by one have become SWE: "The gang shook down ("extorted money from") leading politicians." "The shakedown ("extortion") was revealed only yesterday." "The shakedown ('testing') cruise revealed several weaknesses."

shall　Except in questions starting with "Shall I (*we*)," *shall* is, if not dead, moribund. Only a few purists try to obey the old rules, which were not based on actual use and were never consistently followed. For the pure at heart, these are the rules in simplified form:

	Simple Future	*Determination or Promise*
I, we	shall	will
you, he she, it, they, Jones	will	shall

she　Although no scholar has convincingly explained why, for at least two thousand years people have used a feminine gender pronoun for a ship. So: "My yacht is the *Mark Twain*. She . . ." Some owners, more or less affectionately, call their cars "she," probably never "he."

She　See HE, SHE.

shell　See BULLET/CARTRIDGE/ROUND/SHELL . . .

shenanigans　Suppose that you witness some high-spirited behavior, a practical joke or a trick or two, a little drinking, and a great deal of semi-innocent fun. Suppose that you had to invent a word to cover all that. You probably wouldn't come up with *shenanigans*, but you might not find a better one. Nobody is certain where *shenanigans* came from – the Irish, maybe – but in the absence of an equally descriptive term, the word has deservedly reached SWE status.

ship　See BOAT/SHIP; SHE.

ships that pass in the night　Cliché. Longfellow wrote that many possibly compatible people meet like "Ships that pass in the night, and speak each other in passing,/Only a signal shown and a distant voice in the darkness." The metaphor is excellent and worth repeating – but not over and over (and not misquoted as "two ships passing in the night").

shod　The past tense of the verb *shoe*. The past participle is *shod*, *shoed*, or *shodden* (take your choice). The sports commentator who said that a locker-room attendant has "enough football shoes to shod a centipede" offered an amusing comparison but should have said "to *shoe*" if he followed SWE usage.

shop Generally used as an intransitive verb, as in "He shops on the Miracle Mile" or "She shops for Swiss chocolate," *shop* is now SWE as transitive also: "He shops the stores on the Miracle Mile." Used in this way, the emphasis is on both looking and buying, but *shops on* (*in*, *at*) stresses the buying.

shore See BANK/SHORE.

shortly In SWE this word is not used when "briefly" is meant. "He spoke shortly" probably means "curtly," and "He may speak shortly" probably means "soon." To avoid ambiguity, SWE chooses *briefly*, *curtly*, or *soon* – whichever is intended.

shot See BULLET/CARTRIDGE/ROUND/SHELL/SHOT.

should/would Pupils were once taught to say, "I should like to have one" rather than "I would . . ." But times have changed. Now *should* is used mainly for "ought to": "I should go to Denver tomorrow." Less frequent uses are illustrated in "I should think so," "We should ('are likely to') get there before dark," "If Mr. Clayton should ('does') call, tell him . . ."

show up Once considered only informal, *show up* is now SWE in these senses: come, arrive – "He showed up at noon"; reveal faults – "The official report showed him up as a liar"; be revealed clearly – "Her courage shows up best in her battle against cancer." *Show up* is probably still FF for "outdo, defeat": "I showed him up in the pole vault."

shuttle back and forth *Shuttle* means "move back and forth." The other three words are unnecessary.

[*sic*] Usually enclosed in brackets (not parentheses) and italicized (underlined) because it is a foreign word, *sic* follows or is included in a quotation. It means "That's really the way it is printed. I'm not responsible for this stupid mistake." Example: "Shakespeare's home-town of Avon-on-Stratford [*sic*] was . . ."

sick at (*to*) one's stomach SWE uses both. However, one is *sick with* a cold, and *sick of* ("tired of") the rainy weather.

sick (for "morbid") *Sick humor* and *sick joke* are SWE terms in which *sick* means "morbid, unwholesome." See also BLACK HUMOR/SICK HUMOR; MORBID.

sick/sickly A *sick* person may be temporarily ill, as with a cold. A *sickly* person has one or more enduring illnesses, or is sick much or most of the time. See also *ill/sick*.

sidewalk See PAVEMENT/SIDEWALK.

sideways, sidewise See EDGEWAYS, EDGEWISE/ENDWAYS . . . ; -WISE.

sight See CITE/SIGHT/SITE.

sillily SWE: short for "in a silly way." But the word looks and sounds odd, and for some people is hard to say. SWE must choose here between verbiage and oddity, or borrow the still FF "He behaved silly," recommended by SANE.

similar See CORRESPONDING/SIMILAR.

similar(ly) to SWE checks to see whether *like* will be equally clear.

(for the) simple reason that *Obvious* may be better than *simple* here. Or the whole phrase may be replaced by *because* or *only because*: "We stopped feeding birds for the simple reason that (or *because*) squirrels and raccoons were eating most of the seed."

simple/simplistic A *simple* solution and a *simplistic* solution are not the same. The simplistic one is actually oversimplified. The word implies that the person offering such a solution is not aware of or chooses to disregard some of the complexities.

simulate See DISSIMULATE/SIMULATE.

since See BECAUSE/SINCE.

singlehanded(ly) Although the adverb *singlehandedly* still exists, many respected authors use the less cumbersome *singlehanded* instead: "Singlehanded, Fred installed the garage door opener." SANE approves.

sink down Because sinking can be only downward, SWE deletes *down*.

sinus A *sinus* is one of several cranial cavities. SWE writes, "His sinuses were bothering him again," not "His sinus were . . . " Sinus is not an ailment. One does not get treatment or take medication for sinus, but for sinusitis or a sinus infection.

Sir See DAME/SIR.

sit See SET/SIT.

sitcom Well on the way to replacing *situation comedy*. It follows the frequently traveled path of *mob*, which Jonathan Swift decried as a replacement of *mobile vulgus*. (The language survived the shortening.)

site See CITE/SIGHT/SITE.

size/sized With *large*, *small*, and similar words, *sized* appears in SWE more often than *size*: "large-sized brushes." Often, however, as in that example, it can be omitted.

skeptical See CYNICAL/SKEPTICAL.

skim See SCAN/SKIM.

skirt around "Senator Raddles skirted around the issue but never quite discussed it." To *skirt* is to "go around" or "go along the edge of." SWE omits *around*.

slacks (verb with) SWE: "This pair of slacks *is* new." "These slacks *are* new." Verbs with *hose* ("legwear"), *stockings*, *pants*, and *trousers* are similar. See also *pair*.

slander See DEFAMATION/LIBEL/SLANDER.

SLANG William Lyon Phelps, a nineteenth-century professor of English at Yale, wrote: "Our slang's piquant as catsup. I decry it / Not as a condiment, but as an entire diet." Slang originates in various ways, as these outworn words reveal. *Vamoose* is a variant of Spanish *vamos*, "Let's go." *Square* ("an ultraconservative person") is a poetic or at least metaphorical way to say that the person lacks the smooth-running qualities of a wheel; *wheel* itself ("an important person") emphasizes in another way this century's idol. Some slang expressions are only overused ordinary terms, such as *drop dead*. A few, like *punk* or *moll*, have been borrowed from the argot of crime; thieves' language has been notably inventive for centuries, perhaps as a protective device. The jargon of an occupation or a sport, when used in another context, is often slang but may become SWE; *hit a homer* is good baseball talk, but when used to mean in business "succeed in an undertaking," it becomes slang. Much slang results from teenagers' wish to break away from the supposed conservatism (linguistic and other) of their elders, and from the attempt, also observable in some of their younger siblings, to create a secret language that only the initiated can understand.

Slang has four major weaknesses, writers of SWE believe, and for that reason they, like Phelps, use it mainly as a "condiment." One weakness is that it is a transitory language; a grandfather, using the slang of his youth, has difficulty in conversing with his grandson, who uses today's slang. The second, and related, weakness is that slang may not be understood even by others of the same generation. Third, the endless repetition of any expression, slang or not, becomes tiresome, and the users of slang tend to repeat endlessly. Finally, most slang expressions are not precise. For example, *real cool* (a 1950ish term that earlier was *real George* and still earlier *swell*, and later became *ba-ad* and will be something else when you read this) signified vague approval but suggested no reason for the approval, no identification of the good quality. The constant use of such easy and inexact terms leads to shoddy thinking and contributes to mental debilitation. You know, like, man, that's the name of the game.

In its place, though, if not overused, slang may be valuable. Its place is almost always an informal one (FF) – at a party or picnic, on the beach, at a ball game, in conversation with close friends. But occasionally in SWE a slang term may lend force, on a few occasions a surprising or even poetic effect.

SLANTING   Slanting is the rhetorical device of omitting whatever material may harm one's cause and selecting materials and words that favor it or are hurtful to the opposing view. For example, here are headlines from two newspapers with differing political and economic views. Both headlines were used for the same story: "Congressional Leaders Threaten New Taxes." "Congressional Leaders Promise Tax Reforms." Note *threaten* vs. *promise* and the unpleasantness of *new taxes* in contrast to supposedly good *tax reforms*.

slattern/sloven/slut   A *slattern* is an extremely unkempt woman. A *sloven* is an extremely untidy man or woman. A *slut* is a woman, often but not necessarily untidy, who is considered sexually immoral or promiscuous.

slaughter   See ANNIHILATE, DESTROY, FLAY . . .

slay   **1.** If it weren't for headline writers, who like its brevity, this word might have become obsolete, but they have kept it as vigorous as the descendants of Cain. The principal parts are *slay, slew, slain.* **2.** With the meaning of "greatly amuse," as in "His funny stories slay me," *slay* is FF. See also ANNIHILATE, DESTROY, FLAY . . .

sleek/slick   Both words convey the idea of smoothness, but *sleek* is more often figurative for "well-groomed, well-fed, thriving, polished in manner." *Slick* most often means "slippery," but also may mean "shrewd" or "tricky," especially in informal usage: "a slick trader." It may also mean "superficially attractive."

sleeper   Flexner says that in the 1930s *sleeper* for "unexpected success" was first applied to a movie. It has since become rather frequent in regard to horses, investments, politicians, athletic teams, and many other things. It occurs at times in SWE.

sleight/slight   *Sleight,* meaning "skill, dexterity" or "cunning, craftiness" appears most often in the expression *sleight of hand.* For other meanings, *slight* is the accepted spelling.

slick   See SLEEK/SLICK.

slob   *Slob* is a contemptuous word for a person who is crude, uninformed, and slovenly. Sitting in his T-shirt the slob guzzles beer while he takes part vicariously in a television wrestling match. When the female slob is in the kitchen, she wears a dirty housecoat, ignores the sinkful of dishes, and sets on the grimy table an open can of beans and a couple of beers. People who pride themselves on their standard English sometimes need a word for such persons, but most dictionaries call *slob* informal or slang. It's a good, understandable word and should be SWE. A word ought not to be called nonstandard because its surroundings or its meaning is unpleasant.

slow drawl   Redundant. By definition a drawl is a slow manner of speaking.

slow/slowly   Both *slow* and *slowly* may be used as adverbs. In fact, *slow* is the older. So both "Go slow" and "Go slowly" are SWE. Euphony may sometimes determine the choice. "The two deer slowly went behind the trees" sounds better to most people than "went slow." *Slow* is more likely in short sentences, *slowly* in long, especially in writing. Similar comments apply to *loud, loudly; quick, quickly;* and *soft, softly.*

small   See LIMITED/LTD./SMALL.

smaller, smallest   See LEAST, LESS/LITTLER, LITTLEST/SMALLER, SMALLEST.

smash   See ANNIHILATE, DESTROY, FLAY . . .

smell (and its synonyms)   Pleasant: *aroma, bouquet, fragrance,* PERFUME, SAVOR; neutral: *odor, smell;* unpleasant: *stench, stink. Odor* and *smell* are general words. Sometimes they need to be qualified with adjectives such as *strong* or *flowerlike,* or be replaced by another of the words listed above. *Aroma* often means a spicy or savory smell, especially one that fills a considerable area: "the aroma of Grandma's kitchen." *Fragrance* refers to a light, perhaps flowery smell, as does *perfume*. *Bouquet* usually applies to wine. *Savor* combines the senses of taste and smell, emphasizing the former. *Stench* is stiffer than *stink*. Both appear in SWE.

smell (verb)   See also FEEL (GOOD/WELL; BAD/BADLY).

smog   Blends involve combining two words, a practice popularized several decades ago by *Time*. Some blends are meant mainly to amuse, as *infanticipating* ("expecting a baby") perhaps is. Some blends are useful and become standard, as is true of *brunch* (although the imitations *linner* and *lupper* have little value and have never caught on). Like *brunch, smog* ("a combination of smoke and fog, as well as pollutants and sometimes sunlight") has become SWE.

snide   Either not listed or else labeled as slang in older dictionaries, *snide* is now an SWE adjective for "derogatory" or "slyly insinuating." More rarely it is a noun meaning "a dishonest person or act" or "a counterfeit."

snooty   George Orwell said that a bourgeois belief he had encountered in his youth could be summarized "The lower classes smell." People who figuratively tilt their noses up to reduce such a smell are described as "snooty." It's a picturesque word, occasionally a good SWE substitute for *disdainful* or *haughty*.

snow job   FF (slang), rare in SWE, for "flattery intended to persuade": "Dillard tried a snow job on me, but I held my ground."

snuck   *Snuck* is FF for *sneaked*.

so (in comparisons)   "It was *so* hot yesterday!" Conservatives call such sentences "unfinished comparisons" and recommend completion, possibly "It was so hot yesterday that every newspaper ran pictures of eggs frying on sidewalks." Another interpretation is that *so* in such a sentence is an intensifier, like *very* or *extremely*. In this case, no completion is necessary. However, most writers use *so* as an intensifier mainly in informal contexts. The male chauvinists say that it sounds feminine: "It's *so* lovely!" With some exceptions, SWE avoids unfinished comparisons.

so as   Redundant when followed by an infinitive, as in "We crossed the road (so as) to see the cows." FF when followed by a clause: "We crossed the road so as we could see the cows."

so . . . as/as . . . as   See AS . . . AS/SO . . . AS.

so . . . so   In student writing, *so . . . so* sentences are marked almost as frequently as *and . . . and* sentences. *So* is especially overused in the sense of "for that reason": "My parents could not afford to send me to college, so I had to find other sources of money, so I . . . " Revising the sentence is usually the best remedy: "Because my parents could not afford to send me to college, I . . . The first thing I tried was . . . "

so/so that "They rose early so (or *so that*) they would not miss the plane." Both are used in SWE, with *so* increasing in frequency, although conservative writers and editors still favor *so that*.

soar Journalists tell us often that prices (the inflation rate, humidity, temperature, or what-have-you) soars. Unless the increase is remarkably large and rapid, *soar* may be too strong. One dictionary definition: "climb swiftly or powerfully."

so-called SWE uses *so-called* only when some people actually do use a designation that may be undeserved or unsuitable: "A so-called moral victory is neither moral nor a victory." Note that no quotation marks are needed around *moral victory*. When SWE does use the apologetic marks, it deletes *so-called*. SWE hyphenates *so-called* when it comes before the modified noun, as in "her so-called uncle," but not after: "her uncle, at least so called."

sociable/social For the meaning "friendly, affable, eager to converse," *sociable* is more common in SWE, but *social* is also used. An old-fashioned name for a lawn party or other informal gathering is *social,* which old-timers often called a *sociable*: "an ice-cream social (*sociable*)." Both forms are FF and geographically limited.

social disease This euphemism has been largely replaced in SWE by the more frank *venereal disease* or the specific name.

soft/softly See SLOW/SLOWLY.

software See HARDWARE/LIVEWARE/SOFTWARE.

softwood See HARDWOOD/SOFTWOOD.

soliloquy See MONOLOG(UE)/SOLILOQUY.

some See A/SOME.

some (adverb) "The farmer bought some sixty feeder calves." *Some* in this adverbial use, meaning "about," is SWE.

some/somewhat FF (dialectal or informal): "He's some better today," "The temperature has dropped some." SWE substitutes *somewhat*.

some thing vs. something/some time vs. sometime *Something* and *sometime* are the forms almost always needed. *Some thing* is standard when a contrast is intended: "This time don't bring me some live animal; bring me some *thing*." *Some time* is standard when time is what is being talked about, as in "Some time is what we need" or "I have some time to spare."

somebody/someone Interchangeable. Each is singular. A verb and a pronoun with it are also normally singular in SWE usage: "Somebody is certain to lose his (*her*) wager." *Somebody . . . they (their*), however, has been endorsed by some groups within the National Council of Teachers of English, to the dismay of many members. In FF, *somebody . . . they (their*), is almost universal. See also THEIR, THEM, THEY.

sometime See OCCASIONAL/SOMETIME; SOME THING VS. SOMETHING . . .

sooner I. In the sense of "rather," *sooner* is SWE: "He would sooner vote for a crocodile than for Brown." **2.** After *no sooner, than* rather than *when* is the usual SWE preference: "She had no sooner reached cruising altitude than her radio went dead."

sore FF for "annoyed, angry": "Don't get sore about this."

sort of See KIND OF/SORT OF.

soul As an adjective for "black in origin, rooted in the black experience," this word is SWE but slightly informal: "soul food (*music, sister*)."

sound out In the sense of "learn the opinion or attitude of," *sound out* is SWE: "They sounded out the provost before they asked for the president's approval."

southerly See EASTERLY/EASTERN.

souvenir See REMEMBRANCE/REMINDER/SOUVENIR.

spaded/spayed *Spay* means "remove the ovaries of an animal": "We took Queenie to the veterinarian to be spayed (not *spaded*).

spark SWE in the sense of "serve as the immediate cause of": "The assassination of a relatively unimportant man sparked World War I." (The spark is usually not the real, underlying cause.)

spat (noun) SWE: "A short-lasting quarrel over a small matter." As a rule a few spats between a couple do not lead to divorce, and *spat* is too light a word to apply to disagreements between nations. The same definition and comments apply to *tiff*. See also ROW; RUCKUS. For the verb see SPIT/SPITTED.

spayed See SPADED/SPAYED.

speak to (*with*) Often interchanged, although it is logical to use *to* for one-sided speaking, *with* when two or more persons are conversing: "The captain spoke to his crew to inform them of the new danger." "The captain spoke with the first mate, frankly exchanging opinions." A similar distinction is usually drawn between *talk to* and *talk with*.

spearhead Overused, by journalists especially, for "direct, lead, take charge of."

special Some merchants have given *special* a bad reputation. "Today's Special" at the lunch counter may be last night's dinner warmed over or disguised. The "Special Markdown" on the used-car lot may indeed be a marked-down price – say, by two hundred dollars after being marked up by three hundred. What is special about a "special invitation to subscribe"? Some things in life are indeed special, but it's not always easy to recognize them. In SWE, context shows specifically what is special, unusual, exceptional, or distinctive. See also ESPECIAL/SPECIAL.

specially See ESPECIALLY/SPECIALLY.

specie/species *Specie* is coined money (not paper). In rare instances its plural, *species,* is used: "the species of England and France." Even in such a sentence, however, *specie* is probable. *Species* ordinarily means "a kind" and is most often used in biology for a classification ranking below *genus*: "a rare species of butterfly." In *Homo sapiens,*

Homo represents the genus, *sapiens* the species. Both the singular and plural are *species*. FF: "a specie," "one specie."

SPECIFICITY   See **ABSTRACT AND GENERAL WORDS**.

specimen   See EXAMPLE/SAMPLE.

spectators   See AUDIENCE/CONGREGATION/SPECTATORS.

spell   The verb *spell* meaning "take over a job for a short time" is SWE: "to spell the helmsman." So is the noun *spell* as in "a short spell," "a warm spell," "did a spell in prison," although the noun use is most likely in informal contexts.

spell out   Although Bernstein calls *spell out* "a tired old workhorse," it is still frequent in SWE in the sense of "state explicitly": "Even some IRS officials cannot clearly spell out the implications of this new tax regulation." *Spell out in detail* is redundant.

spend time   See KILL TIME/PASS TIME/SPEND TIME.

sphere   See REALM/SPHERE/WORLD.

spick-and-span   Sometimes people classify words as slang or informal simply because they *sound* informal. This is true of *spick-and-span*. Its first recorded use is in the admired translation of Plutarch's *Lives* by Sir Thomas North in 1579 or 1580, and many other reputable writers have used it since. But Morris in 1975 reported that the term was still "generally regarded as close to slang." Sir Thomas North deserves more respect. The term is SWE.

spiral   "Prices are spiraling once more," a news story said. Perhaps it is easy to guess the direction of this spiral, but ordinarily the context should make clear whether downward or upward is meant. A spiral may go either way. We may climb or descend a spiral staircase.

spire/steeple   A church or other building may have a spire, a steeple, or a spire on top of a steeple. A steeple is a tower, sometimes containing bells. A spire is normally slimmer and may be either hollow or solid.

spit   See EXPECTORATE/SPIT.

spit/spitted   **1.** Yes, *spitted* is one past tense of *spit,* but only in the sense of "thrust a rod through": "He spitted the dressed chicken and suspended it over the fire." **2.** In the sense of "expectorate," both *spat* and *spit* are SWE for the past tense, with *spat* perhaps more frequent.

splutter/sputter   Interchangeable. *Splutter* is the newer word, perhaps a blend of *sputter* with *splash*. (One person with a good ear says that *splutter* "sounds wetter than sputter.")

spoof   As both noun and verb, the word is SWE to refer to a parody or gentle ridicule: "a spoof of modern literary criticism," "a comic opera that spoofs the grand solemnity of Wagner."

sprain/strain   A *sprain* is a painful wrenching or tearing of ligaments – for instance, in the ankle or shoulder. *Strain* usually results from overuse or overexertion and is customarily applied to muscles or ligaments that are extended too far but are not torn. Emotional and mental strain also exist, but most of us need not worry often about the latter.

spray/spume Sometimes an ocean wave strikes a rock as it pounds ashore, sending water high in droplets. These are *spray,* as are the droplets blown from a fountain by the wind. If you look out to sea, you may see foam or froth atop some of the waves, or churning around on the surface. This is *spume.*

sprint/spurt (running) A *sprint* lasts longer than a spurt. For example, a one-hundred-meter dash is often called a *sprint.* Near the end of a longer run, a good runner has conserved enough strength to sprint for the final fifty or more meters. A *spurt* is a short burst of speed, perhaps faster − while it lasts − than the same runner's sprint would be.

spume See SPRAY/SPUME.

spurious See ARTIFICIAL/ERSATZ/FAKE . . .

spurt See SPRINT/SPURT.

sputter See SPLUTTER/SPUTTER.

square FF (outmoded slang) for a person looked on by the speaker as old-fashioned, "out of it," "not with it," "not hip or even hep."

square miles SWE distinguishes between *square miles* and *miles square.* Nine square miles of land could be, for example, 3×3 miles or $4\frac{1}{2} \times 2$. Nine miles square, however, would be nine miles on each side; $9 \times 9 = 81$ square miles. Obviously the same distinction is made between *square inches* and *inches square,* and so on.

squoze Sometimes used humorously in SWE, *squoze* is FF for *squeezed,* by analogy with *froze.*

stabilize When manufacturers or other businesspeople refer to stabilizing prices, they often have no interest in keeping them steady. They overuse (and misuse) *stabilize* to mean "to prevent from going down." OPEC oil ministers, for instance, apparently used an Arabic equivalent of that word each time they raised the price during the 1970s.

staid/stayed The adjective (meaning "dignified, sedate") is *staid*: "The attorney's staid manner was comforting."

stalactite/stalagmite In a cave a *stalagmite* builds from the base upward, but a *stalactite* hangs down from the roof like an icicle. An old mnemonic device: the stala*ctite* is *tight* against the ceiling.

stalemate Headline: "Wage Stalemate to Be Broken Soon." In chess a *stalemate* or a checkmate ends the game. Each is impossible to break, remove, overcome. It's as final as nuclear winter. The headline writer could, however, have written "Wage Stalemate to Be Averted" or "Wage Agreement Near."

stall In the sense of "delay," the verb *stall* was labeled slang in many dictionaries early in this century, but now is SWE in sentences such as "He stalled to catch his breath." In athletic and other contexts it is also used as a noun or a modifier: "The team has gone into a stall," "a stall offense." *Stall for time,* although widely used, is redundant, because *for time* is implicit in *stall.*

stammer/stutter To *stammer* is to speak hesitantly and with pauses and occasional repetitions: "I – I find – I find it – it's hard to – to talk about it." High emotion is the usual cause, but embarrassment or failure to remember may also be at fault. To *stutter* is ordinarily to repeat sounds (less often whole words): "B-b-but Bob-Bob d-d-didn't tell me." *Stutter* is the term used in this sense by speech therapists.

stamp/stomp 1. Often interchanged, although *stomp* suggests heavier, more violent action. People, especially women, usually stamp their feet, but a large, cruel man may stomp on a fallen opponent. Large animals may stomp around, but a pony delicately stamps a front hoof. 2. *Stamp out* is usual for "eliminate": "stamping out use of illicit drugs."

stance Related to *stand, stance* basically means "a standing position" but has been legitimately extended to "an intellectual or emotional position." SWE avoids, however, statements in which the idea of "standing" is absurd, as in "My stance is that we should stage a sitdown strike."

stanch/staunch Used interchangeably in SWE, although some people prefer *stanch* as the verb: "to stanch the flow of blood," and *staunch* as the adjective: "a staunch friend." That distinction is useful.

stand in line/stand on line The usual idiom is *stand in line,* but *stand on line* is frequently spoken – less frequently written – in parts of the eastern United States.

stanza/verse In popular use, a *verse* is the same as a *stanza.* To literary scholars, however, a verse is a single line, and a stanza is a group of lines, often rhyming in a patterned way. *Verse* is also used to distinguish poetic writing from *prose.*

starboard See LEE/PORT/STARBOARD . . .

state of the art This term originated in the 1960s and quickly became SWE. It is used both as a noun and (usually hyphenated) as an adjective, especially in referring to the most advanced developments in a technology, a science, or education: "The state of the art in computer technology changes before there is time to describe it in print." "This state-of-the-art metal detector . . . "

state See also SAY.

stationary/stationery *Stationary* means "not moving": "a stationary engine." *Stationery* is material for writing, especially paper. Children are sometimes told that they can remember the distinction by thinking of the *er* in *stationery* and in *letter.*

statue/stature/statute The stone man or woman standing in the park is a *statue.* He or she may have a *stature* of about twelve feet. A local *statute* makes it illegal to deface a statue.

statuesque/statuelike Both mean "similar to a statue," but *statuelike* is more literal, recalling the hardness and immobility of a real statue. *Statuesque* refers more to graceful appearance, stateliness, or superb proportions. Actress Grace Kelly was often described as "a statuesque blonde," but her easy movements and expressive face were certainly not statuelike.

staunch See STANCH/STAUNCH.

stay home SWE in the United States, but some conservatives prefer the British *stay at home,* arguing that *home* cannot be used as an adverb. Words, however, keep jumping over fences.

stay/stop If you *stop* at a hotel or motel, do you only pause there – perhaps for a meal – or do you spend the night? Because of possible ambiguity, SWE writers generally use *stay* for an overnight or longer sojourn. In FF, *stop* is frequent.

stayed See STAID/STAYED.

steal See ROB/STEAL.

steeple See SPIRE/STEEPLE.

sterling (silver) Not synonymous with *pure. Sterling* silver is 92.5 percent silver, 7.5 percent copper or other metal. A person of "sterling character," it may possibly be inferred, is highly praiseworthy, but like the rest of us has a little alloy to prevent excessive softness.

stewardess The modern preference is for *(flight) attendant* or *steward,* regardless of sex. See also -ESS.

stick up for FF for "uphold, defend, side with": "Louise always sticks up for her husband."

still and all This phrase is almost meaningless. SWE settles for *still, yet, anyhow,* or *nevertheless.*

still continue, still remain, still stay SWE omits *still.*

stomp See STAMP/STOMP.

stone See ROCK/STONE.

stonewall (verb) Popularized by denizens of the Nixon White House to mean "insist that one knows nothing about a subject," *stonewall* (like *at this point in time*) has become fairly well established in journalistic and other writing.

stop by *Stop by* is now SWE for "come for a brief visit." See also STAY/STOP.

straddle (an issue) SWE in the sense of "appear to favor both sides." Some politicians have straddled issues of corporate greed by speaking publicly about helping "us little fellows" against the "giants," but then quietly voting for bills that help generous campaign contributors.

straightened/straitened *Straightened* means "make straight" or "put-in-order": "She straightened her stockings." *Straitened* means "narrowed, squeezed." A financially straitened person is squeezed financially, "feels the pinch," is "in financial straits."

strain See SPRAIN/STRAIN.

straitjacket/straitlaced Preferably not *straight-*. A strait, such as the Strait of Gibraltar, squeezes water between land masses. A *straitjacket* squeezes the person inside it, and a *straitlaced* person is figuratively squeezed by a narrow interpretation of morality, as women used to be squeezed by laced corsets.

strange See ODD/PECULIAR/QUAINT . . .

strangled to death If you have been *strangled,* you're dead.

strata/stratums The usual plural of *stratum,* meaning "layer," as in "a stratum of rock," is *strata,* although *stratums* is occasionally seen.

stutter See STAMMER/STUTTER.

subconscious/unconscious To a psychologist, *subconscious* refers to what goes on, in human thought and emotions, that a person is not aware of: "strong soldiers of hate and love fighting it out in his subconscious." *Unconscious* in ordinary use means "temporarily without consciousness" or "involuntary": "knocked unconscious by his opponent," "unconscious sneering tone."

subject Perhaps for some legal or legalistic reason, police reports frequently refer to a person as a *subject.* The word is vague enough to cover all races, ages, and genders, and may conceivably include such nonpersons as monkeys or dogs. The result is sometimes amusing, as in this quotation from an Indiana police blotter: "A subject was reported to be throwing objects into the street." SWE, unless preparing police reports, uses a more specific word to refer to a person: *boy, woman, young person, man in a checkered jacket,* and so on.

subject matter "The subject matter of the discussion was . . . " *Subject* alone is usually enough, although the two words may be needed in expressions such as "the subject matter of this course."

subject/topic Often interchangeable: "the subject (*topic*) of discussion." Some writers, however, consider it useful to regard topics as divisions of a subject. Thus the subject "polar exploration" can yield a large number of topics, such as the Peary expedition, the question of who really reached the Pole first, or some recent exploratory techniques.

SUBJECTIVE COMPLEMENT See IT'S I/IT'S ME.

subsequent to *After* is more concise.

subsist See EXIST/SUBSIST.

substitute See REPLACE/SUBSTITUTE.

success See GOOD BENEFIT/GOOD SUCCESS.

such a 1. With occasional exceptions, SWE avoids unfinished comparisons, as in "It was such a hard job!" SWE might complete that like this: "It was such a hard job that we had to call for help." 2. In *no such a thing,* the *a* is unnecessary. See also *so (in comparisons).*

suffer from/suffer with Both are SWE, although "suffer from arthritis" (or other ailment) is more likely.

sufficiency *A sufficiency of* is wordy for *enough.*

sufficient number Instead of *a sufficient number* (or *amount*) *of,* SWE prefers *enough, ample,* or *sufficient.*

sufficiently Usually followed by an adjective and an infinitive, or an adjective and *for*: "The engine is sufficiently powerful to lift five tons," " . . . sufficiently powerful for the tasks you described." Wordy: " . . . sufficiently powerful that it will perform the tasks you described."

suggest *Suggest* is standard when what is said is tentative, when it is presented as one possible solution. Sometimes a stronger word is suitable, for example, *advocate, assert, declare, predict, recommend.*

summarize See RECAPITULATE/REPEAT/SUMMARIZE.

summary See PARAPHRASE/SUMMARY. 229

super Overused FF adjective or exclamation for anything favorable – perhaps often for *exceptional, great, marvelous,* or any other word of high or ecstatic praise.

supersede (Note the spelling.) *Supersede* does not indicate superiority. When one person (*regulation,* and so on) supersedes another, he, she, or it replaces the other and may or may not be better. However, in some instances something is superseded when it becomes obsolete.

supersonic/ultrasonic *Supersonic* means "beyond the speed of sound": "This plane flies at supersonic speed." *Ultrasonic* refers not to speed but to acoustic frequencies – those above the range audible to most people: "Dogs can hear ultrasonic whistles." Such sounds are above twenty thousand cycles per second.

supine See PRONE/PROSTRATE/SUPINE . . .

supplement See AUGMENT/SUPPLEMENT.

supplemental inflatable restraints Hoity-toity. A General Motors advertisement says that "supplemental inflatable restraints" are available. Quick, G.M., the air bags!

supporter See PROPONENT/SUPPORTER.

suppose See CALCULATE/RECKON/SUPPOSE.

suppose(d) to *Supposed to* is SWE in "Mr. Bedrosian is supposed to ("is expected to, has promised to") call this afternoon." *Suppose to* in such a sentence is FF.

supreme sacrifice As in "For his country he paid the supreme sacrifice." Criticized as "stock pathos" in some stylebooks, and certainly not to be used often. It is true and forgivable, though, in writing about people who gave their lives for causes they considered worthy. Sometimes it is used ironically, as in referring to a person who abstained from smoking for a day, or to someone who missed a rock concert.

sure/surely "I sure like pistachio ice cream" is FF, with *sure* used as an adverb. SWE requires *surely,* as in "The candidates surely will soon begin to discuss the issues." *Sure enough* is SWE, although informal in tone, in "Sure enough, the gun was loaded" or similar sentences.

suspect (verb)/suspicion 1. Illogical: "Drugs are suspected of being involved in the murders." Better: "Sellers (or *Users*) of drugs are suspected . . . " Despite the lack of logic, sentences like the first sometimes occur in SWE. **2.** *Suspicion* as a verb is FF (dialectal). The SWE verb for "to be suspicious of" is *suspect*.

sustain   Some stylebooks assert that *sustain an injury* is inferior to *suffer an injury,* but the expression is used so frequently in SWE that it may no longer be condemned. *Sustain a loss* is almost never criticized.

swallow down   In SWE, *down* is deleted here. In FF, however, Mama says to her reluctant little patient, "Swallow it down, honey," even though she knows that swallowing up is unlikely. (Granted, a whale and a wolf, respectively, swallowed *up* Jonah and a grandmother. But maybe their anatomy isn't like the little patient's.)

swap   A few years ago, many people would have called *swap* a good word in horse-trading but too informal for international exchanges. However, when the Reagan administration was interested in trading arms for Americans held hostage, *swap* was in constant use by the media, including the most reputable. So horse-traders and *swap* now find themselves in select company. Consider the word SWE.

SWEEPING GENERALIZATION   A sweeping generalization is an inclusive statement that cannot be proved but that often can be at least partly disproved: "Women are not good liars." "Mexicans are short." A statement containing one of these words is often a sweeping generalization: *all, no* or *none, everybody* or *nobody, always, never:* "All Swedes (Poles, or you name them) are brilliant." "No women are great artists." "Always distrust a cross-eyed man." "It never rains but it pours." Seldom, if ever, is a sweeping generalization appropriate. "All generalizations are false, including this one."

swell   Obsolescent slang word intended to praise. See also LOUSY; SUPER.

swoon (verb)   **1.** Still SWE, *swoon* is now usually replaced by *faint* for the meaning "lose consciousness." **2.** It is also SWE for "become ecstatic about": "Teenagers in the 1940s swooned over Frank Sinatra."

sympathy   See EMPATHY/SYMPATHY.

syndrome   Too often used by people who do not know that a syndrome to a doctor is a group of symptoms that, taken together, characterize a disease. So a *syndrome* is not a "disease." One doesn't say, "My husband is in the hospital with a syndrome." Outside medicine a syndrome is a group of signs indicating an undesirable condition. The Super Bowl Weekend syndrome, for example, has been caricatured as massive sandwiches, huge dishes of popcorn, six-packs of beer, and five men staring hypnotized at a television screen. It is inaccurate to refer to something as a syndrome if only one symptom is observable. Dubious: "a Vince Lombardi syndrome."

synthetic   See ARTIFICIAL/ERSATZ/FAKE . . .

T

taciturn See LACONIC/RETICENT/TACITURN.

tacky SWE, *tacky* has in recent years added to its meaning of "physically shabby, dowdy" a more figurative sense: "inconsiderate, unworthy, undeserved, cheap": "a tacky remark."

tact see DIPLOMACY/TACT.

tad/tad bit Dictionaries agree that *tad* is informal for "a small boy" or "a small child." But in recent years the word has been used widely to mean "little": "Move it just a tad." And *tad bit* has been trying to compete with *little bit*, as in "a tad bit noisy." These are still FF.

tailor-made See CUSTOM, CUSTOM-BUILT.

take A dozen or more clichés start with *take*. Here is a bit of nonsense using several of them: "Why don't we take time by the forelock, take the bit in our teeth, take the bull by the horns, and take the enemy by storm? That would take the wind out of their sails." "Maybe so, but I'd rather take cognizance of the situation and take to my heels."

take for example FF if *take* has no clearly indicated object, as in "Take, for example, the parents can't agree on the baby's name." SWE says, "For example, some parents cannot . . ." or "Consider as an example parents who cannot . . ." or "Take, for example, new parents who cannot . . ."

take in Has moved from FF to SWE in the sense of "attend, go to, see, hear": "While in St. Louis they took in a Cardinal-Cub game."

take into consideration *Consider* is often enough.

take off FF or shakily SWE in the sense of "depart, leave": "They took off for Vancouver by car." It is solidly SWE, though, for the taking off of an airplane.

take on SWE for "hire" or "combat": "The factory took on new employees." "The new champion said he would take on any qualified opponent." FF for "scold" or "show excitement": "Ma really took on whenever Pa came home drunk." "Laurie took on over Gina's diamond bracelet and then took off after its donor."

take part See PARTAKE.

take place See OCCUR/TAKE PLACE.

take sick FF (regional) for *become* (*get*) *sick* (*ill*), *take sick* sometimes appears in SWE.

talent See GENIUS/TALENT.

talk (noun) *Talk* is SWE for reference to informal remarks such as a coach's pep talk or to any other rather conversational, not fully prepared oral presentation. For more formal occasions, *address*, *lecture*, or *speech* is appropriate. See also ADDRESS/LECTURE.

talk to/talk with See SPEAK TO.

tall See HIGH/LOFTY/TALL.

target This word often contributes to brevity. *Target date* is obviously shorter and less awkward than *the date by which completion of the task is hoped for*. But *target* is used too often in contexts where it is neither appropriate nor helpful. Often more accurate: *quota, goal, objective. Targeted* can often be omitted, as in "the targeted objective."

task (verb) This is a vogue word, as in "This office is tasked with the responsibility for . . . " Although nouns are often made into verbs, such transformation is desirable only when no existing verb does the job. In our example, *has* or *has been assigned* or *is responsible for* would be the usual SWE preference.

teacher See EDUCATOR.

technic/technique Interchangeable for "method of doing something," but few people use *technic*. However, *technics* is frequent in SWE for "the theory or study of a process or an act" or "technical methods or details."

technician See ENGINEER/SCIENTIST/TECHNICIAN.

teeming *Teeming* means "swarming": "a pond teeming with carp." Dubious: "Savannah and Charleston are teeming with history." Exaggerated: "Nashville, Indiana, is teeming with art dealers." For the first, *rich in* may be more suitable. For the second, perhaps "has almost a dozen art dealers."

teen-age(d) See MIDDLE-AGE(D)/TEEN-AGE(D).

telecast/televise The verbs are interchangeable: "PBS will telecast (or *televise*) the debate." *Televise* has become more frequent. The past tense and past participle of *telecast* may be either *telecast* or *telecasted*, usually the former. *Telecast*, but not *televise*, may be a noun: "The telecast can be seen on CBS."

tell it like it is FF. Not yet old, but already tired, for "be honest about it, face the facts, be realistic."

tell tales out of school Cliché. SANE recommends *tattle*.

temblor *Temblor*, based on a Spanish verb for "shake," is standard – not *tremblor*, even though the earth "trembles" during an earthquake.

temerity/timidity/timorousness *Temerity* is boldness, audacity: "She had the temerity to say that my mascara was too thick." *Timidity* is almost the opposite: "timidity, shyness, fear." *Timorousness* also involves fear or shyness, but hesitation, too.

temperature See FEVER/TEMPERATURE.

tempo Refers to relative speed or characteristic rhythm – not to something not moving. Poor: "The tempo of the international situation has changed." This would be improved if *discussions* or another action word replaced *situation*.

temporal/temporary *Temporal* is sometimes misused for *temporary*. *Temporal* is in contrast to *spiritual* or *eternal*; it means "pertaining to this life": "Ministers tell us that we think too much of temporal life, not enough of the hereafter." *Temporary* means "not expected to last long": "Some 'temporary' buildings were moved to college campuses after World War II and are still in use there."

tend to   Shortened from *attend, tend* is SWE in "tend the sick," "tend bar," "tend the store," and similar expressions. Conservatives, however, object to "tend to business," "tend to a child," and the like, preferring *attend to.* SWE usage is divided. Since the choice is not clear and not really important, follow your own preference.

tender (verb)   See OFFER/TENDER.

tenet   See DOGMA/TENET.

term as   SWE usually omits *as* in sentences such as "We termed him (as) recalcitrant." "He was termed (as) a traitor."

terminate   Often high-flown for "end."

terrible/terribly   Conservatives say – accurately – that *terrible* and its adverb have degenerated from "filling with terror" to mean "bad" or "painful": "My leg cramp was terrible" or to "very" as in "We are terribly happy." There is little chance to reclaim the meanings. Today, to express the similar meaning of *terrible*, we must rely on a substitute such as *terror-filled, terrifying, frightening*, or the much weaker *scary.*

tetchy/touchy   Interchangeable, although *tetchy* is unlikely in serious contexts. A variant of *tetchy* is *techy.*

than (in incomplete comparisons)   SWE avoids unfinished comparisons such as "He liked movies more than his mother." An added *do, does*, or *did* generally makes the intended meaning clear.

than any/than anyone   Suppose that Walter, seven feet tall, is the tallest member of a basketball team. He is not taller than any member, because he *is* a member. He is taller than any *other* member of the team. He is taller than anyone *else* on the team. The principle: In using *any* or *anyone* in comparing things or people belonging to the same group, logic requires *any other* and *anyone else.* (In FF, *other* and *else* are often left out.) See also OTHER.

than I (*he, she, we, they*)/than me (*him, her, us, them*)   SWE: "He argued more successfully than I." The meaning is "than I did," with *I* the subject of a shortened clause. Similarly, "He worked harder than I (*she, we, they*)." Usually FF, but found now and then in informal SWE: "He argued more successfully than me (*her, us, them*)." SWE: "His remarks hurt my sister more than me." The meaning is that he hurt me, although he hurt my sister more. *Me* is an object of *hurt.* Similarly, "His remarks hurt her more than us (*them*)." FF: "His remarks hurt my sister more than Clara and I." In "He called her more often than I [did]" and "He called her more often than (he called) me," the words shown here in parentheses are often added to prevent misunderstanding, but are not grammatically necessary.

than what   In many sentences, such as "Hamburger costs more than what it did last year," *what* is unneeded.

than whom   SWE usually avoids the expression because of its awkwardness. When used, it is generally in sentences such as "Senator

Clancy, than whom no more loyal follower of the president could be found, was . . ." (Grammatically, *than who* would be required, like *she* in "worked harder than she (did)," but centuries of usage have established *than whom*.)

thank you in advance Somewhat discourteous, for this phrase suggests that the writer does not want to take the trouble to write another letter to express his gratitude.

thanks to SWE in sentences such as "Thanks to an early winter storm, the school bus driver could not make his rounds."

that (adverb) Yes, *that* can be an adverb, although usually it is a pronoun or an adjective. In "You won't need an overcoat, it's not that cold," *that* modifies *cold*. The use is SWE, but more frequent in informal contexts. *This* may similarly be employed adverbially.

that of SWE: "The upholstery of the sofa is better than that of the chair." (*That of* is needed. Else *upholstery* would be compared with *chair*.) Illogical: "One of the more interesting sports in Minnesota is that of curling." (*That of* should be omitted. The sport is curling.) *That of* is not followed by a possessive case, which would create a double possessive; not "the theory was that of Mrs. Dipple's" but ". . . that of Mrs. Dipple." Still better: "The theory was Mrs. Dipple's."

that (omission of) *That* may be omitted before a following clause if no lack of clarity results. SWE: "He said (that) he would need more time." Dubious: "I want to point out my opponent was . . . ," which needs *that* before *my opponent* to prevent momentary misreading.

that (position of) "The coach said on Friday he would start Hanson at center." First note the meaning when you insert *that* after *said*. Then note the difference when you place it after *Friday*. Draw your own conclusion.

that (referring to a clause) See WHICH (REFERRING TO A CLAUSE).

that there/this here Why are *that there book* and *this here book* FF, while *that book there* and *this book here* are SWE? The reason is that *there* and *here* are customarily adverbs, but in *that there book* or *this here book* they seem to be adjectives modifying *book*. In *that book there* or *this book here*, however, those words have the clearly adverbial meanings of "in that place" or "in this place." We can say "that book in that place" but not "that in that place book." In most sentences, of course, *there* and *here* are not needed at all. *That book* and *this book* suffice.

that/which In introducing clauses *that* and *which* can often be interchanged. However, many careful writers use *that* with restrictive clauses (essential to the meaning of the sentence) and *which* with nonrestrictive (helpful but not essential). Restrictive: "All eggs that are cracked must be discarded." (Note that the meaning changes if *that are cracked* is omitted.) Nonrestrictive: "All eggs, which are high in cholesterol, are excluded from this diet." (The clause adds but is not essential to the basic meaning.) *Which* is also sometimes useful in a sentence that would otherwise be overburdened with *that*'s.

that's for sure (*certain, real*) Widely used in popular speech, apparently in the mistaken belief that *for* adds emphasis. SWE drops *for*: *that's sure (certain, real)*.

thaw See MELT/THAW.

theft See BURGLARY/HOLDUP/ROBBERY.

their, them, they SWE generally avoids *their, them*, or *they* to refer to *anybody, anyone, each, everybody, everyone, no one, many a person, a person, somebody*, or other singular pronouns or nouns. Instead it uses *he, him, his, she, her, hers* as appropriate. Informal: "Everybody thinks that such an accident can't happen to them, but they are wrong." SWE most often substitutes *him* and *he*, or recasts: "Most people think that such an accident cannot happen to them, but they are wrong."

their/there/they're Their: *belonging to them* – "their house"; there: *in that place* – "Look over there! There it is!"; they're: *they are* – "They're late."

theirs Never use an apostrophe in *theirs*. It is not to be confused with *there's*, meaning "there is."

then too Overused and sometimes inexact. Dubious: "I hope to make the football team; then too I plan to go out for basketball." More clear: "I am trying out for the football team, and in the winter I plan to go out for basketball."

thence, thenceforth See HENCE, HENCEFORTH.

theory See OPINION/THEORY.

therapy May include both physical and mental treatment, but ordinarily not surgery.

there is (*are, was, were*) **1.** Sentences beginning with one of these forms are sometimes unnecessarily wordy. For example, "There are three swans in the pool," although not objectionable, is a word longer than "Three swans are in the pool." Besides, *there* is a colorless, almost meaningless word, but *swans* immediately creates a picture. **2.** Grammatically, *there* as in 1 is called an expletive, meaning "a filler word." It is not the subject. The subject in the example is *swans*, which requires the verb *are* rather than *is*. Similarly, "There *were* three swans," "There *is* one swan," "There *are* ten pies left," "There *is* no pie left," "There *were* ten pies left." **3.** In a sentence such as "There were only two swans got into the water," the *there* construction is FF. SWE would phrase it in either of these ways: "There were only two swans that got into the water" or preferably "Only two swans got into the water."

therefor, therefore, thereof, thereto, theretofore Useful in law and sometimes in business, but except for *therefore* these words are obsolescent or obsolete elsewhere. (*Therefore* is in general use meaning "for that reason." The legalistic *therefor* means "for that thing"

235

or "for those things": "purchased said property and paid therefor the sum of ten thousand dollars.") See also HEREOF/HERETOFORE/HEREUNTO . . .

these kind See KIND OF, SORT OF.

they (indefinite) English lacks a pronoun like the French *on*, which can be used indefinitely to mean "people," "most people," "the inhabitants," "everyone," or "some people." Speakers of English try to overcome the deficiency by using *they*, but then conservatives ask the unanswerable question, "Who are *they* in 'They say that the murderer will never be known' or 'They have cold winters in Montana'?" *They* survives the implied criticism and frequently, even in reputable publications, does serve as our equivalent of French *on*. Often, though, writers of SWE prefer a clear, specific replacement, such as "Townspeople say . . ." or "Montanans have cold winters," but sometimes turn reluctantly to the indefinite *they*.

they're See THEIR/THEM/THEY.

think to 1. FF (regional) for "remember to": "She didn't think to bring her pipe wrenches." 2. SWE for "expect to": "Before he noticed that the rope was frayed, he had thought to use it to climb over the wall."

thing An essential word, but when a more specific one fits the context, SWE gives *thing* a rest.

thinking Overused for *opinion*: "What is your thinking about this?"

Third World This "world" includes undeveloped or developing countries, especially those in Asia and Africa but sometimes also in South or Central America, that are not clearly allied with either Communist or non-Communist powers.

this (for *a*) FF: "There was this man who could stand on his head for two hours." SWE: ". . . a man," unless there has been an earlier reference to him.

this, that (reference) SWE makes sure that readers can immediately understand what *this* or *that* represents. Dubious: "She wanted to buy either the plain or the plaid shirt, but this was difficult." (Does *this* mean the buying or the deciding?) "City officials are making plans for the construction of a new library. That cannot be done quickly." (The planning or the construction, or both?)

this See also the entries for *that*.

thither See HITHER/THITHER/WHITHER.

thoroughbred See PUREBRED/THOROUGHBRED.

thoroughfare Although it survives in "America the Beautiful" in the line "A thoroughfare for freedom beat," the word can be confusing. It can mean either a highway or a street connecting two other streets, and the sign "No Thoroughfare" is equivalent to "Dead End." Because of possible misunderstanding, SWE rarely uses it.

thoroughly (completely) satisfied Usually *satisfied* can stand alone.

those kind See KIND OF, SORT OF.

though See ALTHOUGH.

thousand "Several thousand immigrants" refers to an entire group, "several thousand of the immigrants" to part of a larger group. See also MILLION.

thrash/thresh SWE generally uses *thrash* for "flog, beat," and *thresh* with reference to harvesting grain. See also ANNIHILATE, DESTROY, FLAY . . .

thresh See THRASH/THRESH.

thrice Now rare for "three times."

thrifty In SWE, people can be thrifty but things cannot. The word means "frugal, wisely economical." Inanimate things cannot be wise or unwise. Used dubiously in advertising: "the thrifty flour (*soft drink*, and so on)." See also ECONOMICAL/FRUGAL/THRIFTY . . .

throe/throw *Throe* refers to spasm, struggle, or pain (often emotional). Its Old English ancestor is a verb meaning "to suffer." SWE: "in the throes (not *throws!*) of despair."

through In the sense of "completed, finished," as in "When Congress was through amending, the bill was unrecognizable," *through* is SWE. Conservative editors, however, consider too informal *through* in sentences such as "Our relationship is over. We are through" or "The injury finished his career. He was through." The distinction seems too trivial to worry about, although 25 percent of the AHD usage panel do so.

through thick and thin This cliché was clearer when, as in Chaucer's day, *thick* was understood as short for "thicket" and *thin* meant "open space."

throughout Because of the redundancy, SWE avoids using *throughout* with any word meaning "all" or "whole"; not "She sewed shirts throughout the entire day" but ". . . throughout the day."

throw See THROE/THROW.

thrust As in "the thrust of this proposal" or even "this plan has thrust," the word has only vague meaning but a strong suggestion of the masculine power that many executives and politicians admire. It is SWE.

thus/thusly **1.** *Thus* is one of many adverbs with no *-ly*, so *thusly* is never needed. **2.** *Thus* is a rather stiff word, often better replaced by *so* or *as a result* or *that is why*. *Therefore* also is sometimes possible but is equally stiff.

tied Redundant: "Both (or *The two*) teams are tied." Obviously if one team is tied with the other, both are included. Similarly redundant: "All three teams are tied." SWE says: "The three teams are tied."

tie-in This term is overused for "connection" but useful in specific meanings. For example, businesspeople talk about tie-in sales of one product with another. Newspaper editors or television news directors may be interested in tie-ins between news events.

tight(ly) **1.** In "Screw the lid on (*tight* or *tightly*)," either may be used. *Tight* is both an adjective and an adverb. **2.** "Sleep tight" is

237

standard, although most likely in informal contexts. Never "Sleep tightly."

till, until Interchangeable. Note that *till* has no apostrophe. A short form of *until*, written *'til*, appears mainly in verse of a bygone day.

tiller See HELM/RUDDER/TILLER.

tilting at windmills The nearsighted Don Quixote rode with his lance to attack windmills, which he thought were huge, fearsome knights. Note that the phrase uses *at*, not *with*, as it is sometimes mistranslated. Note, too, that until a better metaphor for opposing imaginary enemies is found, the phrase suits well, even though it has become a cliché.

timber/timbre In American use *timber* ordinarily refers to large growing trees (which become *lumber* after they are cut down and sawed into boards). *Timbre* refers to the quality (not pitch or loudness) of a speaking or singing voice or of a musical instrument: "Two violins may differ slightly or greatly in timbre."

times less "Scientific tests show that Brand X is three times less strong than Brand Y." Third-grade arithmetic teaches children that *times* refers to multiplying, not dividing. Usual SWE: "Brand X is only one third as strong" or "Brand Y is three times as strong."

timidity See TEMERITY/TIMIDITY/TIMOROUSNESS.

tinker's dam(n) SWE writers take their choice, *dam* or *damn*, according to their choice of conflicting etymologies: (1) In mending metal pots, tinkers used a bit of cloth or clay – a sort of dam – to hold the solder in place until it set. (2) Tinkers swore a great deal.

tiny little, wee small Authors of children's books are justified in using expressions such as "tiny little rosebud" or "wee small children" because many children like repetition and reinforcement. But writers for adults need not put one *little* word after another. Similar comments apply to *big huge* and the like.

-tion "The installation of new evaporation instrumentation seems a confirmation of the corporation's intention of remaining in contention." SWE dislikes many *-tion* words close together. It lets verbs do more of the work: "The installing of new evaporating equipment suggests that the corporation intends to continue fighting for a larger share of the market."

tirade See HARANGUE/TIRADE.

tired cliché So it is.

'tis Once used in not very good verse, and now almost never. Same comment: *'twas, 'twere, 'twill*.

titanic Even bigger than *gigantic* and stronger too. But the sinking of the *Titanic* in 1912, with the loss of 1,517 lives, gave the word a bad connotation.

to SWE omits unless really needed. In "Where is she going to?" it deletes *to*. See also **PREPOSITION AT END**.

to all intents and purposes A shortened version of a legal phrase, but still too long, since *practically, in practice,* or *in effect* says the same thing.

to be (omission of)   FF (dialectal): "The rug needs vacuumed," "The engine needs worked on." SWE: ". . . needs to be vacuumed (*worked on,* and so on)." Apparently *need* is the verb most often mistreated in this way.

to me   Except after verbs like *seem, to me* is FF for "in my opinion." FF: "Sandy Koufax to me was the smartest pitcher of that decade." SWE: "Sandy Koufax in my opinion was . . ."

to we the people   Because the Preamble to the U.S. Constitution begins "We the people," some of the descendants of those people believe that the phrase is inviolable. Even congressmen have been heard to say "to (*with, from,* and so on) we the people." In the Constitution, however, *we* is the subject of a sentence, not an object of a preposition. SWE says, "We the people are . . . ," "to us the people," "may hurt us the people."

to wit   Except in law, *to wit* has been replaced by *as follows* or *the following.*

together with   See ALONG WITH, AS WELL AS, IN ADDITION TO . . .

tome   Not generally applied to an ordinary book but to one volume in a series or, especially, to a sizable scholarly work or an unusually large book of any sort.

tomfoolery   SWE, equivalent to *foolish behavior* or *shenanigans.* OED traces *tomfool* to 1356–1357, *tomfoolery* to 1840. Age may deserve respect.

ton   SWE: "a two ton (or *two-ton*) truck," "It weighs two tons," "two tons of coal." British and sometimes American: "two ton of coal" (infrequent in SWE). Incidentally, an American ton is 2,000 pounds; a British ton, 2,240.

tony   Once a favorable adjective meaning "aristocratic," the word is now used as a pejorative similar to "hightoned, pretentious, showy": "lives on the toniest street in town." It is infrequent in SWE, but possible in lightly critical remarks.

too   1. Although *too* in the sense of "very" is now seldom declaimed against, as it once was, it sometimes seems a bit silly, as in "Prospects for peace do not look too good." *Too* usually means "more than enough," and obviously prospects for peace could not be more than enough. Other examples of questionable usage: "She doesn't sing too well." "Glisson is a good fielder, but he doesn't hit too well." See also NOT . . . TOO. 2. *Too* is weak as a sentence opener, in the sense of *further* or *furthermore*: "Too, girls usually have more verbal facility than boys have." 3. A few conservatives still object to *too* before a past participle, saying that *too much alarmed* is preferable to *too alarmed.* SWE accepts both.

top   Headline writers' love of three-letter words has led to overuse of *top*. Possible substitutes: *chief, foremost, highest, leading, main, most important, primary.*

topic See SUBJECT/TOPIC.

tornado See CYCLONE/TORNADO.

tortuous/torturous *Tortuous* means "crooked, unpleasantly winding": "a tortuous road," "tortuous reasoning," "the tortuous path to a presidential nomination." *Torturous* is associated with *torture*, extreme pain: "Visits to a modern dentist are seldom as torturous as they once were."

total (verb) In the sense of "demolish (an *automobile*)," *was totaled* is useful to claim adjusters to indicate that a vehicle would cost more to repair than its worth. Dictionaries still list this meaning of *total* as slang or informal, but the verb is appearing more and more in SWE, especially in newspaper accounts of accidents.

total of Often can be deleted. The words may be used to avoid starting a sentence with a figure: "A total of 1,415 dressed turkeys were (not *was*) shipped."

toted/totted *Toted* is a pleasant SWE informality: "They toted their gear into camp." *Totted*, past tense of the verb *tot* derived from *total*, is usually followed by *up*: "We totted ("totaled") up the day's receipts." *Toted (up)* is sometimes substituted in FF.

touchy See TETCHY/TOUCHY.

tough As a synonym for *difficult* or *unfortunate, tough* is knocking on the doors of SWE but is not always admitted. "It's tough to get a job now." "Yes, it's tough to be out of work these days."

toward, towards Interchangeable, with *toward* extending its lead.

track/tract In referring to land, you could be on the right *tract*, but otherwise you are likely to be on the right *track*. Trains run and autos or horses race on tracks, and animals leave tracks in the snow. Some evangelists may leave religious tracts with us.

trade See OCCUPATION/PROFESSION/TRADE.

tragedy, tragic Junior spills his chocolate milk, messing up the new carpet – unfortunate, but not *tragic*. Joan's date doesn't show up – maybe a good riddance, but not a *tragedy*. Aside from special literary definitions, a *tragedy* is a disastrous event with lasting and often fatal consequences. It may be only personal and familial but possibly may reach international proportions.

trained expert See QUALIFIED EXPERT.

traipse Flesch is rightly puzzled about why this four-hundred-year-old verb for "stroll aimlessly" is still labeled informal, and suggests that it may be because the word suggests "unbusinesslike meandering." A word should not be excluded from any context simply because it doesn't sound businesslike. People who *traipse* are probably not businesslike, anyway, but they're still people. The verb should be SWE, and in the minds of some editors it is.

transient/transitory Although almost synonymous, *transient* is more likely with concrete things, *transitory* with abstract: "transient guests," "the transient sands of a windswept shore"; "transitory grandeur (*beauty, hopes*, and the like)."

translucent/transparent See DIAPHANOUS/TRANSLUCENT/TRANSPAR-
ENT; OPAQUE/TRANSLUCENT.

transpire In science, to *transpire* is to give off vapor. In SWE general
use it means "to come to light, to become known": "It transpired
that Clark had been robbing the till." Some people misinterpreted
sentences like that to mean "it happened that . . ." So arose a
controversy that still goes on. May or may not *transpire* mean "to
happen"? Correspondents have written erudite and witty letters to
the (London) *Times* favoring one side or the other. The conservative
AHD usage panel voted against, 62–38 percent; editors might split
50–50. The issue is not earthshaking, does not affect clarity. Most
things that happen do become known to someone. SWE writers
choose the side they prefer.

treachery/treason Although sometimes used interchangeably for
"betrayal of trust," the words are often differentiated in SWE. The
victim of *treachery* is ordinarily a person, small group, company, or
the like, but the victim of *treason* is one's government, sovereign,
nation, fellow citizens. As a result, treason is certainly a crime, but
treachery is not unless clearly illegal activity is present.

trek This Afrikaans word for a journey by ox-drawn cart or wagon
suggests that the noun or verb should be used for something slow,
long, arduous. Dubious: "a trek to the neighborhood supermarket."

trendy A good word for "following a trend." It is SWE, a favorite
of the *New York Times Magazine*.

trigger (verb) *Trigger* is SWE in the sense of "activate, serve as the
impulse to," but perhaps is overused. See also SPARK.

TRITE EXPRESSIONS Expressions that become trite are generally
somewhat figurative. If not, they are likely to be a set combination
of modifier and noun. When first used, they may have been startlingly appropriate; imitators of the phrasemaker picked up the expression; their own hearers and readers borrowed it in turn. Because
of overexposure it lost its verve, like ginger ale spread over the
bottom of a saucer.

It is impossible to list all the trite expressions. Some are mentioned
elsewhere in this book. Here is a small, random assortment of others:

abysmal ignorance	days of old (olden days)
beat a retreat	every waking hour
better half	fair sex
blind justice	Father Time
blushing bride	generous to a fault
brutally murdered	grateful earth
busy as bees	the Grim Reaper
charming hostess	hoary with age
clear as crystal	honeyed words
crack of dawn	host of friends
dark secret	icy wastes

immaculately dressed	primrose path
the last one on earth to	quick as a flash
manly chest	rolling prairie
Mother Earth	roar of battle
motherly advice	ruby lips
nestling in the valley	streamlined efficiency
off the beaten track	stubborn pride (. . . as a mule)
pluck up courage	throw caution to the winds
point with pride	walk on air
pretty as a picture	white as a sheet

242   **trip**   FF (slang) for "a prolonged hallucination": "I had a bad LSD trip last week." Informal: *ego trip, guilt trip.*

triumphal/triumphant   *Triumphal* ordinarily involves things and celebrations: "triumphal banners, processions," "the triumphal march in *Aïda.*" *Triumphant* also is celebratory but usually with reference to people: "triumphant team members hugging one another," "triumphant voices."

trivial   See ACADEMIC; PALTRY/PETTY/TRIVIAL.

-trix   Along with another feminine ending, *-ess, -trix* is dying out. For example, *aviatrix* has been largely superseded by the generic *aviator.*

troop/troupe   *Troupe* is used almost solely for an itinerant group of entertainers.

trooper/trouper   The first is a mounted soldier or police officer; his horse has usually been replaced by a motor vehicle. A *trouper* is one of a troupe of entertainers.

troublous   Obsolescent for *troublesome*, as in "We live in troublous times."

trousers   The word requires a plural verb.

truism/truth   A *truism* is a *truth* but is so obvious that perhaps it need not be stated: "It is a truism that formal weddings are expensive." An author, however, may write a sentence like that to introduce a topic, and go on to add some fresh comments.

trustee/trusty   The plurals of these nouns are *trustees* and *trusties*. A trustee is (1) a person authorized to administer property or affairs for someone else, or (2) a member of the governing board of a college or other institution. A *trusty* is most often a prisoner given unusual privileges, degree of freedom, or responsibility. Trustees of a university are not flattered when students or alumni write about them as trusties.

try (noun)   Although *try* is normally a verb, its noun use is also SWE in expressions such as "make a good try."

try (verb)   News story: "Identities given by the Vietnamese as those of dead Americans will try to be confirmed." No. Identities cannot try anything. In using *try*, SWE shows who or what is making the attempt. The example could be written, "American investigators will try to confirm . . ."

try/attempt, endeavor, strive   *Try* is a workhorse, patient and unassuming. *Attempt, endeavor,* and *strive* can be rather pretentious. (To show this, Evans suggested substituting one of the other words in "If at first you don't succeed, try, try again.") *Endeavor* is the most formal of the three synonyms and suggests continued effort. *Strive* is the most vigorous, suggesting strenuous, conscientious work on a difficult task.

try and/try to   SWE treats *try to* as more logical than *try and*. We *try to do* something (one action), but *try and do* seems to imply two actions, trying and doing. *Try and* is FF.

tummy   A word that children like, *tummy* is cutie-pie as a name for an adult abdomen: "Tuck in your tummy with a Tutweiler." It is sometimes used in SWE for a light touch.

tumult/turmoil   The two are often used interchangeably. If the disorder is noisy, or if large numbers of people are involved, *tumult* is the more likely.

turbid/turgid   *Turbid* means "muddy," "dark with soot, smoke, or fog." Figuratively: "muddled, confused, in turmoil": "a prostitute's turbid life." *Turgid* means "swollen, inflated" and by extension "overornate in language or style": "the turgid styles of some Victorian writers."

twice as many . . . than   Not customary in SWE: "Twice as many cases of flu were reported locally in 1988 than in 1987." SWE usually replaces *than* with *as*. The construction is similar to *twice as large as*.

twins   Seldom if ever is *both* needed with *twins*. In "Both twins like ice cream," SWE replaces *Both* with *The*, although *both* may add a little emphasis. In "pair of twins," *pair of* is ordinarily expendable. However, *pairs of* or *sets of* is needed in "Their children are a girl, a boy, and two pairs of twins" (or ". . . twin boys and twin girls," and so on). To indicate a boy and a girl, either *a mixed pair of twins* or *mixed twins* is customary.

two first, two last   See FIRST TWO/TWO FIRST.

tycoon   Now SWE for "powerful businessman."

type of   SWE: "this type of architecture," "one type of quince." FF: "this type architecture," "an old type sewing machine."

243

U

ugly as sin   This is not only a cliché but an inaccurate one. Most "sin" is on the surface temptingly attractive, like Heinrich Heine's devil: "a handsome, charming man . . . obliging and courtly . . . who speaks well of Church and State."

ultrasonic   See SUPERSONIC/ULTRASONIC.

unabridged   See ABRIDGED/UNABRIDGED.

unalienable   Despite being in the Declaration of Independence, *unalienable* has been largely superseded by *inalienable*.

unanimous   A member of a president's cabinet: "The nomination was unanimous by almost everybody." That's like saying that something is perfect except for the imperfections, or that a bin is full except for the third that is empty. *Nearly unanimous*, however, is logical.

unauthorized trespassers   A hand-lettered sign on a fence: "Unauthorized Trespassers Will Be Persecuted." Since all trespassers are unauthorized, that modifier should have been deleted. See also PERSECUTE/PROSECUTE.

unaware(s)   Because *unaware* can be either adjective or adverb, why bother with the *s*? "They were unaware of . . ." (adjective), ". . . caught us unaware" (adverb).

uncomparable   See INCOMPARABLE/UNCOMPARABLE.

unconscious   See SUBCONSCIOUS/UNCONSCIOUS.

under water/underwater   To modify a noun, SWE uses *underwater*: "the underwater scenery at Silver Springs." Otherwise it uses two words: "They could see fish swimming ten feet under water."

underlay/underlie   See OVERLAY/OVERLIE.

understand   See COMPREHEND/UNDERSTAND.

underwhelm   *Overwhelm* is derived from an Old English word for "to turn over." A person may be overwhelmed if he or she is figuratively turned upside down. *Underwhelm* is a humorous variant meaning "not excited, not turned upside down." It is not yet SWE, but deserving. It is easily understood and provides a light touch.

undue, unduly   These words mean "excessive, excessively, or unwarranted" and are omitted in SWE if something else in the sentence suggests excess: "She overpraised him (unduly)." "His (undue) alarm was not warranted."

unexceptionable/unexceptional   *Unexceptionable* means "beyond reproach, beyond objection": "Few people live completely unexceptionable lives." *Unexceptional* may mean either "common, ordinary, usual" or "without any exceptions": "Our day was routine, completely unexceptional." "Your adherence to this diet must be unexceptional. Eat nothing not listed here."

unfavorable   See OPTIMISTIC/PESSIMISTIC; FAVORABLE/UNFAVORABLE.

UNFINISHED COMPARISONS   "Our trucks are sturdier." "This toothpaste makes teeth whiter." "The analgesic that works faster." Sturdier, whiter, or faster than what? An advertising writer likes such unfinished comparisons because they imply what cannot be proved: that Ford trucks are sturdier than Chevrolets, Aim will make your teeth whiter than Crest, and so on. In all writing, not just advertising, SWE users check to be sure that they show what is being compared with what. See also SO (IN COMPARISONS); SUCH A.

unflappable British slang for a World War II air-raid warning was *flap*; from that came *unflappable* ("not capable of being alarmed.") The word crossed the ocean and in recent years has become an SWE synonym for *calm* or *imperturbable*.

uninterested See DISINTERESTED/UNINTERESTED.

unique The language needs a word meaning "pertaining to the only one of its kind": "She made a beautiful but unique dress." Common usage, although not most SWE usage, has weakened the word to mean no more than "unusual." As a result, to express the example unmistakably we must write, "She made a beautiful dress that was the only one of its kind" or ". . . dress unlike any ever seen before." In its strict meaning, nothing can be *more, less, rather, somewhat,* or *very unique.* SANE pleads for restoration of a unique heritage. See also **COMPARISON OF ABSOLUTES.**

United Kingdom See BRITISH ISLES/ENGLAND/GREAT BRITAIN . . .

universal(ly) Earth is not the universe. Phrases such as *universally believed* cannot be used honestly, because who knows what is believed in other galaxies? But despite the illogicality, the phrases are SWE.

universal panacea See PANACEA/REMEDY.

unknown Probably there is no person not known to someone else. Almost always, then, a person should be described as *unidentified* rather than *unknown.* With reference to things, such as sums of money or itineraries, some may accurately be called "unknown": total losses in a forest fire, for example, may be incalculable and therefore never known. SWE checks, though, to see whether *undecided, undisclosed, uncertain, unannounced, undetermined,* or some other such word may be more accurate.

unless and until SWE generally finds that one of the conjunctions will suffice.

unless/without FF (regional and illogical) says, "People cannot sneak up on a Doberman without he knows it." SWE says, ". . . without his knowing it" or "unless they are extraordinarily cautious." Note that SWE does not use *without,* a preposition, as a conjunction. FF: "You can't get to the Frobishers without you ford a stream."

unorganized See DISORGANIZED/UNORGANIZED.

unprecedented If something is truly unprecedented, it has no precedent. It or something much like it has never happened before. SWE seldom uses it for "strange, uncommon, rare." A drouth, for example, is unprecedented only if the region has never before been so dry for so long. See also UNIQUE.

unqualified See DISQUALIFIED/UNQUALIFIED.

unseemly This is a slightly old-fashioned word for "in poor taste, inappropriate."

unthinkable Nothing is unthinkable (or *inconceivable*) if anyone has ever thought it. But despite this illogicality, *unthinkable* and *inconceivable* are SWE.

until See *till, until; unless and until.*

untold wealth The meaning is not "concealed wealth" but "wealth so great that it has not been counted and perhaps cannot be." (One meaning of *tell* is "count," as in "telling her beads.")

unwieldy (Note the spelling.) The word is an adjective: "three unwieldy bags of cabbage." (The opposite, *wieldy*, is also SWE but is seldom seen or heard. People are more likely to talk about things hard to handle rather than easy.)

up 1. Redundant: *Up* can be omitted after a verb if it does not affect the meaning. For example, in "I picked up the scissors and opened up the package," the first *up* is needed but not the second. Ordinarily *up* can be deleted after *open, close, add, divide, settle, finish, hurry,* and many other verbs. **2.** With *until, till, to:* SWE usually omits *up* in phrases such as "up until 1991." **3.** Informal SWE: Large dictionaries list various phrases using *up* in SWE, especially in informal contexts; for example, *up to you, up to mischief, not up to it.* More likely in FF are *hard up, on the up and up.* **4.** As a verb: The verb *up* is part of the jargon of card-playing: "up the ante, upped the bid," and as a figure of speech has moved into other contexts, including international diplomacy: "Once again Iran upped its demands." Athletics coaches, like military officers in fiction, may say, "Up, men, and go get 'em!" or "Up and at 'em!" in both of which *up* has the force of a verb. Elsewhere: "Restaurants are again upping the price of coffee." (Incidentally, they seem never to *down* the price.) FF: "She upped and hit him."

up to the hilt Cliché. An unpleasant metaphor suggesting the depth to which a dagger may be plunged. Unwisely used in gentler contexts such as "up to the hilt in party preparations."

upcoming As a synonym of *forthcoming* or *approaching, upcoming* is up and coming. Now SWE, despite William Safire's remark that the word reminds him of food being regurgitated.

upon See ON/UPON.

uppity A delightful FF (slang) word for "snooty" or "snobbish." "She gave him an uppity look before she noticed how handsome he was." Sometimes appears in SWE.

upshot See FINAL COMPLETION.

uptight FF. As used by some blacks, hippies, and others in the 1960s and 1970s, *uptight* meant any of several things: "tense," "nervous," "angry," "without money," "having a closed mind," "too conventional," "intimate," or "OK." The chameleonic word has not yet decided on the color(s) it prefers. Even aging hippies cannot always be sure about which definition is intended, although intonation and context give useful hints.

upward revision Used by semantically sensitive politicians and businesspeople to mean "It will cost you more."

upward(s) *Upward* is usual in the United States as both adjective and adverb: "an upward trend," "moved slowly upward."

us men/we men   SWE uses *we men* as a subject and generally as a predicate nominative: "We men sometimes disagreed." "It was we men who disagreed." In the second example, *us men* may sometimes occur in light SWE. *Us men* is the form used as an object: "Their unkind words hurt us men." "Some of us men wanted revenge." Obviously, the same principles apply to *we (us) women, boys, girls*, or *teddy bears*.

usage/use   Although these words are sometimes used interchangeably as nouns, *usage* is customary with regard to the ways that language is spoken or written: "modern English usage." It may apply also to other customary practices: "according to the usages of the Roman Catholic Church." In other senses *use* is much more frequent: "the use of this tool," "a medicine in wide use." *Usage* in such expressions sounds stilted, comparable to *wastage* when *waste* is meant.

use to/used to   Without *did* or another auxiliary verb, *used to* is SWE: "Australians used to resent references to early convict-settlers." In such sentences it attaches the meaning "formerly" and indicates past time. In statements such as "She became used to his bragging," it means "accustomed to." With *did, didn't,* or less frequently other auxiliaries, *use to* is customary, although some SWE writers prefer to avoid the construction. "Did they use to come here?" "They didn't use to come here." For the latter, "They used not to come here" is also frequent.

user-friendly   SWE. A computer term, long needed in other contexts but now overworked, as in an advertisement that calls milk "the user-friendly food."

utilize   The response to "May I utilize your facility?" is likely to be "What?" "May I use your bathroom?" will probably bring "First door on the right." SWE tries to avoid highfalutin words, especially in everyday contexts.

V

vacillating   See AMBIVALENT.

VAGUENESS   *Vague* means "not specific." "She felt uncomfortable" is vague. Did some part of her body hurt, was she embarrassed, or did she have only undefinable feelings that something was wrong? "The room was long" is vague. Was it fifteen feet long, thirty, as long as half a football field, or what? At times there is no need for precision. In "The flames leaped high above the roofs of the little houses," dimensions for *high* and *little* would detract from the effect: "The flames leaped ten or eleven feet above the roofs of the houses, which averaged twenty by thirty feet in size." Amateur writers, however, are much more often vague than overprecise.

valuable/valued   A *valuable* item has monetary value or is useful. A *valued* possession is prized by its owner. It may have only sentimental value; it is not necessarily costly or even useful. For example, an old snapshot may be valued but not valuable in dollars. *Valuable,* however, may sometimes be appropriately modified: "valuable as a reminder of the family's earlier poverty."

vanity See ARROGANCE/CONCEIT/HAUGHTINESS . . .

variety See BRAND/KIND/VARIETY.

variously "The robber was described variously as dark-haired and thirty, and red-haired and forty." Only two descriptions are given, but *variously* implies several. SWE may say "described as either . . . or . . . ," or "described by some witnesses as . . . and by others as . . . "

vault See SAFE/VAULT.

venal/venial "The venal governor became a multimillionaire in two terms, although his salary was only $75,000 a year." A person is *venal* if corruptible, mercenary to an excessive degree. "Such kissing is only a venial sin if it is a sin at all, the priest told her." An act is *venial* if it is forgivable, not really a very serious transgression. In contrast, a *mortal* sin, such as suicide, causes spiritual death.

verbal See ORAL/VERBAL.

verbiage/verbosity Both signify wordiness. They are sometimes used interchangeably in SWE. However, *verbiage* generally refers to the wordiness of a piece of writing or speaking: "the verbiage of her legal opinions." *Verbosity* is more likely to refer to the wordiness of the speaker or writer: "the notorious verbosity of Senator Glickens." Rarely, *verbiage* means one's choice of words, one's manner of expression: "her clear, impeccable verbiage." Since the unfavorable meaning is much better known, this use may be misinterpreted.

verdict Technically, a jury but not a judge may bring in a *verdict.* The judge can make a decision, ruling, or finding, and can pronounce a sentence.

vermin The word refers to harmful or annoying insects as well as small animals such as rats and mice. Once the word was used as a singular, "A vermin was caught," but now is regarded as plural: "Vermin (not *vermins*) were keeping us awake every night."

verse See POETRY/VERSE; STANZA/VERSE.

verve/vim Both refer to energy and liveliness. *Verve* adds the idea of enthusiasm and is often used to describe style in literature or other artistic endeavors. *Vim* emphasizes physical vigor; in fact, *vim* and *vigor* are often teamed up – needlessly.

very Overused. An apocryphal story is told of a young writer with inherited wealth whose literary agent advised him to use *very* less often. A few days later the writer cabled the agent from a cruise ship, "Thank you very, very, very (84 more *very*'s) much." SWE favors *much, very much,* or another adverb rather than *very* alone before past participles showing physical states: *much worn, badly burned, very much strengthened.* Usage here, however, is not consistent.

via In Latin, *via* means "by way of." Conservatives like to preserve that meaning: "to Denver via St. Louis." In general, SWE follows the conservative preference, but some good writers use *via* for "by means of": "via private automobile," "via telephone," or even "became rich via oil-drilling." *By* is simpler and unpretentious.

viable The basic meaning is "capable of surviving," but that has been supplemented by "practicable, workable" and then has moved on to something almost as vague as "good." As a result of so much weakening, *viable* often needs to be replaced by a more precisely defined term, as context demands.

vice/vise Something considered evil is a *vice*: "the twin vices of drunkenness and gambling." "Vice isn't nice." A *vise* is a tool to hold something tightly, as a carpenter's vise holds a piece of wood or metal. Dictionaries list *vice* as an alternative spelling, but SWE (in this instance tool catalogs and books on carpentry) almost invariably use *vise* for the tool.

249

vicious See ABANDONED/DEPRAVED/VICIOUS.

victim See MARTYR/VICTIM.

vim See VERVE/VIM.

violin See FIDDLE/VIOLIN.

virile In SWE, not applied to women. (The ancestral word is Latin *vir* ("man"). The word does not refer solely to sexuality but also to strength, physical endurance, or the like.

virus In SWE one is not "hospitalized with a virus" (that sounds much too cozy), although the expression is common in FF. Nor, obviously, is one "hospitalized with a germ." Viruses and germs cause diseases but are not themselves diseases. One can, however, be "hospitalized *by* a virus."

vis-à-vis Sometimes used in FF but not in SWE for "about, concerning": "What do you think vis-à-vis Poland?" Today's SWE uses it most often in the sense of "compared with, in relation to," as in "What is your opinion of Senator Ream's revised bill, vis-à-vis her original proposal?"

vise See VICE/VISE.

visionary *Prophetic* has good connotations, *visionary* usually bad. A visionary scheme is an imaginative one that farsighted people believe has almost no chance of success. Sometimes, however, a visionary person is able to turn visions into reality, as the inventors of airplanes and radios did.

visit with Informal, now SWE, for "chat with," but may also mean "pay a visit to." You need not be with your friend when you visit with him, however; you may do so by telephone.

viz. An obsolescent abbreviation for *videlicet,* meaning "namely," *viz.* is still used in some reference books or legal documents but almost never elsewhere.

vocation See AVOCATION/VOCATION.

VOICE (of verbs) See **PASSIVE VOICE**.

vow Appropriate in a solemn context, *vow* refers to an earnest promise, an oath, not something trivial. Dubious: "I'm going to eat all the candy," she vowed.

wages (verb with) According to the King James usage in Acts 6:23, "The wages of sin is death," but modern English prefers a plural verb. See also SALARY/WAGES.

250 **wait for/wait on** In SWE a clerk or waiter *waits on* customers in a store or restaurant. The customers sometimes need to *wait for* help or *wait for* someone to come to them. *Wait on*, then, means "to serve," and *wait for*, "await." In FF, *wait on* is often used in both senses.

waive/wave *Waive* is used only in the sense of "relinquish voluntarily" or, less often, "postpone": "Cline waived his right to trial by jury." "The legislative committee waived action until next year." An arm gesture is a *wave*. A flag waves, a woman waves her hair, and water has waves.

wander See MEANDER/WANDER.

want *Want* is FF when followed by a noun clause: "Do you want I should go now?" "He wanted that we should wait." SWE uses a noun or noun equivalent: "Do you want me to go now?" "He wanted us to wait."

want for FF in expressions such as "Your mother wants for you to ride to town." SWE deletes *for*.

want in (*off, out*) FF for "want to come in (*get off, go out*)," these expressions have not become SWE perhaps because they seem to use prepositions as objects, although some grammarians explain that here *in*, *off*, and *out* are simply elliptical for "to come in" and so on.

want to "You want to study hard for Professor Warner's tests." *Want to* for "should" or "must" is FF.

want/wish Often interchangeable, *want* is more likely for physical things and *wish* for abstract or remote things: "He wanted some rye bread." "He wished immortality." Some people regard *wish* as slightly prissy.

ward off See AVERT/AVOID/PREVENT.

wave See WAIVE/WAVE.

wax (verb) For "become" or "grow," as in "He waxed eloquent," *wax* seems old-fashioned.

way (adverb) FF. A shortening of *away*, used by Stephen Foster in the line "Way (or '*Way*) down upon the Swanee River" from his song "My Old Kentucky Home." It is also used in conversation by countless others in expressions such as "way off in the distance," "That's way too hard."

(the) way   In sentences such as "He played it the way the old violinist had taught him," many users of SWE prefer *in the way* or *as* instead of *the way*.

way in which   Often *in which* can be deleted: "The general explained the way (in which) he wanted his subordinates to respond."

way out   This FF expression (persistent hippie slang) is often intended to praise or to describe something extraordinary, almost unbelievable: "Way out, man!" "That chick is way out!" "Allen's poetry is way out." Appears occasionally in SWE but lacks specificity.

way/weigh (nautical)   Seamen *weigh* ("raise") anchor, and soon the ship gets under *way*.

way(s)   SWE avoids "a ways" as illogical, but in FF "a long ways off" and the like frequently occur.

ways and means   Maybe a House of Representatives committee really deals with both, but probably few of its members can tell which is which. We ordinary folk can get by with either one.

we (editorial, royal, and presidential)   An editorial that presents the opinion(s) of a newspaper rightly uses *we* (as in "we believe") unless it is signed by one person. When *we* is used to mean all the people, a distinction such as "we Americans" is necessary. A king, queen, or pope customarily has used *we* to refer to the singular self, and U.S. presidents have used it ambiguously to refer to self, self and staff, the whole government, all Americans, or everybody in the world – which one often not specified.

we (reference)   "In America we follow the precepts of Christianity." Who are *we*? All Americans, some Americans, most Americans? Users of SWE try to make clear the meaning of *we* or any other pronoun. The example should probably begin with "*Many* (*some* or *most*) *Americans*." (In the same example, *the precepts* may also be questioned. All the Christian precepts? Most? Some? Selected ones of?)

wealthy   See AFFLUENT/OPULENT/RICH . . .

WEASEL WORDS   Theodore Roosevelt popularized this term for words that are slippery and elusive in meaning, that are slightly misleading, and that leave their users a way to escape if cornered. In "Savings up to 50 percent," the weasel words are *up to*, which here can mean anything from below 1 up to 50 percent. On seeing "All prices reduced," the weasel-word watcher asks, "Reduced from what?" "Compare our prices and save" – two good bits of advice, certainly, but compare with what and save how much? "Priced as low as (or *starting at*) $12.95" – and how high do the prices go? "Swish fights bad breath" – but who wins? "Water-resistant" – not to be confused with *waterproof*. "Doctors recommend ___" – which doctors, witch doctors?

wedding   See MARRIAGE/NUPTIALS/WEDDING.

wee small   See TINY LITTLE/WEE SMALL.

weigh (nautical)   See WAY/WEIGH.

weird   Dictionaries define *weird* as "supernatural" or "highly un-usual." The word is overused (FF) to describe almost anything at all out of the ordinary: "I had a weird day." "What a weird blouse!"

weirdo   FF (slang, but moving toward SWE for an unusually strange person whom one holds in contempt.

well and good   "Everything seems well and good." SWE generally settles for "All is well" or "Everything seems (or *looks*) good." See also GOOD/WELL.

well-nigh   Has been well-nigh replaced by *nearly*.

westerly   See EASTERLY/EASTERN.

wharf   See DOCK/PIER/WHARF.

what (verb with)   *What* may be singular or plural according to its context: "What sounds like a bird is actually a chipmunk." "What sound like birds are actually chipmunks." "She is wearing what seems to be a split skirt." "She is wearing what seem to be green tights."

what all, who all   Once considered regional but now more wide-spread, *what all* and *who all* are intensive forms of *what* and *who*, asking in effect, "What are all the things?" and "Who are all the people?": "What all did you talk about?" "Who all were at the dance?" Still found only infrequently in SWE.

what it's all about   FF. Cliché, beloved of sports commentators, for "the most important thing," or something similar: "Defense – that's what this game is all about."

what ever/whatever (in questions)   Although *whatever* is SWE in most instances, as in "Tell me whatever you can" or "Whatever you say will be held against you," in questions such as "What ever became of Kenneth Mahoney?" the two-word form is standard.

What's the matter?   SWE, but somewhat informal, for "What's wrong?" Used frequently by Shakespeare, but usually in a different sense.

whatsoever at all   "I felt no pain whatsoever at all" is redundant. SWE deletes *whatsoever*, *at all*, or both.

when, as, and if   To introduce a clause, SWE ordinarily chooses one, not all three.

when, where (in definitions)   A thing is not a when or a where. "A leopard is when a cat has spots" is not SWE, although comparable sentences occur often in FF. SWE: "A leopard is a large, spotted, wild member of the cat family" or "A leopard is a spotted cat."

whence   See HENCE/THENCE/WHENCE.

where (for *when* or *that*)   "Where full payment is impossible, credit terms may be arranged." In this statement, probably place (as sug-gested by *where*) is not really involved. SWE prefers *when* or *if* unless the reference is to place.

> FF: "I saw in the paper where oil has been found in Wyoming."
> SWE: ". . . that oil . . ."

where (in definitions) See WHEN, WHERE.

where . . . at (or *to*) See PREPOSITIONS.

where I'm coming from FF for "what I believe, what I insist on, what I'm trying to do." Sometimes results in odd sentences like this of Senator Robert Dole in 1988: "We need to keep a Republican in the White House, and that's where I'm coming from."

whereabouts (verb with) **1.** "Used with a singular or plural v[erb]," RHD says. However, a plural verb is essential when two or more persons may be in different places: "Their whereabouts ('locations') are unknown." **2.** (adverb) In sentences such as "Whereabouts is she now?" the word is only a long substitute for *where* and is not likely in SWE.

whereas Useful in legal documents and formal resolutions as a short way of saying "because it is a fact that." Today used only seldom elsewhere because it seems stilted.

whereby, wherefore, wherein, whereof Legalese for (respectively) "by which," "for that reason," "in which," "of which."

whether or not A few conservatives still insist that *or not* must accompany each *whether*, but most now grant that the chief use of *or not* is for emphasis, and only occasionally for clarity. Optional use: "Tell me whether (or not) you will be there." For emphasis: "I must know whether or not you will be there." For clarity: "You will be there whether you like it or not."

which Not used in SWE to refer to persons; not "the man which" but "the man who (*that, whom*)."

which (referring to a clause) "Marie asked her brother for some advice, which seldom happened." Such sentences are not uncommon in conversation, and usually not misunderstood, but are questioned in SWE. *Which* is intended to mean that Marie's asking was rare but seems to say that the advice seldom happened. Ambiguous: "She was not noted for her beauty, which was surprising." In using *this* or *that* to refer to a clause, SWE checks for clarity just as it does for *which*.

WHICHMIRE James Thurber coined this word for long, *which*-filled sentences in which even conscientious readers, which all writers hope for but which not everybody is, may become mired as in a swamp which they cannot get out of, for which they can't be blamed. Remedies: Cut irrelevancies. Shorten a clause to a phrase or a word. Divide the long sentences into two or three shorter ones, maybe like this: James Thurber coined this word for long, unclear *which*-filled sentences. Even conscientious readers may become mired in a verbal swamp created by too much whichcraft.

while See ALTHOUGH/WHILE.

whilst Frequent for *while* in Great Britain, but almost unknown in the United States.

whip(ped) cream The SWE form is *whipped*, simply because the cream has been whipped.

253

whiskey/whisky Scotch or Canadian *whisky*, Irish or American *whiskey*.

whither See HITHER/THITHER/WHITHER.

who else's See ELSE'S.

who/whom *Whom*, almost never used in FF, is a leading trouble-maker for those striving to master SWE. Here we will concentrate on formal style. Use *whom* (1) as object of a preposition: "To whom should we address the complaint?" "The complaint came from whom?" (2) as object of a verb: "She called whom?" "Whom did she call?" (object of *did call*). "Tell me whom she called" (object of *called*). *Who* is used as the subject of a sentence or clause: "Who is coming?" "Tell me who is coming." "Who shall I say is coming?" (subject of *is coming*). "I called Gomez, who I felt should be consulted" (subject of *should be consulted*; *I felt* is a clause on its own). Suggestions: (1) Make up several sentences closely resembling these examples. Repeat them *aloud* until all seem natural to you. (2) If in doubt, choose *who*. "Tell me who she called" may be excused as conversational English, but "Whom is calling" sounds idiotic. See also DOG WHO; WHOEVER/WHOMEVER.

whoever/whomever The same principles apply to these words as to *who*, *whom*: use *whoever* as a subject, *whomever* as an object. Consider the function of the word in the clause of which it is a part, and ignore the rest of the sentence. Examples of formal use: "Whoever comes to our door is a friend" (subject of *comes*). "Tell whoever comes to our door to go away" (subject of *comes*). "Tell whomever you see that we are having a party" (object of *see*). "For whomever you invite there will be a welcome" (object of *invite*). "For whoever is invited there is a welcome" (subject of *is invited*).

whole other "That's a whole other problem" is FF. SWE: "That's an entirely (or *wholly*) different problem." FF: "That's a whole nother problem" (*whole* splits the word *another*).

whom See WHO/WHOM.

who's/whose SWE uses *who's* only when it is replaceable by *who is* or *who has*: "Who's ('Who is') in the penalty box?" "Who's ('Who has') been charged with the penalty?" "Whose fault was it?" (*Who is* or *who has* will not fit there.)

whose else See ELSE'S.

whose/of which May *whose* be used to refer to animals and things, not just to people? Yes, according to SWE. "The flowers, whose scent is more noticeable at night . . ." is preferable to the awkward "The flowers, of which the scent . . ." See also DOG WHO.

widow/wife Newspaper people have sometimes debated whether an obituary writer should say that a deceased man is survived by his *widow* or his *wife*. The decision is not always the same. Obviously, she has now become his widow, but some journalists argue that in the few days of transition, *wife* is the kinder choice. Except possibly for the obituary, the surviving woman is a widow. However, in references to her past married life, SWE calls her the wife of so-and-so. Similar comments apply to *husband/widower*.

widow woman   FF. Of course a widow is a woman! Delete *woman*, says SWE.

wieldy   See UNWIELDY.

wiggle/wriggle   Often used interchangeably, *wriggle* is customary for a writhing, snakelike motion that results in a change of location, but *wiggle* is more often a back-and-forth movement in approximately the same spot: "The snake wriggled away from the dog." "Can you wiggle your ears?"

win (noun)   "The team desperately needs a win" is standard on the sports page. Now the noun use has moved into SWE with reference to musical, political, and other competitions: "To stay in the race, Senator Read needs a win in the New York primary."

win out   SWE asks, "Is *out* necessary?"

windward   See LEE/PORT/STARBOARD . . .

-wise   Long established in such words as *sidewise, lengthwise, crosswise*, and *likewise, -wise* has become an overworked combining form and sometimes an object of ridicule late in the twentieth century. It has shown up in such possibly useful forms as *timewise* ("in regard to elapsed time") but also in such absurd combinations as *jumping-ability-wise, movie-acting-wise, word processor-wise*, and "It's been a difficult season, *competitivewise*" or "We're really in a hole *heightwise*." *Wise*wise it must be said that SWE considers it unwise to overuse *-wise*.

wish I was (were)   If I am in Louisville but would rather be in Paducah, "I wish I were in Paducah" is standard. We wish for something that is contrary to fact. See also IF I WERE/IF I WAS.

wish   See WANT/WISH.

wishful thinking   A cliché, but how else can you say "thinking that something is true but not realizing that you are only wishing it to be true"? Frequent in SWE.

with   If a sentence containing *with* seems awkward, SWE checks to see whether a substitute may help; for example, "With increasing use of cocaine by young people, a solution to the entire drug problem becomes even more urgent than before." The *with* phrase is not accurately related to the rest of the sentence. Here SWE substitutes *Because of* for *With*.

with bated breath   Cliché, *bated* is archaic for "reduced." SWE reasons, "If few modern people understand the word, why use it?"

with telling effect   A dying cliché for "highly effective."

with the exception (intention, purpose, and so on)   Many phrases using *with the . . . of* can be shortened. "Everybody with the exception of two girls decided to stay" becomes "Everybody except two girls . . ." "He accepted the job with the intention of resigning after one year" becomes "He accepted the job, intending to . . ."

255

within the framework of Pretentious. Often *in* or *in relation to* can substitute.

without See UNLESS/WITHOUT.

witness As a verb this is often pretentious for "see" or "go to." Stuffed shirts witness a basketball game; basketball fans go to or see the game, or even enjoy it.

woman See LADY/WOMAN.

womanize SWE, as is the noun *womanizer*. The verb may mean either "give feminine characteristics to" or "pursue women excessively for sexual purposes." (Why are there no comparable *manize* and *manizer*?)

womanlike See LADYLIKE/WOMANLIKE, WOMANLY.

womanly See EFFEMINATE/FEMALE/FEMININE . . .

wont Old-fashioned for "custom" or "habit": "He rose at six, as was his wont."

workaholic SWE. Clearly modeled on *alcoholic* and meaning "a person addicted to work," *workaholic* is a valuable addition to the language. Wayne Oates, who probably coined it, also coined *workaholism*, for what lazy people consider a disease from which a workaholic suffers.

world of Overused for *much*, *plenty of*, etc., in phrases such as "a world of time," "a world of difficulty," "worlds of problems."

world See REALM/SPHERE/WORLD.

worn-out See OUTWORN/WORN-OUT.

worry See ANXIETY/APPREHENSION/CARE . . .

worse (*worst*) comes to worst The four-hundred-year-old idiom is "if worst comes to worst." Logic calls for "if worse comes to worst." Who can argue successfully with tradition or logic? SWE uses both forms or ducks the question and says "if worse changes to worst."

worsen Once dialectal but now SWE for "to become worse" or (less often): "to make worse": "The pain worsened." "Scrubbing floors worsened the pain in her back."

worst way 1. FF and sometimes unclear as an expression of intensity: "She wanted Joe in the worst way." SWE might substitute "She longed for Joe" or "She intensely wanted to hold Joe in her arms again." 2. Expressions such as "What she needed in the worst way was sympathy" seem illogical. *Most* is more likely in SWE. 3. A newspaper's advertising consultant understandably advised a garage owner to change the wording of this proposed ad: "We want to repair your car in the worst way possible." SWE finds few, if any, uses for that expression.

worth while/worthwhile A rule of thumb: one word when used before a noun, two words after the verb: "a worthwhile plan," "The plan is worth while." If the expression makes sense when *one's* or *your* is inserted between *worth* and *while*, two words are SWE. Strunk and White caution that both words are rather vague. They recommend something more precise, such as *promising*, *worth reading*, or *worth trying*.

worthless See INVALUABLE/PRICELESS.

worthy The Nine Worthies discussed in medieval times included persons such as Charlemagne and Alexander the Great. But the term has lost repute, and to talk today of someone as "a worthy" is ironic and disparaging, perhaps humorously so. Charles Dickens contributed to the pejoration in his *Sketches by Boz*: "stirring the taproom fire and . . . taking part in the conversation of the worthies assembled around it." The adjective *worthy*, though, has kept its reputability.

would Although *would* may indicate customary or frequent action, as in "He would prepare the same breakfast," *would* is unnecessary with a specific time phrase such as *each day* or *every month*. SWE often changes "Each day he would prepare the same breakfast" to "Each day he prepared the same breakfast."

would be Announcer: "A player is down on the twenty-yard line. That would be Scott Graham." SWE prefers *is*.

would See SHOULD/WOULD.

wrack See RACK/WRACK.

wriggle See WIGGLE/WRIGGLE.

X

Xmas Infrequent in SWE, except in advertising, *Xmas* for *Christmas* is frowned on and regarded by many people as mostly commercial, and irreverent at that. The accusation of commercialism is well founded, but not the other. *X* was the first letter in the old Greek name for Christ and was often used to represent His name.

Y

Yankee Has four meanings: (1) a New Englander; (2) to some Southerners any Northerner (often with *damn* or *dam* as an inseparable prefix); (3) to foreigners any resident of the United States, to whom the term may be applied affectionately, indifferently, or hostilely; (4) a member of a baseball team. It occurs occasionally in SWE for any of the above definitions.

ye As in "Ye Olde Clocke Shoppe," *ye* is not only overused but also based on misinformation. An Old English symbol for *th,* called a "thorn," looks somewhat like a *y,* and later printers confused the two. So this *ye* is simply *the* and should be so pronounced.

Yiddish See HEBREW/ISRAELI/JEWISH . . .

yon Somewhat old-fashioned. Shakespeare used it in "Yon Cassius has a lean and hungry look." It is still heard occasionally in *hither and yon. Yonder* has the same meaning, "over there," but is also infrequently heard and rarely appears in SWE.

you No longer regarded as unsatisfactory in addressing the reader, except in highly impersonal prose. SWE avoids, however, mixing *one* with *you*. Not SWE: "One must be sure that you do not come down too hard on the floor." See also ONE (IMPERSONAL).

you all Generally considered only a Southern expression, as in "Y'all come," *you all,* as well as *all of you,* is actually SWE in all parts of the country, used to emphasize the inclusiveness of *you:* "You all know that most television programs are now recorded." Robert Gorrell has said that in one small town some newcomers were considered uncouth because they used *you all* and *we all* instead of the "correct" *you-uns* and *we-uns.*

You can say that again Tiresome FF substitute for "I agree." Similar is "You took the words right out of my mouth."

you know Especially overused in speaking, *you know* usually has no more meaning than the *uh* that signifies hesitation. Hearing excessive *you know*'s irritates many people and makes them doubt the speaker's intelligence. One such listener is reported to have inserted a quick "No, I don't" after each *you know* used by a friend. (She lost the friend.)

young/youthful Often interchangeable, *young* is more likely to refer to actual age, *youthful* to appearance or actions: "a young man, about twenty-two," "She still has a youthful figure."

your earliest convenience Old-fashioned phrase, once widely used in business letters or duns: "Please remit at your earliest convenience." Today *immediately* or a similar word is probable.

yummy Most dictionaries say that *yummy* is slang, and it must be admitted that the word is unlikely in a letter to a corporation president unless to praise his company's candy bars. But even though not SWE, *yummy* is a wonderful word to use in talking to children or in complimenting Aunt Mabel for her should-be-famous fried chicken.

Z

zap An FF verb or exclamation that became widely used during the computer games craze when trillions of "baddies" were zapped. Vague in meaning – perhaps "obliterate, shoot down, cripple, kill, turn off, turn on," or what you will. It appears occasionally in SWE.

zeal/zest *Zeal* is keen desire, enthusiasm. It implies a cause or goal: "zeal to become a nurse," "zeal to reduce the probability of war." *Zest* emphasizes enjoyment, gusto: "zest for life," "zest for gourmet food."

zero See AUGHT/NAUGHT.

zilch FF (slang). SWE prefers *nothing, none,* or *zero.*

zip (noun)   Marginally SWE, this word sounds as zippy as its name. Much more lively than *alacrity,* and more suggestive of quick movement than *vim* or *vigor. Energy* has little zip, either; it suggests Con Edison.

LAST
DANCE

ALSO BY JOHN FEINSTEIN

Next Man Up

Let Me Tell You a Story *(with Red Auerbach)*

Caddy for Life

Open

The Punch

The Last Amateurs

The Majors

A March to Madness

A Civil War

A Good Walk Spoiled

Play Ball

Hard Courts

Forever's Team

A Season Inside

A Season on the Brink

Last Shot
(A Final Four Mystery)

Running Mates
(A Mystery)

Winter Games
(A Mystery)

LAST DANCE

Behind the Scenes at the Final Four

JOHN FEINSTEIN

Little, Brown and Company

New York   Boston

Little, Brown and Company
Time Warner Book Group
1271 Avenue of the Americas, New York, NY 10020
Visit our Web site at www.twbookmark.com

First Edition: February 2006

Library of Congress Cataloging-in-Publication Data

Feinstein, John.
   Last dance : behind the scenes at the Final Four / John Feinstein —
1st ed.
       p. cm.
   Includes index.
   ISBN-13: 978-0-316-16030-8 (hardcover)
   ISBN-10: 0-316-16030-X (hardcover)
   1. NCAA Basketball Tournament — History.   2. NCAA Basketball
Tournament — Anecdotes.   3. Basketball — Tournaments — United
States — History.   I. Title.

GV885.49.N37F45   2006
796.323'63'0973 — dc22   2005028478

10 9 8 7 6 5 4 3 2 1

Q-FF

Printed in the United States of America

This is for Esther Newberg, who is a wonderful agent, a better friend, and the world's absolute worst sport. Which is part of her charm.

Contents

LAST DANCE

Introduction

Mike Krzyzewski

THERE WAS A TIME, a few years back, when it was very difficult for me to go to the Final Four when my team didn't make it there. Part of it, no doubt, was the disappointment I felt because we weren't still playing. I'm probably spoiled because we've made the Final Four on ten occasions since 1986, although I can honestly tell you that I have *never* taken getting there for granted. Each trip is special.

This past year, after we lost in the round of sixteen to Michigan State, I decided to make the trip to St. Louis. There were some meetings I felt I should attend and some people I wanted to see. As it turned out, making the trip was one of the best things I've done in a long time.

On Sunday morning I attended a new event that the National Association of Basketball Coaches started recently called the Past Presidents Brunch. It is, as you might have guessed, a brunch for all past presidents of the NABC. I was president in 1992, so I was invited.

When I sat down, I found myself next to Bill Foster. I have been given a lot of credit through the years for the success of Duke basketball. What a lot of people don't realize is that the

3

foundation our program is built on was put in place by Bill Foster. In 1974 he became Duke's coach after the worst season in school history. The program was in shambles and Bill had to rebuild in what was, without question, the toughest basketball conference in America. North Carolina State had just won the national championship, North Carolina was coached by Dean Smith, Maryland was strong under Lefty Driesell, and Terry Holland was just arriving to build Virginia into a power. Within four years, Bill turned the program completely around. He recruited players such as Jim Spanarkel, Mike Gminski, Gene Banks, and Kenny Dennard. In 1978 Duke won the ACC Tournament and, with no seniors in the starting lineup (back then, that actually meant something), went all the way to the national championship game before losing to Kentucky.

My first truly great recruiting class included Johnny Dawkins, Mark Alarie, Jay Bilas, and David Henderson. All of them have told me they have memories of that '78 team, that they admired guys like Spanarkel and Gminski and Banks and Dennard, and that those players and that team first put Duke on their radar. If I don't recruit those four players, I'm probably not the coach at Duke today. If Bill Foster hadn't built the team and the program he did, I probably would not have gotten those four players. At that brunch I had a chance to sit and really talk to Bill about what he had to overcome and to tell him how much I appreciated what he had built. I got to look him in the eye and tell him that I honestly believed he deserved at least some of the credit for all that Duke has accomplished in the past twenty years. I think — I hope — that meant something to him.

As I was leaving the brunch, I ran into Marv Harshman. Like Bill Foster, Harshman is retired now, but years ago he was a great coach at the University of Washington. In fact, the first

NCAA Tournament game I coached was against a Marv Harshman–coached Washington team in 1984. We lost. Marv and I joked about the fact that he had started me on the road to having the most NCAA Tournament wins of any coach — with a loss.

I walked out of the brunch with a big smile on my face. Being in that room with so many of my colleagues from so many years and so many games was great. But to run into Foster and Harshman, two men who played a role in my life and were great coaches long before anyone thought to ask me to do a commercial for anything, was a great reminder to me of what the Final Four is all about. It is much bigger than the four teams and coaches who have the honor of playing in it in a given year. It has far more scope than three basketball games. It is about much more than wins and losses — although the wins and losses that occur will be remembered forever by the participants.

The Final Four is about understanding how lucky we all are to be part of college basketball. It is about people like me remembering how important Bill Foster and Marv Harshman are, not to mention John Wooden and Big House Gaines and Bill Russell and Bill Bradley and Dean Smith and John Thompson. And so many others. There's a tendency during the course of a basketball season for a coach to crawl into the cocoon of his team and the day-to-day, game-to-game pressures. Sometimes in April I feel a little bit like someone who has been locked in a cave all winter and I find myself blinking at the glare of Life Beyond Basketball. When I'm not still coaching at the Final Four — and, believe me, I prefer the years when I *am* still coaching — being there is a bridge back to reality. I'm reminded there's more to basketball than our practices, our games, and our rivalries. In spite of what some people might believe, Duke-Carolina is not the game's only great rivalry, although it is a pretty damn good one.

My first memories of the Final Four go back to listening to games on the radio as a kid growing up in Chicago. I always watched the Big Ten game of the week on television when I was young and I often went to games in the old Chicago Stadium. For some reason, a game I saw there between Duke and Notre Dame sticks out in my memory. Maybe there was some fate involved in that.

The first team I really remember well, though, is the Loyola of Chicago team that won the national championship in 1963. Those games, particularly the championship game against Cincinnati, stand out. I remember having the sense that what Loyola had done was a big deal even though I couldn't actually watch the games.

When I played at Army for Bob Knight in the late '60s, the National Invitation Tournament was as big a deal in our minds as the NCAAs were. My three years as a college player coincided with Lew Alcindor's three years at UCLA. (Alcindor, of course, later became Kareem Abdul-Jabbar.) I remember it sort of being accepted that no one was going to beat UCLA. We had very good teams at Army and we badly wanted to win a championship. In 1968 we were 20–4 and invited to the NCAAs. We knew we weren't going to beat UCLA and Alcindor, but we honestly thought we could win the NIT. So, Coach Knight decided to take the NIT bid. Unfortunately, we lost to Notre Dame (on St. Patrick's Day, as I am constantly reminded even now). The next year we went back to the NIT and shocked South Carolina, which had been ranked number two in the national polls for a lot of the season, in the quarterfinals before losing in the semis to Boston College.

My first Final Four was in 1973. I was still in the army but back home on leave in March. I had already talked to Coach Knight about joining his staff when I got out of the army the following year and I flew to St. Louis to watch Indiana play UCLA in the semifinals. I remember thinking *then* how big the event was and how amazing it was to stand in the lobby of the coaches' hotel and watch the parade of famous coaches as they came and went during the weekend. I didn't get to see Bill Walton shoot 21 of 22 for UCLA because I had to report back to my unit soon after the semifinals. I'm not sure if I'm right about this, but I don't think I would have been able to stay even if Indiana had won on Saturday.

A little more than a year later, I went to work for Coach Knight as a graduate assistant. That was the first year [1975] that he coached a team that went undefeated in the regular season. Unfortunately, Scott May broke his leg in February, and even though he was able to come back and play in the tournament, he wasn't the same player and we weren't the same team. We lost in the regional final to Kentucky, 92–90. To this day, I think Coach Knight would tell you that was his most disappointing loss because, with Scott healthy, that was probably his best team. Of course, Indiana, led by Scott, did go undefeated the next season and won the 1976 national championship.

I wasn't around — except as a spectator — when Indiana won that year in Philadelphia. By then I was back at Army as the head coach. I loved coaching at my alma mater, but deep down I knew I wanted to do what Coach Knight had done: take a team to the Final Four and win a national championship. The days when that was even remotely possible at Army were gone. The Vietnam War and big money coming into the NBA had changed recruiting at Army — even more so for football than basketball — and we had to set more realistic goals, such as getting to the postseason and getting into a conference where we could compete. The players I coached during my five years at Army are still among my closest friends today. But I knew there was going to come a time when, if I was successful, I was going to have to consider moving on.

That time came in 1980 when Tom Butters surprised me (and shocked the basketball world) by offering me the job at Duke. Had I known what the first three years were going to be like, I might have thought twice. I had to learn on the job how to coach — and recruit — in the ACC. Dean Smith was at his absolute zenith as a coach. My first game at Duke was against North Carolina in the old Big Four Tournament in Greensboro. Carolina had James Worthy and Sam Perkins and Al Wood on the court, and Dean had already gotten a commitment from a high school senior we knew was pretty good named Michael Jordan. They lost to Indiana in the national championship game that season. A year later, with Jordan, they were national champions. We were 10–17, the worst record in Duke history.

At the same time that I went to Duke, another young coach whom I knew pretty well took the North Carolina State job: Jim Valvano. Jimmy and I had coached against each other while I was at Army and he was at Iona. He had taken Iona to back-to-back NCAA Tournaments, and in 1980, his last year at Iona, my final year at Army, his team was the last one to beat Louisville, which won the national championship. They beat them by 17 in Madison Square Garden and Jimmy had his players cut down the nets. He said he was practicing for the day when he coached a team that cut down the nets at the Final Four. Typical Jimmy.

Of course, in his third year at State — my third year at Duke — Jimmy and his team did cut down the nets at the Final

Four in Albuquerque. While Jimmy and State were becoming national champions, we had improved from 10–17 to 11–17. We lost our last game that season to Virginia, 109–66. A lot of Duke people thought I was going to make a great coach — back at Army, where they thought I belonged.

I still remember that Final Four pretty vividly. Specifically, like a lot of people, I remember the semifinal game between Houston and Louisville. There was a stretch in the second half when it seemed as if every single play took place above the rim. Every player on the court appeared capable of jumping out of the building. They all looked like future NBA All-Stars. It was Roger Valdiserri, the longtime Notre Dame SID [sports information director], who famously commented after the game, "Welcome to basketball in the twenty-first century." I wasn't that much different from most people in New Mexico's Pit that day, in that I was awed by what I saw. The difference was, I was the coach at a school that had recent Final Four history — 1978 — and my goal as a coach was someday to be down on that floor coaching on Final Four Saturday. That's what was scary to me. I knew my team was a long way from being able to compete with what I was watching. It was one of the few times when I wondered if my dream of coaching in a Final Four might not come true.

A year later my four freshmen starters had become sophomores and we went 24–10. We beat North Carolina — with Jordan, Perkins, and Brad Daugherty — in the ACC Tournament semifinals and ended up losing to Washington and Marv Harshman in the NCAA Tournament. In 1986 we made it to the Final Four and beat a great Kansas team to get to Monday night. We lost that championship game to Louisville, 72–69, and if there is a game in my career I look back on with regret, it's that one. I just don't believe I gave my players as much help as I could have if I'd had more Final Four experience at that point. They were tired after the Kansas game, very tired, and I didn't find ways to use the bench early in the game to keep them fresh enough for the finish. Those four kids — Dawkins, Alarie, Bilas, and Henderson — deserved to win the national championship. I know they all feel as if they somehow came up short by not winning that night, but I've always felt that if anyone came up short, it was me. I do think they know that the three national championships we've won since would not have happened if not for them. That's why I honestly believe they have been national champions — because 1991, 1992, and 2001 could not have happened if not for 1986.

That 1986 team began a run that, as I look back on it now, was remarkable. We went to seven Final Fours in nine years. We upset number one seeds in the regional final in 1988 [Temple], 1989 [Georgetown], and 1990 [Connecticut]. In 1992 Christian Laettner hit the shot everyone remembers in Philadelphia to beat Kentucky. In 1994 we beat another number one seed [Purdue] in another regional final. I still remember Pete Gaudet, who was my associate coach throughout that run, joking after we beat UConn that he was going to have to withdraw from the annual coaches' golf tournament at the Final Four *again*. I told him I hoped he never got to play in it again.

When I was in St. Louis last year, I kept hearing people talk about all the pressure that was on Roy Williams because he hadn't won a national championship yet. I remember thinking how unfair that was. Roy was in his fifth Final Four last year — four with Kansas, one with North Carolina. No coach should feel pressure when his team is in the Final Four. He should feel great that his team is still playing on the last weekend of the season and be able to enjoy what they've accomplished. That doesn't mean you don't put everything you have into trying to win it all, because there is no feeling quite like cutting down the nets on Monday night. But getting to the Final Four should always be something you get to celebrate, not something that creates pressure. When I walk around at a Final Four, I'm constantly reminded how lucky you have to be to get to *one*. I see people like Lefty Driesell and Gene Keady and Norm Stewart and John Chaney, each of them a great basketball coach. They all made multiple regional finals; they all built programs that were excellent year in and year out for many years. None of them ever coached in a Final Four.

To get to one, you have to have a number of ingredients. You have to have been able to recruit very good players, you have to have a very patient family, you need excellent assistants, and you need luck. You need to keep key players healthy and, most of the time, you need to win at least one game that you probably deserve to lose. In 1986, when we were the number one seed in the eastern regional, we trailed number sixteen seed Mississippi Valley State with ten minutes left to play. We easily could have lost that game, but Johnny Dawkins made just enough plays to pull us through. Everyone remembers Christian Laettner's first buzzer-beater against Connecticut in 1990 that put us in that year's Final Four. A lot of people (not UConn fans, I know that) have forgotten that Tate George came within an inch or two of intercepting Bobby Hurley's pass downcourt just before the inbounds play that set up Christian's shot. We certainly could have lost to Kentucky in the regional final in 1992, and Quin Snyder's Missouri team easily could have taken us out in the second round in 2001. We managed to win and ended up winning the national title.

My point is this: I'm not sure you have to be a great coach to get to the Final Four. Probably you have to be a good one who catches a few key breaks — during the tournament, during the season, during a career. Sometimes I wonder where I would have ended up if I hadn't listened to Tom Rogers, my officer rep at Army, when I asked him if he thought I should take the Iowa State job when it was offered in 1980. "I think you need to follow this Duke thing through to the end," Colonel Rogers said. I guess it's fair to say he gave me good advice.

I was fortunate to have teachers in my life like Coach Knight, Henry Iba, and Pete Newell. All won national championships and all enjoyed counseling younger coaches. I hope now that I'm an older coach who has won national championships that I can do for some young coaches what my mentors did for me. When I think back now to 1983, I realize how fortunate I've been to have had players good enough to put us in a position to compete for championships.

Every time we've made the Final Four has been a thrill. There's no question I got a little bit spoiled when we had our run and made it seven times in nine years. It wasn't that I took getting there for granted, it was that I thought we would keep on going. When we didn't go for four straight seasons, it made getting back in 1999 that much sweeter. Not going really bothered me at first, especially in 1998, when we had a big lead in the regional final and lost to Kentucky. But what I have come to realize — finally, I'm a little slow sometimes figuring things out — is that you don't have to sulk when your team doesn't make the Final Four. There is too much about the weekend to enjoy, even when you aren't coaching.

Organizing a dinner for my former players and coaches is one of the better things I've done during my coaching career. To begin with, it's a lot of fun and it gives me a chance to spend time with guys who have been an important part of my life whom I don't get to see often. I think it's something everyone involved looks forward to. What's best about it is something I realized this year while we were all sitting around the restaurant, telling old stories and laughing at one another. By setting up this dinner, I have guaranteed myself one thing at every Final Four: regardless of what happens to my basketball team during that season, I will always have my team with me at the Final Four.

Some years I will coach my team. Other years I will drink wine with my team. But one way or the other, I'll always have my team with me. That's a pretty good deal for an old coach.

I'm already looking forward to Indianapolis. I'll be there with my team or with my team.

1

One Shining Moment

ROY WILLIAMS HAD THOUGHT ABOUT IT, planned it, even talked about it. He had told his children that when the moment came he knew just what he was going to do: throw his arms up in the air and walk around the court, arms raised in victory. But now, with the moment finally at hand, he knew that wasn't going to happen. He was looking at the clock and then at the court, the court and then the clock. He saw one final shot go up, knowing that even if it went in, it wouldn't change the outcome. It missed and Sean May had the ball in his hands, standing under the basket. Williams's eyes went back to the clock. Two . . . one . . .

And then there was bedlam. Williams had the sense that celebrations were breaking out all over the court, that his players were diving on top of one another, giving full vent to the emotions that had been pent up inside them for an entire basketball season. At that moment, one that he had waited for so long, the thought of raising his arms in triumph never crossed Williams's mind. There was an unshakable feeling of complete satisfaction, but also a coach's calm resolve to finish a job.

He took off his glasses, just as he did at every time-out, because he needed the glasses only for distance and when he looked his players in the eyes while speaking to them, he didn't want the glasses to blur his vision of their faces. Now he wanted to look into the eyes of the players and coaches from Illinois. He knew — from personal experience — that there was nothing he could say to make them feel any better at that moment, but he had always prided himself on handling victory and defeat with equal grace.

But May found him before he could find Coach Bruce Weber. He had a huge grin on his face, the kind of pure joy rarely seen in elite athletes. He had told Williams and his teammates that when North Carolina won the national championship, he was going to be the first one to hug Williams. Now he was fulfilling his promise. Williams was tingling as he hugged May, but he couldn't linger. He got untangled and began shaking hands with the kids in the orange and white uniforms. These were faces he had seen before, the blank stares that come when someone has put a lifetime into achieving something and been right on the doorstep of that achievement only to see it slide away. "New Orleans," he said. "I saw the faces of my Kansas players in New Orleans right after we lost to Syracuse. I wanted to say, 'I know how you feel' — because I did — but I knew it would be meaningless."

He settled for congratulating them on their season and on a great game. He knew they didn't hear a word he was saying. He found himself looking for Bruce Weber, because he wanted to say to him what Mike Krzyzewski had said to him in 1991 in Indianapolis, what Jim Boeheim had said to him in 2003 in New Orleans: your time will come. In '91, in just his third year as a head coach, he had no trouble believing it. Twelve years later it had been a lot more difficult. Weber was where Williams had been in '91. He had just completed his second season at Illinois.

And yet for him, the loss had to be tougher than the first time for Williams. Illinois had been ranked number one in the country since December. It had come within one victory of going undefeated in the regular season. It had matched the all-time NCAA record for wins — thirty-seven — coming into the final, and playing in St. Louis, a three-hour car ride from campus, this had clearly been Illinois' Final Four.

But someone had written the wrong ending to the Illini's script. The culprit had been Williams and his North Carolina team. Even though the circumstances had been different back in 1991, Williams knew what Weber was thinking and feeling. His Kansas team had been very good that season. It had entered the NCAA Tournament as a third seed in the southeast regional and had peaked at the right time, upsetting Indiana, Arkansas, and North Carolina en route to the championship game. Losing that night to Duke had hurt because he had believed his team was good enough to win and, well, because it was Duke — and if you are a graduate of North Carolina, losing to Duke always hurts. But deep down he had understood that it was Krzyzewski's time. Like ·Dean Smith, his own mentor, Krzyzewski had endured questions about why he seemed able to get to the Final Four but couldn't win that last game. Indianapolis had been Krzyzewski's fifth Final Four and his third title game. It had taken Smith seven Final Fours and four appearances on the last night of the season before he had, at last, cut the final net.

Williams had been on the bench that night in 1982 when Smith finally won his first national championship. He was thirty-one, in his third year as an assistant coach at his alma mater, making less than $10,000 a year and living his dream. He adored Dean Smith, thought him the best coach and the best man he had ever known. When Smith finally won that title, answering all those who said he couldn't win or wondered why he hadn't won, Williams cried. Smith was dry-eyed. Remarkably, Williams's career arc had, in many ways, mimicked those of his mentor and of his mentor's greatest rival, Krzyzewski. He had taken Kansas to the Final Four on four occasions and had twice reached the final. But, like Smith and Krzyzewski, he didn't win right away.

Like Smith and Krzyzewski, he had become defensive about being so successful without having achieved the ultimate success. Smith had actually had studies done to prove that it was statistically more difficult to reach multiple Final Fours than it was to win one. Krzyzewski became snappish when people asked about the monkey on his back. "There's no monkey on my back," he said repeatedly when the subject came up.

He was right. It was a gorilla.

Williams had inherited the gorilla. He was, without question, the BCNTHWTNC — Best Coach Never to Have Won the National Championship. In his fourteen seasons at Kansas, he had won more games than any coach in the history of the game had won in his first fourteen seasons. After the trip to the final in 1991, Kansas was a perennial power. In 1992 the Jayhawks spent the entire season ranked in the top five and went into the NCAA Tournament as the number one seed in the midwest regional, almost certain, most people believed, to return to the Final Four, very possibly to a rematch with Duke.

Except that, as often happens in the NCAA Tournament, Kansas was upset — in the second round by the University of Texas at El Paso. UTEP was coached by Don Haskins, who had coached the Miners to the most famous Final Four victory ever in 1966 when his team (then known as Texas Western) had upset all-powerful Kentucky in the title game. Kentucky, under Adolph Rupp, started five white players. Haskins started five black players. Books, documentaries, and movies still commemorate that game to this day. Haskins never again reached the Final Four after 1966, but on a Sunday afternoon in 1992, closing in on the end of his long career, Haskins's team upset Kansas and brought about a spate of stories reminding people about 1966 all over again.

Later that week, walking through an airport, Williams was stopped by a stranger. He girded himself for the words of comfort and sympathy he knew would come. "Don't worry, Coach, you'll get 'em next year." Or the dreaded "You had a great season anyway." This time, though, that wasn't what he got: "Do you realize what you've done to me?" the man shouted. "I had you guys winning the whole thing. You've completely ruined my bracket!"

Few people on earth are more polite than Roy Williams. Every once in a while, though, he cracks. This was one of those moments. "Ruined your bracket!" he shouted. "You think I care about your bracket? This is about my *life*."

That's what the NCAA Tournament does to college basketball coaches. Fairly or unfairly, they are judged almost solely on how their teams perform in March. A coach can win every game he plays during the regular season and it won't matter a bit unless his team wins in March — and, nowadays, in the first week in April, since the event dubbed "March Madness" now stretches further into the year. In fact, if a coach is highly successful in the regular season or even in the early rounds of the NCAA Tournament but can't win the whole thing, he is likely to be more scrutinized than a coach whose team is consistently decent but almost never very good or great.

Among elite coaches, there are numerous examples of this.

When Gary Williams arrived at Maryland in 1989, the basketball program at his alma mater was in complete shambles. It had been rocked by the 1986 cocaine-induced death of superstar Len Bias and then set back further by the school's decision to hire a high school coach who broke NCAA rules and then lied to investigators about breaking those rules. Less than a year after Williams took over, the school was hammered by the NCAA, given two years' probation because of Coach Bob Wade's transgressions, and quickly plummeted to the bottom of the Atlantic Coast Conference.

Williams dug in, started from square one, and by 1994 had the Terrapins not only back in the NCAA Tournament but, after a second-round upset of number two seed Massachusetts, back in the Sweet Sixteen for the first time since Bias's death. Celebrations broke out on campus. Williams was lionized. "It was as if we'd made the Final Four," he said. "It was one of the great feelings I've ever had in coaching." Maryland lost to Michigan the following week, but no one really cared. There was nothing but happiness in what people had taken to calling Garyland.

A year later the Terrapins made the Sweet Sixteen again — and lost to Connecticut. In 1998 they were there again, losing to Arizona. A year later same round, a loss to St. John's. There was no more joy in Garyland. People began referring to Williams as a "round of sixteen coach." There was no sweetness in that phrase. Williams wondered if they might be right. But he relentlessly pushed forward, and in 2001 his team won in the round of sixteen. Then they upset top-seeded Stanford in the regional final and — presto — Williams and Maryland were in the Final Four. Even a loss to archrival Duke a week later couldn't dull the sense of accomplishment. A year later Maryland made it back to the Final Four — and won the championship.

"The second time was entirely different than the first," Gary Williams remembered. "The first time there was this feeling that you were already a success because you were there. The second time, we would have felt like failures if we hadn't won the whole thing."

Roy Williams knew all about that feeling. Like Gary Williams, he remembered that first trip as a joyride, even after losing the championship game. Two years later a loss in the semifinals was mitigated by the fact that it was to Dean Smith, his old boss and mentor. It took nine years to get back. There were all sorts of near misses — most notably in 1997, when Kansas spent most of the season ranked number one in the country only to lose in the Not-So-Sweet-Sixteen to Arizona, which went on to win the title.

It was after that loss that Williams started telling people that winning the national championship wasn't so important to him. Yes, he wanted to win it. Yes, he would compete with every fiber in his being to try to win it. But if he didn't, he would be happy to walk away someday and just go coach his grandchildren. No doubt he believed it, because if he hadn't willed himself to believe it, he might never have slept at night. But no one else believed it, for the simple reason that no one gets to be as good at anything as Roy Williams was at coaching without burning to be the champion at the end of a season. At least once.

Anyone who had been there in 1982 on the night when Dean Smith finally won his first title on his seventh trip to the Final Four knew exactly how much Smith had wanted to win the minute he opened his mouth at his postgame press conference. "I guess we proved a very bright writer from Charlotte wrong tonight" were his very first words. Many — if not most — in the room looked at one another as if to say, "What the hell is he talking about?"

Those who knew Smith understood exactly what he was talking about. In 1980 Frank Barrows, a gifted feature writer for the *Charlotte Observer*, had written a lengthy story examining why Smith's program won with such remarkable consistency but couldn't win the national championship. Barrows's conclusion was that the very system that made the Tar Heels so good year in and year out prevented them from rising to the highest level when the pressure was greatest, in March. The Tar Heels, impeccably prepared by Smith for every game they played, were always good in November, good in December, good in January, good in February, good in March. But in March you had to be great. He noted that the two most spectacular college point guards of the 1970s were Michigan State's Earvin (Magic) Johnson and North Carolina's Phil Ford. "It would be impossible," Barrows wrote, "for a player at North Carolina to be nicknamed Magic. It simply wouldn't be allowed."

Barrows was right about that. In fact, in December of 1978, Michigan State and Johnson had played and lost at North Carolina. Johnson, as Smith often pointed out, turned the ball over eight times that night. But in March, North Carolina was eliminated in the second round of the NCAA Tournament by Pennsylvania. Michigan State — which beat Pennsylvania by 32 points in the semifinals — won the national title. Carolina had been the better team in December. Michigan State had been the great team in March.

Now, having finally won the title, Smith's first thought as he stood before the nation's media was of Barrows. "It was an immature comment," he said. "I always liked Frank. But I thought he was wrong about our system."

Whether Barrows was right or wrong wasn't the issue. The issue was whether Dean Smith, Hall of Fame coach, could win the national championship. The answer was yes, he could. And you can be damn sure that no matter how dry-eyed he was right then, there were few moments in his career more satisfying to Smith than that one.

Twenty-three years later, sitting in the stands in the Edward Jones Dome in St. Louis, Smith may have felt better for Williams than he had for himself on that night in New Orleans. As those final seconds ticked down, he didn't cry the way Williams had cried for him in New Orleans, but he did feel a surge of relief both for his onetime pupil and for his school. Three years earlier North Carolina had suffered through an unthinkable 8–20 season, a nadir that had led to Williams's return in the spring of 2003. By then, Williams had been to two more Final Fours (2002 and 2003) and had lost twice more, first to Gary Williams's Maryland team in the semifinals and then in a memorable final to Syracuse with rumors swirling everywhere that Williams was about to leave Kansas for his alma mater.

He had been offered the job in 2000 when Bill Guthridge, who had attempted to do the impossible in following Smith, retired. Guthridge had gone to two Final Fours in three years and, in return, had been pilloried by most of the school's fans. They all wanted Ol' Roy to come back, ride in on a white horse, and restore the Tar Heels to glory. Or at the very least, beat Duke. Guthridge had been 2–6 against the Blue Devils. That was unacceptable. But to the amazement of everyone in the college game, Williams had said no — no to North Carolina, no to Dean Smith, no to the shocked Carolina faithful who were ready to build a statue of him the minute he returned. He was adored in Kansas, abhorred in North Carolina. Some took to simply referring to him as "that man who coaches Kansas."

He became the Lord Voldemort of North Carolina: He Who Must Not Be Named.

Matt Doherty, who had played for Smith and coached under Williams, became the coach. He had one good year, winning 26 games, and then the program collapsed. It wasn't because Doherty couldn't recruit — he had recruited all five players who started in the '05 championship game — but those players turned on him and Dean Smith's famous Carolina "family" became dysfunctional.

Enter Williams. Or more accurately, reenter Williams. This time when Smith asked him to come home, he couldn't say no. The pain of being an outcast in his home state at his own school and among his close friends had worn on him. Three years after saying he would never leave Kansas, Williams left Kansas. He was greeted as a returning hero in North Carolina. All was forgiven. Not so in Kansas: he became the Voldemort of the Plains.

He walked into a team filled with talented but in some cases underachieving players. People began predicting an immediate return to greatness for Carolina in 2004. Seeing the predictions, Williams shook his head and said, "Ol' Roy isn't that good." Maybe not, but he was pretty damn good. Carolina returned to the NCAA Tournament that year and lost in the second round to Texas. Some found the season disappointing. Others saw it as a start. Williams recruited one of the top high school players in the country, Marvin Williams, and added him to what was now one of the more experienced teams in the nation, led by juniors Sean May, Raymond Felton, and the mercurial Rashad McCants.

There had been ups and downs throughout the season, but the Tar Heels had come together when it mattered. They had survived a one-point game in the round of sixteen against Villanova and had come from five points down at halftime in the semifinals against Michigan State to set up the championship game that made the most sense: Illinois, ranked number one almost the entire season, against Carolina, ranked number two at the end of the regular season and considered by those who watched basketball the most talented team in the country.

"I just wish people would stop saying we have the most talent," Dean Smith said on the eve of the final.

Very few coaches are comfortable in the role of favorite, but Smith had made an art form out of creating reasons why his team was the underdog. His approach had been best described years earlier by his old friend and rival Lefty Driesell, who once said of him, "Dean Smith's the only man in history who's won eight hundred games [879 to be exact] and been the underdog in every one of them."

In 1981, having reached his sixth Final Four, Smith found himself facing a Virginia team led by Ralph Sampson that had beaten Carolina twice during the regular season. "I think it's obvious," he said, "that they have a psychological advantage because they beat us twice. They've got to be very confident that they can beat us again since they've already done it."

Carolina won and faced Indiana in the final — a team it had beaten during the regular season. That didn't sway Smith. "I don't think there's any doubt Indiana has the psychological advantage," he said at the Sunday press conference. "Since we beat them, they'll want revenge."

Indiana won. Twenty-four years later, Smith was still upset about two quick fouls called in the first half on James Worthy, his star player. "Booker Turner," he said, remembering the referee who called both fouls. "On the second one, the ball wasn't even across midcourt and he called James for trying to get position under the basket. I'm not saying that cost us the game, but . . ."

"I am," Roy Williams said. "It certainly made it almost impossible for us to have a chance. Booker Turner. Wow. Maybe Coach Smith has forgiven him [he hasn't], but I certainly haven't."

On the eve of Williams's third championship game, his old coach didn't want people to see a loss as his failure. "Illinois is awfully good," he said. "They haven't won thirty-seven games because they were lucky."

No, they hadn't. The final was everything that makes college basketball special and the Final Four unique: two teams with one chance to make history. Most players who reach the championship game get only one opportunity to play on the most important Monday night there is on the sports calendar. Since the retirement in 1975 of the legendary John Wooden ended UCLA's dynasty, in which the Bruins won ten championships in twelve years, only a handful of players have been in more than one final. North Carolina played in the title game in 1981 and 1982, Houston went to back-to-back finals in 1983 and 1984, and Georgetown played in 1982, 1984, and 1985. Between 1990 and 1994, Duke played in four championship games in five seasons. Kentucky played in three straight title games between 1996 and 1998, and Duke was in the final again in both 1999 and 2001. That's a handful of players, perhaps 50 — out of about 750 who have suited up on Monday night since 1976 — who have gotten more than one chance. Among those players, only those who played for North Carolina in 1981, Duke in 1990, and Kentucky in 1997 came back after a loss in the final to win the championship a year later. All of which means that, as a player, one must assume there won't be a second chance.

That's what makes the championship game so intense. It is always a matchup of two teams that believe it is their destiny to win. More often than not they have had dominant seasons and had to win five games in the crucible of single-elimination play to get to the final game. On Saturday, in the semifinals, they have beaten teams that undoubtedly arrived in the Final Four city believing *they* were teams of destiny. That was certainly true of Illinois and North Carolina. The Illini were 37–1. They had overcome a 15-point deficit against Arizona in the last four minutes of their regional final, then had pulled away from a Louisville team that had also come from way behind to win its regional final. North Carolina was 32–4. It had trailed Michigan State by 5 points at halftime in the semifinals and then had turned the game into a blowout in the second half.

Two superb teams. But only one could win the national championship. The other would leave with an empty feeling — one that would never completely go away, regardless of how many games it had won en route to the final.

Jay Bilas, now a star analyst for both CBS and ESPN, was the starting center for Duke when it faced Louisville in the championship game in 1986. That Duke team was very much like this Illinois team. It had a dream season, winning thirty-seven games. Four of Duke's starters in that game were seniors, so there was no doubt that this was their one and only chance at a national title. It was a tired team, too, having played a draining semifinal on Saturday against Kansas. The game was decided, in the end, when Louisville's Pervis Ellison grabbed an airball by teammate Jeff Hall and scored what turned out to be the winning basket.

"What I can't forget is the feeling right after the game was over," Bilas said. "To sit there and realize you'd been so close and you hadn't closed the deal. There were all sorts of reasons why we didn't win that game, but none of them really matter. We lost. There aren't many days that go by when I don't think about that night. We did a lot of great things that year. In fact, if you go back and look, people were talking about us being one of the great teams of all time. Then we lost in the final and all of that went away. We were just another good team that came up short in the end. I'd be lying if I said that doesn't still hurt.

"Every year, when the championship game ends, I find myself looking at the players on the losing team. Not the coaches — they'll have other chances — but the players. I know how they feel, especially when it's a close game decided by a play or two at the finish. I know they're going to live with the feeling they've got in their stomachs right then for the rest of their lives. It'll always be there. You can talk all you want about how great your season was, the last memory is the one you carry inside you wherever you go, whatever you do, the rest of your life."

Carolina was in control of the game most of the night. Sean May simply wouldn't allow the Illini any sort of inside game and they took to flinging up three-point shots — by game's end they would attempt forty — and one shot after another chipped paint off the rim. But in the game's final minutes, Illinois showed its resiliency once more, rallying to tie the game at 70 after trailing by as many as 15 points. In the last two minutes, just when people were beginning to wonder if Williams was going to be denied yet again, it was Marvin Williams, the freshman — the one key player in the Carolina lineup Williams had recruited — who made the game's biggest play. After Rashad McCants had twisted to the basket and thrown up one of the worst shots ever seen in a championship game, an underhand flip that didn't come close to the rim, Williams came flying in from the outside to slam home the rebound.

That basket, with 1:13 left, was the game-winner. Illinois had chances but never scored again. Raymond Felton sealed the game with free throws. "After Raymond made the last one, I knew we had done it," Williams said. "I just kept going back and forth from the court to the clock. I saw the last shot miss; I saw Sean with the ball. I may have thought for a split second about throwing my arms up, but then I realized I didn't want to do that. I knew how Bruce [Weber] felt at that moment. I wanted to make sure I saw all the Illinois people before I celebrated."

And so, after May finally let him go, Williams looked around and realized that he hadn't seen Weber yet. In all the commotion, he had started to leave the floor, thinking Williams was going to join his team in the on-court party that had broken out. It wasn't hard to pick out Weber — he was wearing a bright orange jacket — so when Williams saw him leaving the court, he broke into a sprint. He caught him in the runway just before he got under the stands.

"You had a great year," he told Weber over the din. "You will be back here. Your time will come, you're a great basketball coach."

Weber smiled and thanked him as they shook hands. Williams knew his words, though heartfelt, were hollow at that moment. Because there's absolutely no guarantee that you will get back or that your moment will actually come.

"When you make the Final Four the first time, there's no doubt that you're going back," Digger Phelps, the former Notre Dame coach, often says. "At that moment, you're at the pinnacle of your career. You're a Final Four coach. You've built to that point. The question isn't if you're coming back, it's *when* you're coming back."

Phelps took Notre Dame to the Final Four in 1978 at the age of thirty-six. The Irish lost in the semifinals to Duke, rallying from 14 points down to have a shot to tie in the final seconds before losing. "We never figured out how to guard [Mike] Gminski," he said twenty-seven years later. "During the game, Bill Laimbeer says to me, 'We should be beating these guys, Coach.' I said, 'If you got an occasional stop on Gminski, we might beat them.'"

They never figured Gminski out. Disappointing as it was, Phelps knew he'd be back. He was wrong. He coached thirteen more seasons at Notre Dame and never made it back. The Duke team that beat Notre Dame that day lost the final to Kentucky. All five starters were underclassmen. As they left the court that night, the players heard their fans chanting, "We'll be back." They weren't. Nor was Bill Foster, who had coached them from last place in the ACC in 1977 to the championship game in 1978.

And so, while there was plenty of reason for Weber to believe he would be back at the pinnacle of his sport again in the future, there was no guarantee. The only guarantee for anyone who plays or coaches in the Final Four is that the memories will stay with you forever — one way or the other.

2

The Lobby

THE THREE BASKETBALL GAMES that decide the national championship are only a small part of what goes on during a Final Four. The event has evolved into a weeklong gathering of the entire basketball world. For years, the National Association of Basketball Coaches has held its annual convention during the Final Four, meaning that coaches gather from all over the country. The famous ones come and so do the not-so-famous. Retired coaches come and so do fired coaches. Coaches looking for work come and so do those who haven't worked for a while but still, deep down, wish they were.

The coaches — almost two thousand of them when you include all the college and high school coaches who gather at the Final Four site — are only one of the groups that show up. Because the Final Four has become one of *the* events in the cult of American sports — ranking behind only the Super Bowl as a gathering place for the sports world — thousands of people pour into the city where the Final Four is being held. More than 1,400 accredited media cover the event — and that doesn't include the 375 people sent by CBS or those who are turned down by the NCAA when they request credentials. Almost anyone with something to sell, from movie stars to shoe-company hucksters to ticket scalpers, shows up. Fans of the four teams show up and so do corporate high rollers willing to pay almost anything to get a ticket so they can say they were in the building when the national championship was decided.

For five days the city is transformed. The streets are jammed with people, many of them in the colors of the four teams that are playing. An entire brigade of men in sweatsuits can be seen on street corners and in hotel lobbies. Many are coaches, some are scalpers, others are hangers-on who want to corner a coach to tell him about the great player they can help him "acquire." Celebrity-spotting goes on constantly. Autograph seekers pour into the hotel designated for the coaches convention, hoping to spot Mike Krzyzewski or Jim Calhoun but happy to talk to Billy Tubbs or Rick Majerus.

"That's one of the problems nowadays," said Jim Boeheim, the Syracuse coach who has won one national championship and been to three Final Fours. "When I first started coming to the Final Four back in the seventies, we would stand around in the lobby for hours and hours and just talk basketball. You can't do that anymore. There are too many people who want something from you. If it isn't an autograph seeker, it's a ticket scalper. If it isn't a ticket scalper, it's someone from a radio show who just wants 'five minutes' of your time. If it isn't a radio producer, it's a coach who needs work or wants a recommendation. It never seems to stop."

There is no doubting the exponential growth of the Final Four, in every way. It began in 1939 as the National Collegiate Basketball Championship. In those days, it wasn't even the most important basketball tournament — the National Invitation Tournament was. Teams often played in both events — in 1950

City College of New York won them both — and winning the NIT carried as much prestige as winning the National Collegiate Championship until well into the 1950s. As late as 1970, it was not completely unheard-of for a team to turn down a chance to play in the NCAA Tournament to play in the NIT. In 1968 Bob Knight, then the coach at Army, chose the NIT over the NCAAs because he believed his team had a chance to win it — in part because the NIT was played in New York, forty-five minutes from West Point, in part because Lew Alcindor and UCLA were playing in the NCAAs. Army lost in the first round of the NIT to Notre Dame on St. Patrick's Day. Two years later Marquette coach Al McGuire was unhappy about the regional his team was being sent to by the NCAA basketball committee and turned them down, choosing to go to the NIT. The Warriors won the tournament.

The NCAA Tournament became a monolith in stages. The UCLA dynasty, which began in 1964, was a starting point. Texas Western's historic victory over Kentucky in 1966 — the only year between 1964 and 1973 when UCLA did not win the championship — was another touchstone. In 1968 NBC televised the semifinals and the championship game, marking the first time the tournament was on network TV. (The NIT final had already been on CBS for years by then.) In 1971 the finals were held in a dome for the first time — the Houston Astrodome. Then, in 1973 NBC took the championship game to prime time, moving it to Monday night for the first time. The gamble paid off when Bill Walton shot 21 of 22 from the field and scored 44 points, leading UCLA to an easy victory over Memphis State and its seventh straight title. Six years after that, Michigan State — led by Magic Johnson — and Indiana State — starring Larry Bird — met in what was the highest-rated final of all time. Earlier that same season a new cable TV network had been launched, one that was devoted to sports twenty-four hours a day. Desperate for programming, ESPN began televising any and all college basketball games it could gain the rights to. That included persuading the NCAA to allow it to televise first-round NCAA Tournament games and round-of-sixteen games — all the games that were played on weekdays, when NBC had no interest in televising them. Searching for a color commentator who would sound a little different, the fledgling network hired a recently fired coach named Dick Vitale to work many of its games.

Three years later CBS paid an astonishing $16 million a year to wrest the TV rights away from NBC, which had been paying $4 million a year. One of the first things CBS did was hire Billy Packer, who had been working for NBC as its lead color commentator since 1975. In fact, the team of Packer, play-by-play man Dick Enberg, and Al McGuire had become the face of college basketball. The notion that the trio would no longer be calling the Final Four was a major concern to those who followed college basketball closely. McGuire had retired as the coach at Marquette in 1977, dramatically exiting the coaching stage by winning the national championship after he had announced he was retiring at the age of forty-eight. NBC initially hired him to work out of the production truck, but Packer suggested using a three-man booth for basketball — it had been used previously in football and baseball — and his sharp exchanges with McGuire, aided by Enberg's skills as a smooth traffic cop, quickly made them the game's most identifiable spokesmen.

CBS was aware of that. Enberg and McGuire were both under contract to NBC. Packer's contract was up and CBS grabbed him. Because there were few people at the network who knew very much about college basketball, Packer was given far-ranging authority. NBC still had most conferences under regular-season contracts, so Packer was dispatched to piece together a schedule for the network to televise before the tournament began. Together with Len DeLuca, then a CBS executive, Packer also came up with the idea of turning the entire basketball season into a promotional vehicle for the NCAA Tournament and, specifically, the Final Four. They called the concept "The Road to the Final Four" — the obvious point being that four teams would travel the country to end the season in the Final Four city. That year the city was New Orleans and, on occasion, the announcers would call it "the Road to New Orleans."

Even with a relatively weak regular-season schedule, CBS was able to begin selling the fact that it was now the network of the NCAA Tournament and, more important, the Final Four. There was no way to replace the magic of Enberg-Packer-McGuire, but the "road" concept allowed CBS to establish its own identity. Packer and DeLuca came up with a second idea to promote the fact that the tournament was now on CBS: televising the announcement of the tournament field. Up until then, the names of the teams in the field, where they were going to play, and who they were going to play against had simply been released to the wire services on the Sunday afternoon prior to the start of the tournament. The schools that qualified were called by NCAA staffers and told they had been invited to the tournament and where they were going the first weekend so that plane reservations could be made.

Packer and DeLuca decided to turn the unveiling of the field into a televison show. They asked the basketball committee to allow CBS to come to Kansas City (which was then NCAA headquarters) and announce the field on television once it had been selected and seeded. If nothing else, the network knew that all the teams with a chance to be in the tournament would be glued to their TV sets at the appointed hour. The idea proved golden. Simple as it sounds, it changed college basketball. Instead of being the day the bids went out, the second Sunday in March became Selection Sunday. These days Selection Sunday has become almost a national holiday for basketball fans. Most sports sections around the country count down to Selection Sunday the way kids count down to Christmas. People gather around their TV sets, brackets in hand, ready to fill in the names of what has now become a sixty-five-team field.

Almost from the minute the field is announced, people begin dissecting it, trying to figure out why certain teams were left out, why some were seeded higher than expected, why others are lower. CBS now unveils the brackets during an hour-long show that is not only rife with commercials but in which each regional has a sponsor or, as the network likes to call it in this age of euphemism, a "corporate champion." ESPN, which has evolved in the past twenty-six years into one of the most powerful entities in sports, televises a selection show of its own concurrent with the CBS show. As soon as a bracket goes up, the ESPN panel — led all these years later by Vitale, now the most famous personality in college basketball — begins analyzing the teams and their chances.

CBS got very lucky during its first four years as the network of the Final Four. Each of those seasons produced a championship game that was a classic, each in a different way. In 1982 North Carolina beat Georgetown, 63–62. The winning shot was made by a freshman named Michael Jordan and the game ended memorably when Georgetown's Fred Brown accidentally threw the ball right to North Carolina's James Worthy. The next year

North Carolina State, a huge underdog, beat Houston, 54–52, as the buzzer was sounding on a dunk by Lorenzo Charles, who caught a desperation airball thrown up by teammate Dereck Whittenburg and, in one motion, slammed the ball home for the stunning victory. To this day, the tape of State coach Jim Valvano racing around the court looking for someone to hug is one of the signature moments of the college game. The 1984 final was a match of the two schools that had lost at the buzzer the previous two years: Georgetown and Houston. It did not produce a classic finish, but it was a matchup between the two best centers of the time: Hakeem Olajuwon of Houston and Patrick Ewing of Georgetown. Ewing had a better supporting cast and Georgetown finally got its title for Coach John Thompson. Houston, in spite of three straight appearances in the Final Four with Olajuwon, was never able to do the same for Coach Guy V. Lewis.

And then came 1985, another watershed year for the tournament. Beginning in 1975, the basketball committee — the group of athletic directors and conference commissioners assigned to oversee all aspects of the tournament, including, most notably, team selection and negotiation of the TV contract — had started to expand the field. The tournament had started in 1939 as an eight-team event. It then expanded to sixteen teams and in 1956 to twenty-five teams. That odd number meant that seven conference champions received a bye into the round of sixteen, one of the reasons why UCLA had to play only two games to reach the Final Four in nine of its ten championship seasons under John Wooden.

In 1975 the committee expanded the field to thirty-two teams and, for the first time, allowed more than one team from a conference to be invited, still keeping a cap (at two) on the number that could go from one league. The expansion meant that everyone had to play a first-round game and turned the first weekend into an event, since all the top seeds had to play. The success of the expanded tournament led to more expansion: in 1978 the field was increased to forty teams, creating another round for sixteen teams, with the eight winners joining the other twenty-four teams in what was now the second round. Two years later the field grew to forty-eight and all limits on the number of teams that could be invited from a conference were abandoned. The ACC placed five teams in the field that year. Over the next five years, the committee kept inching up the number of teams — it went to fifty-two teams, then fifty-three. Finally, prior to the 1985 tournament, after much debate, the field was expanded to sixty-four teams. That meant there were no first-round byes and everyone had to play six games to win the national championship. It took four wins to get to the Final Four.

The opening two days of the tournament — still on ESPN in those days, with thirty-two games played in about thirty-six hours — became an annual festival of basketball. Vitale worked in the studio those two days, coming on between games and during halftimes to do analysis and make picks. His sometimes outrageous statements became something basketball fans looked forward to. No one could ever accuse Vitale of not going out on a limb.

The wisdom of expanding to a sixty-four-team field, with the tournament champion having to win six times straight in the ruthless single-elimination model, was proved conclusively in 1985. Because of the expansion, Villanova got into the tournament that year as the number eight seed in what was then called the southeast region. The Wildcats had to play their opening game against Dayton — at Dayton. They barely survived, winning 51–49. But soon they got on a roll, upsetting number two seed Michigan in the second round, then beating Maryland and North Carolina to get to the Final Four. The victory over North Carolina was especially sweet for Coach Rollie Massimino because his team had lost regional finals twice to ACC schools: Duke in 1978 and North Carolina in 1982. In the final seconds of the game, North Carolina coach Dean Smith ordered his players not to foul since the game was out of reach and Massimino was able to stand in front of his bench and soak in the fact that his team was — at last — going to the Final Four.

"Everyone who coaches should have a moment like that," he said later. "To be able to stand on the court those last few seconds and realize it has happened, that you're going to the Final Four, is just an amazing feeling. I have to thank Dean for having the class not to foul. It allowed me to have a few of the sweetest seconds of my entire life."

The next weekend was even sweeter. Villanova beat Memphis State in the semifinals, meaning it got to face Georgetown, the defending national champion, in the final. Outside of the Villanova locker room, there probably weren't half a dozen people who thought Villanova had a chance. The Hoyas were still led by Ewing and he had superb players around him. They had absolutely destroyed St. John's, generally considered the second-best team in the country, in the semifinals and most looked at Monday night as little more than a coronation for Georgetown. The Hoyas were a virtual lock to become the first school since Wooden's retirement to win back-to-back championships.

But the Wildcats had other ideas. They had lost two close games to Georgetown during the regular season and had the advantage of knowing how to play them and knowing they could play with them. "Not only were we not intimidated," Massimino said years later, "we were very confident. We thought we should have beaten them in the regular season and now we were on a roll. We'd won five straight games against good teams. There was no doubt in our mind we could win."

The game was the last one played in college basketball without a shot clock. Before every game, Massimino would write a number on the blackboard for his team that told his players how many points they needed to score to win the game. On Monday, April 1, 1985, the number he wrote on the board was 65. That meant, he believed, if his team scored at least 65 points, it would win the game. He almost never got the number wrong.

Villanova went out and played what is now called by most "the perfect game." In an era when shooting more than 50 percent from the field during a game was considered very good — fantastic against Georgetown's vaunted defense — Villanova shot 79.3 percent. In the second half, slowing the game to their pace, the Wildcats made 9 of 10 shots, the only miss being a tip-in attempt by center Ed Pinckney. They made all their free throws down the stretch and won the game, 66–64, in what is arguably the greatest upset in the history of college basketball. Twenty years later that game is still discussed, written about, and dissected. It has been the subject of documentaries and lengthy magazine pieces, chronicling the ups and (many) downs of those who took part that night.

Gary McLain, the point guard who handled the Georgetown press so well that night, sold a story to *Sports Illustrated* two years after the game saying he had a cocaine habit during that season, often played games high, and was high when the team went to the White House after winning the championship. Massimino, a hero in Philadelphia in 1985, left town a pariah seven years later because he had alienated many people in the wake of the championship.

But nothing could change what had happened that night and what that game had done for college basketball. It clearly established one lasting and unequivocal fact: in an event where one loss ends your season, anything can happen. No game is an absolute certainty, especially in the Final Four. N.C. State over Houston had made the notion that any team can win plausible; Villanova-Georgetown cemented it as fact. The Final Four had become established forever by then as an event, a part of Americana just like the World Series, the Super Bowl, and the Masters golf tournament. It transcends sports. Basketball fans follow the game from November to March. Nonbasketball fans pay attention in March, and almost everyone knows something about the Final Four.

The tournament now has two nicknames: fans and marketers refer to it as "March Madness," another phrase trademarked by the NCAA. To players and coaches it has become "the Dance," just as Major League Baseball is known as "the Show." Everyone wants to dance in March. Sixty-five teams get to dance, but only four — the Final Four — get to the last dance, college basketball's Holy Grail.

Although only four teams get to the last dance, the rest of the college basketball world comes to watch them show off their routines. Throughout the week, there are several hubs of activity. One is the hotel that is headquarters for the National Association of Basketball Coaches (NABC), better known simply as the coaches' hotel. Another is the hotel where the basketball committee and the NCAA's corporate VIPs stay along with the media. Another is wherever CBS is headquartered, and another is the shopping mall where ESPN places its set for the week. The number of people who congregate for a glimpse of Dick Vitale is staggering.

More often than not, the teams stay at hotels that are away from the hoopla. Occasionally a coach keeps his team in the downtown hotel it is assigned to — Boeheim did it in New Orleans in 2003, and his team won — but most of the time coaches want their players someplace where the hotel lobby does not resemble Times Square on New Year's Eve most of the time. "I try to make it clear to my guys that we're going to the Final Four for two reasons," said Connecticut coach Jim Calhoun, undefeated in two trips to the last weekend. "The first is as a reward for getting there, to have a good time, to soak the whole thing in. We get in on Wednesday and we spend two solid days seeing the town, going sightseeing, having fun. By Friday, though, it's time to start dealing with the second reason: winning a championship. They understand that there's time for fun and then time for work. I think not doing both would be a mistake."

A lot of coaches don't see it that way. Bob Knight, who won three championships in five trips to the Final Four while at Indiana, would always bring his team in at the last possible moment, and when they arrived it was strictly business until the moment they left. In fact, Knight may be the last coach not to arrive at a Final Four until Friday. In 1987 he scheduled his team's departure so that it would land in New Orleans in time to go straight to practice and the team's Friday press conference. Except there was a problem: the plane hit headwinds and Knight and his players were late for the press conference. Not that they minded. The Hoosiers won the championship, Knight's third title, when Keith Smart hit a baseline jumper with five seconds left to beat Syracuse, 74–73.

Knight was so thrilled with the victory that he told his players and coaches that the bus for the airport would be leaving at 7:00 A.M. and anyone who was late would be left behind. Two of his assistants, Dan Dakich and Murry Bartow, decided there wasn't much point in going to bed for very long. "We figured we would sleep when we got home," Bartow remembered.

They went out celebrating until the wee hours of the morning. They got back to the room they were sharing and fell into their beds, setting an alarm for 6:30 so they could wake up and catch the bus. But the alarm didn't go off. "One of us woke up at about 6:55," Bartow said. "We were scared to death. We just ran into clothes, stuffed our things into our suitcases, and raced out the door. We got downstairs just in time to see the bus pulling away. Fortunately, we knew, with the one-way streets, the bus had to circle the hotel, so we sprinted to the other side and got there just as the bus pulled up to a red light. We were waving our arms to make sure Coach Knight could see us. The light turned green; the bus hesitated for just a second and then took off. I guess he figured, we were late, he wasn't stopping."

Fortunately, the two bedraggled young coaches were able to hail a cab and get to the airport. They found the gate where Indiana's charter was leaving from and were sitting on the plane when the bus pulled up with the team. Needless to say, there was a good deal of snickering as the players walked by them to their seats. "Coach Knight got on the plane, looked at us, and never said a word," Bartow said. "I think Dan and I were half expecting him to tell us to get off."

The joys of victory.

The place to be for most of the week for those who are not part of one of the four teams playing is the coaches' hotel, even if it is not quite as much fun today as it once was for the coaches.

"Years ago, going to the Final Four was almost like going to a weeklong coaches clinic," Maryland coach Gary Williams said. "You would walk through the lobby and there were coaches everywhere talking basketball. Now, it's a zoo. You can't walk five feet without someone asking you for something."

For the famous coaches, the toughest things are autograph seekers, many of them professional memorabilia collectors, and the radio producers who camp out in the lobby and look to grab the first familiar face they can find. The "radio row" at the Final Four isn't as big as the one at the Super Bowl, where it seems that every one of the 412 all-sports radio stations set up headquarters for the week. But it is still very big, with probably close to a hundred radio stations — some small, some national — trying to round up guests during the week. Not only do the producers try to grab anyone and everyone they can, but they won't hesitate to better-deal a coach if they see an opportunity. In New Orleans a couple of years ago, a producer from a syndicated network had just collared Lefty Driesell, one of three men to have coached four different schools into the NCAA Tournament, and was taking him up an escalator to where his network was set up. Just as they reached the escalator, the producer spotted Arizona coach Lute Olson walking past him.

"Coach Olson," he said, introducing himself, "can we grab you sometime for five minutes?"

Olson looked at his watch. "I can do it right now," he said. "Then I have to go to a meeting."

Olson was completely unaware that the producer had Driesell in hand. "Great," the producer said. Without missing a beat, he turned to Driesell and said, "Coach, can we get back to you later?"

To his everlasting credit, Driesell said, "Absolutely not," and turned and walked away.

"It's not like I need to go on with the guy," Driesell said. "He asked me to do him a favor. I understand Lute's a bigger name than I am now, but you don't treat people that way."

Except sometimes on radio row.

The coaches' lobby is also the hub of most Final Four rumors. March is the time of year when coaches get hired and fired, and there are always jobs open or about to open when the basketball world arrives in the Final Four city. Some of the rumors are crazy. In 2003, after Matt Doherty had been fired as the coach at North Carolina, one lobby rumor had it that if Roy Williams didn't take the job, Dean Smith was going to come back and coach. In 2005 Digger Phelps half jokingly said over dinner to some friends that if DePaul coach Dave Leitao left to take the Virginia job — a rumor that later proved true — he would come back to coach at DePaul after a fifteen-year absence from the profession.

"It's a sleeping giant," Phelps said. "I almost took the job back in '97. I told them then that they should try to get into the Big East. Well, now they're in the Big East. I think the job could be exactly like the Fordham job was when I was there."

Phelps's first head coaching job was at Fordham thirty-four years ago. He was twenty-nine and he led the little school from the Bronx to its greatest season. The Rams went 26–3, upset Notre Dame before a sellout crowd in Madison Square Garden, and reached the Sweet Sixteen of the NCAA Tournament before losing to Villanova. That year — and the win over Notre Dame — springboarded Phelps into the Notre Dame job. Even though he took the Irish to the Final Four and numerous NCAA Tournaments, he never had a year quite as glorious as that first one at Fordham.

Phelps is sixty-three now and lives a very comfortable life as an analyst for ESPN. There is a part of every old coach that wants to coach again. But the likelihood of late-night ruminations, rife with nostalgia about his early days as a coach, leading to actually taking a job was just about nil. Nonetheless, the rumor was all over the lobby the next morning: Leitao to Virginia, Digger to DePaul.

One of the most famous lobby rumors, one that had some truth to it, took place in 1988 when the Final Four was held in Kansas City. UCLA had fired Walt Hazzard as its coach, and all sorts of names were being floated as his successor. On Wednesday evening, while the coaches were checking in to the hotel and registering for the convention, word began to make its way around the lobby: Dick Vitale was reporting on ESPN that Jim Valvano was going to be the next coach at UCLA.

At the time, Valvano was one of the biggest names in coaching. He had won one of the most improbable national championship game upsets in history in 1983, North Carolina State over Houston. Valvano was thirty-seven at the time and had one of the most electric personalities the sport had ever seen. He was smart and he was funny and he could really coach. He became an instant star, hosting TV shows, doing the sports on *CBS Morning News,* flying from coaching a game one day to doing TV analysis at another game the next. In 1985 and 1986 N.C. State made it back to the round of eight, each time falling a step short of another Final Four. In 1988 the Wolfpack had finished second in the ACC but had lost to Duke in the conference tournament semifinals and then been shocked in the first round of the tournament by Murray State.

Valvano was restless. Perhaps the answer was to become the coach of the basketball program that had more tradition than any other. No one had been able to follow John Wooden since his retirement in 1975 with any consistent success. Maybe Valvano could be the one to do it.

Vitale had the story right — almost. Valvano had, in fact, interviewed earlier in the week with UCLA's chancellor, Charles Young, and athletic director, Pete Dalis. It was one of those clandestine meetings that academics like to arrange.

"Check in to the hotel under an assumed name," Dalis told Valvano.

"How about Biff, would that be a good name?" answered Valvano, never one to take things quite as seriously as most people do.

The meeting between Young, Dalis, and Biff actually went well. Valvano liked Young. It would be hard to say no to UCLA under any circumstances, even though Valvano knew his family — wife Pam and three daughters — would be less than thrilled with the idea of moving to California. Valvano agreed to come back and visit the campus later in the week after going to Kansas City, where he had several Final Four obligations. By the time he reached Kansas City on Thursday morning, half the media covering the Final Four were camped out in the lobby waiting for him because of Vitale's report.

Valvano was stunned that the story had gotten out so quickly. He shouldn't have been. Valvano was under contract to Nike at the time. Nike's basketball guy was Sonny Vaccaro, a Valvano confidant. Vitale also worked for Nike and was also close to Vaccaro. Biff's trip to L.A. went from Valvano to Vaccaro to Vitale to the world. Valvano wouldn't comment in the lobby that day, fueling even more speculation that he was going to UCLA.

"I'll bet anyone here dinner he'll be the coach by the end of the week," Vitale kept telling people.

He would have lost his bet. Valvano's family put its foot down. What's more, Valvano had a half-million-dollar buyout in the contract he had signed at N.C. State two years earlier.

By Friday there was another rumor in the lobby: Valvano was out, Mike Krzyzewski was in.

That one was really wrong. Krzyzewski had already told UCLA he wasn't interested. Larry Brown, who was coaching Kansas in the Final Four — and to the national championship — was interested in the job. He had already coached UCLA once. He flew to Los Angeles the following week and agreed in principle to take the job. Then he changed his mind and stayed at Kansas — until a month later, when he left to become the coach of the San Antonio Spurs.

No one in the lobby ever mentioned the name of Pepperdine coach Jim Harrick. He got the job.

In 2005 the hottest job on the market was the one at Virginia. Pete Gillen had resigned at the end of the season after seven years that had produced one trip to the NCAA Tournament, in 2001. Everyone in basketball had known all season that Gillen was gone unless Virginia made the NCAA Tournament. Once the Cavaliers lost to Duke in the ACC Tournament quarterfinals to finish their season at 14–15, everyone knew Gillen was out.

All sorts of names had been floated during the season. At the top of Athletic Director Craig Littlepage's list was Kentucky coach Tubby Smith. Clearly, Smith would be an ideal choice: he was a superb coach with a national championship (1998) on his résumé. He was African American, and Littlepage believed it was time for Virginia to seriously consider hiring an African American to coach basketball. He was also expensive: Kentucky was paying him $2.1 million a year. Virginia would probably have to top that. There were rumors that some boosters were willing to come up with the money if that's what it would take to get Smith, but it was also possible that once they came up with the money, Smith would just use the offer to get an extension, and perhaps a raise, at Kentucky.

The family that was putting up the money for the naming rights for Virginia's new arena — the John Paul Jones Arena — had connections to Memphis coach John Calipari. But Calipari, who also made a lot of money, wasn't likely to leave a school in a weakened league (four schools were pulling out of Conference USA to join the Big East) to take over a team that had just finished eleventh in the ACC.

Mike Montgomery, the former Stanford coach who had been a candidate for the Virginia job in 1990, was mentioned. No, Montgomery wasn't walking away from $3 million a year to coach the Golden State Warriors. Notre Dame coach Mike Brey had been considered a candidate early on. Brey had grown up in the Washington, D.C., area, graduated from George Washington University, and been an assistant coach at Duke for eight years. He knew the area and the ACC well. What's more, with the Big East expanding to add Louisville, DePaul, Marquette, Cincinnati, and South Florida, the league — with sixteen teams — would become the most brutal and deep in college basketball. Recruiting against the new schools wouldn't be easy, since no one had ever mistaken any of them for Harvard or Yale when it came to admissions standards. But with Notre Dame struggling for a second straight season to make the NCAA Tournament (the Irish were eventually one of the last teams taken off the board by the basketball committee), Brey's luster had faded a bit by the time Gillen resigned.

Not so Texas coach Rick Barnes, whose team had been in the Final Four in 2003. Barnes had actually taken the Virginia job in

1990 before changing his mind and returning to Providence. Barnes played golf with Fred Barakat, the ACC's associate commissioner, the week before the Final Four when Barakat was in Austin during the regional held there. Barakat asked Barnes if he would be interested in the Virginia job. Barnes was adamant: no, not interested. For one thing, he had what he thought was a potentially great team at Texas for the 2005–'06 season. For another, one of the reasons he had left Clemson after the 1998 season was the constant frustration of trying to compete with Duke and North Carolina. None of that had changed. If anything, the league, now expanded to twelve teams, was tougher than when Barnes had left.

Rumors work in funny ways. By the time the basketball world gathered in St. Louis, a few days after the Barnes-Barakat round of golf, the word was that Barnes and Barakat had played golf and that Barakat had asked Barnes if he would consider the Virginia job. All of which was true. But the rumor left out one thing: Barnes's lack of interest. On Wednesday evening, as coaches started to gather at the Millennium Hotel in the shadow of the Arch, Barnes was the hot name for the Virginia job.

It was going to be a busy week for Littlepage. As a member of the basketball committee — and the already selected chairman for 2006 — he had a full schedule of meetings and parties, not to mention the team practices and the games. As Virginia's athletic director, he was constantly being asked about the status of his search for a new coach. "I told everyone I wasn't going to make any decisions until after I got back from here," he said, sitting in the lobby of his hotel early one morning. "No one wants to believe me. It's a better story if there's something going on."

Of course it was. Who ever heard of a lobby rumor that began: "Hey, did you hear about Virginia? Nothing's happening?"

Which may explain why Littlepage began every conversation with an approaching reporter with a question of his own: "What have you heard?"

He was pretty certain that everyone in town had heard something. He was absolutely right.

3

Getting There

GETTING TO THE FINAL FOUR is easy. Getting into the Final Four is far more difficult. In 2005 the Edward Jones Dome was configured to seat 47,500 people — about 20,000 less than its capacity for St. Louis Rams games. Even with all that empty space, many of the seats sold by the NCAA are so far from the floor that the tickets say "distant view" on them so that those who buy them know what they are getting — or not getting — when they arrive at their seats many miles from the playing floor. No one complains.

Ticket distribution for the Final Four breaks down this way:

- Forty percent of the tickets go to the four participating teams, meaning that in 2005 North Carolina, Illinois, Louisville, and Michigan State each received a little more than 4,700 tickets apiece to give to their biggest boosters.
- Ten percent of the tickets go to the local organizing committee.
- Eight percent of the tickets go to the National Association of Basketball Coaches.
- Eight percent of the tickets go to the Division 1 athletic directors.

- Six percent go to the NCAA.
- Six percent go to CBS, most of those seats going to corporate clients.
- Twenty-two percent go to the general public — meaning that if you were not connected to someone in the groups who controlled the other 78 percent of the tickets, a little more than 10,000 tickets were available, most of them distant view, for each game.

The Final Four actually does better than some other major events when it comes to getting the public into the building. At the Super Bowl each year — with far more tickets available — the public has access to about a thousand tickets. Those tickets cost $500. At the Final Four, tickets downstairs cost $85 and upstairs they cost $65 — a bargain by today's standards. If you really want to get into the games and you aren't a coach, an athletic director, or someone with ties to CBS, the NCAA, or the local organizing committee and if you don't get a ticket through the public lottery, you can still get in: it will just cost you about $2,500. In many cases, those tickets are sold by scalpers and ticket agencies who have connections to the groups that get the tickets. They can be seen on the streets of the Final Four city, cell phones in hand, offering tickets at prices that rise each day leading up to semifinal Saturday, then begin to drop before Monday's game because fans from Saturday's losing teams are willing to sell their tickets at any price.

"If you don't get your price by Saturday, you're in a lot of trouble," one scalper said on Saturday afternoon in St. Louis. He was standing on a street corner, holding four tickets that he said were "prime." They were, in fact, downstairs, about twenty rows up behind one of the baskets. Not exactly where the corporate titans or CBS's best clients would be sitting, but good seats nonetheless. The scalper had been asking for $3,000 a ticket earlier in the week. "I had twelve to begin with," he said. "I sold four at two thousand dollars each and four at three thousand dollars each."

Now it was a little more than three hours before tip-off of the first game and he was getting nervous. "I don't even bother with tickets for Monday," he said. "Most people are smart enough to know there's no need to buy a Monday ticket before the games Saturday because there will be so many tickets floating around Saturday night and Sunday. I keep two on hand, just in case someone gets desperate at the last minute. More often than not, I end up eating them or just going to the game myself. But if I sell all my Saturday tickets, I'm way ahead." His asking price for the last four tickets had dropped considerably: "Give me two grand and all four of them are yours right now," he said.

The money to be made by selling Final Four tickets has become the subject of considerable controversy. The NABC has taken a lot of hits over the years because of coaches scalping tickets. Most are smart enough not to make the sale themselves. You won't see coaches standing on a corner, holding tickets in one hand, a cell phone in the other. But some of the tickets being sold may have belonged to coaches originally.

"The excuse we get a lot is that someone gave his tickets to a friend or a relative and that person did the scalping," said Jim Haney, who has been executive director of the NABC since 1992. "That's why we tell them now that if the tickets fall into the wrong hands, *they* are responsible, no matter how far removed they might be from the actual sale."

The NABC is very sensitive to the issue of ticket scalping and has taken some strong measures in recent years to clean it up. "The ADs get as many tickets as we do, but theirs are distributed very early, so even if someone does sell a ticket, it isn't as likely to be discussed in the public domain," Haney said. "Our tickets are picked up at the Final Four. Our lobby tends to be the hub of activity for much of the week. If something goes on, it will be heard about, talked about, written about. We understand that our image takes a hit when this happens. Every year I've done this job, the one story that's an automatic in the local paper in the Final Four city is on scalping, and a lot of it is about coaches."

Sure enough, on Wednesday morning of Final Four week, the *St. Louis Post-Dispatch* had a story on A-1 of the newspaper about the scramble for tickets, scalping, and the history of coaches as scalpers.

Several years ago the NABC and the NCAA came up with a new system to try to cut down on the scalping they knew was going on early and often, especially among coaches who weren't making the kind of money the famous coaches make today. Under the new system, every ticket is assigned to a specific coach and he is responsible for what happens to those tickets. Coaches have to pick up the tickets themselves. On several occasions in recent years, Harvard coach Frank Sullivan, who didn't want to stay for the weekend, has flown into the Final Four city, picked up his tickets, and then given them to his two assistants so they can see the games. "It seems ridiculous," Sullivan said. "But given what has gone on, I understand it."

If someone's tickets show up in the wrong place — on eBay, in a scalper's hands, in the hands of someone in the arena who brags that he paid $5,000 for them — Haney contacts the coach to tell him he has a problem. The coach is then invited, if he wishes, to write a letter to the basketball committee, explaining what happened. "There's very little slack cut," Haney said. "In

2004 we had forty-five tickets show up in places where they didn't belong. All forty-five coaches involved were told they would not receive tickets for the next five years."

What's more, those tickets were not given to other coaches waiting in line; they were taken out of the coaches' allotment. "When we made this deal with the NCAA, they actually gave us seven hundred more tickets," Haney said. "But it was on the condition that we would lose any tickets that got scalped. We get them back — but only after the coach involved is allowed tickets again."

The most embarrassing moment for the coaches in St. Louis came when a coach was caught scalping a ticket on a street corner and ended up being chased by police — with a TV camera crew recording the entire incident. "The good news is the guy wasn't an NABC member," Haney said with a sigh. "He didn't get his tickets through us. He was a junior college coach from Iowa trying to make some extra money by buying and selling a couple of tickets. But of course the story goes out that a coach was caught on camera scalping tickets and everyone just nods their heads knowingly. Even when we're innocent, we're often judged guilty."

The other way to get into the Final Four is to play or coach your way in. As anyone who has ever done so successfully can tell you, it isn't easy. In 2005 there were 326 teams competing in Division 1 college basketball. Realistically, no more than a hundred have the financing or the tradition it takes to put together a team that can win four games in the NCAA Tournament. If you are a member of the ACC, the Big East, the Big Ten, the Big 12, the Southeastern

Conference, the Pacific-10, Conference USA, the Atlantic 10, or the Mountain West Conference, it is possible, based on the tradition of the league, the finances of the league, and the exposure the league receives on television, to reach the Final Four. There are a handful of schools not from those power conferences — Gonzaga comes to mind right away — that, if everything falls into place, can make a run at the Final Four. Some smaller schools have proven that they can make the Sweet Sixteen: Butler, Valparaiso, and Creighton have reached the second week in recent years. In 2005 Wisconsin-Milwaukee carried the banner of the nonpower schools in the round of sixteen after upsetting Alabama and Boston College, two schools from the power leagues. The dream ended in the round of sixteen against number one Illinois.

The last true nonpower school to make the Final Four was Pennsylvania in 1979. Since then, only one school not currently in one of the nine power conferences has made it to the Final Four: Houston, which appeared three straight years from 1982 to 1984. Back then, Houston was part of the now-defunct Southwest Conference, which included schools such as Texas, Arkansas, and Texas Tech, which are all part of power conferences now. Houston got left out in all the shuffling and is part of the struggling Western Athletic Conference. When Nevada–Las Vegas made three appearances between 1987 and 1991 (winning the title in 1990), it was part of the Big West. It is now a member of the Mountain West and in the thirteenth year of a rebuilding program that started when legendary coach Jerry Tarkanian was forced out while the school was on NCAA probation.

Among those hundred schools, perhaps twenty-five have a legitimate shot in a given year to reach the Final Four. Some schools haven't been in forever. Northwestern won the national championship in 1942 and hasn't even been in the tournament again since. No one expects Air Force, a member of the Mountain West, to reach the Final Four in the near future. Just getting the school into the tournament in 2004 — for the first time in forty-two years — was enough to earn Joe Scott national Coach of the Year votes. Few people consider schools like South Florida (moving from Conference USA to the Big East in the fall of 2005), Duquesne (Atlantic 10), or Texas A&M likely Final Four teams anytime soon. But that doesn't mean it can't happen for those schools. When John Calipari took the job at Massachusetts in 1988, the school was perhaps the worst Division 1 program in the country. It hadn't tasted anything approaching glory since Julius Erving's departure in 1971, and the best Erving had been able to do was get the team into the NIT. It took Calipari four years to get UMass into the NCAA Tournament and eight years to get into the Final Four. He was able to parlay that success into a gigantic contract to coach the New Jersey Nets in the NBA.

Calipari's success at UMass illustrates why colleges will pay millions of dollars if they believe they have found the right coach. It also helps explain why coaches who win games but get into hot water with the NCAA police can always find work. When Calipari left Massachusetts, soon after its appearance in the Final Four, the school was under investigation for a number of violations, most of them involving star center Marcus Camby. Eventually UMass was forced to "vacate" its Final Four appearance — meaning that, technically, only three teams took part in the 1996 Final Four — and return the money it received from the tournament that year, about $600,000. But that didn't matter. No one cares that UMass's appearance was "vacated." And the money the school made from TV appearances, alumni contributions, and increased admissions applications made the penalty more than worthwhile.

Four years later, when the NBA gig didn't work out, Calipari was a hot commodity because of what he had achieved at Massachusetts and he signed a seven-figure deal to coach at Memphis University. Calipari's not the only coach — by any means — to have a run-in with the NCAA police after winning lots of games and then surface at another school: Eddie Sutton went from Kentucky (which was still on probation for violations on his watch) to Oklahoma State; Jerry Tarkanian went from Long Beach State to Nevada–Las Vegas and then survived several investigations while at Vegas before finally being forced to resign in 1992. He was, naturally, hired soon after at Fresno State. Jim Boeheim not only survived sanctions at Syracuse but went on to win a national championship and be elected to the Basketball Hall of Fame. Norm Ellenberger and Tates Locke both went through major NCAA investigations and coached again. Locke even wrote a book describing how he got caught while at Clemson (the book was titled *Caught in the Net*) and, after a stint in the NBA, returned to be the head coach at Indiana State.

Most coaches who get nailed by the NCAA aren't like Locke. They all claim innocence, either blaming the violations on overzealous assistants, the NCAA's infractions committee, or the media — sometimes all three. Very rarely is a head coach heard to say, "I was in charge, it's my fault." Tarkanian sued the NCAA — successfully — not so much because he was innocent but because the NCAA was incompetent. He is also responsible for perhaps the best line ever to describe NCAA justice. When an air express envelope containing $10,000 fell open while en route from the Kentucky basketball office to the father of a recruit in 1988, Tarkanian said, "The NCAA is so mad at Kentucky, it's going to put Cleveland State on probation for another three years."

Cleveland State, a decided nonpower, had enjoyed a brief spasm of glory in 1986 when it upset Indiana in the first round of the NCAA Tournament and reached the round of sixteen. Soon after, the school was on probation and Coach Kevin Mackey was out of work. Cleveland State doesn't drive TV ratings. Its presence in the round of sixteen, while a remarkable story, certainly didn't put any smiles on CBS faces. Think about it: did CBS want Indiana and Bob Knight playing that year, or Cleveland State and Kevin Mackey? Does CBS — and its corporate partner, the NCAA — want Kentucky on probation and off TV? Of course not. That's why when the big-time schools get caught, the NCAA enforcement committee immediately starts talking about how "cooperative" the school has been while it explains why it has been given only a slap on the wrist. The NCAA even went so far, in 1990, as to postpone a major school's sanctions. Nevada–Las Vegas had just won the national championship and was scheduled to be banned from the next season's tournament for major violations. In one of its more bizarre rulings, the NCAA announced that UNLV would be allowed to participate in the 1991 tournament and then be banned in 1992. Some media pundits (okay, me) began referring to CBS that season as "the official network of the Runnin' Rebels." Watching CBS that season — UNLV was, needless to say, on frequently — one might have confused Vegas with Harvard and Tarkanian with Father Flanagan. To be fair, Tarkanian had some Father Flanagan in him. He reveled in taking players who had been in trouble elsewhere and turning them into productive players in his program. He was probably more honest than 99 percent of college coaches about what he did and why he did it. When he was once asked why he took so many transfers, he answered, "Because their cars are already paid for."

That kind of one-liner and the constant presence of NCAA investigators on his campus obscured just how good a coach Tarkanian was. He took UNLV to four Final Fours, won a national championship, and was one of the better defensive coaches of all time. His good friend John Thompson once said of him, "I really don't care how he gets his players or where he gets them from. What I know for sure is that all of them play very hard on defense on every possession."

Tarkanian's brilliance as a coach is best evidenced by what has happened at UNLV since his departure. The school hasn't been back to the Sweet Sixteen, much less the Final Four, and has gone through six coaches who have an overall record of 232–159. Tarkanian went on to Fresno State, where he rebuilt the program, took it from nowhere to the NCAAs — and then had to leave after a number of players were arrested on various charges and reports surfaced that term papers were being written for players. Of course, if Tark had been sixty when all this happened instead of seventy, you can bet someone else would have hired him. His overall record of 778–202, the sixth-best winning percentage in history, is more than worthy of the Hall of Fame. Don't expect him to be giving his induction speech anytime soon.

Of course, the ideal for a school is a coach who wins big and does so with a clean record. In thirty-six years at North Carolina, Dean Smith won two national championships, went to eleven Final Fours, and graduated most of his players. In twenty-five years at Duke, Mike Krzyzewski has won three national titles, been to ten Final Fours, and graduated most of his players. Bob Knight's numbers can certainly stand up to those two: in twenty-nine years at Indiana, he won three championships, reached five Final Fours, and had most of his players graduate. Knight had other issues: getting arrested in Puerto Rico, throwing chairs, choking players, grabbing students who made the mistake of calling him "Knight," tossing the occasional potted plant over the head of an elderly secretary. Even so, he remains an icon in the sport and had no trouble finding work at Texas Tech after being fired at Indiana.

Krzyzewski and Smith were bitter rivals when they coached against each other. Smith was a godlike figure in North Carolina when Krzyzewski arrived at Duke in 1980. His shadow grew even longer when he won his first national championship in 1982 while Krzyzewski was struggling to a 10–17 record in his second season at Duke. A year later, when Jim Valvano won the national championship at North Carolina State while Duke was going 11–17, Krzyzewski appeared to be completely overwhelmed, surrounded on Tobacco Road by an icon and a rock star. Smith was only fifty-one and had the best program in the sport. Valvano was thirty-seven and was the most popular and in-demand person in the sport. Krzyzewski was 38–47 and had most Duke people screaming for his head.

To his credit, he never panicked and he never lost his sense of humor. During his second season at Duke, he made a recruiting visit to the home of a talented six-foot-ten kid from Oklahoma named Mark Acres. As he made his pitch to Acres and his parents, Krzyzewski quickly became convinced that he wasn't getting through, that what he was selling they weren't buying. Still, he had to go through with the ritual, make the best effort he could, especially since Acres would probably be the best player on his team the day he arrived on campus. Throughout the evening, Acres's mother never once opened her mouth, never asked a question, never made a comment. Finally, Krzyzewski turned to her and asked if there was anything she wanted to know about Duke or if she had any questions at all. Mrs. Acres shook her head and said, "No, I don't need to ask any questions because the only thing that matters is that Mark go to school someplace where he can be close to God."

Krzyzewski paused a moment and then, feeling pretty certain he wasn't getting the kid regardless of how he responded, said, "Well, you know, if Mark comes to Duke, God will be coaching eight miles down the road at Chapel Hill."

The Acres family didn't get the joke. It didn't really matter. Mark went to Oral Roberts.

Other moments during those early years weren't as amusing. Krzyzewski's third season at Duke ended with a humiliating 109–66 loss to Virginia in the ACC Tournament. Duke had a superb freshman class that year: Johnny Dawkins, Mark Alarie, Jay Bilas, David Henderson, and Weldon Williams. The first four would be starters on the 1986 team that would win thirty-seven games and play for the national championship. But as freshmen, they simply weren't ready for the ACC. After the loss to Virginia, all of them wondered if their coach would survive as the pressure on him to compete with North Carolina, eight miles to the south, and North Carolina State, twenty miles east, continued to build.

"I can remember saying to my father, if they fire Coach K, where will I go to school?" Bilas said. "I had picked him far more than the school. If they had fired him, I'm sure I would have left."

Krzyzewski was wondering about his future in the wee hours of the morning after the Virginia loss. Bobby Dwyer, then his top assistant, had put together a small group of people to go out and eat if only to get him out of his room, where his wife,

Mickie, was in tears. Also he wanted to get him away from the hotel and the prying eyes of angry alumni. They ended up in a Denny's in the middle of a driving rainstorm at about 3:00 A.M. It was Johnny Moore, Duke's assistant sports information director, who raised his water glass and said, "Here's to forgetting tonight."

To which Krzyzewski famously answered: "Here's to *never* forgetting tonight."

When Dwyer suggested a little later that there might still be time to get in on the recruitment of Tom Sheehey, then a high school senior who would end up playing at Virginia, Krzyzewski shook his head. "We aren't recruiting Tom Sheehey. We aren't recruiting anyone else this year. We've got [Tommy] Amaker coming in to play the point. If we can't win with Amaker and the freshmen we have now, we *should* be fired."

They won. The next season Duke went 24–10 and got back to the Dance. Two years later the Blue Devils won thirty-seven games and played in the final. Krzyzewski didn't get fired. Duke ended up going to seven of nine Final Fours, including five straight, a string surpassed only by UCLA's eleven in twelve years. In 1991 Krzyzewski won his first title. A year later he won again. Suddenly, he had won more national championships than God, who was still coaching eight miles down the road in Chapel Hill. Smith caught up a year later but by then the battle lines had been drawn. Many of the same Duke people who had screamed at athletic director Tom Butters for not firing Krzyzewski in 1983 were now insisting he was clearly a better coach than Dean Smith. Carolina people certainly didn't want to hear that. One of sport's most intense rivalries became even more intense.

The Krzyzewski-Smith rivalry may have been best summed

up by a scene that took place in the building named for Smith — the Dean E. Smith Center, aka the Deandome — in 1993. Early in the game, both Smith and Krzyzewski were up on every call, clearly wired by the importance of the occasion. Lenny Wirtz, the veteran referee, finally called them both to midcourt. "Look, guys, I know it's a big game, but you have to let us make the calls. Don't be up on every whistle, okay? Give us some space to work."

"Lenny, you don't understand," Krzyzewski said with a smile. "There are twenty-one thousand people in here and they're all against me. You three [the officials] are the only ones I can talk to."

Wirtz smiled at the joke. Not Smith. "Lenny, don't let him do that," he said. "He's trying to get you on his side."

Krzyzewski waved his hand at Smith in disgust and stalked back to his bench. Turning to his coaches, he said, "If I ever start to act like him, don't ask any questions, just get a gun and shoot me."

Now it is Duke, and Krzyzewski, who, in the minds of other coaches, gets all the calls. Even in 2005 en route to winning the national championship, Roy Williams told Gary Williams in a private moment that the only reason his team's two games with Duke (they split) had each gone down to the final play was the officiating. Gary Williams didn't disagree. To this day, he remains convinced that Duke's 22-point comeback against his team in the 2001 Final Four was a direct result of the officiating. For his part, Krzyzewski believes that calls went against his team down the stretch in 2004 in a Final Four game against Connecticut because the officials were determined to prove that Duke *didn't* get all the calls.

And Connecticut coach Jim Calhoun, who has won two national titles? He still hasn't completely gotten over the fifth foul called on Nadev Henefeld in the 1990 regional final against

Duke or the officiating in general in 1998 when his team faced North Carolina in Greensboro in another regional final. "The only good thing about the game in Greensboro," he says now, "is it helped make us the team we became in 1999 [when UConn won the national championship]. Back then, though, it hurt because we were one step short of the Final Four . . . again."

The loss to North Carolina was, in fact, Calhoun and UConn's third trip to a regional final — and their third loss. That Calhoun had Connecticut on the doorstep of the Final Four was, in itself, an amazing story. He had taken the job at Connecticut in 1986 after a very successful career at Northeastern University despite many of his friends and colleagues telling him that the move was career suicide. Connecticut was buried in a Big East dominated at the time by Georgetown, Syracuse, St. John's, and Villanova. Three of the four men coaching at those schools then — Georgetown's John Thompson, Syracuse's Jim Boeheim, and Lou Carnesecca at St. John's — are now in the Hall of Fame. Villanova's Rollie Massimino should probably be there but made some enemies along the way that have kept him out. Consider his record against Carnesecca's: Massimino — 515 career wins; five trips to the Elite Eight; one Final Four; one national championship; Carnesecca — 526 wins, three trips to the Elite Eight, one Final Four. Many would say edge to Massimino; others would call it dead even. But everyone loved Looey Carnesecca. Not everyone loved Massimino.

Calhoun took over at UConn at a time when many alumni were saying the school had to get out of the Big East, find a conference where it could compete. Calhoun believed that conference was the Big East. In 1988 the Huskies showed progress by winning the NIT. But a year later they were in the NIT again, and the grumbling began. It all changed the next season. Connecticut won thirty-one games and the Big East title and came within a buzzer-beating Christian Laettner jump shot of going to the Final Four. Calhoun became a hero at Connecticut, much the same way Gary Williams had become a hero at Maryland after taking the Terrapins from the bottom of the ACC in 1993 to the Sweet Sixteen in 1994. If the round of sixteen was Williams's stumbling block, the round of eight became the wall that Calhoun couldn't get through. And just as Williams began to hear whispers that he was nothing more than a "round of sixteen" coach, Calhoun heard people saying he couldn't take UConn to the promised land of the Final Four.

"Some of it was a little bit frustrating," he said. "I mean, we lose in '90 at the buzzer in overtime on a near-miraculous shot. We lose a great game to UCLA in '95 and they go on and win the tournament. We lost to Carolina in '98 on what was basically a home court for them. But the bottom line was the same: we hadn't gotten there."

Like almost anyone who gets into the coaching business, Calhoun had fantasized as a young coach about taking a team to the Final Four. He had started attending the coaches convention as an up-and-coming young coach in the early 1970s and still remembers the awe he felt when he saw the game's icons in the lobby and around town. "I still remember in 1975, I was in my fourth year at Northeastern, very young, still learning my way around the game," he said. "We were in San Diego. UCLA was playing Kentucky in the final; John Wooden's last game. At some point during the day I went to the hotel's hot tub. When I got up there, Bill Musselman was sitting there. We sat there and just chatted for a few minutes. Now, back then, I thought Bill Musselman was a very big deal. He was the coach at Minnesota, and even though he was controversial, he was very successful. So, I thought sitting in a hot tub and talking to him was kind of cool.

"But then, as I was walking out, I felt someone tugging on my arm. I turned around and it was Adolph Rupp, as in *the* Adolph Rupp. He says to me, 'Boy, are you in basketball?' I said, 'Yes, sir, I am. My name is Jim Calhoun and I'm the coach at Northeastern University.'

"Rupp looks at me and says, 'Well, I have no idea what that is or where that is, but I want to ask you a question.' I said, 'Yes, sir, anything. What is it?'

"And he says, 'Do you think our boys can win tonight?' As if my opinion was somehow going to affect the outcome."

Rupp's boys didn't win. Wooden won his tenth title and walked off into the sunset.

Thirty years later Calhoun is now one of the icons the young coaches stare at in the lobby. His team finally broke through in 1999, not only reaching the Final Four but winning the national championship with a stirring victory over top-ranked Duke in the title game. Five years later Calhoun and Connecticut won a second championship. Now Calhoun has two national titles and more than 700 wins, and was voted into the Hall of Fame in 2005. He was voted in along with longtime rival Jim Boeheim of Syracuse, who first reached the Final Four in 1987 — eleven years after he became a head coach. Sixteen years and two more trips to the Final Four later, Boeheim won a national championship.

Like Calhoun, Boeheim remembers his early days as a young coach standing around the lobby watching the stars go by. "To me, the Final Four back then was like going to a nonstop coaching clinic," he said. "Guys would stand around the lobby all day and all night and talk basketball — I mean the game itself. You could grab someone and ask them to show you how they ran a certain offense or defense and they'd grab a piece of paper and draw it for you. I loved the lobby. Now it's completely different. If you want to sit around and tell stories, you have to go to the sneaker suites because at least there all the hangers-on can't get to you. It's still fun, but it's not the same."

The sneaker suites — which are suites paid for by the various sneaker companies who help fund college basketball generally and big-time coaches specifically — have evolved during the past ten to fifteen years because of the logjam in the lobby. Coaches who are paid by a sneaker company can go to the company's suite and escape the crowds. They can bring guests, and most of the time, a Nike coach will be welcomed in the Reebok or the Adidas suite because those companies know that someday a coach who is with Nike might very well be with them.

Among the truly famous coaches, Boeheim and Calhoun are two of the few regularly seen in the lobby. Most look for back doors or try to put their head down and get to an elevator as quickly as possible. In St. Louis, Mike Krzyzewski had all of his nonofficial meals in his room because he knew there was no way he could go to the coffee shop and eat in peace. Coaches who have an opening on their staff are even more wary of the lobby. Maryland coach Gary Williams skipped the '05 Final Four completely because he had two openings on his staff and knew he would be besieged, not only by coaches looking for work but by friends or representatives of out-of-work coaches campaigning on their behalf.

"It isn't just that you don't want to have to deal with all the people," Williams said. "It's that it is so depressing to have guys come up to you asking for the chance to interview for a job and you know you aren't going to hire them. You feel badly for them and it's really awkward to have to say to them, 'You know, I've got some other guys in mind.' You see the look on their face — because they know what that means — and you feel badly for them." He smiled. "Then there are guys who don't get what you're saying, and that's even worse."

The kind of guy Williams is talking about might be embodied in Tom Abatemarco. It can be argued that Abatemarco has coached at more places than just about anyone in the profession. He has been an assistant at Iona, Maryland, Virginia Tech, North Carolina State (where he helped Jim Valvano win the national championship in 1983), Utah, Colorado, and Cincinnati, and had head coaching stints at Lamar, Drake, and Sacramento State. These days Abatemarco works for the Sacramento Kings, part-time as a coach with their WNBA team, part-time as a marketing person, and part-time as a radio personality. "I'm happy doing what I'm doing right now," he said, sitting in the lobby of the Millennium. "I really don't want to get back into college coaching. Too much work." He paused. "Well, maybe I'd go back for the right job." Another pause. "You know, I really think I could help Gary. He needs someone who can recruit."

Abatemarco could always recruit. He is renowned for his workaholic approach. When Iona was recruiting Jeff Ruland in the mid-1970s, most people gave the small school in suburban New York little chance of getting the six-ten star, given that almost every basketball power in the country was also recruiting him. Abatemarco began staking out Ruland's house. Knowing that recruiting rules prevented him from making contact with Ruland at his home, he began leaving daily messages for him on the windshield of his car.

"Great game last night, Jeff, you really ate that guy up. I'll call you later."

"How's that drop step move you've been working on coming along? You look a lot more comfortable in the post than I've ever seen you."

"Tell your mom that new outfit looked terrific on her."

In recruiting, relentlessness can pay off. Especially if you are relentless and different. Ruland signed with Iona and led the Gaels to back-to-back NCAA Tournaments — putting Jim Valvano in position to get the North Carolina State job after Ruland led the Gaels to 29 victories in his junior year. Abatemarco went with Valvano to N.C. State, where he was part of the national championship and became famous for writing 484 letters (that's not a made-up number) to Chris Washburn. Proving that coaches can get carried away by a recruiting success, Valvano called Washburn's decision to go to N.C. State "the biggest thrill of my coaching career."

This came a year after he had won the national championship.

No one ever had a better Final Four than Jim Valvano and N.C. State in Albuquerque in 1983. N.C. State was, in some ways, the classic Cinderella team. The Wolfpack had struggled after losing their best shooter, Dereck Whittenburg, to a broken foot midway through the season. They finished tied for third in the ACC and went into the ACC Tournament knowing they had to at least reach the final to have a chance to get into the NCAAs. They beat Wake Forest in a close game. Then they upset North Carolina — led by Michael Jordan and Sam Perkins — in overtime and then, in the final, not knowing if they needed to win or not to make the NCAA Tournament, they beat Virginia and national Player of the Year Ralph Sampson. It was a terrific run, and it got the Wolfpack into the tournament as a number six seed in the west regional. They should have lost in the first round to Pepperdine, but the Waves missed free throws late in regulation and State survived in double overtime and advanced. They should have lost in the second round to UNLV, but the Rebels missed free throws late and State survived, by one point, and advanced. The Wolfpack beat Utah relatively easily in the round of sixteen and then shocked Virginia again in the regional final. Tim Mullen — not Sampson — took the last shot of that game with State leading by one. It clanged off the back rim into Sampson's hands. He dunked ferociously — one second after the buzzer sounded.

State had survived and advanced to the Final Four. On Saturday, State played Georgia in what was generally considered the preliminary game prior to the main event between Houston and Louisville, the game that would decide the national championship. Houston had been dubbed "Phi Slama Jama" early in the season by Thomas Bonk of the *Houston Chronicle* and the Cougars lived up to their nickname in the Louisville game. The Cardinals, who had been given the name "Doctors of Dunk" in 1980 when they won the national championship, stayed with them for most of the day, the two teams playing at a pace and with a grace and a high-flying elegance no one in the building could remember seeing in a college basketball game. After Houston had pulled away late to win, Roger Valdiserri, the longtime sports information director at Notre Dame, summed up the way most people felt when he said, "Welcome to basketball in the twenty-first century." He proved to be prophetic.

Sitting in the stands that afternoon with all the other coaches, Mike Krzyzewski felt overwhelmed. This was a few weeks after the 109–66 loss to Virginia. "I sat and watched what those two teams could do and thought to myself, 'How am I ever going to get our program to the point where we can compete with teams like this?' I just couldn't believe basketball could be played above the rim for an entire game that way. Beyond that, I wondered how my team could possibly get to that level. I just wondered if I was in over my head."

Krzyzewski's concerns were long-term. Valvano's were far more immediate. He had forty-eight hours to get his team to that level. Almost no one on the planet thought there was any way State could win the game. Krzyzewski, who knew firsthand how good a coach Valvano was, didn't think it could be done. "Houston looked to me to be playing a different sport than anyone else," he said. Dave Kindred, the distinguished columnist of the *Washington Post*, wrote, "Trees will tap-dance and elephants will drive at Indy before N.C. State wins this game."

By nine o'clock mountain time on Monday night, the trees were dancing and the elephants were warming up their engines. Valvano slowed the game to a walk, and when Houston got the lead late, he went into his fouling act. This was an upset that could not happen today because there is a 35-second shot clock that makes it difficult for coaches to control the tempo the way Valvano did that night. What's more, the "double-bonus" rule, in which all fouls in a half after ten result in two shots, would have worked against State, not only in the championship game but in the Pepperdine game, the UNLV game, and the Virginia game. But that was then, not now, and Valvano squeezed everything he could out of his team and the rules of the game. Houston kept missing one-and-one opportunities and State ended up with the ball in the final minute with the score tied at 52.

If Valvano still had a time-out left, he would have used it because his team was in offensive chaos. Houston was attacking on the perimeter, and with the clock winding down, Whittenburg had to chase down a pass near midcourt. Afraid the clock was about to run out, he turned and launched a shot from thirty-five feet that had absolutely no chance to go in. Suddenly, seemingly from nowhere, Lorenzo Charles, the unheralded sophomore forward who was in the lineup to rebound and play defense while the three seniors — Whittenburg, Sidney Lowe, and Thurl Bailey — did most of the scoring, rose up above everyone clustered around the basket. The ball went right to him a couple of feet short of the rim and in one motion he caught it and dunked it as the buzzer sounded.

It was a scene straight out of *Hoosiers* — except that the movie hadn't been made yet. The entire building went into a state of shock. The Houston players sat on the floor staring into space, not believing they had lost the game and the national title that they thought they had won on Saturday. Valvano simply began running. Later, as part of the speeches he was paid a lot of money to give, he would describe his sprint in great detail. "Dereck Whittenburg had been my designated hugger all season," he said. "But I couldn't find him. He was mobbed. So I'm running around in circles, looking for someone to hug."

Before he was through, Valvano had hugged almost everyone in the state of New Mexico. The victory made him into a media star because he was smart and funny and approachable. Whenever he did clinics as a young coach, Valvano would tell the kids that his dream as a coach was to "cut the last net at the Final Four." When he finished speaking, he would make the campers pick him up on their shoulders so he could cut down one of the nets on the court where he was speaking. Camp directors learned to come prepared with scissors and another net whenever Valvano was the speaker. He was so good, he was worth the inconvenience.

Now he had cut the last net for real. He cowrote a book, *Too Soon to Quit,* in which he explained his philosophy of survive and advance. He hosted TV shows; he did a pilot for a variety show in Hollywood; he coached State on a Saturday and did the color for NBC on a Sunday; he spoke to corporations all over the country; he regularly flew to New York on Sunday night so he could do the sports on the CBS morning show on Monday morning. He was everywhere.

Everywhere except with his basketball team and his family — the two most important things in his life. He had dreamed all his life about winning a national championship. Then, out of nowhere, at the age of thirty-seven, he did it. It wasn't until later that he began to figure out what happened to him in the aftermath of the title. "I had done coaching," he said. "I never dreamed of being Wooden and winning ten; I never dreamed of being Dean [Smith] and contending every single year. I dreamed of winning *one.* I dreamed of that feeling I had that night in Albuquerque. The next thing I knew, I had done it. And I woke up the next morning and it wasn't so much Peggy Lee ["Is That All There Is?"] as 'What do I do next?' There wasn't really one thing I wanted to do, so I tried everything. And I still couldn't find anything that really mattered to me."

Valvano drifted. Because of all the attention he and State had received in the wake of the national championship, there were lots of players who wanted to go to school there. Valvano was now in a position much like Dean Smith in that he was selecting players as much as he was recruiting them. They recruited him. Krzyzewski can still remember the frustration he felt trying to recruit a six-foot-six shooter named Walker Lambiotte. He was convinced Duke was perfect for Lambiotte: he was a good student, Duke's motion offense would get him good shots consistently, and he thought he had connected with the kid. He had. But there was one problem.

"My dad thought V was the coolest guy he'd ever met," Lambiotte said years later. "Don't get me wrong, I liked him too. But once my dad hung out with V, it was sort of a given I would go to State."

That was about all Valvano had to do in recruiting at that point: show up and be cool. Or if the situation called for it, be funny. Or poignant. He put together a video to show to recruits and their families that began with him dribbling a ball from darkness to light and quoting Carl Sandburg on following dreams.

There was, however, a hitch: coaching had become a part-time occupation for Valvano because of all the other things he was trying. He didn't pay close attention to the kind of kids his assistants were bringing to him and he didn't spend that much time with them once they were at N.C. State. The program began to flounder — not so much on the court as off. State was good enough to make it back to the regional finals in both 1985 and 1986, but there were cracks. They became fissures when a book alleging all sorts of wrongdoing in the program came out in 1989. The book was badly flawed, full of mistakes. Even the facts that appeared to be accurate were suspect because the source, a former manager, had been paid for his information. But there was just enough truth and near-truth in the book to cause the NCAA to investigate Valvano's program. Most of what they found had been caused by sloppiness, but it didn't matter. Valvano was responsible. He was forced to resign following the 1990 season.

He was bitter and angry and believed that some in the media, whom he had treated so well through the years, had turned on him. What he failed to understand — or refused to understand — was that he had let his program slide, that he hadn't been paying enough attention. Often during his later years at State, Valvano would sit up late at night in his office, unable to sleep the way most coaches can't sleep after games. He would order a pizza, open a bottle of wine, and tell funny stories until the wee hours of the morning. Then, after almost everyone else had gone to bed, he would sit with his last glass of wine and a cold slice of pizza and say, "I still can't figure out what I want to be when I grow up."

One night Valvano's wife, Pam, finally called him at about 3:00 A.M. and demanded he come home. Valvano got in the car, drove home, changed into pajamas, and went to sleep. An hour later he woke from a restless sleep, realizing he had forgotten to tape his morning radio show. Every morning, Valvano did a five-minute radio bit on one of the local stations. He would tape it before he left the office, picking up a special phone line installed for him and leaving his five-minute spiel on a tape at the station so it would be waiting for the morning show producer when he arrived at 5:00 A.M.

"So I got out of bed, jumped in the car, and drove back to campus. About a block away, I ran a light. There was no one on the road — except for a cop I didn't see. He pulls me over. When he sees that it's me he says, 'Coach, how much have you had to drink?' I'm thinking, I had my last glass of wine more than two hours ago, but I could flunk a Breathalyzer. I mean, who knows with those things? So, I just tell the cop what happened: I was in bed, forgot my radio show and I'm driving back to tape it. He gives me this 'yeah, right' look. And then I remember what I'm wearing. I get out of the car and I say, 'Look, Officer, I'm wearing my PAJAMAS!' He starts laughing, tells me not to run any more lights, and lets me go. I seriously considered wearing pajamas to drive home every night after that."

Valvano could handle almost anything that happened in his life with laughter. Until the book. Until the NCAA came to town. Until he had to resign.

And until he found out he had cancer. Everyone knows the story now: back pains, a trip to the doctor, tests, and a doctor showing him an X-ray that revealed his back to be absolutely covered with cancerous cells. That was in June of 1992. On April 28, 1993, Valvano died. But not before he finally found the next thing he had been looking for since the national championship: cancer. It was cancer that gave his life direction again. Knowing he was going to die, Valvano worked feverishly to set up the V Foundation to fight cancer and to raise money for cancer research, enlisting friends in coaching and in the media. Led publicly by Mike Krzyzewski and Dick Vitale, the foundation has raised more than $50 million since his death.

Valvano was forty-seven when he died, ten years after his glorious run around the court at the Pit on that amazing night in Albuquerque. He is still a part of every Final Four. You can't turn on an NCAA Tournament game without seeing Valvano sprinting around the court; coaches still tell stories about him in the lobby and in the sneaker suites. They talk about the dance contest he won the night before the semifinals in Albuquerque. They retell stories Valvano used to tell.

"Remember the one about the dog?" someone will say. And even though almost everyone in the room has heard it, someone will retell the story about the State alumnus who threatened to kill Valvano's dog after his first season if he didn't beat North Carolina the next year. "But I don't have a dog," Valvano protested.

"No matter," the alum replied.

The next day when Valvano went to the front door to get his newspaper, there was a basket on top of the newspaper. Underneath the blanket, according to Valvano, was the cutest puppy he had ever seen. "And around the puppy's neck," he would say, "was a note. It said, 'Don't get too attached.'"

They've all heard the story. They all know it is probably apocryphal. But they all laugh and drink another toast to V. Who will always be a part of the Final Four.

4

Legends

THERE HAVE BEEN MANY PEOPLE who have achieved legendary status during the sixty-seven-year history of the NCAA Tournament. Players such as Lew Alcindor, Bill Walton, Bill Russell, Christian Laettner, and David Thompson all have a place in the pantheon along with countless others — some, such as Chris Webber and Fred Brown, for reasons they would rather not remember. Adolph Rupp won four titles as a coach, Bob Knight and Mike Krzyzewski have each won three, and Don Haskins won arguably the most important game ever played: the 1966 championship game when his Texas Western team, starting five black players, beat Rupp and Kentucky, three years before Rupp first successfully recruited a black player.

But there is one name that has to stand above all the others, one name that probably defines the sport more than any other: John Wooden. The numbers alone are staggering. His UCLA teams won ten championships in twelve years, including seven in a row from 1967 to 1973. If not for an extraordinary performance by North Carolina State's David Thompson in the semifinals in 1974, UCLA would have won nine straight titles. No other school has ever won more than two in a row, and only one

(Duke, 1991–92) has achieved that feat since Wooden retired in 1975.

"The funny thing is, I really never planned to retire in 1975," Wooden says now. "I thought I would coach for another two or three years, and I think with the players we had in the program and the ones that I had recruited to be freshmen in the fall of 1975, we would have had a good chance to win again, or at the very least contend, during that time."

Wooden retired on the spur of the moment. After losing to N.C. State in 1974, UCLA was not expected to be the power in 1975 that it had been the previous eight years. Bill Walton had graduated, unable to match Alcindor's three national titles because of the loss to State. But UCLA made it back to the Final Four and found itself facing a very good Louisville team in the semifinals. This was a difficult game for Wooden because Louisville was coached by Denny Crum, who had been his top assistant during the glory years in the 1960s when the program had ascended to dominance. Crum had become Louisville's coach in 1971 and had taken the Cardinals to the Final Four in his first season, before losing to UCLA. There was no real tug for Wooden then because getting to the Final Four was a big deal for Crum, and UCLA, led by Walton, was loaded. Now it was different. Crum had put together a superb team, and most people thought the semifinal matchup was a toss-up.

They were right. The game ended up in overtime and Louisville led, 74–73, with twenty seconds to go when a senior guard named Terry Howard was fouled. Howard had grown up in Louisville and had been a hotshot player in high school. He had been a starter for two years at Louisville but as a senior had become the backup point guard. He was a fabulous free throw shooter. As he stepped to the line on that Saturday, he was 28 for

28 from there for the season. If he made both foul shots, it would be almost impossible for UCLA to rally, since there was no three-point shot at the time. Howard missed the front end of the one-and-one. UCLA rebounded and Richard Washington hit a jumper with three seconds to go to win the game, 75–74.

Wooden wasn't sure how to feel. He was, of course, thrilled to win the game. But he knew how crushing the loss was for Crum. "I spent a few moments with Denny and, elated as I felt, I couldn't help but feel awful for him," he said. "As I walked across the court to do the postgame television interview, the thought crossed my mind for the first time. I thought, 'Now's the time to quit.' I'm not exactly sure why I thought it at that moment, but I did. I went into the locker room and I told my team that I was as proud of them as any team I had ever coached, that they had listened well all season and had been a joy to teach. Then I said to them, 'I can't think of a better group to have worked with as the last team I'll ever teach.'

"I'm not sure if they understood right away what I was saying. But then when I went into the press conference and said it, everyone knew what I was saying. I knew it was the right thing because as soon as I said it, I felt satisfied and pleased."

Wooden believed his team would beat Kentucky in the final. "I thought they were very big and they were very good," he said. "But I believed we would give them trouble with our quickness." His analysis proved correct. UCLA beat Kentucky in the championship game and Wooden retired, at the age of sixty-three, with a résumé that will never be equaled. It was important to him that he leave the program in good shape. "We had very good players and I wanted to be sure I didn't leave the cupboard bare for the next coach," he said. "I'm very proud of the fact that we won the league championship the first four years after I retired."

In fact, UCLA went back to the Final Four under Gene Bartow the next year — extending its Final Four streak to ten straight years — only to lose to Indiana. The minute the Bruins lost that game, UCLA fans began pining for Wooden's return. Bartow had coached Memphis State into the national championship game in 1973, losing to Walton's 44-point performance in the first championship game played on Monday night, and took UCLA to the Final Four in his first year on the job. But he wasn't Wooden. Tormented by that, Bartow fled the next year when he was offered the chance to start a brand-new program at the University of Alabama at Birmingham. He built a very solid program at UAB and became the first in a long line of coaches who couldn't be Wooden: Gary Cunningham, Larry Brown, Larry Farmer, Walt Hazzard, Jim Harrick, Steve Lavin, and Ben Howland have all sat in Wooden's chair since Bartow's departure. Brown reached the national championship game in 1980 and left a year later to return to coaching in the NBA. Hazzard won the NIT in 1985, his first season on the job, and wanted to hang a banner that said NIT CHAMPIONS in the rafters of Pauley Pavilion along with the ten national championship banners won by Wooden. That idea was swiftly rejected by the school's powers that be.

Harrick did hang a banner, in 1995 winning UCLA's only national title since Wooden's departure. He was gone from the school eighteen months later, after being accused of filing improper expense reports. Lavin reached the Sweet Sixteen five times in six years and was considered an utter failure. There is nothing sweet about the round of sixteen at UCLA. Lavin was under fire the entire time he coached there and was booted in 2003 after the Bruins had a miserable season and failed even to reach the tournament. Howland, who had brought great success to Pitt, was hired to replace him and managed to get the Bruins back into the tournament in his second season, although they lost in the first round to Texas Tech.

Wooden is ninety-four now. He has difficulty walking but still attends every UCLA home game, keeps a close eye on the team, and has firm opinions about his old school and about the tournament that he put his signature on in the 1960s and '70s. "I'm very pleased with what Ben has done so far," he said last season. "They've got a very young team, two freshmen starters, four of them playing, and they're getting better with every game. Of course, the difficulty is that times have changed so much. I think if Ben could count on all four of them being here for the next four years, I would feel very confident that we would contend again during that period. But now there are no guarantees for anyone that will be the case.

"I think college basketball and the NCAA Tournament are like almost anything else: bigger doesn't mean better. In many ways, it means not as good. Having said that, I would like to see the tournament format changed so that every Division 1 team gets to participate. It could be done by adding one weekend to the tournament and by shortening the regular season by a week. Maybe that's the Indiana boy in me coming out because for so long that was the way the high school tournament was conducted in Indiana. I think it would be very exciting and I also think it would lead to a more equitable way of dividing up the money. I think I figured out that a team losing in the first round would get fifty-seven thousand dollars. To a lot of those smaller schools, that would be a lot of money. I don't think the power schools and power conferences should control as much of the money as they do."

Wooden says he first began arguing for an open tournament while he was still coaching. The idea has become more in vogue in recent years, especially in the coaching fraternity, because there is so much pressure on coaches to get into the tournament. Of course, the tournament *is* just about open already since thirty of the thirty-one Division 1 conferences have tournaments. Only the Ivy League doesn't. That means, in theory, any team in the other thirty conferences goes into March with a chance to play in and win the NCAA Tournament, since the school that wins the conference tournament gets an automatic bid to the Dance. Almost every year at least one sub-.500 team gets on a roll in its conference tournament and ends up in the field of sixty-five. In 2005 Oakland University (of Michigan) won its conference tournament and took a 13–18 record into the NCAAs.

Opening up the tournament would take away all meaning from the regular season. It would also take away the suspense of Selection Sunday, when everyone in the college basketball world sits around trying to figure out which bubble teams will make the field and which won't. And it would render making the Dance meaningless, since everyone would play in it.

The tournament and the Final Four *have* changed radically since Wooden first took UCLA to the national semifinals in 1962. He won his first title in 1964 in Kansas City at the old Municipal Auditorium, which seated a little more than 10,000 people. "No one even called it 'the Final Four' in those days," Wooden remembered. "In '64, everyone involved in the tournament — all the teams, the coaches, the media — stayed in the same hotel, the Muhlbach, which was right across the street from the arena. It seemed back then as if everyone knew everyone. We were like a little club, everyone who was in college basketball.

"I still remember on the day of the championship game I was in the lobby talking to some people [imagine a coach in the championship game standing around a hotel lobby on game day in 2005] and a coach I had met earlier in the season from Czechoslovakia came up to me. He had been traveling in our country, watching different teams practice to try to learn more about the game. He had watched us and a number of other teams, including Duke, who we were playing that night. He said to me, 'Coach Wooden, I have seen you and I have seen Duke. They are big and they are good. But UCLA, they are a *team*.' He counted on his fingers — 'One, two, three, four, five.' Then he took his five fingers and made a fist. 'Together, your five become one. This is why you win.' I never forgot that."

UCLA's one beat Duke's five, 98–83, that night for Wooden's first title. A year later the Bruins beat Michigan in the championship, led by Gail Goodrich's 42 points. That was the year Bill Bradley led Princeton to the Final Four. The Tigers lost to Michigan in the semifinals but then beat Wichita State in the consolation game with Bradley scoring 58 points — still the record for points scored in a Final Four game. In fact, Bradley — not Goodrich — was selected as the Most Outstanding Player of that year's Final Four. (Austin Carr of Notre Dame holds the record of 61 points scored in a tournament game, in 1970.) Somehow, through time, Bradley's performance has overshadowed Goodrich's. So has Bill Walton's 44-point night in the 1973 championship game, in part because Walton shot a stunning 21 of 22 from the field.

"I always tell Bill that what Gail did was more amazing than what he did," Wooden said, chuckling. "Bill was six foot eleven and was able to take most of his shots close to the basket. Gail was under six feet tall and dominated that game. I get a kick out of teasing Bill about that because I'm probably the only one who will do it."

Wooden continued to attend the Final Four after his retirement, always bringing his wife, Nell, who had been at his side every time he went to the Final Four, with or without his team, dating back to when he first arrived at UCLA. From 1976 to 1984 the Woodens became staples of the lobby scene, usually holding court in a corner as younger coaches would gather around to hear the great man talk. "What I remember about meeting him as a young coach is the way he acted as if you were just as important, if not more important, than he was," Mike Krzyzewski said. "He would look you in the eye, make sure to remember your name, and acted genuinely interested in whatever you were asking or wanted to talk about. I've always tried to remember that as I've gone up the coaching ladder."

Wooden enjoyed spending time with his colleagues, young and old, but he couldn't bring himself to go after the 1984 Final Four in Seattle. The reason: he would have had to go alone. Everyone knew Nell Wooden was extremely sick during that week in Seattle. She and her husband still camped out in the lobby and greeted friends, but Nell was in a wheelchair. "Deep down, I think I knew it would be her last time," John Wooden said. "But I don't think I ever admitted it to myself."

Late one night, after the Woodens had spent several hours talking to friends and coaches and passersby, they said good night to everyone and John Wooden began pushing his wife across the vast lobby of the Seattle Hilton, which was the coaches' headquarters that year. The lobby was still crowded and, as often happens when Wooden crosses a room or a lobby, people stopped what they were doing to watch the great man. At that moment, what they saw was heartbreaking: Wooden pushing his wife's wheelchair, everyone knowing that her time was short.

To this day, no one is certain how it began, but someone started to clap. Then others did the same thing. By the time the Woodens had reached the elevators, everyone in the lobby was turned in their direction, clapping. It was one of those unrehearsed moments that become remarkable ones. Both Woodens turned in the direction of the applause and smiled. Wooden waved his hand in thanks. He knew what the message was, and as touched as he was, it was also very sad. "To be honest, I barely remember it now," he said. "That was a very difficult Final Four for me. No one actually said good-bye, but that's what people were doing."

Nell Wooden died nine months later. When the Final Four was held that spring in Lexington, Kentucky, John Wooden wasn't there, absent for the first time in thirty-six years. "I just couldn't go without Nell," he said. "I had never been to a Final Four without her, and the thought of being there alone was more than I could bear. In the years after that, I just didn't have any enthusiasm to go without her. It would not have been the same."

It wasn't until 1995 that Wooden returned to the Final Four, again in Seattle. It was an offer from Microsoft to come speak and the presence of UCLA — back for the first time in fifteen years — that brought him there. "If UCLA had not been playing, I might have gone up and given the speech and then gone home," he said. "But needless to say, since my school was playing in the games, I wanted to stay and watch them compete."

They competed very well, winning their first national championship in the twenty years since Wooden's retirement. The Bruins' victory in the final was especially impressive since point guard Tyus Edney, their catalyst all season, had been injured in the semifinals and could play only three minutes. Cameron Dollar, his backup, stepped in and played admirably against Arkansas in the championship game and UCLA won its eleventh national title. Wooden was delighted. He did not attend the Final Four in 2005, because he had a commitment to go to a high school all-star game at Notre Dame earlier that week, and trying to do both would have been a little too much for him.

"I enjoy the idea of going back," he said. "But at my age it isn't as easy to do as when I was younger, especially since everywhere you go now is a mob scene. I can honestly say the thing I miss most about not coaching is practice. I always enjoyed that so much because I felt like that was when I was teaching. Four years ago, the McDonald's [high school all-America] game was in Durham and Mike [Krzyzewski] invited me to [Duke's] practice. I really liked his practice. No wasted motion or time. A clear plan about what was to be done that day. I remember sitting there thinking, 'The only thing that would be more fun than watching this practice would be to run it.' They were getting ready to leave the next day for the Final Four and Mike asked me to speak to the team. I told the players that if they worried about the score, they were making a mistake. If they just worked as hard as they could on every possession, they would be fine in the end. That Saturday, they came from twenty-two points down [against Maryland] to win and I felt as if, one way or the other, they had proved that what I was saying was accurate."

Wooden clearly enjoyed his ten championships, but when asked for his most special moments, he doesn't talk about a specific victory or a specific team. "There's no question that the first time you take a team to the Final Four, it is very special," he said. "Even if it wasn't called that the first time we went. There is a great feeling of accomplishment, especially when it takes you as long as it took me [fourteen seasons at UCLA] to get there. And, of course, you always remember the first one.

"But the moments that make me smile the most are a little different. I remember after one of our championships, I think it was the year we beat Jacksonville in the final [1970], a reporter asked Curtis Rowe about the role race played on our team. Curtis looked at him and said, 'Obviously you don't know our coach,' and walked away. The other one I remember very well came the next year when we beat Villanova in the Astrodome. I'd had to discipline Sidney Wicks during the season and it was tough on both of us. Late in the game, when we had things under control, he was fouled. As he was walking to the foul line, he detoured over to the bench, put his arm around me, and said, 'Coach, before it gets crazy, I just want you to know, I really think you're something.' That meant a great deal to me."

No one has meant more to the Final Four than John Wooden.

But what if there hadn't been a Wooden? Who would be considered the greatest college coach of all time? Statistically, Adolph Rupp comes next, with four national titles, but fairly or unfairly, Rupp has been shunted by most people behind three other men who became dominant figures much later than Rupp and, for the most part, after Wooden exited the stage. Alphabetically, the three are Bob Knight, Mike Krzyzewski, and Dean Smith. Knight won three national titles at Indiana (1976, 1981, and 1987) and has been to five Final Fours. Krzyzewski has won three championships at Duke (1991, 1992, and 2001) and reached ten Final Fours. Smith won two titles at North Carolina but reached eleven Final Fours, one fewer than Wooden. Smith has won more games — 879 — than any college coach in history, three more than Rupp and, at the start of the 2005–2006 season, twenty-five more than Knight. Krzyzewski surpassed Smith (sixty-six to sixty-five) in all-time NCAA Tournament victories in 2005, a number that is a tad deceiving because a team can play as many as six tournament games in a year now. During Wooden's heyday, a team like UCLA never played more than four tournament games. Wooden won forty-seven tournament games — forty-one of them (UCLA played five games in 1975) en route to his ten championships.

How you rank the next four after Wooden is purely subjective and, in truth, not that important. All four have very clear legacies, and the three who came after Rupp have clear ties to one another: Krzyzewski played for Knight at Army and got his first job as an assistant coach when he got out of the army working as a graduate assistant coach for Knight in 1974. When he became Duke's coach in 1980, his great rival for seventeen years was the legend working eight miles down the road from him, Dean Smith. The relationship between the three men has always been complicated. Knight and Smith are peers. Smith, who turned seventy-five at the end of February 2006, is almost ten years older than Knight (sixty-five in October 2005), but their head-coaching careers began only four years apart — Smith in 1961 at North Carolina, Knight in 1965 at Army. They met twice in the NCAA Tournament and Knight inflicted two very painful defeats on Smith, beating him in the national championship game in 1981 and then in a stunning upset in the round of sixteen in 1984.

"The one in '84 hurt a lot because we had a great team," Smith said. "We had Michael [Jordan] and Sam [Perkins] and Kenny [Smith] and Matt [Doherty]."

Knight has often said that if that Indiana team had played that North Carolina team ten times, Carolina would have won nine times. But Indiana won the only one that mattered because they didn't play ten times, they played once. Even though the Hoosiers lost a round later to Virginia, that remains one of Knight's most satisfying victories.

The NCAA Tournament committee is always looking for matchups with a little pizzazz on the opening weekend of the tournament, and in 1997 it came up with a made-for-TV dream game. In the first round Smith was going to tie Rupp's record for victories. That meant he would break the record in the second round with a victory. Who would make a better final hurdle than Bob Knight and Indiana? The seedings worked well: North Carolina was a number one seed. Indiana was placed in an eight-nine game against Colorado, the winner to play the Tar Heels. There was one problem: Indiana failed to show up. Colorado blew the Hoosiers out and Knight was so angry and embarrassed that he walked three miles back to his hotel room on a frigid night rather than ride on the bus with his team. Smith got his historic victory against . . . Colorado.

Knight and Smith have always been friendly with each other. They have played golf together through the years, and both say all the right things about each other publicly — and mean most of them. Each respects the other greatly, and they enjoy talking basketball with each other. But the two men could hardly be more different: Smith never curses. Knight always curses. Knight has never smoked and rarely drinks anything stronger than sangria mixed with soda. Smith smoked constantly until 1987, when his doctor ordered him to quit, and likes a good glass of scotch. Smith is happiest away from the public eye; Knight craves it — though he constantly denies that fact. Both were backup players on great teams. Knight was part of a national championship team at Ohio State in 1960 and played on Final Four teams the next two years. Smith played thirty-seven seconds in Kansas's victory in the 1952 national championship game (a fact he later had added to the box score since his name did not appear on the original) and was on the 1953 team that lost in the championship game. Both had to become great coaches to surpass their old teammates — and did.

Krzyzewski was recruited by Knight out of Weber High School in Chicago while Knight was an assistant coach under Tates Locke at West Point. He has often told the story about how uninterested he was in going to Army or into the military until his parents all but shamed him into it, wondering aloud while standing in their kitchen how they could have raised a son who would pass up the chance to go to a great college *and* serve his country. By the time Krzyzewski arrived at Army, Knight was the head coach, since Locke had left to take the job at Miami (Ohio). He was a three-year starter at point guard for Knight and his captain as a senior. Even though Knight made Krzyzewski miserable — as he has done for everyone who has ever played for him — on many occasions Krzyzewski knew how his coach felt about him, especially during his junior year, when his father died midway through the season of a heart attack and Knight flew home with him and stayed several days to make sure he and his mother and older brother were doing all right.

"Under the definition of the term 'tough love' in the dictionary is his picture," Krzyzewski says now, looking back. "He's never been an easy person to deal with, and I don't think he's ever wanted to be an easy person to deal with. But if he's on your side, he's very definitely on your side."

Knight was never close to his father, in large part because he was nearly deaf and it was difficult for the two of them to communicate. Krzyzewski never saw his father very much because he was always working. Each went into the adult world subconsciously searching for a father figure. Knight became close to a number of older coaches who mentored him at an early age: Pete Newell, Henry Iba, Clair Bee, Joe Lapchick, Red Auerbach. Krzyzewski had Knight early in his career and then also became very close to Newell and Iba.

As close as Knight and Krzyzewski were at times, there have frequently been skirmishes between them. Some of the early ones were directly connected to Krzyzewski's choice of girlfriend — later, wife. Mickie Marsh was an airline stewardess (they were still called that in the sixties) when she met Krzyzewski, then a West Point cadet. They started dating and Mickie began coming to games whenever she could. During Mike's senior year, she showed up when Army played at Princeton, a game the Cadets ended up losing in overtime. She and a friend stayed over so that she could spend some time with Mike the next morning before the team bused home. They were eating an early breakfast in the hotel dining room when Knight walked in. Seeing his captain with his girlfriend, just a few hours after a brutal loss, was more than Knight could handle.

"I'm sure he assumed Mickie had spent the night with me — which she hadn't," Krzyzewski said years later. "I knew that was against the rules. But he went crazy, screaming at me about not caring about the team or my teammates. He told me I was off the team and I couldn't ride the bus back to Army, I had to get home by myself."

Krzyzewski managed to get to a bus terminal and back to West Point. During the ride, he was furious with his coach for assuming the worst about him. When he got back he went straight to Knight's office to tell him how unfair he had been and how much he *did* care about his team and his teammates. Knight decided that having to sit in the bus station alone was punishment enough and relented.

Several years later, preparing to leave the army, Krzyzewski went to Bloomington, Indiana, for a job interview with his old coach, who was rapidly becoming an icon at Indiana, having taken the Hoosiers to the Final Four in his second season there. Krzyzewski and Mickie, now his wife, were invited to Knight's house to talk about the job. "It became pretty obvious that Knight wanted to talk to Mike alone," Mickie Krzyzewski said. "But I didn't want to leave the room. I thought Knight was fascinating. He was so smart and so driven. I could see he and Mike had a lot in common, although there were also obvious differences."

Knight kept dropping hints to his wife, Nancy, to clear the room. Mickie kept putting him off. No, she didn't want a tour of the house. No, she didn't want to see the backyard. She was fine sitting right where she was. Finally, Knight, clearly exasperated, stood up, pointed at Mike, and said, "You come with me." He pointed at Mickie and Nancy. "You stay here," he said. He stalked off to the back porch, with Krzyzewski trailing him. When they were outside, Knight turned to his old captain and said, "Mike, I think you have every quality needed to be a head coach — the whole package. But I gotta tell you something. Your wife is a pain in the ass."

Years later Mickie Krzyzewski proudly retold the story.

Krzyzewski got the job at Indiana even though his wife was a pain in the ass, and a year later he became the head coach at Army at the age of twenty-seven. It was Knight who recommended him for the job and played a role in his getting it even though he had not left Army on the best of terms with the brass. Five years later Krzyzewski's name was being mentioned for a number of big-time jobs. One was Iowa State. The other was Duke. Knight had mentioned Krzyzewski to Duke athletic director Tom Butters when Butters called looking for advice, but the person he was really pushing for the Duke job was Bob Weltlich, another of his ex-assistants who was a good deal older than Krzyzewski.

"Iowa State was a couple of weeks ahead of Duke in their process because Duke had gone to the final eight that year," Krzyzewski said. "I went through all the interviews there, and the next thing I know, they're offering me the job. I didn't know what to do. Duke had interviewed me once and Tom [Butters] had said he would be in touch. I knew he had other guys to talk to."

Krzyzewski called Knight and asked him what he thought he should do. Knight was firm. "Mike," he said, "I don't think you can afford to say no to Iowa State."

Krzyzewski was torn. He knew Iowa State was a good job in a good league, a clear step up from Army. But he knew the job he really wanted was Duke. He also suspected that Knight had a little bit of an agenda in telling him to take the Iowa State job. "Weltlich was ahead of me in the pecking order," Krzyzewski said. "He was older. I think Coach wanted him to get the Duke job. He thought it was his turn."

Still confused, Krzyzewski went to Tom Rogers, an army colonel who had once been Knight's officer representative and now served the same role for Krzyzewski. At the military academies, officer representatives (better known as O-reps) work with varsity teams to help with logistics — such as helping players put together schedules or find tutors — and often become close to the coaches they work with. Krzyzewski trusted Rogers implicitly. He asked him what he thought. "I think," Rogers told him, "you need to see this Duke thing through."

Krzyzewski liked that answer. "Which told me it was what I needed to do," he said. "Deep down, that was what I wanted to do. If it hadn't been, I would have just taken Knight's advice."

And the course of basketball history would have changed. Butters has often told the story about how he came to choose Krzyzewski. He had interviewed several more-experienced coaches — including Weltlich — but couldn't get Krzyzewski out of his mind. When he brought him to campus for a second interview, he was convinced he was the right choice. "But how did I justify hiring a coach who had just gone 9–17 at *Army* to coach an ACC team that had just played in the final eight?" he said. "I couldn't bring myself to pull the trigger."

Butters sent Krzyzewski back to the airport. Steve Vacendak, who had played on Final Four teams at Duke in the mid-sixties, now Butters's assistant, came in to ask how the interview had gone. Butters told him that it had gone great, that he was convinced Krzyzewski would be a great coach. "So, you offered him the job?" Vacendak said.

"No, I didn't. I'm afraid of what people will say if we hire him."

Vacendak looked his boss in the eye. "Since when are you afraid of what people are going to say? If you think he's that good, how can you let him get away?"

In a scene straight out of a movie, Butters made a snap decision. "You're right," he said. "Go out to the airport and bring him back here."

Krzyzewski was on a pay phone in the airport, telling Mickie he thought he had done everything right but hadn't gotten the job, when he saw Vacendak approaching. "Tom wants you to come back," he told him, and hustled the stunned young coach into his car. The next day Krzyzewski was introduced as Duke's new coach.

It was Vince Taylor, then a sophomore guard, who summed up the national reaction best: "What the hell is a Krzyzewski?" he asked.

Years later Taylor, now an assistant coach with the Minnesota Timberwolves, laughs about the comment. "It was the first thing that came into my head," he said. "I mean, not only had I never heard of the guy, but there was no way I could pronounce his name." (For the record, it is *je-JEV-skee.*)

The first few years were difficult for the young coach and for the boss who hired him based on a gut feeling. Duke was 38–47 the first three seasons while its two most bitter rivals were winning national championships — North Carolina in 1982 and North Carolina State in 1983. In those days, when Duke fans talked about making the Final Four they were talking about the semifinals of the ACC Tournament — a place Duke didn't go until Krzyzewski's fourth season.

That was the year Duke basketball was reborn, the Blue Devils going 24–10. It was also the winter when Krzyzewski's rivalry with Dean Smith bloomed into a full-blooded two-way vendetta. What started it was the teams' first meeting that season, in Cameron Indoor Stadium. North Carolina, led by Michael Jordan and Sam Perkins, won a taut game decided in the final seconds. At one point during the game, Smith accused the people working the scorer's table of intentionally failing to get the officials' attention to allow his team to substitute. Late in the game a frustrated Krzyzewski drew a technical foul, screaming at the officials about their performance. When it was over, Krzyzewski insisted in his press conference that there was a double standard in the ACC: one set of rules for North Carolina and Smith, another set of rules for everyone else. Smith was furious and said so. Krzyzewski didn't back off until twenty years later.

That was after Smith had retired and Krzyzewski and Duke had become the ACC's dominant — and most hated — program. All the things Carolina had been in the eighties, Duke had become. "And more if you think about it," Smith said. "We won three ACC Tournaments in a row, but never *five*. We were on top in a completely different era, especially in terms of media. No sports talk shows. No Internet. None of the crazy rumors that fly around now when you are everyone's target. At times it was tough for us, but we used it to our advantage, too. I can imagine how difficult it has been for Mike."

It has at times been difficult, Krzyzewski admits that. But being on top has given him a different appreciation for North Carolina and for Smith. "Back then [1984] I was looking at it strictly from my perspective," he said. "I thought my kids were getting the short end and I said so. But there's a tendency to not appreciate sometimes that the other guy is just very good. The reason Carolina won all those close games was because they had a great coach and great players. My guess — now — is that there were very few games that they won because of the officiating. Very few. It is a lot easier for me to see that now that I've been on that side of the fence."

Krzyzewski and Smith will never be close friends, but each can now appreciate the other. Smith even commented late in his career that the program Krzyzewski built probably pushed him to be a better coach. "You make the extra phone call," he said. "You work a little harder. The last thing you want to do is lose to the guy right down the street from you."

The 1984 season was one in which Smith, Krzyzewski, and Knight formed a fascinating triangle. After Krzyzewski's outburst, his team played North Carolina twice more, losing in double overtime in Chapel Hill, then bouncing back a week later to beat the Tar Heels in the ACC Tournament, a victory that probably announced the arrival of Duke and Krzyzewski as important factors in the ACC again. Carolina went on from there to play Indiana in the NCAA Tournament round of sixteen, suffering what might have been the most stunning loss in Smith's thirty-six-year head-coaching career.

The Final Four was in Seattle that year and Smith arrived at a rent-a-car counter only to be told that because he had made his reservation so late, the only car available was a compact. Smith shrugged as he signed the contracts. "I did wait until the last minute," he said. "I was sort of counting on traveling around out here on a bus . . . with my team."

It would be seven more years before Smith would get to go to a Final Four again with his team. By then, Duke and Krzyzewski were in their fifth Final Four in six seasons. But they still hadn't won.

By the time Smith and Krzyzewski arrived at the 1991 Final Four together — Duke to play heavily favored Nevada–Las Vegas, North Carolina to play Kansas — Bob Knight had won three national championships. He had been hired at Indiana in 1971, after six years at Army, when he was still only thirty years old. Two years later the Hoosiers reached the Final Four, losing there to (of course) UCLA and Wooden. In 1975 Knight had a superb team that cruised through the regular season undefeated. But star forward Scott May was injured in February, and even though he came back to play in the tournament, neither he nor Indiana was the same and the Hoosiers lost to Kentucky in the regional final. That was the Kentucky team that went on to lose to UCLA in Wooden's final game.

To say that Knight takes losing hard is like saying that Watergate created some problems for Richard Nixon. Knight rages at defeat, in part because he honestly believes his team should win every game if the players do everything he tells them to. But it also infuriates him to think that people around the country are waking up in the morning and saying, "Hey, look, Knight lost" — even though 99.99 percent of the people alive have far too much going on in their lives to be concerned about how Bob Knight's team is doing other than to note a score. Deep down, Knight believes he knows and understands basketball better than anyone ever has because he learned from the masters of the game — Newell, Lapchick, Bee, Iba, Auerbach — and because his intellect allows him to see things about the game others do not. He might very well be right. But he is never going to match Wooden's ten titles, and that galls him. Having lost to Wooden in the Final Four in 1973, he would have loved nothing more than the opportunity to ruin his farewell by beating him in the championship game in 1975.

He never got the chance.

A year later Indiana went through the regular season undefeated again. This time everyone stayed healthy and the Hoosiers beat Michigan in the national championship game in Philadelphia — in spite of shooting guard Bobby Wilkerson getting hurt in the final — and walked away with a 32–0 record and the national title. No team has gone undefeated since, a source of great pride to Knight. But even as he walked out of the Philadelphia Spectrum that night on top of the college basketball world, Knight could not completely enjoy the accomplishment. He was with his close friend Bob Hammel, then the sports editor of the

Bloomington Herald-Telephone. Hammel became so close to Knight through the years that Indiana's players gave him two nicknames: "the shadow," because Knight was almost never seen without him, especially on road trips, and "Pravda," because he was, for all intents and purposes, the official Bob Knight news agency.

As the two men left the Spectrum that night Hammel was overjoyed for his friend. "You did it," he said. "You went undefeated and you won the national championship!"

Knight's response was almost glum: "Shoulda been two," he said, thinking back to the '75 team that — healthy — was probably better than the one that had just been crowned champions.

Many, if not most, great coaches are that way. The victories are quickly forgotten; the defeats linger. It is part of what makes them great. It also frequently makes them less-than-happy people.

"It took getting sick and not being able to coach to make me understand how lucky I had been," Mike Krzyzewski said, referring to his 1995 season, lost to postoperative back troubles and a complete breakdown that landed him in the hospital in January. "Until then I was always thinking about the next thing. We won national championships and I enjoyed them for a few hours, maybe a few days. Then it was on to the next thing."

Krzyzewski's first national title was completely unexpected. Nevada–Las Vegas had hammered Duke in the national championship game in 1990 and had all its starters back. The Rebels were being fitted for immortality by the time they arrived in Indianapolis a year later with a 34–0 record. Duke was a surprise Final Four team that year, having lost three seniors off the 1990 team. But Krzyzewski had added a superb freshman named Grant Hill to his team, and Christian Laettner and Bobby Hurley had emerged as stars. When Krzyzewski looked at the tape of the game a year earlier, painful as it was, he was convinced his team could win the game.

North Carolina played Kansas in the opening semifinal that afternoon. To some, this was almost an intrasquad game. Roy Williams had worked for Dean Smith for ten years before getting the Kansas job in 1988 and did everything almost exactly the same way Smith did. Kansas's victory was a mild surprise, but the shocking part of the day came when Smith was ejected in the final minute by referee Pete Pavia. Smith was angry with Pavia for giving him a technical foul in the first half and frustrated because his team was about to lose. When one of his players fouled out late, Pavia told Smith he needed a sub.

"How much time do I have?" Smith asked.

"I knew exactly how much time I had, of course," Smith said years later. (By rule he had thirty seconds.) "But I was upset with Pete's approach. I was being sarcastic and Pete decided that was enough."

Pavia, who died of cancer in 1993, said later that he knew Smith was being sarcastic and decided to call him on it. Smith's assistant Bill Guthridge was so upset about what happened that he had to be kept away from Pavia in the hallway under the stands when the game ended.

Krzyzewski, in the locker room, waiting for the game to end, really didn't care that Smith had been tossed or why. "All I knew was that when I realized Kansas had won, I felt this little shudder of relief," he said. "The thought that flashed through my head was 'Okay, even if we don't win, our archrival isn't going to win, either.' It occurred to me that if I had that thought, the players had to have it, too. I walked into the locker room and said, 'Fellas, we all know Carolina just lost. Maybe you feel like that relieves a little bit of pressure. I understand why you feel that way. Now, think about it for another second and then flush it. What just happened doesn't matter. What happens next is what matters.'"

What happened next was one of the great upsets in the history of college basketball. Laettner and Hurley were brilliant and, as Krzyzewski had told his players, UNLV got tight in a close game. The Rebels had been so dominant that they hadn't played a game all year decided in the final minute. Duke had played in close games all season. Hurley made a clutch three-pointer with Vegas up 76–71 and 2:14 left in the game, and Laettner made the two free throws that won the game with twelve seconds left. Vegas superstar Larry Johnson passed up an open three in the last frantic seconds and the game ended with Anderson Hunt hurling a desperation shot at the buzzer that was way off the mark.

As the building went nuts and his players jumped into one another's arms, Krzyzewski ran onto the court, palms down, trying to calm everyone down. "Stop it," he kept saying. "Stop it. We haven't won anything yet!"

"I was angry at that moment," he said years later. "I thought my guys should understand that winning on Saturday isn't the goal. We'd been down that road before — in '86 and in '90 — and lost on Monday. All I wanted to do right then was get in the locker room and tell them in no uncertain terms that we were only halfway to our goal."

Krzyzewski was something of a dervish the next two days. He screamed at Greg Koubek and Marty Clark for wearing newly acquired cowboy hats on the bus to practice on Sunday. He told the team that day that they had better stop acting as if they had won the national championship by beating UNLV on Saturday, or they would surely lose it to Kansas on Monday. "I felt as if I hadn't done enough to get them ready to play against Louisville after we had beaten Kansas in '86," he said. "The loss to Vegas [in 1990] was different. We had no chance to win that game. But '86, if I had been a little more experienced, I think we could have — should have — won. I wasn't going to make the same mistake twice. I knew we were tired mentally and physically, but that didn't matter. We had to find a way to get through forty more minutes."

They did. Krzyzewski rested Laettner at key junctures, Hurley made several huge shots, and Grant Hill made one of the most spectacular dunks in Final Four history early on to set the tone. Duke won, 72–65. Jay Bilas, who had been the starting center on that 1986 team that had lost to Louisville, was an assistant coach at the time. "There's one moment I remember better than anything else that happened that night," he said. "In the final seconds, we got a dunk that wrapped up the game. There might have been fifteen seconds left and Coach K turned away from the court so that he was looking right where I was sitting. He just closed his eyes, clenched his fists, and, almost under his breath, said, 'National championship — *yes!*' I'll never forget that because I was so happy for him."

Duke went on to win the title again a year later, becoming the first — and only — team since Wooden's retirement to win back-to-back titles. In the semifinals, the Blue Devils beat Indiana. Knight took that defeat fairly hard. He and Krzyzewski didn't speak to each other again for almost ten years.

5

Storytellers

EVERY FINAL FOUR WEEK has a rhythm to it, almost like a Shakespearean play in five acts: there is the prologue, early arrivals beginning to trickle into the host city while last-second preparations are still going on, whether they involve putting up WELCOME FINAL FOUR! signs on anything that isn't moving on the city streets, making sure every last banner that *isn't* Final Four–related is taken down in the building where the games will be played, or being certain that the team hotels are overrun with security. Act two usually comes on Wednesday and Thursday, when most of the core participants arrive: teams, coaches for the convention, most media members. Act three is Friday. Fans begin to stream into town, most of them proudly wearing their school's colors so they are easy to identify as they choke the streets looking for parties or pep rallies. Act four is Saturday — game day — when everyone finds creative ways to kill time until the late-afternoon tip-off of the first semifinal reminds everyone why they're here, that there are actually basketball games to be played. And then act five, when the city begins to quiet. By Sunday evening, half the fans are gone and only two teams remain, quietly waiting for Monday night's climactic scene that, in the minds of those involved, will end with all the pathos of *Hamlet*. Someone will lie figuratively bleeding to death onstage while a triumphant army arrives to survey everything that has gone on. Good night, Sweet Prince, indeed.

There are a few people who understand the five acts better than most, because they have lived them over and over for years. In that sense, for them, the Final Four is more like *Groundhog Day* than Shakespeare. Unlike the Bill Murray character, though, they look forward each year to the alarm going off at 6:00 A.M. to start the cycle anew.

Shortly before the Friday afternoon practices began in St. Louis for the 2005 Final Four, Rich Clarkson stood at the baseline of the court inside the Edward Jones Dome, looking around with just a bit of wonderment in his eyes as thousands and thousands of fans poured into the building to watch *practice*. "First Final Four I went to, I think the building seated a little more than ten thousand and they couldn't fill it," he said, laughing. "Of course, that was a few years ago."

Fifty-three years ago, to be precise, when the Final Four, then known only as the National Collegiate Basketball Championship, was played on the campus of the University of Washington in the Hec Edmundson Pavilion. Clarkson was a freshman at the University of Kansas back then, an aspiring young photographer who had persuaded Kansas coach Phog Allen to let him travel with the team that season. "I had to have a roommate on the road," he said. "There were eleven players on the team, so I was assigned to room with the guy generally considered to be the eleventh player."

That eleventh player was Dean Smith, then a Kansas junior. "What I remember about Dean was that the game would start with him sitting on the end of the bench," Clarkson said. "By halftime, he had usually manipulated himself so that he was sitting next to Doc Allen [Allen was an osteopath] and [assistant coach] Dick Harp. I don't think there was anyone on the team back then who wasn't convinced that Dean was going to end up as a coach."

Clarkson had first met Phog Allen as a boy growing up in Lawrence, Kansas. He and his friends frequently played in a series of tunnels that ran underneath the Kansas campus. "One day we heard noises at the end of one of the tunnels and followed it," he said. "We popped out in old Robinson Gym. The team was practicing. We hid out for a little while, but when there was a break, we just walked out into the gym. Doc Allen came over and asked us if we were basketball fans. We said we were. He said, 'In that case, there's someone here watching practice who you should meet.' He walked us over to an older gentleman who was sitting on a chair and said, 'Boys, I'd like you to meet James Naismith.' The inventor of basketball was visiting Doc Allen, his old pupil."

Naismith was not the most famous person Clarkson met as a boy. When he was in junior high school, his two fascinations were aviation and journalism. He combined the two by starting an aviation newspaper. He frequently wrote to famous people in the aviation industry, asking for photos or press releases to put in the newspaper. One of the people he interviewed for the paper — the *Lawrence Aviation News* — was Dr. William Simpson, the chairman of the aeronautical engineering department at Kansas. One afternoon Clarkson got a call from Simpson saying he should come by his office right away. Clarkson showed up and found that Simpson had a visitor.

"Rich, I'd like you to meet Orville Wright," Simpson said.

Clarkson ran home after meeting Wright to write a story for

his newspaper and to tell his parents what had happened. "My father was pretty impressed," he said. "He asked me if I had gotten Orville Wright's autograph. I drew myself up, I think I was eleven or twelve at the time, and I said, 'Dad, a journalist doesn't ask for autographs.' Looking back on it now, I probably should have broken the rule that one time."

It was in high school that Clarkson fell in love with photography, specifically, photojournalism. He went to Kansas intending to become an air force pilot but found out after he had signed up for ROTC that his eyes weren't strong enough to allow him to fly. So, the man whose eyes weren't good enough to fly a plane instead used his eyes to take pictures that have become a part of basketball history. The moment that John Wooden talks about remembering so vividly, when Sidney Wicks put his arm around him to thank him at the end of the 1971 championship game, is one that Wooden can see not only in his mind's eye but in the picture Clarkson gave him of the coach and the once-wayward player.

"I always enjoyed looking for the out-of-the-ordinary picture," Clarkson said. "When I was at Kansas, I divided the game into two parts. In the first half, I would be taking pictures for the AP, the *Kansas City Star,* the *Topeka Capital,* and Acme Pictures. I'd file all of them at halftime. Those were your more routine game shots. Then in the second half I'd just shoot for the *Lawrence Daily World* and I'd look for things that were a little more interesting."

Clarkson made enough money working for all those publications to buy his own camera equipment. When he went to that first Final Four in 1952, he remembers being one of six photographers shooting the championship game. "I think I was the only one who shot the awards ceremony, because everyone else had to leave early to file," he said.

He was back at the Final Four with Kansas in 1953, when it was held in Kansas City. "That was a lot different than Seattle," he said. "Especially with KU playing, it was a very tough ticket. You could feel the excitement in town. I remember [former NCAA executive director] Walter Byers once saying that the best way to guarantee a sellout was to go to Kansas City. Everyone stayed in the Muhlbach and there was a tunnel that went under the street to Municipal Auditorium. It was about a two-hundred-yard walk from the hotel lobby to courtside."

Clarkson didn't get to go back until 1957. Kansas didn't make the last weekend his junior or senior year and then he was in the air force, fulfilling his ROTC commitment, after college. It was while he was in the air force that he began doing freelance work for a relatively new magazine called *Sports Illustrated*. "My first assignment was to shoot Wilt Chamberlain when he was a sophomore at Kansas," he said. "I got him to sit in a folding chair and bend over to tie his shoes to try to give people an idea of just how huge he was. The magazine opened the story with a full page of that photo."

Clarkson was able to get passes to leave the air force base to work for *SI* in return for supplying the base commander with tickets to Kansas games. He returned to the Final Four in 1957, shooting the historic triple-overtime game between Kansas and North Carolina in which the Tar Heels outlasted Kansas and Chamberlain, 54–53. "That was one time when I remember making a conscious effort not to think about the game," he said. "Obviously I was pulling for Kansas, but I couldn't get emotionally involved. When I look around today during a game and see all the security and people watching every move the photographers make, I laugh. I remember in those days I'd just walk right over and shoot the players and coaches in the huddle during time-outs. You could go anywhere you wanted."

Clarkson's first *Sports Illustrated* cover came in 1964, a picture taken during the UCLA-Duke championship game. The cover wasn't supposed to be Clarkson's. It was supposed to be Hy Peskin's. Peskin was *SI*'s star photographer at the time and had made a deal with a camera company to take photos of him taking the cover photo during the championship game. The only problem was that the magazine editors liked what Clarkson filed better and chose one of his photos for the cover.

Clarkson has known all the great coaches of the past fifty years. When Bob Knight wrote his autobiography, he asked Clarkson to shoot the cover. The two men had first met when Clarkson and writer Pat Putnam had been assigned to do a piece during Knight's second year at Indiana. "By the end of the week I was eating dinner at his house," Clarkson said. "In '76, when they went to Philadelphia for the Final Four, Bob let me in the locker room before the game to take pictures. He did it again in '81, when they won the second time."

Clarkson remembers going to a victory dinner with Knight and a group of his friends in 1976. John Havlicek, the Boston Celtics Hall of Famer who had been Knight's college teammate, was in the group. Walking into the restaurant, Havlicek spotted Curry Kirkpatrick, then with *Sports Illustrated*, eating at a table across the room. Knowing that a *Sports Illustrated* photographer was in the Knight group, Havlicek assumed that Knight would be friendly with a writer from the same magazine. What he didn't know was that Kirkpatrick had written a story earlier that year that had enraged Knight. When Havlicek suggested to Knight that they invite Kirkpatrick to join them, Knight said, "You bring that son of a bitch over here and I'll kill him."

Victory never mellowed Bob Knight.

During the nearly ten years that Knight and Mike Krzyzewski

weren't speaking, Clarkson photographed each on several occasions. "Without fail, acting as if they didn't really care, they would both bring up the other one," he said. "As in 'I saw you had a photo of Mike in the magazine last month' or something like that. The fact that they cared about each other was still very apparent."

Clarkson also knew Adolph Rupp, a fellow Kansan, quite well. "First time I was sent by the magazine to shoot him, Kentucky was still playing in the old Memorial Gym," he said. "The benches were at either end of the court. I thought it would be nice to sit in front of the bench, since I wouldn't be on the court, and shoot Rupp from there. The SID said absolutely not. I went to see Rupp in his office. He started screaming: 'I know why you're here, you're just here to make a fool out of me and I'm not going to have it!'

"I said, 'Coach, I'd never want to do that. Why, you helped launch my career as a photographer.'"

Rupp looked at Clarkson as if he had lost his mind. "Do you remember coming to Lawrence to visit your sister one time and you wanted to get your picture taken with Doc Allen? Your sister and my mom were friends, and she called me and asked me to come out and take the picture."

Rupp stared at Clarkson in disbelief for a second. "That was you?" he said. "I remember that. Okay, you can do whatever you want."

Rupp appears in what may be Clarkson's most famous picture. It was shot moments after Kentucky had lost to Texas Western in the 1966 championship game, the so-called *Brown v. Board of Education* final, and it shows Rupp and his players on their bench, clearly in shock over the outcome. "Hard to believe that game was almost forty years ago," he said. "I can still see the look on Rupp's face when I took that picture."

Nowadays, Clarkson, who is seventy-two, is a Final Four institution. St. Louis was his fiftieth, and the NCAA put together a series of his photos to show on the giant message boards in the dome throughout the weekend. "It's a little embarrassing," he said, smiling. "But it's also very nice." Like everyone else who has seen the event grow from small-town sideshow to massive three-ring circus, Clarkson finds it all just a little bit amazing. "If anyone ever tells you they dreamed it would become *this*," he said, gesturing around the dome as more than 30,000 people watched the Friday practices, "they're lying. In some ways it isn't as much fun, because we've lost the intimacy we had years ago. But seeing what it has become is a great thing. I feel proud to have been a small part of it."

Not far from where Clarkson stood setting up camera positions for the next day, Billy Packer sat watching each of the four teams practice. He was seated in the second row, a few feet behind where he would be sitting the next day as the analyst on CBS's telecast of the semifinals. It would be his thirty-first consecutive Final Four — seven with NBC, the last twenty-four with CBS. Packer has been an analyst for so long now that many — if not most — who listen to him have no idea that he was a star on Wake Forest's first (and only) Final Four team in 1962.

"Of course, back then it wasn't even that big a deal to us," he said. "The big deal was winning the ACC Tournament; that was the way you earned your spurs in those days. Once we won the ACCs, they told us there was this other tournament we were going to play in because we won. That was fine with us and we tried to win, but it wasn't the same thing." He smiled. "I remember they gave us watches when it was over. I think half the guys on my team pawned them. First year we went [1961], we lost to St. Joseph's in the regionals. The next year when we won the ACC Tournament again, we were a little more psyched-up for the NCAAs because of what had happened the year before. But I remember when we beat Villanova to win the regional, we didn't celebrate the way we did when we won the ACCs. It just wasn't the same."

Wake Forest ended up playing UCLA in the consolation game that year after losing to Ohio State. (The Bruins had lost to Cincinnati.) "We didn't even know it at the time, but because we won that game, the ACC got a first-round bye the next year — which it kept until the tournament expanded in '75 and everyone had to play a first-round game."

Packer was aware of the NCAA Tournament growing up in Bethlehem, Pennsylvania. His dad coached at Lehigh, and Packer remembers getting out of school early on a fall day in 1954 because La Salle, which had won the 1954 national championship, was coming to town to scrimmage his dad's team. "I remember thinking Tom Gola was an amazing player," he said. "I was thirteen at the time, not even that much of a fan yet, but I was awed by Gola. The next spring, La Salle was back in the Final Four and I listened on the radio because it wasn't on TV. The guy doing the game kept talking about this guy Russell who kept blocking Tom Gola's shots. I'm thinking, 'That's impossible, no one can do that to Gola. Who the hell is this guy Russell?' Think about that, I was a basketball fan, this is the Final Four, and I had never *heard* of Bill Russell."

Russell and his San Francisco team went on to win that year and again the next. Even then Russell wasn't that big a star. He played on the 1956 Olympic team and then joined the Boston Celtics, whom he ended up leading to eleven NBA titles over the next thirteen seasons. "I remember telling Bob Cousy the story about never having heard of Russell before the '55 Final Four," Packer said. "He laughed and said, 'First time I laid eyes on him was in the layup line before his first game.' These days, Russell probably wouldn't have gone to college for more than a year. He'd have been in the NBA."

Packer coached briefly after graduating from Wake Forest, before getting out of basketball and into business. His TV career began soon after that when he was asked to do the ACC Game of the Week. People quickly noticed his ability to break a game down, and he and his partner, the late Jim Thacker, became one of the most popular duos on TV. In 1974 he was asked to do early-round tournament games by TVS, which still shared the TV rights in those days with NBC and the NCAA. A year later Scotty Connell, NBC's executive producer, called Packer the week before the tournament began and said, "We thought you did well last year; you feel like working for us again this year?" Packer said that was fine with him, they agreed he would be paid $750 a game, and he was told to report to Tuscaloosa for the first weekend of the tournament.

"I checked in to the hotel and the clerk said, 'Mr. Gowdy has already checked in.' It had never occurred to me that I'd be working with Curt Gowdy. That was when it first occurred to me that maybe they really liked what I was doing."

Back then Gowdy was *the* name in play-by-play at NBC. If Gowdy did an event, it was a big deal. If you worked with Gowdy, it was really a big deal. In what would prove to be an ironic twist, Packer's first game on NBC was Kentucky-Marquette. Al McGuire, who would become both his broadcast partner and best friend, was Marquette's coach. "Kentucky had [Rick] Robey and [Mike] Phillips," Packer said. "They were both huge. Early in the game Al was up bitching every time they did anything, trying to get them in foul trouble. The officials were calling nothing. Finally, Al just turned to [assistant coach] Hank Raymonds and said, 'You go ahead and coach. This is over.' He was right. He knew if the officials let Robey and Phillips play, there was no way his team could win."

At the end of the first weekend, Connell called again and asked if Packer would go to Portland for the regionals. It was the same way a week later when the Final Four went to San Diego. "That was the first time I had been there since I played in it in '62," he said. "It still didn't strike me as being that big an event."

Packer hasn't missed a Final Four since. In 1978 NBC hired McGuire, who had retired the previous season after leading Marquette to the national championship, and, unsure about what he would bring to the broadcast, initially put him in the truck to help break down replays. By then Dick Enberg was the play-by-play man. After the first game they did together, Packer suggested that McGuire sit with him and Enberg, creating basketball's first three-man booth. "Al was a natural right from the start," Packer said. "He saw things in the game other people didn't and he wasn't afraid to say what he was thinking. I've never been afraid to speak my mind, either. I think that's why we worked well together."

They worked together so well that, with Enberg acting as their moderator, they became the face of college basketball. They were Dick Vitale before there was Dick Vitale. When Enberg-Packer-McGuire came to town to do a game, it was a big deal. "You have to remember that this was still when there wasn't very much college basketball on TV," Packer said. "Even when ESPN did start [in 1979] they weren't in any homes, so our games were still the standard."

The era of the NBC three came to a crashing halt in 1981 when CBS shocked the sports world with its massive $48 million, three-year bid for the tournament rights. Enberg and McGuire were still under contract to NBC, but Packer wasn't. CBS quickly hired him and early on began asking him for ways it could make an impact on the sport, especially since NBC was still doing regular-season games with Enberg and McGuire. "One thing I came up with [along with Len DeLuca] was the idea of the selection show," he said. "That was the whole idea behind the 'Road to the Final Four' concept. To get here, you have to go down a lot of different roads during a long, hard winter, and the teams come from a lot of different places and backgrounds. We wanted to remind people of that by showing them the entire field going into the bracket because the tournament isn't just about the powerhouses, it's about the little guys, too."

Packer has now worked the Final Four with five different play-by-play men: Gowdy, Enberg, Gary Bender, Brent Musburger, and Jim Nantz. He has been the one absolute for CBS since the beginning. There are very few people in basketball who don't respect his knowledge of the game, his work ethic, or his ability to break down what is happening in a game on the fly. And yet he isn't nearly as popular with most fans as Vitale and, to many, is a remote, often difficult person to deal with. Packer makes no apologies for any of this. He has always been outspoken and does not enjoy being around masses of people the way Vitale so clearly does.

As he watched Illinois practice on Friday — with at least two-thirds of the crowd dressed in the school's blue and orange colors — Packer was fuming about a story in the local paper that implied that he and Vitale didn't like each other.

"It's funny how sometimes people try to make a big deal out of Dick and I not being friends," he said. "We haven't spent much time together through the years, but that's because our paths don't cross that much and because, to be honest, when I'm on the road, I don't go out much. I'd rather stay in my room, relax, and prepare. All that means is that Dick and I are different, nothing more, nothing less. He does things one way and it works for him, and I do things another and it works for me. The thing I enjoy the most about this job is preparing and then having a really good game.

"I've learned lessons as I've gotten older. I know now that no one at CBS really wants my input beyond showing up and doing my job. It took a while for me to figure that out. I should have figured it out sooner because I remember Al telling me, 'Billy, the TV people don't want you in their business.' In other words — do your job and shut up."

Packer's not likely to shut up. He still bridles when he hears people talk about Indiana State–Michigan State (Bird vs. Magic) in 1979 being a turning point in the game's history. "It was a bad game," he said, shaking his head in disbelief when the myth was brought up again. "Go back and look at the tape. Bird didn't play well and Michigan State was in control because it had a much better team. Magic had Greg Kelser, Bird didn't have anyone close to that level playing with him. The reason the game is so big in people's minds is because of what Magic and Bird became later, not because of the game itself."

Even so, the game remains the highest-rated college basketball game in history. "There's no question it had the buildup," he said. "Indiana State was undefeated and a lot of people [Packer included] had questioned them during the season because of the conference they played in. Magic was already a big star because of his flair. So people watched. That doesn't mean it was a good game."

Packer is sixty-four now and very comfortable with his role.

He has made lots of money in business and doesn't need to work. But like so many people, he still gets a rush from being courtside, especially for a great game. He readily admits that he still misses McGuire, who died of cancer in 2001 at the age of seventy-two. CBS hired McGuire during the 1990s after his NBC contract ran out, and later hired Enberg. The three were even reunited for a game. "That was a lot of fun," Packer said. "It was almost as if we had never stopped working together."

While Packer is talking about McGuire he looks up to see Enberg approaching. These days Enberg, who looks considerably younger than sixty-eight, does a lot of essays and commentaries for CBS in addition to the play-by-play work he still does. He has also written a one-man play based on the musings of McGuire. He and Packer greet each other with the warmth of men who have shared something special. In this case it isn't just their work; it's their friendship with McGuire.

"We both end a lot of sentences by saying, 'Well, like Al used to say . . . ,'" Enberg said, laughing. Enberg spoke at McGuire's funeral and it was while he was putting together his eulogy that he was struck by the number of wise and funny things McGuire had said to him through the years. That was when the idea came to him to try to write a one-man play. Appropriately, the play was produced and performed in Milwaukee, which is where McGuire made his major mark on the game, as the coach at Marquette. In 1977, on the eve of the national championship game against North Carolina, McGuire talked about retiring to look for "seashells and balloons." Then he walked out of the press conference, got on his motorcycle, and tooled around downtown Atlanta for several hours. It is probable that he is the only coach in history to show up for the national championship game on a motorcycle.

"One of the reasons we got along is because neither one of us was afraid to tell people what we thought," Packer said. "The difference is I make people mad. Al could criticize them and they wouldn't get mad at him. Maybe it was because they knew he was right."

Even after NBC lost the rights to the NCAA Tournament, McGuire continued hosting a one-hour show that would air on Final Four Sunday. It became a tradition that the two coaches in the championship game would show up on Sunday morning to tape an interview with McGuire that would air as part of the show that afternoon. As soon as the interview was over, McGuire would give each coach the same piece of advice: "Tomorrow night, when you walk onto the floor, stop for a minute. Look around, soak it in. Because at that moment, you will be at the pinnacle of your profession, coaching in the one game every coach aspires to coach in. Take it all in, take a deep breath, and then go to work."

The only coach who ever refused to be part of McGuire's Sunday show was John Thompson, not because he had any problem with McGuire but because that was Thompson's way: if everyone else did something one way, he tended to do the opposite. So, in 1985, prior to the Villanova-Georgetown game, McGuire ended the show by interviewing Thompson's towel. Thompson always kept a large white towel draped over his right shoulder during a game, partly because he was superstitious but also because he tended to perspire heavily during games. McGuire took a white towel, draped it over a chair, and asked the towel questions while the credits ran. It might have been his best pre-championship interview ever.

Packer and Enberg both agreed that only Al could have pulled off that trick.

North Carolina was coming out onto the court at that moment and Roy Williams walked over to say hello to everyone from CBS. As various producers and directors gathered around Williams to pay their respects, too, they blocked Packer's view of the court. "For crying out loud," he shouted, "can't you people let a guy get some work done here!"

He was kidding. Sort of.

One person who would agree with Packer's assessment of his relationship with Dick Vitale was Vitale. "Billy's right, we're just different," he said. "He's vanilla and I'm Thirty-one Flavors."

For Vitale, Final Four week was completely different than it was for Packer. For one thing, he wouldn't be calling the games, something he had made peace with years ago, even if he might wish it different. "I learned a long time ago not to worry about things you can't control," he said. "When I was coaching I always dreamed of running one of the big-time programs: a UCLA or North Carolina or Indiana or Duke. But it didn't happen that way for me. I got to coach at Rutgers and Detroit. I made the best of it, and in the end, my life could not have worked out better."

One of the things that is difficult for people to understand about Vitale is that what you see on TV is what you get in real life. The one-eyed bald whack job who overflows with enthusiasm about everything, every single minute he is on the air, is no different from the guy sitting in a room with one other person. Vitale doesn't like things, he *loves* them. It is simply who he is, who he has been, dating back to his coaching career, which peaked when he took the University of Detroit to the Sweet Sixteen in 1977. The Titans lost to Michigan in that game, 86–81, but Vitale still remembers all the details.

"We had three future NBA guys on that team [Terry Duerod, John Long, and Terry Tyler], but they had size on us," he said. "What kills me is we had a six-ten junior college player who had to sit out that year because of a technicality. He was at Robert Morris, and the year he left they became a four-year school. So, instead of being eligible for us that year, he had to sit out! I wore a maize-and-blue jacket for the game in honor of Michigan. Imagine what it meant to our school with the city campus to be in the round of sixteen playing Michigan." (It should be noted here that every Vitale sentence should probably be punctuated with an exclamation point.) "I looked around that night and thought, 'This is what I always wanted to do, this is a long way from East Rutherford High School.[!!!!]'"

Vitale had grown up in New Jersey, gone to Seton Hall, and started his coaching career in local high schools. His first Final Four trip was on a whim. "I had a buddy, Tom Ramsten, a high school coach like me, and there was an all-night diner we'd go to and we'd just sit there and draw up plays," he said. "One year, I think it was 1967, we're sitting there and at four o'clock in the morning we said, let's drive to Louisville — which is where it was that year. We just got in the car and drove. Getting tickets wasn't a problem. We hung out the whole weekend, saw all the famous coaches walking through the lobby, and went to the games. I was awed by the whole thing. I just kept thinking, 'Someday I want to be a part of this.'"

Of course, he never dreamed how he would become part of it. Vitale was hired as an assistant coach by Dick Lloyd at Rutgers in 1971 and played a key role in recruiting the players whom Tom Young took to the Final Four in 1976. "People told me I was crazy," he said, repeating one of his favorite phrases. "I just believed if we worked hard enough, we could be on equal footing with the big-time programs. My buddies would say to me, 'Dick, you're at Rutgers. Calm down. It doesn't happen like that.'"

Vitale wasn't at Rutgers when it did happen for the Scarlet Knights. He was at Detroit, where he had been hired as head coach. "I think I made seventeen thousand dollars my first year," he said. "My whole pitch to the people there was 'Don't accept mediocrity.' We can play with Michigan and Michigan State, we just have to find the right kid for Detroit. I went out and told the guys if they wanted grass, we were in the wrong place. But if they wanted a big city, if they wanted to be watched by the top execs at General Motors and Ford, we were it."

The pitch worked. Detroit got one of the NCAA's thirty-two bids in 1977 by beating Marquette — which would go on to win the national championship — at Marquette on the last day of the regular season. Vitale did a madcap dance at midcourt after the buzzer, one that no doubt would have been replayed about a million times in today's media world. When his team made it to the round of sixteen, Vitale milked the moment for all it was worth. He had photos taken before the game with Curt Gowdy and John Wooden (who were broadcasting the game) and took Michigan to the last minute. It made him a star. The Detroit Pistons, fighting consistent mediocrity and lack of interest at the time, needed a coach — one who might sell a few tickets. Vitale had become a big name in Detroit. They offered him the job and he jumped.

"Most of my friends told me I was crazy to do it," he said. "I remember Jimmy Valvano saying, 'Dick, you're made for college, your enthusiasm won't play in the pros.' I can still hear those words. I have to admit a lot of it was money. I'd gotten up to twenty-five thousand dollars at Detroit being coach and athletic director. This was for four times as much. That was hard to turn down."

Early in his second season with the Pistons, Vitale was fired. The Pistons went 30–52 his first season and were 4–8 on November 8 when he got what he came to call "the ziggy," Vitalese for being fired. Looking back now, he understands it was the best thing that ever happened to him — for a number of reasons. Back then, it hurt. "I felt like a failure," he said. "Maybe that's why I defend coaches so ardently and get in trouble for it now, because I remember how it felt when it happened to me. I still remember, around my neighborhood, people who had been my friends wouldn't even look at me. On Sundays, after mass, we would always have coffee and doughnuts. When I was coaching, there was always a group of people around me wanting to hear stories, wanting to know about our last game or about different players or coaches. Now, I'm standing all alone with my wife. One Sunday I finally walked over to a group and said, 'Hey, can anyone here at least say hello to me? Am I a complete pariah because I got fired? Have I got bubonic plague or something?'"

Vitale's assumption was that he would end up back in college coaching. He had a record of success there that would attract someone. He was only thirty-nine when the Pistons fired him. But a man named Scotty Connell intervened. It can be argued that Connell is the most important person in the history of college basketball announcing. While he was at NBC, he hired Billy Packer and Al McGuire. In 1979 he left NBC to become the first executive producer of college basketball for a new cable network called ESPN. The idea, outlandish at the time, was to broadcast sports twenty-four hours a day. Since there was little college basketball on network TV at the time and there were many games, the sport became an outpost for ESPN, a place where it had a chance to make its mark.

Connell had been the producer for NBC on the night Detroit

lost to Michigan. He had heard Vitale speak, seen his act. He thought his combination of enthusiasm and outrageousness could work for a start-up entity pleading for attention. He called Vitale, newly out of work, and asked if he wanted to try his hand at doing a few games. "I had nothing else to do at the time," Vitale said. "Scotty seemed to think I might be good at it. I figured I'd give it a shot."

That shot changed Vitale's life and the course of college basketball history. "Putting aside all the great things that have happened to me, I am convinced of one thing absolutely," Vitale said. "If I had gone back into coaching, I would have been dead by fifty. I mean that. Almost for sure, my marriage would not have lasted. I still remember my second year at Detroit, I managed to convince Michigan to come in and play in our Christmas tournament. This was huge for us. First round, they played Western Michigan while we played Eastern Michigan. We were going to play them in the finals and it was going to be a big deal. Except we lost at the buzzer. I still remember that Christmas. It was miserable. I just sat and watched tape and didn't talk to anyone. I don't know how my wife put up with it. If I'd gone back into coaching, even if I hadn't been dead, there's no way my marriage would have survived, no matter how patient she was."

Vitale made his ESPN debut on December 5, 1979, doing color on a game between Wisconsin and DePaul. His partner that night was a man named Joe Boyle, who was by trade a hockey play-by-play man. In fact, that was the only college basketball game he ever did for the network, making him the answer to a trivia question: Who worked with Dick Vitale on his first night as a broadcaster?

Vitale quickly became a cult figure at ESPN. The network wasn't in that many homes at the time, but it began acquiring games that people wanted to watch. Then it made a deal with the NCAA to televise early-round games of the tournament. Rather than attach Vitale to one tournament site, Connell made the decision to put him in the studio so he could be on all the time, talking at halftime and between games about what was going on. Vitale's outrageous comments and predictions became a part of the tournament to basketball fans, most famously when he promised to stand on his head if Austin Peay beat Illinois in a first-round game in 1987 — then did after Austin Peay pulled off the upset.

"It worked out well, though," he said, laughing. "Austin Peay asked me to come out and speak at their banquet that year. I actually made money on the deal."

Vitale was soon making a lot of money in a lot of places. As ESPN grew, so did his popularity. He began doing commercials, speaking for huge fees (up to $50,000 and more nowadays), and endorsing everything from pizza to sneakers. College students in particular loved him, especially when he came to their place to do a game and engaged in pregame shooting contests or allowed himself to be passed up through the stands. Much to the horror of many basketball purists, he became the number one face and voice of college basketball. To those who enjoyed Packer's steady, solid analysis, Vitale's screaming endorsement of anything and everyone he met was anathema to their ears. Vitale doesn't so much break down a game as surround it — he talks about his family, every coach, most of the players, numerous fans, writers, people he met overseas during the summer, the hockey lockout, and every restaurant he has ever set foot in. If you don't know Vitale, it is easy to think he is simply sucking up to people. It really isn't true: he simply likes almost everyone he meets.

"I've had times where people who have ripped me have come

up to say something and I greet them and I'm friendly to them," he said. "My wife will say, 'That guy ripped you, why are you nice to him?' I say, 'Why not? The guy is doing a job; he has an opinion. I may not like it, but so what? Life is too short to make enemies. Making friends is a lot more fun.'"

That approach, and his genuine enthusiasm and willingness to try almost anything, has made Vitale the most famous person in college basketball — period. Some can't stand listening to him, many more clearly love him, but all know him. He has been criticized, sometimes justifiably, for defending any and all coaches. He doesn't apologize for it. "Whenever I watch a losing coach, it reminds me of why I'm lucky I never got back into coaching," he said. "The worst thing is that phony postgame handshake. I wish they'd cut that out. If guys really want to do it, fine, but most of the time you lose you just want to get out of there. Whenever a guy gets fired, I bleed for him. For one thing, I know it is almost impossible for a guy who gets fired from a big-time job to get back to that level and how hard it is going to be going back down a level or two. I'm lucky I never had to do it."

Vitale's Final Four weekend is filled to the brim. He makes appearances for corporations, gives speeches, does several-times-a-day bits from ESPN's set (complete with screaming, adoring fans in the background), and probably signs more autographs than every other coach in town combined. In 2005 he had hernia surgery in early March and there was some question about whether he would be well enough to make it to his twenty-first consecutive Final Four. "Some people told me, 'Don't do it, Dick, you can miss one year,'" he said. "I said, 'Are you kidding? Miss the Final Four! Miss my favorite weekend of the year? No way, baby!'"

It should be thus forevermore.

6

Partying

BY THURSDAY AFTERNOON, the events surrounding the Final Four are well under way. The teams are in town and off practicing at secret locations. They are required to show up at the arena on Friday for a practice that is open to the public, but even that won't be real. All will schedule their real workouts away from the arena and then spend their fifty required minutes on the court getting accustomed to the shooting backgrounds, having dunk contests, and perhaps scrimmaging a little bit.

It didn't used to be that way. Only in the past dozen years have teams taken to scheduling an extra practice on Friday. "I remember when we were in Seattle in 1984, our workout in the Kingdome was very much the real deal," said Terry Holland, who twice took Virginia to the Final Four and was later chairman of the basketball committee. "We were the last team to practice that day and they were having some kind of cookout inside the dome that night. When they started turning on the grills, the place was just filled with smoke. Our kids were coughing, having trouble breathing. I started screaming at [basketball committee member] Dick Shrider that this was ridiculous; how were we supposed to practice for a Final Four game when we couldn't breathe?"

That's not likely to be a problem nowadays. And if someone did schedule a cookout inside one of the domes, the coach whose team couldn't breathe would probably just see it as a convenient excuse to get his team away from the required appearance a little bit early. One thing coaches really don't like about the Final Four is being forced to do everything the NCAA demands. Most are used to being unquestioned dictators in their worlds, and all of a sudden, on the most important weekend of their lives, they are being told what to do.

"I remember my first one, in 1982, they made us go to this meeting," said John Thompson, the former Georgetown coach who made three Final Fours (and reached the final each time) and won the national championship in 1984. "First of all, I didn't like being told that I had to go to a meeting. Then we get in there and they're telling us, 'You will wear this pin on the bench,' and, 'When you are introduced, you will walk down and shake hands with the other coach,' and on and on like that. I'm sitting there thinking, 'Let's just play the damn games and stop all this nonsense.'"

Nonsense is part of the Final Four, whether it is the lengthy Friday afternoon meeting Thompson was referring to that remains mandatory for head coaches — all coaches, no assistants may attend in their place — or the hijinks in the coaches' lobby or all the various official parties throughout the week. On Thursday night the NCAA throws something called the "salute" dinner, which is appropriate since it is the NCAA saluting itself. The salute dinner is also mandatory for the coaches, who are each asked to get up and speak briefly. It is one of those good news/bad news jokes: On the one hand, you are thrilled to be one of the four guys still coaching. On the other hand, because you are coaching, you have a lot better things to do than stand up in front of several hundred people and tell them how glad you are to be there.

South Carolina coach Dave Odom, who has been to the final eight (at Wake Forest) but never the Final Four, may have spoken for all coaches as he walked out of the dinner one year: "My dream is to go to that dinner some year because they force me to go," he said.

Everywhere you turn during Final Four week there are parties. The U.S. Basketball Writers Association, for whom the Final Four is a convention much the way it is for the coaches, has its annual dinner for board members, past presidents, and USBWA Hall of Fame members on Thursday night, too. The main reason it is held on Thursday is that the writers all know there is no way they will be invited to the salute dinner — which is fine with most of them. CBS throws all sorts of parties as well. There's a Wednesday night dinner thrown by the public relations staff; then a Friday night party, usually in a bar, for anyone who has ever coached; and then the big Sunday night dinner for CBS execs and members of the basketball committee. The coaches association has its official dinner on Sunday night but now also has a Sunday breakfast for all its past presidents and is planning to add in 2006 a predinner event for any coach who has ever taken a team to the Final Four.

And on and on. The best party of the 2005 Final Four had absolutely nothing to do with ex-presidents or Hall of Famers or salutes or CBS or the basketball committee. It was put together by Frank Sullivan, the longtime coach at Harvard, in honor of his buddy Tom Brennan, who was retiring at the age of fifty-five after nineteen years as the head coach at the University of Vermont. Sullivan invited about a hundred people to a bar far removed from downtown St. Louis — "It was the best I could do for the money I had," he said — and close to three hundred people showed up. Brennan had told Sullivan that there was absolutely no way he was going to speak and then spoke emotionally for fifteen minutes.

Brennan is one of college basketball's true Runyonesque characters. He was an assistant coach early in his career under Rollie Massimino at Villanova and later coached at Yale for four years before taking the job at Vermont in 1986. During his first three seasons there he was 14–68 — and didn't get fired. "How many schools in the country would not fire you with a record like that?" Brennan said. "When I say the people at Vermont took me in, I mean it; they really took me in."

Brennan survived at Vermont in part because the school is never going to hire and fire the way big-time schools do, but also because he became one of the most popular people on campus before he became a winner. Most coaches have to win to be popular; Brennan was an exception. He built a solid program and also became a radio talk show host. On a whim, a local radio station asked him in 1991 if he wanted to do the sports for a week or two while their regular sports host was away. Brennan figured what the heck and did it for yucks. The chemistry he quickly developed with the show's host, Steve Cormier, was so good that Cormier asked him if he would be interested in cohosting the show. Fourteen years later *Corm and the Coach* was syndicated throughout the state and got higher ratings than either Howard Stern or Don Imus in the morning drive.

Brennan is a natural behind the microphone. He's smart, well read, and quick-witted. He has as many opinions on who should be governor of Vermont as he does on who should start for the Catamounts at point guard. In the spring of 2000 he had recruited a very good point guard from Rhode Island named

T. J. Sorrentine, a hard-nosed little player with great range who he thought would give his program a boost. That same spring he also signed a local kid named Taylor Coppenrath. "His main asset," Brennan said, "was that he was six-nine. I thought if we redshirted him a year, worked with him, he could help us down the line."

Vermont lost eleven straight games the next season while Coppenrath was sitting out, and Brennan was tempted to play him because by then he had an inkling the kid might be a little better than just someone who could help down the line. A year later, with Sorrentine at point guard and Coppenrath starting as a redshirt freshman at center, Vermont won the regular-season title in the America East Conference and was 21–7 before crashing in the first round of the conference tournament. "I thought maybe I'd blown my best chance to ever make a postseason tournament," Brennan said. "I mean any postseason tournament. We would have walked to the NIT if they had taken us."

Sadly, the NIT would rather have an eighth-place team from the ACC or the Big East than a regular-season champion from a one-bid league whose players and coaches would be willing to walk to New York for a chance to play. The Catamounts stayed home. Then Sorrentine broke his wrist in preseason that fall and had to be medically redshirted.

But the dream didn't die. Coppenrath was emerging as a star. During his freshman season he had scored 33 points in a game at Binghamton. Brennan was beside himself. "Taylor," he said, "you remind me of Larry Bird. You can be Bird!"

Coppenrath, who is the classic strong, silent type, shook his head at Brennan and said, "Coach, don't be ridiculous."

Three nights later he scored 3 points at Albany. "Hey, Taylor," Brennan said, "Bird never got held to three, you know."

He had cooled it with the Bird talk after that, but Coppenrath kept getting better. In March of 2002, after finishing second behind Boston University during the regular season, the Catamounts made it to the championship game, to be played at BU. After the semifinals, BU coach Dennis Wolff congratulated Brennan on the win and told him he looked forward to seeing him in six days in Boston (the America East final is played six days after the semifinals to accommodate — surprise — ESPN) and had one request: "No calls this week."

Brennan laughed. One of his favorite tricks in his guise as talk show host was to call opposing coaches on the air very early in the morning and wake them up. "Anyone else but Tom, you would have to kill the guy," Wolff said over the din of the Brennan farewell party. "From Tom you accept it and laugh it off."

Brennan called Wolff that week. Then on Saturday his team went into Boston and beat Wolff's team on a last-second jumper by a kid named David Hehn, who grew up in Canada but somehow became a basketball player instead of a hockey player. For the first time in history, Vermont was in the Dance. The entire state went nuts. Getting snowed in in Denver en route to Salt Lake City for the first round couldn't dampen the joy, nor could a one-sided loss to Arizona. "Hey, I did my job," Brennan said. "I won the press conference."

A year later, even though Coppenrath missed three weeks with an injury late in the season, Vermont won the conference tournament again — Coppenrath coming back to play in the final and scoring 43 points. It was that night, during the victory celebration at his house, that Brennan decided to quit. "I looked around and I saw how happy everyone was," he said. "I knew it couldn't possibly get better than this. Taylor and T.J. and the other rising seniors [five in all] had one more year and I wanted to coach them and go out with them. I felt completely satisfied. I don't think you can be a good coach if you're satisfied. It was time to go."

He made the announcement before the season began in the fall. By then, he and Coppenrath and Vermont were getting more national publicity than most highly ranked teams: a feature in *Sports Illustrated,* an ESPN camera crew trailing them for days at a time, a *USA Today* cover story. "No one loves Tommy Brennan more than me," Brennan said at one point, "and *I'm* getting sick of me."

Along with the attention and the yucks came pressure. Vermont was now supposed to be good. It was supposed to dominate the league. A close loss in the opener at Kansas actually left Brennan frustrated. "The officials got us," he said. Then he caught himself. "Whoever thought the day would come when I'd be upset about losing a close game at Kansas. Wow."

There were some off nights and a couple of disappointing losses early, but the Catamounts did dominate the league. The toughest weekend for Brennan was the first two rounds of the conference tournament, held in Binghamton. Because Vermont was the top seed, the championship game would be played in Burlington, in 3,200-seat Patrick Gym, a building that had once been all but empty for home games and was now sold out every night. "I knew if we got back to Patrick, we weren't losing there," Brennan said. "But it made me nervous to think we might stumble before we got there. When we won our semi, I was more relieved than I'd ever been after a win. And exhausted. I was so tired I let Lynn [his wife] drive home. I never do that."

He was right about playing in Patrick. Vermont blew out Northeastern. Midway through the second half, the chants began: "Thank-you, Bren-nan." The crowd was saying good-bye and thank you. Brennan cried on the bench. The next morning Dennis Wolff called to congratulate him. "I'm proud of you," he said. "But what was all that crying about?"

"We were up thirty," Brennan said. "I had nothing else to do."

There was a great sense of anticipation later that afternoon when the team gathered for the NCAA tournament selection show. Because it had played a tough nonconference schedule, Vermont had been in the top thirty in the vaunted RPI (Ratings Percentage Index) rankings all season. The RPI is supposed to rank teams based not only on record but on whom they have played and where they have played them. The members of the basketball committee reference the RPI all the time, insisting it is only part of how they seed the field — except when they want to back up something they've done. Then they cite the RPI. Based on the RPI, Vermont should have been seeded somewhere between seventh and tenth in its regional. Everyone waited to see where the team would fall in the draw, and then it popped on the screen: number four (in the so-called Austin regional) Syracuse against number thirteen Vermont — a Friday game in Worcester, Massachusetts.

"Number thirteen!" Brennan screamed. "How in the world can we be a number thirteen?"

Easy. They weren't from a power conference. The basketball committee takes care of power teams first and foremost. Of course, Syracuse and Coach Jim Boeheim, certainly a power team from a power conference, weren't thrilled, either. "First of all, I knew they were good," Boeheim said later. "Second, playing in Worcester, I knew half the state would be there."

Brennan told his team that week that the days of going to the NCAA Tournament and making videos and soaking it in were over. This was the last chance for the five seniors and for him.

They would go down to Worcester to win. On Tuesday, Brennan had Boeheim on the radio show.

"I really like to look at tape right after a game," Boeheim said. "I can't sleep anyway, and that way you look at it while it's still fresh in your mind. How about you, T.B., do you do that?"

"Yeah, I look at tape after games sometimes," Brennan answered. "If there's tape of the game on in the bar where I'm drinking, I'll look at it."

As it turned out, Boeheim wasn't far wrong about half the state of Vermont showing up. Maybe it was two-thirds. A lot of people thought that Syracuse, which had closed the season hot, had a chance to get to St. Louis. The Orange never got out of Worcester. Jesse Agel, Brennan's longtime assistant coach, came up with a game plan that slowed the pace, taking advantage of the fact that Syracuse rarely attacks defensively out of its 2–3 zone defense. The game rocked back and forth through regulation and into overtime, with Worcester's DCU Center in an absolute uproar. With a little more than a minute left in overtime and Vermont clinging to a 56–55 lead, Sorrentine stood thirty feet from the basket, dribbling down the shot clock. Brennan waved him over near the bench and, over the din, yelled, "Run red, TJ!"

"Red" was an end-of-the-shot-clock play in which Sorrentine would try to penetrate, bringing the defense to him, and then slide the ball to Coppenrath. Sorrentine shook his head. "It's okay, Coach," he said. "I got it."

Even in what might have been the most tense moment of his coaching life, Brennan couldn't help but laugh. "Not the first time he's overruled me," he said later. "And with good reason, I might add."

Sorrentine waited until the shot clock was under ten seconds then shouted, "Run the play," for the benefit of the Syracuse defenders, who backpedaled just a tad, expecting Sorrentine to make some kind of move to the basket. Instead, he took one dribble and let fly from 27 feet. "I didn't realize I was that far out," he said later, smiling. "But when it left my hand it felt good."

It *was* good. And even though there was still work to do in the final minute, Sorrentine's shot was the dagger in Syracuse's heart. Gerry McNamara, who had made seven three-point shots in the national championship game as a freshman in 2003, missed the last shot, an off-balance three that went wide, and Vermont had pulled the upset, 60–57. It was one of those games and moments that bring people back to the NCAA Tournament year after year. For Vermont this was the national championship. Brennan had been wrong a year earlier: it *could* get better — and it had. "I just hope I can make it back here for the game Sunday," Brennan joked in the postgame bedlam. "I'm going to do some partying tonight." He shook his head in disbelief. "Never, never did I dream a moment like this." He stopped and pinched himself. "Just wanted to be sure I wasn't dreaming it now.

"Boy, would I love to be Coppenrath and Sorrentine right now. Young, single, and . . . them."

Within the hour, an equally stunning upset would take place in Indianapolis: Bucknell, another school that had never won an NCAA Tournament game, representing a league (the Patriot) that had never won an NCAA Tournament game, shocked third-seeded Kansas. Pat Flannery, the coach of the Bison, who had graduated from the school in 1980, had dealt with heart problems in 2004 and had been forced to leave the team for two games in 2005 because of stress. The victory over Kansas was his moment to pinch himself. There would be no parties for him in St. Louis (he wasn't retiring), but everywhere he turned there were congratulations. "It was as if everyone in my profession suddenly knew who I was," he said. "What a great feeling."

Both teams lost very respectably in the second round: Vermont to a Michigan State team that would make it to the Final Four; Bucknell to Wisconsin. Those games almost didn't matter. The Vermont and Bucknell teams of 2005 will gather for years to come to replay a memorable season — and one night each will remember forever.

"The best thing," Brennan said at his farewell, "is that so many people have enjoyed it. When we got home, it was as if everyone in the entire state couldn't stop smiling. There's this tremendous feeling of 'We really did something special,' and —"

He was interrupted by a loud voice calling his name. "Hey, Brennan!"

Stalking through the crowd came Roland Vincent Massimino, who knows something about improbable wins, having coached Villanova's miracle in 1985. The night before, Brennan and Sullivan and a number of Massimino's former assistants had stayed up late regaling one another with stories about the old days. This was Massimino's first Final Four since 1985. He had been through a lot since then: leaving Villanova in 1992 for Nevada–Las Vegas after alienating a lot of people at the school, being forced out at UNLV, and then going on to seven unsuccessful years at Cleveland State. He was seventy-two now, living in Florida again but — amazingly — planning to coach one more time. He had agreed to coach a start-up program at a tiny NAIA school in West Palm Beach. "My wife and I went to see some Division 2 games this season," Massimino said. "She says to me, 'Rollie, these teams aren't very good.' I said, 'Sweetheart, these guys are four levels up from where I'm about to coach.'"

Massimino is one of those people who needs to coach the way

most people need to breathe. He also needs to give people a hard time. It is his way. The night before, his ex-assistants had finally had a chance to get even. Sometime about two o'clock in the morning, Massimino had claimed he needed to go home, that he was tired. Jay Wright, who is now Villanova's head coach but, like Brennan and Sullivan, once suffered working for Massimino, stopped him. "You aren't going anywhere," he said. "You killed us for years. Tonight we get to kill you."

Massimino stayed. "You were such a pain to work for," Brennan told him. "You made us miserable."

"And how'd it work out?" Massimino shot back. "Did you become a pretty good coach or not?"

In a twist of fate, the stroke of midnight had marked exactly twenty years since the night that Massimino's Villanova team had stunned Georgetown, the seemingly unbeatable defending national champion, 66–64, in what is still considered the greatest championship game upset of all time — more remarkable even than NC State over Houston.

"Upset! Upset! I still get angry when I hear that," Massimino had said the night before. "We played 'em twice in the regular season and should have beaten 'em both times! If we hadn't won that game, I'd a killed my guys. They knew they could do it and they knew how to do it. That's why we did it."

Shooting a stunning 79 percent for the game — including 9 of 10 in the second half — didn't hurt, either. "Look at the shots we got," Massimino said. "We took shots we could make in our sleep all night."

Now, after all the battles and the controversy, Massimino had come home. Villanova, at Wright's behest, had thrown a twenty-year anniversary party for Massimino and the team in January and a banner honoring Massimino had been raised to the rafters in the Pavilion, Villanova's home court. Now he was finally back at the Final Four and loving every second of it. He thrashed his way through people and made it to Brennan, who assumed he had come to say good-bye and give him one more hug before leaving.

He was right . . . sort of. "CNN just called," he reported to Brennan. "They want me to come on in an hour."

"Okay, I understand," Brennan said. "It's great that you came. . . ."

Massimino was waving his arms to indicate that Brennan didn't understand what he was saying. "I need your tie," he said. "I can't go on TV without a tie. Gimme the tie."

Once an assistant, always an assistant. Brennan dutifully pulled the tie off and handed it to Massimino, who then rewarded him with a hug and a kiss on the cheek. "You know I love you," he said softly.

"I love you, too, Coach," Brennan said.

Massimino stalked away.

"I really like that tie," Brennan said. "And I'll never see it again."

It was dark by the time the party for Brennan began to break up. The city was now teeming with people. In addition to the teams, the coaches, and the media, fans had come pouring into downtown — all looking for a good time. Radio row at the coaches' hotel was chockablock with celebrities, some moving from one show to another — especially if they had something to promote. Dick Vitale had finished his on-air duties for the night and was at a corporate gig that featured a Dick Vitale sound-alike contest. In the coaches' lobby, one could see such current coaching stars as Jim Boeheim and Jim Calhoun talking to people while ex-stars like John Thompson, Jerry Tarkanian, and Lefty Driesell also made the rounds. Billy Tubbs, who had coached Oklahoma into the national championship game in 1988, wandered into the bar and spotted several old friends. Tubbs had retired from Oklahoma, then unretired to come back as athletic director at Lamar University and, a year earlier, had fired his coach — Mike Deane — and hired himself to replace Deane.

"I did a nationwide search for the best possible replacement," he said. "The search found me."

When Tubbs was coaching at Oklahoma, he was famous for two things: running up scores on weak teams and his absolute dead-on Jack Nicholson sound-alike voice. One year, after the Sooners had beaten a completely overmatched opponent by 90 points, someone asked Tubbs what he said to the other coach during the postgame handshake after a 90-point blowout. "I said, Can you come back next year?" Tubbs said.

Rarely did someone get in the last line on Tubbs. An exception was Rick Brewer, the longtime sports information director at North Carolina, who for many years was the moderator of the Final Four press conferences. In fact, Brewer was the last moderator to actually refer to the players as "players" rather than "student-athletes," as the NCAA handbook insists they be called. During the Sunday press conference in 1988 prior to the championship game between Kansas and Oklahoma, someone asked Tubbs if he thought perhaps God wanted Kansas to win the title, given that the Jayhawks had been a sixth seed in their bracket and were now in the final.

Sounding exactly like Nicholson, Tubbs said, "What number does God wear?"

Without missing a beat, Brewer said, "Twenty-three," cracking up everyone in the room — including Tubbs — because at that point in his career most people believed that Michael Jordan *was* God.

Brewer's exchanges with Duke coach Mike Krzyzewski in years that Duke made the Final Four were also frequently memorable.

"Coach, what do you like best about coaching at Duke?" someone once asked.

"Well, it *is* ten miles from the University of North Carolina," Brewer said, in his best nasal Dean Smith–like voice.

"And I like it there anyway," Krzyzewski said quickly.

Brewer, who most people believe was there when UNC first opened its doors in 1789, does an absolutely perfect imitation of Smith. Once, someone made the mistake of telling Smith just how good Brewer's imitation was. Surprised, even though his nasal Kansas twang has been mimicked throughout the ACC forever, Smith turned to Brewer and said, "Rick, do *you* do me?"

Flustered for once, Brewer finally threw up his hands and said, "Coach, *everybody* does you."

Another oft-imitated ex-coach was stalking the lobby late Friday evening, one of the easiest people to identify in all of sports: John Thompson, the Hall of Fame Georgetown coach turned radio talk show host. Thompson is six foot ten and must weigh 350 pounds. When he was coaching, he often said that he believed he intimidated people because "I'm big, I'm black, and I'm loud."

Make that very loud. Thompson became a coaching icon by taking a small Jesuit school from nowhere to the national championship. When he was hired in 1972 — he was a high school coach at the time — the university president, Reverend Robert Henle, told him that if he could take Georgetown to the NIT once every two or three years, everyone at the school would be very happy. In his third season Thompson and Georgetown reached the NCAA Tournament. In 1980 the Hoyas came within seconds of reaching the Final Four before losing to Iowa in the east regional final. A year later Patrick Ewing enrolled, and the Hoyas played in the national championship game three of his four years there.

But it was hardly seashells and balloons being around Georgetown's program. Thompson was, by his own admission, paranoid and secretive. His teams practiced behind doors chained shut to keep people out. When the team traveled, even the athletic director didn't know where it was staying. Thompson's very close relationship with Sonny Vaccaro, then the guru of Nike basketball, which paid the coach very big money, led to accusations that Vaccaro was funneling players to him. Thompson and Georgetown played a ludicrously easy nonconference schedule, except for the occasional game put on by Thompson's friend Russ Potts, a former athletic director turned promoter. To say there were whispers among coaches about exactly how Potts got Thompson to play some of those games is an understatement.

Thompson was frequently confrontational. When someone asked him at the 1982 Final Four how he felt about being the first African American to coach in the event, he went off. "I resent the hell out of that question," he said. "Because the implication is that I am the first black man capable of coaching a team to the Final Four, and that's far from the truth. I'm just the first one given the opportunity to do so."

That was the trouble with Thompson: on the one hand, he made you crazy with all his rules and his paranoia and his assistant coaches' prowling the locker room after games just in case someone asked a player a "nonbasketball question." He once complained to a reporter who had asked two players what they planned to do when they finished playing basketball. "Are you implying," he thundered, "that because they are black they won't know what to do when they aren't playing basketball anymore?"

On the other hand, he was as smart and as interesting as anyone in the game. His opinions were as big as he was, and when he chose to share them, not listening was a mistake. After Ewing graduated (and he did graduate), Georgetown continued to be very competitive, but not as good as with Ewing. The Hoyas made the round of eight in 1987, 1989, and 1996 but haven't made the Final Four since. Thompson was selected to coach the U.S. Olympic team in 1988 but did a poor job of picking players (too many defenders, not enough shooters), and when the United States lost to the Soviet Union in the semifinals and settled for a bronze medal, some of the spark went out of Thompson. He continued coaching until halfway through the season in 1999, when he abruptly resigned, talking about going through a divorce and being tired but never fully explaining his sudden departure. Longtime assistant coach Craig Esherick took over and the program nosedived, not even making it into the Big East Tournament in 2004. Two weeks after saying there was no way Esherick would be fired, the president of Georgetown fired him, eventually hiring Thompson's son John Thompson III to try to bring the program back to the kind of glory days it had seen under his father.

In the meantime, Thompson was reborn as a radio talk show host in Washington. Because of who he was (he had been elected to the Hall of Fame in 1998), he could get almost anyone in sports on his show. Those who knew him could see the changes in him. Old enemies became friends. Thompson and Morgan Wootten, the great high school coach, whom Thompson hadn't spoken to for more than twenty years, dating to his days in the high school ranks, became almost cuddly when talking to each other on the air.

"The media exaggerated the hell out of our rivalry, didn't they, Morgan?" Thompson would say.

"Boy, they sure did, John."

Once, when asked why he had never recruited any of the great players Wootten had at DeMatha, Thompson said: "There are some people on earth you can live apart from."

Thompson readily admitted that being out of coaching had changed his outlook on life and on people. "It's almost as if you spent your whole life working in a flower garden but never noticed there were any flowers," he said. "I know how corny that sounds, but it's true. When I was coaching, it was all about the competition, about trying to win, about trying to get an edge and making sure no one got an edge on you. I *was* paranoid — except when there were people who were actually out to get me.

"When I first got the Georgetown job, I was obsessed with knocking down barriers. When Father Henle told me the NIT was fine, part of me understood that, because when I was at Providence in the sixties, the NIT was still a big deal. Twice we turned down the NCAA to go to the NIT. But that was a different time. I told Father Henle if the NCAA was the place to be, that was where we would be. When I first started coming to the Final Four in the seventies, I often thought about wanting to coach in it, but back then I was still learning. I can remember sitting in the lobby and listening to Big House Gaines [the legendary coach at Winston-Salem State] telling stories, and feeling as if I was in a life seminar. Now I sit with him and I see these young coaches walk by without even noticing him, and I want to grab them and say, 'Boy, do you know who this is? Do you know this is a Hall of Fame coach?'

"I remember when we got to New Orleans in '82, being shocked when I walked out on the court for Friday practice. I was used to closed practice, I mean no one in the gym. Now there are people roaring and yelling and screaming. It helped me understand the significance of the event and the moment. But that didn't mean I had time to sit around and think about it or talk about it. And then I had these people running at me, telling me to go to meetings and wear pins and the like. I did not deal with that well."

The '82 championship game between North Carolina and Georgetown is one of the most remembered games ever played: it was Dean Smith, still seeking his first championship, taking on his star pupil, Thompson. The two men had become friends when Thompson was a high school coach, and Thompson had been an assistant coach for Smith during the 1976 Olympics. Now Thompson and his team, led by Ewing, were the last roadblock between Smith and a championship.

"I remember not wanting to let myself get caught up in the friendship during the game," Thompson said. "I didn't want to look down at him. Early in the game, Patrick went to the foul line and I heard Dean saying to the referee, 'Now, it's okay with me if he goes over ten seconds. You don't have to call that.' I felt better when I heard that because I thought, 'Okay, he's playing one of his mind games, that means he wants to kick my butt, so it's okay for me to try to kick his.'"

Ewing was a notoriously deliberate free throw shooter, frequently timed by observers as going well over the ten-second time limit. No one in basketball can ever remember a ten-second violation being called on a free throw shooter. It was never called on Ewing. Thompson recognized his mentor's putting the thought into the heads of the officials early, and it helped him forget friendship until the game was over.

That game ended famously: Michael Jordan making the winning jump shot that announced his arrival as a superstar and Georgetown's Fred Brown getting confused on the ensuing possession and throwing the ball directly to North Carolina's James Worthy to deny the Hoyas a chance to win the game. Thompson hugged and consoled Brown on the court when it was over, and he was put on a pedestal by many for reacting that way — a pedestal he still laughs about.

"I'm glad I did what I did," he said. "But I could just as easily have said, 'Fred, what the f—— were you thinking about out there,' and it would not have changed one bit the way I felt about Fred or the way he felt about me. God knows I've jumped players for mistakes. As it was, something inside me told me there was no sense jumping him, because the game was over, the season was over. So I consoled him — as I probably would have done in the locker room later if I had jumped him. That's the way coaching is. What I did was not a great act of humanitarianism, the way it has been made out to be. It was an instinctive coaching act that could easily have been different."

Georgetown won the national championship two years later, and Brown was the first player to come to the bench to hug Thompson when the victory over Houston was assured. As disappointing as the loss to Villanova was a year later, Thompson felt a sense of completion after the '84 title. "I wanted to prove I could do it," he said. "I wanted to prove *we* [African Americans] could do it. Once that barrier was down, the hunger was still there, but it wasn't quite the same.

"Now, not coaching, I'm completely different. I see more things and enjoy more things. I can be relaxed around people. I like going to games now and talking to people, old friends and even old enemies. I like being here [at the Final Four] because I still like the games and I like seeing my friends, especially now, because I have a lot more of them than when I was coaching."

As Thompson spoke, Gene Keady walked by. He had just completed his twenty-fifth — and final — season at Purdue, the school more or less forcing him into retirement when his once-proud program slipped. Keady had been a remarkably consistent winner at Purdue and had twice taken teams to the final eight. But he never reached the Final Four, a fact that will probably keep him out of the Hall of Fame. Thompson and Keady exchanged warm greetings and small talk before Keady moved on.

"I feel a certain emptiness when I see Gene," Thompson said softly. "The man is a much better coach than a lot of guys who have been to the Final Four or even won national championships. But the way our profession works, they judge you on things like that. It's not fair, but it's a fact of the lives we've chosen to lead."

Just outside the entrance to the hotel sat another coach who had been close to the Final Four on multiple occasions without ever getting to coach on the last weekend: Lefty Driesell. Driesell reached the round of eight four times — twice at Davidson — and then twice more at Maryland. Driesell coached four places during a forty-year college coaching career: Davidson, Maryland, James Madison, and Georgia State. In all four places he inherited floundering programs and took them to heights they had never been to before. He is one of only four men in history (Eddie Sutton, Jim Harrick, and Rick Pitino are the others) to coach four different schools into the NCAA Tournament. In all, he won 786 games before retiring at midseason — much like Thompson — in 2003 because, at seventy-one, he felt burned out.

Now, at seventy-three, he looked ready to coach again as he smoked a cigar just outside the hotel entrance while passersby stopped to shake his hand and tell him how much they missed seeing him on the sidelines. "Someone offers me a million dollars, I'll come back," he said. "But I ain't taking any job where I have to go stay in motels by the side of the road in the middle of nowhere. I'm done with that."

Driesell is honest enough to admit it bothers him that he's not in the Hall of Fame. "Last time I was on the ballot, they didn't even have my résumé right," he said. "They left Georgia State off it completely. You think that makes me feel good about my chances?"

Driesell belongs in the Hall of Fame even though he didn't reach the Final Four. There is recent precedent: Temple coach John Chaney was elected because he had a superb record even without a Final Four trip and because there was a sense that his contributions to the game went beyond wins and losses.

The same is true of Driesell. He helped make the ACC in the 1970s by building a program at Maryland that made the league relevant outside the state of North Carolina. He was involved in some of the great games in the history of the sport, most notably the classic 1974 ACC Tournament final against North Carolina State. Maryland was led by Tom McMillen, Len Elmore, and John Lucas; State by the incomparable David Thompson, seven-foot-four Tom Burleson, and five-six Monty Towe. With no shot clock and no three-point shot, the game was tied at 86 at the end of regulation. State finally won, 103–100, in overtime and Lucas sat on the scorer's table and cried during the awards ceremony after missing a late free throw. That scene caused the ACC to excuse the runner-up from future awards ceremonies, a wise move later copied by the NCAA.

After the game Driesell walked out of the Greensboro Coliseum and climbed onto the State bus just before it pulled out. "I just wanna tell y'all I'm proud of you," he said. "I have a great team and they played great and you guys beat us. Now you *better* go out and win the national championship."

State coach Norman Sloan said years later that Driesell's getting on the bus might have been the classiest move he ever witnessed as a coach. The Wolfpack did win the title that year, upsetting UCLA and Bill Walton in the national semifinals in double overtime.

Sadly, Driesell left Maryland under a cloud in 1986, forced out in the wake of the cocaine-induced death of Len Bias, who died the morning after he was chosen by the Boston Celtics with the second pick in the NBA draft. It took Maryland years to recover from the Bias tragedy, and Driesell's career was never the same, even though he coached successfully at James Madison and Georgia State. In 2001 he put together a team at Georgia State, a commuter school in downtown Atlanta, that won thirty games, including an upset of Wisconsin in the first round of the NCAA Tournament. When someone asked him after the game about coaching at a "mid-major" school, his answer was classic Driesell: "Mid-major?" he repeated. "I ain't never been mid anything. Ask Wisconsin if we're a mid-major."

That was his last hurrah. Georgia State lost in the second round to his old school, Maryland, and hasn't been back on the national map since. Driesell has been a Hall of Fame finalist but still isn't in, despite all the victories at all the different places and all the color he brought to the game. There will always be people who will blame him for Bias's death and people who won't let him forget the famous "UCLA of the East" line he delivered in 1969 when he was introduced as Maryland's new coach.

"We will be the UCLA of the East," he declared, thus setting the bar impossibly high for himself and his program. Maryland had great success in Driesell's seventeen seasons there, but no one was going to come close to matching Wooden, ever. The line was hung around Driesell's neck like an albatross every time the Terrapins lost in March, as they inevitably did. Driesell, with his country Virginia accent, inspired love in some and ridicule in others. He was as entertaining as anyone in the game, never afraid to speak his mind to anyone at any time.

In 1982, after his Maryland team had lost four starters — including Buck Williams and Albert King, both taken in the top ten picks in the NBA draft — he took a young team into North Carolina to play the Tar Heels, who were led by James Worthy, Sam Perkins, and a freshman named Michael Jordan. To make the situation even more impossible, Driesell's best player, center Charles Pittman, was injured. "If I was smart like Dean, I'd tell y'all we ain't got no chance," Driesell said the day before the game. "But I ain't that smart. I think we're going to go in there and whip 'em."

Remarkably, they almost did, losing in the final minute when Worthy stole the ball from point guard Reggie Jackson with Maryland leading by one and trying to kill the clock. When Dean Smith was asked how a depleted Maryland team could walk into Chapel Hill and come within seconds of a stunning upset, he shrugged and said, "You can always play one great game without a key player."

Smith has made this comment thousands of times, about both his team and opponents. He believes a team will rise to the occasion for one game after a critical injury. But when the comment was repeated to Driesell, he took it as an insult, that Smith was refusing to give his team credit for a gutsy effort. "Dean's got

Perkins, Jordan, and Worthy," he said. "I got a bunch of freshmen and I come in here and almost whip him, and that's all he can say? That ain't right."

At season's end, Maryland had struggled to get into the NIT; North Carolina had won the national championship. That spring, at the ACC meetings, Smith showed up for the coaches meeting with newspaper clippings from the Maryland game in Chapel Hill. Highlighted in yellow were Driesell's comments. "Lefty, I'm very disappointed you would say all this . . . ," Smith began.

Driesell exploded, telling Smith he had a lot of nerve complaining about something like that when he had just won the national title and he (Driesell) had been through an awful season. Still angry, Driesell wrote Smith a note when he returned home, telling him he would not shake hands with him — win or lose — after they played the following season. Smith, every bit as stubborn as Driesell, wrote back that he would always shake hands with an opposing coach following a game.

Naturally, the game in Chapel Hill the next year went to the final play. In an absolutely brilliant coaching move, Driesell put his son, Chuck, a little-used benchwarmer, in the game at the finish and called a play for him rather than for leading scorer Adrian Branch or Bias, then a freshman. The play worked perfectly. Chuck Driesell was wide-open under the basket. No mortal on the court had any chance to get near him before he laid the ball in for the winning basket. Unfortunately for Maryland, Carolina was playing four mortals and Michael Jordan. From the top of the key, Jordan flew in behind Driesell and deflected the ball away at the last possible second as the buzzer sounded.

The Carolina players sprinted off the court. Driesell sprinted after the officials, demanding a call: a foul, goaltending, ball out-of-bounds to Maryland — *something*. Smith sprinted after Driesell to shake his hand. When Driesell turned and saw Smith coming at him, hand extended, he didn't see good sportsmanship; he saw taunting. He slapped at Smith's extended hand. A step behind Smith, his longtime lieutenant and close friend Bill Guthridge saw Driesell swing his hand at Smith's hand and lost *his* temper. He put his head down and rushed at Driesell. Behind Driesell, one of his assistants, Mel Cartwright, saw Guthridge coming and turned to pick up a chair.

The only reason there wasn't a full-scale riot was that Rick Brewer, UNC's sports information director, tackled Guthridge before he could get to Driesell, wrestling him away long enough to allow others to intervene. Who knows what would have happened if Brewer hadn't stepped in.

Now, twenty-two years later, it is all different. Smith has spoken up on Driesell's behalf to try to get him into the Hall of Fame. Guthridge, who succeeded Smith as Carolina's coach in 1997, talks fondly about the good old days when Lefty was at Maryland. All three will tell you with absolute straight faces that their rivalry was largely a media creation. However, in 2001, after his thirty-win season at Georgia State, a friend suggested to Driesell in the coaches' lobby at the Final Four that he might surpass Smith as the all-time winningest coach if he could hang on for about four more seasons.

"Never happen," Driesell said.

"Why not?"

"'Cause if I ever got close, Dean would come back."

7

March to the Arch

THE FOUR TEAMS WHO MADE IT to St. Louis in 2005 had varied Final Four histories, ranging from North Carolina's three national championships to Illinois's zero, without so much as an appearance in the championship game. The Illini had reached the Final Four in 1989 under Coach Lou Henson, only to lose on a basket just before the buzzer to fellow Big Ten school Michigan, which went on to win the title on Monday. Not long after that trip to the last weekend, the Illini found themselves under investigation by the NCAA.

The other three schools had more memories and happier ones. North Carolina was in its fifteenth Final Four. It had won the national championship in 1957 under Frank McGuire and in 1982 and 1993 under Dean Smith. The Tar Heels had been in the Final Four four times since that third championship but hadn't advanced beyond Saturday. Carolina had been in three of the most memorable championship games ever played: in '57 they had beaten Kansas and Wilt Chamberlain in triple over-time; in '82 Michael Jordan had hit what proved to be the winning shot against Georgetown; and in '93 Michigan had been denied a chance to tie the game in the final seconds when Chris Webber called a time-out his team didn't have.

Michigan State, Carolina's opponent in the second of Saturday's semifinals, had won two national championships. The first, in 1979, had been the Magic vs. Larry game — the highest-rated game in the television history of the tournament, even if Billy Packer insists that the game wasn't any good. The second had come in 2000 in the middle of a three-year run when Coach Tom Izzo took the Spartans to the Final Four three straight times: losing to Duke in the '99 semifinals, beating Wisconsin and Florida for the title in 2000, losing to Arizona in the semis a year later. The Spartans were now back, having come through the Austin regional as a fifth seed by upsetting Duke in the regional semis, then beating Kentucky in an extraordinary double-overtime game in the final.

Finally there was Louisville. The Cardinals also had plenty of Final Four history. Between 1972 and 1986 they had reached it six times under Denny Crum, winning titles in 1980 and 1986. But they had not been back since their 1986 victory, even though the MOP of that Final Four had been Pervis Ellison, then a freshman. The Cardinals didn't even make the tournament a year later and had been deep into the event only once in the ensuing eighteen seasons, in 1997, when they were crushed by North Carolina in the east regional final. Crum, in spite of his Hall of Fame credentials, had been more or less forced into retirement after the 2001 season, and the school had ardently and successfully pursued Rick Pitino as their coach.

This was an interesting choice, given that Pitino had been the King of Kentucky from 1989 to 1997, rebuilding the tarnished University of Kentucky program after an NCAA investigation and probation to regain the status that most Kentucky fans considered a birthright: perennial national contender. The Wildcats had reached at least the round of eight in five of Pitino's last six seasons, had gone to three Final Fours and two title games, and had been national champions in 1996. Pitino left in 1997 after his team lost a classic national championship game to Arizona in overtime, lured by money ($10 million a year) and absolute power to take over the Boston Celtics.

When Pitino took over the Celtics, it looked as if the team would end up with the number one pick in that year's NBA draft, and everyone knew that pick would be Tim Duncan, the precocious six-foot-ten Wake Forest center. Except that the Celtics, even with the most Ping-Pong balls in the lottery, didn't get the number one pick, the San Antonio Spurs did. Things might have been different if the Ping-Pong balls had bounced differently, but Pitino ended up failing miserably in Boston, making one personnel mistake after another. That failure did not taint him as a college coach, however, and when he resigned from the Celtics early in 2001, it seemed as if half the colleges in the country were lined up to hire him.

Pitino finally chose Louisville, a decision that sent shock waves through the state of Kentucky. UK fans had been willing to forgive Pitino for leaving for the Celtics. After all, the nomadic coach — he had gone from Boston University to the New York Knicks [as an assistant] to Providence College to the Knicks as head coach and then to Kentucky, all in a ten-year stretch — had stayed at Kentucky for eight seasons and brought glory back to the school. Leaving for the NBA was forgivable. But coaching another college? No, unacceptable. And coaching at Louisville, the in-state archrival of the Wildcats? Pitino became Judas and Benedict Arnold rolled into one.

That didn't really bother Pitino. He was coaching at a place with basketball history, knowing he would be able to recruit good players and rebuild the program. Within two years the Cardinals were back in the top twenty-five in the polls and back in the NCAA Tournament. But even with high-seeded teams, they had not advanced beyond the second round. The 2005 team appeared to be Pitino's best, led by Francisco Garcia and Taquan Dean, both outstanding shooters. What's more, Garcia was a superb lock-up defender. Louisville finished the regular season on a roll, and some thought they might be a number one seed. The committee somehow made them a number four seed but helped them out by placing them in the same regional with the weakest of the number one seeds — Washington. Louisville beat Washington easily in the round of sixteen, then produced a memorable comeback against West Virginia, which had gone from not in the field going into the Big East Tournament to upsets of Wake Forest (in double overtime) and Texas Tech to reach the final of the Albuquerque regional. Louisville overcame a superb shooting performance by the Mountaineers to win in overtime, meaning Pitino had coached three different schools (Providence, Kentucky, and Louisville) to the Final Four — the first coach in history to do so.

Clearly, Pitino was a coach headed for the Hall of Fame. In fact, the case could easily be made that three of the four coaches in St. Louis — Pitino, Izzo, and Roy Williams — already had Hall of Fame credentials. They had been to a combined fourteen Final Fours and five championship games, and Pitino and Izzo each had a national title. Bruce Weber had been at Illinois for only two years. And yet, to many, his team was the favorite. The Illini bused into St. Louis under cover of darkness late Wednesday night.

As the bus made its way from Champaign-Urbana across Illinois, fans were everywhere — standing by the side of the road, hanging good-luck signs from overpasses, waving at the players as the bus whizzed by them. Even when a drenching thunderstorm hit the middle of the state, people stood outside to watch the bus go by. No one had enjoyed a more remarkable season than the Illini. When Weber had been hired two years earlier to replace Bill Self after Self left for Kansas, many Illinois fans were skeptical about the hire. Weber had been a longtime assistant to Gene Keady at Purdue and had not gotten his first chance to be a head coach until he was forty-two years old. He had been very successful in four years at Southern Illinois, but there was a tendency among fans of the giant state school to look down at Southern Illinois as if it were a minor league franchise of some kind. Even though Weber took the Salukis to the Sweet Sixteen in 2002, people wondered why the school hadn't hired a "big time" coach to replace Self.

The first season hadn't been easy. At one point Weber showed up for a game dressed in black because he wanted people to understand that Self was "dead and gone" at Illinois. The team came together late in the season and made it to the Sweet Sixteen before losing to Duke. With four starters back, the following season began with high hopes, especially because there appeared to be a route to the Final Four that wouldn't involve getting on a single airplane if the Illini could be a high seed: first weekend in Indianapolis, second in Chicago, and then the Final Four in St. Louis, about a three-hour drive from campus.

"The phrase 'March to the Arch' [the official motto of the St. Louis organizing committee] has been stuck in my head all season," Weber said.

Illinois lost only once in the regular season, on a buzzer-beating three-point shot at Ohio State in the regular-season finale. That loss comforted Bob Knight and the members of the 1976 Indiana team, since no one has gone undefeated since Indiana in 1976. Indiana coaches, players, and fans everywhere take great pride in that fact. In 1991 Nevada–Las Vegas made it to the Final Four with a record of 34–0. When the Rebels, the defending champions, were upset in the semifinals by Duke, Quinn Buckner, who had been Indiana's captain in 1976, went on a local TV show and said gleefully, "There's a lot of teams that have won one title in a row. Not a lot of them have gone undefeated, though, have they?"

If Illinois had been the team to match Indiana's feat, it would have been especially painful for Knight and Indiana fans. Not only were the two teams from the same conference, not only did the two states border each other, but Knight and Illinois coach Lou Henson had feuded openly throughout the 1980s. Knight had done everything but come out and publicly accuse Henson of being a cheat (he whispered it to anyone who would listen), and Henson had called Knight a bully. There had been games that had ended without handshakes, and Knight had once famously said that he didn't believe Henson could "coach lions to eat red meat." Knight was among those Illinois people held responsible for the investigation that had landed Illinois on probation in the early 1990s. Knight had no problem with their thinking that.

Illinois wasn't going to go undefeated. In his coaching exile in Lubbock, Texas, Knight no doubt raised a glass of sangria in tribute to Ohio State — his alma mater — on the night the Buckeyes beat the Illini. Illinois had gone on to win the Big Ten Tournament and three NCAA games before running into a buzz saw in a hot Arizona team in the regional final in Chicago, which was, for all intents and purposes, an Illinois home game. Arizona appeared completely unbothered by the thousands in blue and orange for thirty-six minutes, leading by 15 points with four minutes to play. It looked as if the "March to the Arch" was going to end one step shy of the goal. Somehow Illinois rallied, burying numerous three-point shots, while Arizona completely lost its composure. Illinois outscored Arizona 20–5 in those frantic final minutes. The miracle comeback completely convinced Illinois fans that theirs was a team of destiny — that this was, at least, their year.

Of course, every year all four teams arrive at the Final Four convinced they are that year's team of destiny. All of them have won at least four games in a row and, almost always, all have had a narrow escape along the way. North Carolina had needed a fortuitous call in the final minute against Villanova to ensure its victory in the Sweet Sixteen and had gone to the final minute before escaping a hard-nosed Wisconsin team. Michigan State had blown a lead against Kentucky, the game being tied by a miracle three-pointer just before the buzzer that required close to ten minutes for TV replay to confirm it was good, and then had come from behind to win in double overtime. And Louisville had been down 22 in the first half against West Virginia before it had rallied to win in overtime.

Four teams marched to the Arch convinced they were going to march out with the trophy in their hands. Only one of them could be right.

Through the years, the Final Four has become a gathering place not just for coaches but for players, many of whom have left the basketball world to go on to other things. But they still love the game and the feeling of the event they played in when they were young and convinced they would play forever.

Among the ex-players making the trip to St. Louis, perhaps no one was happier to see his alma mater reach the final weekend again than Terry Howard. "I've lived in Louisville my whole life," he said. "Grew up more of a UK [Kentucky] fan because my mom and dad were UK fans, but I always liked Louisville. I've had two [of five] children go to Louisville and, of course, it's my school. The only thing better for me than having Louisville in the Final Four would be to have Louisville and UK both there."

That had almost happened in 2005, Kentucky losing in double overtime in the regional final to Michigan State. The only time it actually happened was in 1975, Terry Howard's senior year at Louisville. Howard had been a star as a high school senior, a sweet-shooting point guard with the kind of quickness with the ball that brought recruiters running. "Pretty much every basketball school in the country offered me a scholarship," Howard said. "Except for UCLA. Coach Wooden said I could come as a freshman and walk on and then he'd find me a scholarship as a sophomore. I really didn't want to do that."

Howard eventually narrowed his list to Kansas, Alabama, Maryland, Kentucky, and Louisville. He was tempted by Maryland coach Lefty Driesell because he liked the idea of being part of "the UCLA of the East." He also liked Alabama coach C. M. Newton a lot. And, as one might expect, he was in awe of Kentucky coach Adolph Rupp. "For a long time I thought that I would go to Kentucky," he said. "I even made a verbal commitment to Coach Rupp on the telephone. But I couldn't really get away from Pete Maravich. He was my hero. I wanted to be like him. I didn't think I'd be able to do that at Kentucky."

Maravich was a senior at LSU in 1970, the same year that

Howard was a senior at Westport High School. Maravich had become a legend playing for his father, averaging an astounding 44 points a game, racing down the court on every possession, long floppy hair flying, socks drooping, and either shooting the ball or making some kind of spectacular pass — frequently behind his back or between his legs. "I just loved watching Pete play," Howard said. "Anytime they played anywhere close to us, we went to see them. I liked putting the ball behind my back and between my legs. I had a feeling Coach Rupp wouldn't approve of that sort of thing."

There was another factor: race. "The Southeastern Conference was still, for the most part, all-white," Howard said. "My senior year I think there was one black playing in the league, Wendell Hudson at Alabama. I spent my summers playing over at Shawnee High School against all the black kids in town. I was friends with a lot of them and I enjoyed the style of play — up and down — a lot more than the SEC, which was walk-it-up basketball most of the time. I knew Coach Rupp had started to recruit blacks because I played against Tom Payne [Rupp's first black recruit] and he was a year ahead of me in high school. But Louisville had black players and it was in the Missouri Valley Conference, which was far more integrated. I thought I would enjoy that style of play a lot more."

When Howard called Rupp and his top assistant, Joe B. Hall, to tell them he had changed his mind and was going to go to Louisville, they were stunned. "They just couldn't understand the idea of going to U of L over UK," he said. "I could see why they felt that way."

Freshmen weren't eligible to play on the varsity in the fall of 1970, so Howard played on the freshman team. At the end of that season, Louisville hired Denny Crum, who had been

Wooden's top assistant at UCLA, to take over the program. Howard went into his sophomore season expecting big things — the Cardinals were a talented, veteran team — but never got to play because he came down with viral meningitis. Louisville ended up in the Final Four that year, playing (and losing to) UCLA in Los Angeles. Howard didn't even get to make the trip because he was hit with appendicitis on the day the team left.

It was all different the next year. He was healthy and started as a redshirt sophomore along with three other sophomores and a junior. "We were young, but we were talented," he said. "We kept getting better as the season went on."

Early in that season Louisville played in the Rainbow Classic in Hawaii. The Cardinals reached the final and played North Carolina. Late in a close game, Dean Smith went to his four-corner offense, spreading the floor and letting guards George Karl and Steve Previs handle the ball, running the clock down (there was no shot clock) and either getting fouled or getting an open layup on seemingly every possession.

"We got home and put in the four corners the first day we were back," Howard remembered. "I was the point guard and I was our best foul shooter. That meant the last few minutes of the game, the ball was going to be in my hands. I loved it."

Louisville was an NIT team in 1973 (there were still only twenty-five NCAA bids back then) and reached the round of sixteen in 1974. At the start of the '74–'75 season, *Sports Illustrated* picked the Cardinals number one because they were both experienced and deep. The only problem for Howard was that he had become part of the team's depth — going from two-year starter to the bench. "Denny always believed that if two guys were close, he played the younger guy," Howard said. "Phil Bond was a sophomore and he was very good. Denny came to me before the season and told me I was still going to get my minutes and I would be in at the end of the game and that it really didn't matter. But it did matter. I'd been a starter for two years, it was my last year — I wanted to start. But I certainly couldn't argue with the results."

Howard remains close to Crum thirty years later. His oldest son, Todd, played for Crum before hurting his knee and is now the top assistant coach at IUPUI, the city school in Indianapolis cosponsored by Indiana and Purdue. "I loved playing for Denny," he said. "He was amazing. He never used [profane] language even in the heat of the battle and I never saw him anything but cool at the end of a tight game. I remember he liked to say, 'Fellas, if you do this, I can't guarantee we'll win, but if you *don't* do it, I guarantee you we won't win.'"

Howard shook off the disappointment of not starting and became an invaluable third guard, taking over the offense and the basketball whenever a game was close in the final minutes. The reason was simple: he never missed a free throw. "I wanted the ball at the end and I wanted people to foul me," he said. "Denny had a thing where we all had to make ten free throws in a row at the end of practice before we'd leave. Sometimes I'd shoot them left-handed because I knew I wasn't going to miss with either hand. Almost every free throw I shot that year was at the end of a close game when I knew I had to make the shot for us to win.'"

Louisville rolled through the NCAA Tournament that year, reaching the midwest regional final against Maryland. That Maryland team may have been Lefty Driesell's best: it had dominated the ACC during the regular season and was led by John Lucas, who would be the first pick in the NBA draft a year later, and stars Brad Davis, Steve Sheppard, and Mo Howard. Louisville crushed the Terrapins, 96–82, leading from start to finish. "We were primed for that game because we knew how good Maryland was," Howard said. "I was ready for it because Lefty had recruited me and, even though I liked him, I wanted to beat him. Of course, I didn't have to make any crucial free throws because there weren't any to make at the end of the game."

The victory put Louisville into the Final Four, played in San Diego that year. The Cardinals would play UCLA — the team they had lost to in 1972 — while Syracuse played Kentucky in the other game. "Having UK there made it all the better, especially since we had never gotten to play against them. We were convinced that we were going to play them in the final."

Rupp had refused to schedule Louisville. Joe B. Hall, who succeeded him in 1973, had followed his lead. It was not until 1983, when the Kentucky state legislature voted to require the two schools to play each other, that they began playing annually during the regular season. As luck would have it, the teams met in the NCAA Tournament in the spring of 1983, with Louisville winning the game in overtime. This was ten years earlier, and the Cardinals wanted to play Kentucky almost as much as they wanted to beat UCLA.

"We were convinced we would beat UCLA," Howard said. "We thought we were better than they were."

UCLA had finally had its seven-year string of titles ended in 1974 when North Carolina State, led by David Thompson, beat the Bruins in the semifinals, aided by the fact that the Final Four that year was in Greensboro, about sixty miles from N.C. State's campus. Bill Walton had graduated, and even though UCLA was back in the Final Four, led by Richard Washington, David Meyers, and Marques Johnson, the Bruins didn't carry the aura they had in the past.

Both Kentucky and Louisville flew to San Diego a day earlier than usual back then (Wednesday) in order to get acclimated to the time change. Both coaches asked the NCAA to find a place to practice on Thursday since the San Diego Sports Arena, the Final Four site, wasn't available until Friday. "We showed up Thursday afternoon to practice at some high school, and as we're getting off the bus, we see another bus pull up," Howard said. "It was Kentucky. Somehow, the NCAA people had gotten confused and thought we were Kentucky, or Kentucky was Louisville. Anyway, they'd booked us both for the same place at the same time. They didn't realize we were two different teams."

One can only imagine if two teams, not to mention archrivals, ever had the same thing occur today at a Final Four. Imagine Mike Krzyzewski and Roy Williams getting off their buses and seeing each other. Or Jim Calhoun and Gary Williams. Blood might be spilled. In 1975 Joe Hall and Denny Crum flipped a coin. Kentucky won the toss and practiced first while Louisville sat around and watched. "Yup, we watched," Howard said. "And when they were done, their coaches stayed and watched us. I guess you could say it was a different time."

On Saturday, Kentucky beat Syracuse easily in the first game. Then UCLA and Louisville played what those who were there remember as one of the great NCAA Tournament games ever played. It was back and forth the entire afternoon. They ended up in overtime. As always, Howard was in for the endgame, handling the ball for the Cardinals. With the clock under thirty seconds in overtime, Louisville led by one and the ball was in Howard's hands. "For some reason, as loud as it was, I could hear Coach Wooden yelling at his players, 'Don't foul Howard! Don't foul Howard!' He was actually up off the bench because he didn't want them to foul me."

But with the clock winding down and Howard not wanting to relinquish the ball, UCLA finally fouled. There were twenty seconds left. Howard looked over and saw Wooden clap his free hand against the ever-present rolled-up program he held in his left hand. "I was completely confident," Howard said. "This is what I did."

At that moment, Howard had attempted 28 free throws during the season and had made all 28. It was a one-and-one, meaning he had to make the first shot to get the second. The three-point shot was still twelve years away from being voted into existence, so if Howard made both shots, UCLA would need to score twice: one possession would not be enough. "It didn't feel any different than any other free throw I'd shot all season," Howard said. "I remember walking to the line. Pete Trgovich was to my right. Marques Johnson or Richard Washington walked past me and said something about not making it, but I'd heard that a million times; it was standard stuff.

"The one thing that surprised me was that Coach Wooden didn't call time-out to try to freeze me. I thought he would. Maybe he outthought me by not calling it because, to be honest, I was expecting it. But I went up there and did everything exactly the way I always did. The shot felt good out of my hand. Nothing felt different."

But the shot was different: it spun out of the basket. Teammates later told Howard that they thought the ball had actually gone into the basket before it popped out. "I've never watched it," Howard admitted. "It comes on just about every year, Final Four time; someone shows it as one of the great games, but I've never sat down and watched it. Doubt if I ever will."

Of course, the game wasn't over at that point. In fact, Louisville still led by one. UCLA came down the court and ran the clock down, and Washington hit a difficult 10-foot baseline jumper with three seconds to go. That was the ball game. Howard doesn't remember very much about the immediate aftermath. "I just remember the locker room was very quiet," he said. "There just wasn't much for anyone to say. My wife [Rhonda] was eight months pregnant with our second son at the time, so we just went out to eat. We saw a lot of Kentucky fans in the restaurant. To tell you the truth, they couldn't have been nicer. When we got back to the room, there were a lot of messages. I remember C. M. Newton had called, and some of the folks from NBC had called, too. The messages were the same: keep your head up, you had a great career — that kind of thing.

"I think that was the hardest part, knowing I wouldn't get another chance."

Louisville did have one game left to play — the consolation game against Syracuse. "We had a shootaround on Sunday and I just felt like I had to make some free throws," Howard said. "I made eighty-seven straight. Of course, the next night we won pretty easily and I didn't have to shoot any. The last free throw of my career was a miss."

Howard still has a box full of letters that he received after the game. Virtually all of them were encouraging. The one that meant the most to him came from John Wooden. "He reminded me that he always said that a game isn't decided by one player or one play," he said. "It was our team that was in a position to win and our team that lost. Richard Washington had to hit a tough shot to beat us. It was great of him to write."

He paused. "I still wish I'd made the shot."

Howard had a brief fling as a pro. He actually got to go to training camp with his hero, Pete Maravich, because he was signed as a free agent by the New Orleans Jazz. He played in two exhibition games with the Jazz, got cut, had a quick shot in Philadelphia — "Two days," he said — and then played in South America before going to work, first in real estate, then in sporting goods, and now back in real estate development.

"I can honestly tell you there's not a day that goes by that the free throw doesn't come up in some way," he said. "I was in a meeting today and someone mentioned I had played at Louisville. The guy we were meeting with looked at me and said, 'You aren't the guy who . . . ?'

"I said, 'Missed the free throw against UCLA. Yup, that was me.' It's the easiest way to handle it. That way, people don't feel awkward. Sometimes they'll just say, 'You played in the Final Four, right?' And I just nod and say I was on the '75 team. If they ask me more, I tell them.

"I've never gotten to the point where I can't talk about it or won't talk about it. I understand why people bring it up. I'm honored to have played on that team and in that game and to think that Denny wanted me to have the ball in that situation. Sometimes it's tough. I've seen it listed among the ten worst moments in Final Four history. A couple of years ago someone did a story on Gary Anderson, the kicker up in Minnesota, and me, because he had missed a field goal in the conference championship game after not missing all season. They called them the two most surprising misses in history or something."

Anderson's kick came in 1999 with the Vikings leading the Atlanta Falcons, 17–10, and less than two minutes to play. It was a relatively easy kick, 37 yards, and Anderson hadn't missed all year. But he missed the kick. The Falcons drove the length of the field for a tying touchdown and won in overtime to go to the Super Bowl. There was a difference between Anderson and Howard: Anderson got to kick again. He kicked in the NFL for four more years and, in his final season at the age of forty-four, kicked a game-winning 46-yard field goal for the Tennessee Titans in the final seconds of a playoff game against the Baltimore Ravens.

Not surprisingly, Howard identifies with others who have had inglorious Final Four moments: Georgetown's Fred Brown; Syracuse's Derrick Coleman (who missed two late free throws with his team leading Indiana in 1987); Chris Webber. "Even with those guys there's a difference," he said. "Fred Brown got to come back two years later and win. Coleman and Webber have both had long pro careers. I just had to go on with my life."

He's done it quite well: five children (his daughter is now a manager at Louisville), a successful business, and a love of basketball that keeps him playing in rec leagues even today at fifty-two. Every year he makes the trip to the Final Four, where people still point fingers at him and say, "Are you the guy . . . ?"

"The one I remember the most was maybe a year or so after I graduated," he said. "Of course, now I look quite a bit different than thirty years ago. Back then, it seemed like everywhere I went people would point or whisper or say something. I was working in real estate and I was out somewhere working sales around a lake, quite a few miles out in the country. I went into a place to get something to eat. It was one of those places with a bunch of old boys sitting around a stove. When I walked in, their mouths dropped open. I'd seen it before, so I just said, 'Yes, I'm the guy.' One of them looked at me and said, 'You know, it's really too bad about that shot. I guess it just spinded out.'"

It spinded out. Thirty years later Terry Howard — and many, many others — haven't forgotten.

8

Refs

ON FRIDAY MORNING Hank Nichols walked briskly through the lobby of the Renaissance Hotel en route to a meeting. By now, many fans were staking out the Renaissance, which was directly across the street from the Edward Jones Dome, knowing that many of the sport's famous names were bound to show up at some point since this was the hotel where the NCAA basketball committee was staying, meaning that many of the weekend's meetings would be held in the building.

No one stopped Nichols for an autograph. As he stepped outside and lit a Merit cigarette, a line of autograph seekers who had just besieged Jim Boeheim moments earlier didn't even glance at Nichols. Which was exactly the way he wanted it.

To those in college basketball, he is one of the most familiar and important people in the game. But as the Friday morning scene proved, very few of the general public could pick him out of a lineup. In real life, he is Dr. Henry Nichols, distinguished professor of business administration at Villanova University. In his basketball life, he is Hank Nichols, longtime referee and, for the past seventeen years, the guru of all NCAA basketball officials. "When I was offered the job, I told my father about it,"

Nichols said. "He did some officiating years ago and he said to me, 'Henry, they want you to try to straighten out the officiating? That's perfect — you'll have a job for life, because it will never happen.'"

That was in 1988, and in 2005 Nichols would be the first to admit that his officials — everyone in the game refers to the referees as "Hank's guys" — are far from perfect. "But we've come a long way," Nichols said. "I know fans don't appreciate that, but we have. Guys are trained better today, they learn, they go to schools, and we get on 'em when they screw up. When I first started working, all I had were [old-time refs] Jim Hernjak and Steve Honzo saying to me, 'Kid, you don't want to make that call.'"

Nichols, who is sixty-six now, grew up in Morganton, North Carolina, the town best known as the home of Senator Sam Ervin Jr., the man who presided over the Senate Watergate hearings. He and his older brother, Bob, were both good athletes, both basketball players. "Bob was four years older than me," Nichols said. "After he graduated from high school, he ended up going to a prep school for a year and we played against each other one night, guarded each other, in fact. My dad refereed the game. Bob fouled out. For years he claimed that was proof that Dad favored me because I was the baby."

The baby ended up at Villanova and, after graduating in 1959, spent a couple of years in the marines because of an ROTC commitment before briefly playing minor league baseball in the Cincinnati Reds' farm system. When he realized he wasn't going to make it to the big leagues, he followed Bob to Buffalo and became a coach and teacher at DeSales High School. "In the winter of '65 Bob and I were both looking for ways to make some money on the side and he said, 'Hey, let's take the refs' test, we'd be good at it.' I'm sure the fact that my dad had done it influenced him. But we did and I started working high school games, making maybe five or ten bucks a game. But I liked it and when I went 2–17 one year at DeSales, I realized I was probably better at reffing than at coaching."

By 1969 Nichols was working college games, assigned out of the ECAC, which at the time ruled college basketball on the East Coast. He had gone back to school by then to get both his master's and his PhD, in educational administration and counseling. He had met Hubie Brown when Brown was coaching at Niagara. When Brown went to Duke as an assistant coach for Bucky Waters, he invited Nichols to work a scrimmage between Duke and Jacksonville. "Jacksonville had Artis Gilmore, Pembrook Burrows III, and Rex Morgan," Nichols remembered. "They were the best team I'd ever seen." (They went on to play in the national championship game in 1970.) Out of that experience came the chance to work games at Duke's summer camp, which led to a recommendation to ACC officiating supervisor Norval Neve. By the early '70s, Nichols was working in both the ACC and the ECAC and rising rapidly. He had a good feel for the game and the players and made it clear who was in charge. Nichols was famous among players for almost never calling a charge. Often when a player would try to take one, Nichols would call the block and then just look down at the player who had tried to take the charge as if to say, "Not happening tonight, son."

Nichols worked his first ACC championship game in 1974, the famous North Carolina State–Maryland game. Late in the game several players began jostling with one another just prior to an inbounds play. Showing his understanding for what he was a part of at that moment, Nichols jumped in between the players, pointed his finger at everyone involved, and said, "Stop it right now. You will not do that in *this* game."

A year later he was assigned to his first Final Four and got to work the championship game. According to Nichols, he got lucky that night — thanks to his partner, Bob Wortman. "It's probably fair to say I was a little hopped up," he said. "It was my first final *and* it was John Wooden's last game. Early in the game [UCLA star] David Meyers slammed the ball down in frustration over a call and I teed him up. Wooden couldn't believe it. He got up and started to argue with me. I'm not sure what would have happened, but I think if we had gotten into it, I might have ended up teeing him up, too. That wouldn't have been good, to tee John Wooden up in his last game. Fortunately for me, Bob Wortman got to Wooden before I did and got him calmed down. I'll always be grateful to him for that."

Nichols eventually worked ten Final Fours and six championship games and became one of the most respected officials in the game. Throughout the time that he was a referee, Nichols continued to teach at Villanova. In 1987 Dave Gavitt, who had been the chairman of the basketball committee, came to him with an idea. "Dave was like a lot of people in the game who thought we needed to make officiating more consistent," Nichols said. "It was too regionalized, too different from league to league. A foul in the ACC wasn't a foul in the Big Ten. We needed more good officials and we needed it to be more consistent. He wanted me to supervise officiating across the country and help pick the guys who would work the tournament. The timing was good. I was forty-eight. I enjoyed working the games, but the travel was wearing me out. And there were times when I had people calling me a c—— and I'd say to myself, 'I'm an educator. I don't need to be talked to this way.' The offer was really a godsend, perfect timing."

Nichols continued to work selected games the first four years on the job so he could meet younger officials and give some of them an up-close look at how he worked and what he expected. The last game he worked was late in 1990: James Madison against Old Dominion, with Lefty Driesell coaching JMU. He went out with Lefty's voice ringing in his ears.

Every year, Nichols begins the season by doing seminars — they used to be in person, but now they're done by video — for both coaches and officials. Both are told what calls are going to be emphasized during the season: It might be calling three seconds more often, or hand-checking. Coaches might be warned that officials are going to give them less rope before giving them a technical foul. Of course, in the end, everyone winds up refereeing the way they're most comfortable. "You put it out there, you try to get the guys to be consistent, but you know they're going to ref the way they want to ref," Nichols said. "I can't blame them; that's probably what I would have done, too."

What coaches ask for constantly and what Nichols tries to give them is consistency. "I know what makes coaches crazy more than anything is when a charge on one play isn't a charge on the next," Nichols said. "Or if guys change the way they officiate late in the game. A foul should be a foul — first minute or last. That doesn't mean it always happens that way."

Nichols's biggest job each year is choosing ninety-six officials to work the NCAA Tournament. The process begins in February, when each conference nominates officials it believes should be selected to work the tournament. In many cases, if not most, Nichols is familiar with the officials and he tries, through watching games on television and going to them in person, to keep abreast of how officials are working during the season. "Referees are like players," he said. "Some get better, some lose a step. Sometimes a good official has a bad year. Sometimes a guy you didn't think was very good shows improvement. I try, as best I can, to know how a guy is reffing *now*. But there's no doubt some of it is on reputation and on the word of the supervisors."

Occasionally if Nichols isn't familiar with someone's work, he will call the supervisor to ask about him. There are also times, he says, when he makes a mistake and underrates an official. "There was a guy named Steve Olson," he said. "He was nominated one year and I left him out. Just didn't think he was good enough. Then I saw him several times the next year and he was very much good enough. I had just missed on him. When I saw him that season, I told him, 'I made a mistake last year leaving you out.'"

Like most good officials, Nichols always told coaches when he realized he had blown a call. "One year I had LSU-Kentucky in the regionals," he said. "There was a block/charge and I called it for Kentucky, and as soon as I had signaled the foul I knew I'd gotten it wrong. A minute later Dale Brown called time and said, 'Hank, can I talk to you?' I knew what it was about. I said, 'Send your captain.' He didn't bother. Next time by the bench I said what I always said in those situations: 'I owe you one, but I'll never pay.'"

Which was his way of saying he was sorry while letting the coach know he didn't believe in make-up calls. A make-up call is perhaps the worst thing an official can do because it usually means he has now made two bad calls instead of one.

Once Nichols has the nominations from the conferences, he puts together a list of who he thinks should work the tournament and takes it with him to Indianapolis when the basketball committee meets to select the field. He usually meets with the committee on Thursday morning to show the members his list and, in some cases, explain why certain officials are on the list and some aren't. He then meets again during the weekend with the officials subcommittee, which in 2005 consisted of Southern University athletic director Floyd Kerr, George Mason athletic director Tom O'Connor, Princeton athletic director Gary Walters, and Mid-Continent Conference commissioner John LeCrone.

"Occasionally they or the staff might catch a conflict problem," he said. "They might, just as an example, remind me that Duke Edsall [an ACC official who has worked the Final Four in the past] is the brother of Randy Edsall, the Connecticut football coach. I know most of them already, but every once in a while when I start assigning games, they'll catch one."

Nichols does not begin assigning games until he has the bracket, which is usually about 3:30 on Sunday afternoon. He is paid to know the game, so there are certain first-round games he looks at as potentially more difficult than others and tries to make sure to have at least one or two experienced officials on that game. In 2005 he sensed that Vermont-Syracuse would be a difficult game and put Verne Harris, who has worked the last two national championship games, on that crew.

"You try to mix it up, regardless," he said. "You want the younger guys with veterans. Some games, like that one, you say, 'Okay, let's make sure we've got one of our best guys there.'"

Twelve officials go to each site. Only six, plus a standby, remain for the second round. Which six will remain is decided before the first round, in part because Nichols doesn't want officials competing to get noticed so they can advance and in part because it is easier logistically to tell officials in advance how long they will be staying at a site. But not working the second round does not mean an official can't advance to the round of sixteen.

"We like to tell guys that not getting a second-round game doesn't mean they can't advance. We just have to make decisions Sunday and then it is up to them to ref their way into the second week. It happens sometimes, just as sometimes guys we expect to advance don't work as well and don't advance."

Nichols knows that every time he selects one referee, he disappoints another. "This is not a science," he said. "It's an art and sometimes you choose the wrong colors. All we can do is make our best guess as to who will do the best job."

Once Nichols has gone through the bracket on Sunday afternoon and put together teams of three referees per game, he presents it to the committee and staff for a last look to make sure he hasn't missed anything. Then, at about the same time the bracket is going up, staff members begin calling officials to tell them they've been selected and where they are going. "Then it's up to us to make our travel plans," said Reggie Greenwood, a veteran referee who had consistently been selected for the tournament prior to 2005 but had never made the Final Four. In 2005 he made it. Why? "Because he reffed better," Nichols said. "He's worked at it and gotten better. He deserved it."

Once the tournament begins, the officials are graded by Nichols, who travels to as many sites as he can; by evaluators who are assigned to sites; and by the committee members at each site. They all fill out a form on each official in which they are asked to "strongly recommend" him for advancement, "recommend," or "not recommend." It is rare for someone who is not "strongly recommended" by all or most of the evaluators to advance. The exceptions usually come when Nichols has seen a game and believes the official has done better than the evaluators rated him or thinks there may be a particular reason why he didn't grade as well as others.

From a field of ninety-six the first week, the list is narrowed to thirty-six the second week — nine at each site — everyone working one game. As with the first weekend, being assigned a round-of-sixteen game as opposed to a round-of-eight game does not mean you can't advance to the Final Four. Who advances is decided early Monday morning after a teleconference involving Nichols, the committee, and the staff. The same process takes place during the second week with ten officials — nine to work the games plus a standby — selected for the Final Four. Every official who has worked gets a call on Monday morning.

"They either tell you, 'Thanks very much for all your hard work,' or, 'We'd like you to go to . . . ,' wherever it is you're going," said Tim Higgins, who has been a college referee for twenty-six years and has worked twelve Final Fours. "It's a tough call when they just give you the thank-you, but you understand. When I get that call, I always just resolve myself to work a little harder next year."

Higgins got that call in 2005 after the regionals. He thought he had done good work but he also understood that Nichols can't just pick the same nine guys for the Final Four every year. "Hank's got to do a juggling act," Higgins said. "We all understand that."

In fact, Nichols readily admits that he has to be aware of geography, of who works for what conference, and experience. "I like to bring in at least one new guy every year," he said. "It's important to extend the Final Four pool so that as guys get older, there are younger guys to step in." In 2005 Reggie Greenwood and Mike Shouse were the new guys. Shouse worked Illinois-Louisville; Greenwood had Michigan State–North Carolina.

The standby official in 2005 was Larry Rose, meaning he sat at the scorer's table through all three games for two reasons: to be ready to jump on the court if one of the officials was injured and to keep track of the game to prevent his partners from making a mistake.

"It's the hardest job in officiating," Rose said. "For one thing, you are so close to working the Final Four, but you aren't actually out there. We're all competitors, we all want to feel like we're part of the game. For another, you have to stay in the game mentally because if you don't, you will miss something and embarrass your buddies."

During the North Carolina–Michigan State game, Greenwood, Bob Donato, and Randy McCall got confused about who was supposed to shoot a free throw. Rose, paying close attention, noticed that they put the wrong shooter on the line for the Spartans. "Soon as I saw it, I said to the scorer, 'Hit the horn,'" Rose said. "He said, 'What, what?' I said, 'Hit the horn!' He wouldn't do it. So the kid shoots the first shot. Fortunately, the error is still correctable at that point because no time has gone off the clock, so I stood up and started waving my arms. That's when they saw me and we got it fixed."

Needless to say, the other three officials were grateful to Rose. "They know the game is going to be evaluated, and if someone [probably Nichols] sees that the wrong shooter took free throws, that will hurt them in the future," he said. "They were ready to kiss me when they got back to the locker room. I told them a handshake would be fine."

Rose has worked six Final Fours. He is a high school vice principal in southwestern Virginia not far from where he grew up. He was a good enough baseball player to be offered a partial scholarship to what was then Hampton Institute (now Hampton University). To pay for the nonscholarship part of his tuition, he had to have a work-study job. "I was assigned to referee intramural basketball games for work-study," he said. "Right from the beginning I enjoyed it. I felt like I was part of the action even when I wasn't actually playing in the game."

He continued officiating after college, working his way up from high school to the Central Collegiate Athletic Association before being hired by Fred Barakat to work in the ACC in 1982. "Fred started me out slowly," he said. "I was like a lot of young officials who needed to be brought along. I worked a lot of games with Lenny Wirtz early on, which was a blessing."

Wirtz is a legendary figure among ACC people: coaches, players, officials, and fans. Short, hyper, and intense, Wirtz was once the commissioner of the Ladies Professional Golf Association Tour. "He was the best because he was the most consistent official who ever lived," Tim Higgins said. "We all say we treat every game the same. Lenny actually did it."

Fans hated Wirtz because he was less likely to be influenced by a home crowd than most officials. Dean Smith was frequently frustrated by Wirtz because he would shake off his protestations with a laugh and keep working. "Lenny and I have been together for twenty-five years," Smith said one night. "I think we're entitled to a divorce." When Rick Barnes was coaching at Clemson, he decided one night to get thrown out of a game that he knew his team wasn't going to win in order to make a point. He screamed at Wirtz. He cursed at him. He came on the court and pointed his finger in Wirtz's face. "Rick," Wirtz said, "do what you want, say what you want. I know what you're doing and I'm not throwing you out."

Rose learned from Wirtz and worked his way up through the ACC officiating hierarchy. In 1990 he was selected for his first

Final Four — as the standby. "Fred told me later that Hank told him I deserved to work," he said. "But the ACC had two teams [Duke and Georgia Tech] there, so I couldn't work any of the games. Back then I was just thrilled to be there, to be considered one of the top ten guys."

Three years later he got the call saying he had been selected to work. He did the Michigan-Kentucky game in the Superdome — a game that went into overtime — and came home feeling as if he had climbed the mountain. "People look at you differently when you have been a Final Four ref," he said. "It becomes part of your résumé. I remember I worked at the Portsmouth Invitational [a postseason camp for college seniors that is scouted by the NBA] and before my first game the announcer said, 'And let's welcome back from working the Final Four, Larry Rose!' That was a great feeling."

Like most officials, Rose gets along with the majority of the coaches he works with (referees almost always say they work "for" coaches). "I remember I had Kentucky-Stanford in '98 [national semifinals], and Tubby Smith, who almost never says anything, jumped up on a call and said, 'What kind of a bullshit call was that?'" Rose said. "Then he realized I was standing almost right next to him. He said, 'Larry, I'm so sorry, I didn't mean it.' I said, 'Sure you did, Tubby, but I'm not teeing you up for *that* in a Final Four game.' I think he was shocked because I was laughing. You have to give coaches some rope under that kind of pressure."

One night at Maryland, Rose almost tripped over Gary Williams while running down the court because Williams was a couple of feet inbounds, screaming instructions at his players. "I said, 'Gary, get out of my way so I can work the game.' He said, 'Hey, Larry, that's my court you're working on.' I said, 'Right now, Gary, it's *my* court.' He just laughed."

Nichols always counsels his officials before a Final Four game on how to deal with the coaches. He reminds them that, just as for them, this is the biggest stage in the game for the coaches. "He's almost like a coach when he talks to us," Rose said. "He talks about how the teams play, what to look for, and reminds us to try to understand how hyper the coaches may be, especially early. The first part of the game is critical for everyone. I've always found that once I get the first call out of the way and get it right, I calm down and I'm okay."

Rose has now worked in the last sixteen NCAA Tournaments and has always made it at least to the regionals. But he has never worked a championship game. "I know part of it is that the ACC almost always has a team there," he said. "It's a little bit of a catch-22. Being in the ACC has made me the referee that I am and allowed me to handle pressure. I would never have made it to the Final Four at all if I hadn't worked in the ACC all these years. But because the league is so strong, it makes it harder for me to get the final. I'd like to think one day I will."

Tim Higgins got the final the very first year he made it to the Final Four, 1988. "I was floored, completely shocked," he said. "I was still in shock that I was there at all and then Hank announces in the meeting that I'm the ref on the final." (The officials in every game are designated as the referee, umpire 1, and umpire 2 — the ref being the ultimate authority in any disputes.)

The officials' meeting on Final Four weekend is held on Saturday morning. Until a few years ago all nine officials who were working would meet with Nichols and he would begin by announcing the assignments for the weekend. That has now changed. The three who work on Monday night don't fly in until late Sunday or early Monday. That takes some of the tension out of the Saturday meeting because the seven officials (including the standby) in the room all know their assignments before they arrive.

"It's good for a lot of reasons," Higgins said. "For one thing, whether guys admit it or not, it's a letdown to be in the room and find out you've got a semi instead of the final. We all want the final, just like players and coaches want to be in the final. For another, there's just no good that comes from getting in on Friday and then having nothing to do until Monday. It just makes you more tense about it all. The funny thing is, when I work a Final Four game with someone who is doing it for the first time, I always say, 'Treat it like just another game.' Which is silly because it isn't just another game. The minute you walk out there it feels different because it *is* different."

Higgins began officiating in 1972 after getting out of the army, "to get some beer money." He started working high school games in New Jersey — where he had grown up and gone to college at Fairleigh Dickinson — and got his big break when the Big East came into existence in 1979. Twenty-six years later he and Jim Burr, another perennial Final Four ref, are the only two men who worked the first year of the league's existence who are still working.

"I always tell people this is the best part-time job in America," he said. "For one thing, it forces you to stay in shape. For another thing, I really enjoy the friendships. For another, in terms of business, there's nothing I could do that could be better. Guys I deal with see me working on television all the time. It's invaluable."

Higgins owns his own business selling commercial building supplies and has offices in both Manhattan and Brooklyn. He has worked every NCAA Tournament since 1985. He still remembers being shocked when Nichols announced that he would be working the 1988 final. "There was a moment of shock, then a

John Wooden (with trophy) and the 1971 UCLA Bruins,
perhaps his most difficult and gratifying team. (© ASUCLA Photography)

Mike Krzyzewski. He always brings his team to the Final Four, one way or another. (© Duke University Photography)

The committee at work. Very serious stuff. (Courtesy NCAA)

Jim Valvano. They still tell his stories long into the night. (© ESPN)

Endless enthusiasm. Dick Vitale (right) speaks . . . and speaks . . .
(© ESPN)

Tom Brennan. No one enjoyed the Final Four more.

(© Sally McCay/ University of Vermont)

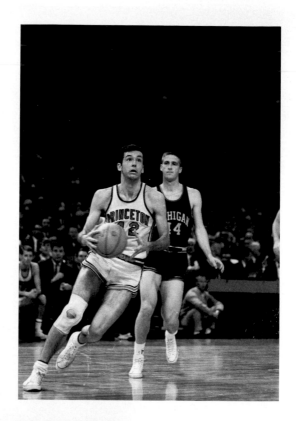

Bill Bradley. The Final Four's first Rhodes Scholar. (© Rich Clarkson / Sports Illustrated)

Clay Buckley. The last of the Buckley dynasty, he finally got the family the ultimate victory. (© Duke University Photography)

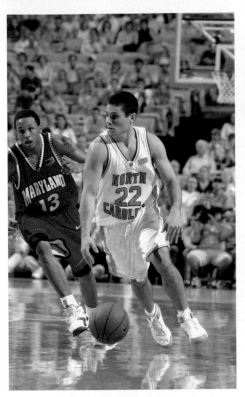

Wes Miller. Savoring every moment . . . on and off the court. (© Jeffrey A. Camarati / UNC Athletic Communications)

Sean May. Complete satisfaction: the MOP Award and the first hug by Roy Williams. (© Jeffrey A. Camarati / UNC Athletic Communications)

Three champions: Dean Smith, Michael Jordan, and Roy Williams. (© Jeffrey A. Camarati / UNC Athletic Communications)

Roy Williams. The final net was his, at long last. (© Jeffrey A. Camarati / UNC Athletic Communications)

moment of being thrilled," he said. "And then I thought, 'Oh boy, Tim, you better not screw this up.'"

One of the reasons Higgins has succeeded is that he has a self-deprecating way of working a game. He is not one of those officials who has to prove he is in charge. He looks and sounds like Barney Rubble, as opposed to some of his colleagues, who want to be Fred Flintstone and give all the orders. "I always tell coaches that I don't tee them up, they tee themselves up," he said. "I don't do it unless there's no choice."

Higgins had the chance early in his career to work with — and learn from — Nichols. "He was great at defusing bad situations," Higgins said. "One night he and I and a guy named Dave Pollock have Georgetown-Syracuse in the [Carrier] Dome. This was back when that was one of *the* games every year. I called a bad foul against Syracuse, really a terrible call, putting [Patrick] Ewing on the line for two shots. The place was going crazy. They're throwing things, screaming profanities. [Jim] Boeheim is angry; [John] Thompson is angry. I mean, it's chaos. Hank goes down to talk to the two coaches. I'm standing there with Pollock and I said, 'Should we go help?' and he just says to me, 'Timmy, let the big dog eat. Hank's got it under control.'"

In 1990 Higgins was assigned to work the Final Four in Denver. He and his wife, Kathy, took a drive to the Air Force Academy to spend the day with an old friend who was teaching there. They toured the campus and finally walked into the chapel. "We sat down for about a minute and the guy behind me turns to his wife and says, 'Oh no, not f—— Higgins!' I mean, I hear that all the time on the court, but not usually in church!"

Nichols and the tournament committee take great pains to keep the names of the Final Four officials secret until the minute they walk on the floor. One reason for this is that certain officials have reputations for working games a certain way — calling more fouls, fewer fouls — and the NCAA doesn't want gamblers to know who is working in advance. It is also a matter of principle: the officials are supposed to be faceless — even though, as Higgins's story about the Air Force Academy clearly illustrates, they aren't — so the NCAA doesn't want their names in the newspaper or on TV in advance of the games. Of course, by Thursday anyone who wants to find out who the officials are can. One reporter and Nichols have an annual ritual whereby the reporter names all the officials for Nichols and Nichols just shakes his head and says, "Next year, you won't find out."

Higgins takes it a step further. "In 1992 they literally tried to sneak us into Minneapolis in the middle of the night," he said. "They took us out a side door of the airport and through a back door of the hotel. I gave the front desk clerk my name and he said, 'Oh yes, Mr. Higgins,' and handed me *twenty-three* phone messages, most of them from people I knew looking for tickets. Some secret."

The officials are given first-class treatment throughout the tournament, perhaps in part because they aren't paid very much. The first weekend they are paid $700 a game; the second, $850; and the third, $1,000. "You make the Final Four, you lose money," Larry Rose said. "They don't pay for your wife or if you want to bring children or anyone else. So, if it's a big deal to you — which it is — you probably lose money on the whole thing." In fact, the official who makes the most money at the Final Four is the standby. The nine officials who work the games get paid for one game; the standby gets paid for three.

"It is nice when they take you to and from the games with a police escort," Higgins said, laughing. "Sometimes I think, 'How cool a thing is this, me getting a police escort.' In Tampa a few years ago we told our escort we wanted him to find a restaurant for us after the game where there would be no fans, because we really didn't want to rehash the game with people who were either very happy or very sad. We get dressed and the cops take us to a biker bar. Wasn't a soul in there without a tattoo. But no one bothered us."

Higgins didn't make a thirteenth Final Four in 2005. He worked the Louisville–West Virginia regional final and hoped to get the call but didn't. "I'm really okay with it," he said. "Disappointed, of course. But look, I've been to twelve. I think there are fifty referees out there — I mean it, fifty — who are worthy of working the Final Four who have never been to one. I sat home and watched on TV and rooted for all the guys to do well because they're my friends. If they do well, we all do well. I really think how the guys do in the Final Four sets the tone for all of us for next season because the whole basketball world is watching and all of us are being judged on how the guys who are there are doing."

The single most famous call in Final Four history was John Clougherty's foul call in overtime that put Michigan's Rumeal Robinson at the line with Seton Hall, up by one and 1.8 seconds to play in the 1989 final. Robinson made both shots and Michigan won the game. What made the call controversial was that Robinson passed the ball and yet Clougherty called the foul when there was clearly no advantage gained because of the contact. Officials are counseled over and over not to anticipate plays (Clougherty thought Robinson was going to shoot when he saw the contact) and not to put someone at the line unless the contact creates a disadvantage for the player who has been hit. Clougherty, one of the best officials of the past twenty-five years, who worked eleven Final Fours, will always be remembered most for one call.

Recently, there hasn't been one call that outraged people, but there was one game that is still argued about and discussed: Duke-Connecticut in the 2004 semifinals. It was a matchup of two Hall of Fame coaches, Mike Krzyzewski and Jim Calhoun, who both have reputations for working the officials. Krzyzewski's approach to officials was best described years ago by an ACC ref who said, "Mike's like a football coach. If you take a possession away from him, you better have a damn good reason why you did it." Larry Rose, who likes Calhoun, says of him, "If you let him, he will talk to you all night."

Nichols always advises his officials to be sure not to "referee the coaches." What he means is that they can't react every time a coach complains about a call, because the best ones — and in the Final Four you are almost always dealing with top-of-the-line coaches — will see that they can get you to react and just keep after you. That's what happened in the Duke-UConn game. After UConn center Emeka Okafor picked up two quick fouls, Calhoun was up screaming. For the next few minutes, UConn got every call. When *his* centers got in foul trouble, Krzyzewski began barking. Sure enough, the calls turned the other way. By halftime Nichols was so exasperated, he did something he had never done in seventeen years as the supervisor: he went into the locker room to talk to his officials.

"I just told them they had to take control of the game," he said. "They were letting the coaches control the game. They had to make their calls and stick by them and forget the coaches. I reminded them that they had whistles around their necks for a reason. They did better the second half."

That is Nichols's story and he's sticking to it. The consensus was that the officials ruined what should have been a great game. Even Calhoun, whose team won, said afterward, "It would have been nice to have been able to see what these two teams could do if they'd been allowed to play."

Nichols shrugs when the subject comes up and insists it wasn't all that bad. The three officials — Ted Hillary, Olandis Poole, and David Hall — were nowhere to be found at the 2005 Final Four.

Hank Nichols was there. Because, just as his father predicted, he was still working on trying to get the officials straightened out. "We've come a long way," he said. "But there's always work to be done."

9

Players

WHILE THE COACHES ARE A CONSTANT at the Final Four, coming back year after year to trade stories and talk about the old days, a player's involvement in the event is far shorter. The absolute maximum number of times a player can participate in a Final Four is, of course, four. Technically, if a player redshirts, he could be on the bench (though not eligible to play) for a fifth year. But that's it. The list of players who have been to four Final Fours isn't very long: Clay Buckley, Greg Koubek, Christian Laettner, and Brian Davis. All went to Duke during the period from 1988 through 1992, when Duke reached five straight Final Fours. When UCLA went to ten straight, from 1967 to 1976, freshmen were not eligible to play. (The freshman class of 1973 was the first to be eligible, but none of them played in that year's Final Four.) Cincinnati also went to five straight Final Fours in the 1960s, before freshmen could play.

Most players dream of being in one Final Four. Only a handful get to play in more than one. Most arrive at a Final Four understanding that chances are good they will never play in another, especially these days, when so many players jump to the pros prior to their senior year.

"It's actually something you don't want to think about when you're there," said Jay Bilas, whose one and only Final Four was in 1986 as a Duke senior. "There's enough pressure as is, without thinking to yourself, 'Okay, this is it. I'll never get this chance again.' But the thought is definitely there. That's why I never feel all that bad for the coaches when they lose. They can have other chances; they can spend twenty-five or thirty years trying to get back again, and often do. It isn't true of the players."

Bilas is forty now, a very popular and well-compensated television analyst who also has a law degree and works during the off-season in a law firm in Charlotte. He's married with two children, and his adult life has been, by just about any standard, a complete success.

And he still hasn't gotten over losing the 1986 national championship game to Louisville. "It's the difference between being remembered and being forgotten," he said. "We won thirty-seven games that season, and people were writing and saying we were one of the best teams of all time. Now when I see lists of the best teams of the last twenty years, we aren't even in the top ten. That's for one reason: we lost. It doesn't change the bond you had with your teammates or take away the good memories of the fun times, but it leaves you with a little hole that you know can't be filled. I can still hear Bob Knight speaking to our team the day before the final, saying, 'Boys, don't hold anything back in this game, because no one remembers the team that loses.'

"In 1991 I was an assistant coach when we won the national championship. Tommy Amaker [the point guard on the '86 team] was there, too. The night we won, Johnny Dawkins, who was still playing in the NBA at the time, called Tommy and me and said, 'Does this make up for '86?' And we both said the same thing: 'Nothing can ever make up for '86.' I don't want to be overly melodramatic. We've all gone and lived productive lives and we still have a great time when we get together, but it's still there — whether we talk about it or not.

"I remember in '91 when the game was over, I stood on the court and watched our players celebrate. I was happy for them because it occurred to me that whenever they got together in the future, they would have this memory rather than the empty one we had after our last game. But that's what makes the Final Four what it is. Everyone watching understands what's at stake for the players, because most of them get only the one chance."

Greg Anthony got two chances. Unlike Bilas, he got to celebrate, got to be part of a national championship team in 1990, when Nevada–Las Vegas hammered Duke, 103–73, in the championship game. Most people virtually conceded the national title to UNLV the next year, and the Rebels arrived in Indianapolis 34–0 and seemingly primed to be the first team since Wooden's retirement to win back-to-back titles. Except they never got back to the final. They were stunned by Duke, 79–77, in the semifinals. When Anthony, who went on to play in the NBA and now works for ESPN, thinks about his college career, he thinks first about the title lost, not the title won.

"I guess it's human nature to think that way," he said. "When we won, it seemed too easy because we won the final by thirty. So losing the next year never really crossed our minds. When we did lose, it was a complete shock. I'm not sure I'm completely over that shock yet."

Many players who have been on teams that have lost in the Final Four remember being in a kind of shock, which meant they didn't understand right away how long the loss would linger. "I remember getting back to my hotel room and thinking,

'Gee, it's too bad we lost, but I'll have a couple more chances before my career is over,'" said Jeff Capel, who was a Duke freshman in 1994 when Scotty Thurman hit a late three-point shot to give Arkansas the championship, denying Duke a third title in four years. "At that point in time, you went to Duke, you just figured the Final Four was part of your schedule every year."

Capel did make it back to the Final Four in 1997 as a senior — to play in an all-star game held that weekend. During his last three seasons, Duke won one NCAA Tournament game and didn't reach the round of sixteen. "Being the son of a coach, I think I have an understanding that nothing is guaranteed — even things you once thought were," he said. "But when you're young, even if you think you understand that, you don't."

Capel is now a very young coach — he was hired as the head coach at Virginia Commonwealth when he was twenty-seven and took the school to the NCAAs in his second season. But he understands that even success doesn't mean you'll get to coach forever. His father — Jeff Capel Jr. — had great success at Old Dominion, winning (among other games) one of the great first-round games ever played, when his team (as a number fourteen seed) upset Villanova in three overtimes in 1993. When the school stopped going to the postseason, Old Dominion started looking for a new coach.

"It was very tough to see my dad go through that," Capel said. "I had come to the Final Four with him a couple of times, and the saddest thing to me was to see the coaches in the lobby who were looking for work or had just been fired. I never dreamed that would happen to him. I love what I'm doing now and it is great fun to be here and see people, but I'm very conscious of how quickly things can change — whether you're playing or coaching."

*   *   *

There weren't any members of the Buckley family in St. Louis. That was surprising only because over a period of four decades, from the '60s to the '90s, a Buckley played in at least one Final Four. In fact, Jay Buckley, his brother Bruce, and his son, Clay, played in a total of seven Final Fours, beginning with Jay's appearance in 1963 as a Duke junior and ending in 1991, when Clay was the co-captain of Duke's first national championship team.

"It took a long time for the family to get one, but we finally did," Jay Buckley said. "I think we were all beginning to wonder if it was going to happen."

How many families can claim to have three different members who not only played college basketball but made their final appearance in the national championship game? That's what the Buckleys did. Jay Buckley's last college game was the 1964 title game: Duke's loss to UCLA. Bruce, thirteen years younger than Jay, played his last college game for North Carolina in 1977, when the Tar Heels lost the final to Marquette. It was Clay who finally got it right in 1991 when Duke beat Kansas in his last game.

"Of course, it took us four tries," Clay said, alluding to the fact that the four Duke teams he played on all reached the Final Four. "Looking back, it's amazing to think that we did that. Every good team's goal at the start of a season is the Final Four. We actually lived up to it. But if we hadn't won in '91 and I had finished my career without a championship, I'm honestly not sure I would be able to watch the Final Four right now. To be that close and to never win would have been very difficult."

His father and uncle say they have no such trouble. Regrets — they have a few. But they still watch. "I was lucky to, in effect, have a second chance with Clay," Jay Buckley said. "It was certainly different, being a father and watching, but it was a great feeling, especially that last night in Indianapolis when they beat Kansas."

Jay was the best of the three Final Four Buckleys, a six-ten center from Bladensburg, Maryland, who was recruited by everyone in the country when he was a senior at Bladensburg High School in 1960. He was a good enough player to attract the attention of Red Auerbach. The great Celtics coach lived in Washington and kept a close eye on most players from the D.C. area. When Buckley was a senior, Auerbach tried to persuade him to go to Harvard. "In those days they still had the territorial draft in the NBA," Buckley said. "If I'd have gone to Harvard, I would have been in the Celtics' territory and they would have had first shot at me when I graduated. I was flattered and my grades were good enough. But in the end [then assistant coach] Bucky Waters convinced me that [then coach] Vic Bubas was building a powerhouse. I wanted to be a part of it."

He was, playing alongside three-time All-American Art Heyman and future NBA star Jeff Mullins. The Duke class of '64 has the distinction of never having lost a game to North Carolina (7–0 in three years of eligibility) and reached the Final Four in both 1963 and 1964. "Of course, back then winning the ACC Tournament was such a big deal because you had to win to get into the tournament, so in a very real way, you had to win *seven* games in a row to win a national championship — three in the ACC Tournament and then four in the NCAAs," he said. "I remember the Final Four being back-to-back nights and the feeling of exhaustion you had when it was over."

Buckley scored 25 points against Michigan in the semifinals in 1964, and he and his teammates honestly thought they were going to win the national championship the next night. "I really think watching UCLA play Kansas State in the second semi was a mistake," Buckley said. "It wasn't a very good game. Neither team played well. We looked at UCLA and they weren't very tall, they weren't powerful. We just thought they were a team from California that probably wouldn't do all that well in the ACC."

Duke led the game early, but UCLA's quickness and shooting wore the Blue Devils out, and the Bruins won going away, 98–83, for John Wooden's first championship. "Of course, now the loss doesn't look as bad, given what Wooden went on to accomplish," Buckley said. "It stung back then, though. I can't say it doesn't still sting a little bit today." Jay Buckley was drafted by the Los Angeles Lakers, but he had been offered a fellowship in physics at Johns Hopkins. "The fellowship was worth more than the Lakers offered," he said. He went on to get a PhD and become an astrophysicist. A *true* "student-athlete."

Like his older brother, Bruce played at Bladensburg High School. He was eight years old when Jay played his last college game and still remembers not seeing his brother's great game against Michigan. "My sister was in a play at school," he said. "I went with my mom. I don't think the game was even on TV where we were. We got home and people were phoning to tell us what Jay had done. In those days you didn't even think about actually going. My dad had died when Jay was a freshman. My mom was a librarian with six kids. We weren't likely to go caravaning around the country to watch Jay play."

If Bucky Waters was responsible for Jay going to Duke, he was also responsible — at least in part — for Bruce not going to

Duke. By the time Bruce was a high school senior in 1973, Waters was completing his fourth season as Duke's head coach. The Blue Devils had gone 12–14 and rumors were rife he was going to be fired. "I just felt like it was an unstable situation there," Bruce said. "Carolina, with Dean, was anything but unstable. I thought I would fit in there."

He was right on both counts: Waters resigned in September of what would have been Bruce's freshman season, and the Duke program fell into chaos. The athletic director, Carl James, actually tried to hire Adolph Rupp, who had just been forced into retirement at Kentucky. Rupp was ready to take the job — a press conference had even been scheduled — when the director of his business operations died suddenly and he had to stay in Lexington. Duke ended up promoting Neill McGeachy to interim coach and it wasn't until 1978, a year after Buckley graduated, that Bill Foster got the program back on the map.

Bruce Buckley was never a starter at North Carolina, but he played consistent minutes off the bench and was a contributor throughout his career. As a senior, he spelled Mike O'Koren, then a heralded freshman, at the small forward spot. Carolina was an NCAA Tournament team in 1975, losing to Syracuse in the round of sixteen, and 1976, losing to Alabama in the first round. Finally, in Buckley's senior year, the Tar Heels got on a roll. "We just kept winning close games," Buckley remembered. "In the ACC final against Virginia, Phil [Ford] fouled out and John [Kuester] had to run the four corners the last few minutes and he did a great job. Then we had to come from behind in the first round of the tournament against Purdue and then from way behind against Notre Dame."

Ford was hurt late in the Notre Dame game, hyperextending his right elbow when he took a hard fall running the four corners.

It was probably the four corners as much as any one thing that eventually led to the shot clock in college basketball. "Even as players, we had mixed emotions about it," Buckley said. "It wasn't exactly a fun way to play, but it was certainly a very effective way to play."

North Carolina played Kentucky in the east regional final with three future pros injured: Ford, with a hurt elbow; Walter Davis, with an injured finger; and Tom LaGarde, who had torn an Achilles tendon and was on the bench in street clothes. Ford and Davis both played. The Tar Heels won, to reach Smith's fifth Final Four. Then they beat UNLV in the semifinals, with O'Koren scoring 31 points. That was the second game of the semifinal doubleheader. In the opener, Marquette's Jerome Whitehead scored at the buzzer to beat UNC-Charlotte. "I remember when we went down there, people were saying we were going to play Charlotte in the final," Buckley said. "We didn't want that, because they were the in-state rival and they would have had so much to prove since we never played them. The funny thing is, we were standing in the tunnel, waiting for the game to end. There were no Telscreens in those days. We couldn't even see the scoreboard. We just heard this huge roar, and a minute later the guy says, 'Okay, you can go out now.' We ran out to warm up and we didn't even know who had won the game."

Carolina fell behind again in the championship game but rallied to tie with twelve minutes left. Buckley was on the court when the Tar Heels made their run. When they got the ball back with the score tied, Smith signaled for the four corners. Buckley isn't sure if he noticed O'Koren reporting to the scorer's table to come back in or if he learned later that he was there. "I know he was getting ready to come back in for me," he said.

Carolina was running the four corners at that stage not to kill the clock but to try to lure Marquette out of its zone. "I was just trying to change sides of the court to go set a screen," Buckley remembered. "I wasn't running a backdoor cut or anything. But [Steve] Krafcisin saw me open and passed me the ball. I was right near the basket and there was no one around me, so I just went up and shot. To tell the truth, I was kind of surprised to get the ball and to find myself open. Except I wasn't quite as open as I seemed to be. Someone came flying at me. I wasn't sure if it was Whitehead or [Bo] Ellis, but he blocked the shot."

It was Ellis, who made a spectacular play and started a fast break the other way. Marquette took the lead and Carolina never caught up. "Obviously, I wish things had happened differently," Buckley said. "My life was never tied up in basketball. I wasn't all that emotional about playing my last college game, although I do remember that waiting from Saturday to Monday was terrible. It was as if I could feel the energy draining from my legs each hour that went by. I was planning to go to law school and move on. But, of course, I wish I'd seen Ellis or maybe passed or maybe that Steve hadn't passed me the ball when I wasn't really looking for it. I know that play didn't decide the game, because there was a lot of time left, but I think about it sometimes. What I really remember, though, is the locker room after the game. That's such an emotional moment. I remember the seniors each getting up and giving a little speech after the last game the three years prior, and now suddenly it was my turn. I didn't say much, but I know there was a lot of hugging and crying."

One person pulling hard for Carolina that night was Duke graduate Jay Buckley. He had been disappointed when his brother decided to go to Carolina, but he understood. "Duke was in flux," he said. "Plus, Dean was great to our entire family, especially my mom. It was tough to argue with the decision." He laughed. "I never hated Carolina the way some Duke people do. I think part of it is that I never lost to them, but I also think there's an understanding among players that if someone is a rival, it's because you respect them. If you don't respect them, where's the rivalry? Even when I was playing, if an ACC team was playing outside the league, I pulled for the ACC team. I still do — even Maryland, which can be hard sometimes because living here [in suburban Washington, not far from the Maryland campus], surrounded by Maryland fans who hate Duke, it can be tough at times."

The brothers have an agreement now that whenever Duke plays Carolina, the loser calls the winner after the game to offer congratulations. They chat about the game, and that's pretty much the end of it. "I remember a couple of years after I graduated, Carolina beat a pretty good Duke team by about twenty and I called Jay and gave it to him pretty good," Bruce said. "Well, the next week in the ACC Tournament, Duke turned around and won by twenty and I got the same phone call. We decided after that to tone it down a little bit."

When Jay's son, Clay, grew to be a six-foot-nine prospect, there wasn't much doubt where he would go to college. By then, Duke was well beyond the troubles of the early 1970s, not only stabilized by Mike Krzyzewski but turned into a national power. "I wasn't pressured to go to Duke — I was brainwashed," Clay said. "My dad always took me down to reunions and to games. I got my first recruiting letter from Coach K when I was in the seventh grade. But I never hated Carolina. For one thing, I always heard about how great Coach Smith had been to my uncle and to my grandmother. For another, whenever I've encountered people from there, they've been people I've liked."

In fact, when Clay first went to Duke's basketball camp as a six-five eighth-grader, he found himself on the same plane with a group of kids who were obviously basketball players. "Are you guys going to the camp?" he asked. Sure are, they said, you just come with us when we get off the plane. Clay followed the other kids and found himself getting on a bus. "I was confused because I thought my dad had said that one of the coaches from the camp was going to meet me," he said. "But these guys were older, they knew what they were doing, so I got on the bus."

They arrived at what was clearly a college campus, but not one that looked familiar to Buckley. He suspected something was wrong as he lined up to register, then knew something was wrong when he saw kids who had already registered coming out the door wearing brand-new T-shirts that read, CAROLINA BAS-KETBALL CAMP.

"I got out of line and ducked inside, wondering how in the world I could get myself over to Duke," he said. "The first person I saw was [then Carolina assistant] Eddie Fogler. He recognized me and said, 'Clay, I think you're in the wrong place.'" (Even when players are in the eighth grade, coaches know these things.) "He couldn't have been nicer. He got me to a phone, where I called my parents and they made arrangements to get me picked up."

Buckley did receive one recruiting letter from Dean Smith. "It said, 'I know you're inclined to go to Duke, but if you change your mind and want to go to a *real* school, you know where to find us.'"

Like his uncle, Clay was never a starter, and when he did play, he was a dirty-work guy. "It's amazing the number of screens you can set in the motion offense," he said, laughing. "The funny thing is, I play old-man's basketball [rec league] now, and I'm great at trailing the fast break and shooting the three-pointer. Coach K would be amazed if he saw me."

Buckley is now a successful executive at AOL, but he still loves basketball. "I never thought of myself as an NBA player," he said. "I went to college to be as good a college player as I could possibly be, and even though I was never a star, I loved my college experience. I have to admit there would be an emptiness if we hadn't won in '91. My sophomore year, when we lost to Seton Hall in Seattle, I think there was a feeling that maybe we'd missed our best chance. Danny [Ferry] was graduating, and none of us knew how good Christian [Laettner] was going to become. Even my senior year when we started to play really well, we knew we were going to have to go through Vegas to win, and they had just killed us the year before."

Most Duke people talk now about how confident they were going into the UNLV game. Buckley says they may not have been quite as confident as they sound now. "I think Coach K did a great job of convincing us we could play with them," he said. "But there was still doubt; there had to be. They were 34–0 and no one had really challenged them all year. But I still remember early in the second half seeing some of their guys yelling at one another on the court, and we all kind of looked at each other because Coach K had said, 'When it's close, they're going to start bickering with one another. They're going to get frustrated.' Which is exactly what happened."

North Carolina was in that Final Four and had just lost to Kansas in the game in which Pete Pavia ejected Dean Smith. The Carolina fans, their team eliminated, many of them angry with the Duke fans for taunting Smith as he left, were pulling zealously for UNLV. One exception was Bruce Buckley. "Oh, I definitely wanted Duke to win," he said. "For one thing, I respect what Krzyzewski's built there. For another, I wanted to see Clay win. I didn't want it to end for him the way it did for Jay and for me."

It didn't. It ended with a 72–65 victory over Kansas. Clay Buckley didn't score in the game. That really didn't matter. He can remember vividly everything about that night — including the look in his father's eyes. "It's funny," he said. "I know Jay [Bilas] always says he looks at the losers after the championship game because he knows they're feeling what he felt back in '86. I always look at the winners. I try to look into their eyes to see if they really understand what they just did and how much it is going to mean to them down the road, or if they're just into chest pounding and making sure people are looking at them. I'm not sure these days what the answer is — different with different guys, I guess — but I'd love to go and tell them to savor that moment, really savor it, because they're part of a very lucky few who get to have it."

Even in a family that played in seven Final Fours, that moment came only once.

Making the Final Four is special for everyone, but never the same for a coach as it is for a player. Some of it has to do with age, some of it with the camaraderie of being part of a team instead of coaching one. For one assistant coach, Michigan State's Doug Wojcik, being in the Final Four had great meaning — because he had just missed making it as a player and wondered if he would ever have another chance to get there.

Wojcik came out of Wheeling, West Virginia, in 1982, just wanting to play college basketball somewhere — anywhere. "I wasn't exactly highly recruited," he said. "I had a friend named Mike Sonnefeld who had gone to Navy, and he encouraged me to try to go there. But Navy wasn't all that interested in me. Years later I saw my recruiting file: they thought of me as a marginal prospect at best."

Encouraged by Sonnefeld and his high school coach, Skip Prosser (who had attended the Merchant Marine Academy), Wojcik kept after Navy until Jim Leary, one of the assistant coaches, told him the school might be willing to send him to the academy's prep school for a year. "That was actually great for me because I was very skinny and needed a year to fill out."

Even filled out, Wojcik wasn't slated to play much at Navy until another point guard, Willie Jett, flunked out of school. He became friends as a plebe with another skinny freshman named David Robinson. "David was only six-seven that year and he really didn't know how to play," Wojcik said. "But you could see he had amazing athletic ability."

A year later Robinson had grown six inches. He was seven-one and was rapidly becoming the kind of player that you *never* see at a military academy. Wojcik had become the starting point guard. The Mids made the tournament that season (1985) and faced LSU in a first-round game in Dayton, Ohio. No one from LSU knew what league Navy played in. The players said they had heard something about Navy having "a big center," but that was about all they knew. Navy won, 78–55. The game was summed up by a moment in the second half when LSU coach Dale Brown jumped up to tell one of his players, "You take number ten and tell Mike to take Wojcik."

Wojcik *was* number ten.

A year later the Mids were back in the tournament and were sent to Syracuse to play Tulsa in the first round, the winner to play Syracuse *at* Syracuse in the second round. Most people were already anticipating a Syracuse-Indiana game in the Sweet Sixteen. It never came close to happening. Cleveland State shocked Indi-

ana in the first round, and Navy beat both Tulsa and Syracuse —
Syracuse by a dozen (the game wasn't that close in reality) in a
game Jim Boeheim still says was one of the most stunning losses
of his coaching career. Navy then beat Cleveland State in the
round of sixteen and found itself one step away from the Final
Four. The opponent was Duke.

This was not the Duke that has now become the target for most
college basketball programs. This was not the Mike Krzyzewski
who has now become the Coach K of American Express fame
(or infamy, depending on your point of view). But it was
Krzyzewski's first great Duke team, led by Johnny Dawkins,
Mark Alarie, David Henderson, and Jay Bilas. "All I know,"
Wojcik said, "is they were much too good for us."

Perhaps the 71–50 final margin had something to do with the
pregame pep talk Krzyzewski, Army class of 1969, gave his
team. After telling his players how much he respected Navy and
how remarkable it was for a Navy basketball team to be in the
Elite Eight, he told them that if they did not *kill* Navy, he would
never speak to them again. They took him seriously. The moment Wojcik, and most who saw the game, remembers most
vividly came midway through the second half when Wojcik
stepped into the lane to try to stop a driving Dawkins and
Dawkins simply jumped *over* him and dunked the ball. "I can
still see his feet in my face," Wojcik said almost twenty years
later. It was at that point that the Duke students began chanting,
"Abandon ship," in the direction of the Navy bench.

Robinson and Wojcik still had one more year left. But Vernon
Butler and Kylor Whitaker, both outstanding shooters, had
graduated. Coach Paul Evans left to take the job at Pittsburgh.
The Mids — with Robinson on the cover of *Sports Illustrated*'s
preseason basketball issue — made it back to the tournament

but lost in the first round to Michigan in spite of Robinson's 50 points.

The season still had memorable moments. Robinson and Wojcik played their final home game in Halsey Field House against Army in front of a standing-room-only crowd, Midshipmen almost literally hanging from the rafters to watch. Army had a great guard named Kevin Houston, a shooter with amazing range. This was the first year of the three-point shot, and Houston took full advantage, torching Wojcik and Navy for 38 points. "By then, Kevin and I had become friends," Wojcik said. "There's always a bond between guys from Army and Navy. I was pleading with him during the game, 'Please stop it, my entire family is here, all my friends. It's my last home game.'" Houston never stopped shooting, but Navy managed to rally late to win in overtime.

Wojcik knew he wanted to follow in Prosser's footsteps and coach when he graduated, but he had a five-year commitment to the navy. He served on the USS *William Simms* (the *Billy Simms* to everyone on board) and then came back to the academy as an assistant coach in 1992. After the graduation of Robinson and Wojcik and Evans's departure, Navy basketball had fallen into disarray. Working for Don DeVoe, Wojcik was part of the rebuilding. Navy went to three NCAA Tournaments between 1994 and 1998, and everyone agreed that the dogged recruiting of Wojcik and fellow assistant Emmett Davis was a key reason for the turnaround. When Dino Gaudio was the coach at Army, he frequently told Wojcik that he would gladly recommend him for any job in the country — if only to get him away from Navy. "It seemed like any place we went to recruit, Doug or Emmett had already been there," said Gaudio, now Prosser's top assistant at Wake Forest.

Wojcik finally took a job in 1999 with Matt Doherty at Notre Dame. He then went with Doherty to North Carolina and helped recruit the class that included Sean May, Raymond Felton, and Rashad McCants, only to watch everything fall apart during Doherty's last two seasons. When Doherty was fired, Wojcik was hired almost immediately by Tom Izzo at Michigan State. During his first year there, he was offered the chance to return to Navy and succeed the retiring DeVoe as head coach.

"For a long time I always thought that would be where I'd end up again when the right time came," he said. "I still love the place and I always will. But when I met with [Navy Athletic Director] Chet Gladchuk, I just didn't feel that comfortable with the conversation. I mean, he was talking to me about how great the weather is in Annapolis. I *lived* there for twelve years, I know all about the weather there. I wanted to know what he was thinking about doing to help a new coach improve Navy basketball. I talked to Tom [Izzo] about it and he said to be patient, maybe wait a year and see what happens."

Wojcik knew that Izzo assistants had landed good jobs in the past: Stan Heath is now at Arkansas, Brian Gregory is at Dayton, and Tom Crean has already taken Marquette to the Final Four. As tough as it was to say no to his alma mater, he decided to wait. The decision proved correct: soon after the regular season ended, Wojcik was named the coach at Tulsa, a school that has become a coaching cradle in recent years: Nolan Richardson, Tubby Smith, Bill Self, and Buzz Peterson have all coached there. As excited as he was about finally becoming a head coach eighteen years after playing his last game at Navy, Wojcik felt as if he had unfinished business at Michigan State.

"We felt this team had a lot of potential going into the season," he said. "If I'm leaving, I want to leave on an up note."

When the draw came out with Michigan State as the fifth seed in the so-called Austin regional, most people thought Wojcik would be starting work at Tulsa after the first weekend of the tournament. Old Dominion was a tough first-round opponent, and then would come a game with Syracuse, one of the hotter teams around.

Old Dominion proved to be difficult; the Spartans trailed midway through the second half before rallying to win. Syracuse did not — the Orange were upset by Vermont. Even though the Catamounts showed up wanting very much to beat Michigan State, their dreams had all come true in the Syracuse game two nights earlier. They hung around for most of the game, but Michigan State was in control down the stretch and won, 72–61.

That put the Spartans into the round of sixteen against Duke. For all his coaching accomplishments, Izzo had never beaten Mike Krzyzewski, losing to him in the 1999 Final Four and four times in the regular season. Wojcik had his own Duke memories: the Dawkins dunk in '86 and a 2–7 record against the Blue Devils during his three years in Chapel Hill. Still, he believed Michigan State had the quickness at guard and the strength up front to give this Duke team trouble. He was right. The Spartans won, again with relative ease, 78–68. Then they beat Kentucky in the double-overtime classic. All of a sudden, nineteen years after the "abandon ship" game, Doug Wojcik found himself in the Final Four.

"I can finally say I'm getting to do something David [Robinson] never did," he said with a laugh. "I now have exactly one thing on my basketball résumé he doesn't have. This will be an emotional weekend for me, regardless of what happens, because I know now that my last game here is coming soon. Win or lose, it will be tough to say good-bye to these players and to Tom. I always say that Skip [Prosser] is my coaching father. Tom's my coaching older brother. It will be tough leaving. But it's time."

Most people expect that someday Johnny Dawkins will succeed Krzyzewski as Duke's coach. If and when he does, he and Wojcik may very well meet again. "My guess," Wojcik said, "is that he can probably still dunk on me."

10

The Committee

IF THERE IS ONE GROUP OF PEOPLE at the Final Four that tries to stay under the radar as much as the referees, it would probably be the nine men and one woman who are in charge of the event. Technically, they are called the NCAA Men's Basketball Committee. To everyone involved in the sport, they are simply "the committee."

Being appointed to the committee is not quite as big a deal as becoming a Supreme Court justice, but the perks are just about as good. And although one is actually on the committee for only five years, those perks tend to last a lifetime. Very few former committee members pass up the chance to attend the Final Four — they all receive two tickets for life — and they are all quickly handed passes upon their arrival that allow them access to anything and everything Final Four–related.

"The one thing you have to give up," said George Washington athletic director Jack Kvancz, "is the police escort to the games. That's a killer, getting back on those shuttle buses with the regular people."

The reverence paid committee members sometimes borders on the ludicrous. The committee chairman (Iowa athletic director

Bob Bowlsby in 2004 and 2005) is frequently referred to by those interviewing him as "Mr. Chairman," as if he were a member of Congress, not simply someone leading a group charged with picking teams for a basketball tournament. The committee members are wined and dined throughout Final Four week. During the games, several committee members sit at the scorer's table wearing headsets to monitor the CBS broadcast. When the committee and the network meet during the summer, CBS often is handed a list of things that the committee wasn't happy with during the previous season's broadcasts. The complaints can range from too many mentions of the NBA (seriously) to referring to the "N-C-A-A" as the "N-C-double A." That is most definitely a no-no.

"That was a Walter Byers thing," Tom Jernstedt said, laughing, one morning in St. Louis. "He always insisted that people say both a's, and I guess we've stuck to it."

More than anyone else, Jernstedt is charged with keeping the committee members happy and moving forward with the job of putting on the tournament. Jernstedt has worked for the N-C-A-A since 1973. He grew up in the tiny town of Carlton, Oregon (pop. 1,054), and played football and basketball in high school. After graduating from Oregon, he went to work for an investment firm in San Francisco and was bored out of his mind. When he was offered the chance to come back to Oregon as the facilities manager in 1970, he jumped at it. "I was making fourteen thousand dollars a year and being provided with a car in San Francisco," he said. "At Oregon they offered me six thousand and no car. I took it in a heartbeat."

He met a number of people with NCAA connections when the school hosted the NCAA Track and Field Championships in 1972, and a year later was offered a job working as an administrator at NCAA headquarters. He wasn't sure if that was the right move, since his goal was to be an athletic director, but a number of people — including UCLA athletic director J. D. Morgan — told him this was a way to "spread his wings." He began working for Walter Byers in 1973, and thirty-two years later he is probably the second-most powerful man in the NCAA, behind only President Myles Brand. He has worked with the basketball committee ever since he arrived and has seen huge changes in the committee and the tournament it runs.

"When I first got there, it was a six-man committee," he said. "We didn't even bring people to headquarters [then outside of Kansas City] to select the field, we did it by conference call. I can remember some loud arguments even then, especially between J. D. Morgan and [then North Carolina State athletic director] Willis Casey. You were talking about some strong-willed people there."

Jernstedt was there when the decision was made to expand from twenty-five to thirty-two teams for the 1975 tournament and watched as the tournament kept growing until it got to sixty-four teams in 1985. "There was always debate on the committee about whether we were expanding too fast," he said. "Everyone wanted to be careful not to overtax the field. The guy who really pushed to go to sixty-four was [former Duke coach and Sun Belt Conference commissioner] Vic Bubas. Wayne Duke was the chairman at the time, and in the end he was the one who brought everyone along to get it done."

Duke was the Big Ten commissioner when he was on the committee — having once been Walter Byers's assistant, and only employee, at the NCAA — and was one of the people who played a major role not only in expanding the tournament but in agreeing to put the Final Four into domes. "That was something else Vic Bubas pushed for," Duke said. "We were all a little wary about it because the first time we tried it in the Astrodome [1971], it didn't work very well. Too many bad seats. Even the good seats were bad seats. But Vic kept saying if we were better prepared, if we let the people know that the seats upstairs were going to be less than perfect and far away, that it would work because it would allow so many more people to be part of the event. In the end, we decided to try it and he was right."

The second dome Final Four was in 1982 in New Orleans. That year marked the beginning of many new things. It was the first year of the CBS contract, the beginning of the dome era, and the first year when there was no consolation game for the Saturday losers.

"Thank goodness we finally convinced them to eliminate that game," said Dean Smith, echoing the sentiment of most coaches.

The last consolation game in the history of the tournament was played under the eeriest of circumstances. It was March 30, 1981, the day that John Hinckley shot Ronald Reagan outside a hotel in Washington, D.C. The national championship game between North Carolina and Indiana was scheduled to be played that night, with Virginia and LSU playing in the consolation game beforehand. Word reached Philadelphia before noon that the president had been shot.

"What I remember is that we were told initially that the president had not been hurt that badly," Duke said. "At first we thought we would hear back pretty quickly saying he was okay and there was no reason not to go ahead and play the games. But as the afternoon went on, it started to become apparent that it wasn't quite that simple, because he was still in surgery. That's when I got the committee together and said, 'We have to start considering alternative plans.' We decided to get together at the arena with the school presidents and the athletic directors, too."

Dave Gavitt was also on the committee at the time. He was then the commissioner of the Big East, but prior to that he had been a coach at both Dartmouth and Providence and had coached in the Final Four in 1973. "The sense I had was that Dave, as an ex-coach who knew something about the pressures of the Final Four, should be our liaison with the coaches," Duke said. "Of course, nothing Dave had been through could prepare them for a situation like this."

The only significant group that Duke decided not to consult was NBC. "This could not be about TV," he said. "Obviously, if something serious was going on with the president, they had to cover that anyway. But if there was doubt, one way or the other, I wanted the decision to be about what was right for the country and the event, not what was right for TV."

Two other important people were not consulted that day: Virginia coach Terry Holland and LSU coach Dale Brown. "I remember seeing Dale at some point during the day and saying to him, 'Why are we playing this game?'" Holland said. "He felt the same way. But they told us to show up and play, so we showed up and played. I know we won, but that's about all I know. I'm not sure there were a thousand people actually watching the game. None of us wanted to be there."

That is true of all consolation games, which is why all postseason tournaments have now eliminated them. Once, the NCAA made teams that lost in the regional semifinals play a consolation game. Those games were mercifully ended after the 1975 tournament. "We lost to Syracuse in the round of sixteen that year," Dean Smith said. "Then we had to come back and play the consolation game at ten o'clock on Saturday morning. Boy, was that depressing."

Virginia-LSU was even worse than that. The Philadelphia Spectrum was not only all but empty except for a small cadre of fans from LSU and Virginia, but it was almost silent. There were no cheers, because the game was meaningless and those few people watching were aware of what was going on down in Washington. "What was strangest about it," Holland said, "is that we were out there playing while the committee was behind closed doors deciding whether to play the championship game."

Several alternative plans were discussed: postpone the game for twenty-four hours, postpone it for a week, or even declare co-champions and send everyone home. "I remember thinking neither Bob [Knight] nor I would want to do that," said Smith, who at that point had not yet won a national championship. "In the end, we all wanted to play but we had to wait for a signal from Washington."

The signal finally came about two hours before tip-off, with Virginia and LSU still playing: the president was out of surgery and appeared to be doing okay. "We were in touch with the White House at that stage," Jernstedt remembered. "If they had told us to shut it down, obviously we would have. But the message to us was that they wanted us to play. So we did."

Indiana won the game, and Smith would later joke that maybe the co-championship would not have been such a bad idea after all.

The work done by the committee and how it does that work have changed radically since the days of a six-man committee and a Sunday conference call to pick the field. These days the committee consists of ten people, a mix of athletic directors and conference commissioners. There are always ex-coaches involved, although some coaches say not enough. One of the ex-coaches who became an athletic director and sat on the committee is Holland. He disagrees with the notion that more coaches are needed. "Some of the best guys I worked with and who have been on the committee were guys who didn't coach basketball," he said. "Maybe they worked harder because of that, I'm not sure. But I don't think we have a problem there."

The committee now meets several times a year: once in July to review the previous year's tournament and make any rule changes for the coming year; once in December to plan for the upcoming tournament; once in February to stage a "mock" selection of the field; and then in March to pick the field. The July and December meetings usually take place in good weather near good golf courses — certainly a coincidence. The February and March meetings are held in Indianapolis, which is where NCAA headquarters are now. Throughout the basketball season, the committee chairman holds a monthly conference call with basketball writers, which usually centers on how much weight the committee is going to give to the RPI; how many teams from certain conferences may be selected; how much emphasis will be placed on strength of schedule, on road wins, and on and on. No matter what the chairman says, everything usually changes by Selection Sunday.

To say that the committee's March meeting is taken seriously is a little bit like saying summits involving the future of world peace are taken seriously. The ten members fly in on Wednesday evening and check into the Westin Hotel in downtown Indianapolis. They are then taken to the top floor of the hotel, which is, for all intents and purposes, sealed off for the rest of the week.

No one can get onto the floor without credentials. Security patrols the hallways, and committee members are told not to leave the building unless they are in absolute need of a walk to clear their mind.

"One thing that isn't a problem is food," said Jack Kvancz, who was on the committee from 1998 to 2003. "They will bring you anything you want."

Especially ice cream. As Jernstedt remembers it, Arnie Ferrin, the former Utah athletic director, and Cedric Dempsey, then at Arizona but later president of the NCAA, were the ones who started the tradition of ending each evening with endless supplies of ice cream. "It started kind of innocently," Jernstedt said. "But then it became a tradition. It was as if no one could go to bed until they'd had their ice cream."

Nowadays most committee members go to Indianapolis fully prepared to gain five pounds while they are there. "There's a workout room you can use," Holland said. "But it doesn't do much good."

Each day becomes a bit more tense. On Thursday morning the group gathers formally for the first time. The members sit around a long table in a conference room along with Jernstedt and several key staff members, including Jernstedt's lieutenant, Greg Shaheen, and Bill Hancock, who handled all NCAA media through the 2005 tournament. For years Hancock was the "board master." Whenever a team had to be moved from one of the three large boards set up in the room, it was Hancock's job to do it. No one else was allowed to touch the board.

"My first year, we were talking about some kind of bracketing problem," Kvancz remembered. "I got very animated about something and I got up, went to the board, and I was about to say, 'Move this team here and that team there' — and I touched the Velcro strips with their names on them up on the board to make my point. Everyone started screaming, 'Don't touch the board, only Hancock touches the board!'"

Sadly, that tradition went away in 2005, when everything was put on computer so that someone can now press a button and move a team from one screen to another. But the principles remain the same: there are three screens (formerly boards). On one are the teams already in the field. On another are those not yet in but under discussion. On the third are those considered out. The middle board, the one with teams under discussion, is called the "cross-country board," in honor of Willis Casey. It was Casey who came up with the three-board concept. Since he was a former cross-country coach, the board where teams are, in effect, moving from one place to another (out to in, or in to out) is called the cross-country board.

The first thing the committee members do is make a list of the thirty-four teams they believe belong in the tournament. It should be remembered that even though there are sixty-five teams in the field, the committee's number to select is thirty-four since thirty-one of the bids go automatically to conference champions. Any team that appears on nine of the ten lists (which are actually submitted prior to the members' arrival in Indianapolis) is in the field and is placed on the "in" board. All the other teams that are named but don't get nine votes go on Willis Casey's cross-country board. Then the discussion begins. According to most who have served on the committee, things get a little more heated each day.

"The funny thing is, in the end, if you put thirty-four teams on your list, you're probably going to have thirty-two of the teams that get in eventually," Kvancz said. "Or maybe thirty-one or thirty-three or all thirty-four. But you have to go through the process. There are usually anywhere from eighteen to twenty-five teams that go in right away on the first ballot. There may be as many as six to eight more that get in fairly easily. Then you really get down to it for the last two or three spots."

As the weekend goes on, some teams eliminate themselves. In 2005 Maryland was on the cross-country board on Thursday morning. When it lost that afternoon to Clemson in the first round of the ACC Tournament, it was moved to the "out" board. Other teams move to the out board as spots dry up. For example, if a regular-season champion that is worthy of an at-large bid loses in a conference tournament, that takes up an at-large spot. In 2005 both Notre Dame and Miami of Ohio were on the cross-country board with at-large spots still open until Utah and Pacific lost conference championship games on Saturday night, meaning those two schools needed at-large bids to get into the field. Their losses eliminated Notre Dame and Miami.

By Saturday, heated arguments begin to break out. Charles Harris, then the commissioner of the Mid-Eastern Athletic Conference, got into the habit of jumping from his seat and doing push-ups at especially tense moments. Sometimes members would simply get up and leave the room in order to cool off. In 1984 Gene Corrigan, then the Notre Dame athletic director and one of the calmer men ever to sit on the committee, was so incensed that Dayton was being left out of the field that he got up in mid-argument on Saturday night and said, "I just don't want to speak to any of you anymore. This is just plain wrong."

The next morning, when everyone had calmed down, Dayton was placed in the bracket. The good news for Corrigan was that the Flyers made him look good by making it to the final eight. The bad news is that one of the last teams left out of the field that year was Notre Dame. "Me and my big mouth," he joked later.

Four years earlier, in 1980, UCLA was the topic of a heated discussion. The Bruins, under Coach Larry Brown, had started the season very poorly but had rallied late to put themselves onto the cross-country board. The sentiment in the room was that they belonged in the field based on their strong finish. Russ Potts, then the athletic director at Southern Methodist (and now a state senator in Virginia) kept insisting that the pro-UCLA members were basing too much of their feeling on UCLA's history. "This isn't the sixties or seventies, fellas," he kept saying. "Wooden isn't the coach. They just aren't that good."

Potts finally went for a walk. While he was gone, Wayne Duke, the chairman, decided it was time to end the UCLA conversation and vote. When Potts walked back into the room, UCLA was in the bracket, scheduled to play a first-round game against Texas A&M. Potts blew up.

"Russ, calm down," Duke said. "We put you down as a no vote, and UCLA still got in."

"I understand that," Potts said. "But you've got them playing Texas A&M." (A&M was a heated SMU rival and fellow member of the Southwest Conference.)

"So?"

"So, all those damn Aggies are going to kill me for letting you guys pair them against UCLA. They don't want to play *them!*"

"But you said they weren't even good enough to be in the tournament."

"I know I said that. But that was *before* they were in the tournament."

Eventually, after some bracket shuffling, UCLA played Old Dominion. The Bruins won that game and then upset number one seed DePaul in the west regional and ended up in the national championship game. Of course, its second-place finish was eventually "vacated" for NCAA rules violations, meaning it does not appear in any of the official records for the tournament that year. So, in a sense, Potts got his way.

Twenty years later a similar argument took place involving one of the sport's glamour teams: North Carolina. Like UCLA in 1980, the Tar Heels had struggled during the season. They had lost in the first round of the ACC Tournament to Wake Forest and had an 18–13 record. Their credentials were almost identical to another ACC team, Virginia. The conversation went back and forth. Carolina had been in the tournament for twenty-five consecutive seasons. The question many committee members was asking was whether they would even be under serious consideration if they weren't North Carolina.

Finally, Jack Kvancz turned to Les Robinson, the athletic director at Citadel, but formerly the coach at North Carolina State and a graduate there. Each committee member is assigned three conferences to follow during the season. He is expected to watch as many games involving teams from that conference as possible so he will know and understand the teams in great detail when questions are asked about them. One of Robinson's conferences that year was the ACC.

"When it comes right down to it, Les," Kvancz said, asking what is often the ultimate tiebreaker question, "who has a better team, Carolina or Virginia?"

Robinson paused for a moment and smiled. "You guys know it kills me to say this," he said. "But I think Carolina's better."

That was enough for Kvancz. "I said right then and there, 'Carolina must be better,' because there's no way Les is going to vote for them unless he has to."

Carolina was voted in as an eighth seed and almost matched what UCLA had done in 1980, upsetting number one seed

Stanford in the second round en route to the Final Four. The Tar Heels lost in the semifinals to Florida. Their finish, however, was not vacated.

Almost every year the longest and most heated discussions take place on Saturday night, when the field is almost always complete or virtually complete. Often committee members will ask for a "nitty-gritty" on a team. That means the members are shown every detail available: RPI, road wins, record in the last ten games, quality of cheerleaders — okay, there is nothing on the cheerleaders, but that's the *only* detail left out. Sunday is used to finalize seeding and to put the teams in brackets and then, finally, to spend the last hour briefing the chairman on what questions he should expect when he is interviewed on TV and radio and by the print media after the field has been unveiled. By Saturday evening in 2005, there were six unfilled spots in the field, with the committee understanding that the number could be sliced if heavily favored Utah and Pacific were to lose their conference championship games that night.

The teams still on the cross-country board who were under discussion were Northern Iowa, Iowa, UCLA, UAB, Miami (Ohio), Notre Dame, St. Joseph's, and George Washington. Earlier in the day Georgetown, Memphis, and New Mexico had been moved to the "out" board as the number of at-large spots available began to shrink because of the results in conference tournaments. Georgia Tech, which had been a "bubble" team (bubble being one of the most overused sports terms of the twenty-first century, along with "red zone" in football) going into the week, had played its way into an at-large bid with two wins in the ACC Tournament. So had North Carolina State. West Virginia had done the same thing in the Big East Tournament.

Exit Georgetown, exit New Mexico, exit Memphis. The latter

two could still get in by winning their conference tournaments. Memphis almost pulled it off, losing to Louisville in the final seconds of the Conference USA championship game. That was good news for the bubble teams. A Memphis victory would have taken away another spot.

As the day progressed, Iowa, UCLA, and UAB made their way — after lengthy discussion — from the cross-country board into the bracket. Northern Iowa, Miami, and Notre Dame were considered the leading contenders for the three spots still left at that moment, with St. Joe's on hold pending the outcome of its championship game in the Atlantic 10 with George Washington. If the Hawks won, GW would go onto the cross-country board as a possible at-large team, perhaps bumping one of the three teams under discussion.

On Saturday night everything changed as the evening wore on. George Washington won the A-10 final with relative ease. St. Joseph's went off the board. Northern Iowa was voted in, leaving Miami and Notre Dame needing wins from Utah and Pacific. When both lost — to New Mexico and Utah State, respectively — Miami and Notre Dame were finished. They would go where all teams blown off the bubble go: the NIT, or National Invitation Tournament, now known among major teams as the Not Invited Tournament. In fact, at major conference tournaments like the ACC, Big East, and Big 12, fans who suspect that an opponent is headed for the NIT will chant those letters tauntingly in the final seconds of a lost game.

Once the thirty-four at-large teams are chosen and the sixty-five-team field is decided, the teams must be placed into four brackets and seeded. In its own way, this is as much of a task as picking the field. There is always controversy about who receives the four number one seeds, and that was certainly the case in

2005, when the committee plucked Washington from a group of several candidates to be the fourth top seed, along with Illinois, North Carolina, and Duke. The problem, several committee members admitted later, was that they were all caught off guard when Kentucky — which had been slotted in the third of the four number one spots — was upset in the SEC Tournament final by Florida on Sunday afternoon. By midafternoon on Sunday, everyone on the committee except for the chairman, who stays behind, is thinking about getting to the airport for a flight home. They have all been locked up in the hotel since Wednesday and they all know they are facing three more weeks during which they will be on the road most of the time.

There is also the ongoing issue of those conferences that play their tournament finals on Sunday, such as the ACC, the Big Ten, the Big 12, and the SEC — all major conferences in which the outcome of the final frequently affects seeding and can knock an at-large team out of the tournament if a low-ranked team plays its way to the conference championship. The reason these finals are played on Sunday is simple: ESPN and CBS pay the conferences a lot of money to play on Sunday. In 2004, when everyone sprinted for the door, the Big 12 final was still going on. Oklahoma State beat Texas Tech and, in the minds of many, played its way into a number one seed. When the field was unveiled, Oklahoma State was the number two seed in the east regional, behind St. Joseph's. An argument could be made for either team being the top seed. But when Bowlsby said in the post-unveiling interview that one of the reasons Oklahoma State did not move up to number one after its victory was that the Big 12 title game was played too late to make a switch, many people were — justifiably — incredulous. Bowlsby then went on to criticize the conference for playing late on Sunday, a rather remarkable statement since he is the athletic director at Iowa, a Big Ten member that readily gobbles up the money CBS pays the league to play on that same Sunday.

With all the money the NCAA spends on the committee — the hotels the members stay in during meetings are not exactly $39-a-night motels, and none of them would recognize a coach-class seat if it hit him in the head — the notion that they would simply break off their talks to get to the airport at the most crucial moments of their decision-making process stunned people.

Of course, Bowlsby's faux pas was nothing compared with what had happened to Jim Livengood in 2003. Livengood is the athletic director at Arizona, one of the truly decent men in college athletics, the rare athletic director who doesn't break into spin-speak whenever he is asked a question on a subject other than the weather. He was the committee chairman that year. For whatever reason, the committee had a very bad year in 2003. For one thing, it placed Brigham Young in a bracket where it would have to play a second-round game on Sunday. BYU is a Mormon school and has always made it clear that it will not play on a Sunday. The committee members simply forgot, causing an embarrassing scramble on Monday in which they were forced to switch BYU with another team to another bracket at another site.

The other problem was Kentucky and Arizona. There are years when separating the top two seeds from the others is difficult. In 2005, for example, Illinois was a clear-cut number one seed in the field, with only one loss — a buzzer-beater at Ohio State — all season. North Carolina was almost as clearly the number two seed in spite of a loss in the ACC Tournament. The next six to eight teams were all pretty even (although no one making mock brackets had Washington as a number one seed and no one had Louisville as a number four; most people had the Cardinals as a one or two).

In 2003 Kentucky and Arizona had clearly distanced themselves from everyone else during the regular season. At that time the committee did not seed the number one seeds. It simply produced four number one seeds, placed them in brackets, and never told anyone who was considered number one in the field, who was number two, and so on down the line. When the brackets went up that night, everyone gasped: Arizona and Kentucky had been bracketed to meet in the national semifinals. How was that possible? How could the committee look in such detail at what every team had accomplished and not seed these two teams to meet in the championship game?

CBS always gets first crack at the chairman once it has revealed the bracket to the country, another perk it receives in return for the $6 billion it is paying over eleven years, a contract that extends now through the 2011 tournament. Jim Nantz and Billy Packer, on-site at one of those Sunday championships Bowlsby so dislikes, question the chairman along with the studio crew led by Greg Gumbel. When it was Packer's turn, he looked ready to jump through the screen to ask Livengood how in the world Kentucky and Arizona could be placed in the same half of the overall bracket.

One could not help feeling sorry for Livengood. In the hour-long briefing with his fellow committee members to prep him for his TV appearances, no one had brought up the Arizona-Kentucky question. There was a reason for that: no one had noticed.

"We just blew it," Kvancz said later. "We sat there and looked at the four brackets and somehow, because the four brackets were up there side by side, not one half together and the other half together, we all missed it. Everyone was responsible and then poor Jim was the one who got stuck trying to explain something that was unexplainable."

Caught off guard, Livengood tried to get out of the question by talking about how well qualified all four number one seeds were (although a lot of people also took issue with Texas being a top seed over Kansas) and how hard the committee had worked. Packer wasn't buying. He again demanded to know how this could have happened. Finally, Livengood blurted out, "You know, it isn't our job to project matchups."

It is difficult to come up with an analogy to explain what Livengood said at that moment. It was a little bit like a pilot saying it wasn't his job to fly the plane or a hockey goalie saying it wasn't his job to stop pucks. Perhaps it was like a comedian saying it wasn't his job to be funny.

When all the talk and bluster and hoo-ha about RPIs and schedules and good wins and bad wins is over, the basketball committee has two basic jobs:

1. Select the field.
2. Seed the field.

What is the purpose of seeding? To project matchups.

If you don't want to project matchups, why seed the field? Just throw all sixty-five teams into a hat and begin drawing out names. If the top two teams come out to play in the first round, let them play — you aren't projecting matchups. But if you are seeding a field, lining up the number one seed in a bracket to play the number sixteen seed and working your way toward a matchup of the number one and number two seeds in the regional final if both teams keep winning, then you are — say it all together — projecting matchups.

It is difficult to be too harsh on Livengood, because he is a good man and because, as Kvancz pointed out, the entire committee was responsible for the screwup. The committee was taken off the hook a tiny bit when Kentucky and Arizona were upset by Marquette and Kansas in their regional finals. But that didn't change what had happened, and everyone knew it. That summer the committee voted to seed the four number ones so it would be impossible for the top two seeds to meet before the championship game. Thus, in 2005 there was no way that Illinois and North Carolina could meet before Monday night, April 4, in St. Louis.

That was a good thing.

However, in its infinite wisdom, the committee — partly, no doubt, to hide its embarrassment over the Arizona-Kentucky fiasco — announced that from now on, each regional would be named for the city it was being played in rather than by the simple geographic names — east, south, midwest, west — that had been traditional. So, instead of going to the east regional in 2005, North Carolina was sent to the "Syracuse regional." Illinois didn't go to the midwest; it went to the "Chicago regional."

This is confusing and silly and completely unnecessary.

Of course, it makes perfect sense to the committee. That makes ten people in the world who feel that way.

Making honest mistakes, especially under the pressures that are part of selection weekend, is both understandable and forgivable. It happens. We all make mistakes. Having said that, what the committee did five years ago when it created the "opening round" game — to use the committee's euphemism — was neither a mistake nor forgivable. It was done in the name of greed by men who clearly cared only about their own interests.

The problem began with the breakup of the Western Athletic Conference. The WAC had grown out of control, with sixteen schools spread out from Texas to Hawaii, and it was finally decided that eight of the schools should break off and form their own league, the Mountain West Conference. Since the MWC met the various criteria for an automatic tournament bid, beginning in 2001 there would be thirty-one conferences eligible for automatic bids instead of thirty. Which meant, logically, that the number of at-large bids would drop from thirty-four to thirty-three.

Anyone who knows anything about the history of the NCAA Tournament understands that the true magic of the event lies in the upsets that occur during the first week, whether it is Vitale standing on his head because Austin Peay beats Illinois or Bryce Drew beating the buzzer on the swinging-gate play so that Valparaiso can beat Mississippi, or Vermont beating Syracuse and Bucknell beating Kansas in 2005. Those games have produced indelible memories because they involved little-schools-that-could shocking power schools from power conferences. To fans of Vermont, beating Syracuse was every bit as big a moment as winning the national title was for North Carolina fans. Perhaps bigger, because it may never happen again.

All the schools that produce those moments are from the so-called one-bid conferences, the leagues where everyone knows that each year only the conference champion, the winner of the automatic bid, is going to the tournament. Regardless of what its RPI number was in 2005, Vermont was not going to get an at-large bid if it had lost in the America East Conference Tournament. "We were in the twenties in the RPI rankings all season," Coach Tom Brennan said. "That means, worst case, based on the numbers, we should be an eighth seed — maybe a nine or ten because we're not in a big conference. What were we? A thirteen! What's that tell you? It tells you we don't get in if we don't have the automatic bid."

Brennan's right. As a number thirteen seed, Vermont was ranked by the committee behind every at-large team in the field. The lowest-seeded at-large teams were eleventh seeds.

There are some coaches in power conferences who chafe at the automatic bids, saying the tournament should just be the sixty-four best teams in the country. They're wrong. If the tournament was the best sixty-four teams in the country, then sixty of the teams would come from the ACC, the Big East, the Big Ten, the Big 12, the Southeast Conference, the Pacific-10, and the Atlantic 10. Conference USA might get a bid or two, the Missouri Valley might get an occasional bid, and the Mountain West might sneak in a team every now and then. The America East? No way. The Patriot League — Bucknell's conference — no chance. Ivy League, SWAC, Mid-Continent (Valparaiso), and the Big Sky? Long gone. A major first-round upset would consist of the seventh-place team in the ACC upsetting the second-place team from the Big 12. So what? One school with unlimited resources beating another school with unlimited resources.

The committee is smart enough to understand that the one-bid leagues are a crucial part of the tournament. That doesn't mean they treat them fairly or well. Vermont should have been much higher than a thirteenth seed in 2005, just as Holy Cross should have been higher than a fourteenth seed in 2003. Even though committee members are assigned to follow the smaller conferences during the season, there isn't as much access to their games on TV and most committee members just don't care enough about how they seed those teams. At one point, a sub-committee on bracketing the teams on the thirteenth to sixteenth lines was formed, but it didn't help much, either. The little guys are allowed into the room, but they are expected to keep quiet, know their place, and pull an occasional upset so the committee can take bows and tell people how well the system works. The system does work, but it is more an accident of luck and fate than anything else.

When the committee was faced with the possibility of losing an at-large bid for the 2001 tournament, panic set in. Bids equal money. Each team that receives a bid to the tournament is paid one "unit" of the tournament's profits, which in 2005 was worth $300,000. Each time a team advances through a round, it receives another unit. That means an at-large bid is worth at least $300,000 and can be worth a good deal more should the team win a game or two — which can happen and has happened with teams that get in at the last minute. Witness Dayton in 1984, Virginia that same year (all the way to the Final Four), or, more recently, North Carolina in 2000.

The committee was being pushed hard by the big-money conference commissioners not to lose an at-large bid. Two of the men pushing hard were Roy Kramer, then of the Southeast Conference, and Jim Delany of the Big Ten — both former chairmen of the committee. Both also pushed to make sure that the committee chairman would always be from a big-money conference. In 2003 Kvancz, athletic director from George Washington, was supposed to be in line to become chairman in his last year on the committee. At the last minute, because of some backroom maneuvering, Jim Livengood from Arizona ended up as chairman. Which probably worked out for Kvancz, because it was Livengood instead of him left to answer all the questions about the mistakes the committee made that year in bracketing.

Pushed by Delany and Kramer, the committee decided to keep thirty-four at-large bids, as if that were some kind of magic number. It couldn't simply declare a league that met the criteria for an automatic bid no longer eligible for one, so it increased the number of teams in the tournament to sixty-five — thirty-one automatic bids, thirty-four at-large. How, then, do you get from sixty-five to sixty-four? Easy: send two automatic-bid teams from smaller conferences to, in effect, play off for the last spot in the sixty-four-team field. The committee smartly selected Dayton, a true college basketball hotbed, as the site of the play-in game and christened it the "opening round" game.

In other words, it created a second tier of teams, consisting of two schools among sixty-five. It made these two into second-class citizens, forcing them to play on Tuesday, then fly to another site, and play a number one seed on Friday. The losing team in Dayton never gets to go to a true tournament site. It doesn't get to take part in the day-before practices or the press conferences that are part of the Dance. They are in the Dance, but they end up dancing alone in an empty room with no one to talk to about their experience. To add financial insult to injury, the winning team in the play-in game isn't even credited with a financial unit for the victory. It's a win, but the NCAA doesn't really count it as a win. It is as if you've gotten into the Dance by winning your conference tournament and then you're told you have to go win another game to *really* be in the Dance.

It is insulting and it is demeaning and, in many cases, it denies kids whose greatest dream is to step on court in a packed building to take on a big-name team in the NCAA Tournament that chance. In 2005 the play-in game matched Oakland University (from Detroit) playing in its first-ever NCAA Tournament against Alabama A&M. There are two predominantly black conferences that have automatic NCAA Tournament bids: the Southwestern Athletic and the Mid-Eastern Athletic. In five years of play-in games, there has always been one school from a predominantly black conference involved — never two, because the committee knows it would get killed politically if it sent both schools to the play-in game even if they were the two weakest teams in the field.

A year earlier, in 2004, the play-in game matched Lehigh from the Patriot League against Florida A&M from the MEAC. Lehigh was a great story. In 2002 it had won five games. Under Billy Taylor, a bright young coach, the school had turned its basketball fortunes around and in 2004 had gone from worst (in 2002) to first in the Patriot League and had won the conference tournament. Because of television, the Patriot League final that year was played on Sunday afternoon: bid day. A few hours after they had hugged one another on the floor of Stabler Arena and cut down the nets, the Lehigh players learned they weren't actually going to the Dance; they were going to Dayton. The next day they flew to Dayton, practiced, tried to learn about Florida A&M, and, forty-eight hours after the most emotional game of their lives, had to try to play Florida A&M in front of seven thousand neutral fans (a good crowd but a quiet one). They lost. Forty-eight hours after thinking they had made the big time, they went home having never seen the big time.

"It was a letdown," Taylor said later. "We had this great moment, winning the championship game, feeling that accomplishment, and then we sat there that night and saw we were going to Dayton. It really took away any chance to savor what we had done."

Lehigh was a senior-dominated team, meaning the seniors had no chance to come back and try to make it to the round of sixty-four, and the underclassmen were unlikely to get another chance, either. They still had their conference title and an NCAA banner to hang in their arena, but not the memories that come with going to a true tournament site.

The committee members say they will not take away the thirty-fourth at-large bid. Okay, fine. What should be done then is that the thirty-third and thirty-fourth at-large teams should be sent to the play-in game. Sending two teams from major conferences means sending schools that will almost certainly be back in the tournament again soon; sending to Dayton players and coaches for whom playing at a true tournament site isn't nearly as big a deal as it is for Lehigh or Alabama A&M or Florida A&M or Oakland. For example, in 2005 the committee could easily have matched Iowa and UCLA — two of the last teams into the field. That would have been Big Ten vs. Pac-10. It would have been a far more glamorous TV matchup; it would have sold more tickets in Dayton, and the likelihood is that the players from the losing team would make the tournament again next year or the year after. Instead of putting the winner of the game into a number sixteen seed and feeding it to a number one, you put the winner into an eleventh or twelfth seed and match it up accordingly with a number six or a number five in the first round.

"It does make sense to do it that way," said Kvancz, who was part of the committee that created the play-in game. "I can see the argument. I don't think you will get a majority of the committee to see it that way."

Translation: the committee is always dominated and controlled by the major conferences. Perhaps if the entire committee — instead of one or two representatives — made the trip to Dayton and then went into the losing locker room after the game, they might feel differently.

11

Friday

FOR THOSE WHO ARE PART of the Final Four, Friday is when it begins to *feel* like a Final Four. The town is full; fans are everywhere; there isn't a restaurant reservation to be had. And for the first time, everyone gets a look inside the place where the games will be played.

Like most modern arenas and stadiums, the Edward Jones Dome is named after a corporation that pays a lot of money to stick its name all over the building. Once, it was named after an airline that went bankrupt (TWA) and is now named after an investment firm. The building is only ten years old, which means it was *built* with the idea of being used for basketball. So the seats sold for a basketball game — 47,754 for the Final Four — are not all as far away as in some of the older domes.

"In the Astrodome everyone was about five miles away," former committee chairman Wayne Duke remembered about 1971. "Going there probably set us back ten years in terms of domes. Everyone was wary for a while after that."

There are many people who will tell you that the best day of the Final Four is Friday. For one thing, people without the connections or the money to buy tickets for the actual games can walk in for free and watch the four practices. This has become a tradition to the point where most coaches allow their players to stage dunking contests during the last five minutes of their fifty-minute workouts for the specific purpose of entertaining the crowd.

"Not something you normally write into your practice plan," said Roy Williams, who *did* write it into his.

The unofficial attendance for the Friday practices in St. Louis for the 2005 Final Four was 31,000 — higher than the total season attendance for some Division 1 teams. It appeared to most people on the floor that at least 80 percent of those fans were from Illinois. They covered the building in blue and orange and went completely crazy when the Illini took the floor. "It felt like we were going out there to play a home game," said Luther Head, one of the trio of star guards who had formed the heart and soul of Illinois' remarkable season. "I mean, you don't usually run out there for practice and get a standing ovation."

The presence of so many Illinois fans may have been even more surprising to the players from the other three teams. "It was actually kind of overwhelming to run out of the tunnel and see how many people were there *and* how many of them were Illinois fans," said North Carolina walk-on guard Wes Miller. "We're so used to seeing Carolina fans everywhere we travel that to go to a place and see that many people from another school was kind of shocking."

When Carolina had gone through its open practice in Charlotte on the day before its first-round game against Oakland — the survivor of the dreaded play-in game — the Charlotte Coliseum had probably close to 10,000 Carolina fans watching. Even though Duke has become one of the strongest national programs under Mike Krzyzewski, the number of fans in the state who pull for "Carolina" — no one ever adds the "North" — dwarfs the number of Duke fans. Which makes sense: UNC is the public school in the state, it has a long and storied basketball tradition, and most of the people who go to school there come from the state and remain there after graduation. Duke, which has about 30 percent as many undergraduates, draws its student body from around the country and only a sliver of them stay after graduation. Most of the great players who have come from North Carolina — Michael Jordan, James Worthy, Jerry Stackhouse, Antawn Jamison, Brad Daugherty, Bobby Jones, Phil Ford, Walter Davis — have gone to North Carolina. The most notable exceptions are the great David Thompson and Tommy Burleson, who led North Carolina State to the national championship in 1974. The best in-state players to play at Duke? Probably Stuart Yarbrough, who played for Vic Bubas in the 1960s, and Kenny Dennard, who was on Bill Foster's Final Four team in 1978. The only highly touted player from the state Krzyzewski had successfully recruited was Shavlik Randolph, who was notable as a Duke player in that he was an oft-injured bust who left after his junior season in 2005 even though he had no chance of being drafted.

Wes Miller was one of those Final Four stories that should make people smile regardless of where they are from or which team they follow. Miller was the ultimate gym rat, a kid judged too small to be a Division 1 basketball player when he was in high school. Listed at five foot eleven and 185 pounds but looking smaller, Miller almost willed himself into a college scholarship. He left his home in Charlotte and played for three seasons at New Hampton Prep School in New Hampshire, where he roomed with Rashad McCants, who was as touted as Miller was unnoticed. But during his fifth year of high school (a lot of athletes spend an extra year in high school these days), he did attract some D-1 coaches because of his shooting ability and his willingness to do anything on the court to help his team win. He ended up going to James Madison and played solid backup minutes as a freshman, averaging 17 minutes per night and 4.1 points a game.

But the JMU program was in disarray. Sherman Dillard, the coach who had recruited Miller, was barely hanging on to his job (he was fired in 2004), and Miller's old friend McCants was urging him to transfer to North Carolina and try out as a walk-on. Most big-time teams have walk-ons these days, but Carolina has a genuine walk-on tradition. Dean Smith always encouraged good students to try out for his team, and frequently walk-ons would work their way into playing real minutes and receiving scholarships before they graduated. Having grown up in the state as a Carolina fan, Miller was aware of this. Even though it meant giving up his scholarship, he decided to transfer. He sat out the '03–'04 season, then became eligible to play the following year.

Miller had no illusions about where he would fit in as a Tar Heel. "My most important job is to run the blue [backup] team in practice," he said. "I try every day to make [starting point guard] Raymond [Felton] work as hard as I can. The minutes I get in the games are just a bonus." Miller's statistics for the season were a reflection of that. Coming into the Final Four, he had played in twenty-three of the team's thirty-five games, a total of 91 minutes, scoring 26 points and being credited with 12 assists and 4 rebounds. Almost all of that had come late in games, with Carolina in control of the outcome. But he was an important member of the team, in part because of what he contributed in practice but also because he got along well with everyone — including the sometimes moody McCants and the far less moody Sean May, the team's best player, who was his road roommate and a close friend.

On Thursday night Miller had talked to Mike Roberts, a high school teammate who had been on the Indiana team that reached the national championship game in 2002. Roberts had told Miller to make sure to look around all week and realize that he was going through a once-in-a-lifetime experience. He had told him to make sure to enjoy Friday because that was the fun day, the chance to play in front of a lot of people, with no pressure.

The focus at the Final Four is — naturally — on the coaches and the star players. But the backup players, the ones on the end of the bench, are just as thrilled to be there and find being a part of it just as memorable. "When we got out on the court and started doing our stretching, I was literally tingling with excitement," Miller said. "My whole life I dreamed of being on a Final Four team, but that was all it really was — a dream. Most of the time I heard I wasn't a D-1 player; and if I was, it would be low D-1 — not a team that would get to the Final Four. When I was at James Madison, the dream for us was to win our conference tournament and play in the first round of the tournament. Now I was on a team that had won four games but knew it still had work to do."

Roy Williams had reminded his players of that in the locker room before they practiced. They had accomplished a lot during the season already, but they had two more games to win. "Have fun, enjoy being here, but go out there prepared to work," he said. "I want forty-five hard minutes and then you guys can do whatever you want the last five. But give me forty-five first."

Carolina had arrived at the arena on the same bus it had taken on every road trip within the ACC all season. Williams, who is as superstitious as any coach, had the bus driven to St. Louis from Chapel Hill so his team could ride on it throughout the Final Four. He had been to four Final Fours at Kansas without a championship. He wasn't taking any chances.

During the forty-five minutes of real practice, it occurred to Miller that this was the time when he was most likely to make a real contribution if Carolina was to win. He was running Michigan State's offense for the blue team and he wanted to be sure that he helped the first team prepare for what they were going to see the next night. He was fully aware that once the game began, his major role would be as a cheerleader. Miller remembered hearing cheers during the Charlotte practice when he had drilled a couple of three-point shots. The next day he had gotten into the Oakland game with Carolina in control and made a three — his fifth of the season — in the late going. "That was a big thrill," he said. "Actually scoring in an NCAA Tournament game."

Now Miller could only hope that his team might get enough of a lead late to allow him to make it into a Final Four game. The good news was, unlike Dean Smith in 1952, he would not be left out of the box score if he got into the game. He hit a couple of threes during practice, which didn't seem to impress the St. Louis crowd as much as it had impressed the folks in Charlotte. That was okay with him. He was on the court practicing at the Final Four in front of more than 30,000 people. "In all," he said, "it was pretty cool."

When the Tar Heels began their dunking contest, Miller grabbed May's video camera and became the cameraman/play-by-play announcer. "I'm vertically challenged," he said. "This is the best role for me."

A good role player always knows his role — in practice or in a game.

* * *

Wes Miller was not, by any stretch of the imagination, the first player or coach to find going through the Friday practice at the Final Four emotional. Billy Hahn, who played at Maryland for four years under Lefty Driesell and then coached there later in his career for twelve seasons as Gary Williams's top assistant, remembers the chill that ran through him walking down the steps to the court in Minneapolis when Maryland went out to practice before the 2001 Final Four.

"It just hit me all of a sudden as we went down the steps," he said. "I've been in basketball all my life. I've watched the Final Four on television; I've come to it for years and seen all the games. Now I'm *in* the Final Four. Those kids walking onto the court are kids I recruited, I coached. It was just an unbelievable feeling. I got very emotional."

Williams wasn't as emotional at that moment, but he was aware of the road he had traveled to get there. "If you coach in college, I don't care what level you are at or whether you are an assistant or a head coach, the Final Four is the Holy Grail. Right or wrong, it is. We all talk about how we shouldn't judge our careers on making the Final Four or on winning it, but every single one of us wants to be there. To finally get there, to walk out on that court to run practice, was a big deal."

He smiled. "I had friends tell me to savor the moment on Friday because I didn't have to coach a game. I tried. I couldn't do it. I was too uptight."

One thing that has changed about Friday is getting into the building. Before 9/11, since there was no charge to get into practice and no tickets, people just walked in and found seats. Now, with post-9/11 security in place, everyone has to go through metal detectors or get wanded or both; there are limits on what can be brought into the arena; and anyone who doesn't have proper ID — including players and coaches — isn't going to get in.

That's a lot different from New Orleans in 1982, which was Roy Williams's first Final Four as a North Carolina assistant coach. "I had gotten into the habit during the season of eating a candy bar before every game," he said. "It started with the Wake Forest game. I had a candy bar before the game and we won. Superstitious as I am, I kept making sure I ate one before every game. Sometimes a manager would get me one, or I'd just go get one at a concession stand.

"Now we're in the national championship game against Georgetown and I get into the Superdome and I realize I forgot to stop and get a candy bar someplace. None of the managers have one. I go up to the concession stands, and they're not selling candy bars. Well, I've *got* to have a candy bar. If I don't have one and we lose, I'll never forgive myself. In those days we really didn't have any kind of credentials. We'd just all kind of come into the building off the bus, the guards would nod at us and wish us luck, and that was it.

"So, I go to one of the dome exits and I explain who I am, that I have to go out for a few minutes and will he be sure to remember me and let me back in. He says he will. I go out and it takes me a while, but I find a candy bar finally. I go racing back, it's maybe an hour or so before the game now, and I go to the same entrance. The guy's not there. He's been moved or something, and the guy in his place is looking at me like 'Yeah, sure, you're a coach and you went out for a candy bar.' I'm panicked. I'm thinking, 'Oh God, we're playing the national championship game in an hour and I can't get back in the building.' There were no cell phones. Finally, while I'm trying to talk this guard into letting me in, please, before Coach Smith kills me, another guard comes by and recognizes me. He tells the other guy it's okay, that I really am a coach, and I get back in."

In 2005 Williams would not have gotten back in. "That's true," he said. "Because I wouldn't have had my cell phone with me since you aren't allowed to bring them in these days."

One person who could relate to what Wes Miller was feeling as he went through practice on Friday was District Court Judge T. Bruce Bell of Lexington, Kentucky. Or as he was known during his days as a walk-on player at Duke, "Juice."

Bruce Bell is, almost without question, the only son of a Final Four referee ever to play on a Final Four team. Bell's father, Tommy Bell, who practiced law in Lexington throughout his adult life, was a top college basketball referee and one of the best-known referees in the history of the National Football League. In fact, it can be argued that Tommy Bell refereed the most important game in the history of pro football: Super Bowl III, the game in which the upstart New York Jets — 17-point underdogs — stunned the Baltimore Colts, 16–7. That was the last game played before the American Football League became a part of the NFL, and Jets quarterback Joe Namath had expressed pregame concern about having an NFL referee working the game. Late in the game Namath made a point of telling Bell that he had done an excellent job. "How can you say that, Joe?" Bell replied. "*My* team is losing."

Tommy Bell was a Kentucky basketball season-ticket holder, and his son grew up a fanatic UK supporter. He was a good high school basketball player, but not good enough to be recruited by

Kentucky or any of the other power basketball schools. At his father's urging, thinking he would follow him into law, he chose Duke, hoping he might be able to at least walk on to the team there, given that the Blue Devils had been struggling for several years. He was right. He made the team as a walk-on and became a starter during his junior season when starting point guard Tate Armstrong (a member of the '76 Olympic team who later played in the NBA) broke a wrist and his backup, Steve Gray, struggled. In Duke's last home game that season, Bell was matched against North Carolina's Phil Ford, who would later be the second pick in the NBA draft and the rookie of the year.

"Little bit of a mismatch," Bell said, laughing. "I remember I thought I'd stolen the ball from him once and then I heard the whistle. The guys all said later, 'What were the chances anyone was going to believe you stole the ball from Phil Ford without fouling?' I'm telling you, dang it, I stole it clean."

Bell really does say *dang it*. His teammates always delighted in mimicking his high-pitched voice and still mimic it every chance they get, regardless of how many people now refer to him as Your Honor. Naturally, they refer to him now as "Judge Juice."

Bell didn't play very much as a senior. Two transfers, John Harrell and Bob Bender, became eligible and took most of the minutes. That was the season when Duke exploded onto the national consciousness again, going from last place in the ACC to the national championship game, where, as luck would have it, they played Kentucky. Even though Kentucky, led by Jack Givens's 41 points, won the game, Bell doesn't remember the loss as much as he remembers the ride.

"To go from where we had been to be in the Final Four was just beyond amazing," he said. "We had high hopes when we started the season because we knew we were better with [Gene]

Banks and [Kenny] Dennard plus Harrell and Bender. But it wasn't until February really that we started to understand just how good we were."

Bell was the only senior on that team. On senior night he stood alone at center court while his teammates and schoolmates stood and cheered for him for three solid minutes. He still has a picture of that moment in his house. Duke went on to win the ACC Tournament for the first time in twelve years to get back to the NCAA Tournament for the first time in just as long. "Imagine that," Bell said. "Nowadays it's unthinkable for Duke not to be in the tournament. Back then, just getting back in set off wild celebrating on campus. When we beat Villanova to get to the Final Four, none of us could really believe it."

The Final Four was in St. Louis for the second time in five years, although it would not return again until 2005. Duke beat Notre Dame in the semifinals to set up the meeting with Kentucky. "I just couldn't believe my college career was going to end against Kentucky," Bell said. "And it was for the national championship. Of course, Givens just killed us. He did the same thing in my last high school game, too. I still have nightmares about him."

That night was probably the highlight of Givens's life. He had a relatively brief NBA career and landed a job as a color commentator for the Orlando Magic. But in 2004 he was arrested and charged with sexual battery and lewd molestation in a case involving a fourteen-year-old girl. Givens denied the charges, and the court case was still pending (he was acquitted in the fall) when college basketball returned to the scene of his finest hour in 2005. By then, Bell was a judge, a season-ticket holder for both Kentucky and Duke basketball games, and had two sons who had gone to Duke. And yet it can be argued that in a different way, St. Louis was as much a highlight for him — even though he never played a second in the national championship game — as it was for Givens.

"I still get chills whenever I think about that weekend," he said. "The connection I still feel to all those guys is amazing. It's been twenty-seven years, but we're *still* teammates. We have an e-mail circle that will get started sometimes on a topic and just go on for days. I remember after we lost the Kentucky game, we came back in the locker room and I asked Coach [Bill] Foster if I could say the postgame prayer because it was my last game. During the prayer I said, 'I love everyone in this room.' I know men aren't supposed to say things like that, but that's the way I felt at that moment. I still feel that way about all of them today — whether they like it or not."

Bell finally did get to see his school win the national championship in 1991. He and Rob Hardy, also a walk-on for the '78 Duke team, rented a limo and made the trip to Indianapolis when Duke played Kansas in the championship game. "I'd been in Dallas when they lost to Louisville and that was disappointing, but I just had a feeling this was going to be their time," Bell said. "When they won, it was a great feeling because I felt I was part of it. That's one thing Mike [Krzyzewski] has done well. He's tried to make everyone feel they're a part of the program, even those of us who didn't play for him. I know he's not the only coach who does that, but it still feels great to go back to a game at Duke and feel as if I'm a part, even a very small part, of all that's gone on."

These days there are people around Lexington who have no idea that the Honorable Judge Bell once played for Duke, now the team Kentucky fans love to hate most. "I play it kind of low-key," Bell said. "But if it comes up, I say, 'Yes, I played for Duke — on the team that lost to Kentucky in '78.' That seems to calm things down." He smiled. "Of course, every now and then I can't resist bringing up '92."

That was the year Christian Laettner hit the shot at the buzzer to beat Kentucky in the east regional final, a game Kentucky fans still rant about even though the Wildcats evened the score in '98 in the south regional final, rallying from 17 points down to beat Duke. In each case, the winner went on to win the national championship.

As thrilling as it has been to see his alma mater win three national titles, Bell's fondest memories are still of '78. "I'm not sure a Final Four team ever had more fun than we did," he said. "Maybe the pressure got to us a little bit in the Kentucky game when we walked out on the floor and realized we were in the national championship game. But until then, it was nothing but a joyride."

He smiled. "To tell you the truth, it still is."

While the four teams went through their paces in the dome, rumors continued to swirl around the coaches' hotel. By Friday afternoon it is just about impossible to walk from one end of the lobby to the other without being accosted by someone who has a rumor to spread, tickets to sell, or a story to tell. Someone spotted Buzz Peterson, the recently fired coach at Tennessee, strolling down a sidewalk with Coastal Carolina athletic director Moose Koegel. Within minutes word passed through the lobby: Peterson is going to Coastal Carolina. That one turned out to be true. He was named the following week.

The Virginia job was still the one creating the most stir. Terry Holland walked into the coaches' lobby and was set upon like bugs at a light because of his Virginia connections. Holland swore he knew nothing and fled for an elevator — then spent ten minutes waiting because the elevators simply couldn't keep up with the traffic trying to go up and down.

There were two theories flying around the lobby: One was that Craig Littlepage wanted to hire DePaul's Dave Leitao, that he had wanted a minority coach all along and that all the big names that had swirled about earlier — Rick Barnes of Texas, Mike Montgomery of the Golden State Warriors, Mike Brey of Notre Dame — were nothing but smoke screens. Perhaps that was true, but Barnes had been approached by ACC Associate Commissioner Fred Barakat the week before. The "Digger Phelps to DePaul" rumor still had life, too.

Theory number two was entirely different: it had Littlepage meeting with South Carolina coach Dave Odom. The two men were old friends. In fact, they had been assistant coaches together under Holland at Virginia. South Carolina athletic director Mike McGee was retiring, and there was talk that Odom, whose team had just won the NIT, might be a little nervous at the age of sixty-two about a new boss. He certainly had ties to Virginia and to the ACC, having gone from Holland's staff to Wake Forest, where he had been the head coach for twelve years.

Odom made the mistake of showing up in the lobby late that afternoon. "It just isn't true," he insisted. "I'm not going to Virginia."

Of course, that comment convinced everyone that a press conference was imminent.

While Odom was issuing denials, Mike Krzyzewski was arriving at the hotel. No one tries to be more low-key at the Final Four than Krzyzewski — except when he brings his team with him, which he had done for ten of the past twenty seasons.

Krzyzewski is now the most visible coach in the sport. His mentor, Bob Knight, once held that role and has also won three national titles, but because he is now coaching in Lubbock, Texas, and hasn't had a team in the Final Four since 1992 (when it lost to Duke), Knight isn't as visible as he once was. The only other active coach with more than one title is Connecticut's Jim Calhoun — who beat Krzyzewski en route to both his championships — but he has been to eight fewer Final Fours.

Krzyzewski is also a lightning rod, within his profession and among basketball fans. There are people who see Duke as the model for what a big-time college program should be: a good academic school that recruits kids who actually go to class and graduate and who can also play well enough to make the team a consistent national contender. Duke has had academic All-Americans under Krzyzewski as well as basketball All-Americans. Duke plays in one of the game's great settings, Cameron Indoor Stadium; it is part of one of the sport's great rivalries, Duke–North Carolina; and it is a member of one of the great basketball conferences, the ACC. It has a beautiful campus and a coach many national corporations have sought as a spokesman.

The perfect college basketball program.

All of which makes many people nauseous. For every college basketball fan who loves Duke, there are probably at least five who can't stand the place, the idea of the place, or the sainted coach. Where once North Carolina was the target throughout the ACC, Duke now is. Dean Smith makes the point that Duke faces far more vitriol than his team did when it was dominant in the 1970s and 1980s because back then there was no sports talk radio, no Internet rife with crazy rumors, no *USA Today*, no ESPN, and nothing approaching the obsession with sports that exists today.

Duke has now won six of the last seven ACC Tournaments and would have won all seven if not for a stunning collapse in the 2004 final against Maryland. It is a sign of Duke's dominance that Maryland fans were more excited about that game than they were about Maryland's victory in the 2002 national championship game. "I think for a lot of people, it *was* bigger," Gary Williams said. "Indiana [the team Maryland beat in the title game] isn't Duke. To beat them in the ACC final was very definitely a big deal for us. I'd be lying if I said it wasn't."

Williams's relationship with Krzyzewski in many ways symbolizes the way basketball people feel about him. Williams can rant about Krzyzewski and Duke at length: Duke gets all the calls from the officials; the officials were the reason Duke came from 22 points down in the 2001 Final Four to beat Maryland; the ACC schedule is set up to help Duke; the school isn't as hard academically, especially for basketball players, as people say it is; the media are all intimidated by Krzyzewski's aura. In the next sentence, he will tell you that no one is a better coach than Krzyzewski, that winning one ACC Tournament made him understand how amazing it is to have won five in a row, that one of the most touching moments in his career came in 2002 when Krzyzewski sent him a fax prior to the Final Four wishing him luck and telling him he thought Maryland had the best team. "Showed a lot of class," Williams said. "Especially given some of the battles we've had."

Williams and many of his fellow coaches were ready to do battle — though not to his face — with him again by the time Krzyzewski parked his car in the basement of the Millennium and sent his fund-raiser and right-hand-man Mike Cragg to check in for him at the front desk so he could avoid the lobby.

"Mike can't walk through that lobby," NABC executive director Jim Haney said. "I've been with him. If he tried to walk from the front desk to the elevator, it could easily take him three hours."

Which is why Krzyzewski would have breakfast in his room all weekend and slip out through the basement to go to the events he was scheduled to attend. The latest Krzyzewski-related battleground was an American Express commercial that had been airing during the tournament. It was one of the "My Life"–themed commercials that the credit card company had started with Robert De Niro walking around New York City. In this one, Krzyzewski talks about coaching and his relationships with players and coaches. The line that had some coaches losing their minds is: "I don't consider myself a coach, I consider myself a leader of men."

Hyperbole? Of course. That's what commercials are. But in the hypercompetitive world of college basketball coaching — and recruiting — seeing over and over on national television a competitor being portrayed as some kind of saint or icon was more than some coaches could bear. Krzyzewski had done a lot of national commercials before this one. In fact, he had been part of a very funny one for Allstate in which a group of men playing hoops in a driveway re-create the famous Laettner shot against Kentucky. As the shot drops through, Krzyzewski charges out of the bushes and begins hugging everyone, then disappears as quickly as he appeared, leaving the players staring at one another.

No one objected to that one, or others. But this one put people over the edge. "Unfair recruiting advantage!" they screamed, though not on the record. The most honest response came from Jim Calhoun: "As someone who recruits against Mike, I hate it," he said. "And if I had been offered the exact same thing, I'd have taken it in an instant."

Krzyzewski knew what was being said. He knew a lot of it was jealousy and almost all of it was out of his control. "When I hear the things people say about me and about our program, I know there's really only one way to stop all of it," he said. "Stop winning. I certainly don't want to do that. I worry sometimes because I don't think it's fair what the players have to hear sometimes and I do think sometimes the officiating goes the other way because guys are trying to prove that we *don't* get all the calls. But if that's what comes with winning, I'll deal with it. It's better than losing and having everyone talk about what a bunch of great guys we are."

Krzyzewski's entire weekend was planned. He had NABC meetings to go to. He would attend the Past Presidents Brunch on Sunday. On Saturday night he would gather a group of his ex-players and ex-coaches for dinner. The only thing he did all weekend that wasn't carefully planned was get up on Sunday morning to go to church. Pope John Paul II had died on Saturday and Krzyzewski, being both Catholic and Polish, felt it was important to attend a service that morning. He walked by himself to an early-morning Mass at a church near the hotel. One of the things many who deify him and many who crucify him miss about Krzyzewski is that he is intensely emotional and sentimental. The pope's death, even though it had been expected for weeks, was a very sad moment for him. As he was walking out of church, he bumped into Cliff Ellis, the former coach at Auburn and Clemson. He was surprised to see Ellis because he knew he wasn't Catholic.

"Cliff," he said as they shook hands. "A Catholic Mass?"

"I thought the pope was a great man," Ellis said. "I wanted to pay tribute to him."

Krzyzewski's eyes welled with tears, and he and Ellis hugged briefly. Then it was time to go back to being Coach K. He had a luncheon to get to.

12

The Senator and the Icon

IT MIGHT WELL HAVE BEEN that the most nervous man in St. Louis on Friday night was someone who would not be coaching, playing, or officiating when the games began on Saturday. He would simply be watching.

Dean Smith was always in his element when he was coaching. He readily admitted that since his retirement, watching North Carolina play had been very difficult for him. "I try to watch at home," he said. "But I get so nervous that sometimes I just turn it off. Sitting in the arena will be very hard — especially if things aren't going well."

Standing outside a St. Louis restaurant on Friday night, Smith, who had turned seventy-four on February 28, appeared relaxed after a good dinner. He wasn't. "I just wish," he said, "that everyone would stop saying we have the most talent."

There was a reason people were saying that North Carolina had the most talent: it did. It wasn't as if the other teams didn't have talent, too, but none of them had four players who would be among the first fourteen chosen in the NBA draft in June, including one — freshman Marvin Williams — who didn't even start but would be the second player selected. "Illinois is very good," Smith said. "Louisville can really shoot. Michigan State plays great defense."

All true. But Smith was doing what he had always done during his remarkable thirty-six-year career as the head coach at North Carolina: lowering expectations for his team. And there was no mistaking that the Tar Heels were very much his team. He still had an office in the building named in his honor in 1986 when it opened — the Dean E. Smith Center — and he had played a central role in all the machinations that had gone on involving the coaching job since his surprise retirement in October of 1997. It had taken until April 2003 to bring Roy Williams back home to North Carolina. Smith had very much wanted his longtime number one assistant, Bill Guthridge, to succeed him and to succeed as his successor. He had done both, taking Carolina to the Final Four in two of the three years he had been the coach. That wasn't good enough for Carolina fans, who frequently pointed out that the 1998 team had been built around Vince Carter and Antawn Jamison — both Smith recruits — and the 2000 team had struggled during the regular season before finding itself in time to make the Final Four after squeezing into the tournament as an eighth seed. What no doubt bothered the Carolina faithful as much as anything was his team's 2–6 record against Duke.

Of course, that record did lead to a great Guthridge line at the annual postseason banquet in 2000: "Duke beat us three times this year," Guthridge said. "They beat us in Chapel Hill, they beat us in Durham, and they beat us home from the NCAA Tournament."

Touché. The Blue Devils had lost to Florida in the round of sixteen.

Guthridge's decision to retire that June had set off dancing in the streets of Chapel Hill. Now, everyone said, Roy Williams would return from the plains of Kansas, march into town on his white horse, and lead the Tar Heels back to glory. Except that Williams wasn't quite ready to climb into that saddle. To the shock of everyone — including Smith — he turned the job down to stay at Kansas, feeling as if there was still more to be done there. Turning down the job wasn't a mistake: in fact, in many ways, Williams should have been applauded for his loyalty to the people he had spent twelve years with. "The hardest thing I've ever done in my life," Williams said later, "was say no to Coach Smith."

Williams made one critical error during the entire affair: when he called his press conference to announce that he was staying at Kansas, he declared that the next press conference he held like this would be to announce his retirement. He had violated the first rule of coaching: never say never.

While they celebrated in Kansas, people in North Carolina were hurt and angry. When negotiations with another Carolina prodigal son, Larry Brown, fell apart, and when Eddie Fogler also said he wasn't interested in the job, Smith and athletic director Dick Baddour finally turned to Matt Doherty. At another time, in another place, Doherty might have been the perfect choice. He had been a very good player on very good Carolina teams, a starter on the 1982 national championship team when he was a sophomore. He had worked on Wall Street for a while after graduation before deciding that his true passion was still basketball. Williams had hired him at Kansas, and in the spring of 1999 he got his first head-coaching job, taking over a long-dormant Notre Dame program.

Doherty did excellent work his first season. The Irish just missed making the NCAA Tournament — they hadn't been since 1990 — and reached the NIT final. Perhaps if Williams had taken the Carolina job, Doherty, who was still only thirty-eight, could have spent the next ten seasons coaching the Irish, waiting his turn to coach his alma mater. Now, quite suddenly, one year into his career as a head coach, it was Doherty's turn at Carolina. He almost had to take the job — the next person on the list was Randy Weil, the coach at North Carolina–Asheville.

He accepted Baddour's offer, but on one condition: he had to be allowed to bring his assistant coaches with him from Notre Dame. They had all left other jobs a year earlier to work for him, and he didn't want to leave them behind, where their future would depend on the whims of a new coach. It was exactly the kind of loyalty Doherty had been taught by Smith and Williams — but in this case it backfired. Smith had announced during Guthridge's retirement press conference that all three of his assistants — Phil Ford, Dave Hanners, and Pat Sullivan, each (of course) a North Carolina graduate — would be on the staff of the new coach. Now Smith had to scramble to find the three ex-coaches jobs within the athletic department. He also insisted that all three still appear in the next season's media guide.

Doherty made other changes: office personnel were moved around, longtime secretaries were reassigned. There is one thing you simply cannot do at North Carolina: anger Dean Smith. Doherty had done that. Smith and Guthridge moved to an office in the basement of the Dean E. Smith Center, and all was not well on the good ship *Carolina*. Dave Odom, who was still at Wake Forest at the time, got a sense of how difficult things were when Kansas came to play at Wake Forest early that season. Odom called Bill Guthridge to tell him that if he and Coach Smith wanted to come to the game to see their old pal Roy, he would make arrangements to get them in through a back door and stash them in a box where they wouldn't have to deal with the public. Then they could be whisked down to the locker room after the game. Guthridge thanked Odom for the offer and said he would get back to him. The day before the game he called back.

"We can't make it," he said. "Dean has some other commitments."

Odom was shocked. No one would have expected such a schism in the Carolina family. When he saw Williams at the shootaround on game day, he told him that he had invited Smith and Guthridge to the game. Williams just shook his head and said, "This has been really, really hard."

It got worse before it got better. Doherty's first season started well. The Tar Heels won at Duke in January and were ranked number one in the country in early February. But they faded in March, losing the ACC Tournament final by an embarrassing 26 points to Duke and then getting bounced in the second round of the NCAA Tournament by Penn State. This was basketball, not football. Star guard Joe Forte jumped to the NBA in the spring, and Doherty had a bare cupboard the next season. Carolina went an astonishing 8–20; astonishing because this was a school that had reached the NCAA Tournament a mind-boggling twenty-seven years in a row. The season began with losses at home to Hampton and Davidson, and things only got worse after that. There was a 112–79 loss at Maryland; an 86–54 loss at Connecticut; and, worst of all, an 87–58 loss at home to Duke.

The glimmer of hope was in Doherty's recruiting class: Raymond Felton, a jetlike point guard; Rashad McCants, a wonderful shooting wing guard; and Sean May, the son of former Indiana star Scott May, a six-foot-nine widebody with soft hands who came to Carolina largely because an embittered Bob

Knight told May's father he would never speak to him again if he allowed his son to go to Indiana.

Led by the three freshmen, Carolina became competitive again the next season, going 19–16 and reaching the NIT quarterfinals. There were encouraging moments: a win at home over Duke, an upset of defending national champion Maryland in the first round of the ACC Tournament. But there was also insurrection inside the team. The young players thought Doherty was too harsh, too quick to jump them in practice. Rumor had it that Felton had left school one night and driven home, only to be talked into coming back by Phil Ford.

True or untrue, there was certainly dissension. Shortly after the season ended, even though Carolina had won eleven more games in 2003 than 2002, Doherty was fired. It was a bitter moment for Smith, because firing one of his own went against everything he had ever preached or stood for. And even though it was Baddour who technically pulled the trigger, everyone knew it couldn't have happened without Smith's approval. Once again the question became: Will Roy come home?

At the time, Williams was busy taking Kansas to the national championship game. Those who liked to read the Roy tea leaves were sure he was going to take the job. He kept saying he was only focused on this Kansas team and not thinking beyond that. If he wasn't going, wouldn't he just say he wasn't going? In Kansas they were convinced Roy wasn't going anywhere; after all, he had promised in 2000 that he would never leave.

Kansas lost the national championship game to Syracuse. Williams, who curses more than Smith (who never curses) but less than 99 percent of his coaching colleagues, used a profanity on the air when CBS's Bonnie Bernstein asked him about the North Carolina job a few minutes after the loss. "Right now, I don't give a shit about the University of North Carolina," Williams said. "I only care about the brokenhearted kids sitting in my locker room."

He meant every word. A week later he was the new coach at North Carolina. Now he became Lord Voldemort in Kansas — which was unfair, given what he had done there in fifteen seasons — but at least partly because of what he had said three years earlier. Williams is a sensitive soul. The things being said about him in Kansas in 2003 were as crushing as the things said about him in North Carolina in 2000. The irony was this: if he hadn't been such a good coach, people wouldn't have cared so much.

Dean Smith breathed a sigh of relief on that April day in 2003 when Roy came home. Doherty had left very good players behind, and Smith knew Williams could recruit and could coach. Carolina's record against Duke since his retirement was 4–13. That was unacceptable. Smith is almost obsessive about Duke. That is understandable to some extent, because the schools are archrivals, but a little surprising since Smith had great success against Duke, winning 59 times to 35 losses.

Smith never liked the way the Duke students behaved. He thought their antics went too far at times, and there was nothing he enjoyed more than winning in Cameron Indoor Stadium. Vic Bubas was his first great rival in coaching and Mike Krzyzewski his last. Everything about Duke brought out the competitor in Smith, once described by columnist Mark Whicker (a North Carolina graduate) as "the only man I've ever met who would compete with you in an interview."

It was true. Smith has always tried to deflect personal questions. His father was a teacher and a coach who coached what is believed to have been the first integrated high school team in the state of Kansas. Dean was a good athlete as a kid — he played football, basketball, and baseball — and went to Kansas to play for Phog Allen, expecting to major in math and go on to teach and coach high school just like his father. He was never a starter for Allen, but by his junior year he was helping the coaches teach the younger guys the plays. It was apparent to everyone that he had a knack for teaching and coaching.

Kansas made it to the Final Four in Smith's junior year, 1952. The Final Four that year was in Seattle at the Hec Edmundson Pavilion on the University of Washington's campus, which seated 10,000 people. "I was the eleventh man on the team," Smith remembered, laughing. "My job was to take our tickets — we each had two — and see if I could sell them. It wasn't easy. I think the face value was about five or six dollars each. I'm not sure I got that much for them. It wasn't a very big event out there."

Kansas won the national championship, beating St. John's in the final game. With a comfortable lead, Phog Allen got Smith into the game. "Thirty-seven seconds," Smith said. "And then they left me out of the box score."

It wasn't until years later that the box score was amended to include Smith. The following year Kansas again made the Final Four and played Indiana for the title. "Because it was in Kansas City, we were scrambling for tickets," Smith said. "We all had friends and family who wanted to come. We thought we'd win; playing there was like having a home-court advantage. But Indiana was better than we were."

Smith did a stint in the air force after college — meeting Red Auerbach and Adolph Rupp in Germany when the two legends conducted a clinic at the base where he was stationed — and was then hired by Bob Spear as the first assistant basketball coach at the newly opened Air Force Academy. It was during the 1957 Final Four that he met Frank McGuire, who was then the coach at North Carolina. In those days, even the participating coaches hung out with one another, and Spear introduced his protégé to McGuire, who was impressed enough to offer him a job as his top assistant. "I felt guilty because I was rooting for Kansas to beat them in the championship game and I knew Frank was going to offer me a job," he said. "I guess that was the last time I ever rooted against North Carolina in anything."

He was McGuire's assistant for four years and always accompanied his boss on recruiting trips to New York and trips to the Final Four. "Traveling with Frank was a great experience," Smith said. "He knew everyone, he knew what restaurants to go to. He was just a lot of fun to be around."

The most important thing Smith did as an assistant coach had nothing to do with basketball. Not long after he arrived in Chapel Hill, he began attending the Binkley Baptist Church and became friendly with the pastor there, Dr. Robert Seymour. It was Seymour who pointed out to him that Chapel Hill's restaurants were segregated and that it might take someone who had the clout of the North Carolina basketball program to put an end to that tradition. Soon after, Smith walked into a well-known local restaurant with a member of the church who happened to be black. The two men sat down at a table, daring the restaurant's management to say something. No one said anything. Everyone knew that Smith was Frank McGuire's assistant coach. That was the beginning of the end of segregation in Chapel Hill restaurants.

Twenty-three years later, Seymour told that story to a reporter whom Smith had reluctantly agreed to cooperate with on a newspaper profile. "I wish you'd write about the players and not me," he had said when first approached. He finally agreed because the reporter told him he had been assigned to write the story with or without Smith's cooperation. When the reporter asked Smith about the restaurant story, Smith was clearly perturbed. "Who told you that story?" he asked.

When he heard that it was Seymour, he shook his head. "I wish he hadn't done that."

"Why?" he was asked. "Aren't you proud of what you did?"

"I did what I thought was the right thing," Smith said. "I don't think you should take bows in life for doing the right thing. You should just do it."

No story says more about Dean Smith.

A lot of Frank McGuire's success was built around recruiting in New York City, his hometown. According to Auerbach, McGuire's genius lay in whom he brought to the house with him on recruiting visits: "The priest of the local parish and the local police captain," Auerbach said. "Especially when he was recruiting an Irish Catholic kid. He knew just how to get to the parents."

McGuire left for the NBA after the 1961 season, and Smith was named his successor at the age of thirty. As has been frequently chronicled, he struggled his first few seasons. Saddled with an NCAA probation left over from McGuire and the fact that Duke and Wake Forest were both national powers, Smith was 66–47 his first five seasons, certainly respectable but not what was wanted or expected at North Carolina. He was famously hanged in effigy by students after a loss in 1965 to Wake Forest — an effigy that a furious Billy Cunningham tore down as the team got off the bus and saw what the students had done.

"I don't remember much about that," Smith has said. "But I do remember Billy tearing it down."

Several days later Smith got his first victory over Duke and Vic Bubas. In 1967 he won his first ACC Tournament title and went to his first Final Four. He did it again the next year and in 1969 — three in a row for both the ACC Tournament and the Final Four. This was in the midst of the UCLA run, and the one time Carolina reached the title game it was overwhelmed by UCLA and Lew Alcindor. After the three straight Final Fours, Smith's legend grew and Carolina became the dominant program in the ACC. Even so, it wasn't until 1982, when Michael Jordan hit his famous shot against Georgetown, that Smith finally won a national title — on his seventh trip.

"I really noticed a big change in the event between the time we went to Los Angeles in 1972 and the next time we went when it was in Atlanta in 1977," he said. "In '72 I don't remember that we even had press conferences. We just stood outside the locker room and talked. I really felt as if it had doubled in size by the time we went back in '77."

They were still playing a consolation game in 1967. After North Carolina lost in the semifinals to Dayton, it had to play Louisville in the consolation game. "I just told the players to be on time for the game," Smith said. "We didn't practice, do a scouting report, or anything. The game just didn't matter once we had lost to Dayton." As it turned out, Smith, an absolute stickler for being on time, almost missed the start of the game. "I never took consolation games seriously because I didn't think they should be played," he said. "When we got into town that week, I ran into Al McGuire. He had forgotten to make a hotel reservation. I told him he could stay in my room for the week. On the day of the consolation game I went to lunch with Al and [his ex-boss] Bob Spear and Don Donoher [whose Dayton team was playing in the final that night]. We got to talking and I lost track of the time. I finally looked at my watch and said, 'Oh God, I have to get to the game.'"

That is the difference between McGuire and Smith. McGuire would have let the game start without him. Smith made it to the arena before tip-off.

In 1982 the NCAA finally got rid of the consolation games Smith hated so much. Carolina avoided playing in the consolation game in 1977 by beating UNLV in the semifinals to get to the championship game against Marquette. It can be argued that getting to that game was one of the great achievements of Smith's career, because no fewer than three starters — Tom La-Garde, Walter Davis, and the great Phil Ford — were injured during Carolina's run, which included a huge comeback in the round of sixteen against Notre Dame. "On St. Patrick's Day," Smith liked to point out when the subject of the Irish's lack of luck late in that game came up.

Marquette was also a surprise finalist. It had just squeezed into the tournament at the last possible moment, and some wondered if the Warriors would have been invited if Al McGuire hadn't announced that he was retiring at season's end. As had been the pattern throughout the tournament, Carolina fell behind, then rallied, tying the game with a little more than eight minutes to go. When the Tar Heels got the ball back with the score tied, Smith immediately went to his famed four corners. Even with an injured hand, no one ran the offense the way Ford did, and Smith saw this as Carolina's chance to pull Marquette out of its zone and to wear down the Warriors by chasing Ford. As soon as Carolina got the ball back, Smith sent star freshman Mike O'Koren to the scorer's table to check back into the game.

O'Koren had scored 31 points in the semifinals and was being given a brief rest. In his place was Bruce Buckley. With Ford running the four corners, assistant coach Eddie Fogler leaned over and asked Smith if he wanted to call time to get O'Koren, who was quicker than Buckley, back into the game. Smith said no — at least in part because he would never do that to a senior. It can be argued that Smith's greatest strength as a person — his loyalty — might have been his only failing as a coach.

Buckley made a move toward the basket and Steve Krafcisin passed him the ball for what looked like an open layup. But Bo Ellis, Marquette's brilliant center, came flying in from out of nowhere to block the shot. "At the time I thought it was goaltending," Smith said years later. "But when I saw the tape, I realized Ellis just made a great play."

The block led to a layup at the other end. Carolina never got even again. Marquette won the game, 67–59.

"I've never regretted it," Smith said. "First, it would have been wrong to do that to Bruce. Second, it took a great play to stop us from scoring."

Smith insists he still has fond memories of that Final Four. "I was president of the coaches association that year," he said. "But because we were playing, I didn't have to go to all the meetings."

Carolina continued to be hugely successful after winning the national title in 1982 but wasn't quite as dominant as it had been. The Tar Heels, who had been to seven Final Fours in sixteen seasons from 1967 to 1982, didn't go back until 1991. By then, Mike Krzyzewski — whose early years at Duke had been even shakier than Smith's start at Carolina — was there for the fifth time in six years. That was the year Duke finally won, and then it won again the next year. When North Carolina came to Cameron Indoor Stadium the next season, the Duke students all arrived wearing T-shirts that had a picture of Smith with the caption "I Want to Be Like Mike." This was soon after a Michael Jordan commercial had come out with the slogan "I Want to Be Like Mike."

The students were referencing a different Mike than the one in the commercial. Smith graciously accepted one of the shirts when it was offered to him and then went on to win the national championship that year, evening the score with Mike at 2–2. He reached the Final Four twice more — in 1995 and 1997 — but by then some of the joy of coaching was gone. In the aftermath of the '93 championship he had brought in a great freshman class: Rasheed Wallace, Jerry Stackhouse, and Jeff McInnis, the first two arguably the best high school players in the country that season.

But as often happens in sports, more can be less. The championship team lost only one starter, but he was crucial: George Lynch, the unquestioned leader of the team even if he wasn't the best or most talented player. Wallace and Stackhouse were instantly resentful of Smith's loyalty to more experienced players, and the team was rife with dissension and underperformed the entire year, losing in the second round of the NCAAs to Boston College. A year later, led by Wallace and Stackhouse, they reached the Final Four, at which point both sophomores bolted for the NBA. McInnis stuck around for one more season, and Carolina was again — by its standards — mediocre, again going out in the second round of the tournament.

During the 1997 season, Smith admitted that retiring had crossed his mind the previous season. He would never say it, because it would have sounded like a put-down to his players, but coaching Wallace, Stackhouse, McInnis, and many of the "modern players" wasn't as much fun as coaching Charlie Scott or

Bobby Jones or James Worthy or Michael Jordan, among others. Carolina rallied from a poor start in '97 to win the ACC Tournament and reach the Final Four. In the second round of the tournament, Smith broke Adolph Rupp's all-time record of 876 victories when the Tar Heels beat Colorado. Even so, Smith was exhausted by season's end. "I *am* tired right now," he admitted a few weeks after the season. "I'm sixty-six. I don't bounce back as fast as I did. But I think by October I'll be fresh again and want to coach. If I'm not, like I've always said, that's when I'll retire."

October came. The freshness didn't. A few days before the start of practice, Smith stunned the basketball world by retiring, handing the reins to Guthridge. What happened over the next seven seasons — even with Guthridge's two Final Four trips — was very tough for Smith to take. There was open bickering inside his cherished "Carolina family." Even with Williams back, all didn't go well right away. Carolina did make it back to the NCAA Tournament and did beat Smith's first employer, the Air Force Academy, in the first round. But then Texas took the Tar Heels out in the second round. The only good news about the early exit was that none of the three star sophomores — May, Felton, and McCants — had done enough to make themselves guaranteed lottery picks in the NBA draft. If Felton or McCants had been locks, they almost certainly would have left. Instead, all three returned, as did Jawad Williams, who would be a senior. Roy Williams added a superb freshman, Marvin Williams, and Carolina came into '04–'05 looking loaded. The team had lived up to the hype, winning the ACC regular-season title and earning a number one seed, even after being upset in the ACC Tournament by Georgia Tech, an event Roy Williams used to work McCants back into the playing rotation after he had missed three weeks with an "intestinal disorder."

Now the Tar Heels were back in the Final Four. But with most people convinced that at least two of the juniors *and* Marvin Williams were bound for the NBA draft, there was a now-or-not-for-a-while feeling around the team. Williams had been to four Final Fours at Kansas. Always protective, Smith had called North Carolina SID Steve Kirschner to tell him he needed to mention in his game notes that Williams's percentage after sixteen years as a coach was the best in history. Kirschner *had* mentioned it. Smith wanted it in the notes for *every* game.

Smith had first attended a Final Four forty-eight years earlier. He hadn't missed many since. The argument could be made that this would be the most difficult one he had ever attended.

Bill Bradley had been to a lot fewer Final Fours than Dean Smith — to be precise, he had been four times: once in 1961, when he and several of his high school buddies made the trip from Crystal City, Missouri, to Kansas City to see Ohio State play Cincinnati in the national championship game; once in 1965, when he and his Princeton teammates made the trip from New Jersey to Portland, Oregon, as the east regional champions; once in 1966, as an Oxford Rhodes scholar on a break from his studies; and once in 1998, when he was about to run for president of the United States and made the trip to San Antonio as a visiting professor at Stanford to watch Stanford play Kentucky in the semifinals.

"I've only been four times," Bradley said. "But I can honestly say I had four very different experiences."

Bill Bradley served three terms in the U.S. Senate and ran for president in 2000, losing the Democratic nomination to Al Gore. He also scored 58 points against Wichita State in the consolation game of the 1965 Final Four — still the Final Four record for points in a game, a record surpassed in the history of the *tournament* just once, by Notre Dame's Austin Carr, who scored 61 in a first-round game in 1970.

"What I remember about that [consolation] game was the beginning," Bradley said. "Every time I passed the ball to a teammate who I thought had a good shot, the ball would come back to me. I'm thinking, 'What's going on here, why are they passing up open shots?' Finally Coach [Butch] van Breda Kolff calls time and says to me in the huddle, 'Bill, this is your last game, will you please shoot the damn ball!' So I did what I was told."

It wasn't until years later, when he was retired from the Senate and politics and was spending most of his time speaking and writing, that Bradley got a sense of just how good he had been that night. "Some guy came in [to his New York City office] with a bunch of memorabilia that he wanted me to sign. One of the things he had was the box score from that game. I'd never really looked at it, but when I did, I think my line was twenty-two of twenty-nine from the field and fourteen of fifteen from the line. I looked at it and thought, 'Hey, I guess I was pretty good that night.'"

Bill Bradley was good on a lot of nights, from high school through Princeton through his ten-year career with the New York Knicks. His first basketball hero was Wilt Chamberlain, who arrived at the University of Kansas just when Bradley was beginning to emerge as a standout player. "During his sophomore year, I was in the eighth grade," Bradley said. "I kept a scrapbook on him. Everything he did, I put it in the scrapbook. I still remember them losing the final in triple overtime to North Carolina and how disappointing that was to me."

Bradley became a star in high school and was recruited by all the basketball power schools. In those days, high school players didn't make final decisions on college until the end of their senior seasons. Bradley's senior year at Crystal City High School ended with a huge disappointment when the school lost the state championship game by one point. "We were down one in the final seconds and I managed to steal the ball," Bradley said. "One of my teammates broke ahead of everyone and I passed him the ball. He had an open layup at the buzzer — and missed."

The teammate was Tom Haley. "He became Rabbit Angstrom," Bradley said, a reference to the famous Updike character who never got over his days as a high school star. "He just couldn't get past it. He dropped out of college, went into the military, and then came back to Crystal City. To this day — forty-four years later — I think people still bring it up to him all the time." Haley did have one moment of stardom, though, when Bradley ran for president. Looking for a boyhood friend, many members of the media found Haley to ask him about his old teammate. "I was happy that my running did something positive for him," Bradley said, laughing. "I think he enjoyed it."

Perhaps because of his team's near miss in the championship game, Bradley decided to go to Duke, where Vic Bubas was building a power. He'd had a chance to witness the national championship game shortly after his high school career ended. "The finals were in Kansas City again that year, and some of my friends and I drove up there and went to the final. I don't even know how we got the tickets but I don't remember that it was a big problem. I *do* remember that we somehow got down to the hallway where the Ohio State players were walking from their locker room to the court. I remember standing there watching them and seeing Jerry Lucas, who would later be a teammate on our '73 championship team, and John Havlicek, who would be the toughest guy I ever played against, going out onto the court. Of course, I had no idea I'd be connected to them later. I just remember being surprised when Cincinnati beat them. Ohio State had won the year before and I think we all thought they'd win again.

"I knew I wanted to go to school someplace where I could play for the national championship. Duke had Art Heyman and Jack Marin and seemed to be building a team that could win a championship. That's what I wanted to do. The fact that it was a good school helped, but I was driven by the idea of a national championship."

Basketball history changed when two things happened: First, Bradley broke a foot and "got a look at life without basketball." Second, he went on a summer trip — "thirteen girls and me" — to England and visited Oxford. "Fell in love with the place," he said. "Fell in love with the whole idea of the place. That was when I first heard of the Rhodes scholarship. I read someplace that Princeton had produced more Rhodes scholars than any other school. So, at the last possible second, I changed my mind and decided to go to Princeton."

This was long before the NCAA had come up with the one-sided idea of the "letter of intent," which basketball players are now allowed to sign almost a year before they are scheduled to enroll in school. If a player changes his mind because he hears about the Rhodes scholarship or, more likely, because the coach who recruited him leaves to take another job, he can't simply decide to go elsewhere. If he doesn't go to the school with whom he "signed" (imagine a "student" signing a contract with a college), he must sit out one year before he can play. Coaches who change jobs aren't required to sit out a year before they coach again; athletes are.

In 1961 Bradley could change his mind. He knew that the Ivy League wasn't as powerful as the ACC and that most years the league champion lost in the first round of the NCAA Tournament. But he remembered seeing Yale's Johnny Lee on the cover of *Sports Illustrated* when he was a high school freshman, so he figured the quality of ball couldn't be all that bad.

"A lot of the basketball cognoscenti said I had given up on winning the national championship when I decided to go to Princeton," he said. "I didn't see it that way. I still wanted to win it. I became a recruiter. I talked to kids when they came to campus; I went and *visited* kids [which was still legal then] to tell them to come to Princeton. We got some very good players: Ed Hummer and Gary Walters were the best. Then we added Don Rodenbach and became a very solid team. Our center my senior year was a six-nine walk-on named Robby Brown. He had some qualms about the morality of winning, but he was a pretty good player anyway."

Princeton improved each year Bradley was there and went into the '64–'65 season thinking it had a chance to do something special. Bradley, Michigan's Cazzie Russell, and UCLA's Gail Goodrich were considered the three best players in the country, and Princeton had already attracted a good deal of attention because it was winning with smart kids and because its best player had already said he would pass up his rookie year in the NBA if he got a Rhodes scholarship. In December the Tigers faced Michigan and Russell in the semifinals of the Holiday Festival in New York. In those days there was no bigger in-season tournament. It was an eight-team tournament, and almost without fail, several of the teams were nationally ranked. Princeton-Michigan in the semifinals was a complete sellout: 18,499 packed into the old Madison Square Garden.

"I remember what the building seated," Bradley said. "I know it was sold out. But since that game I've had at least twenty-two thousand people come up to me and say they were there that night."

Those who were there saw Bradley and his teammates dominate Michigan, which was ranked number one in the country, for thirty-six minutes. The Tigers led by twelve when Bradley fouled out. Once he was gone, the game changed completely, and Russell hit a shot in the final seconds to give Michigan a one-point win.

"It was disappointing, very disappointing," Bradley said. "But I think our attitude was 'We had the number one team in the country on the ropes for thirty-six minutes, we're good enough to play with anyone.' Our goal was to play them again because we knew if we did, it would be in the Final Four."

It wasn't called the Final Four back then, but the goal was the same: Princeton wanted to win the east regional championship and get to Portland. In those days, only twenty-three teams made the tournament and they never traveled outside their own geographic region. Princeton had to play a first-round game — fourteen teams played in the first round while nine teams had byes. The Tigers beat Penn State to get to the regional in College Park, Maryland, and then beat ACC champion North Carolina State in the round of sixteen. Providence won the second game, 81–73, over St. Joseph's. The Princeton players had stayed to watch the second game. They were stunned when the Providence players cut the net down after their win.

"It was as if they thought they were already in the Final Four," Bradley said. "We took note of that."

To put it mildly. The next night — in those days the regionals and the final four (no caps back then) were played on Friday and

Saturday — Princeton put on one of the most stunning basketball clinics ever seen. "I think there was one stretch where we hit eighteen of twenty shots," Bradley said. "It was the way you dream about playing basketball. I can still see most of the plays in that game in my mind's eye very clearly. I can remember Don Roth, who later became the treasurer of the World Bank, throwing a perfect pass to Ed Hummer for a dunk. The feeling of satisfaction was just incredible." Princeton won the game by the remarkable final score of 109–69, a score Bradley can still pull out of the air on command.

"I remember we cut down the nets and really celebrated," he said. "All the games and all the teams I played on, that was, without question, one of the two or three best performances I was ever part of. It was a great high.

"And then, on Monday, we all went to class."

Bradley's memories of the Final Four are vivid, but not quite as satisfying as the regionals. "We flew out on Thursday to play on Friday," he said. "I don't think we even went to the arena to practice. Princeton was very tight. We stayed in some motel that didn't have any beds in the rooms — just pullout couches. It was the classic fleabag motel. Really awful. Here we are, getting ready to try to win a national championship and we're sleeping on pullout couches. We couldn't believe it."

Nowadays, the NCAA is so flush with its network billions that it pays the expenses for all sixty-five teams to travel to game sites as well as their hotel bills. It has been a long time since any team playing in the opening round, much less the Final Four, has stayed in a motel with only pullout couches for beds. Back then, the schools received a per diem of $25 a day for each player — probably enough for a decent hotel room but apparently not enough to get Bradley and his teammates a real bed to sleep on.

"When we got to the arena, I think it hit us for the first time that this was a big deal," Bradley said. "We're playing Michigan again and UCLA is playing Wichita State in the second game. Michigan had been ranked number one all year, and UCLA was the defending champion. We started out very nervous. They got ahead and stayed ahead. We made a run in the second half, but then I got the fouling disease again and fouled out. I think we were down three or four when I fouled out." Michigan ended up winning the game, 93–76. It might well have been losing that made Bradley realize how important the game was to him.

"It was crushing," he said. "I think we all believed we were going to win the national championship. To sit in that locker room and realize we weren't was about as difficult as anything I can remember. People tell me now how great the next night was [when he scored the 58], and I explain to them that it wasn't. Yes, I played well; we played well but we didn't meet our goal. Our goal was to win, not finish third.

"After the game, Henry Iba came into the locker room to see me. I had played for him on the '64 Olympic team. He said I'd had a great game and a great career. It was really nice of him, but it all felt pretty empty right then. I don't think we even stayed for the championship game. In some ways, it almost felt as if we weren't there, it was all over so quickly. We flew home the next day and went back to school. That was it."

Bradley has never seen a film or tape of that game — because there is none. The game wasn't on TV, and in those days teams didn't routinely tape — or film — games the way they do now. "A couple of grainy highlights," he said. "That's it. Fortunately, most of it is still inside my head."

The Princeton players missed a second remarkable performance in the Michigan-UCLA game, Gail Goodrich's 42 points, which led UCLA to its second straight title. John Wooden still calls that the greatest individual performance he witnessed in the Final Four. Between the two of them, Bradley and Goodrich scored exactly 100 points that night. Their paths would cross again in the NBA finals a few years later when Goodrich played for the Lakers and Bradley for the Knicks and the teams played each other for the championship three times in four seasons.

Bradley returned to the Final Four a year later on a break from Oxford and was in the building in College Park on the night Texas Western beat Kentucky in what has become the most famous and arguably the most important Final Four game ever played. For Bradley, the return to Maryland's Cole Field House was bittersweet. The night when he and his teammates had cut down the nets in that same building felt more like a lifetime ago than just a year.

Bradley graduated from Oxford and joined the New York Knicks the following season. In a twist of fate, it was an injury to Cazzie Russell that elevated him to the starting lineup and turned the Knicks into a championship team. With Russell coming off the bench to lift the team offensively at key moments, the Knicks won their first title in 1970 and won again three years later. They haven't won an NBA title since. "I don't go to see them play very often even though I work right here [in Manhattan] now," Bradley said. "I really have trouble watching the NBA game. So much of the time the offense consists of two guys running the pick-and-roll or a big guy pitching and catching with someone shooting a three-point shot. I really think the three-point shot has damaged the game a great deal. You have four guys playing and six guys watching most of the time.

"I was taught that you play the game with your feet. Now the game is played with the chest; it's all about strength. It looks more like sumo wrestling than basketball to me, and I find it more or less unwatchable. I try to watch the finals or pick one team I like every year just to keep up with it, but it's very, very hard. It's just a boring game to watch. Every year I'll try to go to one game, put my toe in the water to see if it's warmed up at all. It's still freezing."

Bradley didn't return to the Final Four for thirty-two years after 1966. For ten years he was playing in the NBA and soon after that he launched his political career. In 1998 he was teaching at Stanford and got involved with Mike Montgomery's team. Most of the players knew he had been a U.S. senator and had played in the NBA. But they had little clue that he had been one of college basketball's great players. "One of the kids, Mark Madsen, had read *A Sense of Where You Are* [Princeton professor John McPhee's legendary book on Bradley and the '65 Princeton team], so he knew. But that was about it. Still, they were smart kids, real students, and I enjoyed the way they played. I started going to practices, got to know Mike very well, and for the first time in years I became a real fan."

Stanford made the Final Four that year, for the first time since 1942, and Bradley, who was doing some commentary for CBS News, got to go as part of his role for the network. "But I was there as a fan," he said. "I was devastated when they lost to Kentucky because I liked the kids so much. Still, it was fun to feel passionate about the game that way again. I enjoyed it."

He hasn't been back since, but does sit down to watch the games on television. He enjoys the college game more than the NBA because he sees passion in it. "It just has more human drama," he said. "I follow the first round, looking for those upsets that happen. I still remember the Princeton-Georgetown game in '89 and how beautifully Princeton played all night and thinking [Princeton center] Kit Mueller got fouled on that last play. You see mental blunders, you see how much it means to the kids. I find myself flashing back to '65 and remembering how much it meant to all of us.

"I really don't follow Princeton closely, to be honest. I might sit down and watch a big game in which I think we have a chance, but that's about it. I loved [Pete] Carril and I like it when they play well, but I guess life moves on."

Bradley did go back to Princeton in the winter of 2005 for a fortieth reunion of the 1965 team. Every member of the team and van Breda Kolff, now eighty-five, made it back. "It was very emotional to see everyone all together again," he said. "It's amazing how clear my memories are of that season."

Bradley's devotion to the game he played so well is still apparent when he talks about it. He sounds almost angry when discussing what he sees as the fall of the NBA, the commercialization of the college game, the lack of passion he sees so often. And, he says, he still thinks basketball is an excellent window into someone's soul.

"I think I can learn more about a person's character by playing basketball with them than by sitting down and interviewing them for an hour," he said. "Not that I play very often these days. A few years ago I was looking to hire a state director in New Jersey. I was interviewing a guy named Kevin Rigby and we were down at the Jersey Shore. We were walking on the beach, talking, and we came on some people playing half-court. We stopped and got into a three-on-three game. Kevin was a perfect teammate: passed the ball, played hard, knew how to box out. When the game was over, I said, 'Kevin, you're hired.' He was one of the best people I ever had work for me."

Nowadays, Bradley stays busy speaking and writing and traveling. He says he has no plans to run for public office again, even though there are many Democrats who would like to see him run for president in 2008. He still believes, even with all the changes in the game since his playing days, that character and heart are as important as talent. "You have to have some degree of physical skill," Bradley said. "We had that in '65. I've heard people say that we won because we were smarter than other teams. I really don't believe that. I believe we won because we had more heart than other teams, that we cared about what we were doing. I still believe once you reach a certain talent level, the difference between teams is in their character. [John] Wooden's teams had great talent, but they had character, too. They were so well prepared that he didn't even coach very much during the games. They knew how to play and they went out and played. Seeing basketball played the right way is still something I find beautiful. That's why Stanford was so much fun in '98.

"It may be why I think back to our team so often. I can still see so much of it so clearly. And all these years later, it still looks great to me."

13

Saturday

THE WAITING BEGINS on Saturday — for everyone. Thursday and Friday are all about getting into town, finding your way around, and, for the teams, going through practices and tape sessions and (sometimes) a little sightseeing.

Saturday, though, everyone waits. The first game doesn't start until 6:07 eastern time — an hour earlier in St. Louis because of the different time zone — and no one, especially the teams, wants to do very much. Each goes through a brief shootaround in the morning and then returns to its hotel, all with orders from the coaches to "stay off your feet."

All of the teams have been through this during the regular season, especially nowadays when so many college basketball games don't start until nine o'clock — for television, of course, which is the ultimate dictator of all starting times in college basketball, as in most sports. When the Final Four was last played in St. Louis, in 1978, the first semifinal began at 12:30 local time and the second one was over by just after five o'clock — almost the exact same time that the games would now begin.

"It was a lot harder waiting at the Final Four than any other time during the season," Wes Miller said. "It wasn't anything new, but that was part of the problem. Sean [May] and I had been roommates the whole tournament, and by the time we got to St. Louis, we had ordered every movie there was to order from every hotel we'd been in. On Saturday we spent a lot of time arguing about whether it was worth ordering a movie for the third time or not. We finally ended up not ordering anything. Instead, Sean tried to sleep — which wasn't working — and I walked around the room in circles, playing with a deck of cards or flipping TV channels. It was a long four hours between our morning meal and our pregame meal."

Most teams eat a pregame meal four hours before tip-off. Once, everyone ate the same thing for the pregame meal: steak. The last thing you wanted to do was eat anything that was heavy, like pasta or pancakes. Then, about twenty years ago, someone discovered the concept of carbo-loading and now most pregame meals consist of pasta and pancakes. Many coaches serve pasta at 8:00 A.M. pregame meals when their teams play at noon.

"It's all probably ridiculous," said Texas coach Rick Barnes, whose team made the Final Four in 2003. "During the summer all the guys eat is McDonald's and Burger King, and that's probably when they play their best basketball."

Barnes was in the lobby Saturday morning, killing time like everyone else. He had just finished his eighteenth season as a head coach — one year at George Mason, six at Providence, four at Clemson, and seven at Texas. He had won twenty games in his one season at George Mason and built programs that consistently made the tournament at his next three stops. But he had never been past the Sweet Sixteen until his Texas team made its run in 2003.

"Sometimes it's still hard for me to believe that I actually got to the point in my career where I coached a team in this event,"

Barnes said. "It seems like it was about fifteen minutes ago that I was a twenty-two-year-old assistant coach at Davidson making twenty-five hundred dollars a year, and now I've been a head coach for almost twenty years. I remember early in my career I looked at the guys coaching in the Final Four and they were like gods to me. Dean Smith, are you kidding me? I grew up in North Carolina. Jim Valvano? Coach Wooden? I can't even call him John Wooden, he's just Coach Wooden to me."

Given Barnes's roots, it is ironic that he and Smith came close to a fight during the 1995 ACC Tournament. Barnes was an ACC rookie coach trying to rebuild a sputtering Clemson program. The overmatched Tigers played North Carolina in the first round of the ACC Tournament, and as expected, the game was a blowout. But a couple of chippy plays late in the game angered Smith, who began yelling at one of Barnes's players, Iker Iturbe. Barnes told Smith that if he had a problem with one of his players to yell at *him* — which he did. The two men ended up having to be held apart by referee Rick Hartzell while Smith yelled at Barnes, twenty-two years his junior, "Go ahead and hit me."

The incident made Barnes a pariah in most of North Carolina but seemed to establish what he wanted to: that Clemson wasn't simply going to be rolled by the ACC's powers anymore. In 1997, after a loss at Duke, Barnes showed up the next morning in Greensboro at the office of Fred Barakat, the ACC's officiating supervisor, insisting he had tapes that proved Clemson got the short end when it played Duke and Carolina. His team made it to the Sweet Sixteen that year, losing in double overtime to Minnesota, which went on to the Final Four. A year later Barnes took the Texas job, in large part because he believed no matter what he did at Clemson, jumping over the league's two superpowers would be virtually impossible.

He quickly built Texas into a perennial contender in the Big 12, where Kansas and Roy Williams were just about as big an obstacle as Duke and North Carolina. When Texas beat Connecticut and Michigan State to win the south regional in 2003, Barnes found himself in a place he had never really dreamed of reaching. "I remember all the phone calls and notes," he said. "It was great. But the amazing thing is the phone call that really got to me was from Amp Davis."

Amp Davis had played on Barnes's George Mason team, his first real problem as a head coach. The two clashed almost from the day Barnes took over the program: over conditioning, over class attendance, over just about everything. "He spent more time in my office being lectured than any player I've ever coached," Barnes said. "The fact that either one of us made it through that season was a miracle."

Davis played well in the second half of the season, made it to class, and became one of the team's leaders. On the night Texas beat Michigan State, Barnes got home and found a message from Amp Davis. "When I called him, he was crying," Barnes said. "He said he felt as if he were a part of it in a small way, that he knew he'd never play in a Final Four, but now he felt like he was part of a Final Four. By the time I hung up, I was crying, too."

Having been once, Barnes yearns to go back. He had thought his 2005 team had a chance to make an impact in the tournament until P. J. Tucker, his best player, was declared academically ineligible for the second semester. "It's very hard to go the first time and not feel totally fulfilled, whether you're a player or a coach," Barnes said. "Part of it is there's so much to do during the week, you just feel like you don't get time to prepare for a basketball game. It didn't really hit me that we had a game to play until

I walked on the practice floor on Friday and I heard my assistants talking about what we were going to do to try to stop [Syracuse's] Carmelo Anthony. Even then, I caught myself looking around the [New Orleans Super] dome thinking, 'This is a long way from Davidson.'"

The manner in which Barnes got his first two coaching jobs is legendary among his colleagues. In 1977, having just graduated from Lenoir-Rhyne College in the western corner of North Carolina, he got a friend to set up an interview with Davidson coach Eddie Biedenbach for a part-time coaching position. The appointment was for nine o'clock in the morning. Not wanting to be late, Barnes was there at eight. Eleven hours later he was still sitting in the unair-conditioned gym. The assistants had told him they expected Biedenbach back at any moment throughout the day. They had left at six. An hour later Barnes decided that eleven hours was enough and was getting up to leave when Biedenbach walked into the gym. When he saw Barnes, a look of horror crossed his face. "You're Rick Barnes, aren't you?" he said. Barnes was so tired by then that he wasn't 100 percent certain who he was, but he nodded his head. "Oh God, I completely forgot," Biedenbach said. "Come on in."

Thirty minutes later Barnes had the job. Two years later, when Joe Harrington was hired at George Mason and was looking for an assistant coach — he could hire only one full-time assistant — Biedenbach's assistants, Tom Abatemarco and John Kochan, told him he was crazy not to hire Barnes. "They told me he was the hardest-working young coach they'd ever seen," Harrington said. "They said he was in the office every morning at five o'clock. I decided to call their bluff. I set my alarm one morning and called the Davidson basketball office. Someone picked up the phone and I said, 'Is this Rick Barnes?' He said, 'Yes, it is.' I said, 'Rick, this is Joe Harrington at George Mason. You're hired.'"

Eight years later, when Harrington left George Mason to take the job at Long Beach State, George Mason athletic director Jack Kvancz hired Barnes. By then he had worked at Alabama for Wimp Sanderson and at Ohio State for Gary Williams. "I learned a lot from both of them," Barnes said. "Of course, my wife has never completely forgiven Gary because he taught me how to curse."

Barnes has cursed more than a few times but has now won 363 games as a head coach and been to the Final Four. "Once you've been, you want to go back and you want to win," he said. "Most coaches don't win the first time they go. I guess Jim Calhoun's the exception, but he had a great team that was on a mission — and he's a Hall of Fame coach. I'm fifty now. I know I'm on the back nine of my coaching career. I want to win the thing once so I can retire someday with a smile on my face."

Coaches who have won once would tell Barnes it isn't that simple. Two of them were in the lobby Saturday afternoon taking bows and telling stories. Word had started to circulate that morning that when the Hall of Fame announced its class of 2005, Jim Calhoun and Jim Boeheim would be two of the people going in. Calhoun had been a finalist a year earlier and had somehow not been selected. His second national championship — which he won on the night the Hall announced he had *not* been chosen — made it impossible for him not to get in. Boeheim had been winning more than twenty games a year at Syracuse for close to thirty years. He had been to three Final Fours and three national championship games, and in 2003 his team had beaten Barnes's Texas team and Roy Williams's Kansas team to win the national title.

Boeheim had coached in the Big East from the day the league began play in 1979. Calhoun had coached at Northeastern and had taken over a moribund Connecticut program in 1986. They had competed against each other for nineteen years. They had both survived prostate cancer and returned to coach. Boeheim had been ridiculed early in his career as someone who recruited great talent but couldn't harness it. Syracuse had spent a year on probation in the early 1990s and had bounced back to reach the championship game in 1996. Calhoun had been hailed as a savior at UConn and then been questioned when he couldn't get to the Final Four. Some of his key players had had brushes with the law, including star point guard Khalid El-Amin, arrested on drug charges soon after the 1999 national championship, but he had come through it all standing.

Now Calhoun and Boeheim would go into the Hall of Fame together. Both spent a good deal of time accepting congratulations.

"It's still almost an adjustment for me to realize that this is where my career is now," Calhoun said. "I still remember when I first came here, being openmouthed walking through the lobby, seeing people like John Wooden and Dean Smith and Louie Carnesecca. It sort of hits you at moments like this that now you're one of the guys people are looking at. It's a nice feeling." He smiled. "It's also an old feeling."

Boeheim may be the most ridiculed great coach in history. He played at Syracuse — as a walk-on — on very good teams alongside Dave Bing in the 1960s and succeeded Roy Danforth when Danforth left to take the Tulane job after getting Syracuse to the Final Four in 1975. "Even though we'd been to a Final Four, I really didn't think we had a national program back then," he said. "We were pretty good but we weren't at the level where I thought of us in the same sentence as the true national powers. The Big East changed all that. When we became part of the league, it gave us a chance to be a national power."

Many people (including this author) have made fun of Boeheim through the years because he always appeared to be in pain on the bench during his early years as a coach. He has a nasal voice that makes him sound as if he's whining when he's not. As he acknowledged, he had some very good teams in the '80s that suffered some frustrating losses and some embarrassing ones — not the least of which was a second-round loss to Navy in the Carrier Dome in 1986. "They *did* have David Robinson," Boeheim pointed out.

Nevertheless, to be a national power playing on your home court and lose to a team filled with future naval officers was embarrassing. A year later Syracuse and Boeheim bounced back, upsetting North Carolina in the east regional final to make the Final Four. "The feeling of relief was unbelievable after the years of not getting there," Boeheim said. "It just felt great."

Even so, there was a moment in the postgame press conference when Boeheim was talking about Carolina's late rally and the mistakes his team had made that almost cost them the lead. Finally, center Rony Seikaly, sitting on the podium next to Boeheim, said, "Hey, Coach, cool it, man — we won!"

Boeheim laughed.

A week later Syracuse easily beat Providence, coached by former Boeheim assistant Rick Pitino, in the semifinals but then lost to Indiana in the final on Keith Smart's off-balance jump shot from the corner with five seconds left. Boeheim never forgot what Bob Knight said to him when they shook hands that night: "You'll be back."

He was — nine years later — only to lose to Pitino, who by then had become the King of Kentucky. The third time was the charm. "The road from zero national championships to one is miles and miles and miles long," Boeheim said. "From one to two is a few yards. I always knew my life would change if we ever won, but I never dreamed how much. It isn't as if I can do no wrong now, but it certainly makes up for a lot of things. We lose the way we did to Vermont this year with a senior team, I'm getting killed right now. As it is, people are disappointed, but they can still talk about '03. And we'll have other chances. We'll be pretty good again down the road."

Boeheim has strong opinions about the way the tournament is run. He believed that the best team had not made it to St. Louis. "I think Arizona was the best team," he said. "They had Illinois by fifteen *in Chicago*. That was a home court for Illinois. There's no way Arizona loses that game if it is played any place that's even a little bit neutral. I'm not knocking Illinois, it was a great comeback, but it just isn't fair that way. They don't have to keep teams at home to sell tickets. We would have played in Austin this year, and there were thirty thousand people in Syracuse to see North Carolina, Wisconsin, North Carolina State, and Villanova. The tournament has gotten that big. They say they keep high seeds home so teams don't have to travel as much. If you look at it, teams are traveling just as much — it's just different teams traveling.

"The advantage of being a number one seed should be that you play the number sixteen seed first and then the eight-nine winner and so on. It should *not* be that you get some kind of home-court advantage. This should be a neutral-court tournament — for everybody. And I say that as someone who has benefited from home court or near home courts in the past. It's just not right."

Boeheim is one of the few big-time coaches who never leaves the Final Four until after the championship game. "I still love the whole thing," he said. "I love going to the games, I love being here. The lobby's not the same. I miss staying up late at night and just listening to coaches talk basketball and hearing guys like Jimmy V. tell stories. But I still love coming here and being a part of it. I love all of it."

A radio guy walked up to Boeheim, wanting to know if he had "just a couple minutes."

Boeheim smiled his wry smile. "Okay," he said. "Maybe I don't love *all* of it."

The only coach among the four still working who had not previously been in a Final Four was Bruce Weber. He had been a late bloomer as a head coach, not getting his first job until he was forty-two, when Southern Illinois hired him in 1998. Weber might have lacked experience compared with the other three Final Four coaches, but he didn't lack smarts. On the Monday of Final Four week, he had called Jim Calhoun — the last coach to win the championship in his first trip to the Final Four. Winning the Final Four in your first trip isn't impossible — after all, you have to win only two games — but it doesn't happen often. Since Don Haskins did it in the *Brown v. Board of Education* game in 1966, it has happened eight times — Norm Sloan in '74, Jud Heathcote in '79, Jim Valvano in '83, Rollie Massimino in '85, Steve Fisher in '89, Jim Harrick in '95, Tubby Smith in '98, and Calhoun in '99. Interestingly, only Fisher ('92 and '93) and Calhoun returned, and only Calhoun won a second time.

Calhoun's advice to Weber was simple and direct: "You divide the week into two parts," he told him. "The first part is to celebrate the achievement of getting there. Let the kids get out and see the town, let them enjoy themselves and realize that being in the Final Four is a big deal. But then, at some point late Thursday or early Friday, you have to let them know that it's time to work. They've had their playtime, now there is a job to do: there are still two more games to be won and then you can celebrate for as long as you want. But playtime is over. The key is making sure when you walk on the court Saturday night, your team is as well prepared mentally and physically as it has ever been to play a game."

That doesn't always happen. Many coaches admit that, especially the first time, the hoopla and demands of Final Four week can overwhelm them. "The first time we went [Dallas '86] I honestly think I spent more time on ticket requests than on preparing my team," Mike Krzyzewski said. "It happens whenever you go, but especially the first time, people come out of the woodwork and want to be there. On the one hand, you understand it and appreciate it. On the other hand, you have to find a way to get away from it, or you'll show up unprepared."

Calhoun agrees with that but thinks there can be an advantage to being a first-timer. "You're almost an innocent," he said. "Yes, the demands can overwhelm you. I felt that a little bit in '99. But in a way there's less pressure because by getting there, you've already answered that one big question — 'Can he coach a Final Four team?' — and until you get there and don't win, no one is asking the other question — 'Can you win the Final Four?' — because you haven't lost one yet. In a sense, that first time you're playing with house money. When you go back a few times and haven't won it yet, then you start to feel the pressure."

Jim Boeheim agreed. "If you have a program where you can get there more than once, after a while you feel like you *should* win at least once," he said. "I know I felt that. I'm sure Roy feels it. We all say the same thing when we haven't won it yet — Dean [Smith] said it, Mike [Krzyzewski] said it, I said it, and now Roy is saying it: 'It isn't that big a deal, I won't be a better coach if I win it, I'm not losing sleep over it.' You know what? We're all wrong. It *is* a big deal and you just can't know how big a deal it is until it happens." He smiled. "It's a little bit like parenting. People can describe it to you all you want, but you can't understand it until you experience it."

In a sense, it was good for Roy Williams to be coaching a different team and school in this Final Four than in the past. His players were certainly aware of his last-weekend failures at Kansas, but they hadn't lived them with him, hadn't been there to feel the acute disappointment. They had dealt with their own set of crises: the three seniors on the team had been freshmen during the 8–20 year, and the seniors and the juniors had lived through the Doherty-to-Williams coaching change. In fact, the media rarely brought up to the players the question of Williams's winning a Final Four. That would not have been the case had he still been at Kansas.

In an experienced Final Four group of coaches, Williams was making his fifth appearance, as was Rick Pitino, and Tom Izzo his fourth. But Pitino and Izzo each had a title. Williams was also the most superstitious coach in the group. Since his team had bused from Chapel Hill to Charlotte for the first weekend of the tournament and been successful, Williams had had the same bus driven up to Syracuse. Now it was in St. Louis. Carolina had an off-season trip scheduled for the Bahamas. One had to wonder how Williams would get the bus *there* if they won in St. Louis.

"One thing I think has really changed in the last ten years is that there's no clear-cut favorite or clear-cut underdog any-more," Boeheim said on Saturday afternoon as he prepared to leave for the arena. "You go back ten or fifteen years ago, there was almost always one team people were saying should win and there was almost always one team most people didn't think could win. Look at these four teams. Sure, you have to give an edge to Carolina and to Illinois, but will anyone be shocked if Louisville and Michigan State win tonight? I don't think so. You get here, you're playing well. Everyone going out there tonight thinks they're going to win."

A lot of coaches were walking over to the arena, a ten- or fifteen-minute jaunt from the hotel. Others were taking buses that would drop them at the front door. One ex-coach waiting for a bus was George Raveling, who had coached successfully at Washington State, Iowa, and Southern California before leaving coaching in 1994 after health problems. He did some radio and TV work and then became the honcho of Nike basketball, tak-ing over after Sonny Vaccaro, who had first come up with the idea of paying coaches a lot of money to put themselves and their teams in Nike gear, jumped to Adidas. (Vaccaro has since jumped again, to Reebok.) Raveling once worked at Maryland for Lefty Driesell and was an assistant coach to Bob Knight at the '84 Olympics and to John Thompson at the '88 Olympics. So he has plenty of stories to tell about people in basketball.

But his most interesting story has nothing to do with basket-ball or basketball coaches.

That's because sitting in George Raveling's house are the original notes from which Martin Luther King Jr. read his "I Have a Dream" speech in Washington, D.C., on August 28,

1963. Raveling was a young assistant coach at the time, having grown up in Washington, from where he had gone on to play at Villanova. He was home in Washington on the day of the rally and was planning to attend. He was walking around the Mall early in the morning with a friend when someone walked up and asked him if he might be available to serve as one of Dr. King's bodyguards that afternoon. Raveling is six foot five and in those days was a lean twenty-four-year-old still in basketball-playing shape. "I guess they didn't have anything formal the way they do nowadays and they just wanted some big guys to be around Dr. King," he said. "I said yes, sure I'd do it, and the guy told me to report someplace at a specific time. We walked onto the podium with Dr. King, and I just stood behind him with several other guys while he was speaking.

"It wasn't hard to tell that something extraordinary was going on. I listened in awe while he spoke. When it was over, he just started to walk away and I noticed he had left his speech notes sitting there on the lectern. I picked them up and I said, 'Dr. King, do you want these?' He said, 'No, you can go ahead and keep them. Maybe they'll be worth something someday.'"

Raveling laughed at the memory. "I read through them later, they're pretty readable, and nowhere did I find the words 'I Have a Dream.' That must have just come to him while he was speaking, I guess. A few years ago someone offered me six million dollars for them and I said no. I'm hanging on to them. Someday I'll give them to my son. If he wants to sell them, he can. But I won't do it."

Raveling was one of the first African American coaches to have consistent success, taking all three schools he coached to the NCAA Tournament. He never got past the Sweet Sixteen and didn't achieve the fame or notoriety of John Thompson or, later, Nolan Richardson, African American coaches who went to multiple Final Fours and won the national championship. But he is one of basketball's most respected and best-liked figures, someone who knows everyone and is known by everyone. When he was still coaching, he was consistently one of the captains of the "all-lobby" team, the unofficial group put together every year by observers consisting of those who spent the most time hanging out in the lobby.

"It was how you learned," Raveling said. "John [Thompson] and I used to argue every year about who the all-lobby captain was, because it was almost always one of us. Now I have to spend a lot of time up in the [Nike] suite. It isn't the same. Times change."

They certainly do. Having been where he was on that August afternoon in 1963, Raveling can certainly attest to that.

What may be the most amazing thing about major sporting events post-9/11 is that everyone does eventually get into the building. People are allowed to arrive earlier nowadays because security checks make getting in a much more complicated process. Even the players go through security checks, though not nearly as thorough as those performed on everyone else. If you have a lapel pin that shows you are part of a team's official party — players, coaches, managers, trainers, doctors — you are usually waved through pretty quickly.

"It was a lot easier getting in last year than this year," Georgia Tech coach Paul Hewitt said as he waited to go through a security check. In 2004 Hewitt's team played in the championship game. In St. Louis he was just a spectator. "It's a lot harder to go back to watching after you've been in it than it is to watch when you've never been in it," he said. "I can certainly understand why coaches who have been a few times don't want to come when their team isn't in. This isn't easy."

Mike Krzyzewski had skipped Final Fours in the past when Duke didn't make it. Like his mentor, Bob Knight, he found it tough to be there when he wasn't competing, for the same reasons Hewitt found it tough — only more so because of his visibility. "When you've been a few times, people sort of expect you to be there," he said. "So, when you're not, even in a year like this one, where it really wasn't reasonable for us to expect to make it, you know a lot of people are going to ask, 'What went wrong?' Some years that's a legitimate question when you don't make it. Other years it isn't."

Krzyzewski had just completed one of his most gratifying years in coaching. After his team's devastating loss to Connecticut in the 2004 semifinals, he had been rocked by freshman Luol Deng's decision to turn pro. He had expected Deng, who was a good student, to stay at Duke for at least two years or perhaps even three before turning pro. But Deng's family, after hearing that he would be a lottery pick, wanted him to take the money while it was there. Deng ended up being the seventh pick in the draft and had played well in Chicago as a rookie before getting injured.

Krzyzewski had expected to lose one starter, point guard Chris Duhon. When Deng decided not to return, he had lost two. Then, when high school star Sean Livingston, who had been slated to fill Duhon's spot at the point, decided not to go to college at all, Krzyzewski found himself without a point guard and two holes he hadn't counted on. This wasn't brand-new to him — since 1999, when three underclassmen left, Duke has lost more underclassmen to the draft than any other major program. Krzyzewski learned after 1999, when Elton Brand left (as expected) and William Avery and Corey Maggette left (unexpectedly), to try to prepare for early defections. "If they're lottery picks, it's hard for them to say no to that kind of money," Krzyzewski said. "I don't always think it is the best thing for them. But they aren't always going to listen to me."

To some degree, Krzyzewski is a victim of his own success: not only in recruiting top players but in sometimes making them look better than they actually are — at least in terms of pro potential. Mike Dunleavy was taken with the third pick in the draft, Avery (who is now out of the league) the fourteenth pick, and Jason Williams (who was badly hurt in a motorcycle accident and may never play again) second. About the only Duke player who has ever been *under*rated was Carlos Boozer, who didn't go until the second round because he was considered a center in a forward's body. He has become a very good (and wealthy) player.

Duke started the 2004–05 season not picked in the ACC's top three for the first time in years and not picked in the national top ten for the first time in just as long. But with J. J. Redick emerging as a much better all-around player, Shelden Williams becoming a force inside, and Krzyzewski squeezing minutes out of freshmen like DeMarcus Nelson and David McClure, Duke finished a strong third in the ACC and then won the ACC Tournament to finish 25–5 and earn a number one seed in the NCAAs. Some thought Krzyzewski had done his best coaching job even after Michigan State had "upset" the Blue Devils in the round of sixteen. Duke had now reached the sixteens for eight straight seasons. No one else had a string going of longer than three years.

After missing several Final Fours, Krzyzewski had decided

years earlier that he should show up with or without his team. There were meetings he felt he should attend and people he should see. He also decided to pick up on an old Knight tradition by getting all of "his guys" together for dinner one night. Before Knight stopped holding them, Knight's dinners had grown almost massive, because they included ex-players and assistant coaches, old friends, fishing buddies — anyone in town who knew Knight was invited. Krzyzewski's dinners were a little more exclusive: you had to have coached under him or played under him.

"You know, when I first came up with the idea, I didn't give it much thought, it just seemed like a fun thing to do — in part, to take my mind off not having a team to coach during the weekend," he said. "But now, having done them a few times, I realize that they mean a lot more to me than just an enjoyable evening. When I look around during these dinners, I see the people who have shaped my life — outside of my family — and brought me to where I am. These are the guys who had the faith to choose me as their coach — some of them when doing that was a big gamble — and were willing to come work for me, some of them after they played for me, some not. In a sense, it's a way of having my team with me at the Final Four even when that year's team isn't playing. I know that sounds corny, but it's true."

Krzyzewski's dinner was scheduled for 7:30 on Saturday night, just a few minutes before the scheduled tip-off of the North Carolina–Michigan State game. "It was the only time we could get a reservation," he said, smiling.

No doubt that was true. And who would want to eat dinner at, say, 5:30. "We'll drink a toast to Carolina," Krzyzewski said.

He didn't mention what he would say in that toast.

*   *   *

An hour before tip-off of the Louisville-Illinois game, it was quickly becoming apparent that this was going to be a Final Four in which, even playing in a dome, one school would have a home-court advantage. It appeared that almost all of the seats upstairs had been bought by people wearing Illinois blue and orange. Downstairs was divided the way it always is: four sections with the big-bucks fans who had bought their tickets through the school allotments, and then several sections filled with coaches and the NCAA and CBS's corporate guests. Or as they liked to call them at CBS and the NCAA, their "corporate champions."

These matchups may have been as eagerly anticipated as any in recent Final Four history, if only because the previous week-end's regional finals had been so remarkable. North Carolina's victory over Wisconsin had been decided in the final minute, and that had been the most one-sided of the four games. In fact, it was the only one that didn't go into overtime. Louisville had come from 22 points down in the first half to beat West Virginia — the most surprising final eight team in the field — in overtime in the opening game on Saturday. Most people thought that one would be the game of the weekend. Except later that evening, Illinois had pulled its impossible escape against Arizona, coming from 15 points down in the last four minutes and then winning in overtime. Clearly *that* game wouldn't be topped. Only Kentucky–Michigan State (following Carolina's "rout" of Wisconsin on Sunday) went double overtime, reaching overtime after the officials spent more than ten minutes watching replays of Kentucky's Patrick Sparks's shot at the buzzer that (a) hit the rim twice before going in, (b) came either just before or just after the buzzer, and (c) was released with his toe either just on or just off the three-point line.

Remarkably, the officials got the call exactly right after watching the play in super slow-motion from every conceivable angle: Sparks was an inch (maybe less) outside the three-point line and he had released the ball with just about one-tenth of a second left. It can be said, without exaggeration, that millions of people around the country sat transfixed at dinnertime, watching the replay over and over exactly as the officials were watching it.

When overtime began, it was almost impossible to believe that Michigan State could recover and still win the game. The Spartans fell behind, rallied, and then fell behind once more in the second overtime. Again they rallied, and this time they hung on to win what has to be considered one of the great games in tournament history.

That was the backdrop as the Jones Dome began to fill up. With the exception of some seats in the fat-cat Michigan State and North Carolina sections, it was full by the time Illinois and Louisville tipped off. Sitting in his front-row seat on press row, covering the Final Four for a thirty-third straight year, Dick Weiss of the *New York Daily News* was amazed by how he felt as the final seconds ticked off the clock before the player introductions began. "I still get chills," he said. "All these years, all these games, it is still the only event in sports that makes me tingle just before it starts."

A lot of people feel that way about Saturday. It has now become such a big deal for a team just to get there — winning four games is never easy — and the hype throughout the week makes that moment when the games finally begin and the hype ends special. The NCAA tries to choreograph everything. In the "game itinerary" that the teams are given, this line is included:

"After the coaches are introduced, they are to walk to the scorer's table and shake hands." As staged as it all is, the building is still electric, and everyone — even those in the upper reaches of the dome — feels that electricity. Almost everyone feels the exact same thing as the first game begins: *Boy, am I lucky to be here.* Or as Bill Bradley once said of the way he felt before playing in the seventh game of the NBA finals: "There is no place on earth I would rather be at this moment than right here, doing what I'm about to do."

That's the way the Final Four feels just before tip-off on Saturday night.

Sometimes, much like the Super Bowl, the games don't (or can't) live up to the hype. That turned out to be the case in 2005. The games were similar to each other. In the opener, Louisville stayed close to Illinois until almost midway through the second half, trailing by just 50–49 with 10:04 left. But the Illini, a veteran team built around three guards — Dee Brown, Luther Head, and Deron Williams — who kept firing three-point shots all night, finally wore the Cardinals down, outscoring them 22–8 in the game's final 10 minutes. The last five minutes were little more than Louisville shooting threes and fouling to try to slow the game down, to no avail. The final was 72–57. The best moments of the second half came during the (endless — almost three minutes apiece) TV time-outs during which the Illinois band began playing the Michigan State fight song to try to get the Michigan State fans to pull for them — one Big Ten group pulling for another. The tactic worked. The green-and-white-clad fans, who had been watching the game quietly, responded to the familiar music and chimed in with the Illinois fans — not that Illinois really needed more support.

During the second game, the Illinois fans returned the favor, pulling quite noisily for Michigan State. This was for two reasons: the support showed by the Michigan State fans for their team, and — more important — their understanding that their chances of winning the national championship on Monday night would be greatly enhanced if they were to play the Spartans instead of the Tar Heels. For twenty minutes it looked as if they might get their wish. A drive straight to the basket by MSU's Kelvin Torbert through a defense that appeared stuck in cement put Tom Izzo's team ahead, 27–25, with 5:44 left in the half. At halftime it was 38–33, Shannon Brown's layup in the final minute upping the margin to five.

The buzz of upset ran through the building.

It didn't last. Roy Williams decided on his way to the locker room that this was not the time to stay calm, to soothe frazzled nerves. This was the time to let his team have it, to tell his players they were being outplayed, outhustled, and — most of all — outfought in a Final Four game. "I really let them have it," he said later. "I was angry and I needed them to understand why I was angry. We'd worked so hard to get where we were, we couldn't just throw it away without putting it all on the line. If they put it all out there and got beat by a better team, fine. I'm disappointed, but I can live with it. This, I couldn't live with."

Wes Miller hadn't heard his coach this angry very often during the season. Then again, he thought, neither he nor his team had been in this position before. "It was the first time since we got to the point where it was 'lose and go home' where we had played poorly in the first half," he said. "Coach wanted to make sure we understood the consequences of playing another half like that one."

Clearly, they got the message. The Tar Heels scored the first six points of the second half to take the lead, 39–38. The game seesawed to 49–49 with 15:17 left. At that point Carolina exploded, scoring 12 straight points. No one knew it, since there were still twelve minutes to go, but the game was over. A Torbert three made it 61–52, but Sean May answered immediately with a rebound basket and Michigan State never got to within single digits again. Carolina just had too many weapons, especially with senior Jawad Williams, who had struggled for most of the tournament, shooting 9 for 13 and producing 20 points and 8 rebounds. It was tough enough stopping May (22 points), Rashad McCants (17), and Raymond Felton (16 points, 7 assists). Throw in a hot Williams and Michigan State had no chance.

As Carolina pulled away, word reached the Krzyzewski party at Kemoll's Restaurant that their archrivals were in control of the game. "I'd like to propose a toast," Krzyzewski said, holding up a glass of wine. "This is to all of you who have played for me. From here going forward you will always be known as 'Coach K's players BC.'"

Everyone held up their glasses and waited for the punch line. "BC," Krzyzewski repeated. "Before Commercial."

With Carolina comfortably ahead, Wes Miller got in for the game's final minute. This was his turn to tingle. "Coming out of the tunnel was an unbelievable feeling before the game," he said. "We'd played in big places before big crowds in big games during the season. But this just felt different. Then the first half was such a disappointment. But the way we turned it around and then to get into the game was just unbelievable. It's a memory I'll always treasure."

Miller didn't shoot — Williams didn't want his team trying to score at that point — but he made the box score in a Final Four game. At the very least he matched Dean Smith — and he wouldn't have to call the NCAA to tell them to make a correction. He was there when the final box was handed out, just below another walk-on, Charlie Everett, and just above Marvin Williams, who would be the second pick in the NBA draft in a couple of months.

When the game was over — final, 87–71 — Williams was direct with his team again in the locker room: "If you play on Monday night the way you played the first half tonight, we have no chance to win," he said. "If you play the way you did in the second half, there's no one in the country who can beat us. It's that simple."

It was also this simple: Illinois — ranked number one at the end of the regular season — vs. North Carolina — ranked number two at the end of the regular season — for the national championship. It was the first time since 1975 (UCLA vs. Kentucky) that the regular season's top two teams had made it to the championship game.

Louisville and Michigan State had both had memorable seasons. Clearly, though, the better teams had won on Saturday. There was no doubt that the two best teams in the country would play for the title.

There was only one question left now to be answered: which one was the best?

The answer wouldn't come until Monday night.

14

The Long Wait

UNTIL 1968 THE FINAL FOUR WAS, for all intents and purposes, a forty-eight-hour event. Teams would fly in on Thursday, and the semifinals would be played on Friday night. The finals were on Saturday night, and everyone would head home on Sunday morning. Bill Bradley's description of his final college game sums it up well: "We played, took a shower, ate a cheeseburger, and flew home to New Jersey the next morning."

It isn't anything like that anymore. In 1968, the first year that NBC televised the event on network TV (before that it had been syndicated to markets that had an interest), the championship game was moved to Saturday afternoon because it wasn't a big enough event to merit prime time on a network. That made it impossible to play the semifinals on Friday, since the teams would then have only about fourteen hours prior to the finals. So the semifinals were moved to Thursday. Five years later NBC decided to take a chance and move the final to Monday night in prime time. But it still wanted games to be played on Saturday afternoon. So the semifinals were moved into the Saturday afternoon slot occupied by the finals (there were still two games on the last day then, since the consolation game didn't go away until 1982).

Which created what everyone in college basketball now calls the Wait.

It isn't that teams aren't accustomed to having forty-eight hours between games. In fact, the two teams playing for the title have already been through two similar weekends, playing either Thursday/Saturday or Friday/Sunday in their regionals. But this is different. For one thing, as Wes Miller pointed out, there are only so many movies that can be ordered on hotel television systems. For another thing, this is the third straight weekend they have spent away from home, cooped up in a hotel, waiting to play. More than anything, though, is the pressure. Everyone knows what Monday night means. Playing in the championship game is something every player dreams about, every coach wishes for. When it becomes real and you have to wait . . . and wait . . . the forty-eight hours between games feels like an eternity.

"I remember waking up on Sunday morning after we beat UNLV and being ready to go out and play," said Bruce Buckley, recalling his experience with the Wait in 1977 while a North Carolina senior. "Every hour waiting, even if you were lying down, you could just feel the energy draining out of you. After a while you find yourself thinking, 'Are they *ever* going to play this darned game?'"

The players and coaches aren't the only ones who feel that way. A lot of people leave town on Sunday; others stay for the coaches' dinner on Sunday night and leave on Monday morning. If you peruse the coaches' section on Monday night, you aren't likely to see many of the game's stars. Jim Boeheim is always there, and coaches who have a friend in the game might stay. Most of the big shots get out of town on Sunday or early Monday. They have had enough.

"You come in on Wednesday or Thursday and you're usually

happy to see people," Maryland coach Gary Williams said. "You might spend time in the lobby; you talk to old friends. You go out Thursday and Friday and probably stay out too late. By Saturday, you're tired but you want to see the games — even though it's a lot tougher to sit there and watch when you've been in them before. Even so, that's okay. But by Sunday, it's time to go. You know you've got work to do at home. You watch on Saturday and think, 'I need to get our team better so I'm not here watching again next year.' It's fun to go most of the time, but you reach a point where you just feel like you're done."

Williams had taken Maryland to the Final Four in 2001 and 2002. After his team lost in the round of sixteen in 2003, the shock of not getting back to the Final Four didn't hit him until he checked in to his hotel in New Orleans. "For the first time in three years," he said, "I used my real name at check-in. It didn't matter if anyone called. I had no work to do."

The fans of the two losing teams on Saturday usually clear out of town on Sunday, too. The best time to buy tickets for Monday night is right after the games on Saturday, when fans of the two losers come streaming out of the dome looking to dump their Monday tickets. Most accept face value if you simply take the tickets off their hands so they can start planning their escape. Few fans want to stick around and watch the team they have just lost to play for the national title. One of the few exceptions was in 2001, when many Maryland fans stayed in Minneapolis to root heartily and often angrily *against* Duke in the final.

The city was considerably quieter on Sunday — especially in the morning, when most people were still sleeping in since the second game on Saturday didn't end until after eleven o'clock eastern time and clocks were set forward by an hour early Sunday morning for daylight saving time. If you see people on the streets early on Sunday morning at the Final Four, it is for one of three reasons: (1) they're on their way out of town, (2) they still haven't gotten back from Saturday night yet, or (3) they're morning people who can't sleep in no matter how late they've been up the night before.

Other than the players and coaches of the two teams in the final, there is one group that always stays in town until Tuesday morning: the media. Most are happy to do so, even though the weekend can get long for them, too. They arrive on Wednesday and Thursday, and because of the way the event has grown, they have much less to write about than they did years ago, when the event was smaller.

"My first one was in 1970, Cole Field House," said Dick Weiss of the *New York Daily News*. "I can remember after practice on Friday, Coach [John] Wooden came over and just sat in the stands and talked for about half an hour. There couldn't have been more than twenty-five of us there. If you wanted a player one-on-one, you just went and got him."

Like a lot of veteran writers, Weiss understands that times change and that all events in sports have grown to the point where intimacy is nothing more than a memory. Once upon a time, the White House press corps would pile into the Oval Office once a day to chat with the president. To some who have covered basketball for a long time, the growth of the Final Four is something they have mixed emotions about. On the one hand, they're pleased to see their sport appreciated and its popularity has been good for them professionally. On the other hand, they grimace when in the massive Friday press conferences a columnist who hasn't seen a basketball game all season asks Sean May what it means to follow in his father's footsteps as a basketball player, a question May has been answering since high school.

Dick Weiss is known to everyone in basketball — including his wife — as "Hoops" for the simple reason that basketball has been his greatest passion, dating back to his boyhood, when he grew up in Philadelphia following the Big Five. Weiss started going to Big Five games when he was ten, riding the el downtown from Sixty-ninth Street to Thirty-fourth Street with a group of friends from St. Bernadette's CYO, where he first learned the game. In those days Saturday doubleheaders were routine, with the Big Five teams playing not only one another but national teams who wanted to come in and play in the Palestra. Weiss loved the games and the atmosphere and to this day can recite the names of all the great Big Five players of the late '50s and early '60s. "I especially loved the '61 St. Joe's team that Jimmy Lynam was a sophomore on," he said. "I remember them getting to the Final Four and losing to Ohio State in the semifinals but then beating Utah in four overtimes in the consolation game to finish third in the country. That was a big deal.

"Then, a week later, we started hearing stories that the New York District Attorney's Office was investigating several of the players for point shaving. That was the beginning of what I call the Curse of Philadelphia. If you look at the NCAA official record book for 1961, it reads 'vacated' for third place — which is where St. Joe's is supposed to be. Then you go ten years further to 1971 and second place is vacated because of Villanova and Howard Porter."

Howard Porter was the star of the Villanova team that shocked an undefeated (28–0) Penn team in the regional final, beating the Quakers, 90–47, after having lost five straight games to their Big Five rival. Weiss was working at the *Trenton Times* by then, having graduated from Temple in 1969. It was there that he first acquired the "Hoops" nickname from friends because of his devotion to basketball at all levels. In the last game of his senior year, Temple beat Boston College in the NIT final (the NIT was still a big deal back then), ruining Bob Cousy's exit from Boston College as coach but turning Weiss's exit from Temple as a student into a celebration. Weiss was thrilled to be working in Trenton in '71 when the two Philadelphia teams hooked up with a trip to the Final Four at stake.

"It was just shocking the way Villanova dominated them, because Penn was vurry, vurry good." (Like most Philadelphians, Weiss always says *vurry* instead of *very*, and almost always says it twice when describing something.) "We thought they were the Final Four team from the city. The worst part for Penn was that both teams flew home on the same plane. In the meantime, the Villanova students marched on the Penn campus to celebrate. A week later, when they beat Western Kentucky [in double overtime] to get to the championship game, they marched on the Penn campus again."

The marching ended soon after that. UCLA beat Villanova to win its fifth straight title, and shortly thereafter it was revealed that Porter had signed a contract with the American Basketball Association (which at the time was competing with the NBA for players) and had forfeited his eligibility. "The Curse of Philadelphia, part two," Weiss said.

Weiss moved to the *Philadelphia Daily News* in 1974, first covering high schools and later covering both the Big Five and the Philadelphia 76ers. He enjoyed covering the NBA playoffs, but his true love was always college basketball. As a sideline, he ran one of the first basketball camps for girls, to the point where in the 1980s, when women's basketball began to catch on at the college level, it seemed as if every star player had once been one of Weiss's campers.

Not surprisingly, Weiss's favorite Final Four memory is 1985, when Villanova not only won the championship but managed to keep its name in the record books after it was over. "To cover a team that actually won it was a thrill," Weiss said. "I'd be lying if I told you I was unaffected by it. People say a lot of things now about Rollie [Massimino] and what happened afterwards — and a lot of them are true — but the fact is, the guy could really coach and he had built a wonderful program that peaked at just the right moment."

Villanova was no fluke. The Wildcats had reached the final eight in both 1982 and 1983, losing to powerhouses both years: North Carolina with Michael Jordan, James Worthy, and Sam Perkins in '82 and the Hakeem Olajuwon–led Houston team a year later. Their victory in 1985 was one of the great upsets in the history of the Final Four, and Weiss not only got to fly home with the team the next morning but was actually in the victory parade, riding on the same flatbed truck on the ride from the airport to City Hall as the players and coaches. "To see the people lining the streets that way was amazing," he said. "I looked at the players and had to pinch myself because this was a team that barely squeezed into the tournament [eighth seed] and then had to play Dayton at Dayton in the first round. I remember going out there thinking I'd fly someplace else for the weekend after Villanova lost on Friday."

Weiss left the *Philadelphia Daily News* in 1992, the same year that Massimino left Villanova — though the circumstances were different. Massimino fled to UNLV, hoping to start anew after Villanova was never able to climb to the heights of '85 again. Weiss was offered a job by the *New York Daily News* as its national college basketball writer (few papers have a full-time national writer) and agreed to take the job only if the paper allowed him to continue to live in Philadelphia — which he does to this day. It was right around then that Weiss began to feel as if the Final Four had grown out of control.

"I think it was '94 in Charlotte that it really hit me," he said. "The city just couldn't handle the event, it was too big. When President Clinton came, no one could get to the arena. I began to look around and notice a lot of what I call 'event' guys. Some of them came because they had to do TV or radio from the Final Four. Others came because it has become an event, like the Super Bowl or the World Series or the Masters. I knew it was bad when I heard guys complaining before the games started on Saturday that they were actually missing a few days of spring training to be at a basketball game. *Spring training?* Are you kidding me? The NCAA has all these rules about newspapers and TV and radio stations having to have covered a certain number of games during the season to get credentialed. They ought to have that same rule for columnists."

Or perhaps a test of some kind: if you can't name Mike Krzyzewski's three daughters (who have been on TV about as often as David Letterman the past twenty years), you can't cover the Final Four. Or perhaps you should be required to know why Roy Williams always claps for the other team's starters when they're introduced. (Because, as with most things Williams, Dean Smith always did it.) One person who would pass any or all tests is Bill Brill, a proud graduate of the Duke class of 1952, who has covered almost as many Final Fours (forty-eight) as Rich Clarkson. There's no doubting his allegiance to Duke — he retired to Durham in 1992 after a distinguished career as the sports editor and columnist of the *Roanoke Times and World News* — but to simply label Brill a "Duke guy," as many people do, is a great oversimplification. For one thing, his wife, Jane, graduated from North Carolina and Brill has always gotten along well with both Dean Smith and Roy Williams. More important, Brill probably has a better understanding of the basketball tournament historically and in terms of how it has evolved than anyone in the sport — including the members of the committee. In fact, it is a long-standing Saturday night tradition at the ACC Tournament that Brill unveils *his* tournament bracket about eighteen hours before the committee unveils its bracket. Brill is so precise in announcing his brackets, placing teams into specific regional and subregional sites, that in years past there have been occasions when young reporters who don't understand the process have actually believed that Brill's bracket was the real one and began making travel plans before gently being told that the Brill bracket wasn't quite as official as they thought.

Maybe it should be. Brill puts together his bracket based not so much on what he thinks is right as on what he thinks the committee will do — and *should* do, based on past history, all the various rules about who can play whom, RPI/quality wins/road wins, and how a team finishes. Brill sticks to these rules better than the committee does and knows all of them cold. He certainly knew in 2003 that Brigham Young couldn't go in a bracket to play a Sunday game and he also had Arizona and Kentucky opposite each other in the draw. In 2005 he had Kentucky as the fourth number one seed — before its loss on Sunday — and Louisville as a number two. Like everyone else, he was stunned when the committee opted to make Washington a number one and Louisville a number four — and was proved right when Louisville easily beat Washington in the round of sixteen.

Brill usually has almost the same field as the committee — "They get one wrong every now and then," he says, not kidding — and more often than not, his seedings and bracketing are very similar to the committee's. All kidding aside, his bracket often makes more sense than the committee's. Which calls into question all the time and money that is spent by the NCAA on the committee. The group meets four times a year: in the summer to review the previous year's tournament; in December to begin preparing for that season's tournament; in February to put together a "mock" bracket; and then for five days in early March to put the field together. There are ten committee members, innumerable NCAA staffers, reams and reams of computer printouts.

After all of that time and money and hours and hours of staff work, the end result is virtually the same as that produced by a retired sportswriter working by himself, fortified by several beers and cheered on by a few friends during Saturday night dinner at the ACC Tournament.

Perhaps just as silly is the absolute secrecy the committee insists upon during its deliberations. Although the information leaks out every year, committee members don't like to talk about how the teams left out ranked and how early (or late) they were removed from consideration. The committee members insist — quite angrily at times — that politics never enters into the equation. There are all sorts of rules about committee members having to leave the room if the school they work for or even a school from their conference is being discussed in earnest. Are we supposed to believe that the other nine members don't *know* what the missing member thinks? In 2005 the committee was chaired by Iowa athletic director Bob Bowlsby. As luck would have it, three teams from Iowa were on the bubble — Iowa, Iowa State, and Northern Iowa — and all three got into the field. When someone jokingly asked Bowlsby if he was planning to run for governor of Iowa, he didn't even crack a smile: "Obviously I had nothing to do with those three institutions [committee members insist on calling colleges *institutions,* just as they ludicrously insist on calling players *student-athletes*] getting into the field," he said.

Almost undoubtedly he didn't. And just as probably, they all deserved their slots. But by acting as if the future of the planet is at stake when they walk into their conference room, the committee members make people suspicious of their actions. In the past when it has been suggested to them that a pool reporter be allowed to sit in on the deliberations, most committee members have reacted as if someone had suggested they fly coach for the rest of their lives. "Not gonna happen" is the standard answer.

Why not? Congress's deliberations are public and frequently on TV. Murder trials are frequently televised these days. Ten people are selecting sixty-five teams for a basketball tournament. They insist there are no politics involved, that no one is ever given a break — good or bad — that they are America's ten most honorable people. Okay, fine. Let one reporter sit in for the weekend. Specifically, why not let Bill Brill, who probably knows the rules better than anyone on the committee, sit in. Heck, if he had been there in 2003, he might have been able to whisper in someone's ear and the Arizona/Kentucky and Brigham Young debacles would have been avoided. More important, when the committee members report that the presence of Bowlsby as chairman had nothing to do with the Iowa teams getting in or when they say that Charlotte got into the field as a number nine seed in 2002 (when it had been on the bubble) because it deserved that seeding, not because Charlotte athletic director Judy Rose was on the committee, there would be an outsider to vouch for those statements.

Of course, the committee members insist they don't care what people think or that the media frequently speculates on politics influencing their decisions. And then they get angry every March when people question them.

It is all part of the tradition.

If Bill Brill is the Bracket King among the media, then Jim O'Connell is the King of Games. Sunday at the Final Four is tough on O'Connell, who has been the AP's lead college basketball writer since 1987, because there's no game to cover. "It's brutal," said O'Connell — Occ to everyone he knows — "all you've got are those endless press conferences."

If there's one thing everyone — players, coaches, media — agree on, it is that the worst day of the Final Four is Sunday and the worst part of Sunday is the press conferences. Like the rest of the Final Four, it has simply gotten to be too big — and too long. "How is it that we're scheduled to spend more time talking to the media than we are practicing?" Roy Williams asked, noting that he and his players were supposed to be with the media for an hour and forty-five minutes and on the practice floor for ninety minutes.

Years ago, the Sunday press conferences were an hour — and that was plenty. The five starters and the coach would sit up on a podium for thirty minutes and answer the usual desultory questions. Then the players would spread out around the room and talk to writers in small groups — sometimes as few as two or three writers with one player, because a lot of people would stay with the coach, who remained on the podium — and most of the electronic media would have the sound bites they needed and would leave. Now everything is formalized. After the first thirty minutes, the players are taken into separate rooms, where they are put on podiums with microphones. This does four things: makes life easier for TV people, who can set their cameras on the risers in the back of the room rather than scrambling for position if the player is talking more informally; almost guarantees that the answers will be stilted and clichéd, since the player is very aware of the cameras and the microphones being used not only by him but by the questioners; allows the NCAA to put its logo on the backdrop of everyone being interviewed; and gives each moderator the chance to say the NCAA's two favorite words, *student-athlete,* several dozen more times.

In truth, the Sunday press conferences — like most NCAA press conferences — are something out of a *Saturday Night Live* parody. They make a presidential news conference look informal; at least there, the president calls on questioners himself and tends to know many, if not most, of the reporters by name.

The NCAA — surprise — has very strict rules. You may not ask a question until someone brings you one of the roving microphones so that questions can be picked up on the satellite feed sent out by the NCAA, which is second to none when it comes to feeding trite answers to the outside world. You must identify yourself before asking a question, even a follow-up question. This is how the asking and answering of two questions can sound:

MODERATOR: Questions for the student-athletes. Yes, left side, second mike.

REPORTER: Sean, when you first got to North Carolina —

MODERATOR: Identify yourself, please.

REPORTER: Oh, right. Barry Svrluga from the *Washington Post*. . . . Sean, when you first got to North Carolina, the team had just gone 8–20; did you think when you got there, you guys would reach this point either this quickly — or ever?

SEAN MAY: We thought we had a lot of talent, and that talent just had to come together. It took us a while, but we knew we had the potential to get to where we are now.

REPORTER: Just to follow up, was there a game —

MODERATOR: *Identify* yourself, please.

REPORTER: Again?

MODERATOR: Yes.

REPORTER: Barry Svrluga. Sean —

MODERATOR: Please identify your publication also.

REPORTER (sighing): Barry Svrluga, still from the *Washington Post*. To try to follow up, was there a game this season when it hit you that you had turned a corner to becoming a very good basketball team? And Roy [Williams], could you answer the same question after Sean, please?

MODERATOR (interrupting May as he begins his answer): We're only taking questions for the student-athletes now. You can ask Coach Williams the question later.

This isn't even an exaggeration or an aberration. It is, in fact, typical. At least after the games, when everyone is on deadline, the press conferences don't last very long. Even on the Friday practice day the time on the podium is limited to fifteen minutes for the "student-athletes" and fifteen minutes for the coach. Sunday is torture for everybody.

"What you have to do on Sunday is already know from Saturday what you're going to write or who you're going to write about," O'Connell said. "If you just walk in there hoping a story is going to appear magically, you're going to be in a lot of trouble. And you're going to sit through a lot of very boring answers."

Very occasionally a Sunday story will magically appear — though not in recent years. In 1975 John Wooden stunned everyone on Saturday when he announced that the championship game would be his farewell. On Sunday he sat and talked to reporters about his decision and his coaching career. "Maybe twenty guys sitting around at a hotel pool," Dick Weiss remembered. "It was amazing. No moderator, no cameras, no one identifying themselves, just him sitting there talking."

In 1981 Bob Knight had made news late on Saturday night when he got into an altercation with a drunken fan and ended up stuffing him into a trash can. Coming two years after his confrontation with a Puerto Rican policeman at the Pan American Games, Knight, who desperately wanted to be the Olympic coach in 1984, was concerned about the incident overshadowing his quest for a second national championship. Prior to the Sunday press conferences, Knight asked Dean Smith if he would defend him (not about the incident, which Smith obviously hadn't witnessed, but on more general terms) in his press conference. Smith launched into a lengthy diatribe about how Indiana and North Carolina stood for what was right about college basketball, about how he and Knight insisted that players go to class and graduate and play by all of the NCAA rules. (He did make the mistake of referring to his players as *players* rather than *student-athletes*. No doubt he was reprimanded.) One reporter stood up at the end of Smith's monologue and asked him if he was saying that the final matchup was a triumph for truth, justice, and the American way.

Smith smiled. "I didn't say that," he said. "But if you want to write it that way, it would be fine."

In 1986 a shouting match broke out among media members during the Duke press conference. A number of writers had laughed about the brevity of the answers given by the Louisville players and had joked about Milt Wagner, the Cardinals' star guard, commenting that all he and his teammates had known about (first-round opponent) Drexel was that "they're one of those academic-type schools." The Duke players, by contrast, were loquacious and funny. At one point each of the starters was asked if he aspired to play in the NBA: "I'd give my left arm to play in the NBA," Jay Bilas answered. "But I don't think there's much call for one-armed players in that league."

In the back of the room, Mike Lupica, the superb columnist for the *New York Daily News,* and Charlie Pierce, the equally superb feature writer who was then with the *Boston Herald,* began railing at several writers who were praising the wit and charm of the Duke players. Lupica, a close friend of Larry Brown's, was still upset about a couple of critical calls that had gone Duke's way late in its victory over Kansas on Saturday. Pierce was upset because that is just his way. They began telling people that the reaction to the two teams was racial — which didn't really make much sense: Louisville had four black starters, Duke three.

"They're the Cosby kids," Lupica insisted, referring to the then popular TV show in which Bill Cosby played a well-to-do doctor whose kids were good-looking, smart, and spoiled. It got loud, even while the Duke players were still answering questions. The next day those who read newspapers in New York could see a prime example of how the same event could produce radically different viewpoints: Dave Anderson, the Pulitzer Prize–winning *New York Times* columnist, wrote about how remarkable it was to hear a group of players good enough to be 37–2 and in the national championship game express themselves in complete sentences while clearly enjoying the chance to address the nation's media. Lupica wrote about his colleagues wanting to embrace the "white" team and not understanding the backgrounds from which the Louisville players came.

There was a transitory moment in the sport's history during the 1989 Sunday press conferences when Seton Hall's P. J. Carlesimo mentioned that one of the reasons he felt close to Michigan coach Steve Fisher was that "we're both Nike schools." It was a great moment for branding, if not for the sport.

There hasn't been much to write home about — or to write about, period — since the formalization of the press conferences. In 2003 Roy Williams and Jim Boeheim were bombarded with questions about what it would mean to each of them to finally win a national championship: Williams had been in four Final Fours and two title games, Boeheim three and three. The two of them spent so much time insisting it didn't matter that you wondered why either would even bother showing up for the game the next night. The most ludicrous moment of the day came when Tom Izzo, working as a commentator for CBS, said he would readily change his record — which included the 2000 national title — for either Boeheim's or Williams's record. That's a little bit like saying being vice president for two terms is better than being president for one.

"I love being at the Final Four," O'Connell said. "But I don't love the press conferences. I don't think anyone on either side does."

If Weiss sounds like pure Philadelphia when he talks, O'Connell is as New York as it gets. He has a round Irish face, thinning black hair, and a quick smile. Growing up in Queens, he was a St. John's fan, often going to games at nearby Alumni Hall and to the college doubleheaders at Madison Square Garden. "I remember in '71 when Digger [Phelps] had the great Fordham team and beat Notre Dame in the Garden," he said. "Then he went to Notre Dame, and when he came back the next year we all chanted, 'Digger is a mercenary.' Hero to goat, just like that."

He went to St. John's and worked in the sports information office as a student, becoming friends with the legendary Lou Carnesecca. By the time he was a junior, O'Connell knew he didn't want a "regular job." He went to talk to Carnesecca, who set him up to work as a stringer for the Associated Press. He can still remember Gordon White, the *New York Times*'s longtime college basketball writer, showing up for a St. John's game with the first computer anyone had ever seen at a basketball game. "Fans just stood around behind him while he was writing because they had never seen anything like it," he said.

O'Connell worked for two years after graduation as the SID at Fordham, which is where he met his wife, Annie — who to this day is the all-time leading rebounder in women's college basketball history. "She finished with one thousand nine hundred and ninety-nine," O'Connell said. "In her last game she needed thirteen to get to two thousand. They were counting it down on the P.A. With three minutes left she gets the thirteenth rebound, but one of the refs calls her for going over the back — and it's her fifth foul."

That official would have made a great NCAA press conference moderator.

O'Connell begins most answers during his frequent radio appearances by saying, "Deffanaly," as in, "He's deffanaly a great player." Like Weiss, he is an absolute basketball purist. Every November the AP flies him to the Maui Invitational. O'Connell watches all twelve games — four a day for three straight days — writes about all of them, never puts on a short-sleeved shirt, and has never once been on the beach that is about twenty-five yards from the front door of his hotel room. "It's not what I'm there for," he said. "I'm there for two things: to watch basketball and to write about it."

O'Connell has three children, which makes his travel schedule from mid-November to early April difficult. Fortunately, Annie remains as big a fan as her husband, and O'Connell frequently takes the kids to games in the New York area. He loves covering Duke-Carolina but gets just about as much of a buzz covering Wagner–Long Island University. "I just like being in gyms," he said. "When I'm on the road and I'm on my way to a game or at a game, I'm having a great time. I get back to the hotel room, I miss my family."

O'Connell laughed when talk of how big the Final Four has gotten came up. "My first one was '79, Magic vs. Larry in Salt Lake," he said. "I remember the older writers talking about how it had gotten too big *then*. It's deffanaly lost its homey edge, you can't argue that. I miss being in real basketball arenas [the last nondome Final Four was in New Jersey in 1996] and the fact that you can't do real reporting when you're at the event. It's become what I call ASAP journalism. People just wait for the quote sheets."

ASAP (as soon as possible) is a business that has sprung up in the past ten years. At most major events now, ASAP supplies dictationists who transcribe every word of every press conference. The transcripts are handed out within minutes of the end of a press conference. ASAP is a boon to deadline-pressed reporters, especially in this era when TV has pushed starting times deeper and deeper into the night. But it does give many people an easy excuse never to go into a locker room or even attempt anything resembling reporting.

O'Connell has made a career of writing incisive leads with little time to think about what he is going to write. When Kansas won the national championship in 1988 — with the team dubbed "Danny and the Miracles" because Danny Manning was so clearly the team's star — O'Connell's lead that night said: "The one-man team is number one." He is very good at pithy descriptions of some of the basketball people he has dealt with over the years:

JIM BOEHEIM: Cynical, sarcastic, and misunderstood. You spend time with him, you're gonna be surprised because you're gonna like him.

JOHN THOMPSON: Imposing and often right.

DEAN SMITH: Complicated, tough, always finding an angle.

JOHN WOODEN: The man who never lost.

JIM CALHOUN: Intense and funny — often at the same time.

MIKE KRZYZEWSKI: The guy I wish I could be as good as.

ROY WILLIAMS: Dean Jr.

DICK VITALE: I enjoy talking to him on the phone more than listening to him on TV. On the phone, he's just Dick; on TV he's Dickie V.

BILLY PACKER: Honest — never gives in. Does it his way.

HOOPS: My alter soul. If you cut us both open, there would be basketballs bouncing around in there.

BILL BRILL: The guy who knows everything going on and will tell everyone what he knows.

O'Connell would probably describe himself this way: he's the guy who gets home from the Final Four after seeing 150 games in a season and sits down in front of the TV set on Tuesday night and feels lost because there's no basketball game to watch. "I pick up the remote and don't know what to do," he said, laughing. "All there is to watch is baseball. It kills me. For one night every year, I hate baseball."

O'Connell became the AP's lead basketball writer in 1987, succeeding a man named Dick Joyce, who had been on the beat for years. Joyce, a sweet, friendly man, called O'Connell over to his desk after he had been told the job was his. "Kid, I want to show you the key to success in your new job," Joyce said. O'Connell nodded, waiting for a sage piece of advice about how to deal with deadlines or coaches or writing game stories. Joyce led O'Connell over to a desk where newspapers were stacked. He picked up *USA Today* and opened it to the national weather map. Jabbing a finger at a section of the map covered in blue to show cold, and probably snowy, weather, Joyce said: "Stay out of the blue."

O'Connell has heeded that advice. "Except when the Alaska Shootout has a really good field," he said. "Then I have to go — blue or no blue."

15

The Music Stops

IF SUNDAY IS THE DAY when almost nothing happens at the Final Four, Monday is the day when everything happens — late. Very late. It is college basketball's longest day.

Television dictates a 9:22 P.M. eastern time start; in St. Louis that meant 8:22, which is a little better, but not much. The two teams playing in the championship game have now been in the same town and the same hotel for five days. On the biggest day of the players' lives, they have to wait for hours and hours. They can't go out and be tourists; it is too late for that. They don't really want to hear the coaches' scouting reports again. The opponent is always someone they are familiar with. Unlike the old days, when players could meet in the championship game without ever having seen one another play, players see the other top teams on TV constantly. And tapes of virtually every game they have played are available to them. If Raymond Felton didn't know what Dee Brown's game was about, or vice versa, by the time they stepped on the court on Monday night, something was very wrong.

Sean May had managed to get his hands on a DVD of Indiana's victory in the 1976 title game over Michigan. His father had been voted to the All-Tournament team of that Final Four.

He started watching it soon after breakfast on Monday morning, and by the time it was over, most of his teammates had wandered in for a look. "It was cool seeing my dad play in the game I was about to play in," he said later. "It helped get me ready to play."

Beyond that, everyone waited. The teams had their final walk-throughs and shootarounds at the dome in the middle of the day, the building locked up tight until three hours before tip-off, when spectators would be allowed to enter. The town had been taken over, or so it seemed, by Illinois fans. There were occasional pockets of people in baby blue and white walking around, but everywhere one looked was orange and blue. At one point in the afternoon, four fans dressed in orange and blue with their faces painted orange got on an elevator in the official hotel with Jack Kvancz, the George Washington athletic director and former committee member.

"So," Kvancz said with a straight face, "who are you guys pulling for tonight?"

There were still a few meetings going on. The U.S. Basketball Writers Association held its annual awards brunch. Like most of the other events held at the Final Four, this can be a drawn-out affair since almost everyone in basketball with any kind of official title is invited to speak. Most understand that the best speech is a short one: "Thanks for having me — anytime I can help, give me a call." Of course, there is always someone who feels the need to speak for fifteen minutes. The USBWA inducts new members into its Hall of Fame during the brunch. One year, one of the inductees spoke for about fifteen minutes and just when everyone thought he was finishing up, he said: "And so, to begin at the beginning . . ."

There have been some memorable moments at the brunch, too. The USBWA gives an annual "Most Courageous" award, and some of the winners have had remarkable stories to tell. In 1981 the winner was Mark Alcorn, who had been a walk-on at LSU and then had been stricken with cancer. He had come back to be part of the team after beginning cancer treatments. LSU had lost to Indiana in the semifinals that year on Saturday and had to play in the consolation game on Monday afternoon. Even so, Dale Brown brought his entire team to the brunch to be there for Alcorn. Even cynical reporters were moved by the sight of all the Tigers leading the applause for their stricken teammate.

The USBWA also presents what is called the Katha Quinn Award, given to someone in basketball who has greatly aided those who cover the sport. It can be an SID, someone who works for the NCAA, even a reporter. In 2002 the *Washington Post's* Mark Asher, who continued to cover college basketball after kidney and pancreas transplants, was given the award. One NCAA basketball committee chairman, Tom Frericks — the former Dayton athletic director — received the award. As chairman of the committee, Frericks, over the objection of both the NCAA's then media director and most of the committee, took the unheard-of step of agreeing to have committee members actually meet directly with the media. Until then, any requests from the media on issues such as telephone lines, locker-room access, or press conference scheduling had to be funneled through Dave Cawood, who was then the media director. Most of the time the answer to requests was simple and direct: No. When Jim Delany, Frericks's predecessor as committee chairman, was approached by the USBWA with the notion of direct contact, he reacted as if he had been asked to donate both his kidneys to Mark Asher. Out of the question, was his response. "Dave Cawood does a fine job representing the interest of the media to the committee," he wrote.

That was a little bit like saying that Karl Rove did a fine job of representing the interests of the Democratic Party in the White House.

One of Frericks's first acts when he succeeded Delany was to schedule a meeting with the USBWA. The two groups — committee and writers — have met regularly since then and the world has somehow remained spinning on its axis.

Most of the award winners have been very proud to win the Katha. That's because almost all of them knew Katha Quinn. She was St. Johns's SID, and one of the first women to hold that post at a big-time college basketball school. Part of her genius was in persuading writers to see the lovable side of her coach, Lou Carnesecca, as opposed to the paranoid side. "People forget that in 1985 when Louie made the Final Four, he kept his team as far away from Lexington as [Georgetown coach] John Thompson kept his team away," Dick Weiss likes to point out. "Louie was just more charming about it than John. And John never had Katha working for him."

Katha Quinn was one of those SIDs who figured out a way to make the answer yes even when the easy answer was no. Writers loved her for that. They also loved her for her sense of humor — she did a wicked Dean Smith imitation — and because she could drink most of them under the table and be at work ready to go first thing the next morning. There was really nothing that could slow Katha Quinn down.

Except cancer. When she was first stricken in 1987, no one really believed it. Or wanted to. She never stopped working. She would go for chemo in the morning and be at the press table that night. She was thin, she was drawn, she often looked horribly sick, but she was always there. And she was still Katha. She joked about her chemo and talked about all the different wigs she was planning to buy when her hair fell out. "I'm not gonna die," she would snarl at writers. "Louie would never forgive me."

As luck would have it, the USBWA had decided the year before to create an award to give people who had gone out of their way to help writers through the years. When it came time to discuss who the first winner should be, there really wasn't any discussion: Katha.

And so, on that morning of the Kansas-Oklahoma national championship game in Kansas City, the writers gathered for their brunch and went through all their annual rituals. The first class of USBWA Hall of Famers was inducted that year, with six very deserving men being honored. Arizona's Steve Kerr, who had been unrecruited as a high school senior, who had dealt with his father's assassination in Beirut as a college freshman, and who had come back from what had appeared to be a career-ending knee injury, was the Most Courageous winner. Kerr's speech was witty and emotional and most years would have easily been the highlight of the morning.

But that day he was upstaged by a woman who hadn't been sure she would be able to walk to the podium, a woman who was afraid she wouldn't have the strength to get through her speech. He was upstaged by a woman who would not be alive the next time the Final Four was played.

Her speech was, as her good friend Malcolm Moran, then of the *New York Times,* now of *USA Today,* liked to say, "pure Katha."

She was funny — as always — making fun of herself, talking about how she'd always wanted to lose weight but not this way. She told stories about writers and coaches and about *her* coach, Carnesecca, who sat a few feet away with tears streaming down his face. She talked about all the friends she had brought to "her fight" and how very much she loved St. John's and the players she had worked with.

By the time she finished, the room was utterly silent except for the quiet sounds of her friends all crying. People who had never met her before that day were crying, too. The standing ovation — once people collected themselves — lasted several minutes. The applause still rings in the ears of everyone who was there.

Soon after that day, the award she had received was given a name: the Katha Quinn Award. She died on the Sunday before the Final Four in 1989. St. John's dedicated its victory that week to her. Every year when the Katha is presented, those who were in Kansas City in 1988 flash back to that morning. Without fail, they laugh — and cry — all over again.

On Monday afternoon the coaches' hotel feels like a ghost town. The meetings are over. Most of the coaches have gone home. The few that linger are snapped up by the now-desperate radio producers. Even some of the radio people have gone home, knowing that what was *the* sports place to be on Thursday, Friday, and Saturday is now being dismantled. There are even people in the hotel who have no idea that a championship game will be played in town that night. They are here on business that has nothing to do with basketball.

Coaches will tell you that the most trying time before any game is the last few hours before tip-off. "You keep thinking about what you haven't done, that there must be something else to do," said Maryland coach Gary Williams. "Deep down, though, you know there's nothing. You just have to hope the players are ready. If there's any one thing that will drive me out of coaching, it is the waiting around on game day."

Williams was lucky in 2002, the day his Maryland team played for the national championship. His daughter, Kristen, had brought his then eighteen-month-old grandson with her to Atlanta, and since Maryland was staying out near the airport, the little boy spent most of the afternoon pointing out airplanes to his grandfather. "It made the game feel very far away," Williams said. "At least for a little while."

Every coach who reaches the championship game understands that what Al McGuire used to say is true: coaching on Monday night is something to be savored — at least until game time. But that becomes more difficult when you have been there and not yet won. "You reach a point," Jim Boeheim said, "where you don't want to wait anymore. You don't want to answer the questions anymore."

Bruce Weber could savor the day. He could look around and think about how far he had come in eight years to reach this moment in his life. Roy Williams would insist he could savor it, too. But this would be his third Monday night. Like Boeheim, he was tired of waiting. "I never thought that winning the national championship would make me a better coach," he said. "There is no question, though, that it makes you a coach people look at differently."

The players understand that the night is special — sort of. "I think they understand that it's a big deal because it has become such a big-time event," Bill Bradley said. "But I'm not sure there's any way for them to understand the long-term impact it will have on them. The short-term impact they understand: feeling great because they won or awful because they lost. But it takes time to really get a grasp on how much it meant to you to play. I still regret not having gotten to the last game, just as I know there are guys who got there and didn't win who think about it all the time."

Wes Miller, who knew he would play at a critical juncture only if his team was beset by injuries or foul trouble, felt as if he understood the significance of what was to come. "When I was a kid, playing in the Final Four was a dream," he said. "Each step of the way I had to stop and pinch myself to believe I was going through this experience. I felt it on Friday and again on Saturday. There was no question in my mind that running onto the floor on Monday night was going to be unlike anything I'd ever experienced in my life. And I had to take the approach — I think we all had to take the approach — that this was a once-in-a-lifetime thing. It could happen again, but it's certainly not something you can count on, especially after you've seen how tough it is to do once."

Years ago, when the teams ran onto the court for the championship game, Frank Fallon, who was the Final Four's P.A. announcer for twenty-three years, would say the following: "Ladies and gentlemen. On October fifteenth, 326 teams began practicing, each of them pointing for this night. Now, two are left. They are . . ."

It was always a thrilling moment when the names of the two schools were announced, especially by Fallon, who had one of the great P.A. voices of all time. For some reason — no one is quite sure why — that tradition has been abandoned, which is a shame. Still, players and coaches will tell you that there is nothing quite like the feeling of running onto the court on Monday night, knowing you are playing in the last game of the season, knowing you are about to be part of history, one way or the other. "You kind of know you're going to end up on [ESPN] Classic down the road when you play in the final," Shane Battier had said on the eve of his last game at Duke, the 2001 final. "You want it to be a game you can feel proud about having people watch for years to come."

For many years it seemed as if every championship game was a classic or near classic. In fact, from 1982 through 1989, the only game decided before the last minute was the Georgetown-Houston game in 1984, and that was still a compelling matchup: Patrick Ewing and Hakeem Olajuwon squaring off at center. That string ended in 1990, when UNLV beat Duke, 103–73 — the largest margin ever in a final. Since then, finals have blown hot and cold: Duke-Kansas in 1991 was taut until the last thirty seconds; Duke-Michigan a year later was a 20-point blowout. Carolina-Michigan in '93 was memorable because of Chris Webber's time-out that wasn't a time-out because Michigan was out of them, and Scotty Thurman hit the late three for Arkansas in its win over Duke the following year. Then came relatively easy victories for UCLA and Kentucky, followed by Arizona's spellbinding overtime win over Kentucky in 1997.

Since then, there have not been too many games worth remembering. UConn over Duke in '99 was a superb game, Duke over Arizona in '01 was a good one, and Syracuse holding off Kansas in '03 was very good. The others are remembered only by the fans of the teams that won, including UConn's blowout of Georgia Tech in 2004.

No one (except the coach or the fans on the winning side) wants a blowout on Monday night. It is bad for TV ratings, especially on the East Coast, where people simply go to bed if the game isn't competitive. It is bad for the fans in the arena. It is bad for the media, except perhaps some of the print reporters, who can start writing their stories early. Deadlines on Monday night, with the game ending not long before midnight eastern time, are brutal.

"It's hard to be very good when you have to hit the send button the instant the final buzzer sounds," Tony Barnhardt of the *Atlanta Journal-Constitution* said.

Carolina-Illinois had all the makings of a final everyone could feel good about. The two teams had a combined record of 69–5 coming into the game. One of Carolina's four losses had come in its opener against Santa Clara when point guard Raymond Felton didn't play. The other losses had been at Wake Forest, at Duke, and to Georgia Tech in the ACC Tournament. Illinois' only loss had been in the regular-season finale at Ohio State. Carolina was in the championship game for the seventh time; Illinois had never been there before.

The dome filled early. People didn't want to take a chance on having trouble getting in because of security lines, and since no one has very much left to do on Monday afternoon, they tend to arrive early — almost as if getting in the building early will somehow get the game started sooner. It never works out that way.

Like most major sports organizations, the NCAA likes to harp on patriotic themes in the post-9/11 world. No one has commercialized patriotism more than the NFL, but the NCAA isn't all that far behind. The playing of the national anthem featured the unleashing of a bald eagle, which fluttered down to the court a few feet away from where Wes Miller was standing. "It gave me chills," Miller said. "Just to be on the court, to see that eagle land, to be part of it in a small way. I remember I looked over at Coach [Joe] Holladay and he smiled at me as if to say, 'Yeah, this is really cool, isn't it?'"

Moments before they went on the air, Jim Nantz spotted a

flaw in the way Billy Packer's tie was tied and put his microphone under his arm to tighten it for him. Standing a few feet
away, John Thompson, who was doing color on the radio broadcast, laughed as he watched Packer and then the two coaches as
they walked onto the court. "I'll tell you the biggest change in
coaching since I started," he said. "The way coaches dress. How
much do you think Roy's suit cost? I guarantee you it's more
than all the clothes I owned when I started at Georgetown. I
never wanted to wear anything too nice anyway, because I knew I
was just going to sweat right through the damn thing before the
game was over."

Exactly how much Bruce Weber's outfit cost was a different
question. He was wearing a bright Illinois-orange jacket that
looked as if it would glow in the dark. If nothing else, he had to
feel very secure to wear a jacket of that color, knowing millions
of people would be watching him.

There is nothing quite like the tip-off of the national championship game. After all the waiting, all the hype, and all the
pregame pomp, the scripted introductions, and the scripted
coaches' handshake, by the time the players finally walk to center
court and shake hands all around one more time, the building
feels as if it is about to burst. As soon as Ed Corbett threw the
ball up, thousands of flashbulbs went off from cameras around
the building. Fans are allowed to carry very few items into places
where major sports events are being held these days, but cameras
are still okay. It seemed as if about 47,000 of the 47,262 in the
building wanted a picture of the opening tip.

Illinois won the tip and Deron Williams buried a jumper
30 seconds into the game, causing about three-quarters of the
building to explode in orange-and-blue joy. There wasn't any
more of that for the next two minutes as North Carolina raced to

a 9–2 lead. Frequently the championship game begins with a lot of missed shots. But both teams came out looking comfortable and confident in spite of what was at stake. Illinois quickly tied the game, at 9–9, with 15:32 left.

The first critical moment came early. With 12:57 left, Deron Williams started a drive to the basket and Raymond Felton fouled him. It was his second foul. Carolina had played several games without Rashad McCants and had hardly missed a beat. Sean May was invaluable but didn't have to score in huge numbers for his team to win. Felton was the player the Tar Heels could least afford to lose for an extended period of time. That they had lost to Santa Clara when he didn't play was evidence of how key he was to his team's success.

The unwritten rules of college basketball say that when a player picks up his second foul in the first half, he comes out. Once, coaches would let players stay in until they picked up a third foul in the first half, but in the past twenty years that has changed. Rarely does a player stay in the game with two fouls or come back in before halftime unless his team falls way behind. In 1984 Michael Jordan had picked up his second foul early in a round-of-sixteen game against Indiana. Dean Smith took him out and kept him out for the rest of the half. Indiana built a big lead by halftime and Carolina never caught up. It was Jordan's last college game.

Roy Williams learned at Dean Smith's side. One of the reasons Smith believed in taking a player out with two fouls was that you had to show faith in your bench; you had to let the non-starters know that you believed they could step in and play if needed. What's more, Felton's backup was Melvin Scott, a senior, and you always had to have faith in your seniors.

As soon as the whistle blew, Felton knew the foul was on him.

He also knew that Williams's first instinct was going to be to take him out of the game. He made a dash toward the bench where Williams was standing, arms folded.

"Coach, it's okay, I'm all right," Felton said.

"I've heard that before," Williams answered.

Still, he made no move to send in a sub for Felton.

There are, in every coach's life, moments when he has to take a risk, one that involves stepping out of character. In 1982 Dean Smith, who always believed in putting the game — and each season — in the hands of upperclassmen, turned to a freshman as his team came out of the huddle in the final minute of the national championship game against Georgetown. Carolina trailed, 62–61, and Smith knew there was no way the Hoyas were going to allow the ball to get to James Worthy, his best player, anywhere near the basket. He might have instructed Jimmy Black, his senior point guard, to try to create space either for himself or Worthy or even sophomore Sam Perkins.

But deep down, Smith knew that Michael Jordan would be open. And he knew Jordan could make the shot. "Knock it in, Michael," he said to Jordan as his players returned to the court. A few seconds later Black reversed the ball to a wide-open Jordan, who followed his coach's instructions perfectly and drained the shot that won Smith's first national championship. Smith had to go against all his instincts to put the game and the season in the hands of a freshman, but his coaching gut told him that was the moment to do it.

Now Williams let his coaching gut take over. He went against the rules and tradition and left Felton in the game. Carolina led at that moment, 14–12. Williams missed both free throws, and on Carolina's next possession, Felton fed Sean May for a dunk. The game stayed close for the next eight minutes and Felton was careful not to commit his third foul. Then, with Carolina leading, 27–25, he drilled a three-pointer. Dee Brown missed at the other end, and Felton found Jawad Williams open for a three: swish. The lead was 33–25. A minute later Felton fed McCants for another layup and the margin was suddenly 10 and Illinois had to call a time-out. Williams got Felton out for the last minute of the half to make sure he didn't commit a tired foul. McCants hit one more three and at halftime Carolina led, 40–27.

No one had expected either team to build that kind of lead. A year earlier Connecticut's 41–26 halftime lead against Georgia Tech wasn't that big a surprise. This was.

Neither team thought the game was over. Illinois hadn't gotten to 37–1 on good fortune. Carolina had shot 6 of 11 from outside the three-point line, Illinois 5 of 19. The Illini simply had no semblance of an inside game, which had allowed Carolina, normally not a good defensive team against the three-point shot, to extend its defense and make it difficult for Illinois to find open shots. During the break, each coach said essentially the same thing to his players but for different reasons: the first five minutes would be crucial. Williams knew if his team could extend the lead, the game would be over. Weber knew his players needed a jolt of confidence, and closing the gap would do that.

It was Weber who got what he needed: after May opened the half with another basket inside, Illinois went on an 18–7 run, punctuated by Deron Williams's three-pointer with 15:11 to play. The momentum seesawed: every time Illinois crept close, Carolina would stretch the lead, mostly on the strength of May's play inside. He was simply too big and too strong for anyone from Illinois to guard him one-on-one. He was a smart, gifted passer, so when the Illini attempted to double-team him, he would find Felton, Jawad or Marvin Williams, or McCants on the perimeter.

Illinois' inability to handle May was never more evident than during a two-minute stretch after Carolina's lead dwindled to 52–50. First he posted up and powered to the basket for a layup and was fouled. He made the free throw and then hit a short jump shot to push the lead to 57–50. A few seconds later, after Deron Williams had answered with a three-pointer at the other end, he recognized a double-team and fed a wide-open Jawad Williams for a three that stretched the margin back to 60–53. May ended up scoring 10 points and assisting on the Williams three during a 13–5 Carolina run that pushed the margin back to 65–55 with under nine minutes to play.

But as often happens, Carolina forgot how it had kept control of the game. With Illinois putting more and more defenders in the lane to try to deny May the ball, the Tar Heels got jump-shot happy and began to make mistakes. Illinois, showing the re-silience that had gotten it this far, rallied one more time. A three-point shot by Luther Head with 2:40 to go tied the game at 70, and amid the cheers of the Illinois fans you could hear the kind of rumble that goes through an arena when something special is about to happen. One way or the other, this was going to be a memorable championship game, one that was going to show up on Classic for years to come. It was either going to be the story of Illinois' remarkable comeback from a 15-point second-half deficit or the story of Carolina righting the ship at the last possible moment to finally win a title for Roy Williams.

After Head's shot, Williams again stepped out of the Dean Smith school of how to coach a game: he called time-out. In thirty-six years as a head coach, Dean Smith probably didn't call a dozen time-outs that weren't part of the absolute endgame, usually in the final minute. Williams had even joked on Friday that no one in history had taken fewer time-outs than he had. If there was anyone who had done so, it was his old boss and mentor, who now sat directly across from the UNC bench, his face creased with tension.

"I was far more nervous right then than I would have been if I'd been coaching," Smith said. "When you're coaching the game, you don't have time to be nervous. You aren't thinking about what might happen if you lose or if you win. You're focused completely on figuring out what to do right at that moment. When you're just watching, it's a helpless feeling because there's nothing you can do to help."

If he had been at home watching the game on TV, Smith might have turned off the set and paced around for a while, too nervous to watch. But now there was no place for him to go or hide. He had to sit, watch, and hope.

Just as Smith would have been, Williams was completely calm as his players jogged over to the bench for what is euphemistically called a 30-second time-out. (They tend to last almost a minute so that CBS can get in a commercial and reset the game once they return.) "We're fine," Williams told his players in a calm, steady voice. "We've been through this before. We've been in much worse situations than this. Take a deep breath and let's go finish the job."

Calm was just what the Carolina players needed at that moment. The place was in absolute bedlam, the Illinois fans convinced that their destiny was to win. After all, why else had they come from 15 down in four minutes against Arizona? Why else had they just come from 15 down to tie?

The teams traded misses by Williamses — Marvin Williams, whose jump shot never made it to St. Louis, missing for Carolina;

Deron Williams missing for Illinois, a three-point attempt that, had it gone in, might have been a dagger in the heart for the Tar Heels. Carolina came down again and worked the ball around the perimeter. Sean May was trying to post up, but half the population of Illinois appeared to be guarding him. With the shot clock winding down, McCants drove from the left side into a bevy of defenders. There really wasn't time for him to pass, so he forced up a horrible shot, the ball popping high into the air with absolutely no chance to get to the rim, much less the basket.

Luck and talent now came into play. With the ball spinning skyward, Marvin Williams came flying in from the top of the key. He didn't have a chance to think about the moment or be nervous or worry about what was going on around him. He was playing on pure adrenaline and he flew over everyone, grabbed the ball out of the air, and pushed it into the basket before anyone from Illinois could even think to move for it. In some ways it was reminiscent of another freshman, Louisville's Pervis Ellison, grabbing a Jeff Hall airball out of the sky and laying it in during the final minute of his team's victory over Duke in the '86 championship game. In a completely different way it brought back memories of another Carolina freshman, Michael Jordan, burying the jumper against Georgetown twenty-three years earlier.

The Carolina bench went wild. The score was 72–70, but there was still more than a minute left. Illinois pushed downcourt, and Head missed another three — Illinois would end up attempting a mind-boggling 40 three-pointers — and this time it was Jack Ingram of the Illini getting the rebound. Now Weber called time, wanting to be sure his team got a good shot. But his team was out of bullets, perhaps worn out by the comeback and by the fact that it had missed its best chance to take the lead a possession earlier. Deron Williams missed another three, Illinois rebounded again, and Weber called time again.

This time Weber demanded that the ball get inside somehow, someway. Deron Williams tried, but Felton stole his pass to Head, and Williams had to foul him. But Felton made only one of two free throws, and trailing, 73–70, the Illini had one last chance to tie. Now they *had* to shoot a three, and Carolina's entire defense grouped on the perimeter. Head finally forced up a shot from beyond the arc with 16 seconds to go. It hit the back rim and — naturally — May was there for the rebound. He slipped the ball to Felton, who was fouled again with 9 seconds to go.

Carolina was now one free throw from the national championship. Roy Williams almost couldn't look, even though if you glanced at him at that instant, you might have thought he was sitting in an easy chair, reading a book. "If I looked at all calm," he said, "it was because I didn't think Raymond was going to miss another free throw."

He didn't. Both shots went in. Head missed one last time — Illinois missed its last five field-goal attempts, all of them threes — and May grabbed his tenth rebound, the last of his collegiate career. He began looking for Roy Williams because he had told him he wanted the first hug when the game was over. May had played one of the great championship games of all time: 26 points on 10 of 11 shooting, 10 rebounds, 2 key assists, and a blocked shot on a rare Illinois foray inside. Twenty-nine years later, he had actually surpassed his father. He would be voted the Most Outstanding Player of the Final Four.

For Illinois, as is always the case for the loser on Monday night, the defeat was devastating. It never occurs to a team good enough to win five games in the NCAA Tournament that it might lose one step from being remembered forever. "It hurts a lot at the moment when it happens," Jay Bilas said. "But you're in shock a little bit. The real pain doesn't really set in for a while."

The Illini would be celebrated at their school as the first team to reach the championship game, as a team that won as many games as any team in college basketball history (tying Duke 1986, UNLV 1987, and Duke 1999, all teams that also failed to win the national title), and as a team that brought great joy to an entire state in the winter of 2005. Banners would go up in Assembly Hall: Big Ten Champions, Final Four, NCAA Finalist. But the banner they all wanted — and expected — would go to Chapel Hill.

That banner would hang with three others — 1957, 1982, and 1993 — amid the dozens of banners that hang in the Dean Dome. (Carolina hangs so many banners — ACC CHAMPIONS — REGULAR SEASON TIE rates one — that Jim Valvano once joked that he was going to put up banners in Reynolds Coliseum that read NATIONAL CHAMPIONS — ALMOST.)

There was no *almost* in this banner or in this championship. Roy Williams never got around to putting his arms in the air, but he did get to feel the joy that comes with winning your last game and spending an entire summer doing what Mike Krzyzewski calls "a victory lap."

It can be argued that no one has ever been more entitled.

Epilogue

CELEBRATIONS DON'T LAST LONG in college basketball. The best moments for the North Carolina players and
coaches came after they had gone through the seemingly inter-
minable on-court ceremonies: the cutting of the nets (which lost
its romance years ago when the NCAA began providing plat-
forms for people to walk onto), the presentation of the trophy,
and then the playing of the unbearably sappy "One Shining Moment." The only thing that makes playing the song defensible is
that the players and coaches actually enjoy it. At that moment
there are very few things they wouldn't enjoy.

Once Roy Williams had chased down Bruce Weber, he asked
Dick Baddour, his athletic director, if there was any way to get
his wife and children down near the court so he could see them.
"I knew there was no way Wanda was coming out on the court,"
he said. "But I wanted one moment with her and the kids before
we accepted the trophy." When Wanda Williams came downstairs with Scott and Kimberly, they all enjoyed heartfelt hugs.
Williams saw tears in his wife's eyes and felt a little bit choked
up himself. But unlike in the past, when tears had come so easily,
he didn't cry. "I did get a little bit teared up during 'One Shining

Moment,'" he said. "I always made a point to watch that every year when I was home because I wanted to see the looks on the faces of the winners. I would sit there and think, 'I wonder what it is like to feel *that* good.' It was something I wanted to feel — more a dream than a demand — but to stand there did get me pretty emotional."

Once the last notes of the song were played, the Tar Heels escaped to their locker room, where they found both Dean Smith and Michael Jordan waiting. Jordan had flown in for the game and had watched from a luxury box. They had both made their way to the locker room during the awards ceremony and were there when the players came in. Smith's presence was no surprise, as he was often at practice and was frequently seen around the building that bears his name. Williams still slipped on occasion and referred to "Coach Smith's office" while sitting in the chair Smith once occupied. Jordan was another story. None of the players had been born when he hit the shot that beat Georgetown, and even though he still showed up in Chapel Hill on occasion, he was almost a mythical figure to the players.

"Seeing the two of them when we walked in there, arguably the greatest coach and the greatest player of all time, made me realize all over again what we're all part of," Wes Miller said. "Seeing Coach Smith and Coach Williams hug one another made all of us get kind of emotional."

In a sense, those locker-room moments, away from the public eye, are the best for any team that has just won — or lost — a championship. Players who have lost on Monday night talk about how close they felt to their teammates in those few minutes a team is allowed in the locker room before the doors are opened and the TV lights go back on. "I'm not sure I remember a word anyone said," Bruce Buckley recounts. "But I vividly remember

how intensely emotional it was. The hugs and the feeling are something I've carried with me since that night."

"Men aren't supposed to say, 'I love you,' to one another, especially jocks," said Bruce Bell, the only senior on Duke's 1978 team. "But I told everyone in the room that night that I loved them and they said the same thing back to me. It was the right thing to say."

The emotions winners feel are different. There is a glow to a winning Monday night locker room because every goal a team can set prior to a season has been reached. "There's a feeling that, as you go forward in life, no matter what else happens, no one can take this away from you," said Duke assistant coach Johnny Dawkins, who dealt with the emotions of defeat as a player in 1986 and as an assistant in 1999 before finally being part of a Monday night winner in 2001. "You almost can't feel totally satisfied when you've been so close but haven't gotten over that last hump."

There were no humps left for the Tar Heels. No more questions for Roy Williams and a feeling of complete satisfaction for all the assistants and players. Of course, the moment the locker-room door opened, the questions started again. The three juniors — Raymond Felton, Sean May, and Rashad McCants — were asked if they were going to turn pro. So was freshman Marvin Williams. Wes Miller probably should have been insulted that no one asked *him* if he was turning pro. May had turned twenty-one on Saturday and Miller had bought him a bottle of champagne. Now they could truly celebrate.

Everyone knew McCants was leaving; he and Williams had more or less thrashed that out in January. He had played well in the championship game — 14 points — but had been bailed out of long-lasting infamy by Marvin Williams's rebound of his wild shot with the score tied at 70. Most people expected Felton to leave, too. He was a lock top-ten pick and, especially after winning the national championship, was more than ready to make a move. Marvin Williams probably would have liked another year of college. He was only a freshman, and what exactly was there not to like about being a star freshman basketball player at the University of North Carolina? But the way basketball works today, if the NBA says you are a top-five pick, you almost have to go because there is no guarantee you will be as highly sought in another year. There are too many examples of players whose draft status has slipped after another year of college to risk not making the jump when the money is, for all intents and purposes, dumped at your feet.

The only real question mark among Carolina people was May. He had been saying emphatically, both publicly and privately, that he was coming back for his senior year. No one doubted that he meant it. In fact, Rick Brewer, who had worked at North Carolina in sports information and as an associate athletic director since the Civil War, was so certain May would return that he bet on it during the Final Four.

"Even if we win, he's coming back," Brewer said. "He likes college."

No doubt May liked college. But after his performance in the Final Four, a lot of pro scouts who had talked about his being a "tweener" — too small to play the low post in the NBA, not quick enough to play forward — were rethinking that position. May had great hands, great vision, and a great feel for the game. Because he was also the kind of person you wanted on your team, his stock soared. He went from a late-first- or second-round pick to a high- to mid-first-round pick. There was another issue: May had climbed the mountain. He had done it with Felton and

McCants, whom he had arrived with three years earlier. With Felton, McCants, and Marvin Williams gone, Carolina — with May and a great incoming freshman class — would still be very competitive in 2006. But they weren't likely to return to the Final Four. When you've celebrated your twenty-first birthday with national championship champagne, it is awfully hard to think about starting a season with the Sweet Sixteen as a reasonable goal.

May was the last of the four to announce that he was leaving. "That was the one that felt like a kick in the stomach," Roy Williams said. "Obviously, I knew Rashad was going and I suspected Raymond was. Marvin really had to go. But I had thought Sean would come back. I understood the decision completely, but I'd be lying if I didn't say it hurt."

The pain was lessened by the victory lap. Williams had almost come to dread being recognized in airports. "It isn't that people weren't nice," he said. "Most of the time they are. But you really get a little tired of hearing 'Is this the year, Coach?' or 'You think you're finally going to get it done?' It's nice just to have people walk up and say, 'Congratulations, I'm real happy for you.' I think people were happy for me because they knew it wasn't easy. I think a lot of them had felt sorry for me all those years. Now they didn't have to feel that way anymore."

Letters came in from colleagues: Mike Krzyzewski, Gary Williams, and Clemson coach Oliver Purnell wrote letters that were there almost as soon as Williams got home. Jim Boeheim and Jim Calhoun both wrote, too. So did some of his ex-Kansas players. The new president of Duke, Robert Brodhead, also wrote. The letter Williams may have enjoyed the most came not from a friend or a coach or a fan or a relative. It came from Lenny Wirtz, the longtime ACC referee who might have had more on-court duels with Dean Smith than anyone who ever officiated. Wirtz was now retired but he wrote to Williams to tell him how pleased he was for him. Williams was touched by the letter from someone he and his mentor had battled with through the years.

He knew that next season would be different. Four underclassmen gone to the NBA — plus three seniors graduating — would make for a very young team. Four talented freshmen would arrive, but they would be freshmen. There would also be an entirely different feeling at Carolina. Much like Duke in '05, the season would start with lower expectations than normal. "It will be easier to go to practice every day and look up and see that banner," Williams said. "It will help when I get frustrated during the season. But it isn't going to make me want to win any less. I don't see that changing."

That wouldn't change. The great coaches are always hungry for the Next Thing — whatever it may be. Krzyzewski, whose Duke team would enter the '05–'06 season as one of the favorites to win the whole thing much the way Carolina had entered '04–'05 — wants a fourth title as much as he wanted his first. Jim Calhoun — another preseason favorite, at UConn — wants a third. Jim Boeheim and Roy Williams want a second. Gary Williams may want a second more than he wanted a first.

"I always thought if I ever won the national championship, I'd feel less pressure," he said. "I think, if I'm being honest, I feel more pressure now. I feel as if more people are watching what our team does and when we lose, it's a bigger deal than it used to be — because it *is* a bigger deal than it used to be. We miss the NCAA Tournament, and our fans are very unhappy. I understand. I'm unhappy, too. But now, in the back of my mind, I catch myself thinking, 'If I could just win one more, that would be enough.'" He smiled. "Of course, that's not true. It wouldn't be enough."

It is never enough. Because when one Final Four ends, when one city clears out and another — Indianapolis in 2006 — begins to prepare for the next, everyone in basketball looks ahead. They all began again on October 15, 2005. The first goal for each is to get to the Dance. The next goal is Indianapolis. Then comes getting to Monday night to walk onto the court, tingling because they are there, knowing that only two teams who started on October 15 will still be playing on April 3, 2006. Only two get the Last Dance.

And only one will get to hear that sappy song.

Acknowledgments

I HAVE BEEN ACCUSED, on occasion, of being a name-dropper. Actually, I learned the art from perhaps the greatest name-dropper of all time: Dick Schaap, who could begin a sentence by saying something like "One night when I was having dinner with Jack Kennedy, Frank Sinatra, and Muhammad Ali, Billy Crystal stopped by the table. . . ."

I will never be in Dick's class in the name-dropping category (he wanted to call his memoir *Name-Dropping,* but some publishing genius came up with *Flashing Before My Eyes,* which is silly and meaningless), but when I started to think about the acknowledgments for this book, it occurred to me that Dick would be proud of me if he could read them.

Consider the following people I need to thank for taking the time to talk to me about their Final Four experiences: John Wooden, Dean Smith, Roy Williams, Bill Bradley, John Thompson, Jim Calhoun, Jim Boeheim, Gary Williams, Lefty Driesell, Dick Vitale, Billy Packer, and Rick Barnes. I haven't even mentioned Mike Krzyzewski, who not only talked to me at length about his Final Four experiences but agreed to write the introduction for the book. That's a pretty good group of names for starters. There's more: Jay Bilas, Greg Anthony, Jay Buckley, Bruce Buckley, Clay Buckley, Tom Brennan, Rollie Massimino, Jay Wright, Frank Sullivan, Doug Wojcik, Digger Phelps, Dave Odom, Jeff Capel III, Mike Brey, Phil Martelli, Jeff Jones, Jim Larranaga, Ralph Willard, Pat Flannery, Emmett Davis, Jim Crews, Billy Taylor, Fran O'Hanlon, Bill Lange, Jimmy Patsos, Billy Hahn, Tom Abatemarco, George Raveling, Bruce Bell, Johnny Dawkins, Tommy Amaker, Chris Collins, Steve Wojciechowski, Kenny Dennard, Rich Clarkson, Dick Weiss, Jim O'Connell, and Bill Brill. Special thanks to Wes Miller, who agreed to keep a journal for me during North Carolina's trip to St. Louis. I also owe thanks to Jack Kvancz, Gene Corrigan, Wayne Duke, Dave Gavitt, and Terry Holland, who talked to me about their experiences as members of the basketball committee, and to Tom Jernstedt, who is a walking encyclopedia of tournament history. Whether I could have finished this book at all without the help of Bill Hancock is something I seriously doubt. To say he will be missed by those of us who cover the tournament each year is a vast understatement, but if anyone can straighten out the BCS, it is Bill. Thanks also to Steve Kirschner and Rick Brewer at Carolina, to Mike Cragg at Duke, to Bill Bennett at UCLA, and to Bruce Bosley at Vermont. More thanks: to outgoing committee chairman Bob Bowlsby and incoming chairman Craig Littlepage. Also to Hank Nichols and many of his refs, most notably Larry Rose and Tim Higgins, who are Final Four refs every year as far as I'm concerned.

That's the group that played a crucial role in *this* book. Then there are the people who play a critical role in *every* book I write: Esther Newberg, my agent for life, and Michael Pietsch, who truly is a wonderful editor and exhibited great patience on this particular project, especially when my shoulder surgery put the book way behind schedule. Esther and Michael have great assistants: Chris Earle (aka FA/FW) and the precocious Kari Stuart put up with both Esther and with me — which is pretty close to miraculous. They learned, of course, from Andy Barzvi. Michael is aided immeasurably by both Stacey Brody and Zainab Zakari. Heather Fain (Murphy Brown to her friends) has promised to promote this book as she has promoted no other, since her alma mater won the 2005 national title. I'm not certain that Heather Rizzo, Katherine Molina, and Marlena Bittner will be as enthusiastic, but if they're not, Holly Wilkinson will ride in and crack her whip. Extra thanks are owed to Steve Lamont, who copyedited two of my books in a short period of time and saved me from myself on countless occasions. (That's not hyperbole, that's fact.)

Friends (still, I'm pleased to say, a long list): Barbie Drum, Bob and Anne DeStefano, David and Linda Maraniss, Jackson Diehl and Jean Halperin, Lexie Verdon and Steve Barr, Tom and Jill Mickle, Shelley Crist, Jane Brill, Terry and Patti Hanson, Bob Zurfluh, Pete Teeley, Al Hunt, Bob Novak, Vivian Thompson, Phil Hochberg, Wayne Zell, Mike and David Sanders, Bob Whitmore, Andy Dolich, Mary Carillo, Doug and Beth Doughty, David Teel, Beth (Shumway) Brown, Beth Sherry-Downes, Erin Laissen, Bob Socci, Pete Van Poppel, Frank Davinney, Scott Strasemeier, Eric Ruden, Billy Stone, Mike Werteen, Chris Knoche (still a bitter man), Andrew Thompson, Joe Speed, Jack Hecker, the perennially fabulous Dick Hall, Steve (Moose) Stirling, Jim and Tiffany Cantelupe, Derek and Christina Klein, Anthony and Kristen Noto, Roger Breslin, Jim Rome, Travis Rodgers, Jason Stewart, Tony Kornheiser (still angry after all these years), Michael Wilbon, Mark Maske, Ken Denlinger, Matt Rennie, Mike Purkey, Bob Edwards, Tom

Goldman, Jeffrey Katz, Mark Schramm, Kenny and Christina Lewis, Joanie Weiss, Bob Ryan, the soon-to-be-married L. Sandy Genelius, Jennifer Proud-Mearns, David Fay, Frank Hannigan, Mike Butz, Mike Davis, Mary Lopuszynski, Marty Caffey, Jerry Tarde, Mike O'Malley, Larry Dorman, Marsha Edwards, Jay and Natalie Edwards, Len and Gwyn Edwards-Dieterle, Brian and Laurie Edwards, Chris Edwards and John Cutcher, Joe Valerio, Rob Cowan, Andy Kaplan, Chris Svenson, Dennis Satyshur, Billy Andrade, Davis Love III, Jim Furyk, Mike Muehr, Tom Watson, Andy North, Joe Ogilvie, Joe Durant, Bob Low, Don Pooley, John Cook, Jeff Sluman, Peter Jacobsen, Lee Janzen, Brad Faxon, and, of course, Paul Goydos. Norbert Doyle has attended, I believe, every Final Four. Thanks also to my team of orthopods: Eddie McDevitt, Bob Arciero, Gus Mazzocca, and Dean Taylor.

Thanks, as always, to Howard Garfinkel, for understanding, and to Tom Konchalski, the only honest man in the gym, who checked on me constantly after my surgery.

The swimmers: Jeff Roddin, Jason (sorry I can't make it) Crist, John Craig, Mark Pugliese, Carole Kammel, Margot Pettijohn, Susan Williams, Amy Weiss, A. J. Block, Danny Pick, Warren Friedland, Marshall Greer, Tom Denes, Peter Ward, Doug Chestnut, Bob Hansen, Paul Doremus, the peripatetic Penny Bates, and the remarkably patient Mary Dowling. The FWRH group remains intact: Clay Britt, Wally Dicks, and Mike Fell.

The China Doll Gang: Red Auerbach (toughest guy going), Morgan Wootten, Hymie Perlo, Aubre Jones, Sam Jones, Rob Ades, Jack Kvancz (again), Joe McKeown, Stanley Copeland, Reid Collins, Arnie Heft, Pete Dowling, Bob Campbell, Chris (the Rookie) Wallace, Stanley Walker, Harry (the Champ)

Huang, Herman Greenberg, Joe Greenberg, Alvin Miller, Johnny Auerbach, Charles Thornton, Bob Ferry, and the ombudsman, George Solomon. Zang is still there, too.

The Rio gang: Tate Armstrong, Mark Alarie, Clay (LB) Buckley, and secretary to the group, Terry Chili.

The Feinstein Advisory Board: Keith Drum, Frank Mastrandrea, Wes Seeley, and Dave Kindred. Sadly, I didn't consult any of them during the fourth quarter of the Navy-Duke game.

Last, never least, my family: Jim and Arlene; Kacky, Stan, and Ann; Annie, Gregg, Rudy, Gus, and Harry; Jimmy and Brendan. Also Dad and Marcia; Margaret, David, Ethan, and Ben; Bobby, Jennifer, Matthew, and Brian. Danny and Brigid are a joy (most of the time), and Mary Clare Gibbons Feinstein is a remarkable mother, wife, and person. They put up with a lot dealing with a cranky cripple last summer.

My thanks and love to all of them.

John Feinstein
Potomac, Maryland
October 2005

INDEX

About the Author

JOHN FEINSTEIN is the author of a dozen highly acclaimed bestsellers, including books on golf (*Caddy for Life, Open, The Majors, A Good Walk Spoiled*), basketball (*Let Me Tell You a Story, The Punch, The Last Amateurs, A Season on the Brink, A Season Inside, Forever's Team, A March to Madness*), football (*A Civil War: Army vs. Navy, Next Man Up*), and other sports. He contributes to the *Washington Post,* writes a column for America Online, is a contributor to *Golf Digest,* and is a commentator on National Public Radio and Sporting News Radio. He lives in Potomac, Maryland, and Shelter Island, New York, with his wife and their two children.